Acclaim for Evelyn M. Monahan and Rosemary Neidel-Greenlee's

And If I Perish

"An extremely valuable addition to the historical perspective of nursing. . . . I felt as if I were there; I could smell the canvas of the tents and I could feel the scorching heat and the bitter cold. . . . The writer made the nurses and their stories come alive. . . . Quite simply, the entire book [is] outstanding."   —Lt. Col. Mary S. Nelson, USAF, NC, *Military Medicine*

"A laudatory account of the plucky American women—nearly 60,000 of them—who served in and near combat zones in the Mediterranean and European theaters of war from 1942 to 1945. . . . A nice tribute."
—*Kirkus Reviews*

"This compelling book tells the moving stories of World War II heroines who were never recognized, the nurses of the U.S. Army Nurse Corps. They were courageous, tireless, and committed to serving on the front lines of the war. They saved and rebuilt lives, and they gave many of us—including myself—a most valuable gift: hope."
—Senator Daniel K. Inouye, Medal of Honor recipient

"From the onset of the North African campaign until the conquest of Germany, the nurses of the U.S. Army Corps endured the same hardships, danger, overwhelming sacrifices, and risk to life as the soldiers they were destined to save. Heroines all, their story begs to be told."
—Adm. Frances Shea Buckley, former Director,
U.S. Navy Nurse Corps

EVELYN M. MONAHAN AND
ROSEMARY NEIDEL-GREENLEE

And If I Perish

Evelyn M. Monahan, a retired psychologist, served in the Women's Army Corps from 1961 until 1967 as a corpsman and psychiatric technician. She subsequently took her M.Ed. and Ph.D. at Georgia State University and her M.Div. in theology and ethics at Emory University. She worked at the Department of Veterans Affairs from 1980 to 1996.

Rosemary Neidel-Greenlee served in the U.S. Navy Nurse Corps on active duty from 1962 until 1965, and on reserve duty between 1989 and 1991. She has a master's degree in nursing from Emory University, and worked at the Veterans Affairs Medical Center in Atlanta from 1981 to 2002.

ALSO BY EVELYN M. MONAHAN &
ROSEMARY NEIDEL-GREENLEE

All This Hell: U.S. Nurses Imprisoned by the Japanese

Albanian Escape: The True Story of U.S. Army Nurses Behind Enemy Lines
(with Agnes Jensen Mangerich)

And If I Perish

And If I Perish

Frontline U.S. Army Nurses in World War II

EVELYN M. MONAHAN

&

ROSEMARY NEIDEL-GREENLEE

Anchor Books

A DIVISION OF RANDOM HOUSE, INC.

NEW YORK

FIRST ANCHOR BOOKS EDITION, NOVEMBER 2004

Copyright © 2003 by Evelyn M. Monahan and Rosemary Neidel-Greenlee

All rights reserved under International and Pan American Copyright Conventions. Published in the United States by Anchor Books, a division of Random House, Inc., New York, and simultaneously in Canada by Random House of Canada Limited, Toronto. Originally published in hardcover in the United States by Alfred A. Knopf, a division of Random House, Inc., New York, in 2003.

Anchor Books and colophon are registered trademarks of Random House, Inc.

The Library of Congress has cataloged the Knopf edition as follows:
Monahan, Evelyn.
And if I perish / by Evelyn M. Monahan and Rosemary Neidel-Greenlee.—1st ed.
p.   cm.
Includes bibliographical references and index.
1. United States. Army Nurse Corps—History—20th century.   2. World War, 1939–1945—
Medical care—United States.   3. Military nursing—United States—History—20th century.
I. Neidel, Rosemary L., [date]   II. Title.
D807.U6M66   2003
940.54'7573—dc21
2003047463

Anchor ISBN: 1-4000-3129-X

Author photographs © Herbert Kuper
Book design by Robert C. Olsson
Maps by David Lindroth, Inc.

www.anchorbooks.com

Printed in the United States of America
10   9   8   7   6   5   4   3   2   1

To all the women of the Greatest Generation

I will go . . . and if I perish, I perish.

—The Book of Esther, 4:16

CONTENTS

Introduction   3

Prologue   8

PART ONE: THE NORTH AFRICA CAMPAIGN

CHAPTER 1: Operation Torch—U.S Army Nurses in the Invasion
Force: D-Day North Africa—*8 November 1942*   25

CHAPTER 2: Nurses at the Battle of Kasserine Pass: In It All
the Way—*January–February 1943*   56

CHAPTER 3: The Allied Push to Bizerte and Tunis: Perfecting
Combat Medicine—*February–May 1943*   88

CHAPTER 4: Staging for Italy: Needed, 50,000 Army Nurses—
Spring–Summer 1943   120

PART TWO: THE ITALIAN CAMPAIGN

CHAPTER 5: Nurses in the Sicilian Campaign: Tough Enough
for Patton's Army—*10 July–1 September 1943*   149

CHAPTER 6: The Sinking of HMHS *Newfoundland:* Army
Medical Teams at Salerno—*26 August–27 September 1943*   173

CHAPTER 7: From Salerno to the Gustav Line:
Army Nurses Going Where They Are Needed—
29 September 1943–25 January 1944   198

CHAPTER 8: Hell's Half-Acre—The Anzio Beachhead:
And If I Perish . . . —*22 January–15 February 1944*   238

CHAPTER 9: Stalemate at Anzio Beachhead and Monte Cassino:
Nurses Endure with the Rest of the Troops—
12 February–15 May 1944   276

CHAPTER 10: Breakout and Pursuit: The U.S. Army Enters
Rome—*15 May–5 June 1944*   303

PART THREE: THE LIBERATION OF FRANCE

CHAPTER 11: The Invasion of Normandy: Army Nurses in
Northern France—*6 June–21 August 1944*   319

CHAPTER 12: Operation Dragoon and the Battle of the
Rhône Valley: Combat Medicine in Southern France—
15 August–15 September 1944   350

CHAPTER 13: Confronting the Siegfried Line: Medicine Under
Canvas—*15 September–15 December 1944*   373

PART FOUR: THE CONQUEST OF GERMANY

CHAPTER 14: The Battle of the Bulge: Army Nurses Meet the
Challenge—*16 December 1944–15 January 1945*   405

CHAPTER 15: Battle of the Rhineland: Army Nurses Persevere—
15 January–23 March 1945   427

CHAPTER 16: The Surrender of Germany: Army Nurses
at Dachau and Nordhausen—*29 April–8 May 1945*   442

EPILOGUE: Forgetting and Remembering   458

Notes   469

Bibliography   493

Acknowledgments   501

Index   503

And If I Perish

Introduction

THIS BOOK IS ABOUT the women who served on the front lines of World War II as U.S. Army nurses. It contains firsthand, eyewitness accounts of life lived close to, and often within, the line of fire, by female World War II veterans who served in hospitals in combat zones throughout the European and Mediterranean Theaters of War, from the first D-Day in North Africa, through the campaigns in Italy and France, to VE-Day in Germany. We, the authors, have had the privilege to record these women's stories in the last decade of the last century, fifty years after the war, while some were still alive to tell their tales.

For many of you reading this book, this may be the first time you've ever heard that women served anywhere near or in the combat zones of World War II. This ignorance is not hard to understand, since for decades after the war these army nurses were largely ignored. As strange as this may seem today, no one kept records of these women—not the military, nor the U.S. Veterans Administration, nor any historical society. After their return from the war, women veterans were not allowed membership in veteran groups such as the American Legion and the Veterans of Foreign Wars. Many of the women did not speak about their experiences to anyone. Few attended reunions. No one asked them about what happened. Schoolbooks did not mention their service; newspapers, books, radio, film, and television all but overlooked them. As the last century was drawing to a close, World War II's army nurses—who they were, why they volunteered for the front, what they endured, how much they gave to the cause—were destined to be lost to history.

This is where we came in. In 1985, Rosemary Neidel-Greenlee was appointed the first Women Veterans Coordinator, a collateral position at that time, at the Veterans Administration Medical Center (VAMC) in Atlanta. She quickly formed a Women Veterans Committee at the medical center. In 1987, Evelyn Monahan was appointed Women Veterans Coordinator for the VA regional office in Atlanta. With the fiftieth anniversary of World War II fast approaching, we asked the directors of the VAMC and the VA regional office in Atlanta to co-sponsor the first National Salute to Women Veterans of World War II. All three—the Atlanta Chamber of Commerce Military Affairs Task Force, the VAMC Atlanta, and the VA regional office—agreed to support the effort to recognize women veterans of World War II.

It now remained for us to find these women. We hit on the idea of advertising a call in several magazines that have large readerships of veterans: the *Retired Officers Magazine*, *VFW Magazine*, the *Disabled American Veterans Magazine*, *American Legion Magazine*, *Purple Heart Magazine*, and *Delta Sky Magazine*. The magazines agreed to publish, within advertisements announcing the upcoming 1989 National Salute to Women Veterans of World War II, a request to women veterans and their families and friends to contact us via a post office box. The response we got was overwhelming: we were shocked when, about a week after the first announcement appeared in spring 1989, the U.S. Post Office contacted us to say they had approximately a thousand letters waiting for us. We had to pick them up at a loading dock in the back of the post office.

We brought the boxes of letters home and began to read them. They contained sentences such as: "It's about time someone paid attention to the women veterans of World War II" . . ."It's great to finally get to tell our stories" . . . "I'm enclosing the names of women I served with so you can contact them too." By the end of the summer, we had received more than 100,000 letters from women who had served in the military during World War II, their husbands, families, friends, or even their former boyfriends. With a team of thirty volunteers to help, mostly former military women from World War II and the Korean War, we sent out questionnaires to the women who inquired about the National Salute. Like the response to the announcements in the veterans' magazines, the four-page questionnaires streamed back to Atlanta bearing the facts and stories of women who had volunteered to serve their country during World War II.

We used these letters and questionnaires to telephone the respondents and interview them about their experiences. The first woman, a former World War II army nurse who had been a prisoner of war in a Japanese internment camp in the Philippines, asked us: "Do you really want to hear this? No one has ever asked before." Our answer was a firm "Absolutely!"

With those words, we began a journey of more than twelve years to contact, interview, record, and make known the history and personal experiences of the women of the "Greatest Generation" who served in our country's armed forces during World War II. As we listened and talked with these unrecognized heroes of the war, we became more and more convinced that what these women endured, and the spirit in which they bore their burdens, was a national treasure that had to be told to the American people and the world they helped to liberate and keep free.

On 28 October 1989, more than eight hundred women veterans of World War II traveled to Atlanta to attend the first National Salute to Women Veterans of World War II. During the three-day event, women veterans went to reunions of the various branches of the armed forces, visited with each other, were interviewed by local and national news networks including CBS, NBC, ABC, and CNN, and attended a dinner and program given in their honor. Near the end of that evening, women veterans were entertained by a re-creation of a World War II radio program, and danced to the music of the Coca-Cola Spotlight Band. On Sunday morning, a woman army chaplain conducted a memorial service to honor and remember all of the military women of World War II who died before this Salute was held. When the event ended and the veterans returned to their home states, we resumed the interviews and research that continue even as this book makes its appearance. We are honored and humbled to have conducted hundreds of hours of personal interviews with more than seventy of these frontline army nurses.

Over the years, we have become friends with many of these women, as well as other World War II veterans of the Navy Nurse Corps and other women's military branches. In 2001, we were saddened by the death of Colonel Madeline Ullom, a former army nurse and prisoner of war of the Japanese during World War II. It was Colonel Ullom's impassioned speech to Congress in 1982 that prompted the legislature to mandate, for the first time, that each VA medical center and regional office appoint a Women Veterans Coordinator, as well as establish a national Women Veterans Advisory Committee to identify and recommend ways to meet the special needs of America's female veterans. The national advisory committee was a first in the history of American women in the military;

before 1982, there was no government organization to advocate for women veterans. While we are saddened by Madeline's death, we're glad that our book, *All This Hell: U.S. Nurses Imprisoned by the Japanese*, was published in time for Madeline and the other POWs to read. No possible book review could have made us happier than some of the comments of Madeline and other former POWs of the Japanese during World War II. Hearing them tell us that "that's how it really was" made the years of research and writing totally worthwhile.

Over 350,000 American women volunteered to serve in the armed forces during World War II. More than 59,000 of those women were registered nurses, who volunteered to serve in the U.S. Army Nurse Corps. More than half of these women volunteered again to serve in frontline hospitals in overseas war zones. Sixteen were killed as a result of enemy action; more than seventy were held as POWs of the Japanese for more than three years; approximately sixteen hundred of them won awards and decorations, including the Distinguished Service Medal, the Legion of Merit, the Silver Star, the Bronze Star, and the Purple Heart. More than two hundred died while in military service.

We are also humbled and honored to have interviewed the male officers and enlisted men who, along with these army nurses, comprised the staffs of hospital personnel in the field and evacuation hospitals. We interviewed some of the patients, too; the army nurses we spoke with could not have praised these men more highly or admired them more genuinely. Neither could these soldiers have spoken with more respect for and gratitude toward the nurses, who endured the horrors of combat zones in order to give them a better chance for survival should they or their buddies be wounded.

Much has been written about World War II: the battles, the strategies, the causes that led up to its outbreak, and the effects of its aftermath. It is not the purpose of our book to revisit these topics here, though enough of battle strategy and troop movements is given that we try to keep the reader aware of what was happening in the big picture. What we do hope is that this book will acquaint the American people and the world with the heroic contributions made by army nurses, army physicians, and hospital personnel who kept the wounded alive on the front lines in the Mediterranean and European theaters of war.

The superintendent of the U.S. Army Nurse Corps, Colonel Florence Blanchfield, expressed the feelings and commitments of U.S. Army nurses very well when she wrote to the mother of Lieutenant Ellen

Ainsworth, who was killed by enemy action on the Anzio beachhead in Italy in February 1944: "She typifies the very finest in American womanhood. Had she known that it was to be thus, she would still have said, 'I must go. It is my duty.' The nurses are like that in this war. They fear nothing. They beg to go forward as far as possible because they feel they are needed so urgently."[1]

—Evelyn and Rosemary, January 2003

Prologue

Manila, Philippine Islands
Feb. 19, 1941

Dear Mother,

They are sending the Army dependents back to the States, which is as it should be, in case anything happens over here. We will have enough to take care of but there are lots of rumors—of course things look hideous, however, I'm not worrying—which would only impair my mind at present, and we have to be on the job. . . .

I have the colonel's Masonic ring. We never discuss war, as he will not listen to it, and doesn't want me to cross bridges before we get to them, but underneath I know why he gave me the ring. Any Mason who saw the ring would give me a hand in case I needed emergency help. I am to wear it all the time I am in Manila. Let me know if you are getting my letters. I never know when they will get to you, as mines are planted all around us, so that the Japs [sic] can't get into Manila Bay.

Don't worry. I don't as it can't be changed. Maybe things will turn out. You be sure to collect my insurance if I don't get back. I am in good health so far, and in good frame of mind.

Love,
Frances

P.S. Keep personal some things I tell you about the Army. There are plenty of spies here.

When Lieutenant Frances L. Nash took the oath of service in the U.S. Army Nurse Corps on 14 November 1935, there were fewer than 600 U.S. Army nurses on active duty. Seven years later, when she was taken prisoner by the Japanese in the Philippines on 6 May 1942, more than 12,000 women army nurses would be on active duty. All told, by the war's end, 59,000 army nurses would volunteer to serve in World War II. But on that cold November day in 1935 when Nash became an army nurse, she was one of a relatively small number of women who were taking what we now recognize as a major pioneering step for women in the nursing profession and in the military as well.

Frances Nash was typical of the women who volunteered to enter the Army Nurse Corps in the 1930s and 1940s: she was adventurous, independent, and self-reliant. A feisty, Georgia farm girl, Frances had made up her mind early in childhood to be a nurse, and before she had even finished high school, she applied for admission to Grady Memorial Hospital School of Nursing in Atlanta. After high school graduation in 1929, Frances was off to "The Gradys," as Atlanta residents referred to the hospital at the time. She received her nursing diploma in 1932, then stayed on at Grady Memorial as a surgical nurse until she joined the Army Nurse Corps in 1935.

Unfortunately for any young woman considering nursing as a vocation in America during the 1920s and 1930s, prevailing public opinion held that women of good character did not become nurses. Women had served as nurses in every war in the nation's history to that point—from the American Revolution through the Civil War to World War I. Florence Nightingale had done excellent nursing work for the British army during the Crimean War in 1855. Yet most Americans believed that nursing was an unsuitable and somewhat suspect profession for young unmarried women. In her book *From Nightingale to Eagle*, Major Edith A. Aynes remembered her mother's response when, in 1928, Edith informed her that she wanted to become a nurse. After telling her daughter that "nurses were not decent," and that "she would not be able to hold her head up if her daughter became a nurse," Mrs. Aynes stated that "Nursing was emptying bedpans and doing other disgusting things for people."[1]

Not only was nursing considered demeaning physical labor for a young woman, it was also considered a profession that required "unwholesome" mingling of the sexes. In the American society of the day, which was very closed regarding sexuality, the majority of citizens believed that a vocation that often required unmarried women to provide care that could involve exposure to the male genitalia was no place for innocent young women fresh out of high school. In a society with such attitudes, women with "knowledge" of male sex organs were considered aberrant—unfit for marriage and motherhood. Even married women did not discuss sexual matters with unmarried female friends or family, and were lucky to have a married friend with whom to broach the subject.

The undesirability of the vocation was heightened by the fact that nursing often involved rendering personal care and treatment to men and women suffering from taboo illnesses such as venereal disease that were simply not mentioned in polite society. Normal body functions were considered improper topics for conversation with anyone who was not one's personal physician. Thus, a young woman's innocence depended on things she did not do or discuss as well as on things of which she had no "knowledge." Unmarried women with "knowledge" of male anatomy, the sexual nature of marital relations, or venereal diseases were automatically suspect in an atmosphere that treated such topics with the utmost secrecy and reluctance. Knowing of these "sinful" matters was itself proof of indecency.

Aside from this negative public attitude was the additional hardship of the exhausting training nurses had to undergo. Civilian hospitals used nursing students as free labor and required long hours of work on hospital wards. But since a hospital provided room and board at usually no significant cost, many women who were unable to afford a college education decided to enter nursing school in order to get some type of professional training and a means to earn a living.

For Frances Nash and others who graduated from nursing schools in the depression of the 1930s, however, jobs were not easy to find. Hospitals hired very few nursing graduates since the supply of free student labor seemed endless. Most registered nurses—those who had graduated from a three-year nursing school—were forced to seek private duty at a time when few American families could afford to pay for such care. Waiting lists of nurses looking for private duty assignments were often two-hundred-hopefuls-long and the periods between paychecks forced many nurses to seek other work to support themselves. When a private duty job did materialize, it came with twelve-hour shifts and a salary of about two dollars a day. Registered nurses who were lucky enough to be hired by a hospital or clinic found themselves working twelve hours a day and on call for the other twelve hours. In small clinics and rural hospitals run by one or two physicians, one registered nurse was usually the entire nursing staff, working virtually twenty-four hours, seven days a week. When a day off was required, a licensed practical nurse (i.e., a nurse who had not graduated from a nursing school and was not a licensed RN but instead had only ten months to a year's training in more restricted areas) might be brought in for that time, with a quick return of the graduate nurse to her regular relentless hours.

In spite of all these conditions, young women like Frances Nash flocked to nursing schools, and after graduation devoted themselves to their patients' care for an average salary of $70 a month (16¢ per hour) for twelve-hour days and only the occasional day off. In the midst of the long bread lines of the Great Depression, 16 cents an hour sounded like a gold mine to the unemployed, especially given that the national unemployment rate was, on average, 25 percent. In Atlanta, the unemployment rate hovered in the range of 25 to 30 percent for whites, and 70 to 75 percent for blacks, so twenty-one-year-old Frances considered herself quite lucky to land employment at Grady Memorial Hospital in 1932 after graduating from its nursing school.

In the face of staggering unemployment and concerns about a possible approaching war, nursing journals in the 1930s carried advertisements for the U.S. Army and Navy Nurse Corps. Young women like Frances Nash, independent enough to enter the field of nursing despite prevailing public opinion, found it even more daring to join the military nurse corps. If nursing was somewhat unacceptable, military nursing was all the more unacceptable. Still, the military corps promised comparatively good salaries, a chance to serve one's country, travel to distant places, and gain contact with cultures few civilian women would ever see. Only the most adventurous young women would sign up for the military nurse corps, and only the bravest of those would volunteer for duty in the Philippines, a group of islands in the Pacific on the other side of the world, within just a few hours of Japan by air.

FIVE YEARS after volunteering for the U.S. Army Nurse Corps, Frances Nash again volunteered in the late summer of 1940 for a two-year tour of duty in the Philippines. When Frances told her family that she would be leaving for the Philippines, she met the same concerned comments so many other army nurses were hearing as they delivered their "good news" to parents and friends. "Why are you going to the Philippines?

Lt. Frances L. Nash (Courtesy of Mamie Nash Cason)

America is going to be at war soon, and it's going to start in that area."
Like the other nurses who'd chosen a Pacific tour of duty, Frances replied
that she was an army nurse, and if war came to the Philippines, that was
exactly where she should be to take care of casualties.

When Nash and other army nurses arrived in Manila harbor in 1940,
they looked more like debutantes than military nurses. They left the ship
in chiffon dresses accessorized with matching or complementary high
heels, white gloves, and large-brimmed picture hats. Their trunks were
free of khaki, since there was no military uniform for the army nurse of
the day. Instead, they were packed tight with floor-length evening gowns,
fashionable dresses for dinners and cocktail parties, as well as a range of
outfits suitable for a variety of social occasions.

The army imposed two sacrosanct requirements on each nurse who
served in the Philippines: each had to have completed two years of military service in the United States, and each had to be in perfect health.
The health requirements were particularly important since transport

ships bringing supplies and replacements arrived in the Philippines only once every three months. A sick nurse who could not perform her duty meant the nursing staff would be shorthanded for as much as twelve weeks. Added to this concern was the fact that tuberculosis, which was feared everywhere, carried a special peril in tropical climates. The heat and humidity of the Philippines acted as a catalyst for TB, an often deadly disease at that time, increasing the number of cases many times over, and compounding their severity.

Since the end of the Spanish-American War in 1899, there were five army hospitals and one navy hospital in the Philippines to support the American troops. Lieutenant Nash's first duty station was in the heart of downtown Manila at Sternberg General Hospital. The Sternberg, as it was called by most of its staff, consisted of a series of two-story buildings around an enclosed courtyard, in the style of the Spanish architecture that dominated the city. The hospital stood at a busy intersection and was constantly bombarded by the sounds of a large city: fire and police sirens; car horns; screeching brakes; ambulances bringing the sick and injured for medical help to the Sternberg and civilian hospitals; the braying of donkeys and whinnying of horses as they pulled carts between and around motorized vehicles. There was one feature, however, that almost made up for the noise: the Sternberg's staff was within walking distance of the municipal golf and tennis courts, an up-to-date shopping area, the Army & Navy Club, and the old walled city.

Until America's entrance into World War II, the Sternberg was the most modern hospital in the Philippine Islands. It had 450 beds, an officers' ward, an enlisted ward, more than 20 private rooms, a large laboratory area for research of tropical diseases, a barrio ward, excellent operating suites, the most modern X-ray equipment, the services of between fifteen and twenty army nurses, and a civilian physiotherapist and dietician. All military hospitals in the Manila area had to make special arrangements due to the tropical heat and humidity. Nurses on the day shift worked an average of four hours while the afternoon and night shifts worked eight hours each, the one beginning at 1230 and the other at 0030. The shifts were rotated among the nurses to ensure fairness.

Like all working American women at that time, army nurses received much less pay for their labors than their male counterparts. Lieutenant Nash received 50 percent of the salary given to male officers of the same rank. This was due, at least in part, to the fact that Nash's rank as "lieutenant" was not the same as a man's. Nash had what was called "relative

rank," a term that had originated in 1920 when Congress passed the
Army Reorganization Act in recognition of the twenty thousand women
nurses who served during World War I. The act provided that nurses
would have the relative, temporary rank of second lieutenant to major.
Relative rank conveyed the right of women army nurses to wear the military insignia, but without conferring military status or privileges (for
example, nurses did not rate the salute that is the mark of military
respect). The inequities of relative rank extended into the area of military pay.

A nurse such as Nash with the relative rank of second lieutenant
earned $88.60 a month ($70.00 of this amount was base pay, and the
remaining $18.60 was considered a subsistence allowance), while a male
second lieutenant in the army received double that amount—$140.00
base pay and $37.20 subsistence allowance, a total of $177.20 plus additional pay for each dependent.

Since relative rank carried no real military status, nurses were not
considered to be in need of military orientation or training. So these
young women were placed immediately on duty in military hospitals,
dressed in civilian white duty uniforms marked only with the military
insignia they were ordered to wear on their collars.

Although the nation had not adequately equipped or trained its military nurses at the time it sent Frances Nash and the other nurses to
Manila in the summer of 1940, America was, however slowly and incom-
pletely, preparing for the possibility of war there. The number of army
nurses stationed at army hospitals in the Philippines was now nearly one
hundred, double the usual quota. On orders issued the previous winter
from the War Department, dependents of all military personnel serving
in the Philippines had to return to the United States. Navy dependents
sailed back in March 1941, followed by army dependents in May. In June
1941, Frances was transferred to Fort William McKinley, seven miles
from Manila, where she was to set up the surgical unit in what would
become, virtually overnight, a hospital. Fort McKinley had been a dis-
pensary for America's Filipino allies before July 1941, when the Army
Medical Department converted it into a 259-bed hospital.

At the same time, the number of ships leaving the United States for
the Philippines increased threefold. Military personnel and supplies that
used to arrive in those islands once every three months now arrived once
or twice a month. Almost every ship that docked brought more army
nurses to serve in the fabled tropical paradise.

In September and October 1941, the last two convoys carrying army nurses to the Philippines left San Francisco. As usual, the September sailing of the USS *Holbrook* was announced in the local newspapers, but the last two ships to carry army nurses into what would soon be a war zone, the USS *Scott* and the USS *Coolidge*, were silent sailings—without the dubious benefits of a newspaper announcement. Nurses on the *Scott* and the *Coolidge* reached Manila harbor on 28 November 1941, nine days before America would be brought, bloody and angry, into World War II.

It was 7 December 1941 in Hawaii and the United States, but across the international dateline in Manila, it was already Monday, 8 December. Lieutenant Frances Nash and other military nurses awakened to news that would change the world forever: at 0755 Hawaii time, 0355 in the Philippines, naval and air forces of the Empire of Japan attacked the military forces of the United States at Pearl Harbor and sank or damaged most of the U.S. Navy's Pacific Fleet. U.S. forces in Hawaii braced for the Japanese landings they expected to follow the sneak air attack, but Japanese military leaders had other plans.

Less than three hours after the first bombs fell on Pearl Harbor, Japanese planes struck Camp John Hay, an army post 200 miles north of Manila. U.S. Army nurses in and around Manila were issued outdated World War I helmets and gas masks and told to prepare for the hundreds of casualties that would result if and when Japan struck Manila and its adjacent U.S. military bases. At approximately 1215, 192 Japanese warplanes, bombers, dive-bombers, and fighters flew over Clark Field, 70 miles north of Manila, strafing and bombing U.S. planes lined up in symmetrical patterns around the airfield. Only nine hours after the attack on Pearl Harbor, U.S. airpower in the Philippines was virtually destroyed without ever having left the ground.

The first wave of the attack lasted fourteen minutes, and left 85 dead and 350 wounded. Stotsenberg Army Hospital was located across the road from Clark Field, and army nurses—young women in white duty uniforms or civilian clothes—ran across open roads and fields toward the devastation, despite the second wave of Japanese planes that arrived only three minutes after the first attack ended. They were the first in a long line of military nurses who would leave safe cover to run to the aid of America's wounded soldiers in World War II.

After two weeks of intensified bombing and strafing throughout the Philippines, Japanese forces landed at Lingayen Gulf, 130 miles northwest of Manila. The next day, General Douglas MacArthur moved his headquarters to the island of Corregidor and ordered American and Filipino troops to withdraw to the peninsula of Bataan. Most army nurses had never heard of Bataan, but in a matter of weeks it would be in the headlines of newspapers throughout the world.

On Christmas Eve morning 1941, while army nurses were being evacuated from Manila to the Bataan peninsula, Lieutenant Nash was summoned by her commanding officer, Colonel J. W. Duckworth, and given special instructions. "I was told," Nash recalled, "to prepare myself to be taken prisoner. Five years earlier, I would have laughed at the thought of ever receiving such an order, and answering merely, 'Yes, Sir.' " The colonel told Nash that she was to remain behind in Manila until all staff members and supplies had been evacuated. "In case you are cut off, you must prepare to be taken prisoner," Duckworth said again.[2]

Nash spent all of Christmas Eve and Christmas Day working in surgery, and in her spare time, she destroyed any papers that might prove useful to the Japanese. By Christmas night, Japanese troops were drawing closer to Manila, and Nash and other members of the surgical staff were ordered to evacuate to Hospital No. 2 on Bataan. At 2300, they climbed aboard one of the small steamers that were used for transport among the several islands of the Philippines and began their zigzagging trip across Manila Bay. The flames from burning buildings on shore and ships ablaze in the harbor added to the light cast on the bay by a brightly shining moon. What little sleep Nash "got that night, [she] caught stretched out on the top deck, dressed in mechanic's coveralls, helmet and gas mask" at her side. Her pockets were crammed full of narcotics, stimulants, and enough morphine to provide every army nurse a lethal dose as a grim alternative to the manner of death the enemy had been known to inflict on its captives. As long as the nurses continued to be useful in treating casualties and maintain their dignity, the morphine would remain their secret. Many women wore a hairpiece known as a "rat," an elongated roll of hair around which the wearer would wrap her own long hair. Nurses hid the tablets of morphine inside the rat and then placed the rat in their hair, in accordance with the fashion of the day.[3]

During the night, the steamer passed the island of Corregidor and Nash could see fires burning on Malinta Hill. At 1000, the small boat arrived at Bataan's Lamo docks as a blanket of Japanese planes overhead was strafing and bombing the area. Nash spotted a native scoop on the dock where chickens had taken refuge. Without thinking twice, she pushed the chickens out and squeezed herself in. When the raid eased up a little, Nash and her companions hurried into the jungle, crouching as they ran. For almost three hours, Nash sat in her first jungle foxhole while tree rats scurried about taking an occasional shortcut across the jungle's newcomers. "You live a million years in each second in a foxhole," Nash recalled. "There you sit, your mouth open to protect your ear-drums. You test your helmet's chin strap, you absentmindedly brush off the bugs that swarm over you."[4]

From the foxhole, they traveled fifteen miles further into the jungle, where Nash took on the problem of setting up an operating tent under the low-hanging trees. Before she could solve it, Colonel Duckworth's command car arrived with the message that she was to report to Colonel Duckworth at Hospital No. 1. The colonel told Nash he needed her to set up the operating tent for this, the most forward hospital. Nash followed orders. Hundreds of casualties were already lying on litters on the ground, awaiting surgical help, and Nash went to work immediately. She credited her ability to bring order out of chaos to her training and upbringing. "What I was able to do in those horrible days on Bataan I owe to knowledge I gained at Grady Hospital, and to the hard times," she said.[5]

Between Christmas 1941 and the beginning of April 1942, 70,000 sick, starving, and exhausted American and Filipino troops defended Bataan against 250,000 well-fed and battle-hardened Japanese forces. Medical personnel worked day and night caring for thousands of wounded and ill Allied troops, and the wounded Japanese soldiers in their care. Nash recalled, "American medics brought Jap wounded to us. We let them keep all the American socks, underwear and watches they had lined up on their wrists. Made you want to say something bad when you saw the laundry mark on the garment of someone's name you knew. It meant the person was dead."[6]

All of the nurses and medical staff on Bataan worked beyond what might be expected from any human being, but even here, Nash's dedication to duty stood out like a beacon. In his book *Barbed-Wire Surgeon*, Dr. Alfred A. Weinstein, who had practiced medicine in Atlanta before he joined the Army Medical Corps, described some of the unique qualities Nash possessed: "Frances especially was a dynamo, driving the medics with her lashing tongue until they cursed her sullenly under their breath—not openly because they were sure they'd get the back of her hand. A strapping brown-haired comely girl, raised on Georgia-grown pork, black-eyed peas, hominy and grits, she packed a mean wallop."[7]

Japanese strafing of the hospitals happened so often that Colonel Duckworth issued new orders to surgical personnel who always remained at their posts in the operating-room (OR) tent, despite the attacks. "The C.O. finally issued orders to medical personnel to strap patients on OR tables, turn off the anesthesia machines, and go outside and get in a foxhole or hit the ground flat. We were losing too many medical personnel during these raids. The Japanese could see us, but deliberately continued to fire," Nash said. "A dead officer was no good to anyone, and there were no replacements."[8]

The Geneva Conventions redrawn in 1929 stipulated that, in time of war, hospitals were not legitimate military targets. But as a nonsignatory of the Geneva Conventions, and in flagrant disregard for the red cross on the ground that marked the hospital area, Japanese planes bombed Hospital No. 1 at the end of March. The deliberate attack left many dead, and as usual the bodies were collected and taken into the jungle at night to be buried. The chaplain in charge of the burial detail was told to bring back one dog tag from each body and whatever clothes might still be used by the living who had to return to nearby front lines. One evening, Nash walked out to the burial site to remind the chaplain about the clothing. Although she had seen thousands of wounded and dying soldiers, the common grave site had a deep and lasting effect on her. "I never went back again. Too much for me, got to thinking I might be next."[9]

On 6 April, the day after Easter, Japanese planes bombed the hospital again and scored a direct hit on ward tents. The blast from the explosions and shrapnel hit the operating-room area and Nash was knocked down in a corner and covered with medical cabinets and supplies. "When I pulled the cabinets and saline bottles off of me, I was surprised to see that I could walk." The bombs had re-wounded and killed hundreds. Nash was furious when she saw the carnage. "In that raid, several wards were wiped out completely," Nash said. "One of them contained thirty or more head cases, boys without eyes, ears or noses. I had never before been so mad at any individual that I wanted to kill him, as I did the Japs. I was so mad that I wasn't frightened."[10]

Only 65 of the original 1,600 beds in the field hospital at Hospital No. 1 were still standing. All patients who could be moved were transferred to Hospital No. 2, and two nurses who were wounded in the bombing were transferred to Corregidor for further treatment.

On 8 April, as many American troops as possible and all of the army nurses who would be needed to care for new casualties were evacuated to

Corregidor, where Americans would make their final stand in the Philippines. On 9 April 1942, General Edward King surrendered Bataan. American and Filipino troops left behind and all the wounded in the jungle hospitals became prisoners of the Japanese. The surrender made headlines throughout the world, and stories of Corregidor's last stand filled the front pages for weeks to come.

On 6 May 1942, General Jonathan Wainwright surrendered Corregidor, and all American and Filipino troops, including Nash and sixty-six other army nurses, became prisoners of war. It was the first day of thirty-seven months that Nash and her sister nurses would spend as prisoners of the Japanese. They would continue to work as army nurses in the prison camps, caring for sick and wounded internees, while American and Allied forces fought their way back to the Philippines to liberate their comrades. But Nash and her sister nurses, along with imprisoned American soldiers, would not be brought home until the war ended more than three years later.

MEANWHILE, thousands of women at home, knowing the terrible fate that had befallen American nurses in the Philippines, nonetheless began volunteering for the Army Nurse Corps. Both young women fresh out of nursing schools and women with years of experience responded to the call of news stories, recruitment posters, and magazine ads. Many would volunteer twice over: once in the U.S. Army Nurse Corps, they would volunteer again for overseas duty in frontline hospitals. One of these volunteers was Helen Molony, a tall, redheaded nurse from upstate New York. On the day after the Japanese attack on Pearl Harbor, Molony signed up in the U.S. Army Nurse Corps and volunteered for overseas duty.

Recognizing the contributions women had made in World War I, Congress moved quickly to establish the Women's Army Auxiliary Corps (WAAC) in May 1942, and to reestablish the Women's Army Corps (WAC) in June 1943. The U.S. Navy's bill was passed and signed on 30 July 1942, authorizing the Women Accepted for Volunteer Emergency Service (WAVES) and the Marine Corps Women's Reserve. The Coast Guard Women's Reserve (known as SPARs from their motto, *Semper paratus*—Always Ready) was authorized and established on 23 November 1942. After the United States declared war on Japan on 8 December 1941, and Germany declared war on the United States on 11 December 1941,

America began to send its sons and daughters to meet the enemy before they could strike the U.S. homeland again.[11]

Following Pearl Harbor, the American public was understandably outraged against Japan and calling for action in the Pacific. Yet throughout 1942, only a limited number of American troops were sent to the Pacific—sufficient to at best contain, but not defeat, the Japanese. President Franklin Roosevelt was not willing to launch a full-scale attack against Japan in 1942; rather, the United States agreed with Britain that Hitler had to be stopped first. But after months of debate on the pros and cons of invading Europe, the leaders of both the United States and Britain realized they were as yet unprepared to invade Europe. Britain had been humiliatingly routed from France when Paris fell to the Germans in 1940, and was now fighting German and Italian forces in North Africa. Roosevelt was reluctant to send inexperienced U.S. troops into Europe alone without British support. It was finally decided that the United States would invade North Africa. The North African coast would make an excellent launching area for the later invasion of Europe and Britain was amenable to taking part in this action. Thus, French North Africa was chosen as the site for an Allied invasion code-named "Operation Torch." It would be America's first amphibious invasion outside the Pacific and America's first D-Day (the first day of any military operation or amphibious landing) in the European theater of World War II.

U.S. military planners assigned the 48th Surgical Hospital to support U.S. and British troops in the invasion of North Africa. The 48th team included redheaded nurse Helen Molony from upstate New York, now Lieutenant Helen Molony. She, along with fifty-six other army nurses, would land with the invasion forces on D-Day—not a few days after the taking of the beachhead but right alongside the fighting troops on D-Day itself—which was scheduled for 8 November 1942. It was the first time in the nation's history that women nurses would land with assault troops on the initial day of an invasion. These army nurses would share all the dangers of the combat zone without the benefit of full military rank, with little military training, and with only half the salary paid to male officers.

War had overtaken Nash and her sister nurses in the Philippines almost unawares, but army nurses like Lieutenant Molony who followed in Nash's footsteps would go to war knowing what had befallen their predecessors. The nurses who were to land on D-Day in North Africa and those who came after them would travel to the front lines knowing that the Geneva Conventions which were intended to protect hospitals and medical personnel in combat areas could not guarantee that an enemy or wayward shell would not bring them dismemberment or death. Like Second Lieutenant Frances Nash, who clearly accepted that danger when she wrote to her mother, "You be sure to collect my insurance if I don't get back," and like Queen Esther, who had answered her country's call many centuries before, army nurses would give life to the meaning of Esther's words: ". . . I will go . . . and if I perish, I perish."

PART ONE

The North Africa Campaign

In the early morning hours of 8 November 1942, the Allied invasion of North Africa began. The largest amphibious invasion force assembled to date in the history of warfare—107,450 men (combat troops and medical personnel), transported on 111 ships, supported by more than 200 warships—made three separate, almost simultaneous landings on the coasts of Morocco and Algeria.

Landing with the D-Day forces was the 48th Surgical Hospital, including fifty-seven female U.S. Army nurses. The army nurses, unarmed and without the benefit of rigorous military training, climbed down ropes and ladders into landing craft that took them, alongside the fighting men, onto the beaches of French North Africa. This was the first and last time army nurses would land with an invasion force; at no other D-Day in World War II was it to be repeated.

Here is their story.

CHAPTER ONE

Operation Torch—U.S. Army Nurses in the Invasion Force

D-DAY NORTH AFRICA

8 November 1942

I spotted Lt. Vilma Vogler descending a ladder at my side. Our eyes met for a moment in mutual shock, and then we quickly descended into a waiting barge. At that moment she and the other nurses had ceased to be "the women." We were all comrades in equally dangerous footing, trying to survive the insanity of combat.

—*Edward E. Rosenbaum, MD, former captain,*
U.S. Army Medical Corps,
"Wartime Nurses: A Tribute to the
Unsung Veterans," New Choices *(July 1989)*

AN ARTILLERY SHELL exploded sixty yards off the starboard side of HMS *Orbita*. Lieutenant Helen Molony, seated on board in the officers' mess, felt her hand shake as she raised her coffee mug to her mouth. It was early morning, 8 November 1942. A convoy of Allied war- and transport ships, including the *Orbita*, the *Santa Paula*, and the *Monarch of Bermuda*, lay two miles off the coast of Algeria. On board these British ships were not only combat troops but the men and women of the 48th Surgical Hospital, including Lieutenant Molony. She was one of 57 U.S. Army nurses who, along with the hospital's 48 officers and 273

*Lt. Helen M. Molony, 48th Surgical Hospital/
128th Evacuation Hospital (Courtesy of Helen
Molony Reichert)*

enlisted men, were waiting to land, side by side with the combat troops, on the beachheads of Arzew and Oran in Algeria.

The sun had not risen yet and the ships were still under cover of darkness. Molony glanced around the officers' mess. The thunder of artillery had begun an hour earlier, and now, at 0515, she saw that the tables in the mess were crowded with officers, male and female, dressed in combat gear. Aside from the clanking of silverware and an occasional word or two spoken in hushed tones, the large wardroom was strangely quiet. In less than an hour, Molony knew that her part in Operation Torch—the invasion of North Africa—would begin. What she could not know was that her participation in the D-Day invasion would become a landmark in U.S. military history.

Only a few months earlier, in midsummer, the 48th Surgical Hospital had crossed the Atlantic on the USS *Wakefield* as part of what was, at that time, the largest convoy ever to sail from the United States. On 6 August, the 48th Surgical had disembarked at Greenock, Scotland, and taken a one-day train ride to Tidworth Barracks in the area of Shipton-Ballanger and Kangaroo Corners in southern England. The unit remained there for two and a half months, and Molony underwent the closest thing to military training the army nurses would receive, a regimen of hardening exercises of five- and ten-mile hikes, complete with field packs.

For the nurses of the 48th Surgical Hospital, as for all the army nurses sent overseas before July 1943, uniforms presented a definite problem. Before America entered World War II, the sole uniform the U.S. Army nurses had was a white duty nurse's uniform and white nurse's shoes. The only thing military about the uniform was the second lieutenant's gold bar, worn on the right lapel, and the caduceus with an "N" superimposed upon it on the left lapel. The caduceus had been a symbol of the Army Medical Department for decades. Doctors wore the caduceus plain, while nurses had a superimposed "N" for nursing, the dentists a superimposed "D," and veterinarians a superimposed "V."

As for the clothing itself, the army provided blue seersucker dresses for the nurses in combat theaters, but it was obvious that this would not be appropriate for climbing over patients, or for working in cold climates, mud, rain, or mosquito-infested areas. Long pants would at least solve some of the problems presented by cold weather, rain, and mud, but the national consensus at that time held that women did not wear slacks. Hence it would be some time before the army produced pants for women nurses; in the meanwhile, army nurses simply wore men's GI field uniforms or coveralls. Many of them could sew, and those who could helped those who could not in making alterations to male army fatigues so they would more adequately fit the smaller, shorter frames of American women. Shoes presented a separate set of problems. For the smaller army nurses who could not get GI shoes to fit their feet, blisters were a frequent and painful result of marching through the English countryside.

During the weeks of training in England, the women of the 48th Surgical Hospital got to know each other. There was Helen Molony, the tall redhead from upstate New York, who, in the words of friends and family, was "pretty enough to be a movie star." Pretty or not, Molony never had Hollywood in mind for herself and her future. Instead, she trained to become a nurse, and joined the U.S. Army Nurse Corps the day after the Japanese attack on Pearl Harbor. After a few months training at Fort Slocum on Long Island Sound, Molony was moved out to the New York port of embarkation. There she was assigned, along with fifty-six other nurses, to the 48th Surgical Hospital.

There was Ruth Haskell, a thirty-three-year-old divorced mother from Maine, who had left her ten-year-old son, Carl, in the care of his

Lt. Ruth G. Haskell, 48th Surgical
Hospital/128th Evacuation Hospital
(Courtesy of Helen Molony Reichert)

grandparents fourteen months earlier before setting off for Camp Forrest near Tullahoma, Tennessee, for duty as an army nurse. A heavyset woman of medium height with brown hair and intelligent brown eyes, Haskell was determined, self-initiating, and confident.

Quite the opposite of Haskell was the nurse who would become her best friend, Lieutenant Louise Miller. Miller was a fair, petite blond from Selma, Alabama, who lacked something of the assurance that Haskell had in abundance. Unlike Haskell and most of the nurses with the 48th Surgical Hospital, Miller had not volunteered for overseas duty, but had been chosen for the assignment by the chief nurse at Camp Wheeler, Georgia. Miller and Haskell had met on the train to New York. The two were a study in contrasts: the one a slight blonde, the other a sturdy brunette; one a southerner, the other a northerner; one hesitant, the other bold. Miller's soft southern accent stood out in stark contrast to the "down east" Maine accent that shaped Haskell's speech. From the moment the two women met on the train ride to New York, Haskell took the more frightened Miller under her wing, and Miller quickly began calling Haskell "Yankee." Becoming friends with Haskell and other nurses in the unit helped calm the apprehension Miller felt during the two-week trip from Georgia to England.

The 48th Surgical Hospital to which these women were attached was a field hospital, and, as such, designed to be among the "forward" hospitals—those hospitals closest to the fighting troops, including battalion aid stations, division collecting and clearing stations, field hospitals, and evacuation hospitals—rather than to the rear where station and general hospitals would be located. Each type of hospital was designed to perform a different function in an evacuation chain that would be set up to get the wounded off the battlefields and into medical care as quickly and efficiently as possible.

The first link in the chain was the battalion aid station. Battalion aid stations would be located close to frontline combat but far enough away to avoid small-arms fire. They were to be manned by battalion surgeons, medics, and corpsmen who were attached to all army divisions. Battalion aid stations were the first places surgeons would be available to wounded soldiers. Only absolutely lifesaving surgery would be performed here, since the main objective of the battalion aid stations was to stabilize and evacuate casualties brought to them by battlefield medics and litter bearers to hospitals farther back from the front.

Next in the chain of evacuation came the collecting stations, located near the command posts of the regiment they supported. Here, collecting companies would change bandages on incoming wounded, adjust splints, administer plasma, and combat shock while preparing the patient for the next step in the chain. Collecting companies would be units indigenous to infantry divisions; each collecting company would consist of a battalion surgeon or assistant battalion surgeon, medics, litter bearers, and vehicles such as jeeps to evacuate the wounded to field hospitals or evacuation hospitals farther behind the front lines.

Clearing stations would be farther back from the front, usually four to six miles behind the collecting companies. Here, medical personnel would triage the wounded, maintain wards for the care of shock and minor sickness and injuries, and transfer men needing immediate emergency surgery to adjacent field hospital platoons.

Field hospitals would be located close to the clearing stations. Personnel would consist of surgeons, nurses, medics, and litter bearers. Regular personnel were to be augmented with auxiliary surgical teams such as the 2nd Auxiliary Surgical Group, who would bring their special skills to the frontline area. Patients were to remain at field hospitals until they were stabilized, a recovery period that could take anywhere from one to two weeks, after which they would be transported to evacuation hospitals farther behind the frontline area. If necessary, field hospitals could be broken into three platoons in order to serve more battle casualties at three different locations near the front. When field hospitals were split, each of the three platoons would then have only six regularly assigned nurses.

Evacuation hospitals were 400-bed semimobile facilities that were to be located approximately ten to fifteen miles behind the front lines. They were to be staffed by, on average, about 40 army nurses and 38 officers, including doctors; 218 medics; and auxiliary surgical teams. Patients could be kept longer at evacuation hospitals than at field hospitals: those soldiers who recovered within several weeks would be sent back to the front, while patients who needed more recovery time were to be sent farther to the rear, to station or general hospitals. A 750-bed evacuation hospital was a larger version of the 400-bed evac, and thus far less mobile. It was to perform the same duties as the 400-bed evacuation hospital but might be five miles farther behind the front lines.

Farther to the rear and even less mobile than the evacuation hospitals were the station hospitals, set up usually in buildings rather than tents, and located thirty to fifty miles behind the front lines. They were to have bed capacities for 250, 500, or 750 patients. These hospitals would receive patients who needed a longer term of treatment than a field or evacuation hospital could provide, but less than 180 days. If a soldier needed more than six months to recover, he was to be sent back to the States.

General hospitals were designed to be completely nonmobile. They were to be set up in buildings containing 1,000 to 5,000 beds and would be located 70 to 100 miles behind the front lines. These hospitals would have larger staffs to deal with the large patient load and would offer specialized care in such varied areas as orthopedic, thoracic, and facial reconstruction.

The 48th Surgical Hospital was divided into three working units and a headquarters platoon. Lieutenant Alys Salter, a tall, dark-haired nurse in her mid-thirties from Pennsylvania, was the chief nurse of Unit 1, and Lieutenant Leona Henry, a quiet, retiring nurse from Camp Tyson, Tennessee, was made chief nurse of Unit 2. Unit 3—the Mobile Surgical Unit—was composed of six teams from the 2nd Auxiliary Surgical Group.

The 2nd Auxiliary was a special corps of surgeons, surgical nurses, and technicians who were not part of any one hospital. The teams were known as "floaters"; they were to move from hospital to hospital as needed. A team usually comprised a surgeon, a surgical nurse, and a corpsman. The teams of the 2nd Auxiliary Surgical Group were made up of ninety-three of the best surgeons in the country and more than sixty experienced army nurses. These teams were to supplement the surgical staffs of forward hospitals, be they battalion aid stations, division clearing stations, field hospitals, or evacuation hospitals.

The six teams of the 2nd Auxiliary Surgical Group attached to the 48th Surgical Hospital were made up of surgeons chosen for their special expertise in various surgical fields. Each of the six 2nd Auxiliary teams had one nurse, and all six army nurses were led by Chief Nurse Lieutenant Mary Ann Sullivan. The 2nd Aux teams were assigned to the specially designed mobile "operating room" vehicle known as the "Commando Truck." The Commando Truck was a regular 2.5-ton army truck with the back section modified to contain a fixed operating table, cabinets, and lights. The truck would be driven to the places at the front lines where it was needed most, then set up with a large canvas tent covering all but the cab. Dr. Kenneth Lowery, a 2nd Auxiliary Surgical Group surgeon from Ohio, commented on the shortcomings of performing surgery in that vehicle in 1943: "Frosty [Dr. Forrest Lowery, Dr. Lowery's younger brother] and I did a sucking chest wound in the truck and found that we were rather cramped for room." But the truck had its merits. "These units have certain advantages," Dr. Kenneth Lowery said, "the chief of which is the rapidity with which it can be set up and put into operation and, likewise, torn down again."[1]

All six nurses with the mobile surgical unit had years of experience in the surgical suites of large city hospitals, but Chief Nurse Lieutenant Mary Ann Sullivan was the only one with experience in treating war casualties. A year before Pearl Harbor, she had volunteered for the Harvard Medical Red Cross Field Hospital Unit, which had gone to England to work with the British wounded. Her year's experience in London and Dunkirk with battle casualties and bombing victims qualified her to serve as the head of the other American army nurses assigned to the Commando Truck.

On 20 October 1942, the 48th Surgical Hospital returned to Greenock, Scotland, and boarded the *Monarch of Bermuda*, the *Santa Paula*, and the ancient and dirty HMS *Orbita*, the three troopships that had been pushed into service to carry combat troops and supporting medical personnel to the invasion site. At the time that these ships set sail, neither the troops nor the personnel of the 48th Surgical Hospital knew where they were headed. The planned Allied North African invasion was a secret; for security reasons, no one was allowed to know anything about battle strategy more than a few days or hours ahead of time.

Now, in the early morning hours of 8 November, the 48th Surgical Hospital nurses waited with combat troops and medical personnel for their turn to go ashore. The invasion was planned as a surprise attack. It was hoped that the troops and the hospital would land on the beach under the cover of predawn darkness without rousing a response from the French barracks on shore. Molony's hand shook as she held her coffee cup that morning not only out of fear but out of surprise: coming from the shore was the sound of artillery fire. With that sound, she and everyone else realized that a battle was in progress. The United States and Britain had hoped that the French would not oppose the Allied landing on the shores of France's colonies of Morocco and Algeria. However, all hopes of an unopposed landing were now dashed.

That the enemy fire from the shore was coming not from the Germans but from the French was a terrible irony. It was not the Allies' declared Axis enemies—the Germans and the Italians—who were fighting the Allied invasion. Rather, it was the French, allies of the British against the Germans earlier in the war, who were now opposing the British and U.S. troops invading the French colonies of North Africa.

But even as U.S. and British troops began their D-Day landings, military commanders were still not sure how France would respond. This uncertainty was due largely to the armistice France had signed with Germany at Vichy in 1940. In that armistice, which ceded the city of Paris to Germany, the French also agreed to defend their North African colonies—Morocco, Algeria, and Tunisia—from invasions by the Allies.

To complicate matters further, France's African colonies contained several groups with conflicting allegiances. There were the "Vichy French" who, like their leader, Admiral Jean Darlan, felt "honor bound" by France's armistice with Germany to oppose any landings by the Allies. But opposed to the Vichy French as well as the Germans were the "Free French," the resistance forces, whose sympathies lay with the Allies. Meanwhile, the sympathies of native Arabs went with any force that might throw the long-hated French colonizers out of their countries. Thus, Arab sympathies generally lay with the Germans rather than the Americans or the British, both viewed by the Arabs as allies of the French.

Another wrench in the works was the fact that the Americans were teamed with the British—a hated enemy of the French since 3 July 1940. It was on that day that British ships carried out Winston Churchill's order to sink the French fleet in the harbors of Oran and Mers-el-Kebir, Algeria. Churchill feared that after France signed its armistice at Vichy with Germany, the French navy—the fourth largest in the world—would fall into German hands, and thus shift the balance of seapower in the Mediterranean dramatically in favor of Germany.

Prime Minister Churchill could not allow that possibility to become a reality. He therefore presented France with four alternatives: (1) the French could bring the French fleet out of North African harbors and join the Royal Navy against German and Italian forces; (2) the French could sail the French fleet, with reduced French crews, to a British port and the French crews would be repatriated; (3) the French could sail to a French West Indian or U.S. port and decommission the fleet there; or (4) the French could scuttle the ships where they lay in Mers-el-Kebir harbor. The French refused to comply with any of these options. Instead, France promised it would destroy its own ships should Germany try to take over the French fleet. Since the British had grave doubts that the French could foil such an attempt, Churchill reluctantly ordered the British navy to sink the ships. In this one action, 1,297 French sailors lost their lives and Britain made a potential enemy out of its former ally.

The British and Americans had tried to secure French cooperation before D-Day. Less than three weeks before the planned Allied invasion of French North Africa, American general Mark Clark was secretly delivered by submarine on the night of 22 October 1942 to a house on the Algerian coast. There, he met with French general Charles Emmanuel Mast, a trusted representative of General Henri Giraud. General Clark's mission was to get General Mast and his French troops to agree not to fight against Anglo-American troops. In effect, General Clark's diplomatic mission was, in Churchill's words, "The battle to have no battle with the French."[2]

Since the French would undoubtedly not wish to cooperate with the British, they had to be made to believe that what was being planned was a total American operation. Therefore, General Clark's first problem was to hide the three British officers who were accompanying him. The three were dressed in U.S. Army uniforms and told not to speak unless absolutely necessary.

Clark's negotiations lasted more than a dozen hours before he

Europe and North Africa,
November 1942

——— Political boundaries, 1937
••••••• German military advance
to November 1942

0   200 Miles
0   200 Kilometers

returned to England to report back to General Dwight D. Eisenhower. The negotiations were inconclusive; Clark had no clear answer from the French to give to Eisenhower. The Allies did not know if the French would attack an Allied invasion of North Africa or not.

Nonetheless, for the Americans, the die was cast. The invasion would take place as planned, with or without the cooperation of the French.

Now, in the early morning hours of 8 November, the invasion fleet lay waiting off the shores of French North Africa. In the fleet were British ships flying American flags, and British commandos wearing American uniforms. Added to this deception was the fact that President Roosevelt and the American military leaders had misled the French in North Africa into believing the impending invasion would take place in France—not Algeria and Morocco—and many weeks later than the chosen invasion date.

Of course, both General Clark and General Eisenhower feared that cooperation from the French would never be forthcoming if the French were to discover the deceptions the United States had perpetrated on them. Fortunately, the deceptions were going undetected by the French legions on shore until, at one minute past midnight on 8 November, the unmistakable voice of President Franklin D. Roosevelt crackled over the radio waves in French North Africa. "We arrive among you," Roosevelt said to the French citizens and troops of North Africa from Washington, D.C., in words that were being simultaneously translated into French, "with the sole object of crushing your enemies. We assure you that once the menace of Germany and Italy has been removed, we shall quit your territories. I appeal to your realism, to your self-interest, to French national ideals. Do not, I pray you, oppose this great design. Lend us your help wherever you can. . . . "[3]

This midnight radio broadcast was the first notice the French received of the Allied invasion force lying off their shores. It could not have come at a worse time. As the president's speech ended, French artillery shells began firing at the U.S. invasion fleet offshore at Oran, Algeria, a city with a population of approximately 200,000 located about twenty miles west of Arzew. Lights on shore were extinguished. French troops in North Africa were definitely opposing the imminent landings.

After a breakfast that was more companionship than physical nourishment, Molony and the other nurses returned to their cabins and crowded around portholes to watch the first waves of Sixteenth and Eighteenth Infantry Divisions board landing barges. The nurses were glad when

Lieutenant Salter stuck her head into individual cabins and told the girls that the commanding officer, Colonel Merritt G. Ringer, had given his permission for them to go to A Deck and watch troops loading into barges from B Deck. "We were to stay on the starboard side and remain out of the way," Molony remembered. It was hoped that having something to do would keep their minds busy and assuage any jitters they were feeling.[4]

Molony followed Lieutenant Ruth Haskell to A Deck's rail, where both leaned forward for a better view of men climbing into landing barges, and barges pulling away from the ship and heading for shore. Haskell adjusted the straps on her field pack as she tried to forget the nagging back pain that had started after she fell from her top bunk during a rough night in the voyage from Scotland to North Africa. Haskell had decided to say nothing about her back injury, and had elicited her cabin mates' promises to keep her fall a secret, since she did not want to take any chance of being separated from her unit and of not taking part in this historic American invasion.

From their new vantage point, nurses watched two barges being loaded. GIs were filing onto one from the iron ladder that swung out from the side of the ship, while others were climbing down a rope net and filling the second barge that waited there. "We all hoped that when our turn came to leave the ship, we'd get to use the iron ladder," Molony said. "It looked a lot more sturdy than the rope net, and with our packs on our backs, we figured it would be easier."[5]

As the barges pulled away from the ship and headed for shore, the GIs, almost to the man, turned and waved to their comrades still on board, then faced forward and disappeared into a smoke screen being laid down by Allied destroyers. Whenever the screen began to grow thin, a small boat from the destroyers would fire special shells into the thinning areas. As the shells hit the water, thick smoke rose into the air and created a new opaque curtain to hide the landing craft.

In less than an hour, Lieutenant Salter appeared again with additional orders. The nurses would go ashore in groups of five assigned to landing barges carrying two medical officers and twenty enlisted men. "The chief nurse cautioned us to wait until the landing barge rose to the top of the wave before we stepped into it from the bottom of the iron ladder," Molony said. "The barge would be as far as eight feet away from the last rung of the ladder when it bobbed to the bottom of the wave trough. We all realized that with our twenty-six-pound packs, helmets, and extra equipment like surgical instruments and bandages that we carried, we were likely to sink like rocks if we missed the barge and went into the sea." Earlier orders to the nurses and men were designed to cover that eventuality. They were to keep the harnesses on their packs and the straps on their helmets unfastened, and leave their shoes untied, so that if any of them fell into the ocean, they could slip out of their weight quickly.[6]

Like the GIs in the first barges to leave the ship, the nurses and men looked back at their fellows still on deck and received a salute from many soldiers before they turned around to face the bow. The smoke screen hid each barge from the others' view, and the thunder of artillery shells overhead, combined with the roar of their own engines, effectively isolated and cut off each barge from the others. The senior medical officer on each barge shouted further orders to the nurses and men, telling them to crouch lower to avoid enemy fire; to exit the landing craft the moment the bow ramp was lowered; to wade ashore as quickly as possible; and to take whatever cover they could find on the beach.

Suddenly, the barge Haskell was in stopped its forward motion, dropped its bow ramp, and GIs farthest forward disembarked into a cold, choppy sea and began wading toward the beach. Haskell was shocked to see tall men disappear up to their necks in the Mediterranean. She watched as two of the shorter nurses in her party followed the soldiers and sank up to their eyes in cold, gray-green salt water. GIs rushed to their aid, one on each side of the waterlogged nurses, and carried them toward the shore until the water was lower than their chest and they could wade the rest of the way.

Haskell and the other nurses shivered as the frigid November wind hit their wet clothes and drove the cold through their skin to the marrow of their bones. Snipers' bullets bit into the sand around them and made pitting sounds as the nurses ran toward a dilapidated beach shack built on stilts about seventy-five yards from the high-water mark. They took cover beneath the shack and waited for their fellow nurses to join them. When forty minutes passed and no other nurses or doctors appeared, Captain Henry Carney, a tall, dark-haired dentist from New York, walked down the beach to look for them. About an hour later, Carney returned with the nurses, doctors, and medics from another barge. "Is that you, Molony?" Haskell asked as the new arrivals joined them under the beach shack. Molony's red hair hung in damp, straight strings. "How'd you get your hair wet?"

Molony laughed as she crouched on the sand next to Haskell. "If you think I look like a drowned rat, wait till you see Friedlund," Molony said, referring to a fellow nurse, Doris Friedlund. "Our barge got off course and overturned offshore about a mile up the beach. We all got dunked, but Friedlund is so short she almost drowned." As Molony spoke the last word, Doris Friedlund crawled under the beach shack, her usually curly hair as straight as a poker.[7]

Haskell and Molony were still laughing when Salter crawled in beside them and said they were to spend the night on the beach. The fighting had moved inland, but French and Arab snipers were still taking potshots at American military personnel. "It's almost 1700 so you might as well go ahead and eat before you turn in. You'll need all the sleep you can get when we start receiving casualties," Salter told the nurses as she left for the headquarters shack about 150 yards up the beach. C-rations appeared from field packs, and in most instances, two nurses shared one can of food since excitement and anxiety had taken the edge off their appetites. A GI brought them a message before they had finished their meal. They were to walk about 50 yards up the beach where another deserted beach shack had been cleared of snipers.[8]

The nurses trudged through the sand to reach the two-room, run-down beach cottage that would be their shelter for the night. After storing their packs and equipment, they went outside in the failing light of dusk to watch the activity at the shoreline. Landing craft infantry (LCIs) were being unloaded in the harbor, and floodlights on shore were aimed at the boxes of supplies held in the huge, dark caverns of the craft to illuminate the area and help speed the unloading process. Heavy equipment was working along the beach, compacting the sand to make driving inland from the shoreline easier. The bulldozers made a continuous, rhythmic clunking sound as they pounded the loose sand into tightly packed roadways for equipment and supplies that were arriving spasmodically and being sent ahead to combat troops five miles inland. Around 1800, as darkness covered the landing site, all lights illuminating the LCIs were extinguished, and blackout conditions were in effect on the beach.

In the last fading rays of daylight, nurses went inside the tiny beach cottage to sleep. The French and Arab forces had used the cottage in their first defense against the invading U.S. Army, and several defending French and Arab soldiers had died there. American GIs had removed the bodies only fifteen minutes before the nurses' arrival. The floor was littered with spent shells, rotting pieces of uneaten food, scattered bloody rags, and empty rusting cans. Human waste had been scraped out of corners that had been used as privies, but the acrid odor of filth and rotting garbage permeated both rooms.

Their clothes still damp from wading ashore, the nurses lay down on the cold tile floor and tried to sleep. Outside, medics and doctors of the 48th Surgical Hospital settled into foxholes for the night. The nurses could hear the sounds of distant combat. Haskell and Molony looked at the night sky through the shards of broken glass and pieces of wooden window frame above and across the room. Momentary flashes of faint light from distant exploding artillery shells cast an eerie, pale greenish light over the dark night sky every two or three minutes. Accompanying the faint flashes of light was the sound of distant artillery fire, like far-off thunder. In the off-and-on weak flashes of light, objects on the beach appeared in vague shades of gray and black. The nurses had no hope of quiet since a GI had told them that the noise and fireworks were the results of American troops fighting twenty miles away to take Oran from French and Arab troops.

About 2330, a soldier awakened the nurses with a message from Colonel Ringer for Lieutenants Ruth Haskell, Edna Atkins, a native of Green Bay, Wisconsin, and Marie Kelly, a New Yorker, to report to the headquarters shack immediately and to bring all their equipment. Louise Miller helped Haskell get into her field pack. "Take care of yourself, you damned Yankee!" Miller said in her southern drawl. The three nurses followed the GI to Colonel Ringer.[9]

Colonel Ringer and Lieutenant Salter greeted the appointed volunteers with grave news. "All hell's to pay up the line," Colonel Ringer said. "And we have to help. The boys at the battalion aid station can't handle the casualties. They're coming in too fast."[10]

Lieutenant Salter gave each nurse a box of morphine surrettes—a premeasured injectable morphine—and a hypodermic syringe. "Goodness knows what you'll find there," Salter said. "But do as good a job as you can, and at least these will help those God-blessed boys if the pain gets too bad."[11]

Haskell, Kelly, and Atkins left headquarters with Captain Henry Borgmeyer, Captain Blackwell Markham, and two enlisted men. They trudged through deep sand in darkness so profound that visibility was almost zero. They had not gone far when there was a whistling sound past their heads, and a GI in the lead shouted for them to hit the dirt. A sniper was trying to pick them off as they hurried through the night to the battalion aid station. One of the enlisted men cursed the sniper under his breath; after a couple of minutes, the group got to their feet and pushed forward in inky blackness.

After another ten minutes, a large, black object took shape out of the darkness. It was the jeep that would carry them the four miles to the battalion aid station. Haskell climbed on board and Captain Borgmeyer practically tossed the two smaller nurses, Atkins and Kelly, in behind her. The jeep started off with soldiers holding Thompson machine guns perched on each front fender, and another posted at the rear. About every mile, a sentry materialized out of the darkness and he and the jeep's driver exchanged passwords—sign and countersign. On that night, the sign was "Hi, Ho, Silver!"—the command the popular radio hero, The Lone Ranger, would give to spur his horse, Silver—and the countersign spoken by the driver was "Away!"

Finally, they reached the outskirts of Arzew, a port city in northeast Algeria where soldiers of the French Foreign Legion had been garrisoned for more than half a century. Gunshots rang out and several bullets whistled past their heads. Another French sniper had them in his sights. Without a word, everyone in the jeep slid lower in his seat as the vehicle passed quickly through narrow streets lined with the dark silhouettes of palm trees. The distant noise of gunfire could be heard across the city— the almost rhythmic sound of one or two shots, followed immediately by a group of three or four shots, like notes played in staccato. The deadly music instinctively brought a sense of dread to doctors, nurses, and medics who would deal with its aftermath.

The jeep came to a sudden stop in front of a high fence. Passwords were exchanged and a gate swung open to admit the medical team to the compound on foot. Before them was a square, squat, three-story building that had been a civilian hospital before the invasion. They groped their way toward the area where a GI said they would find a door. Seconds later, a soldier pulled back a blanket serving as a blackout curtain, opened a door, and led the group into total darkness.

"The first things that struck you were the odors," Haskell wrote later. "The unmistakable odor of filth and dirt, mixed with the odor of old blood and stale ether. There was a suppressed groan here and another there, and then a voice over in the corner: 'May I have a drink of water?' "[12]

A corpsman switched on his flashlight in the pitch-black room and,

for the first time, nurses and doctors saw the rows upon rows of casualties who awaited their care. Young boys in their teens and twenties lay on
litters on the floor with scarcely enough space between them for the medical team to move and care for the wounded. Many of the stretchers had
pools of blood beside them where dressings applied hours ago could no
longer absorb the flow of blood.

The captain in charge told the nurses that they were to assist in surgery, but their first task was to triage—sort the wounded according to
the severity of their wounds, their need for immediate surgical help, and
their chance for survival and return to the front. An enlisted man was
assigned to each nurse to show her from floor to floor, to follow her
instructions, and to take the worst cases to the second floor for surgery.
In the pitch-black darkness, each team of one medic and one nurse
worked their way from man to man on the crowded floor with flashlights
in hand. As the beams of light lit the faces of the wounded, the nurses
could see the men's features contorted, sometimes hideously so, in pain.
Yet, but for an occasional groan, the men made not a sound, and they
voiced no complaint.

The teams of medics and nurses climbed the stairs to the second floor
and found it cold and infested with large rats. Unlike the windows on the
first floor that were covered with blankets, the windows here were blown
out and open to the frigid air of a November night. As Haskell straddled
a stretcher to move farther into the room, a soldier looked up and asked
for water. The only water the nurses had was what they carried in their
individual canteens, approximately one quart each. They had been told
to be careful with it since no other water would be available until a water
point could be established. Without hesitation, Haskell knelt, lifted the
young boy's head, and gave him a drink from her canteen. As he lay back
on the litter, Haskell asked the soldier where he was hurt. There was a
second or two of silence, then the young man's voice cut across the room.
"Holy cow! An American woman! Where in the world did you come
from?" The boy appeared to be about nineteen or twenty.[13]

The young boy's surprise touched Haskell. "Yes, Sonny!" she said.
"An American woman, a nurse. And there are more than fifty of us over
here to take care of you and your buddies." The young soldier had a bullet wound in the soft tissue of his groin and the dressing had not been
changed because of the high number of casualties. Bits of dirt and shreds
of his trousers were all buried deep in the wound. Large clots of blood

oozed from the edges of the bandage. Haskell told the corpsman that this man should be taken to surgery immediately, and moved on to the others who still needed her attention.[14]

When she had triaged everyone remaining on the second floor, Haskell moved to the third, where she discovered that Atkins and Kelly had already completed their tasks and were standing by the stairs, talking. Haskell joined the conversation; all three nurses agreed that they had never seen anything in any civilian hospital to compare with the casualties they had been treating over the last thirty minutes. Arms, legs, and abdomens had been slashed open, muscles, tendons, and intestines lay spilled on bloodstained stretchers where American soldiers waited their turn for surgery—injuries resulting from hand-to-hand combat in the Allied effort to take Oran from defending Vichy French and Arab troops. Even the worst injuries of accident victims brought into city emergency rooms could not compare with the wounds of combat the women were now seeing. The most seriously wounded were waiting on the second floor for surgery and the three nurses hurried there to help.

As they entered the makeshift operating room, Captain Borgmeyer was rolling up his shirtsleeves in preparation for surgery. Improvisation would be the byword here. Equipment and furnishings were all but non-existent, since 98 percent of the 48th's personal and medical equipment was still aboard ships in the Arzew harbor. The small percentage that had reached the landing site was either soaked with seawater or stranded somewhere along miles of beach. An improvised operating table was set up in the middle of the room and a droplight with a twenty-watt bulb hung above it. Blankets covered the one window in the room in an attempt to keep all light inside. The French had turned off the water to the city before the Americans entered Arzew, and a single rusty spigot that dribbled water into a small hand basin served as a scrub sink where alcohol was used in place of soap and water. A large wooden crate became a stool for the acting anesthetist; one small sterilizer worked by burning alcohol; one scalpel, a handful of surgical clamps, and one pair of surgical scissors were the team's only surgical instruments. There were no surgical gowns, gloves, drapes, or masks. The only thing the medical team had in great supply were casualties—and their own knowledge and skills.

A soldier with a bayonet slash on the inner side of his upper arm was the first patient placed on the OR table. When the arm was flexed at the elbow, the brachialis muscle popped in and out of the wound as if it were designed to do just that. Lieutenant Kelly and a corpsman cut the sleeve out of the patient's shirt and that constituted this soldier's preoperative care.

Fifteen minutes into surgery, the twenty-watt bulb burned out and flashlights provided the only light. A corpsman kept a light focused on the surgical field while Kelly worked as a scrub nurse. She kept her lighted flashlight fastened to the band of her trousers in order to free her hands to work as best she could with the few instruments and tiny sterilizer. There was no anesthesiologist or anesthetist, so Haskell volunteered to administer ether. She had not given anesthesia for years, but neither had anyone else on the medical team. As the hours wore on, Haskell's small hands, unaccustomed to the task of holding the lower jaw in order to keep the airway open and unobstructed when using inhaled ether, became tired and cramped. Captain Carney, the unit's dentist, took her place at the head of the table, and she moved to other OR duties in order to give her hands a rest. After an hour, Haskell relieved Carney, who planned to relieve her every ninety minutes, as long as his services were not needed as an oral surgeon.

Haskell had just sat down on the wooden packing crate to once again take over administering anesthesia when the door opened and Atkins entered to ask Captain Borgmeyer a question. The opened door caused just enough of a breeze to blow the blanket covering the room's only window. In that split second, a shot rang out and Haskell automatically ducked just as the bullet ricocheted off the wall directly behind her. The silence in the room was broken by the curses of the medical personnel trying to save the patient's life. The staff made a series of angry remarks about the sniper, who had just fired into the operating room again even after the window was completely covered. Finally, two quick shots sounded outside, followed by the thud of a heavy object hitting the ground. Word reached the team that the sniper was dead. "I wouldn't have believed it possible to get so much positive exaltation as I did over the death of that sniper," Haskell remembered later.[15]

At 0430 on the morning after they had landed on the beach and four and a half hours after Haskell, Atkins, and Kelly had arrived at the battalion aid station, the last surgery was completed. They then began making rounds of the hospital to see how their patients were doing. A large number of patients still needed surgery, but their conditions were stable and they could wait until sunrise, when the OR teams would have more light to help them operate. New casualties were still arriving, as fighting in Arzew and Oran on D+2 continued.

The corpsmen seemed to have everything under control on the first two floors, so Haskell went immediately to the third floor to see if she could be of help there. "A rat the size of a rabbit scampered past me," she remembered. "Then I heard a low moaning from one corner of the room and I went to investigate. The beam of my flashlight fell on the face of a young boy whose entire left cheek had been blown away. He had also suffered a fractured leg and wounds of his abdomen."

At first Haskell thought she was going to cry as she knelt down next to this critically wounded soldier. Even with the massive facial wound, she could tell he had been a handsome boy. His dark blond hair was wet and sticky with blood; his dark blue eyes looked frightened and the pupils were large and unequal. "I'm going to give you a shot for the pain. In fifteen minutes you should start feeling better." She looked at the two loops of the boy's intestines that were lying outside his body and wondered if they could save him here with so little surgical equipment. She brushed the hair from the young man's forehead. "I'm going to try to move your broken leg to a more comfortable position and then will get you downstairs to surgery." The soldier reached out and squeezed Haskell's hand, and smiled with his eyes as if to say thank you. Haskell felt a warm tear escape and make its way slowly down her cheek.[16]

What young men like this soldier—sons of women like herself—were doing today, had done last night, and would continue to do until the final victory was won, Haskell knew would help ensure the gift of freedom for her own son and countless generations not yet born. For the young soldiers who would never return home, children such as Haskell's ten-year-old son, Carl, would be their spiritual progeny. The freedom for which these men would pay dearly, even with their lives, would be their legacy to the future.

As Haskell moved away from the badly wounded soldier, she stopped to steady herself against the doorjamb of a room she had not noticed on her earlier trip to the floor. She opened the door to make sure there were no wounded inside who needed her help.

Before she could step inside, the strong odors of blood, feces, and decay assaulted her nostrils. In that same instant, the beam of her flashlight fell on the room's inhabitants. A surrealistic tableau loomed before her. Lying on the floor in grotesque positions, arms and legs reaching into the darkness, were the dead bodies of Arabs, French soldiers, and several American boys. She had entered the makeshift morgue where casualties brought in dead had been placed until the firing let up and they could be identified and buried. Haskell swayed as she closed her eyes, leaned against the door, and fought to control a rising wave of nausea. She jumped as a man's hand came to rest on her shoulder and a soft voice cut across the stillness. "Come away from there, ma'am. You don't need that, after the kind of night you put in in surgery." It was the tall young corpsman who had worked with her all night; he led her gently out of the room.[17]

Haskell returned to the second floor and sent two corpsmen to bring the young boy with half a face downstairs for immediate surgery. Then she sat down, weary and heartsick, on the steps, leaned her head against the wall, and dropped off to sleep. Twenty minutes later, her corpsman awakened her. "Come on, miss, there are several new casualties in from the front. Guess we're needed again."

On their way to the OR, Haskell asked if the soldier with the blown-away cheek was in surgery. "No, ma'am. He was dead when we went upstairs to get him." Haskell thought of the terrible morgue she had entered by mistake, and knew that the handsome soldier was now part of its grotesque tableau. She forced herself to think of those who might still be saved.[18]

Everyone on the medical team was busy throughout the morning. They had been working steadily for more than fourteen hours, and on a brief break between patients Haskell wondered why no one from the 48th Surgical Hospital had shown up to relieve them. Finally, at 1400, twelve nurses from the 48th reported to the battalion aid station and took over for Haskell, Atkins, and Kelly. They were told by their replacements that doctors and nurses were quartered in the old French barracks a half-mile away, and they could go there to get some sleep. The three women met Captain Carney at the door, and he led the small group toward their new home. They had not gone far when enemy planes swooped down and strafed the area. Carney shouted for the nurses to follow him into a trench that ran alongside the road. They had no sooner landed and ducked for cover when the unmistakable odor of human excrement enveloped them. To their great disgust, they realized the trench they were in had been used by Arabs as a privy. While they waited uncomfortably for the planes to leave the area, they learned that the beach shacks where they had stayed after the landing had been severely strafed that morning by Italian planes. Luckily, the rest of the 48th's personnel had moved out twenty minutes earlier.

Finally, the planes left and Haskell's group climbed out of the trench and continued toward the French barracks, now occupied by the U.S. invasion force. Formerly housing for officers of the French Foreign Legion, the old building was divided into medium-sized rooms. Five nurses were assigned to each room. Despite the fact that there were no cots or bedding, Haskell, Atkins, and Kelly, exhausted from fourteen hours of caring for severely wounded troops, curled up on the dirty floor and fell fast asleep.

Back at the battalion aid station, Helen Molony and the eleven nurses who had taken over the old civilian hospital were discovering the special hazards of a makeshift hospital set up without supplies to clean out filth and control rats and vermin. Within the first fifteen minutes of reporting for duty, fate stepped in and changed Lieutenant Molony's assignment in the unit. As she walked down the hallway, she stopped by the open door of the makeshift operating room. "I looked into the OR and they were working on a soldier with two compound fractures of his leg. The leg was elevated and the wounds were wide open," Molony remembered. "All of a sudden, the nurse giving anesthesia fainted, and I caught her before she hit the floor. Before I could revive her, the surgeon shouted, 'You come in here and take her place.' I followed orders and that's how I became part of the surgical unit." Molony had worked in maternity in civilian life, but she took to her new duties as if the OR were where she had always been.[19]

Added to these critical conditions was the lack of medical and personal supplies to treat and feed the more than eighty casualties crowded into a building designed by French standards to hold a maximum of seventy-five. Necessity, the mother of invention, forced the nurses and doctors to find creative emergency solutions. "We had a young soldier on the table when we ran out of suture material," Molony said. "One of the nurses got a spool of white thread from her musette bag and they sewed up his bladder with that." Before supplies arrived, long strands of nurses' hair would also stand in for sutures. The hair was soaked in alcohol and used when nothing else was available.[20]

Compounding the problems created by lack of surgical supplies and equipment was the dire need for food and water for the wounded men. Ships in the harbor were still being fired on and were unable to unload their supplies for troops on shore. The only food available was the three days' rations carried in nurses' and corpsmen's field packs. The nurses pooled the food and fed patients who could tolerate beans, hash, or beef stew, and distributed drinking water from their own canteens. Feeding the patients was a slow process. There were only five plates and five spoons in the hospital, and nurses had left their mess kits in the French barracks since C-rations did not require their use. There was no water to wash plates and spoons between patients, so they wiped them with a cloth and used them again until all patients who could eat C-rations had been fed.

Even more pressing than the shortage of food was the rapidly dwindling supply of narcotics and sedatives. Doctors and nurses administered the meager supply as best they could, but it was clear that soon there would be no medications to relieve their patients' pain. This knowledge only added to the distress medical personnel felt at seeing patients lying on bloody litters on filthy floors, covered by blood- and vomit-stained blankets, still dressed in as many of their combat clothes as possible. Even postoperative patients who had undergone chest or abdominal surgery were redressed in their filthy combat clothes. Clothes and dirty blankets were the only protection the wounded had from the frigid November weather. For one patient—a soldier with a spinal cord injury who had lost all feeling below his waist—extra protection was needed. His doctor ordered the posting of a guard at night by the young man's litter to prevent hungry rats from eating the flesh from the patient's legs.

Temporarily bivouacked nearby was the 38th Evacuation Hospital, which had landed late in the day of D+1. The 38th Evac staff, who would not go into operation until two days later, on 11 November, when the unit would move to the Saint-Cloud area, loaned the 48th Surgical Hospital essential equipment and whatever supplies they could spare. The 48th also borrowed from British and U.S. Navy medical units located within a reasonable radius.

On 10 November, after the 48th Surgical Hospital received its first shipment of newly wounded, it was decided that the 2nd Hospital Unit at the civil hospital would care for all critical, nontransportable patients. What had been a battalion aid station would become, then, a hospital for the critically wounded. All other less severely wounded would be moved to the 1st Hospital Unit of the 48th, which had set up a hospital the day before in one of the single-story, whitewashed buildings of the captured French barracks nearby. In the French barracks, a nurse discovered a warehouse filled with the blue capes and red sashes that were part of the French officers' uniform. The nurses decided to use the capes as bedding for themselves on the floors of their rooms, and to stack them on wooden frames of beds found in some of the barracks to afford their patients a little more comfort.

French snipers were still active in the area and they fired shots into the hospital wards at the barracks day and night. On the afternoon of the 10th, Lieutenant Evelyn Hodges, a comely, dark-haired nurse from South Carolina, with a soft southern accent and a sharp Irish temper, was on duty in one of the wards when two bullets whistled past her head. It was the last straw for Hodges, who was appalled that there were soldiers who did not respect the Geneva Conventions. "The very idea!" Hodges shouted, and headed for the door. "Don't they know there are patients in here?" One of the corpsmen grabbed Hodges and pulled her to the floor a split second before a bullet ripped through the wood where her head had been.[21]

In its first forty-eight hours at Arzew, the 48th Surgical Hospital, with little food and water and using improvised and borrowed equipment, cared for 480 casualties.

ABOUT TWENTY MILES west of Arzew lay the city of Oran, the second site in Algeria where Allied troops landed on 8 November 1942. When, on 11 November, the French ceased fighting and surrendered both Oran and Arzew to the Allies, ships carrying the 77th Evacuation Hospital arrived offshore. Because the harbor at Oran was completely blocked by sunken French ships that had been attacked by the British on 3 July 1940, the Allied troopships continued to the port of Mers-el-Kebir, about fifteen miles west of Oran. At Mers-el-Kebir harbor, nurses of the 77th Evac climbed onto trucks and were driven to Oran while medical officers and enlisted men hiked the fifteen miles. The nurses arrived at the civilian hospital in the city and found conditions as bad as those that had greeted the nurses of the 48th at Arzew.

They also found that Oran was a city of paradoxes. From a distance, it looked clean and beautiful. The white stucco houses with their red-tiled roofs clung to the terraced hills that made up the city; minarets and steeples dotted the area like exclamation marks. The inhabitants wore flowing, colorful robes of blue, beige, gold, green, and burgundy. Up close, the picture was not so pretty. The white stucco became dingy gray, and most of the robes and turbans that looked colorful and romantic from a distance were ragged and smelled of unwashed bodies. Bands of Arab children, disheveled and insistent, followed American soldiers begging for *"chocolat"* or *"cigarettes pour Papa!"*

The nurses of the 77th Evacuation Hospital entered Oran's largest civilian hospital to find civilian patients and war wounded lying side by side about the halls and rooms on litters, dirty blankets, or piles of discarded clothing. Patients suffering from dysentery and contagious diseases were placed beside seriously wounded American soldiers. A few wounded French and Arab troops were scattered among the Americans. In accordance with the Geneva Conventions, army nurses gave these men the same medical attention they gave their own troops.

Meanwhile, back at Arzew, on 13 November, two days after the French surrender of Oran and Arzew to the Allies, the 48th's supplies finally arrived, and nurses and corpsmen scrubbed the hospitals and barracks with brushes and GI soap. Dirty blankets, French capes, and the stained and tattered clothes of the patients were thrown out, to be replaced with GI cots, clean blankets, sheets, pillows, pillowcases, and pajamas. Within two days, the hospitals even began to smell good, and engineers had hooked up generators and electric lights that added greatly to the morale of patients and staff alike.

With the surrender of the French to the Allies, French and Arab wounded prisoners of war also had to be cared for in the hospital. The POWs presented several problems, the first of which was security: arrangements had to be made to guard them. A French POW physician was allowed to care for French prisoners, but he too had to be watched closely. Another problem in dealing with the POWs was the language barrier: these casualties arrived at the hospital with medical papers and evacuation tags written in French. Translators became a necessity on the wards and anyone who spoke and read French took on a new aura of importance. The 48th's nurses considered themselves fortunate to have as chief nurse Lieutenant Theresa Archard, who was not only fluent in French but had traveled widely before the war.

Archard, then in her mid-thirties, was born and raised in Massachusetts. She joined the U.S. Army Nurse Corps in January 1941, answering the call of her local Red Cross Chapter. She had signed up for a year and, on 4 December 1941, just before Pearl Harbor, was looking forward to returning to civilian life when her year of service was up in just five weeks. She had planned to get her new Ford Coupe out of storage and head out to explore Arizona and the Yosemite Valley in California. The last place she expected to find herself in November 1942 was in a hospital near the front lines. Archard had not intended to go to war when she signed on with the army and had declared so in writing. "I had signed on the dotted line that, in the event of famine, floods, fire or other disaster, I would be available for duty," Archard wrote later. "War was there too, but I had crossed that out. No war for me. I didn't believe in war."[22]

Yet when Archard left for her first assignment at Camp Shelby, Mississippi, in January 1941, she recalled feeling a strange sense of foreboding. She had left home before for trips to Europe, South America, and the West Indies, but never with any sense of dread. Her foreboding only increased when she saw Camp Shelby in its first days, a tent city in an ocean of mud, with all the chaos of a three-ring circus auditioning acts for the first time. Her fears proved to be prescient when America was attacked at Pearl Harbor. On 11 December 1941, Germany and Italy declared war on the United States and a notice was posted asking nurses to volunteer for overseas service. Archard still thought war insane, but as an American whose country had been attacked, she placed her name on the list for overseas duty.

She had already thought of her mother's likely negative response to her being shipped to a combat zone and had her answer ready. She encouraged fellow nurses to give the same reply to any family opposition to their upcoming overseas assignments. They would say that they had *not* volunteered (although the majority of them had), but rather that they were GI (government issue) and the army could send them anywhere it wanted.[23]

Archard's orders had brought her to French North Africa—a land of deserts, daytime heat that reached 130 degrees, and nighttime cold that chilled to the bone. It was a far cry from Yosemite Valley and the deserts of Arizona, but she was 100 percent sure that this was where she was supposed to be, and completely dedicated to saving the lives of sick and wounded soldiers.

DURING THE LAST weeks of November, bags of U.S. mail arrived in Arzew, providing troops and medical personnel with that all-important contact with home. Lieutenant Haskell was looking forward to receiving at least one letter from all the mail brought in, but as it turned out, she was pleasantly surprised that twenty-eight letters were addressed to her, and the one on top of the stack was from ten-year-old Carl.

A soldier who had been wounded in his leg asked Haskell if she would share some of the "not too personal" mail with him, and she gladly agreed. Of course the best thing would have been for the soldier to get his own word from home, but in a pinch, all news from the United States was welcomed by its sons and daughters. Sharing mail with one's buddies became a regular ritual for Americans fighting overseas.

December 1942 opened with heavy rain and deep mud. Engineers provided crushed gravel to spread on the roads inside the hospital compound and in the hospital and barracks area. Despite the weather, nurses moved out of the barracks and into tents in order to get away from the fleas, bedbugs, and roaches that still inhabited the old buildings. The general feeling among the women was that "it's better to shiver than scratch."

By this time, fighting had moved six hundred miles to the east, as the Allies moved toward their objective, the ports of Tunis and Bizerte in Tunisia, to meet the imminent German threat. The first German forces had landed at an airfield in Tunis, the capital of Tunisia, on 9 November 1942. By the end of November, there were more than fifteen thousand German and fourteen thousand Italian troops in Tunisia, with the sole mission of stopping the advance of American and Allied forces on Bizerte and Tunis, two coastal cities that were ideal for the launching of an Allied invasion of Europe.

With American troops moving swiftly east to Tunisia, the only Americans remaining in Arzew by late November were the 48th Surgical Hospital personnel and patients, engineers who were unloading ships in the harbor, and the First Ranger Division. Colonel Ringer was transferred to command a large hospital in Oran, and Lieutenant Colonel Chester J. Mellies took his place in Arzew as the CO of the 48th Surgical Hospital. The First Ranger Division had returned to Arzew toward the end of November and was stationed near the nurses' barracks. Rangers were appointed to escort nurses the three blocks between the nurses' quarters and the hospital, to and from duty. "There would be a Ranger in front with a rifle, four nurses following him, and a Ranger with a rifle behind the nurses," Molony said.

The Rangers went beyond the call of duty in protecting the 48th's nurses from any possible invasion by an outside force. "The engineers couldn't get in to see the nurses because the Rangers were guarding all gates and wouldn't allow engineers or any other men in to visit with us," Molony recalled. "So we were dating all the Rangers and they were just great."

Molony remembered one Ranger in particular. He was a big, hand-some man who stood a head taller than the five-foot-nine nurse. "He was beautiful and he called me 'little girl.' No one had ever called me 'little girl' before."[24]

Christmas was on its way. Hostilities in Arzew had ceased for the moment as the front moved east. Patients were getting better, and there was more off-duty time. Medical personnel now no longer working eighteen to twenty-four hours a day actually had time for recreation, walks on the beach, and sight-seeing. On or about 28 November, doctors, nurses, and corpsmen organized a sight-seeing trip to Oran. They piled into 2.5-ton trucks for the twenty-five-mile trip to Oran, but before reaching Oran they stopped to visit Sidi-bel-Abbès, the headquarters of the French Foreign Legion. Their first stop was a tour of the historic buildings the legion used for offices. Most of the furniture had been handmade by legionnaires, and large glass cases in the hallways displayed one of each type uniform worn by its members since the legion had been established by Louis-Philippe of France in 1831 to help control French colonial possessions in Africa.

The nurses talked with several of the French officers who were used to shifting alliances, and discovered that most spoke several languages, English included. After the tour of headquarters, three officers showed the Americans around town. Despite the orange trees that lined the roads, and the olive groves and mountains in the distance, Sidi-bel-Abbès was not welcoming to American and Allied troops. Some of the French civilians explained that most of the town's population was pro-Nazi and not happy to have Allied forces on their soil.

The staff of the 48th Surgical Hospital finally reached their destination of Oran later that morning. Unlike the 77th Evac's impression of Oran, the 48th's personnel thought the inhabitants seemed much friendlier. The warmer welcome and beauty of the white houses and apartment buildings clinging to the terraced hillside overlooking the bay seemed inviting.

When the nurses and doctors returned to Arzew that night, it was with a renewed dedication to make Christmas in Arzew one they and their patients would long remember. "One of our nurses came up with the idea of making Christmas stockings out of all the red serge they found in the warehouse in November," Helen Molony remembered. "I think it was Lieutenant Archard's idea to use the red serge and white sheets together so we could make more stockings to give to the troops.

We sewed by hand every chance we got and ended up with more than seven hundred red and white stockings to give out on Christmas Day."[25]

During the first ten days of December, the First Ranger Division was transferred from Arzew to Tunisia, and now with the Rangers no longer guarding the nurses' barracks, the engineers wasted no time in visiting and dating the army nurses. The engineers were quartered in a large nearby house and Molony and two other nurses asked their dates to show them through it.

The house was clean and warm and Molony mentioned what a contrast it was to the nurses' tents. The young man excused himself, ran upstairs, and returned with a bedroll given to him by a naval officer. He explained that he had never used it since the house was warm and comfortable and insisted that Molony accept and use it as her own. She slept in the bedroll for three nights before the young engineer showed up wanting another date. Molony did not want to date him so she insisted on returning the bedroll. Since nurses used a lot of perfume to cover up a lack of soap and water for bathing, three nights in the pretty redhead's care had changed the bedroll forever. "I couldn't sleep in that now," the young engineer said as Molony handed it back to him. "I can smell your perfume and I wouldn't sleep a wink."[26]

As Christmas drew closer, the Red Cross director in Oran provided candy, cigarettes, and a small individual present to stuff into each stocking. This still left Christmas decorations and a tree that would be needed for the traditional Christmas they envisioned thousands of miles away from home. With the help of two or three corpsmen who used old plasma cans as raw material, they cut out ornaments of angels, stars, and snowflakes, using shears and pliers as artists' tools. One patient, who had been an art teacher in civilian life, used paper to fashion candles, holly, and Christmas greetings. He painted them, and when they were hung up in the wards and main lobby of the hospital, they looked so real they almost gave off warmth and shed leaves. Everyone was in the Christmas spirit and eager to add to the celebration.

"Somehow our supply officer came up with enough peanuts, milk, sugar, and chocolate to make more than four hundred pounds of candy," Helen Molony recalled. "Lieutenants Archard and Salter got us nurses to make fudge, peanut brittle, and taffy whenever we were off duty. We had a regular candy factory going for a while. It was a lot of work, but it was also fun."[27]

As their part of the celebration, the corpsmen in the X-ray department provided the heavy tinfoil that was packed around X-ray plates, and nurses and corpsmen cut long strips of foil to decorate the fir tree several GIs managed to supply as their donation to the 48th's Christmas.

On Christmas Eve, midnight mass was held in the foyer of the civilian hospital, which seemed specially constructed for the occasion. Directly across from the front door was a broad set of approximately twelve steps leading to a wide landing. On either side of the landing, a set of stairs led to the second floor. Corpsmen and nurses had decorated the entire area in preparation for Christmas services. Sheets had been draped over the staircase wall and a large cardboard cross, four feet high, was hung in the center of the landing wall and covered with purple bougainvilleas that nurses had hand-sewn into place. Enlisted men with the 48th Surgical Hospital had made the altar under the cross, and the candelabras on it; spotless white hospital sheets covered the altar. Palm trees had been placed on each side of the altar, and floral bouquets sat behind the two candelabras.

Nurses had invited everyone—troops, patients, officers, and enlisted men—to attend mass and a small party with cookies and cocoa that would follow. Litter patients who wanted to attend were placed up front near the altar, while ambulatory patients filled the foyer before mass began. No one could resist second and third glances at the Christmas tree set up to the left of the main door and decorated with handmade ornaments and the tinfoil tinsel made from the heavy foil donated by the X-ray department.

At 2400, the Catholic chaplain, Lieutenant John J. Power, went to the foot of the altar and began midnight mass. The male choir, composed of Catholics, Jews, and Protestants, began singing "Silent Night," and American and Allied soldiers thought of Christmases at home.

"On Christmas morning, Captain Henry J. Carney, dressed in a Santa suit Lieutenant Archard had made by hand, gave out the Christmas stockings we had all worked on," Helen Molony remembered. "The men were like little boys. You would have thought Santa had brought them the bikes they had always wanted. Just the right brand and just the right color."[28]

For many soldiers, it was the first of too many Christmases spent away from home. For the majority, it was the most memorable Christmas they would ever spend. But for some, it was the last Christmas they would ever see.

CHAPTER TWO

Nurses at the Battle of Kasserine Pass

IN IT ALL THE WAY

January–February 1943

It is still disturbing to recall how unprepared our nation was for war and the lack of knowledge that was displayed by the officers of the regular Army Medical Corps about the conduct of other wars. . . . The laboratory for the testing of ideas in World War II was the North African–Mediterranean Theater, not only in medicine and in the care of the wounded, but also in many of the tactical operations.

—*Col. Edward D. Churchill, MD, surgical consultant,*
North African–Mediterranean theater, Surgeon to Soldiers

THE CHRISTMAS celebration the 48th Surgical Hospital and its patients enjoyed in Arzew in 1942 was but a brief lull in the storm. Soon after, the 48th was ordered to move farther east to Constantine, Algeria, to be closer to the troops at the front lines.

The 750-mile trip to Constantine was miserable. It began ten minutes after midnight on 15 January 1943 at Arzew, and ended more than two days later in the darkness of a cold night at a bivouac area outside Constantine. To Lieutenant Helen Molony, it seemed like the middle of nowhere. After arriving in Constantine by train, the 48th Surgical had boarded trucks and wound up the mountains to the bivouac camp outside the city. Climbing down from the back of the British lorry that had carried them from the train station, Molony and her fellow army nurses strained to see through the total blackness, without any success. At

2,000 feet above sea level, the night air was bitterly cold. Bone-tired and freezing, the nurses gravitated into several large groups, drawn by body heat and a shared desire to get warm.

Constantine was not the nurses' final stop; they were headed into Tunisia, where Allied troops were battling the Germans. The capture of Tunisia was the main objective of the Allied invasion of North Africa. The tiny country, only 500 miles long and 150–200 miles wide, contained port cities on the Mediterranean ideal for a future Allied launch into Southern Europe: Tunis, the capital of Tunisia, and Bizerte. Of course, the Allies were not going to reach their objective unopposed: on 9 November 1942, the day after the Allied invasion of North Africa, German troops, led by General Jurgen von Arnim, landed at an airfield in Tunis. They met no French or Arab opposition and set out immediately to counter the Allied advance into Tunisia.

By the end of November, there were more than fifteen thousand German troops in Tunisia, and thousands more were on the way from Libya and Egypt, as Field Marshal Erwin Rommel's forces retreated from the British Eighth Army commanded by General Bernard Law Montgomery. Montgomery had been fighting the Germans in Egypt since 1940, and had finally succeeded in late 1942 in routing Rommel's troops and forcing them to flee to Tunisia.

In addition to German and Italian opposition, Allied troops were challenged every step of the way by an Arab population that aided the Germans whenever possible, and by a rugged terrain of jagged mountains, steep hills, and mine-filled valleys. The weather also proved to be an enemy; when the rainy season began in December, roads and ground turned into thick gluelike mud that mired men and equipment. Conditions were so bad that on 24 December Allied leaders called off any further offensives until the end of the rainy season.

By the second week in January 1943, fighting had resumed in earnest, and it was clear that American and Allied combat troops would need hospitals close to the frontline troops. It was for this mission that the 48th Surgical Hospital had undertaken the two-day trip to Constantine and would continue on into Tunisia.

Now, on the night of 17 January, Molony and the other nurses of the 48th stood in the French Foreign Legion Park outside Constantine. The darkness was so complete they could not see their own hands in front of their faces. Had they not heard the sudden sound of a British soldier's voice, seemingly from nowhere, the women would have thought they

*Nurses of the 48th Surgical Hospital with Protestant chaplain in North
Africa, 1943* (Courtesy of Jesse Flynn)

were alone in the darkness. Shortly thereafter, a second—and this time,
familiar—voice cut through the darkness and across the nurses' muted
conversations. "We'll be here for a night or two at the most," said
Colonel Chester J. Mellies, the 48th's CO. "We'll be moving up front as
soon as possible, in order to support the boys of the First Division.
They're expecting more and heavier fighting against the Jerries and all of
us will be needed." Mellies told the nurses that the 48th Surgical Hospital had received orders to head for Tebessa, an Algerian border town
close to the front. "We'll be moving out," Mellies continued, "so we can
provide better care to troops scattered over a forty-mile area. For now,
we'll take you to your tents so you can get some sleep. I'm sorry your
bedrolls haven't arrived yet, but the boys will get them to you as soon as
they come in."[1]

The nurses' eyes had adjusted to the darkness enough to see the
nearby shapes of large objects. Molony and the others followed the nearest silhouettes across a field that seemed strewn with natural and man-
made obstacles. People stumbled and turned their ankles as they stepped
into shallow holes and tripped over rocks and tent ropes.

The tents provided little warmth against the cold mountain air and,
without bedrolls, sleep would not come easily even to the exhausted.

Molony was pleasantly surprised when Ruth Haskell asked if she
wanted a drink of Scotch to help her warm up. "Sure," Molony said. "But

where in the world did you get Scotch?" Haskell explained that it belonged to Louise Miller and that an air corps friend had given it to Miller before Haskell and Miller got on the train in Oran. The Scotch helped a little, for a short time, but was no real match for the frigid night air. Nurses cuddled two on a cot but there was no way to beat the cold. After midnight, most were walking around inside their tents, stamping their feet and rubbing their arms. Finally, a GI's voice called into their tents to tell them that the bedrolls had arrived. GIs helped nurses carry the bedrolls indoors and place them on their individual cots. Nurses unrolled the bedding and climbed in, clothes and all. In fifteen minutes, sleep blanketed the nurses' tents.[2]

The next morning, as sunlight took the chill out of the air, the nurses began to take stock of their surroundings. The bivouac area was at the top of a high hill that overlooked the ancient city of Constantine stretched out below them. The city had been named for the Roman emperor who had made Christianity a state religion in the fourth century A.D., and the small white stucco houses clinging to the almost perpendicular hillsides reminded the nurses of a scene out of *Tales of the Arabian Nights*. "It sure looks beautiful from here," Ruth Haskell said as she stretched in an attempt to lessen the pain in her back. "Let's ask Lieutenant Salter if we can visit the city and look around."[3]

Thirty minutes later, groups of nurses, each accompanied by a male officer, made their way into the city over the Kantara Bridge. The bridge spanned a deep gorge through which a fast-moving river roared hundreds of feet below. The bridge swung from side to side as the sight-seers made their way across and into Constantine itself. "One misstep on that bridge, or on the cliffs of that city and you'd have been a memory," Molony recalled. "We were told that in the days before the French took over, Arabs would take an unfaithful wife to the highest point and give her a shove into eternity."[4]

The city seemed cleaner than Arzew or Oran; the Arab inhabitants also appeared better fed and clothed than those the nurses had seen when they first arrived in North Africa. In the three hours the colonel had given them to look around, the nurses passed shops that had a few pieces of jewelry and souvenirs for sale, but food or clothing could not be purchased inside the city. As usual, the Germans had cleaned out the town, taking anything they wanted or might find useful.

A little after 1600, the nurses recrossed the Kantara Bridge and climbed the many steps carved into the hillside to where their hospital was bivouacked. After the evening meal, a large group of the 48th was sitting on the ground talking when they heard the sounds of marching feet and male voices speaking in foreign languages. Molony and Haskell walked to the edge of the hill and looked down on a long double column of bedraggled soldiers climbing the steps. "They don't look so good," Molony said. Colonel Mellies walked up behind her and peered at the column. "They're German and Italian prisoners being taken by our allies to the French garrison," he said. Just then, several of the prisoners realized that they were being watched. Italian soldiers grinned, waved, and threw kisses in the nurses' direction, while German POWs glanced stone-faced, then looked away.[5]

As the first prisoners reached the top steps, French guards halted them, and an American enlisted man who spoke Italian went over and talked with a group of prisoners. The conversation, interspersed with much laughter and gesturing, went on about ten minutes. When the captives moved on, Haskell and Molony asked the GI why they were laughing. He explained that the Italians were very glad to be POWs and out of the fighting. "They're tired of being hungry and doing the Germans' dirty work," the young man said. "One of them asked me for a Lucky Strike in perfect English. The guy's from Brooklyn. He was visiting relatives in Italy when the war broke out and they drafted him into the Italian army."[6]

That night of 18 January, the colonel told the nurses that they should start sewing a large cross out of sheets so it could be displayed on the ground near their hospital as they moved up to the front lines. "The Germans have respected the Geneva Conventions so far, so the large cross should offer some protection for us and our patients."[7]

The nurses began sewing fifty-four sheets together. They worked in teams of two, each sewing from an end and meeting in the middle. The cold turned fingers purple and the hours of sewing made fingertips sore and sensitive. The frigid weather and the order for total blackout conditions which forbade a fire or even a candle led Lieutenant Theresa Archard to place a request with the hospital quartermaster for long underwear for the nurses. Nurses in her 2nd Unit had begun to develop bad colds and Archard was determined to get them what was needed to keep warm and healthy. At the same time, she requested shoes for herself, size 7AAA, since the soles on her oxfords were now paper-thin.

Captain Charles A. (Chuck) Ebbert, the hospital's supply expert, delivered an answer to her three hours later, along with a pair of men's shoes that were the closest they had to her size—7EE. He brought three pairs of men's socks with the suggestion that maybe if she put on all three at the same time, she would be able to wear the extra-wide shoes. His news about the long underwear was not as good: there was none to be had. He would keep looking, but he couldn't promise anything. Archard told the nurses they would have to continue wearing the pink-and-blue and pink-and-green pajamas they had purchased in England several months earlier layered underneath their clothing.

Archard followed Captain Ebbert's advice and wore three pairs of socks with her new shoes. Since the water supply was at a minimum—a cupful each day for bathing and laundry—she rotated the layers of socks and allowed herself to think of each new layer as clean.

On 19 January, an advance party from the 48th Surgical Hospital left for Tebessa to set up tents in the wooded hills eleven miles south of the city. This party was assisted by an Allied reconnaissance team that had been instructed to camouflage the nurses' tents and vehicles. The men had taken their orders to conceal the tents to heart, knowing that German fighters and bombers would be combing the area. The 48th Surgical Hospital did not arrive at the camp south of Tebessa until after nightfall on 20 January. The nurses could not possibly have guessed to what lengths the reconnaissance team had gone to hide their tents; in the darkness of night, they could not see anything.

Just as Helen Molony was wondering if the nurses and truck drivers were the only people in the area, a male voice with a distinctly British accent boomed out of the blackness. The voice got closer and Molony could make out a dark silhouette. "If you think you're the only people here, ladies, it's because we've done a great job with camouflage," the soldier said. "Your tents are up ahead and there are already two other hospitals bivouacked here." Everyone agreed that they would have to take this Tommie's word for it, since they could not see any signs of a camp. After being led to their tents, the women set up their bedrolls on cots and turned in for the night.[8]

About 0800 on 21 January, with daylight filtering into the tent, Lieutenant Molony turned on her right side without opening her eyes. She reached down to pull the blankets of her bedroll up over her shoulders and discovered that her blankets were not within arm's reach. She rolled onto her back and felt a small, pointed rock digging into her flesh. "What the hell!" Molony said, opening her eyes and sitting bolt upright. Her eyes caught the corner of her cot above her right shoulder and she looked around the tent in disbelief. Nurses in various stages of awakening were scattered on the rocky ground without the benefit of their blankets. Gravity had taken over during the night, and the women had slipped gradually out of their bedrolls, off their cots, and onto the ground without awakening.

Molony got to her feet and stuck her head through the flaps of the tent. "I don't believe it," she said. "They must think we're mountain goats!" The troops had pitched the tents at an almost forty-five-degree angle against the side of a steep hill and, in morning light, fifty-seven disgruntled nurses were complaining vociferously about the location. Colonel Mellies ordered that the tents be taken down immediately and repitched on more level ground. Three hours later, a happier group of nurses made their way to the chow line and ate like "little pigs."[9]

On Saturday afternoon, 23 January, while the nurses talked and waited in the chow line, a young soldier with the First Infantry Division whom the women had last seen in Arzew materialized over the crest of the hill and walked toward them. A dozen nurses recognized him at once. "Jamie!" they shouted. "How did you get here? Are the rest of the boys with you? Are they okay?"[10]

Yes, Captain William E. Jamison ("Jamie") answered, some of the boys were with him, and yes, they were all okay. The division was reorganizing for a new offensive, and that allowed the men some free time. Of course, Jamie knew few details about the upcoming new offensive because, as usual, for security reasons neither troops nor hospitals were informed about any battle plans or strategic details. Both groups got their orders and information on a strict need-to-know basis only.

And certainly no one knew of the German battle plans that would soon lead to the tremendous defeat of the Americans and British at the now-infamous Battle of Kasserine Pass. In the coming weeks, Field Marshal Erwin Rommel would attack the Allies from southern Tunisia, while General von Arnim would attack from the north, crushing the Allies in a pincer movement at Kasserine Pass—a break in the western Dorsal Mountains and a corridor between Algeria and Tunisia where military vehicles and troops could pass through the mountains and cross the border.

During early January 1943, the Allies had begun moving troops into the Tebessa area. The First Armored Division and the Thirty-fourth Infantry Division, recently arrived from England, were added to the II

Corps. The First Division had traveled from Oran, Algeria, where it had landed during Operation Torch. The Allies had moved Major General Lloyd R. Fredendall's headquarters to Constantine, Algeria, closer to the front lines. American and Allied troops were guarding mountain passes in the eastern Dorsal Mountains, a mountain chain running north-south, paralleling the eastern coast of Tunisia for about two hundred miles. Consequently, the medical support units, including the 48th Surgical Hospital, were moving in the same direction. The medical battalions were organic to the combat units: the 51st, 1st, and 109th Medical Battalions, the 16th Medical Regiment, and the 2nd Medical Supply Depot had accompanied the troops to the front lines. The 9th and 77th Evacuation Hospitals and the 48th Surgical Hospital completed the American medical support for the Allies, and likewise were moving into place.

As Jamie spoke, Lieutenant Ginny Ayres, the primary reason for his visit, rushed toward him. They had started dating in Arzew, and it was clear to everyone who knew them that "these two kids were head-over-heels in love." They exchanged a brief kiss and stood arm-in-arm. When Jamie heard that the 48th had moved closer to the front to support his outfit, he decided to use his free time to find the hospital and spend some time with Ginny. He visited for about an hour while he ate lunch with Ginny and the others. When he left to rejoin his unit en route to its ultimate destination of Tunis, he promised to visit again as soon as he could.[11]

That night, Chief Nurse Lieutenant Salter called the girls of the 1st Unit—including Molony and Haskell—together and told them to get their things packed and to be ready in the morning. Their unit would travel by truck in a British convoy on its way to the front lines near Thala, in Tunisia, in support of Jamie's unit and others who would spearhead the upcoming attack. Thala lay approximately thirty-five miles northeast of Tebessa, about twenty miles inside the Tunisian border.

For the 1st Unit, the trip to Thala would take about fourteen hours, due to the narrow, winding roads, with a ten-minute rest stop every two hours, and a thirty-minute break for a lunch of C-rations. Salter smiled and singled out Ginny Ayres. "Don't look so stricken. At least you got to see Jamie today. That's a lot more than the other girls got." She said goodnight and reminded them to be on time in the morning.[12]

On 24 January, Lieutenants Helen Molony, Ruth Haskell, Genevieve Kruzic, Margaret Hornback, Glenna Whitt, and Louise Miller, along

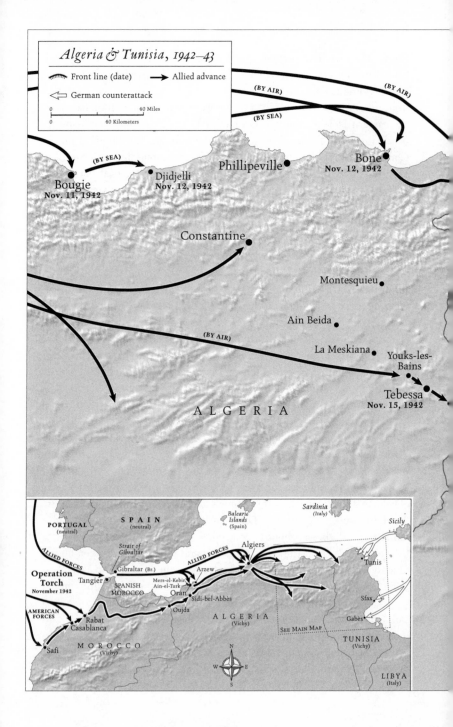

Algeria & Tunisia, 1942–43

Front line (date)   → Allied advance
⇐ German counterattack

0   40 Miles
0   40 Kilometers

(BY AIR)   (BY AIR)

(BY SEA)

Bone
Nov. 12, 1942

Phillipeville

(BY SEA)   Djidjelli
Nov. 12, 1942

Bougie
Nov. 11, 1942

Constantine

Montesquieu

Ain Beida

(BY AIR)   La Meskiana   Youks-les-
Bains

Tebessa
Nov. 15, 1942

A L G E R I A

PORTUGAL
(neutral)

SPAIN
(neutral)

Balearic
Islands
(Spain)

Sardinia
(Italy)

Sicily

ALLIED FORCES

Operation
Torch
November 1942

Strait of
Gibraltar

Gibraltar (Br.)

Tangier

ALLIED FORCES

Algiers

Tunis

AMERICAN
FORCES

SPANISH
MOROCCO

Mers-el-Kebir
Ain-el-Turk

Arzew

Oran

Sidi-bel-Abbès

Sfax

Rabat
Casablanca

Oujda

A L G E R I A
(Vichy)

SEE MAIN MAP

Gabès

Safi

M O R O C C O
(Vichy)

TUNISIA
(Vichy)

N
W   E
S

LIBYA
(Italy)

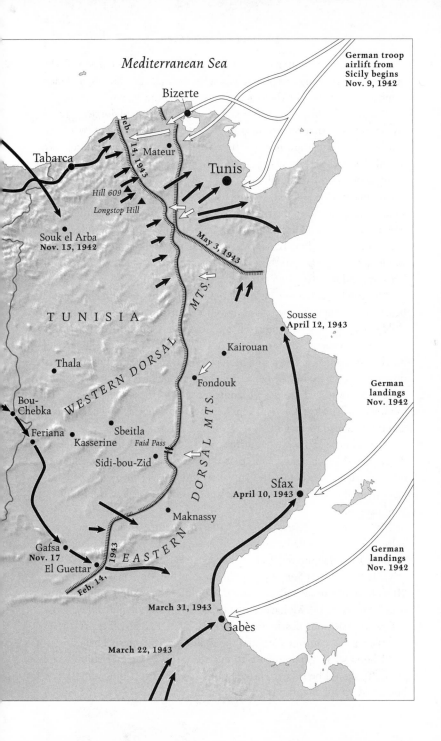

with Chief Nurse Lieutenant Alys Salter, loaded into one truck near the beginning of the long line of vehicles. The other officers, nurses, and men climbed into the rest of the trucks that made up the convoy.

The British officer in charge moved along the line of lorries, giving last-minute instructions to the group. He reminded the members of the convoy that they were going into a very dangerous zone where they would need to be constantly vigilant for enemy planes. The safety of the group depended on each individual being aware of his surroundings. If an enemy plane were sighted, the first truck would stop, the driver would signal with his hand to the truck directly behind him, and so on down the line. Everyone would leave the trucks immediately, run to the side of the road, and hit the dirt. Lunch was planned precisely at noon, and they would not eat again until they reached their destination. He said, "Good-bye now, and may God be with you."[13]

The trucks pulled out onto the highway one by one and the convoy began its journey. The vehicles moved forward like the segments of a child's toy snake, wrapping itself up, down, and around the many hills and wadis (valleys) that comprise the face of northeast Algeria and northwest Tunisia. Lieutenant Molony had asked for and gotten a seat next to the tailgate in case her childhood tendency to carsickness should return. She watched the desert landscape as the truck rolled along. The bumpy conditions of the road kept anyone from catching up on lost sleep and time seemed to drag by.

After almost an hour, the nurses could see a large walled city ahead. They passed a sign announcing that the place was Tebessa, the Algerian city just a few miles before the Tunisian border. The convoy stopped outside the walls while a British soldier went inside to speak with headquarters' personnel.

"What kind of place is Tebessa?" one of the nurses asked. Lieutenant Salter answered immediately and, as always, Molony and Haskell were surprised and delighted with the knowledge Salter carried around so quietly. "It has a lot of religious significance to the Moslems," Salter said. "It's off limits to all military personnel unless they're on official business." She added, "We have about thirty-five mountainous miles to go before we reach our destination at Thala." The British officer returned and the convoy continued around the walled city and on to Thala.[14]

"I hope we're getting close to our rest stop," Doris Friedlund said later. "It should be soon," Haskell said. "We've been riding almost two hours." As if on cue, the truck leading the convoy pulled to the side of the road and stopped. The truck carrying the nurses drove ahead about fifty yards, stopped, and a British soldier lowered the tailgate. "I don't see a gas station," Molony quipped and looked down the road where scores of men were lined up with their backs toward the nurses. "There's not even a bush to hide behind." They milled around for a couple of minutes trying to figure out how thirty nurses dressed in coveralls were going to answer nature's call in the middle of a wide-open, treeless desert, in view of so many GIs about a half a football field away. Lieutenant Haskell came up with a solution: Four nurses held four army blankets up by the corners to form an enclosure for the others. It worked fine, and they planned to use it for all other rest stops.[15]

Once on their way again, the trucks climbed steadily. In time, they passed through areas where large bomb craters and parts of wrecked airplanes marked the sites of earlier combat. A little farther along, they passed an airfield where several American planes lay: twisted hulks, surrounded by scattered pieces. Ten GIs were swarming over the wrecks, salvaging usable parts as replacements for other damaged planes that would fly again into battle.

In another forty minutes, Haskell and Molony spotted long, round metal objects sticking out of the ground about twenty feet from the road. They were equally spaced on both sides of the highway. As they got closer, the women could see that the metal objects were actually small visible portions of U.S. antiaircraft guns which had been dug into holes up and down the road. In a country where roads were few and far between, this strip of highway was very valuable for troop and equipment transport. As the trucks passed by the guns, the nurses could see the helmeted heads of American soldiers down in the holes with their artillery pieces. Their job was to keep the road intact despite attacks by German planes bent on destroying it.

As the nurses' truck passed the first two or three gun emplacements, the men on the ground realized it was carrying women; they climbed out of their holes and whooped, hollered, whistled, and waved. The nurses, now grown accustomed to this attention, smiled, waved back, and blew kisses to the troops.

A mile or two ahead, they could see American engineers working to repair the one railroad track that ran out of Tebessa. The Germans wanted desperately to cut the transportation lines bringing American and Allied troops to the front, and it was up to these artillerymen and engineers to keep those avenues open. All along the sides of the road, behind, between, and around the large guns, Arabs grazed their herds of sheep and goats as if the soldiers were invisible and death was not a bomb or bullet away.

Near dusk, as the nurses watched the convoy snaking along behind, they noticed British Tommies taking the covers off machine guns that were mounted on the truck cabs. "Why are those men taking the covers off the guns?" Kruzic addressed her question to Chief Nurse Salter. "This is a particularly dangerous time of day," Salter replied in a matter-of-fact tone. "German pilots love sunrise and sunset because they can drop right out of the sun and be on top of a convoy before they're sighted. The men are just preparing for any eventuality."[16]

Molony felt a shiver pass through her body. She appreciated Salter's honesty, but the facts only added to the tension she already felt. Like most of her fellow nurses, Molony had faced and worked through the possibility of her death in a combat zone. "If you get hit, you get hit," Molony recalled her feelings. "If you didn't get hit, you thanked goodness. But you knew all the time that you could be killed. You're in a combat zone all the time, and people get killed in combat zones."[17]

As darkness fell, it brought colder temperatures, and despite layers of clothing, the women felt chilled to the bone. In the failing light, the sounds of artillery rumbled in the distance and grew louder as they neared their destination. U.S. First Division forces supported by the First Armored Division of the II Corps were assaulting General von Arnim's German troops near Kairouan Pass about sixty miles east of Thala. Suddenly, the trucks seemed to be climbing a vertical cliff and the road was filled with holes and large rocks. They had entered the foothills of the western Dorsal Mountains.

"Now I know what a milkshake feels like!" Molony said as the nurses were bounced in all directions. Finally the trucks stopped, the tailgates were lowered, and thirty tired and hungry army nurses jumped to the ground and scanned the area as best they could in nighttime blackout conditions. They were glad to hear Major William E. Proffitt Sr.'s voice, since he was with the advance party that had gone ahead to set up the hospital and tents for the personnel. "Are you girls hungry?" he called. One of the nurses shouted, "We'll eat almost anything!" A murmur of agreement rose from twenty-nine famished women.[18]

Major Proffitt warned them that not even a flashlight could be used this close to the front lines and the deep clanking sounds of tanks moving forward underscored his words. The tents were widely dispersed and the cook tent was on a hill about three quarters of a mile away. With their mess kits filled with hot food, they sat down on the cold ground and ate every bite. There was no milk or sugar for the coffee, but it was hot and much appreciated for the warmth it brought to the cold night.

When they finished their meal, the nurses were directed down the hill and up another where their tents were waiting. GIs had already carried the women's bedrolls inside and were busy putting cots together outside in the pale moonlight. Molony and others pitched in and helped assemble the cots, and by about 2130 they were digging holes inside their tents for the two legs of their cots that were on the high side of the hill. "We leveled the cots as best we could since no one wanted a repeat of the roll-out we slept through at Tebessa on our second night," Molony remembered.[19]

The next morning, nurses stumbled outside and searched for the latrine. Next, they looked for the water tank to refill their canteens, and found that it had been hidden behind a large bush. The cook tent had also been successfully camouflaged and nurses followed the sounds of male voices, Sergeant Roberts and his crew, since they knew their presence meant food.

WHILE THE 1ST UNIT of the 48th Surgical Hospital was setting up at Thala, Lieutenant Theresa Archard and the nurses of the 2nd Unit left the Tebessa area by truck convoy on 27 January, headed for their new hospital site. They arrived in Feriana, Tunisia, about forty miles southeast of Tebessa. They were to set up a hospital in an old one-story French barracks.

Archard and her nurses were not looking forward to the assignment. Their first experience with the filthy French barracks and hospital in Arzew led them to expect the worst. Instead, they found these barracks "cleaner than a hound's tooth." German troops had occupied the buildings and had been forced to withdraw in much too big a hurry to do significant damage. True, there were swastikas, ribald comments about American soldiers, and proud German boasts daubed on the walls, but Archard would take that any day compared to the dirt and garbage they had had to clean out in Arzew. There were holes in the roofs, every single windowpane was broken, the stoves did not work, and the weather was cold, but enlisted men and engineers could remedy the situation with cardboard, blankets, and American ingenuity.

On 1 February, the 48th's 1st Unit closed, packed, left Thala, and rejoined the 2nd Unit and mobile unit at Feriana. Doctors, nurses, and corpsmen of both units received casualties from the First Armored and II Corps. The next day, headquarters for the First Armored Division opened at Sbeitla. American and Allied troops continued their drive to a ridge east of Sened, about fifty miles south of Sbeitla, and dug in, in preparation to repel a German attack by the main body of Rommel's troops. The battle was fierce and resulted in many casualties. Hospital personnel were not told the details, but at the high rate that troops and equipment were being sent forward and badly wounded soldiers were being admitted to the hospital, Archard and the others figured they had better be ready for anything.

In their first couple of days at Feriana, twenty-five nurses of the 2nd Unit and six from the Mobile Surgical Unit (the 2nd Auxiliary Surgical Group teams) shared one entire building that was in close proximity to airfields. With all good intentions, Captain Woolbine and a few men of the 16th Medical Battalion built a large fireplace in the center of the nurses' barracks. But the fireplace never did draw right, and apart from smoke and beautiful dancing flames, it gave off little actual heat. GIs nailed the nurses' pup tents over the glassless windows to meet blackout conditions and keep as much wind as possible out of the building. On 2 February, several of the nurses took the time to spread out the large cross they had hand-sewn in Constantine on the ground in front of the barracks.

Less than an hour passed before their good intentions caught the attention of a senior Army Air Forces officer. He entered the barracks shouting at the top of his lungs: "Who the hell put that white cross on the ground out there?" Archard was quick to tell him that Colonel Mellies had ordered them to sew the cross several days ago so it could be used in the field. She felt sure the officer did not know anything about the use of the Red Cross to mark an area as a "safe" hospital zone, but his next statement took her completely by surprise. "I don't know much about the Geneva Conventions," the officer said. "But I do know that what you put out there is no Red Cross. It's a big white cross and a white cross on the ground like that means an airfield is under construction. I ordered some men to take it up and to destroy it. You're lucky you didn't get us killed!"[20]

Archard and the rest of the hospital personnel were dumbfounded. How had Colonel Mellies made such a mistake? Why had the army not supplied them with the correct Red Cross flag to display? The logical conclusion that flashed through Archard's mind was very unnerving.

Most likely, the U.S. Army did not know any more about the Geneva Conventions than Colonel Mellies or the nurses. Being the first and only surgical hospital in the field—the prototype for all others that would follow—definitely had its drawbacks. The 48th Surgical Hospital and the U.S. Army in general were learning hard lessons from their first invasion outside the Pacific. Archard prayed that those who followed them would not have to learn the hard way.

Adding frustration to the nurses' dismay was the realization they would have to hand-sew the proper Red Cross symbol all over again. This time, Archard did some checking on her own and determined that the Red Cross needed to be 100 feet square, with a large red cross in the middle of a white flag. She did the mathematics and told the nurses to start sewing forty sheets into a cross and to back it with 100 yards of unbleached muslin. The enlisted men would paint the center cross bright red. The everyday routine of sewing by hand began all over again.

That same day, Allied forces, including the First Armored Division and the 168th Infantry of the Thirty-fourth Division, attacked the scrubby little town of Sened's railroad station. The tactical importance of Sened's station rested with its location. Sened was the entryway to the southwest corner of the central plain of Tunisia; it also contained the station where several major rail lines converged. Since the Germans were using the railroad as a major supply line, the Allies wanted to gain control of this major station. In addition, the American and Allied troops were fighting their way forward along the route of this railway, all the way to Maknassy, about twenty miles northeast.

The Allies succeeded in capturing Sened railroad station and the troops advanced to within ten miles of Maknassy by noon on 3 February. However, that night, the Allied advance toward the Tunisian coast was stopped and reversed; American troops were ordered to withdraw back through Sened to the town of Gafsa, about twenty-five miles west. It was the opening phase in a series of battles that would soon make the front pages of newspapers throughout the world.

On 4 February, the 1st Unit of the 48th Surgical Hospital closed and moved equipment and personnel back to Thala in response to troop movements on the front lines.

At the 2nd Unit of the 48th Surgical Hospital at Feriana, the 2nd Auxiliary Surgical teams had set up their own operating room. Ten medical officers, led by Lieutenant Colonel John Snyder from Pennsylvania, six surgical nurses led by Lieutenant Mary Ann Sullivan from Boston, and fifty enlisted men worked day and night. They were accepting the most seriously wounded, while other casualties needing surgery went to the unit's operating room, overseen by Lieutenants Amy Nickles and Marie Kelly. The two nurses kept "Maudie," the unit's one sterilizer, working around the clock. Lieutenant Archard insisted that all of the 2nd Unit's nurses rotate on duty in the operating room so that if anything happened to the operating-room nurses, the hospital would not be left without these specialized nurses. She took her orders one step further and made sure that each nurse could perform any other nurse's duties. It was one way to ensure that if any nurse were wounded or killed, those remaining could perform her job.

All of the nurses were relieved when the large Red Cross flag was finally finished and stretched out on the ground between the barracks. Remembering their painfully cold, needle-pricked fingers while sewing the first large white cross, they all agreed that, if anything happened to this flag, they would rather take their chances with German bombs than have to sew another.

In the midst of running a two-hundred-bed hospital with additional patients arriving every day, Archard was confronted with a contentious new problem. Surgeons in the operating room began using sterile equipment as if they were back home at the Mayo Clinic. One surgeon used twenty-four sterile towels in a simple debridement procedure—the surgical removal of dead or damaged tissue from a wound to promote healing. Nurses were working around the clock, after their regular ward duty, to keep the hospital supplied with sterile goods. This was no easy task: the hospital laundry consisted of three fifty-gallon GI cans placed on a homemade firebox—a hole dug in the ground, with several rocks and diesel oil thrown in. The clothes and linen were boiled but no attempt was made to remove the stains. Nurses began to hoard sterile supplies for the wounded and resented doctors' cavalier use of the precious materials.

Archard, always looking out for her nurses, decided that something had to be done. She knew she would not be popular with most of the surgeons for her actions, but she had never been concerned with popularity contests. Archard confronted Colonel Mellies with the situation over sterile supplies, and the colonel went directly to the surgeons. There was no more waste of sterile goods, and when things calmed down, Archard reasoned with the offending surgeons that they could rest when their tour of duty was done, but nurses and corpsmen did not have that luxury, since they were responsible for the physical maintenance of all supplies as well as patient care.

At this time, the 2nd Unit received its first gas gangrene patient. Gas gangrene had been an enemy of combat soldiers throughout history. The spores of the bacteria that cause it (*Bacillus Welchii*, now known as *Clostridium perfringens*) live in soil and infect open wounds. Once in the human body and within the tissue of an injured arm or leg, these bacteria multiply rapidly. Tiny bubbles created by the bacteria form in the damaged muscle and press on small blood vessels, stopping oxygen-carrying blood from nourishing nearby tissue. The lack of oxygen causes necrosis—death to that tissue. Within seventy-two hours, the bacteria release a toxin that travels along nerve pathways to the spinal column and then the brain, causing death to the infected person. Historically, the only treatment available to doctors was amputation of the affected body part. If done in time, this drastic measure would stop the process before the lethal toxin could spread and bring death to its victim.

The gas gangrene patient was an Italian soldier, and his leg needed to be amputated. Since the bacteria that cause gas gangrene can contaminate an operating room and spread to other patients, a separate tent, set up by Lieutenant Amy Nickles, was erected right outside the operating room for the procedure. Following the amputation, the POW was placed in a separate area and a nurse or corpsman stayed with him around the clock. The second gas gangrene patient was an American soldier, also requiring an amputation of his leg. After the operation, he too was placed in the isolated area with the Italian POW. Both patients had been wounded near Sened in a cultivated olive grove where animal fertilizer had been used. These were among the first of thousands of wounded soldiers who would be treated for gangrene before the end of World War II.

In the midst of caring for hundreds of battle casualties, nature presented the hospital personnel with another challenge. That night, a wind- and sandstorm hit the hospital, driving sand into the wards and blowing down several tents. Archard and the others rushed about to see that patients were moved to safe places. The force of the sand hitting their unprotected skin felt like tiny pieces of broken glass as they groped in the darkness to relocate patients. The next morning, all wards had to be thoroughly cleaned again, but nurses and corpsmen were grateful for the temporary lull the sandstorm provided in the arrival of new casualties.

On 10 February, General Ernest M. Cowell, the British director of medical services, visited the hospital to see how the personnel were caring for so many wounded. Lieutenant Archard escorted General Cowell around the hospital, explaining the setup, the types of casualties, and answering his questions. As he was leaving, General Cowell asked Archard if there was anything she needed that he might supply. "Long underwear!" Archard said. "All the nurses would be happy if they could get a set of long underwear to help protect them against the cold. If I give you the nurses' sizes, maybe you can get them for us." Thirty minutes later, Archard delivered the list and General Cowell said he would see what he could do.[21]

Archard forgot about her request until two days later, when Colonel Richard T. Arnest, U.S. Army II Corps surgeon, arrived at the hospital with fire in his eyes. "What do you mean by requesting long underwear from the British?" Arnest demanded. "If you nurses wanted long underwear, you could have had it long ago!" "That's what you think," Archard retorted. "I've been trying to get long underwear for those girls since we were in Arzew. The supply officer says it's impossible." She pulled out the collar of her pink-and-green pajamas from under her uniform. "We've been wearing the pajamas we bought in England months ago."

"I'll see that you get all the clothing you need, but don't ask the British for anything else. It makes us look bad," Arnest said. He stormed off without waiting to hear another word.[22]

The next day, Scripps-Howard news correspondent Ernie Pyle and Eliot Elisofon of *Life* magazine turned up at the hospital to gather information for a story. One of the nurses came to Archard with the message that both men wanted to talk to her. "I'm much too busy to bother with newspapermen," Archard snapped and went about her duties. Both men wrote stories about the medical personnel and patients at "a surgical hospital on the North African front," but neither got to speak with the principal chief nurse.[23]

On 14 February, Valentine's Day, all hell broke loose in Tunisia. At 0400, German forces began their first major offensive against American and Allied forces approximately seventy-five miles from Gafsa at Faid Pass—the one opening in the eastern Dorsal Mountains where troops and vehicles could pass from the coast to the towns inland. Two full battle groups of the German Tenth Panzer Division, including sixty-ton Tiger tanks, were making their way from the east through Faid Pass. Coming at them through the pass from the west were inexperienced American troops with comparatively lightweight Honey tanks that seemed like toys compared to the German Tigers.

Colonel John Waters ordered fifteen Honey tanks into Faid Pass to block the advancing Tigers. The tall, poorly armored Honeys with their 37-millimeter "popguns" were doomed from the start. The German Tiger tanks were armed with 88-millimeter guns that could target and explode the Honeys before the Honeys were even within range to hit the massive Tigers. Even the German Mark IV tanks were better armored than the "cracker box" Honeys, and they carried a 75-millimeter gun that also outdistanced the Honey's 37 millimeter. A single shell into, or glancing off, the Honey's rear sprocket would turn the tank into a fiery coffin. The five-man American crew would scramble as fast as they could to escape the flames, but many who were lucky enough not to die inside the blazing furnace escaped with massive second- and third-degree burns. If they managed to survive the critical days following their injuries, they faced weeks, months, and even years of skin grafts and reconstructive surgery. The wounded were taken to the 48th Surgical Hospital at Feriana.

At Thala, word got around the hospital fast. The boys of the First Division, whom the nurses had known since their landing at Arzew, were fighting up ahead and the hospital was already receiving the first casualties of those battles.

Just before 0700 on 15 February at Thala, Lieutenant Haskell reported to her ward tent for duty, and was told by her corpsman, Corporal Krist, that they had received several wounded tankers. He gestured toward a young second lieutenant and Haskell decided to begin her rounds with him. The soldier was holding one hand under his lower back and appeared to be in considerable pain. "What seems to be the trouble, fella?" Haskell asked. The young man assured Haskell that he did not have a scratch on him, and that he had simply hurt his back getting out of a tank that had been hit and had caught fire. A couple of his boys had been badly hurt and he asked Haskell to check on them. He nodded toward the other side of the tent and asked Haskell to let him know how they were doing.[24]

Haskell walked in their direction, stopped short, and closed her eyes for several seconds. A young soldier lay on the cot before her. The entire surface of his face and chest had been severely burned. The wounds had been treated with sulfadiazine ointment and left uncovered. Through a whitish, greasy layer of medication, the red and black charred second- and third-degree burns looked raw and painful. In the bed next to him was his fellow crewman. This young man's right arm was severely burned

and horribly disfigured. He was trying to strike a match and light a cigarette with his one good hand. Haskell took the match from his hand and
lit the cigarette. The soldier grinned. "Well, where did you come from?"
the young man asked. "It's not such a bad war after all." Haskell smiled.
"Is there anything I can get you?" she asked.[25]

Both of them knew it was a horrible war.

After Haskell made her rounds of the ward, she returned to the young
officer she had spoken with first. He appeared to be asleep, but as she
started to walk away, he reached out and clasped her hand. "How are my
boys doing?" Haskell said they were doing okay. "They're great boys,"
the second lieutenant said. "But there aren't many left after yesterday."
Suddenly he winced as if in great pain. "Where do you hurt?" Haskell
asked. When he did not answer, she rolled him over and rubbed his back
with alcohol. As her hands moved over his lower back, the soldier stiff-
ened. Haskell could imagine his pain since it was in the same area as her
own back injury, and like this soldier, the pain had stopped her in her
tracks a time or two.[26]

Captain Louis G. Kingston, a tall, thin physician from Vermont,
entered the ward tent and walked directly to Haskell and her patient. "A
runner from the battalion aid station just arrived. There are about fifty
more casualties coming to us," he said in a calm, quiet manner. "We'll
just fill all the wards and evacuate them to the rear as soon as we can."
The doctor turned his attention to the lieutenant with the back pain
whom Haskell was taking care of. After examining the young officer and
diagnosing a ruptured vertebral disc, he ordered the young man's back
strapped with adhesive tape. This done, Haskell gave the wounded man a
sedative and he drifted off to sleep.[27]

Haskell and Kingston made the rounds of the tent, then stepped outside for a cigarette.

"And how's your back?" Kingston asked.

"My back, sir?" Haskell asked. Kingston went on to say that he had
known for some time that Haskell's back was giving her trouble and that
when they had time he wanted to examine her. "Sure, sir," Haskell
responded. "As soon as we have time."[28]

As they finished their cigarettes, ambulances began arriving at the
receiving tent, and an hour later all cots were filled and the surgical tent
was operating nonstop. Nurses and corpsmen worked continuously,
changing dressings, giving injections, setting up traction, and applying
plaster casts to broken limbs. When Haskell stepped outside to get sev-

eral rocks to use for weights in traction setups, she could see rows of wounded soldiers lined up on litters along the ground, awaiting their turns in surgery. Several corpsmen were going from patient to patient giving plasma to help ward off shock.

The Germans had scored a victory against the Allies at Faid Pass. In just two days after the German attack on Valentine's Day through the pass, the U.S. First Armored had lost 44 tanks, 59 half-tracks, 26 artillery pieces, and 22 trucks. Two days before the attack, the U.S. 168th Infantry of the Thirty-fourth Division had had a strength of 189 officers and 3,728 enlisted men; by the evening of 15 February, they had 50 officers and 1,000 enlisted men left.[29]

AT 2030 on the fifteenth, First Sergeant Loren Butts (chief administrative enlisted person), a six-foot-tall, sandy-haired soldier from Terra Haute, Indiana, answered the phone at Unit 2 at the hospital in Feriana. The call relayed belated orders for Unit 2 of the 48th Surgical Hospital to retreat: all patients were to be evacuated to the 9th Evacuation Hospital, forty miles to the rear. After evacuation of the patients, the hospital was to close its doors and retreat to Bou Chebka, a town on the Algerian border. The call only confirmed what hospital personnel had already begun to suspect: American troops were beating a retreat from the Germans at Faid Pass. "Traffic—trucks, artillery and tanks—had been going the wrong direction past the hospital for the last hour," Sergeant Butts remembered. "Our orders were to evacuate casualties and follow the retreat as fast as we could move. Just getting ready took hours."[30]

At this point, Butts overheard a discussion between Colonel Mellies and several doctors. "They were afraid that we couldn't take all the patients and would have to leave some behind," Butts recalled. "A doctor and several corpsmen volunteered to remain with the patients, even though they realized it would mean capture by the Germans. In the end, we were able to take all the patients and no one had to stay behind."[31]

Finally, at ten minutes past midnight on 16 February, the convoy was loaded and ready to move out. "I was driving the lead car in the column and Colonel Mellies and a major were riding with me," Butts said. "The road from Feriana to Bou Chebka was very narrow and pockmarked with bomb and shell craters. We were under strict blackout conditions and the only lights on our vehicles were cat-eye slits that gave just enough light to see the vehicle ahead of you. It was a really scary ride. We hadn't gone far when we met Sherman tanks coming down the middle of the road in our direction. They were trying to get to the front, and I was trying to avoid getting run over by staying to the far side of the road. Finally, after the moon went behind some clouds, I couldn't see anything at all and I had no idea where I was.[32]

"In utter desperation," Butts went on, "I switched on my headlights for about five seconds. Just long enough to see that we were about fifteen feet from the edge of a cliff, and to get cursed and yelled at by tank drivers because I had broken blackout conditions. If I hadn't turned my lights on when I did, I could have led our hospital column over a hundred-foot drop. I believe God must have had a hand in my timing even if the tank drivers didn't like it." Butts smiled. "It's one midnight ride I'll never forget."[33]

On 17 February at Bou Chebka, before a single patient could be admitted, the 2nd Unit was again ordered to withdraw further yet to the rear, to Youks-les-Bains in Algeria, another thirty miles to the rear. There, they set up and handled nine hundred patients by midnight.

MEANWHILE, in Thala, the 1st Unit of the 48th Surgical Hospital was inundated with battle casualties and newly wounded were still arriving from the battles at Faid Pass and Kasserine Pass, collectively known as the Battle of Kasserine. Nurses and corpsmen were working twelve- and fourteen-hour shifts, getting only a few hours' sleep, and returning to duty on the overflowing wards. The OR was running continuously.

As Lieutenant Haskell made her way toward her tent on the night of 15 February, a new and severe pain radiated from her lower back and traveled down the back of her right leg. She fought to hold back her tears, and hoped a few hours of sleep would lessen the excruciating pain now wracking her body. She took the codeine Captain Kingston had prescribed and finally fell off to sleep.

By morning, the pain had lessened enough to allow her to get up and carry on as if nothing were wrong. During breakfast, Chief Nurse Salter showed up with some new instructions: "From what I'm told about how things are going at the front, we can expect a good many patients before the day is out. Be on the alert for trouble, and if we get bombed or shelled, head for a foxhole and stay there until you're told it's okay to get out."[34]

As Haskell walked to her duty station, Ward 1A, she could see GIs digging foxholes at regular intervals throughout the hospital compound. A few nurses who had finished their ward work were helping GIs with the digging.

She ran into Corporal Krist as she entered the ward. They exchanged greetings; then Haskell asked if they had any seriously ill patients. He gestured toward a soldier four cots away. "He just came in from the OR. Corporal Calcaterra is staying with him until he reacts from the anesthesia. His cheeks are pretty much blown away, and he has a bullet hole in the roof of his mouth. He got a little too close to a 37 millimeter," Krist said. He gestured toward the other side of the tent. "There are three boys down there with pretty bad burns. Those tankers really get the worst of things."[35]

Haskell began her rounds by stopping to check one young patient who sat with a fixed expression and a thousand-mile stare in his eyes. The soldier was not responding to anything going on around him. Haskell wondered if he were deaf and went to the improvised desk to look up his record. Before she could locate it, a plane flew over the ward. Haskell knew by the steady sound of its engine that it was "one of ours," but the young soldier she had just left reacted as if he were still at Kasserine. He threw back his blankets and began to run toward the door of the tent.

"Krist, Calcaterra, Smiley, stop that boy!" Haskell shouted. "Don't let him get outdoors."

As the soldier reached the tent flap, Krist caught him by one arm and Smiley by the other. "Let me go!" the soldier screamed hysterically. "Can't you hear those planes? Dozens of planes. Get to the slit trenches before they get us!"

"Take it easy, Mac," said Corporal Krist. "That baby is one of ours. Nothing . . . is going to happen. Let's get you back to bed." They spoke to him as they might talk to a child and guided him gently back to safety.[36]

In many ways, seeing a boy whose mind had been shattered by combat was even more difficult than working with shattered bodies. As Haskell made her way back toward the desk, a soldier placed his hand on her arm. The boy had curly blond hair, deep blue eyes, and appeared to be about twenty years old. "Thanks for being gentle with him," the young man said. "We've been in the same company for months. He's usually a quiet guy, but a day ago, when we were catching it pretty bad, he climbed out of his foxhole and started shaking his fist at the German planes." He met Haskell's eyes, then looked down toward his missing right leg. "I'd rather

Lts. Helen M. Molony and Margaret B.
Stanfill, outside their tent in North Africa
(Courtesy of Jesse Flynn)

be like this than like he is." Lieutenant Haskell patted the boy on his shoulder and smiled. "You're both heroes to us, fella," Haskell said. "It's a privilege to take care of all of you." That night when Haskell got off duty, she limped back to her tent.[37]

The next morning, 17 February, her back and leg were so painful that she could not get out of bed. Before she had to deal with the situation, Lieutenant Mary Meyers appeared in her tent. "The jig's up, Ruthie," Meyers, a brunette from Ohio, announced in her flat midwestern accent. "Several people saw you limping last night. Lieutenant Salter said that you and I are going to be admitted. I have an infection under my chin and Kingston ordered bed rest for both of us. I'm going to carry your things to the ward tent you and I will share. Miller and Molony are going to take care of us." Their assignments seemed perfect since Louise Miller and Ruth Haskell, and Helen Molony and Mary Meyers, had been tentmates for months.[38]

Both nurses received immediate medical attention. Haskell was examined, diagnosed with a ruptured intravertebral lumbar disc, and ordered to stay in bed. Hot compresses were started on Meyers's chin. In addition to the dangers of spreading the infection to surgical patients, there was the possibility that an infection located in an area with many blood vessels and in close proximity to the brain might eventually spread to that area. Since doctors were unwilling to take such a chance, Meyers was put on bed rest.

Battle casualties were pouring into the hospital, but no amount of pleading on the part of Meyers and Haskell got them back to duty. Soon, their wall tent was needed for newly arriving battle casualties, and the two patients were moved to a small tent in the hospital area. The opening of the new tent faced the highway and Haskell had a good view of what was going on down the road. She wondered what was happening at the front as she watched a steady flow of olive-drab boxlike military ambulances with large red crosses painted on their sides, roofs, and double back doors arrive at the hospital. As she watched, she realized that the new casualties were not being unloaded, but were still on board as the ambulances departed toward the rear. This strange activity confused her. The more she watched the constant activity, the more anger and frustration she felt at her helplessness.

Finally, after Lieutenant Meyers delivered a convincing argument, the chief nurse let Meyers get out of bed and help, but no amount of pleading from Haskell would persuade the chief nurse to release Haskell from bed rest. As she lay watching the highway through the open tent flaps, she saw huge caravans of camels going past the hospital toward the rear. Haskell was surprised to see that instead of the slow, easy gait she had seen camels use before, these ships of the desert were traveling at a full gallop. Their tall, thin legs and bulging knees stretched forward and back, up and down, like hairy pistons moving at full speed to get their cargo to safety. Clouds of dust swirled around the Arabs while burros pulling carts stacked high with household goods ran beside the tall, ungainly beasts. Behind the camels came an unending line of Arab women carrying family possessions in large bundles balanced on their heads, and small Arab children walking double time to keep up with their families. Haskell counted at least eleven family dogs, barking as they ran

ahead, waiting for their people to catch up, and then running on ahead
again in the fast-moving stream flowing away from the front.

Haskell was curious, but dared not get out of bed. She knew her back
was unstable and did not want to present any more problems to her fellow nurses. Suddenly, a new category of refugee streamed down the highway in front of her tent. The 48th's own patients were being evacuated
and joining the throng that was rushing steadily away from the front
lines.

Just as her curiosity became almost too much to bear, Haskell saw
Major Frederick Mackenbrock, a native of Omaha, Nebraska, and the
unit's chief medical officer, hurrying past her tent toward headquarters.
"Major Mackenbrock!" Haskell called. The good-natured physician
stopped and stuck his head inside the tent. "What's going on?" she asked.
"Does all that activity on the highway mean what I think it does?"

He looked through the swirling dust at the rushing stream of people,
animals, and vehicles. "I'm afraid it does." The American troops were
retreating from Kasserine Pass.[39]

The Germans won the battle begun on 14 February at Faid Pass in the
eastern Dorsal Mountains. They succeeded in keeping the Americans
from going through Faid Pass and on to Bizerte and Tunis, pushing them
out of Tunisia and back to Algeria, through Kasserine Pass in the western
Dorsal Mountains. On the afternoon of 17 February 1943, the Germans
stormed through Kasserine Pass, causing the inexperienced American
troops to break and run in retreat back to Algeria. All told, the Germans
inflicted a massive defeat on inexperienced American forces, causing
6,500 Allied casualties. Personnel of a collecting company of the 109th
Medical Battalion and most of the medical detachment belonging to the
168th Infantry Regiment—10 medical officers and over 100 enlisted
men—were taken prisoner by the Germans. The 47th Armored Medical
Battalion lost one medical officer and four ambulances of casualties were
also captured. The enemy sustained 2,000 of their own casualties.[40]

Haskell could see and hear American tanks, half-tracks, and trucks
moving down the highway and away from the fighting. Their clanking
sounds blended with the shrill high voices of racing camels, the braying
of frightened burros, the barking of excited dogs, and the overwrought
chatter of Arab children and their frightened parents.

Mackenbrock smiled. "Don't worry. We're already evacuating the
patients. I wanted you to stay with the unit. We'll all move out together
when it's time." He offered Haskell a cigarette. "How are you doing?"

"Just fine, sir," Haskell said, "now that I know we're planning to get through this as a team." "Good girl," Mackenbrock said. He lit her cigarette and left to continue his duties.[41]

Most of the nurses dropped in to visit with Haskell for a minute or two. At noon, one of the mess sergeants brought her lunch. About 1500, Lieutenants Miller and Molony showed up and told Haskell that her belongings had been packed, her tent struck, and her bedroll and baggage were with theirs, waiting to be loaded on a truck when the time came.

Suddenly, there was a flurry of dust when two military policemen on motorcycles pulled off the highway near headquarters. Molony and Miller rushed outside to see what was going on. "What the hell are you people doing here?" The taller MP addressed his question to the striking, redheaded Molony. "There's nothing between you and the Germans and they're only fifteen miles away."

"We're taking care of casualties," Molony said. "We're the 48th Surgical Hospital."

"Well, you're about to become prisoners of war or get killed," the MP continued. "You've got to get out of here fast!"

"We don't have any transportation. All our ambulances and trucks are evacuating our patients," Molony said. "We can't leave until they get back."

"That's not soon enough," the tall MP said. He jump-started his motorcycle and looked at his partner. "You stay with them. I'm going to look for some trucks to get these people out of here. You stay here and make sure they get out as soon as the trucks get here." He gunned his motorcycle and disappeared in a cloud of dust.[42]

At about 1645, the tall MP returned with two 2.5-ton trucks. Mattresses were placed in the bed of each truck, and all remaining patients were loaded on board along with the nurses. Lieutenant Salter came to Haskell's tent and told Molony and Miller to get Haskell dressed as quickly as possible. In fifteen minutes, Miller and Molony climbed in the rear of the second truck, and Haskell got into the cab between the driver and Salter. The trucks pulled out onto the highway and took their places between two Sherman tanks.

They moved along at the Sherman's top speed of 28 mph, but the noise from the second tank was a constant distraction. "There must be something wrong with that thing. It's making enough noise for ten tanks," Molony said. Everyone realized there was a very good chance German planes might bomb or strafe them. Night could not fall quickly enough to suit the group as they rolled and clanked toward Youks-les-Bains, the Algerian town about forty miles to the rear. The moon rose full and bright, throwing its light across the countryside, reflecting off tanks and trucks whose occupants wanted nothing more than to remain hidden.

"If German planes come over now, I don't see how they can miss us," Mary Meyers said. "I wish we could turn off the moonlight."

"Well, we can't," Molony said. "So we might as well enjoy it." Without another word, she began to sing Kate Smith's theme song, "When the Moon Comes Over the Mountain." Her voice was clear and on pitch as she sang: " 'When the moon comes over the mountain,/Every beam brings a dream, dear, of you.' "[43]

"How can you sing when we have a good chance of getting killed?" Louise Miller asked.

"All the more reason to sing," Molony said. "Besides, if we all sing, maybe we can drown out the noise those tanks are making." She began again. " 'When the moon comes over the mountain . . . ,' " and several girls joined in.[44]

In the truck's cab, Haskell was fighting nausea and losing the battle. Between the bumps and holes in the road that bounced her back up and down without rest, the effects of codeine, and the dulled but persistent pain, Haskell felt sure she was going to throw up. "I hate to be a pain in the neck," she said to Salter, "but I'm pretty sure I'm going to vomit." For one or two seconds, Salter looked as if she were trying to make a decision. Suddenly she turned toward Haskell. "We don't have time to stop now," the chief nurse said. "Here, use my helmet." She passed her metal helmet to Haskell just in time. Haskell retched and regurgitated into the steel pot as the truck bounced along the rough road. When she'd recovered, Salter took the helmet, rolled down the window of the cab, turned the helmet away from the wind, and let its contents fly. Then she poured a little water from her canteen, sloshed it around in her helmet for a couple of seconds, emptied it out the window, and put the helmet back on her head.[45]

As the hours passed, Haskell and Molony worried about—and prayed for—the officers and enlisted men they had left behind at Thala. Suddenly, they heard the drone of airplane engines in the distance. Nurses had learned to distinguish the sound of a German plane from an American or British engine and they strained, listening in silence. In the pale moonlight, Meyers and Molony broke into smiles. "They're ours!" they said simultaneously, and broke into another chorus of "When the Moon Comes Over the Mountain."[46]

At 2130 on 17 February, both trucks pulled into Youks-les-Bains and all the nurses were surprised to see so many hospital tents in one area.

"It can't be just the 48th," Molony said.

"No, ma'am," the driver said as he let the tailgate down. "There are several hospitals here."

Just then, Lieutenant Mary Francis of the 2nd Unit returned to the truck cab with Lieutenant Salter. "Mary Francis is going to take you to a night nurse's cot for tonight. We'll get you more comfortable in the morning," Salter said to Haskell.

"How are our boys doing?" Haskell asked.

"They're holding for now, at least on this flank," Francis said. "We have nine hundred patients here. The 77th Evac joined us to care for the casualties from Kasserine."[47]

The next morning, Lieutenant Vaughn Fisher, a short, full-figured brunette from Pennsylvania, brought Haskell her breakfast. "What are the patients saying about the retreat?" Haskell asked. Fisher said that the men were angry and frustrated as they had been after every battle, but something new had been added. The retreat had convinced the men that being an American was not enough, that they had to fight smarter than the Jerries if they were not going to be chased out of a position again.[48]

Added to that realization was the men's fervent hope that America would supply them with better equipment. The Honey's 37-millimeter gun was no match for the German Mark IV or Tiger Tanks. Many soldiers told of seeing the shells fired by the Honeys actually bounce off the German tanks and explode in the dirt of a hillside. When the GIs discovered that the shells they were firing were "practice rounds"—shells packed with insufficient powder to cause any real damage, used in training exercises in the States—the men were incredulous. How could their leaders send them into battle with practice shells?

It was clear the United States was less prepared for war than any of these soldiers had been led to believe. In just one day, the tankers had fired as many shells as were allocated for a year's training back in the States. The Battle of Kasserine had gone a long way in teaching green American troops that it would take better equipment and better disciplined soldiers if they were going to defeat the better supplied veteran combat troops of the German army. Rumors had it that General Lloyd R. Fredendall would soon be replaced by a spit-and-polish commander, General George S. Patton.

After breakfast, a medical officer and two enlisted men showed up to move Haskell into a ward tent with the rest of her unit. Haskell asked about the corpsmen of the 1st Unit of the 48th who had been left behind and was told they made it out minutes before the American rear guard turned the old hospital site into the front lines.

Haskell was placed on a cot nearest the tent's stove and was waited on hand and foot by the nurses in her unit. About 1130, Lieutenant Salter turned up at the tent and told Haskell that by some miracle the enlisted men managed to get all their baggage away from Thala safely. Salter sat on the foot of Haskell's cot. "I have something to tell you that you're not going to like." Haskell felt herself stiffen in preparation for bad news. "We've made arrangements to evacuate you to Oran for treatment. If they can help you, you'll eventually be sent back to our unit. If not, you'll be sent back to the States." Haskell's heart sank and she fought to control the tears she felt starting up in her eyes. "I wish we could just keep you here, but we'll be on the move again as soon as there's some change at the front." Salter's eyes and voice were kind. "I hope you'll understand."

Haskell wiped the tears away with the corner of her pajama top. "I'll try to be a good sport," she said, "but, believe me, it hurts more than my back." She swallowed hard and asked for a cigarette to fight back her tears. Salter stood, lit Haskell's cigarette, patted her on the shoulder, and left.[49]

The rest of the day seemed to drag by, as one after another nurses, officers, and corpsmen stopped at the tent to say good-bye and wish Haskell a speedy recovery. Haskell and her comrades knew only too well in their hearts that the possibility of her returning to the unit was about the same as Germany surrendering before the end of February.

Early the next morning, Haskell sent word that she wanted to see Janet Pettingill as soon as possible. Pettingill was from Gardiner, Maine, just six miles from her own home. Their mothers had become friends since their daughters had been sent overseas together. Haskell wanted to make sure that Pettingill did not say anything to her own mother in a letter before Haskell got a chance to let her mother know what was going on. Haskell had never mentioned her injury or back pain in her letters home and she did not want her mom to be frightened.

Around noon, Haskell was placed on a litter and loaded into an ambulance for the trip to the airfield at Youks-les-Bains. Lieutenants Miller and Salter, along with Chaplain Samuel A. C. Grove, rode with her. As they reached the airfield, Haskell momentarily gave in to tears, but regained her composure as they lifted her up and into the plane. Louise Miller, Haskell's tentmate through so many of the dangers of North Africa, watched as the stretcher was strapped into place. Ironically, Louise, the smaller and more "delicate" of the two women, would remain in North Africa, while Ruth, ostensibly the bigger and stronger of the two, was leaving. Louise smiled through tear-filled eyes as the plane's engines turned over and it was time for those not going to Oran to leave. "Good-bye, Yankee," Miller said to Haskell as her voice cracked. "Take good care of yourself."

She bent, kissed Haskell on the cheek, and climbed quickly out of the plane. Lieutenant Salter and Chaplain Grove wished her well and followed Miller.[50]

Now Haskell was alone, the door was closed, and the plane was moving down the runway and into the air. She watched out the window as the plane banked and turned to the left. Scores of hospital tents were stretched out below the wing as far as the eye could see. Haskell knew that somewhere beneath the canvas and large red crosses, her comrades at the 48th Surgical Hospital were working with the wounded, and that each had won the title "Combat Veteran." She watched until the tents looked like so many children's toys and the red crosses could no longer be distinguished.

The door of the cockpit opened and the navigator entered the cabin and stopped at Haskell's litter. He was a solidly built man, with warm, friendly brown eyes. "It's tough luck, girl," he said, and laid a gentle hand on Haskell's shoulder. "But you'll get back."

Haskell knew better, but she appreciated his efforts to comfort her. "It's so hard running out on them like this," she said. "They're mighty swell people, our boys!" She felt the navigator's grip tighten on her shoulder.

"You bet your sweet life they are!" he said. He returned to the cockpit, and Haskell, lulled by the sounds of the plane's engines, fell off to sleep.[51]

CHAPTER THREE

The Allied Push to Bizerte and Tunis

PERFECTING COMBAT MEDICINE

February–May 1943

It was good we were so busy. The wounds were the worst any of us had ever seen. Mine casualties that tore off limbs, blew open abdomens, turned faces to so much red jelly, and left brains oozing out of broken skulls. There was little time to think, and no time to cry.

—*Capt. Theresa Archard, principal chief nurse,*
2nd Unit, 48th Surgical Hospital, G.I. Nightingale

LIEUTENANT THERESA ARCHARD shook her head and blinked in an attempt to clear the sleep from her mind and eyes. It was 18 February 1943, the day after Rommel routed the Allies at Kasserine Pass. As German forces continued to push the Allies back, American and Allied wounded were streaming into the 48th Surgical at Youks-les-Bains, Algeria, in long lines of ambulances and 2.5-ton trucks. Archard, exhausted after twenty-four hours of continuous duty in the hospital, had just gone to bed. She had been asleep only an hour when she felt someone shaking her shoulder gently, and heard a male voice calling her name.

She turned toward the voice and fumbled in the dark for her flashlight.

"Yes. I'm awake," Archard said, as the narrow beam of her flashlight reflected off the face of a corpsman.

"I have a note for you, ma'am." The sergeant handed her an envelope. She sat up, tore the envelope open, and deflected the beam of her light to the enclosed message. "Dear Miss Archard: There is a very sick patient in the operating room who needs special nurses. If this upsets you too much, take the enclosed." The note was signed and had two aspirins with it. Archard felt her blood pressure soar at the surgeon's sarcasm. "Tell the doctor I'm on my way." She put her shoes on quickly and headed for the OR tent.[1]

The sarcasm was all too familiar to Archard. In addition to the pressure that stemmed from caring for an unending stream of battle casualties, she and the other nurses and corpsmen also had to deal with the unreasonable demands and resentments of several physicians. These physicians had "prima donna" attitudes: they insisted that their tents be pitched first at each new hospital site. They were the same surgeons who, three weeks earlier, had been using sterile supplies as if they were unlimited—a practice that, had it not been stopped by Archard's intervention, would have kept nurses and corpsmen on duty virtually twenty-four hours a day.

As chief nurse of the 2nd Unit, Archard's job was to make sure that nurses and corpsmen—herself included—used their time efficiently and got the rest they needed to be able to do their best for every wounded soldier entrusted to their care. She knew that nurses and corpsmen were already taxed to the breaking point in the OR and in the wards; adding needless laundry duty was a senseless drain on precious time and energy best spent elsewhere.

Though Archard had succeeded in ending the physicians' overuse of sterile supplies, it was clear, by the sarcastic tone of the note she had received just in time to awaken her from much-needed sleep, that some of these physicians still expected nurses to be on call an inhuman twenty-four hours a day.

As she reached the OR tent, Archard was determined to withhold her judgment until she knew for certain whether or not a condition existed in the OR and postoperative ward that warranted her being summoned. The night nurse filled her in quickly. "I know he's there, Miss Archard," Lieutenant Amy Brigham said, referring to the patient whose condition prompted the surgeon's note, "but his condition is no worse than a lot of men I've seen. He's getting every bit of the attention he needs. In fact, he's doing so well they are getting ready to move him to the ward."[2]

Archard went directly to the postoperative tent and found things running smoothly. The nurse and two corpsmen on duty were busy and confident that each patient was receiving exactly what he needed. Within minutes, the young man mentioned in the surgeon's note arrived at the ward and was fitted quickly into the routine. Clearly, the surgeon had not checked on conditions in the postoperative ward before writing his biting message. As with his use of twenty-four sterile towels in a simple debridement earlier, the surgeon had acted as if he were back in the States with an unlimited supply of nurses. Archard was leaving the postoperative ward when she ran into Colonel Mellies. "Hello, Tressie, how's everything going?"

Archard, her head pounding and muscles aching from lack of sleep, spoke sharply. "Colonel Mellies, if the 48th Surgical Hospital doesn't want the nurses along, why don't they just say so? They can let the War Department know that women have no place in the front lines with the boys." Known for her forthrightness and take-charge manner, Archard proceeded to tell Colonel Mellies about the unreasonable demands some of the doctors were making on the nurses. "Goodness knows we have nothing but hard work, living like cattle most of the time, dressed in coveralls, washing out of helmets and eating C-rations."

"Tressie, why didn't you say something before?" Colonel Mellies asked. "I had no idea these guys were giving you such a hard time. Believe me, I'll take care of it. From now on, you'll be treated like ladies."[3]

Colonel Mellies put Captain Blackwell Markham in charge of the nurses, and assured Archard that the surgeons' misuse of authority and lack of respect would be rectified. Later, Markham told Archard that at each new site, provided the wounded were taken care of and under canvas, the nurses' tents would be put up first. Under no circumstances would the surgeons' tents be put up before the nurses' tents were pitched.

The next morning, Archard was faced with a new problem. The OR and wards were running smoothly, but the men on the hospital kitchen crew were coping with a real emergency. "We only have dishes for two hundred patients, and with six hundred or more to feed, we can't wash dishes fast enough to get everyone fed while the food's still hot," the mess sergeant complained.

"Aren't there several cases of dishes for the officers' mess that aren't being used?" Archard asked. "There must be enough to feed another hundred patients."

"You can't use the officers' dishes," the mess sergeant said. "I'm responsible for them and if they get broken or lost, they'll bawl me out and take the money out of my pay."

"I'm ordering you to use those dishes," Archard said, taking charge once again of the situation. "You have witnesses. If anything happens, I'll pay for them. There's nothing else around here to spend money on anyway. If the dishes get broken, they can take the money out of my pay. Now get the dishes out and feed these men."[4]

Even with the extra dishes, the kitchen crew worked like beavers to get the patients fed. The ground was uneven and food had to be carried a quarter mile or more to patients' tents.

In the predawn hours of 21 February, a terrible fire erupted in the hospital as day-shift personnel were preparing to take over from the night shift. Corporal Oliver Sorlye from Hudson, South Dakota, remembered that he was facing his last hours on guard duty for the night and had just cleared Sergeant Robert Hardin and his crew to pass through to the kitchen tent where they would start breakfast for hospital personnel and patients. Gerald Taylor, the unit's medical laboratory technician, recalled that he was dressing in the dark, preparing to go to his lab to organize arriving specimens and run tests. Lieutenant Archard was making her way between ward tents to check with the kitchen crew to see if they now had enough dishes to serve all the patients at once. In a split second, a loud explosion ripped through the nighttime silence. The gasoline stove in the kitchen tent had exploded and the large tent quickly went up in flames.

Sorlye, Taylor, Archard, other personnel, and patients closest to the kitchen watched in horror as long fingers of flame clawed at the night sky. Nearby tents were outlined in the yellow and orange light cast by the burning kitchen tent, and Sorlye and Taylor prayed that the sparks, carried by the wind, would not reach other tents. Blackout conditions were destroyed; Archard and the others knew that the fire would be a lighthouse beacon for German planes and artillery. The hospital's red crosses, painted on the tops and sides of the tents, could not be seen at night, leaving personnel and wounded exposed and unprotected.

Enlisted men from among the hospital personnel who were trained to fight fires ran to the burning tent and encircled it. Lessons learned and practiced while still in the States surfaced automatically. Soldiers cut through tent ropes with axes and, as the canvas fell to the ground, shoveled earth onto the flames. In twenty minutes, the fire was out and another tent was being pitched to house the hospital kitchen.

THE TABLES began to turn in favor of the Allies shortly after their defeat at Kasserine. Though Rommel had pushed through Kasserine on

17 February, he did not continue to advance, as expected, to the cities of Tebessa and Thala. Instead, he became cautious and paused to consolidate his forces in case of an Allied counterattack. As Rommel examined captured Allied equipment, he became convinced that the strength of the Allied forces was too great to be defeated by his Afrika Korps, especially since his troops were down to only a one-day supply of ammunition and a six-day supply of food. Rommel withdrew his forces back through Kasserine Pass on 23 February—and with such skill that it was twenty-four hours before the Allies realized what had occurred.

Since the Americans and Allies were unaware of Rommel's decision to withdraw, the Allies continued their own pullback until late afternoon of 23 February. The 2nd Unit of the 48th Surgical Hospital, the mobile unit, and 48th's headquarters closed, moved, and set up at Montesquieu, Algeria, approximately fifty miles farther to the rear, on 22 February.

Operating-room tent of the 48th Surgical Hospital at Montesquieu, Algeria, 1943 (Courtesy of Jesse Flynn)

All patients from the 77th and 9th Evacuation Hospitals were transferred to the 1st Unit of the 48th Surgical Hospital that had moved to a bivouac area three miles west of La Meskiana on 20 February, so the evacuation units could withdraw further to the rear.

The next morning, the 2nd Unit at Montesquieu, about thirty miles north of La Meskiana, began receiving newly wounded battle casualties. The conditions at Montesquieu were in stark contrast to previous sites. Instead of the dust and mud that hospital personnel had contended with before, a field of green grass and yellow and purple wildflowers was the new home for the tent-hospital. Despite springlike surroundings, the work did not change one bit. Wounded soldiers still bled red, and the wounds of battle were as ugly as ever.

Fighting shifted again to the east, and to the southern ridges of the eastern Dorsal Mountains. In mid-March, a new commander was appointed to head the U.S. II Corps: General George S. Patton. With Patton now in charge, the tide of war changed in favor of the Americans and Allies. Part of the reason for this change in fortune was a new and more stringent discipline that Patton imposed upon his new troops.

Corporal Charles Coolidge from Signal Mountain, Tennessee, with the Thirty-sixth Infantry Division recalled an incident that reflected Patton's role as a disciplinarian and his willingness to learn from new information. While Coolidge was walking with his company in a column during training, a jeep pulled alongside them and General Patton jumped out and began talking to Lieutenant Needleman, who was directly behind Coolidge. Coolidge remembered Patton's conversation with the young physician, who was attached to the Thirty-sixth Division. "Patton said, 'Lieutenant, button your chin strap.' Needleman answered, 'Yes, sir, I'll button it. But when you leave, sir, I'll unbutton it, sir.' " Patton repeated his order and Needleman gave the same response. When Patton gave his order the third time, he added, "I'm going to fine you a hundred dollars for insubordination." Coolidge remembered Needleman's response. "Sir, I don't care if you fine me one hundred dollars. I'm a doctor and I can do without the hundred dollars. Don't you know that if I have my chin strap buttoned and a shell hits up here pretty close to us, it will break my neck? So, sir, as soon as you leave, I'm going to unbutton my chin strap again." Without saying another word, Patton turned, got back into his jeep, and disappeared down the road. Two days later, a new order came down telling all GIs to button their chin straps behind their helmets and not under their chins. Needleman was not fined.[5]

March brought several important changes to the 48th Surgical Hospital. With the tide of battle turning against Axis troops in Tunisia, Unit 1 at La Meskiana and Unit 2 at Montesquieu were alerted for future forward moves. On 28 February, the 1st Unit moved from La Meskiana to Youks-les-Bains and set up. On 8 March, in response to new American and Allied advances, the 2nd Unit, the Mobile Surgical Unit, and the headquarters of the 48th Surgical Hospital moved from Montesquieu to Bou Chebka and opened. During the second week in March, hospital personnel received word that Colonel Mellies was to be relieved of command and transferred in a matter of days.

The news was received with genuine grief, and the nurses of the 2nd Unit decided to give their CO a going-away party. The celebration, held at their site a little northwest of Bou Chebka, was a huge success. Nurses wore blue slacks and white shirts they dug out of their bedrolls for the occasion. Lieutenant Cecile Bair—little "Teddy" Bair, who had worn her helmet to bed during the London Blitz while the unit was staging in England—pulled out the red sweater her family had sent her from home. "I've been looking for a special occasion to wear this," Teddy said. "They don't get more special than a party for Colonel Mellies."

The party was one to remember. The supply officer, Captain Chuck Ebbert, following Archard's request, had managed to come up with something special for refreshments. Nurses and officers were treated to white bread and jam sandwiches washed down with lemonade and local red wine. The Catholic chaplain, First Lieutenant John Power, and the Protestant chaplain, Captain "Chappy" Grove, brought the portable church organ and the evening was filled with singing, stories, laughter, and tears. Around 2300, Teddy Bair announced in a loud voice, "Girls, you all line up. We're going to kiss Colonel Mellies good-bye."[6]

Thirty-one nurses with red and blue ribbons in their hair formed a line behind Teddy, and to the cheers and groans of the male officers, each nurse kissed the colonel on the cheek and wished him well.

That same day, 15 March, the new commanding officer, Lieutenant Colonel Norman H. Wiley, arrived at headquarters at Bou Chebka, Algeria, and assumed command of the 48th Surgical Hospital. "Within a week," Archard wrote later, "he had all of us catalogued and most of our numbers, and I don't mean the numbers on our dog tags."[7]

On 19 March, Unit 1 left Youks-les-Bains and moved forward to Feriana in Tunisia, where they set up operations in the French barracks, and were joined by the mobile unit and the 48th headquarters. On 23 March,

Patton launched a major drive from Gafsa to El Guettar and Maknassy, Tunisia. At Feriana, Unit 1 was snowed under with casualties and several nurses and doctors from the 2nd Unit were sent to help.

On 24 March, General Patton paid a visit to Unit 1. The general had a reputation for demanding iron-willed discipline in his troops; Jodie Harmon, a Unit 1 surgical technician from Texas, witnessed the general's hardboiled toughness firsthand. On the day of Patton's visit, Harmon was working in the "postop" ward (World War II's version of the intensive care unit of today), located in the French barracks. Harmon and three other members of his postop team were taking turns eating lunch because they were too busy to eat at the same time. Harmon was the last to stop for a few minutes to eat. He had just sat down on the dirt floor between two patients' cots with his feet toward the main isle and begun on his can of K-rations when the door to the ward opened. "The first thing I saw," Harmon recalled, "was a tall man with bone-handled pistols. He had high-top riding boots, shining like new gold, and riding britches, and of course, bodyguards." Harmon saw the stars on the man's brightly polished helmet and the corpsman immediately recognized him as General Patton.

Patton walked briskly past Harmon, who was "close enough to trip him," and stopped at the cot of a young man at the end of the aisle. Patton took the medical chart hanging at the foot of the cot. He read out the name on the chart and asked the soldier if he were that man. "The soldier was a young guy barely out of his teens and he could hardly whisper," Harmon recalled. "That's when Patton lit into him. He started out with 'No soldier would surrender. The Germans did exactly what they should have done—shot you.' It sure didn't do the kid any good," Harmon said. "He had tried to surrender when the Germans overran his position. He stood up in his foxhole waving a white handkerchief, but it turned out that the Germans weren't taking any prisoners that day. They shot him in the chest and left him for dead." Harmon went on to say that he thought the doctor in the ward at the time, Major Mackenbrock, might stop Patton and tell him he should not be upsetting the patients. "I guess he [Mackenbrock] knew that if he said anything, he would be in trouble," Harmon commented. "Nobody said a word to Patton. He finally turned and left the ward." The incident was a foreshadowing of what was to come later in Sicily when Patton actually struck a hospitalized soldier.[8]

Meanwhile, the 2nd Unit had moved near Bou Chebka on 8 March. Nurses and medical personnel were working twelve-hour shifts for a week taking in casualties from several offenses launched by Patton's II Corps: the Allies occupied Gafsa on 17 March, El Guettar on the 18th, and Sened station on the 21st. Maknassy fell to the Allies on the 22nd.

Between 20 and 26 March 1943, the 48th Surgical Hospital received and treated approximately 1,300 patients, and hospitalized about 400. They evacuated approximately 900 patients to the 9th and 77th Evacuation Hospitals in the rear area, a journey of almost 100 miles to the rear. On 26 March, two surgical teams and nurses from Unit 2 were sent to relieve personnel of the 1st Unit who had been working continuously for 48 hours. On 27 March, the mobile unit, headquarters, and the 2nd Unit of the 48th Surgical moved to 3 miles north of Gafsa, Tunisia, which was about 60 miles south of Bou Chepka. On 28 March, Unit 1 treated 256 battle casualties, hospitalized 42, and evacuated others to the 9th and 77th Evacs farther behind the lines.[9]

Many of the casualties required blood transfusions and donors were sought from American and Allied troops at Tebessa. These casualties were among the worst the 48th's personnel had seen since arriving in North Africa. Lieutenant Archard at Unit 2 recalled one of the most seriously wounded patients, a young soldier named Jimmie who was brought to the hospital with his intestines "just about shot to pieces." Surgeons worked on him for six hours repairing and resecting his colon, then turned him over to the care of the nurses.[10]

Archard appointed three nurses to care for Jimmie, each to work an eight-hour shift around the clock. Jimmie needed specialized care if he were going to live, and each of the three nurses was busy every minute of her tour of duty. The boy's blood pressure had dropped so low that he verged on irreversible shock. Lieutenant Margaret Sramcik, a native of Ohio, took the first shift. Between administering blood transfusions, plasma, and normal saline intravenously, she used a nasogastric tube to suction fluids out of Jimmie's stomach. She also changed his position to guard against pneumonia, and injected him with morphine to dull his pain. It was an intense, full-time job and it went on for days. Finally, Jimmie's blood pressure stabilized; it became high enough to filter blood through his kidneys to remove the impurities from his wounded body. At last, doctors were confident that the young man would live. There would be a great deal of adjustment he would have to make, and they hoped that the colostomy bag attached to his left lower abdomen was temporary, but it would take weeks or even months to know for sure.

"I'm afraid the nurses spoiled him rotten," Archard wrote. "He was twenty, but he looked sixteen, and every nurse adopted him. He was everybody's kid brother."[11]

After the liberation of Gafsa on 18 March, the Germans were on the run, and business at the 48th Surgical slowed enough to allow medical personnel off-duty time away from the hospital. On 20 March, Lieutenant Helen Molony was delighted when Mike, the six-foot-four handsome U.S. Ranger she had dated in Arzew, showed up at Unit 1 with a jeep and an offer to take her to see the walled city of Tebessa.

"Tebessa is off-limits to military personnel," Molony said. She smiled a challenge into the Ranger's brown eyes. "What makes you think you can get in to see it?"

The square-jawed captain grinned like a mischievous little boy. "Trust me," he said. He offered a strong hand and helped the tall redhead into the jeep. "Remember that we Americans are known for our ingenuity."[12]

An hour and a half later, their jeep pulled to a stop at the main entrance to the walled city. Two broad-shouldered MPs, rifles in hand, stood like a stone gate in front of them. "This area is off-limits, Captain," the taller MP called.

Molony fought a desire to smile. She had told her escort that they would not be able to enter Tebessa. Now she could kid him all the way back to the 48th.

"Yes, Sergeant, I know," the captain said in his calm, deep voice. "But this nurse has to get to the hospital immediately. They're waiting for her to report."

Both MPs snapped to attention, saluted, and parted to allow the jeep to pass. Molony could not take her eyes off the captain as she returned the soldiers' salutes and struggled to hide her surprise.

When the jeep was fifty yards into the city, Molony burst out laughing. "I don't think we have a hospital inside Tebessa," she said.

"You and I know that," Mike said. He smiled broadly. "But those MPs don't know that."

"What if we get stopped in here?" Molony said. "What do we say then?"

"Well," Mike's brown eyes were dancing with mischief. "We had better see as much as we can before that happens, because I'm pretty sure they'll show us to the door."[13]

For forty minutes they toured the ancient Algerian city. The Byzantine wall that surrounded Tebessa was thirty feet high and seven feet thick. In more than a dozen evenly spaced locations it was reinforced with square watchtowers that rose twice the height of the wall. Stair-cases stood at regular intervals along the ancient wall, leading to a foot-path that ran along the top, encircling the entire city. In addition to the gate by which they had entered, there were two others, just as massive and also guarded by American MPs.

The native quarter of the city was crisscrossed with narrow streets lined with open-air cafés and small shops. It pulsed with life. Arab men wearing fezzes and burgundy, green, red, beige, and blue turbans sat at tables talking and drinking from small cups. Women, covered from head to toe, hurried by or stood in groups of twos and threes, talking and keeping an eye on their offspring. Naked children, most of them potbel-lied and bowlegged from malnutrition, played along the streets. Skeletal figures of dogs threaded among the young, including themselves in chil-dren's games. The constant music of barking dogs and high-pitched voices of children floated in the air.

More and more Arabs turned their attention toward the slow-moving jeep; the occupants felt themselves change from observers to the ob-served. "I think it's time for us to start back," Mike said. He pointed the jeep toward the gate where they had entered the city.

The same MPs Mike had spoken with on their way in waved them down at the gate. Before either guard could say a word, Mike took control. "Wrong hospital, gentlemen." He saluted and eased the jeep forward. "Keep up the good work." Both MPs snapped to attention and saluted as the jeep drove out of the walled city and took the road to Feriana.[14]

ON 23 MARCH, the First Division held the line against German forces attacking at El Guettar. Despite territorial gains, American and Allied troops were suffering heavy casualties. The next day, all patients with the 2nd Unit of the 48th Surgical Hospital at Bou Chebka were trans-ferred to evacuation hospitals in the rear. The morning after that, Unit 2 and the Mobile Surgical Unit left for the new front lines. Their truck convoy stopped briefly in Feriana to pick up nurses and surgeons loaned to the 1st Unit, then continued with all deliberate speed to their new assignment.

At 1400 on Friday, 26 March, the convoy arrived at its new hospital site, two miles outside Gafsa and twelve miles from the fighting in El Guettar. In stark contrast to the grass and flowers of their last field hospital at Montesquieu, this area was a rock-strewn desert with an almost constant wind blowing dust everywhere. As usual, the hospital arrived expecting to find tents already pitched by the advance team. But Archard was shocked to see the advance team trucks pulled toward the sides of the road, and not one hospital tent erected in the large area that was to be their new home. She went directly to Colonel Wiley and asked why tents were not being pitched so they could receive patients. "There are mines throughout the entire field," Colonel Wiley said. "We're waiting for the engineers to get here and remove them."[15]

When U.S. forces launched the well-known Battle of El Guettar—a major Allied attack in March 1943 from positions near El Guettar toward Gabès, a Tunisian town about seventy-five miles southeast of Gafsa on the east coast—the American advance went well until tanks and troops reached wide and densely planted German minefields. In moving closer to the front, the 48th Surgical Hospital now found itself on one of these fields. Though enemy mines could be painstakingly removed from the limited area where the 48th would set up, they would maim or kill thousands of American soldiers as they pursued the enemy from El Guettar to the coast.

The Allies dubbed the most vicious antipersonnel mine the "Bouncing Betty." It consisted of a canister the size of a No. 10 can of peaches packed with marble-sized steel pellets. It was placed in the earth with only a small, three-pronged detonator exposed. The "Betty" fired when stubbed by an infantryman's toe or set off by a trip wire. The canister would bounce into the air and explode at a height of four feet, scattering its steel projectiles within a radius of fifty feet. The steel fragments tore a path through flesh and bone, creating horrendous wounds. Limbs too mangled to be saved necessitated amputation. Major trauma to abdominal organs often made it impossible for surgeons to save the lives of soldiers so severely wounded.

It took several hours for engineers to clear the mines before the 48th could pitch its hospital tents at Gafsa. The fighting was heavy and fleets of ambulances immediately began arriving: up to twenty were pulling in every hour, delivering as many as eighty nonambulatory wounded at once. As usual, the wounded were first taken to the receiving tent, where they were triaged. Only the most serious cases were admitted; those who could withstand the long trip had their dressings reinforced and were sent to evacuation hospitals in the rear. Behind the receiving tent was the shock ward—tents for soldiers whose conditions were so serious that they could not survive surgery without first having their conditions stabilized with intravenous plasma (the fluid left after the blood cells are removed), whole blood, and normal saline solution.

Now, to save time, doctors and nurses triaged patients on litters on the ground, and rushed the most seriously wounded to shock wards immediately. Dirty, blood-soaked litters were placed directly on the cot beds, and transfusions of whole blood, plasma, or intravenous solutions were started without the patients being changed into clean clothes. Hospital personnel were stunned by how quietly the soldiers lay, in blood-spattered, torn uniforms, waiting patiently for the staff's lifesaving attention. As soon as each man's condition would allow, corpsmen transported him to the operating tent, where ten OR tables were in continuous use and surgical teams worked around the clock.

Sergeant Gilbert Smith, a tall, blond OR technician from Hudson, South Dakota, had worked with Unit 1's surgical personnel from their first days at Arzew; but nothing he had seen before, not even the stress of Kasserine Pass, had demanded more of operating-room personnel than

Lts. Ora White and Gladys Martin outside tent at the 48th Surgical Hospital in North Africa (Courtesy of Jesse Flynn)

the wounded from the battle at El Guettar. Smith and his team—a surgeon, a nurse, and another OR technician—moved from table to table, from patient to patient, stopping only long enough to re-glove.

By now, almost five months after their arrival in North Africa, the team had performed the procedures so often that their movements were as fast, rhythmic, and precise as those of workers on a factory assembly line. There was only one difference: the surgeons, nurses, and OR technicians moved along the line of patients, instead of the line of patients moving. As the surgeon finished operating on a patient, he and the nurse would quickly move to the next table and begin to operate, while Sergeant Smith and the other OR technician would immediately step in to "close" the patient whose surgery was just completed. Taking suturing needles and suture material from his fellow technician, Smith would suture the layers of tissue closed, and then dress the incision. Once the bandages were in place, he and his fellow tech moved forward, assembly-line style, to join their team's surgeon and nurse in working on the next case. This procedure—a medical round-robin of sorts—would go on for twelve, eighteen, or twenty-four hours, until the last casualty had been operated on, was closed, dressed, and on his way to a cot in the postoperative ward. During these long stretches, OR personnel took only a brief break, when they could steal the time, for food—sandwiches and coffee—delivered to the OR tent.[16]

During the long hours of surgery at Gafsa, surgeons amputated scores of arms and legs too mutilated to save, and these discarded limbs were stacked like cordwood behind the tents. Hospital crews appeared each morning to carry off the abandoned remains several miles away where they would dig pits and burn the limbs. The cycle repeated itself each day as American and Allied troops fought their way to Tunis and Bizerte.

With 256 patients received on the first day and 424 on the second, weary medical personnel had their hands full, and equipment was stretched thin. Casualties not in shock were bathed, dressed in pajamas, and fluoroscoped (a type of X-ray that revealed where shell fragments were located in the body). Once the fluoroscope revealed the internal location of shell fragments, the patient's body was marked with iodine. This procedure saved time in the operating rooms.[17]

Archard and her nurses had had the foresight to accumulate along the way packing boxes filled with sterilized supplies. But no one back in Washington at the War Department had foreseen the need for so much specialized equipment, such as the Wangensteen apparatus, necessary for the management of abdominal wounds. The Wangensteen apparatus was a special suction mechanism connected to a small nasogastric tube, the other end of which had been passed through the nose and placed into the stomach and the adjacent small intestine to decompress that area following abdominal or gastrointestinal surgery. With nowhere near enough Wangensteen setups to treat the hundreds of soldiers who required them, nurses improvised their own out of intravenous bottles and extra rubber tubing from used plasma sets. The absence of such apparatus was particularly perplexing to army surgeons since it had been created in 1932 by Dr. Owen Harding Wangensteen, and was in common use in the United States by 1940.

The War Department had not even supplied enough simple, standard equipment, such as stands to support the hundreds of intravenous bottles now in use. Archard devised a way to suspend intravenous bottles without the requisite stands. She ordered corpsmen to sink four extra tent poles parallel to the heads of the cots. Wire was strung on the poles along this parallel line and used to hang the intravenous bottles. "Now string a wire between the tops of the poles and countersink the ends of the wire to add stability," Archard ordered. "That should handle all the IV bottles we need."[18]

Each tent had a double row of sixteen or twenty to twenty-one collapsible cots. There were no tables or chairs; packing crates served as cupboards, desks, and catchalls. Nurses and corpsmen worked eighteen to twenty hours a day. They heated water on a potbellied stove that was in each tent, and bathed patients around the clock, making sure that no soldier went more than one day without a bath and clean pajamas.

One of the problems Archard and her staff faced daily was the need for transfusions of whole blood for severely wounded casualties. All U.S. Army personnel wore two dog tags bearing their names, serial numbers, religion, and blood type. Blood type was listed simply as "A," "B," "AB," or "O." During World War II, people with blood type O were known as universal donors since their blood could be transfused to patients of any blood type.

In North Africa, there was no such thing as a blood bank where whole blood could be refrigerated and stored until it was needed. Even when blood was collected for short-term use, it was under conditions that any civilized country would have considered primitive. One end of a rubber tube was attached to a needle that was inserted into the donor's vein.

The other end of the tubing was then placed into a sterilized bottle that sat on the floor and the blood ran into the bottle by gravity. It was not a closed system, and the opening of the receiving bottle was covered by sterile gauze in an effort to protect blood from airborne contamination. Since there was no refrigeration for storing and preserving blood, blood had to be used within a matter of hours or else be discarded.[19]

Even the availability of "open" bottles was at a premium. Colonel Edward D. Churchill, surgical consultant to the U.S. Army in the Mediterranean theater, was shocked when he visited a British transfusion unit in Cairo in February 1943, and found that the unit was collecting all the beer bottles its men could find in the city, sterilizing each bottle, then filling it with blood for shipment by plane to British casualties in Tunisia and El Alamein.[20]

Medical science had not yet developed the means to send refrigerated blood to the battlefronts where it was needed, nor did it feel under pressure to do so. Civilian and military medicine was all but totally committed to the use of plasma (blood minus red and white blood cells which are removed by centrifugal force in a laboratory process known as "spinning") to treat traumatic shock brought on by loss of blood, and saw no reason to convert to a system that emphasized whole blood.

For the physicians of the day, plasma seemed the quickest and most advantageous treatment for shock and its usual precursor, hemorrhage. Plasma was easy to store and transport since it needed no refrigeration. It was also easy to use, since it did not require blood group typing; it could be administered to anybody regardless of blood type, and no time need be spent in finding donors with identical blood types. Based on findings of plasma lab studies performed on animals and the effectiveness of plasma in the treatment of accident victims in civilian hospitals, the medical community of the day and the American National Red Cross promoted the use of plasma and endorsed its effectiveness to the peacetime United States. Unfortunately, the civilian paradigm was not adequate in wartime since few civilian injuries would equal the horrendous multisystem wounds inflicted in combat.

When America was attacked at Pearl Harbor on 7 December 1941, several medical consultants were in Honolulu to address a conference on military medicine. Among them were Drs. Perrin Long and John J. Moorhead, two men who attested to the increase in the survival rate of critically wounded soldiers, sailors, and marines when whole blood transfusions were used instead of plasma. Despite the evidence presented by these two doctors, no one at the time was championing the use of whole blood rather than plasma in the care of seriously wounded battle casualties.

As the war went on, however, it became clearer and clearer to front-line physicians and surgeons that whole blood produced a better outcome in severely wounded patients. Colonel Churchill and a few other military physicians began to look more closely at why this was the case. Churchill reached the conclusion that shock required more than simply replacing the volume of blood lost with plasma. For all its convenience, plasma was seriously inadequate as a treatment for patients suffering from shock. Plasma did wonders in restoring blood volume in the human body, but it did nothing to make up for the loss of oxygen-carrying red blood cells. Patients treated with plasma would improve for a period of time, but would quickly decline as the lack of red blood cells starved the body of oxygen needed by cells, tissues, and organs. Nothing but whole blood would make up for the loss of red blood cells, yet this very idea went against the leading majority medical opinion of the day.[21]

Armed with new knowledge acquired both firsthand and from surgeons working in the battlefields, Colonel Churchill presented a new medical concept for the treatment of hemorrhage and shock: whole blood. He began lobbying the military and Washington to create a system of collecting, storing, transporting, and administering whole blood as close to the front lines as possible. He concluded that plasma worked fine in getting battle casualties from the front lines to field and evacuation hospitals, but once the patient had reached this point, whole blood transfusions needed to replace the use of plasma at these hospitals.

Lobbying for change in military medical protocol was difficult; Churchill quickly learned that "swimming upstream" against a long-held and entrenched "truth" was no easy task. After six months of trying to change things from the inside, Churchill reached the conclusion that without considerable outside pressure, the military and the American National Red Cross were not about to change their system.

Part of the resistance was due to the fact that the logistics for instituting a whole blood system in military hospitals were formidable. How would whole blood, which needed constant refrigeration, be transported long distances to field hospitals near the front lines, let alone be transported from the United States to overseas theaters of war? In the instances during the early months of World War II in which whole blood was being collected for immediate use from troops and personnel near the front lines, it was often buried underground to keep it cool until needed. In a universal system, digging holes in the ground to preserve the whole blood was simply not practical.

A U.S. Navy surgeon, Lieutenant Henry S. Blake, invented a special box to hold and transport containers of blood under refrigerated conditions. The doctor was disappointed when the navy's Surgeon General saw no particular potential in his invention and declined his offer to have it used regularly in navy medicine. But Lieutenant Blake had enough faith in his box to offer it to the Surgeon General of the U.S. Army. By that time, General Norman T. Kirk had been harangued sufficiently by Colonel Churchill and others to see the potential, and quickly accepted it for army use.

To reach this point of acceptance by the U.S. Army and eventually the U.S. Navy, Colonel Churchill would find it necessary to take his case for the military use of whole blood to the *New York Times*. On 26 August 1943, the paper carried an article entitled "Plasma Alone Not Sufficient." The outcry from an American public fearful for the lives of its sons at the front created the extra pressure needed, when added to the appeals by Churchill and others, to get the American Red Cross to commit to and begin changing its policy and to collect and transport whole blood to military hospitals in the United States and in the theaters of war.[22]

Colonel Churchill's fight to change the outdated thinking of his military superiors and the American Red Cross was eventually successful. However, his hard-won victory would not come in time to help the casualties in Tunisia. Whatever whole blood was used in the Mediterranean theater was collected ad hoc from type O donors willing and able to donate blood. After corpsmen at the 48th Surgical Hospital donated all the blood they could, nurses and doctors volunteered, but were refused on the grounds that there were no replacements for them and they could not be spared. Requests were sent out for donors, and truckloads of quartermaster troops (troops whose primary function was to supply the fighting forces) arrived at the hospital to donate. The process was repeated day after day as new quartermaster troops arrived at the 48th Surgical Hospital and waited their turns to give blood to individual soldiers.

Americans were taking more prisoners now, and wounded German and Italian troops were arriving at the 48th in greater numbers. Italian soldiers were brought in screaming that they were America's friends, while German troops arrived sullen and afraid. Three Americans who spoke fluent German, army nurse Lieutenant Vilma Vogler from Milwaukee, Wisconsin; Catholic chaplain Lieutenant Power; and physician Lieutenant Leonard J. Schwade, were given the extra assignment of reassuring German prisoners that, despite what their superiors had told them, they would be well treated and given the same medical and surgical treatment as American wounded. If it had not been for the guards who had to be posted with Axis prisoners, a visitor to the ward tents would not have been able to distinguish the Axis from American or Allied wounded.

The nights at Gafsa were especially stressful. The hospital was located between an ammunition dump and an airfield, both legitimate targets for German bombers. Flares and antiaircraft tracer fire turned the night sky into a Fourth of July fireworks display, and the constant noise of tanks, vehicles, and troops moving past the hospital to the front made sleeping no easy task. "The noise was nerve-wracking," Archard wrote later. "And in the middle of all of it, we received more than 100 battle fatigue cases."[23]

What was known as "battle fatigue" or "war neurosis" at that time was a psychological ailment resulting from trauma suffered during war. It produced multiple symptoms, including but not limited to hypervigilance (being ever on the alert), irritability, nightmares, flashbacks (a psychological reexperiencing of traumatic events as if they were occurring in the present), and difficulties in forming and maintaining close relationships. This condition has existed for as long as wars have been fought; during the Civil War, it was labeled "soldier's heart"; in World War I, it was called "shell-shock." Today, the condition is recognized as post-traumatic stress disorder (PTSD).

Captain F. R. Hanson was a psychiatrist assigned to the 48th Surgical Hospital to study "war neurosis." Hanson gave orders that soldiers suffering from war neurosis or battle fatigue be put to bed, given large doses of barbiturates, and awakened only for meals and elimination. Archard put Lieutenant Helen English in charge of the two tents with these casualties. When these exhausted soldiers awakened, they saw attractive, red-headed Helen English walking around their tent and not even flinching at the sounds of the heaviest barrage. Most of them decided that if she could take it, so could they, and returned to their frontline units.

The presence of army nurses at the front had another amazing effect on casualties. American boys with amputated limbs, loss of eyesight, and disfiguring facial wounds gauged how their own sweethearts, wives, and families might respond to them by the way these young women reacted to their wounds. Army nurses reassured the wounded men that the women and people who loved them would not change because the war had changed them. The girlfriends of these wounded soldiers would rejoice to have them home and love them just as much as they did when these men were whole. Many a young amputee found the courage to write home about his injuries after being reassured by these American women that his wounds made him no less a man.

For some of the men, their manhood was even more in doubt. They were the soldiers who suffered mine injuries below the waist inflicted by "Bouncing Betties"—the German mines that sent shrapnel into men's thighs, groins, and abdomens. These men were not sure they still had a lot to offer to a future bride or waiting wife. Again, army nurses—young women their own ages or a year or two older—made it clear to these soldiers that if they, the nurses, were in their wives' or girlfriends' places, they would not love these men any less and would want to work any problems out together. Their words and sincerity gave the men the hope they needed to face the future.

Hundreds of battle casualties the 48th received had been treated for less severe wounds at the battalion aid station. After stopping at the 48th's "cafeteria tent," where they were fed and allowed to rest for a few hours, they were loaded into ambulances for the hundred-mile trip to the 77th Evacuation Hospital at Tebessa or the 9th Evacuation Hospital at Youks-les-Bains.

When things slowed down a little at the 48th, visits from Allied officers became a regular event. On 31 March, in addition to the 48th's receiving 430 casualties, Archard was introduced to General T. J. Davis, the adjutant general from Allied Headquarters, who had come to observe the 48th. He appeared to be a good-natured, jovial man and Archard liked him immediately. She showed the general around the wards and invited him to eat with the nurses. When the general asked if there was anything he could get for her, Archard's response took him by surprise. "Do those stars on your shoulders mean anything?" Archard asked.

"Perhaps," the general said. "We could certainly find out."

"In that case, you could get me a sewing machine so we can stop sewing linens and everything else by hand," Archard said.

The general looked a little perplexed. "I'm not sure I know where to look for a sewing machine," he said. "It's a pretty tall order."

Lieutenant Archard stared at the stars on General Davis's shoulders and then looked at her own single silver bar. "You know, General," she said in a matter-of-fact way, " . . . if I had stars on my shoulders and couldn't get what I wanted, I'd send them back to the War Department and be a plain buck private and have some fun."

General Davis smiled in amusement, shook Archard's hand, and said, "I'll certainly see what I can do for you."

Colonel Wiley shook his head when Davis had left. "You know, Lieutenant Archard, generals are always coming in here and promising things, but once they leave, it's a case of out-of-sight, out-of-mind."

"Not General Davis," Archard said. "A man with eyes like his couldn't possibly forget his promise."

"What's his eyes got to do with it?" the colonel asked.

"That man has the most beautiful brown eyes I've ever seen, and I'll get my sewing machine, you just wait and see."

Four days later, Archard received word that there was a package for her. Sergeant David Levine and Private Inkpen—"Squeaky" and "Inky" for short—carried a large packing case to her tent. There was a letter attached to the box and Archard read it aloud to the nurses who had gathered around the crate.

My dear Lt. Archard:

Upon my return to headquarters, I had the good fortune to locate a machine for your hospital which should come to you in the course of a few days . . .

Faithfully yours,
T. J. Davis, Brigadier General, AGD, USA, Adjutant General [24]

Archard sent a formal reply to General Davis, thanking him for his gift, and found herself tempted to add a personal note—"P.S. You have the most beautiful brown eyes I have ever seen." But, as Archard remembered, "Satan was put safely behind me."[25]

On 13 April, with German troops on the run, patients at the 2nd Unit were transported to the 77th and 9th Evacuation Hospitals in the rear, and the unit moved to join Unit 1 in Feriana. On 16 April at 0800, the entire 48th Surgical Hospital—Units 1 and 2, the mobile unit, and headquarters—left in a convoy of ninety-five trucks for the northern city of Tabarca on the Tunisian coast, where they were to set up and care for battle casualties on the new front lines. The 150-mile trip took more than eighteen hours and it was 0200 on 17 April when trucks pulled up in front of the old French barracks in the city. Nurses and medical personnel made their way inside in total blackout conditions. Despite the stench of filth and decay that saturated the area, they stretched out on their newly erected army cots and fell quickly to sleep.

About 0700, they opened their eyes to the dirtiest buildings they had ever seen. Archard stood by her cot and looked around in shocked disbelief. "Of all the dumps we've been in, this was the worst," she wrote. "Until now we hadn't known what dirt was." Human beings and animals had used the floors as latrines, and "there was a horrible stench of decaying flesh in the air."[26]

As Archard left the barracks to find Colonel Wiley, she ran into Lieutenants Molony and Meyers. "We're trying to figure out where that sickening odor is coming from," Molony said. "Something will have to be done about it before we start receiving casualties." She pointed off to the right. "It seems to be coming from that depression over there."[27]

As the three nurses walked toward the site, the nauseating odor filled their mouths and nostrils, triggering a gag reflex. They covered their noses and mouths with handkerchiefs and forced themselves to go forward. When they reached the edge of a ravine, they stood in sheer horror. "Oh, God!" Molony's voice was just above a whisper. They stared in disbelief at hundreds of amputated limbs from German wounded, arms and legs in haphazard piles scattered across a fifteen-foot area in front of them. Single hands and feet were peppered throughout the grotesque mounds of human flesh, and every inch was in various stages of putrefaction and decay. "Let's get out of here," Archard said. "I need to talk with Colonel Wiley."[28]

Five hours later, Colonel Wiley had selected another hospital site four miles from the dirty barracks and foul-smelling ravine. The 48th was under canvas again, set up in green fields with a cork grove along its farthest edge. Twenty miles away, there was fighting, yet hospital personnel were told that they would be receiving fewer patients since a four-hundred-bed evacuation hospital had moved thirty miles to the rear and would take wounded from several sectors.

On 25 April, Archard found it strange that they were receiving so few wounded, and she began asking Colonel Wiley specific questions. Up until this time, the 48th had been a "forward" hospital—that is, one of those field hospitals that moved to positions closest to the front lines. In fact, the 48th handled 90 percent of the wounded and ill soldiers in the

Tunisian campaign. Since it was practical and customary for patients to be delivered to the most forward hospital, Archard asked Wiley why the 48th was no longer receiving heavy numbers of casualties. "Yes," Wiley finally admitted. "We're being reorganized into an evacuation hospital. No more Unit 1 and 2." Their new hospital, farther to the rear, would receive less severe battle casualties that had already been stabilized by treatment at battalion aid stations and forward hospitals. Archard listened as Wiley explained that they would lose several nurses but that it would not happen right away. He also told her not to say anything to her staff until the reorganization became fact. That night, Archard decided to ask for a transfer.[29]

When Lieutenant Bernice Wilbur, chief nurse of the Mediterranean theater, visited the next day, she spoke with the chief nurses of Units 1 and 2, Lieutenants Salter and Archard, individually. Realizing that the reorganized hospital would need only one chief nurse, Archard requested a transfer to another hospital unit. Lieutenant Wilbur left with the assurance that she would consider Archard's comments in her decisions about the coming reorganization.

The North Africa Campaign was winding down, with signs of imminent American/Allied victory. On 15 April 1943, General Omar Bradley took command of the U.S. II Corps, and General George S. Patton took over command of American troops preparing for the invasion of Sicily. With a decline in battle casualties, the 48th Surgical Hospital had fewer patients to care for; therefore, nurses began working a five-hour shift, a far cry from the twelve- to eighteen-hour shifts they worked during the height of combat. The women began spending some time swimming in the bright blue Mediterranean Sea that was within walking distance of the hospital. On 22 April, the final phase of the Tunisian campaign began with an Allied drive north toward Tunis and Bizerte.

On Easter Day—25 April—Father Power and Chaplain Grove conducted services in a large supply tent especially decorated for the occasion. White sheets had been draped against one end of the tent and an altar had been placed in front of it. Large bouquets of yellow forsythia and purple rhododendron stood on either side of the sheet-draped altar, and red roses and Easter lilies were spread on top.

Nurses created their own Easter bonnets by attaching small wildflowers to the netting covering their helmets, and suggested to Lieutenant Ginny Ayres that it was a great time for her and Jamie to get married, since the Easter altar was the perfect background for a wedding. Ayres laughed. "It would take three months to get all the papers through channels," she said. "By then the flowers will be dead and the hospital will be located somewhere else."[30]

Since they could not have a wedding, nurses decided to hold a dance. Engineers laid a wooden floor in the large recreation tent, and a phonograph and donated records provided the music. Officers and GIs from companies stationed nearby showed up to enjoy the music and dance with "a real American woman."

On 1 May, the 48th Surgical Hospital was officially designated the 128th Evacuation Hospital, and several personnel changes began to take shape. About ten miles up the line, the 15th Evacuation Hospital had several openings. Lieutenant Salter was transferred to the 15th to become their new chief nurse, and three other nurses went with her. Archard became the chief nurse of the new 128th Evac Hospital.

The next day, Archard received word that if she went to Constantine, she could probably get some of the clothing her nurses needed so badly. Teddy Bair was down to her last pair of shoes, and size 4½ was not easy to find. With Sergeant John Ford as driver, Lieutenant Archard and Captain Henry Carney left for Constantine, about 170 miles to the west. Carney was to attend a meeting of the Eastern Base Section concerning an upcoming new assignment while Archard visited the supply depot. Colonel Wiley told the travelers that it was extremely unlikely that, with the quieting of the front, the hospital would move in the next few days, so they should take their time and enjoy themselves. Archard, dressed in her good blue uniform, borrowed brown oxfords, and a blue overseas cap, was determined to do just that.

The weather was springlike and wildflowers were everywhere. They passed through Bone and caught a glimpse of the ancient and beautiful cathedral atop one of its many hills. Evidence of the presence of American troops was everywhere in the Algerian town. Homesick soldiers had erected signs along the road: "Brooklyn 2,500 miles; Kansas City 3,100 miles; Miami 2,900 miles."[31]

The highway was in fairly good condition and the group made good time, arriving in Constantine by late afternoon of 3 May. They dropped Captain Carney at the command headquarters for the Eastern Base Section, where he would spend the night and meet them the next afternoon. As they drove on, Sergeant Ford turned to Archard. "Guess you'll be staying at one of the hospitals tonight," he said.

"Not if I can help it," Archard said. "I have a friend here. . . . She is a missionary and her husband is a doctor. I met them when we bivouacked here in January. Take me to the residential area and I'll see if I can find them."[32]

They traveled up and down streets for an hour without success. "I'd better drop you at a hospital, Lieutenant. It's getting late and I still have to find a place for myself for tonight."

"I'm tired of hospitals, Sergeant," Archard said, and she pointed toward the nicest house on the street where a motherly looking French woman was cutting flowers in the front garden. "Maybe she'll put me up for the night. The worst I can get is the 'bum's-rush.' "

Sergeant John Ford, a six-foot, dark-haired soldier from Oklahoma, parked the jeep and watched as Archard walked toward the woman.

"Bonjour, Madame," Archard said in perfect French. "Can you direct me to a hotel for the night? I've just arrived from Tabarca." The small, gray-haired woman stared at Archard without saying a word. Archard continued in French. "I'm an American army nurse, and have come to Constantine to try to get clothing for my nurses."

The phrase "American nurse" seemed to work magic. The woman threw her arms around Archard. "But, my little one, you will remain here for the night," she answered in rapid French. "I am happy to have an American nurse as a guest."

Archard returned to the jeep and smiled broadly at Sergeant Ford. "My luggage, James. I'm spending the night here."

"Why am I not surprised?" Ford said and carried Archard's overnight bag inside the house.[33]

The house was wonderful. Archard had a bedroom to herself, complete with an innerspring mattress and a down pillow, and her own bathroom.

"When you are ready, come to the dining room and we will eat," the woman said as she left to prepare their meal.[34]

Archard was delighted to find a large porcelain tub perched on sturdy claw feet along one bathroom wall. A bar of gardenia-scented soap lay in the soap dish beneath a fluffy pink towel, and there was hot running water. She filled the tub and undressed as steam rose and clouded the mirror above the small round sink.

As she lowered herself slowly into the hot water, Archard closed her eyes and leaned her back against the smooth-curved porcelain. She allowed herself to sink up to her chin in the luxurious touch of perfumed hot water that enveloped her body and surrendered to the feeling of extravagance as she stretched her body almost full-length in the spacious tub. The scent of gardenias was wonderful as she rubbed the bar between her hands, working up a frothy lather, inhaling its fragrance and totally forgetting about the horrors of war.

Forty minutes later, a refreshed and hungry Archard walked into the dining room and was reminded of home by a long mahogany table set with lace doilies, gleaming silver, and beautiful cream-colored china with a small pink hand-painted rose in its center. The matching sideboard held large silver bowls and two uncorked bottles of red wine. For Archard, who had been eating out of mess kits and C-ration cans over the previous five months, it looked like a little piece of heaven.

Dinner started with hot bouillon and good conversation. Madame Gorion and her late husband had been born in France and used to return there each year during the hot African summers. "When you Americans liberate my beloved country, I shall return there again each year," Madame Gorion said.[35]

The next course was a small plate of scrambled eggs with diced potatoes and Archard found it absolutely delicious. When Madame Gorion filled their wineglasses and served the main course, Archard could not believe her eyes. She closed them, and then opened them slowly. Yes, it was steak, and it was accompanied by a salad with artichokes, no larger than Brussels sprouts—tender and succulent—with an absolutely perfect dressing.

"This is too much," Archard said. "I will never be able to repay your hospitality. You must have used the food you had planned to use for days. Now you'll be back to rations just like me."

"It is worth every morsel to have a chance to help an American nurse," Madame Gorion said. "Now eat. We have strawberries and cream for dessert."[36]

The next morning, Sergeant Ford picked up Archard and drove her to the quartermaster's supply depot. Unfortunately, not one article of clothing that Archard needed for her nurses was available, but when the supply officer learned she was with the 48th Surgical Hospital, he opened up his storerooms to her. Archard was allowed to take all the lipstick, face powder, deodorant, cold cream, and facial tissues she wanted. Archard marveled at the wisdom of a War Department that did not supply nurses with long underwear, overalls, or shoes, but did not stint in providing the women with such essentials for frontline duty as lipstick and face powder.

Since Madame Gorion had invited Archard to bring her friends for cake and hot chocolate that afternoon, she stopped by the 26th General

U.S. Army Hospital, and invited Lieutenant Genevieve Kruzic to go with her. Kruzic was in Constantine for shipment to the States for surgery, and Archard figured she could use an afternoon out and a few luxuries. At 1615 on 4 May, the two nurses, Captain Carney, and Sergeant Ford were sitting in Madame Gorion's dining room, enjoying cake, cocoa, and conversation.

The following day, Archard, Carney, and Ford headed back for Tabarca. They picked up a convalescing lieutenant who was hitching a ride back to his unit at the front. By 1200, they had reached Bone and Sergeant Ford suggested that they pull over and eat C-rations for lunch before continuing. "Not I!" said Archard. "Let me out on this corner . . . I'll find a place to eat."[37]

Ten minutes later, a Frenchman Archard spoke with led the small group to a restaurant on a side street where British officers and a few Americans ate. A waiter met them at the door. "The officers, yes, but not the soldier," he said, and blocked their way. Archard raised her right eyebrow and fixed the waiter with "a chief-nurse stare." "Sergeant Ford is a non-commissioned officer," she said. "We are a team."

The waiter stood aside. "But of course, Madame," he said. "Follow me."[38]

They sat down to a steak lunch. By 1430, they were back on the road to Tabarca. Archard dozed off and awakened to Captain Carney's voice. "Where the hell is the hospital? The tents are gone!" The entire site at Tabarca was deserted.

The group drove on in blackout conditions—2100, 2200, 2300—but passed not one vehicle on the road, nor saw one other person. Suddenly Captain Carney sat up straight. "What's that ambulance doing over there?"

Sergeant Ford stopped the jeep and Carney and Archard walked toward the ambulance. As they got closer, they could see by the light of a half-moon that it was hanging by its driver's-side wheels over the edge of a ravine. A dozen or more bullet holes marked one side and glass from the shattered window on the passenger's side of the cab lay in small pieces inside. One of the rear doors was ajar. As Carney approached for a closer look, Archard went to the back to check for patients. In a minute, Carney joined Archard. "The driver is dead. The strafing just about took his head off."

"It also killed the four patients in the back," Archard said. "I doubt if they knew what hit them."

"We can report them to graves registration when we find the hospital," Carney said. "I'm not real sure we can find it in the dark." The sound of artillery in the distance grew louder and the horizon flashed yellow, orange, and greenish-white with explosions, tracer bullets, and flares.

"Maybe we should just spend the night here and start again in the morning," Archard said. "In fact, we should probably stay in the jeep right where it is. There may be mines along the sides of the road." Carney agreed, and it was decided that the four would spend the night in the jeep, in the middle of the road. The sound of artillery continued to shatter the silence while flares and tracer bullets lighted the horizon like lightning in a fierce summer storm. The young patient in their charge placed his head in Archard's lap and fell off to sleep. His companions kept watch, sitting up all night and dozing briefly when they could.[39]

The night seemed endless; the sounds grew louder, and the flashes in the distance grew brighter and lasted longer. Fighting was going on up ahead. The battle was fierce and the combat was near.

Archard watched, shivering with cold, as dawn reached across the night sky, trailing pale pink light in its wake. She leaned toward Captain Carney in the right front seat. "We should probably get started," she said in a low voice, not wanting to wake her patient unless they were about to start moving.

"We can drive a little, and see what we find," Carney said. He shook Sergeant Ford's shoulder. "We're going to drive a little farther ahead and see if the 128th Evac is up there. Try to stay in the middle of the road to avoid mines."

"Yes, sir," Sergeant Ford said. He turned the key and started the vehicle straight ahead. The forward motion awakened Archard's patient and he sat up and wiped the sleep from his eyes. As they followed the road, they could see fighting going on in the valley below. Ahead was a large hill, almost surrounded by a lake. Men were firing into the hill, and others who had taken cover on the hill were fighting back. After traveling a mile further, Archard and Carney decided that instead of traveling toward the combat, it would be better to turn around and retrace their steps. They had no idea where they were, and they longed to see other American and Allied soldiers.

"We only have about two gallons of gas left," Sergeant Ford said. He turned the jeep around. They had gone fifteen miles back when they saw a truck about an eighth of a mile away, moving toward them. Suddenly, a loud explosion filled the air and white smoke all but covered the truck. Sergeant Ford stepped on the gas and they closed with the truck. As they got closer, they realized it was an American vehicle. The jeep stopped and Archard, Ford, and Carney ran forward. Archard could see that the truck had triggered a land mine and that the back of the truck and the trailer it was towing were blown to bits. Three ashen-faced GIs emerged from the cab.

"Are you all right?" Archard asked as she reached the shaken men.

"I think so," a blond-haired corporal said. "That was one hell of a close call."

"You said it, brother," Archard said. "We drove over the same road last night, but weren't heavy enough to trigger the mine."[40]

They talked for ten minutes and the three GIs decided to stay with their wrecked vehicle and wait for someone from their unit to come along on their way to the front. Archard finally convinced her group that it was safe to continue on their trip back to Tabarca. "The middle of the road must be clear or their truck and trailer wouldn't have gotten this far," she reasoned.[41]

After traveling for two miles, they saw a sign pointing to an American clearing station (where the wounded were sorted and sent to the most advantageous hospital for their wounds). There was a collective sigh of relief. They could get coffee, directions, and gasoline to get to the 128th Evac.

No one in the jeep was prepared for the welcome they received from clearing station personnel. GIs surrounded the jeep. "Holy cow! An American woman out here. Hey, guys! There's an army nurse here." Every soldier in the outfit came out to see Archard.

They gave their visitors coffee and powdered eggs while they listened to their stories and asked questions.

"Are you serious?" an incredulous captain asked. "You really don't know what you were watching this morning?" He met Archard's eyes. "You spent the night in no-man's-land. Our guys are fighting to take Mateur [a town about twenty miles from Bizerte], but it's still in German hands. You were wandering around between us and them. You're lucky to be alive!" He told them that the 128th Evac was in Sidi Nsir, about fifteen miles from Mateur, and gave them directions. "There's one hell of a battle going on up there; they're snowed under with casualties. They'll be very happy to see you."[42]

The 128th Evac was alive with activity and overflowing with casualties when Archard and her group arrived in Sidi Nsir just before 1200 on 6 May. Lieutenant Marie Kelly greeted Archard before the jeep rolled to a stop. "We've been receiving patients since last night. A lot of seriously wounded from mines. It's Gafsa, only worse!" Kelly reported.[43]

Archard changed her clothes and got right to work. Lieutenants Vilma Vogler and Gladys Romohr were working in the preoperative tent, talking in German to a small group of German POWs, assuring them that they would receive good care and not be harmed. Archard stopped near Vogler, who was speaking with a young German soldier who seemed to be giving her a piece of his mind. "What's his problem?" Archard asked.

Vogler looked at Archard. "He wants us to know that they are the superior race, and will soon push us out of North Africa." She shook her head. "He has shrapnel in both legs, but he'll be fine. He's sixteen and has been fighting for two years."[44]

Lieutenant Kelly came into the tent and told Archard that a GI with a very serious chest wound needed around-the-clock nursing. Archard assigned Lieutenant Gladys Self from Alabama to "special" the soldier (give one-on-one attention) during the day, and Lieutenant Luella Rodenburg to take over during the night. If he survived, the dark-haired soldier from Georgia would celebrate his twenty-first birthday in two days, and Self and Rodenburg were determined that he would see this birthday and many more. They worked constantly, administering intravenous fluids, clearing suction tubes, and making sure that the oxygen so necessary to serious chest casualties remained in place. Both women knew from experience that most soldiers with serious chest wounds fought to remove the oxygen mask, believing in their confusion that it was suffocating them. Constant vigilance was needed to keep the mask in place. On the morning of the boy's birthday, his condition stabilized and it became clear that he would live.

The Germans fought desperately, but to no avail. Although they inflicted heavy casualties on American and Allied troops, their own losses far outnumbered those they had inflicted on the Allies, and their defeat was imminent.

In just one week, 910 casualties from the Battle of Hill 609 at Mateur were brought to the 128th Evacuation Hospital. Of these, 394, the most seriously wounded, were admitted, while the rest were evacuated to hospitals in the rear.[45]

On 12 May, word reached the 128th that the campaign in North Africa was officially over. German and Italian troops surrendered en masse. General von Arnim was among the prisoners taken by Allied soldiers. On 13 May, General Giovanni Meese, Rommel's successor, surrendered the German Panzer Army, and on 15 May 1943, all fighting in North Africa ceased.

With the cessation of battle and the official end of the North Africa Campaign, it was time to examine the costs and evaluate the lessons learned in the six-month effort. American losses were high: 1,914 killed in action, 872 wounded in action, 1,400 prisoners of war taken, and more than 500 nonbattle casualties and disease cases, for a total of 4,893 casualties.[46]

It was clear from America's first confrontations with German and Italian forces that U.S. military forces had not been adequately trained or equipped for combat. Despite their unpreparedness, Americans doggedly pursued enemy troops all the way to Bizerte, where they finally surrendered. Army doctors, nurses, and corpsmen provided the best medical and surgical care as close to the front lines as possible, despite coming under fire themselves. But another look had to be taken at the standard medical and surgical supplies provided to overseas hospitals—this time with the advice of doctors and nurses who had been there, experienced the inadequacies, and had had to improvise what was needed.

Even though Operation Torch ended in success for the Allies, the United States had experienced serious problems with supply, inferior equipment, and inexperienced troops. It was clear, then, in May 1943, that America was not yet prepared to take part in a joint Allied invasion of France to liberate that country from Germany. Instead, it was decided that a joint invasion of Italy, Germany's weak Axis partner, would be the next Allied move.

The 128th staff were to evacuate their patients and close the hospital as soon as possible. In just two days, all but fifty patients had been transferred and troops and Rangers with the First Division began filtering back from the front. They were men who had crossed the Atlantic with the nurses in August 1942, and for many, it meant reuniting with friends and those who had become their family away from home.

It was during this time, on a day when rain was pouring down, that Archard, while making her way between tents through rivers of mud, looked up to see a kind-looking man with wire-rimmed glasses smiling at her from beneath his rain-soaked helmet. He held out his right hand.

"Hi, Lieutenant, I'm General [Omar] Bradley and I'd like to see your hospital."[47]

Colonel Wiley and Major Proffitt joined the group and Archard dropped back to walk with General Bradley's adjutant. "Do you have much pull with your boss, Captain?" Archard asked.

The young man grinned. "Maybe."

"Well, since the war is over here, why do we still have to wear these heavy helmets? Will you see what you can do for us?"

"Sure," the captain said. "I'll be glad to."[48]

Before General Bradley left the 128th, personnel received word that they could remove their heavy metal helmets, but they had to wear the lighter-weight helmet liners to prevent sunstroke.

In another day, the last patients were evacuated and the 128th Evac staff were told they were to shut down and finally get a couple of weeks of well-deserved rest. Tents were taken down, rolled up, and put on trucks for a move to a bivouac area. They were just about ready to leave when word came to set up and reopen again. One of the nearby evacuation hospitals that was designed to handle 750 patients now had a census of 1,300. The 128th was back in business.

It was the end of the beginning, but resting would have to wait. Less than a month later, and still without a rest, the 128th Evacuation Hospital would begin staging to care for the wounded of the next planned Allied invasion: Sicily.

CHAPTER FOUR

Staging for Italy

NEEDED, 50,000 ARMY NURSES

Spring–Summer 1943

I ask for my boys what every mother has a right to ask—that they be given full and adequate nursing care should the time come when they need it. Only you nurses who have not yet volunteered can give it. . . . You must not forget that you have it in your power to bring back some who otherwise surely will not return.

—*Eleanor Roosevelt, editorial,*
American Journal of Nursing, *August 1942*

O N 9 NOVEMBER 1942—one day after Lieutenants Helen Molony, Theresa Archard, Ruth Haskell, and the other nurses of the 48th Surgical Hospital landed with combat forces in North Africa—twenty-four-year-old Claudine Glidewell raised her right hand before a notary public in Wichita, Kansas, and was sworn into the U.S. Army Nurse Corps. The ceremony followed three days and nights of farewell parties where childhood friends, nursing school buddies, and longtime neighbors wished the pretty blue-eyed blonde well, and sent her off to war with their blessings and best wishes.

Claudine was now one of thousands of young women nurses who had been joining the armed forces in the months following America's entrance into the war in December 1941. In early 1942, the U.S. Army had announced that it would need at least fifty thousand military nurses to care for the wounded and sick of the battles to come, and set out to recruit women to fill this need. And in 1942, it was women—and only women—who were being recruited to fill the posts of army nurses.

There were male nurses in America. In the late 1930s and early 1940s, men were a very small minority in an occupation traditionally dominated by women. Despite the urgent need during wartime for military nurses, male nurses were barred from practicing their profession in the armed forces. During World War I, when seven male registered nurses petitioned Congress for the right to practice nursing within the Army Nurse Corps, the men were advised that ". . . all legislation strictly restricted membership in the Army Nurse Corps to women." The prevailing military opinion of the day was that the duties which naturally comprised a nurse's daily routine, such as bathing patients, emptying bedpans and urinals, and seeing that patients received nutritious meals or special diets, were too menial and degrading to be performed by men who had military status as officers. Some of the registered male nurses who had volunteered or were drafted into the military during World War II were placed in enlisted billets (jobs or positions) as medical technicians. Although the American Nurses Association ascribed to a philosophy that accepted and encouraged the employment of male nurses in both civilian and military life, military tradition and opinion was still firmly against male officers practicing nursing in the armed forces. It would be thirteen years before Second Lieutenant Edward Lyon, a nurse anesthetist from Kings Park, New York, would enter the Army Nurse Corps on 10 October 1955 as the first male nurse on active duty.[1]

Since there was no legal compulsion—no draft—to conscript women into the military nurse corps, the 1901 law that had established the U.S. Army Nurse Corps directed the U.S. Surgeon General to establish and maintain a list of nurses who were qualified to serve during a national emergency. By 1933, the American National Red Cross, though not technically a government agency, was recruiting nurses into a "reserve" from which the government could call the women into service during national emergencies, including war. This official reservoir of nurses from which the U.S. Army and Navy could supplement their nurse corps was referred to as the First Reserve of the American National Red Cross Nursing Service.

With the threat of war in 1940, the American National Red Cross began to recruit nurses for the First Reserve. Although the American National Red Cross is a voluntary agency, it acted as a quasi-governmental agency since it officially held the responsibility for recruiting nurses for the First Reserve, processing their applications, and reviewing their nursing credentials, thus relieving the Army and Navy Nurse Corps of these responsibilities at that time.

On 30 June 1940, the U.S. Army had 942 regular army nurses on active duty. The First Reserve had a list of 15,770 qualified registered nurses who had volunteered to serve in times of emergency or disaster. On 27 May 1941, with global war looming and a declaration of a national emergency by the U.S. government, the American National Red Cross activated these First Reserve nurses. They were called up to serve a one-year tour of active duty with either the U.S. Army or U.S. Navy Nurse Corps. When Japan, Germany, and Italy declared war against the United States in December 1941, the American National Red Cross launched a nationwide search for fifty thousand more nurses. A national appeal went out by radio, posters, pamphlets, magazines, nursing journals, and newspapers for registered nurses to volunteer for wartime duty in the Army and Navy Nurse Corps.

A 1942 Red Cross pamphlet entitled *Uncle Sam Needs Nurses* appealed to the consciences of registered nurses: "You nurses of the country have an inescapable burden to bear. The moral obligation imposed upon you

American National Red Cross photograph used to recruit military nurses for World War II. Left to right: LTJG Mary Brenner, U.S. Navy Nurse Corps; Priscilla Sheldon, American National Red Cross; and Lt. Anna Neidel, U.S. Army Nurse Corps (Authors' archives: Lt. Neidel was Rosemary Neidel-Greenlee's aunt)

by your years of preparation gives you no choice of road to follow. No one else can do your job. It takes years to prepare a nurse and the Army and Navy need you now. The only decision you have to make is where you are needed the most . . . not where you will be safest or your work easiest or your career most promising."[2]

On 12 April, the *Sunday New York Times* ran the following ad: "Needed: 50,000 nurses. Nursing is now a big-time career." The August 1942 *American Journal of Nursing* announced: "Nurses to the colors! Every nurse must serve—with the armed forces or at home. Which is your category? Priorities in nursing to meet the war emergency are here defined by the National Nursing Council for War Service."

In reply, thousands of young and not-so-young female registered nurses joined both the U.S. Army and U.S. Navy Nurse Corps. By 30 June 1943, approximately forty thousand women had been recruited for active duty, and the pressure to serve continued to be applied to civilian nurses. The American Nurses Association ran articles and editorials encouraging nurses to join the military. These volunteers could join either the "Regulars" or the "Reserves": the Regulars took women between the ages of twenty-two and thirty, while the Reserves took women up to the age of forty. For both, the women had to be unmarried, widowed, or divorced; to have graduated from an approved school of nursing as well as from high school; to hold U.S. citizenship or be a citizen of a friendly country; to hold state registration; and to be physically fit and "of good character and general suitability." A recruitment goal of two thousand nurses a month had been set; in some parts of the country local recruitment committees ferreted out civilian nurses who met the criteria and urged them to step forward and serve their country in either the army or the navy since ten thousand more nurses were needed. Thousands of civilian registered nurses did volunteer, passed the qualifications, and entered the military.[3]

Thousands of these volunteers would volunteer again or raise no objection when assigned to serve in frontline hospitals in combat zones all over the world. In the opening months of the war, the young women, with little or no military training, were assigned to field and evacuation hospitals and shipped overseas to live and work in combat zones as few as three miles from the front lines. These women volunteered to serve despite the fact that (as we saw earlier) under the 1920 Army Reorganization Act, the army offered only "relative rank" to military nurses— that is, the army paid women only 50 percent of the salaries paid to male officers of the same rank. Added to the inequity in pay was the fact that U.S. Army nurses, although given the relative rank of officers, did not rate a salute. Despite these inequities, the number of military nurses on active duty steadily increased from the June 1940 level of 942, to 12,475 by June 1942, and 36,607 by June 1943.[4]

If Claudine Glidewell had had her way, she would have signed up for the Army Nurse Corps almost a year earlier, immediately after America entered the war. But obligations at home stood in her way. Claudine's mother, Mrs. Hazel Glidewell, had been a widow for many years; moreover, Mrs. Glidewell had been seriously ill for two months before the Japanese launched their attack on Pearl Harbor. As the oldest of two children and the only daughter, Claudine assumed much of the responsibility for her younger brother, Stuart. Since Pearl Harbor, Stuart had been anxious to enlist in the army but, like his sister, had waited, hoping their mother's health would improve. For the first six months of 1942, Mrs. Glidewell's health was touch and go, and son and daughter considered it their responsibility to remain at home to support their mom.

Claudine was working as one of three nurses for Dr. Everett L. Cooper, Wichita's busiest obstetrician, and business was becoming more hectic with every passing month. Babies were arriving in record numbers from mid-September 1942 onward. The boom in births was beginning, understandably, nine months after the men of America had begun to take leave of their wives for the war. Claudine spent most of her time in the delivery room or on call. Despite the fact that three nurses were in Dr. Cooper's employ, Claudine's easygoing disposition and natural friendliness led to her being requested by name by expectant mothers when they went into labor. After a month of assisting at the births of scores of babies conceived on the eve of their fathers' departures for the war, Claudine decided to sign up for the Army Nurse Corps. Her mother was getting better every day, had resumed most of her household tasks, and with the monthly allotment from her daughter's military pay, and Stuart's help, would be able to get along well financially.

During the last week of October 1942, a letter arrived from the War Department ordering Claudine to report to Fort Riley, Kansas, in two weeks. When she broke the news to her family, Stuart had his own surprise. The twenty-two-year-old had enlisted in the army the previous day, and would leave for basic training before Claudine left for the Army Nurse Corps. Through tears, Mrs. Glidewell assured her children that, with allotments from both of them, she would be able to manage well financially, and otherwise. She told them she would miss them terribly, but was extremely proud that they wanted to serve their country. The evening was filled with reminiscences and laughter until the phone rang and Claudine was called out to assist Dr. Cooper with another delivery.

On Wednesday, 11 November, Claudine, her mother, and several of Stuart's friends from high school said good-bye to Stuart; they hugged and kissed the boy and shook his hand as he boarded a crowded train that carried him off to basic training with the U.S. Army Signal Corps. The next day, Mrs. Glidewell's heart would ache again as she and a half dozen friends accompanied Claudine to the Greyhound bus station. She held her daughter close and whispered through her tears, "I've already told God that I've only loaned my children to the army. He has to bring you back or listen to my complaints for a very long time."

"Honestly, Mom, I'll be fine," Claudine said. "Fort Riley is only one hundred miles away."

As the young woman stepped onto the bus, a familiar voice called out to her, "We'll be praying for you, Claudine." She knew without turning around that the voice belonged to her friend and Sunday school teacher, "Mom" Appleby. She took a window seat and waved to her mother and friends.

Mom Appleby had taught Claudine a lot over the years. As the driver closed the door and eased the bus toward the main road, Claudine could almost hear Mom Appleby advising her: "Always remember to trust in God; to have the courage to let Him watch over you; and for Heaven's sake, don't become a raving maniac when you're afraid."[5]

IF ANYONE HAD told the twenty-eight-year-old, brown-eyed brunette Evelyn "Andy" Anderson on 7 December 1941 that she would have to fight her way into the U.S. Army Nurse Corps, she would have laughed at such an absurd remark. The army had made it clear that they would need at least fifty thousand registered nurses to volunteer for the Army Nurse Corps. Yet when Evelyn Anderson raised her right hand and took the oath for admission, it was after two days of arguments with recruiters and examining physicians as to why being four pounds underweight should not keep her from serving her country as an army nurse. Finally, after many assurances that at five feet three and 107 pounds, she was "not underweight for her family," and that she "had always been thin but healthy," the army issued a waiver for her weight and allowed her to become an army nurse.[6]

On 16 March 1942 the army ordered Anderson to report to Fort George C. Meade in Maryland. Andy worked there as a surgical nurse for three weeks before being directed to report to Camp Shanks, New York, to join the 93rd Evacuation Hospital, which was to sail for an overseas theater of war. A waiver for insufficient body weight not only got a short, thin nurse into the Army Nurse Corps, it got her a ticket to the combat zone and a reservation for frontline military nursing.

AFTER A NEARLY one-hundred-mile trip, the bus from south-central Kansas carrying Claudine Glidewell and another new army nurse, June Gordon, Claudine's best friend, arrived at Fort Riley, in northeastern Kansas. As the bus made its way along the broad, tree-lined streets of the large military post, Claudine, from her window seat, could see neat red-brick houses standing behind the winter-bare branches of beautiful old oaks, hickories, and maples.

Fort Riley, a 100,000-acre military post, had been established in 1853. It was home to thousands of soldiers, including the First Infantry Division. The post included the U.S. Army correctional facility, an airfield, Irwin Army Community Hospital, and a smaller hospital facility called Camp Whitside. In addition to barracks, the post had multiple housing units for families, bachelor officers' quarters, and visiting officers' quarters.

The two station hospitals—Irwin Army and Camp Whitside—served thousands of troops at Fort Riley. Camp Whitside consisted of wards in multiple two-story wooden army buildings that were connected by outside wooden ramps to the nurses' quarters, a mess hall, and other buildings.

Lieutenant Glidewell was assigned to a medical ward where most of her patients were suffering from winter colds and seasonal flu, and the standard treatment was Brown's Cough Mixture and nosedrops administered every four hours. After several weeks at Camp Whitside, as other nurses who had been there longer were sent overseas, Glidewell's responsibilities increased until she was placed in charge of her ward—a long, open room with a center aisle lined by twelve beds on each long wall.

*Lt. Claudine "Speedy" Glidewell,
1943* (Courtesy of Claudine
Glidewell Doyle)

The beds were white and each had a white nightstand at the head on the left side.

One morning, the chief nurse, First Lieutenant Gertrude Ryan, called Glidewell to her office and asked her to "special" a young African-American soldier who was ill with a serious case of pneumonia. In 1942, before penicillin was available, pneumonia was far more likely to prove fatal than it is today. Claudine spent her eight-hour shifts in the young man's private room, changing his position, getting him to cough at regular intervals, administering medication and oxygen, helping him with his meals, and talking to the soldier about his family and getting well. After ten days, the private first class seemed to be out of danger. On what would very likely be one of her last eight-hour shifts specialing this soldier, Claudine was shocked to find that the young man appeared to have had a relapse: his temperature had suddenly soared to 104° Fahrenheit. But on closer inspection, Claudine noted that he did not look feverish and his skin did not feel hot. After twenty minutes of conversation, the patient admitted that he liked talking to Lieutenant Glidewell and did not want to lose her as a private duty nurse. He confessed to holding the thermometer against a hot tube of his bedside radio and promised not to do it again. Glidewell took his temperature and recorded the 98.6°F on his chart. She said good-bye to him that afternoon, convinced that when she returned to duty the next day, he would have been moved to an open ward.

After her shift ended, she met two friends and went to the Post Exchange (PX) to shop, and to the Officers' Club for dinner. When she returned to her quarters that evening, she opened the door to a wonderful and unexpected fragrance, the heady bouquet of dozens of red roses. Two very excited nurses met Claudine at the door, bursting with the news that four dozen red roses had been delivered that day. A card beside one of the vases read: "Thank you for taking such good care of one of our men." It was signed: "Sincerely, Sgt. Joe Lewis." Joe E. Lewis was the reigning heavyweight boxing champion of the world at the time, and a sergeant stationed at Fort Riley. He was also an African-American—or "Negro" or "Colored," as African-Americans were called then. Lewis's extravagant thanks to Claudine, a white nurse, for having crossed the line to give special care to an African-American soldier, underscored the segregation enforced at that time between "Coloreds" and whites in the military.[7]

When America entered the war in 1941, there were an estimated 8,000 female African-American registered nurses in the United States. Yet the U.S. Army set a recruitment quota of only 56 "Colored" nurses, who would be assigned to care only for Negro troops. During World War I, 18 African-American army nurses had served both black and white troops at Camp Sherman, Ohio, and Camp Grant, Illinois, during the influenza epidemic in late 1918. But the army would insist in 1941 that "Colored" troops be administered to by "Colored" nurses only and white troops be cared for by white nurses. In March 1941, the National Association of Colored Graduate Nurses (the American Nurses Association did not accept black nurses into its membership in 1941) initiated a campaign to convince the U.S. Army to increase the quota, but it was not until 1943 that the army raised its quota of African-American nurses to 160. At that time, African-American nurses were stationed at "Colored posts," such as Fort Huachuca, Arizona, and Tuskegee, Alabama. Not until mid-1944 did the army relax its segregation of "Colored" and white caregivers. By July 1945, approximately 500 African-American nurses were serving on active duty. Until segregation restrictions were lifted, white nurses and doctors treated injured and sick black troops stationed at segregated white posts like Fort Riley.[8]

Life at Fort Riley was not all work. The approximately one hundred army nurses were surrounded by thousands of men and the women never wanted for a date or male companionship. One night, Claudine Glidewell agreed to a double–blind date with Artemese Kessler, a former classmate from civilian nursing school. When the two nurses went to the dayroom to greet their escorts, a tall, blond, blue-eyed twenty-six-year-old lieutenant stepped up to Claudine and said, "Hi, I'm Frank Doyle. You're going with me." The four went to the Officers' Club, where Claudine and Lieutenant Doyle danced and talked for hours. Near the end of the evening as they sat together, Frank announced, "I'm going to marry you." Claudine laughed in amusement and disbelief.[9]

By Christmas, the couple had been on a half-dozen dates and Frank was increasingly more a part of Claudine's thoughts. When she developed a severe case of sinusitis two days after Christmas and was hospitalized at Fort Riley's main hospital, Claudine was surprised to learn that Frank had been admitted the night before with an upper respiratory infection. Since Frank was ambulatory and on the Officers' Ward, he was a frequent visitor. During his third visit, while Lieutenant Glidewell was floating in a haze brought on by an injection of morphine for a severe headache due to the sinusitis, Frank asked Claudine to marry him. She accepted without hesitation.

Toward the second week of January 1943, with both back on duty, Claudine received a phone call from Frank. In 1943, no one at Fort Riley, neither soldier nor nurse, had private phones in their rooms. One phone was stationed on each floor in the soldiers' or nurses' quarters and it was connected to the Fort Riley switchboard. When the phone rang, whoever was nearby answered and then tried to find the person being called. When Claudine came to the phone, she learned from Frank that he was leaving Fort Riley and being shipped to Paris, Texas. He asked to see her that night. They met and Frank presented his bride-to-be with an engagement ring that had been a gift from his grandparents. "I hope it's all right," he told Claudine. "It's the only ring I have, and it can be cut down to fit you." They said good-bye that night with the knowledge that Frank was to leave for Texas in a matter of hours, but they had made plans to marry in the spring.[10]

The next morning, Lieutenant Glidewell was called to the phone on her ward. It was Frank. His train was not leaving until that night and he wanted to see Claudine again before he left. As it turned out, she had a half-day off, so the two met in the middle of a snowstorm and took the bus to Manhattan, Kansas, for the day. During the twenty-mile trip, Frank convinced Claudine to marry him that afternoon and they trudged through thick falling snow to the courthouse for a license. At the time, Kansas did not require a blood test or a waiting period, so their next job was to find a man of the cloth to perform the ceremony. There were five ministers in Manhattan, and the Methodist clergyman would be available in midafternoon. That gave the pair enough time to stop by a jewelry store to purchase a wedding ring. They agreed on a gold band encircled by engraved orange blooms.

It was not unusual for women to marry men in the armed forces just before the soldiers left for overseas duty. In a world where the future of couples in love could end with a bullet or a bomb, young people took whatever happiness they could be sure of at the moment. Many of the brides who saw their men off to war either went to live with their parents or the groom's parents until the end of the war. Other civilian wives bonded together and shared apartments or rented houses until their husbands returned. There would be many a young wife who received a telegram from the War Department informing her that her husband had been killed or was missing in action. Many counted themselves lucky if they were pregnant with or had already given birth to their husband's child before he left for the front.

The reverse scenario—that of a young husband receiving news of his wife's death at the front—was a rarity in the 1940s, given that women were not soldiers. Nonetheless, it was a real possibility in the case of military nurses: the families of several army nurses who would later ship out for combat zones with Claudine Glidewell would receive a War Department telegram informing them that the women had been killed by enemy action in a combat area. Yet death was the last thing that concerned Claudine and Frank as they made their way through a Kansas snowstorm to the altar.

Three weeks later, in mid-February, Frank managed a fifteen-day leave and headed to Fort Riley to see his new wife. It was time for Claudine to tell the principal chief nurse of both hospitals at Fort Riley, First Lieutenant Pearl T. Ellis, that she was married. The chief nurse wished Claudine well, but told her that her maiden name could not be changed to her married name on the records. Claudine would remain "Lieutenant Glidewell" for the duration. However, Chief Nurse Ellis did give the new Mrs. Doyle permission to allow Lieutenant Doyle to stay in her room at night. The day after the first night Claudine and Frank spent together as husband and wife, Claudine and three other nurses received orders transferring them to Schick General Hospital in Clinton, Iowa. In the few days the women had left to them before leaving Fort Riley, Claudine managed to take Frank on a weekend trip to Wichita to meet her mother and friends. After returning, Frank spent the next leg of his honeymoon with his wife and three other army nurses in a crowded day coach headed for Clinton.

Given the nature of army barracks life, Claudine and Frank had not been able to spend much time alone together in the first month of their marriage. But once they reached Clinton, they were given a few hours alone. Since Schick General Hospital was brand new and had yet to receive its first patient, the principal chief nurse, First Lieutenant Jessie Locke, gave Lieutenant Glidewell permission to spend her off-duty hours at a hotel in Clinton. The newlyweds walked to the hotel hand-in-hand, looking forward to the novelty of privacy and time alone together, only to find Frank's mother sitting in the lobby waiting to meet her new daughter-in-law. The elder Mrs. Doyle had spent several days on the train from New York with the intent of surprising her son and his new wife. After three days spent with his bride and his mother, Frank boarded the train for Paris, Texas, while Lieutenant Glidewell reported to duty on the isolation ward of Schick General Hospital.

Glidewell was busy creating a nursing care plan for each type of communicable disease patient when the phone rang and she was asked to report to the chief nurse. She hurriedly reported to Lieutenant Locke, fearing she was about to receive bad news about Frank's train to Paris, Texas. Instead, Claudine was shocked to discover that she was being relieved of duty at Schick General and assigned to the 95th Evacuation Hospital, which was preparing to leave for a combat area. Someone had realized at the last minute that no nurses were assigned to the 95th Evac, so orders went out to twelve different army hospitals mobilizing one to six of their nurses for service overseas. The forty-four army nurses named were to join the officers and men of the 95th Evac at Camp Breckenridge, Kentucky.

Within twenty-four hours, Claudine left Clinton, Iowa, for Camp Breckenridge, Kentucky, on 5 March 1943. As was the case with all movements of troops and hospitals, exactly where Claudine and the 95th were headed and when were kept top secret from all, including the men and women of the 95th themselves. Claudine feared she would be shipped overseas before Frank had any knowledge that she had even left Schick General Hospital. At Breckenridge, on breaks between learning to pitch a pup tent and going on several long hikes, Claudine repeatedly placed long-distance calls to Paris, Texas, leaving messages with the switchboard operator for Frank to return her call. The process of placing long-distance phone calls in 1942, in the days before direct dialing and answering machines, was complicated: Claudine would call the switchboard and ask to be connected. Sometimes the call did not connect, or no one picked up, or Frank was unavailable to take the call. If he was unavailable, a message would be left with the switchboard at his camp. For days, Claudine had called and left messages; Frank called back several times only to find Claudine unavailable to take his call. On two or three occasions, Claudine missed Frank's return call by just five or ten minutes. After four days of near-heartbreaking misses, the chief nurse of the 95th Evac, First Lieutenant Blanche F. Sigman, allowed Claudine to leave a class on map reading to run to the orderly room and take her call.

Claudine and Frank talked for almost twenty minutes. It was ironic that Claudine was leaving for the front before Frank, and both remarked on how strange it seemed for a husband to be saying good-bye to his wife, who was being shipped to a combat zone. When each had told the other "I love you" for the third or fourth time, they said good-bye and Claudine clicked for the long-distance operator. In those days, the person who placed the long-distance call had to speak to a long-distance operator after the call was completed to get the charges and pay for the call. The military post where the long-distance call was placed billed the person placing the call. The operator's friendly voice told Claudine that the gentleman had paid for the call and Claudine went back to her map reading class. Three days later, she received a letter from Frank containing four one-dollar bills "to cover the charges"; obviously, Frank had understood that Claudine had arranged to pay for the call. As it turned out, neither had paid: the call had been placed so many times from each direction that the operators forgot who placed it originally and therefore failed to bill either party. Frank and Claudine's phone call was paid through the courtesy and confusion of Bell Telephone.

At Camp Breckenridge, the nurses spent a good amount of time learning how to pack a bedroll. "We were supposed to be able to roll the thing fast so we could clear out quickly in case of a retreat in the war zone," Claudine remembered. "In fact, that's how I got my nickname. I was rolling my bedroll for the third time when two nurses from Sioux City, Iowa, asked if I wanted to go to nearby Evansville, Indiana, to do some last-minute shopping. I shouted back that I'd be with them in a second, and that my middle name used to be 'Speed.' From there on everyone called me 'Speedy.' They even stenciled it on my equipment, duffel bag, bedroll, foot locker—everything had 'Speed' and the last three numbers of my service number stenciled on them."[11]

Nicknames did not stop with Claudine "Speedy" Glidewell. Her closest friends, the two nurses from Sioux City, Iowa, Bernice Walden and Isabelle Wheeler, were affectionately christened and stenciled, respectively, "Hut Sut" after a popular song of the day, and "Bee Wee."

In late March, Chief Nurse Lieutenant Sigman gave Claudine permission to go to Louisville on an overnight pass to visit a friend who had just had a child. Once the L&N train pulled into the railroad station, Claudine caught the bus to St. Matthews and the home of her new godchild. Marge, the child's mother, was waiting with a telegram in her hand when Claudine stepped off the bus. The telegram was short and to the point: "Return at once Stop Blanche Sigman."[12]

Claudine was not the only off-duty member of the 95th to be summarily called back to camp. Military police had gone into Evansville, Indiana, and other nearby towns to gather up all off-duty members of the 95th Evacuation Hospital who were away from camp. The 95th was being mobilized for the front.

Three days later, on 2 April 1943, at 2000, the personnel of the 95th Evac, dressed with full field packs—bedrolls, map cases, musette bags (large military shoulder bags used by both men and women), canteens, and helmets strapped to their pistol belts—boarded a train and left for Camp Shanks, New York. The unit traveled on a private train and the nurses had a Pullman car all to themselves. "Between the excitement of each new experience was the realization that we were off to a combat zone where real bullets, shells, and bombs would bring wounds and death every day," Claudine recalled. "It added flashes of solemnity to the party atmosphere we were living in."[13]

Their train arrived at Camp Shanks on 4 April, and they were the first troops to stay on the post. Like hundreds of other military camps in 1943, Camp Shanks had been thrown up virtually overnight to accommodate the training and movement of troops. Hence, everything was new, muddy, and untried. "The streets in the camp were rivers of mud and the wooden barracks had new army cots complete with new pillows," Claudine remembered. "I'll never forget those pillows. The feathers in them must have come straight from the chickens with no cleaning in between. They stunk to high heaven."[14]

The next day, the nurses discovered that the PX had almost nothing a woman might need or want. In fact, the manager asked them to make a list of things they should stock for the next women who would come through camp. Claudine, Hut, and Bee Wee spent a lot of time trying to

find items on a list that the army had given each to fill. One of the most
difficult items to find were a dozen Curity cloth diapers. Feminine products such as sanitary pads were not stocked at most post exchanges and it
was up to each individual army nurse to make certain she had a good
stand-in—cloth Curity diapers. Where a nurse found and purchased the
dozen diapers was totally the woman's responsibility. The washable cloth
diapers would also double as turbans in the heat and dust of future hospital sites.

U.S. Army nurses of the 95th Evacuation Hospital, 1943. Back row: *Lts.
Adeline "Si" Simonson, June Gordon, Isabelle "Bee Wee" Wheeler, Claudine
"Speedy" Glidewell, Bernice "Hut" Walden.* Kneeling: *Anita Foss and Lillie
"Pete" Peterson* (Courtesy of Claudine Glidewell Doyle)

Most of the 95th's time at Camp Shanks was taken up with immu-
nizations and the issuing of additional equipment. Every member of the
hospital received a full issue of chemically impregnated clothing that was
to be used in case of a poisonous gas attack by the Germans. The military
planners in World War II were quite concerned that the Germans might
employ some of the chemical agents they had used in World War I. The
chemically impregnated clothing was intended to protect military personnel from the effects of chemical agents that could enter the body

through exposed skin. One such agent was mustard gas, which when sprayed or exploded in shells would fall on exposed skin or untreated clothing and cause large balloonlike blisters, nausea, and vomiting. At the least, mustard gas was painful and disfiguring; at worst, it could be lethal. "They also made us carry two 'impregnated' mattress covers in our luggage," Claudine said. "We learned later that they were coverings for dead bodies in the combat zone. We never could figure out why they had to be treated for a gas attack." These impregnated clothes and mattress coverings were treated with a secret formula of chemicals and were to be used for the transport of corpses. Enlisted men referred to such clothes and mattress covers as "pregnant"; all members of the 95th were to turn these materials in to their quartermaster when they reached their frontline destination. "We kidded a lot," said Claudine, "about having to carry our own body bags overseas with us."[15]

After several days at Camp Shanks, the nurses received a thirty-six-hour pass to go into New York City. Bee Wee had not been feeling too well, and when they were getting ready to leave the post, Hut and Claudine noticed that she was covered with pink-red spots. "You've got measles!" Claudine said. "You'll have to stay here and stay in bed. If anyone comes into the room, cover your head up, or they won't let you go overseas with the rest of us."

"How are we going to get her on the ship?" Hut said. "You can see those spots a block away."

"Frank just sent me *Their Hearts Were Young and Gay*," Claudine said, referring to a novel by Cornelia Otis Skinner that was popular that year. "Lucky for us, I read it. Cornelia Otis Skinner and Emily Kimbrough [a well-known actress who was in the stage production] had to cover up a case of measles in the book. We'll do the same thing. Just stay in bed until we get back tomorrow."[16]

On 14 April, Claudine, Hut, and June Gordon met Frank's family at a fancy restaurant in New York City, had dinner, and promised to return the next evening, so Frank's sisters could give Claudine a bridal shower.

The next evening, while Frank's family waited for Claudine and her friends to appear for her bridal shower, Uncle Sam was throwing Claudine a going-away party. The 95th Evacuation Hospital, with full field packs and equipment, were boarding a train that would take them to a ferry, which would take them to a ship that would carry them to war.

At their destination, the Brooklyn Navy Yard, the nurses, doctors, and hospital personnel lined up in alphabetical order on the docks to board the USS *Mariposa*, a former luxury liner that had been refitted as a troopship. They were so heavily laden with field packs, bedrolls, "A" bags (suitcases), and "B" bags (duffel bags) that they were unable to sit down. "If we had sat down," Claudine said, "I'm not sure we could have gotten up again." Whatever extra energy Claudine and Hut had was directed to keeping an eye on Bee Wee and her cosmetically covered-up measles. They were not about to lose a buddy just when they were getting ready to sail.[17]

In addition to the 95th Evac, also boarding the troopship were the 93rd and the 56th Evacuation Hospitals; the 54th Medical Battalion; Army Air Forces officers and enlisted men; tank crews and officers; and the African-American men of the fighter squadron later to be dubbed "The Tuskegee Airmen," led by Lieutenant Colonel Benjamin O. Davis. As a naval officer called the 95th's roll by last name, each person answered with their first name, middle initial, and service number. If the information matched that on the officer's clipboard, the nurse or soldier was allowed to lumber up the gangplank and onto the ship. There were five decks on board, designated "A" through "E." The nurses were assigned quarters in C Deck, midway down into the hold of the ship.

On 15 April, the *Mariposa* sailed out of the Brooklyn Navy Yard alone, without the protection of a convoy, and began zigzagging her way toward what "latrine rumors" said would be North Africa. The nurses believed the comments of male naval officers who said the *Mariposa* was fast enough to outrun any German submarine and did not need to sail in a convoy. They did not add up the sailors' next remarks that the nurses were placed on C Deck "because it's the safest from bombs and torpedoes."[18]

Male officers and nurses were treated like first-class passengers. They were served two meals a day at tables covered with white linen and set with china and heavy silverware. Menus were printed and given out as souvenirs of the voyage. The same group met each day for meals. Claudine shared a table with Hut; Bee Wee; another nurse, Lieutenant Adeline Simonson, nicknamed "Si"; Lt. Neil Hansen, the hospital's adjutant and Bee Wee's steady beau since Camp Breckenridge; and two other officers of the 95th Evac.

The enlisted men were not so fortunate. They were billeted on lower decks, and bivouacked in the empty swimming pool and any other available corners. "Colored" soldiers were completely segregated from white soldiers; not only did the African-Americans have separate quarters, they were only allowed on the upper deck and in the mess hall for meals at different times from the whites.

Three days out to sea, on 19 April, all ships' passengers received a copy of a government-issue booklet, *How to Behave in North Africa*, and were told that they were headed for Casablanca in French Morocco. On 24 April, Lieutenant Claudine "Speedy" Glidewell and the rest of the 95th and 93rd Evacuation Hospitals landed there. The nurses got a quick look at some of the city as they climbed aboard 2.5-ton trucks and rode to what would be the new home for most of the nurses arriving at the port—the Internationale Première on the rue de la Gare. Before the war, the large building had been a boarding school for young French girls. Male officers and enlisted men had to march seven miles to Camp Don Passage, a staging area for American and Allied troops in the area.

Nurses of each hospital shared a large room that was divided into cubicles containing a bed, a chair, and a bureaulike storage cabinet. As soon as Bee Wee, Hut, and Claudine got their bearings and stowed their baggage, they got permission to look around the city.

In the following weeks in Casablanca, U.S. Army nurses met several groups of military nurses from Allied countries. "A group of nurses from the Belgian Congo were very sad about one of their nurses dying from amoebic dysentery and having to be left behind in a cemetery outside of Casablanca," Claudine remembered. The story came back to the nurses of the 95th Evac in earnest when they lined up at the quartermaster's to drop off the chemically impregnated clothing they had been issued in New York. They were told to keep and carry the two mattress-cover body bags.[19]

While in Casablanca, Claudine developed a cough that concerned Chief Nurse Blanche Sigman enough to take her to the 8th Evacuation Hospital, which was operating in the area. The doctors told Sigman that there were some changes in Claudine's chest X-ray, and that if they had shown up in the States, she would never have been sent overseas. Since there were no antibiotics at this time, they followed the standard treatment of the day, issuing Claudine a bottle of Brown's Cough Mixture, and the cough got better.

SIX TEAMS of the 2nd Auxiliary Surgical Group that were assigned to the 48th Surgical Hospital had landed in North Africa on D-Day, 8 November

1942; months later, in March 1943, the rest of the 2nd Auxiliary Surgical Group with its handpicked surgical specialists, experienced surgical nurses, and their enlisted men arrived in Rabat, French Morocco. For the first four days, the nurses were housed at a small hotel, L'Ecole de Jeanne, in the heart of the city. During this stay, Second Lieutenants Laura Ruth Hindman (known as "Ruthie") and Frances A. Miernicke ("Frenchie") learned that the rumors circulating among the natives were that the large group of American women at the hotel were concubines for the U.S. and Allied armies. "We took the rumors in good humor," Ruthie Hindman remembered. "The French Army did travel with concubines, and I guess the natives figured that all armies traveled with those amenities."[20]

Ruthie had earned her RN at the University of Pennsylvania and had joined the U.S. Army Nurse Corps in June 1941 with the idea of serving a year and then returning to civilian nursing. She was on a train heading for her first leave at home in Johnstown, Pennsylvania, on 7 December 1941, when she and the other passengers heard the news break on the train's radio that the Japanese had attacked American forces at Pearl Harbor. When she returned to her hospital at Camp Claiborne, Louisiana, Lieutenant Hindman was told that she was in the Army Nurse Corps not only for the full year she had signed up for, but the duration of the war plus an additional six months. She could not leave in June 1942 when her year was up. Although it had not been her choice to remain in the army, she volunteered for the 2nd Auxiliary Surgical Group, knowing full well that they would be assigned close to the front lines. "People came through Camp Claiborne on the way overseas," Ruthie said. "It didn't take me long to get the itch to go overseas, too. I wanted to be where the action was and I could be of the most help." The chief nurse suggested that, with Ruthie's operating-room experience, she would be a natural for the 2nd Auxiliary Surgical Group.[21]

The 2nd Aux was to be made up of 93 of the best surgeons in the country, 66 experienced army nurses, and 139 enlisted men to assist the doctors and nurses at surgery on the front lines. Second Auxiliary Surgical Group teams were to supplement the surgical staffs of various forward hospitals. The surgical teams would most often be stationed at those hospitals located three to fifteen miles behind the front lines, and would sometimes find themselves in enemy territory if American and Allied troops pulled back on short notice. Ruthie Hindman and Frances Miernicke had volunteered for an assignment that would guarantee them all the action they could stand.

On 22 March 1943, the entire 2nd Aux was transferred to Rabat, where they set up and operated a tent hospital on the Sultan's Racetrack. Each morning the Sultan's Guard, dressed in colorful, flowing materials and mounted on beautiful Arabian stallions, paraded past the racetrack to the accompaniment of trumpets and large drums.

This hospital would prove an interesting and challenging location for doctors and nurses alike. Most surgery performed at the location was to correct the results of training accidents and parachute-jump mishaps. The patient load was low, since the hospital was located approximately nine hundred miles from the front lines. Casualties from the fighting in Tunisia, the battles of El Guettar and Gabès, were taken to hospitals assigned to frontline areas.

Auxiliary surgical groups were composed of individual specialty teams: orthopedic, thoracic, neurological, maxillofacial, ophthalmic, general surgery, and shock. Each specialty team was usually made up of a surgeon—the officer in charge—an assistant surgeon, an anesthetist, an operating-room nurse, and two OR technicians. One physician, one nurse, and two technicians usually comprised a "shock team": a medical team whose specialty was to stabilize a trauma victim in order to prepare him for surgery. The kind and number of specialty teams was based on the number of casualties expected with various types of wounds. Since broken bones from a bullet, shell, land mine, or booby trap were most common, several orthopedic surgical teams had to be assigned to more hospitals in more areas. Head and spinal injuries were relatively fewer than orthopedic injuries; therefore, fewer neurosurgical teams were needed, and these were positioned to serve larger areas in sites where they could receive wounded with spinal and head injuries from several frontline areas.

Rabat was one of the few places where all teams of the 2nd Aux were stationed together for any length of time. Friendships developed among the doctors and nurses who spent their off-duty hours playing gin rummy and sharing bull sessions. Assignments to the front would break the 2nd Aux into its individual teams. These assignments took the teams to specific combat zones or frontline hospitals and could last for days, weeks, or months, depending on the need. During such assignments, team members who traveled, worked, and played together were family in every sense but blood. Frequently, at the end of a particular campaign and before staging for the next assignment, teams were brought back together at 2nd Aux Headquarters—wherever it might be—to share the knowledge they had gained, and to be instructed on any new techniques or procedures that had been developed since their last time together as a surgical group. Such information gathering and sharing was due to the foresight and planning of the commanding officer, Colonel James H. Forsee, MC.

Forsee had determined before leaving the States, during the organization of the 2nd Auxiliary Surgical Group at Lawson General Hospital in Atlanta, that ongoing clinical education and detailed record keeping were critical to the progress of military medicine. Forsee set up periodic returns of the various surgical teams from the front lines to headquarters to ensure that all teams would share the new medical techniques they were rapidly developing ad hoc on the battlefields to treat the war wounded. These periodic returns by the surgical teams were times when members of various teams got to renew friendships and enjoy the closeness of an extended family. After a few days or a week, the teams were reassigned again and would look forward to their next "gathering."

On 9 April, after a few hours of leave in Rabat, Ruthie Hindman returned to her tent to find her belongings packed and orders waiting for her surgical team to leave immediately. Ruthie's team, Orthopedic Team 4, consisted of Major John Adams, a surgeon and graduate of the University of Virginia; Lieutenant Anna Bess Berret, a surgical nurse from Natchez, Mississippi; and Tech Sergeant 5 Theron G. McComb, an enlisted man. Ruthie and Orthopedic Team 4 rushed to catch a flight for Algiers and the British 95th General Hospital.

On 26 April, the 2nd Aux Headquarters was transferred to a dusty, rock-strewn hill southeast of Oran known as "Goat Hill." Battles were still going on in Tunisia, where American and Allied forces were still trying to drive the Germans out of Tunis and Bizerte. The 22nd marked the beginning of the final phase of the Tunisian campaign as the Allied forces battled their way into the northeast corner of Tunisia to capture Mateur and finally Bizerte in the weeks that followed. The 2nd Aux personnel were ordered to put up pup tents for living quarters and lived on C-rations until Colonel Forsee found them a villa in Ain-el-Turk, twenty odd miles southwest of Oran. More teams were sent to frontline hospitals, but the majority of personnel were still waiting for their assignments.

ON 10 MAY 1943, the forty-three nurses of the 16th Evacuation Hospital arrived in Mers-el-Kebir harbor aboard the USAT *John Erickson*. Rather than disembark immediately, the 16th was ordered to wait on board. Fourteen hours later, at 1600, the public address system crackled to life and the ship's captain announced the surrender of all German and Italian troops in North Africa.

Nurses, doctors, and enlisted men of the 16th were assigned to temporary duty at various operating hospitals in the area until 26 May, when Prisoner of War Camp 129 opened at Saint-Barbe-du-Tlelat, Algeria, fourteen miles outside Oran. The 16th Evacuation Hospital was assigned to the POW camp hospital and moved into tents in the barbed-wire-enclosed compound. The camp hospital housed three thousand wounded and ill German and Italian prisoners in need of surgery or suffering from dysentery, malaria, and jaundice.

Running and working in a POW camp hospital brought its own special problems. Since few people in the 16th Evac spoke fluent German or Italian, interpreters were employed on every ward and service. Even medical records that arrived with the POWs had to be translated in order that medical personnel could review their patients' medical histories.

Added to the language problems were problems born of cultural biases: German and Italian soldiers had a strong animosity toward each other. Thus, to avoid outbreaks of hostility between German and Italian POWs, it was necessary to keep the two nationalities separated. Further segregation was necessary among the German soldiers themselves, since men in the *Schutzstaffel* (the notorious elite "Special Services," or SS) and men in the Wehrmacht (regular foot soldiers of the German army) had distinctly different attitudes toward their captors. The SS men were stern and obeyed orders grudgingly, often refusing to cooperate fully with surgeons, nurses, and other medical staff. The SS used their rank and training to order regular German soldiers to be insolent toward and uncooperative with the Americans as well. Separating these different factions was one way to decrease friction and, hopefully, prevent the minor, petty revolts that threatened to disrupt the operation of the camp.

Hot, stagnant summer weather added mightily to the camp's problems. During the 16th Evac's stay in the compound, hot and humid sirocco winds blew steadily for more than two months without rain. The heat was oppressive and unrelenting, with temperatures during the day reaching as high as 132°F, and, of course, there was no air-conditioning in the hospital.

ON 15 MAY, a few days after the Allied defeat of the Germans in North Africa, the nurses of the 95th Evacuation Hospital were issued three days of C-rations, loaded onto trucks, and taken to Camp Don Passage, where they met the enlisted men of the 95th Evac for the first time and ate lunch with them in the crowded mess tent. The next day, the entire hospital loaded onto 2.5-ton trucks and started a two-day journey to their new hospital site, over three hundred miles away in Oujda, French Morocco.

On the first night of their trip, the 95th Evacuation Hospital bivouacked in a deserted field and GIs dug the nurses' latrine about thirty yards from their tents. Lunch and dinner had been C-rations, and by 2030, diarrhea had hit in earnest. Pedestrian traffic to and from all latrines grew heavier as the night wore on. About midnight, Claudine Glidewell ran as fast as she could toward the nurses' latrine. The moon was full and as she neared the canvas surrounding the slit trenches, she saw a GI stagger out the front opening. He pulled himself to attention and shouted, "Halt! Who goes there?"

"We had been given a password to tell the guards, but all I could think of was getting into the latrine," Glidewell remembered. "I never slowed down. I shouted, 'Me!,' and ran into and past the guard, knocking him and his rifle to one side. He didn't try to stop me. I guess he figured there wouldn't be too many German soldiers dressed in red polka-dot pajamas running for the nurses' latrine with a full moon lighting their way."[22]

On 24 May, the 95th Evacuation Hospital opened for business in a large wheat field that backed up to an olive grove. The nurses were quartered five to a pyramidal tent and each group marked their quarters with a small sign out front. Claudine, Bee Wee, Hut, Edna G. Ray, and Anita M. "Foo" Foss shared one tent and named it "Hut Two." Next to them was the "Fall Inn," shared by Si Simonson, Lillie H. "Pete" Peterson, Othelia "Oats" L. Rosten, Dora E. Witte, and Jennette "Jan" Smit.

The Rangers of the 509th Parachute Infantry Regiment were assigned to the 95th Evac for all necessary medical care. After a week, a call went out for nurses to volunteer for training as anesthetists, and Claudine and Si stepped forward. The next unit assigned to the 95th Evac for care was the Eighty-second Airborne Division. The division was taking part in a parachute exhibition for visiting "top brass" when a freak accident landed scores of them in surgery.

"The guys had jumped and were about three hundred feet from the ground when the wind shifted and collapsed about fifty chutes," Claudine remembered. "One by one the troopers hit the ground, breaking ankles, feet, legs, and arms. And one by one Si and I put them to sleep to have their injuries repaired. We'd ask them to count as we gave them Pentothal and most of them never got beyond four."[23]

During off-duty hours, Claudine, Si, and the other two nurse anesthetists prepared sterile packs for surgery and occasionally worked as scrub nurses in the OR. One hot 130° afternoon, General Eisenhower visited the 95th Evacuation Hospital. Lieutenants Glidewell, Simonson, and several other nurses and corpsmen were cleaning up after surgery when Eisenhower paid an unannounced visit to the operating-room tent. "We were all surprised to see him," Glidewell remembered. "He chatted with us for about fifteen minutes in that hot tent. We were all sweating and mopping our faces with handkerchiefs or the sleeves on our OR gowns as we talked. Tents seem to catch and focus the desert heat and everyone was suffering from its effects."[24]

Like Claudine Glidewell, Eisenhower was a Kansan and no stranger to hot weather. The heat of the OR tent, however, would have been extreme even for a Kansas prairie dog. About an hour after the general left, a big truck loaded with narrow-diameter pipe pulled up and parked by the OR tent. As three GIs got out and began unloading the pipe, Glidewell and Simonson went to the door to investigate. "What's all the pipe for?" Glidewell remembered her questions, and a GI's response: "General Eisenhower sent you people a present. Once we get it up and running, you'll love it." "Not unless it's a shower." Glidewell went back to work inside the OR tent. About an hour later, the soldiers had finished their job and a long line of narrow-diameter pipe ran along the top of the OR tent and hooked up to a water supply nearby. One of the GIs opened a valve and water shot through the pipe and out the many holes along its length. It flowed along the canvas roof and down the canvas walls of the large tent, providing the U.S. Army's 1943 version of air-conditioning to a hot and sweating OR crew. "It was wonderful," Glidewell remembered. "It was one of the nicest presents a commanding general could have given to an evacuation hospital set up in a desert."[25]

The 95th Evac's staff had another way to beat the heat. On several sweltering afternoons, nurses, doctors, and enlisted men traveled forty miles by GI trucks to swim at Fort Said. As the French-style bathing suits were more revealing than the nurses were used to, several of them created their own bathing suits out of white Turkish towels and blue bloomers they had purchased at the PX. The bathing suits worked fine

and traveled with the nurses to other beaches in the months and years
that followed.

SINCE TROOPS and equipment were now assembled in North Africa, it
was decided that a joint invasion of Sicily would be the Allies' next blow
against Axis forces. "Operation Husky"—the invasion of Sicily—was
secretly set for July 1943.

On 21 May 1943, Lieutenant Evelyn Anderson, along with the 41
other nurses, 38 officers, and 246 enlisted men of the 400-bed 93rd Evacuation Hospital, left Staging Area #2, nicknamed "Agony Hill," for
Oran, Algeria. All boarded trucks that carried the staff over mountainous roads to a campsite near Mascara, about fifty miles southeast of
Oran. They arrived at 1530 and immediately began setting up the hospital in a wheat field. But just a few weeks after setting up, the 93rd
received word to mobilize for the next planned invasion, which, as yet,
was a secret. "We evacuated our patients," Anderson recalled, "and
began preparing for our move to care for new frontline casualties."[26]

The 93rd Evac began sorting and packing its equipment into "twenty
'cut-down cab-height' vehicles including two ambulances and two 750-
gallon water trucks." With this combat loading, the trucks would be able
to drive off LSTs (landing ship tanks) onto the beaches of the new invasion site, which rumor said would be Sicily.[27]

To make setting up faster, the supply officer divided all ward equipment into twenty-two parts. Each individual part contained all the
equipment needed for one particular ward. Each part was then subdivided into four large chests to facilitate the reconstruction of the ward:
chest 1 contained plasma, saline solution, and medicines; chest 2 was
packed with mess equipment and patient pajamas; chest 3 held soap,
towels, and mosquito bars to support netting around patient beds; and
chest 4 carried mosquito bar spreaders to hold the nets in place. Several
supplemental chests were packed with specific ward equipment and
clearly marked so everything could be found and accessed quickly.
Surgery, X-ray, and laboratory subdivided their equipment in the same
way so that hospital staff could accept and treat the wounded as quickly
and efficiently as possible.

Careful planning by the supply staff even included the placement of
the trucks aboard so that no two similarly loaded trucks were on the
same ship. Troops in the Sicilian invasion would benefit from lessons

learned in supply problems that had occurred during Operation Torch. As a final precaution, hospital personnel were divided so that no one ship carried all the surgeons, all the corpsmen, or all the X-ray or laboratory technicians.

During the first days of July 1943, the staff of the 93rd Evac began loading and boarding ships in preparation for their participation in the invasion of Sicily.

PART TWO

The Italian Campaign

With the cessation of hostilities in North Africa in mid-1943, the Allies turned their sights on Europe. The liberation of France was the objective. But after the battles in North Africa in which the United States experienced serious problems with supply, inferior equipment, and inexperienced troops, it was clear that America was not yet prepared in 1943 to take part in a joint Allied invasion of France. Allied sights turned to Italy instead.

Three invasions—into the island of Sicily on 10 July 1943; the shores of Salerno on 9 September 1943; and the beaches of Anzio on 22 January 1944—comprised the Italian Campaign. Approximately 5,500 U.S. Army nurses served on the front lines in Italy. Many saw some of the roughest combat conditions in the war and earned themselves Purple Hearts, Silver Stars, and Bronze Stars for heroic action in the face of enemy fire. At Anzio—"Hell's Half-Acre"—six army nurses were killed by enemy bombing and shelling.

CHAPTER FIVE

Nurses in the Sicilian Campaign

TOUGH ENOUGH FOR PATTON'S ARMY

10 July–1 September 1943

Every night the Germans came over with planes and we rolled into foxholes. As the flak came through the tents, nurses wore helmets constantly. Everyone was frightened at first, but later paid no attention to it. Bombing and strafing are like thunder and lightning—the thunder scares you and the lightning kills you if it hits. . . .

—*Col. Raymond Scott, MC, U.S. Army,*
"Eleventh Evacuation Hospital in Sicily,"
American Journal of Nursing (*October 1943*)

IN FULL BATTLE DRESS, helmet straps unfastened and dangling at the sides of their faces, Lieutenant Evelyn "Andy" Anderson and the other forty-one nurses of the 93rd Evacuation Hospital stood at the rail of the USAT *Mexico* as she entered the Gulf of Gela, Sicily, on 13 July 1943. Three days before, American and British troops had stormed the beaches of Sicily. Now, the 93rd Evac's nurses were waiting to go ashore. Around them, U.S. Navy ships were firing at an unseen enemy on shore. With each heavy discharge from the ships' big guns, shock waves were set off across the gulf waters. Ships were burning, and "jagged pieces of debris bobbed and floated everywhere," Lieutenant Anderson recalled, "and between the inanimate wood, metal, and tatters of shoes and clothing, the bloated bodies of American soldiers clad in olive drab, floated face-down, bobbing up and down . . ."[1]

Lt. Evelyn "Andy" Anderson of the 93rd Evacuation Hospital (Courtesy of Evelyn Anderson Blank)

After the Allied success of Operation Torch in North Africa in May, General George C. Marshall and the American strategists argued for an invasion of Northern France in the early summer of 1943. But the British favored an invasion of Sicily; they felt that U.S. Army troops were still too green for an invasion of the European continent. Furthermore, the British reasoned that invading and occupying the island of Sicily offered several advantages: it would put Allied troops and equipment within two and a half miles of the toe of the Italian mainland; it would open Allied shipping lanes in the eastern Mediterranean and act as both a land bridge to the European continent and a barrier to enemy shipping across the Mediterranean Sea; it would provide a base of operations for future Allied offensives in the region; and, hopefully, it would shock Italy into surrendering and getting out of World War II. American and Allied soldiers and equipment were already on the coast of Tunisia, a mere ninety miles from the island of Sicily.

In the early morning hours of 10 July 1943, General George S. Patton's Seventh Army landed at three points on Sicily's southwest coast: Scoglitti, Gela, and Licata. It would be a few days later before the evacuation and field hospitals started to arrive. Unlike D-Day North Africa, no nurses went into Sicily alongside the invading troops on the first day, even though the military had wanted nurses there. The commanders who planned Operation Husky—the code name for the invasion of Sicily—had put in requests for army nurses to accompany the troops on D-Day.

The officers recognized the critical value of the services that had been provided by the nurses of the 48th Surgical Hospital who had landed right with troops in North Africa. General Eisenhower turned down the officers' requests.

Eisenhower had strong fears that if the American public discovered that its daughters had gone ashore on D-Day in North Africa, and again in Sicily, there might be such a negative outcry that it would be impossible to assign any army nurses whatsoever to any combat zone.

Although the army nurses of the 48th Surgical Hospital had performed admirably, had done everything that was asked or expected of them, and had done it with courage and willing hearts, Eisenhower would make his decision not as a soldier but as a politician. Awakening the American public to engage in a debate about the role and place of military nurses was one "sleeping dog" Eisenhower intended to let lie.

Now, on D+3, as the ship carrying the 93rd Evacuation Hospital pulled into Gela, smoke and the acrid odor of burning oil and cordite filled the air. It left a metallic taste in the mouths of the nurses. By late afternoon, landing barges carried the 93rd Evac's personnel as close to the beach as possible. Nurses waded ashore, arriving on the beach "sloppy-wet and looking like sad-sacks," Anderson remembered. "It was very different from our arrival at Casablanca." Anderson and the 93rd Evac had arrived in Casablanca on the evening the Allies declared victory in North Africa; a marching band welcomed the newly arrived hospital and celebrated the victory. On the Sicilian beachhead, "there were no welcoming bands—just the roar of navy guns and planes flying overhead."[2]

It was just starting to get dark when GI trucks carried the nurses to the 93rd's bivouac area, a wheat field about a mile away from the small, dirty town of Gela. After a quick meal of K-rations, it was time to turn in. "Our beds that night were bales of straw," Anderson recalled. The next thing they knew, German planes were overhead. "Bombs were falling, and two hit near our straw beds. We ran for foxholes and nearby slit trenches as fast as we could." Anderson jumped into a foxhole and squeezed between two fellow nurses.[3]

The next afternoon, 14 July, forty-two sleepy nurses again climbed aboard trucks and traveled five miles inland to their new hospital site at Gela. The route took them over bomb-scarred roads in scorching heat. "There were wrecked trucks and rotting carcasses of horses and cows all along the narrow roads," Anderson remembered. "The odor of decaying flesh was absolutely nauseating. We covered our noses and mouths with handkerchiefs but it didn't help much. I don't think I'll ever get those pictures and odors completely out of my mind. Even worse were the occasional bloated bodies of dead American soldiers waiting for the graves registration crews to come along and collect them. Somebody's son, brother, or sweetheart, swollen and decaying in the ovenlike heat. You don't forget things like that. You'd like to, but you don't."[4]

When the nurses arrived at the Gela hospital site, it was a carnival of organized chaos. Enlisted men, in groups ranging from four to ten, were putting up the more than seventy large tents that would house the hospital, its patients, and its personnel. Left to their ingenuity, Anderson and her sister nurses put up their own pup tents. "They ranged from an accommodation for four to a bedroll covered with mosquito netting," Anderson said.[5]

The four-hundred-bed 93rd Evacuation Hospital had been assigned to support the veteran First Infantry Division, which had been reinforced with two battalions of Rangers led by Lieutenant Colonel William O. Darby. On 16 July, the 93rd Evac began accepting patients. For more than a week, they worked twelve-hour shifts as battle casualties poured into the hospital. At night, the operating-room tent was lighted by kerosene lamps and surgical teams worked around the clock. Water was scarce and an occasional bath out of one's helmet was considered a luxury. Food for that week consisted totally of C-rations and K-rations, but the menu did not discourage the hundreds of insects that swarmed over, under, and through tents, bedrolls, and clothing. "If anyone was squeamish about bugs, they had to get over it fast," Andy recalled.[6]

General Terry Allen's First Infantry Division with its assigned Rangers were fighting their way up the center of the island to its northwest corner at Palermo; on 22 July, they reached Palermo and turned east toward Messina. Meanwhile, the British Eighth Army was fighting its way up Sicily's eastern coast to Messina. General Patton's plan was to catch German forces in a pincer movement at Messina, trapping the enemy between the U.S. Seventh Army coming at Messina from the western side of the island, and the British Eighth Army coming up the east coast north through Catania. Patton's aim was to prevent German and Axis troops from escaping across the Straits of Messina to Italy.

By the time the 93rd Evacuation Hospital was ordered to move to a new site on 24 July, the staff had treated 544 patients in eight days and evacuated them by air or hospital ship to North Africa for further care. The hospital pulled up stakes at Gela at 1600, piled into GI trucks, and began a harrowing thirteen-hour ride north through narrow mountain roads and along bomb crater–strewn detours. When darkness fell, so did the temperature. "We huddled together and shared our blankets in an attempt to get warm," Andy said. "In the moonlight we could see the bombed-out houses of small towns, and here and there, an American grave detail gathering bodies. We were traveling in complete blackout conditions and several times, going through the mountains, the turns were so sharp that our trucks would have to stop, back up, and then try the hairpin turns. We were all glad we couldn't see the drop-offs. Several GIs had already told us they went straight down for a hundred feet or more. The information didn't make us feel any more relaxed about the trip."[7]

At 0445 on 25 July, the convoy of trucks pulled into their new hospital site on a rocky mountainside at Petralia in north-central Sicily, four miles from the front lines and twenty miles from the northern coast. "Somehow the war seemed less threatening than the possibility of driving off a cliff and never being seen again," Andy remembered. "We got to rest for about two hours. We just stretched out on the ground in our clothes, and most of us actually fell to sleep. We were all so glad to be lying on something that wasn't moving, something you couldn't fall off of and disappear into the night."[8]

At daybreak that morning, the hospital was set up and began receiving battle casualties and sick soldiers. Combat wounds ranged from comparatively simple gunshot wounds to massive head injuries to traumatic amputations. Many of the casualties were the result of land mines the Germans had sewn in dense patterns along and beside roads as they hurriedly retreated toward the port of Messina. Every minute the Germans could gain by slowing the pursuit of American troops meant extra time for German and Axis forces to withdraw themselves and their equipment to the Italian mainland.

General Montgomery's Eighth Army was encountering problems and making slow progress from their landing site at Syracuse up the east coast to their goal of capturing Messina and cutting off the German retreat. Patton was galled that he and his American troops had been denied Sicily's east coast route. Ever since the debacle at Kasserine Pass, the British lacked confidence in American combat troops; hence Montgomery and the Eighth Army had been given the east coast route. As a student of history and a believer in reincarnation, Patton had wanted to follow the east coast that historically had been the route for many victorious invaders. Patton had already pointed out to the British that that

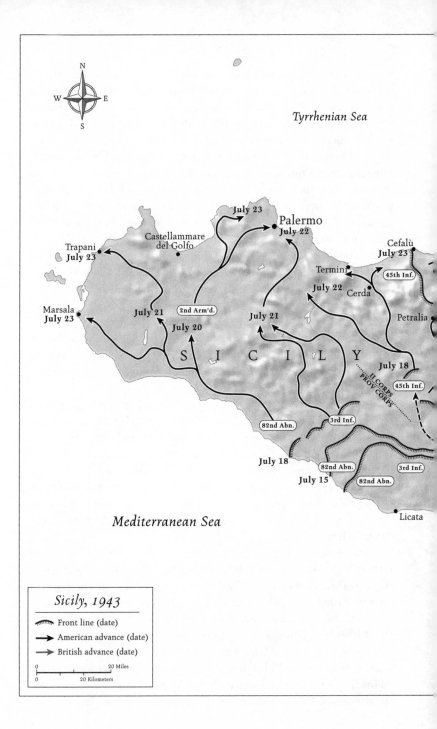

Sicily, 1943

- Front line (date)
- American advance (date)
- British advance (date)

0   20 Miles
0   20 Kilometers

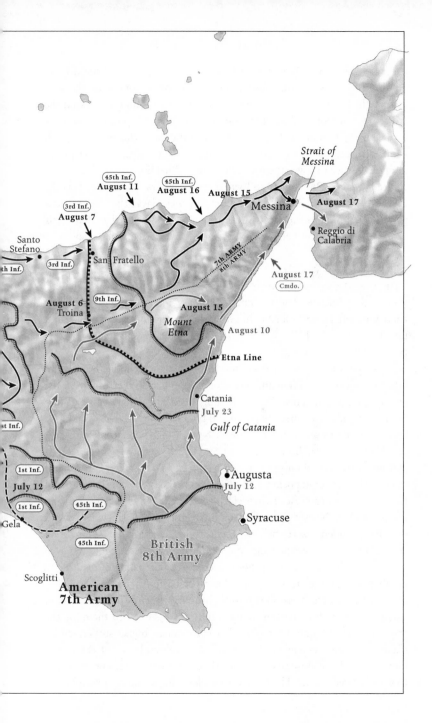

Santo
Stefano

San Fratello

Santo Stefano

(3rd Inf.)
August 7

(45th Inf.)
August 11

(45th Inf.)
August 16

August 15

August 17

Messina

Strait of
Messina

Reggio di
Calabria

7th ARMY
8th ARMY

August 17
(Cmdo.)

August 6
Troina

(9th Inf.)

August 15

Mount
Etna

August 10

Etna Line

Catania
July 23

Gulf of Catania

Augusta
July 12

Syracuse

(1st Inf.)
July 12

(1st Inf.)

Gela

(45th Inf.)

(45th Inf.)

British
8th Army

Scoglitti

American
7th Army

(3rd Inf.)

route held the key to Messina. Not a man to take a perceived slight lying down, Patton was determined that his Seventh Army coming up the west side of the island would beat the British to Messina, and he pressed the troops to move forward quickly. The five U.S. Army hospitals on Sicily—the 11th, 15th, and 93rd Evacuation Hospitals and the 10th and 11th field hospitals—kept up with the rapid American advance by leapfrogging each other to cover the ever-advancing Allied lines.

At 1300 on 25 July, the 93rd Evac received its first patients at Petralia in north-central Sicily. Over the next thirteen days, the 305 hospital personnel, which included just 42 nurses and 38 officers, handled 1,292 wounded and sick soldiers—an average of 100 new casualties a day.[9]

THE 128TH Evacuation Hospital (formerly the 48th Surgical Hospital) remained in Bizerte, Tunisia, until 20 July, when an advance section of their unit left by LSTs for Sicily. On 27 July, two more sections of their unit left Bizerte on LSTs packed with hospital equipment, including 2.5-ton trucks.

The plan was for the nurses to follow in a matter of hours, but several mix-ups in transportation and a lack of shipping space kept them in the crowded staging area near Bizerte harbor for an additional day. Finally, at noon on 28 July, the nurses lined up and boarded an LST that would take them to Sicily to rejoin their hospital. Ninety-nine percent of their personal belongings had been sent ahead, and the nurses, dressed in coveralls and helmets, carried only a musette bag, a gas mask, and a tube of lipstick in their coverall pockets. The lipstick was to keep their lips moist in the hot sun, but the rest of their clothes and belongings were packed and aboard a ship. Nurses were glad to finally be leaving fly-infested and dysentery-ridden Bizerte behind. Lieutenant Helen Molony summed up conditions in Bizerte when she commented, "If these flies get any more brazen, they'll be setting up housekeeping in our hair. I'm glad we're finally getting out of Bizerte. Sicily has to be better than this place."[10]

When the nurses were shown to their quarters below deck, they were surprised to see the Spartan living conditions assigned to them for the trip. "It was just one big room filled with canvas bunks suspended by chains," Molony remembered. "There were rows and rows of three- and four-tier bunks so close to each other that there was barely enough space to walk between them. The tiers were so close that if you bent your knees, they bumped the person in the bunk above you. And to top it all off, the fifty of us had to share two toilets."[11]

The women soon discovered that more than sixty nurses from the 59th Evacuation Hospital were also on board the LST. The 59th would operate a 750-bed hospital to support the 400-bed evacs—one of which was the 128th Evac. The smaller, more mobile evacuation hospitals would be closer to the front lines. Originally, planners called for one 750-bed hospital to support every two 400-bed evacs, but the scarcity of shipping space to move hospital supplies from North Africa to Sicily meant that the 59th Evac would be the only 750-bed hospital on the entire island. All told, the total evacuation, field, station, and general hospital beds in Sicily for an invasion force that would reach 200,000 men would number only 5,000—about one quarter of the beds that would actually be needed. It was the lack of transportation equipment that kept beds, people, and supplies from being moved to where they were needed.[12]

After the nurses were aboard, Lieutenant Archard asked the LST's captain to pull out into the channel so that nurses who had bathing suits in their musette bags could go swimming and get some relief from the oppressive heat. The captain complied, and when the LST stopped in the middle of the channel, he ordered the gangplank lowered. "We had a few nurses who couldn't swim and the crew threw life preservers and rubber rafts into the water around them in addition to tying a rope around each one's waist," Molony said. "All of the crew who didn't have an assignment stood on deck and kept an eye on the women. No group of nurses ever had more willing or better-looking lifeguards."[13]

In a couple of hours, the LST was signaled to return to the harbor and form-up for the convoy to Sicily. As it took its place among the other LCIs, LSTs, corvettes, and destroyers, and pulled out into the Mediterranean Sea, American fighter planes flew overhead like protecting angels. Those angels could protect them from the Germans and Italians, but they could not help one bit with the LST's pitching and tossing, or side-to-side rolling. It did not take long for seasickness to claim the nurses; one by one, they went below to lie in their hammocks.

Unfortunately, the constant roller-coaster motion seemed ten times worse below deck. "We didn't have much choice about going below," Molony said. "There were no benches or chairs on deck, and the metal itself was so hot from the sun that you could have fried an egg on it."[14]

When darkness fell, Archard ordered even the nurses with the strongest stomachs to go below for the night. They protested that they would "rather stay on deck," that it was "too crowded below" and the "cabin smelled awful" from the nurses' vomiting. But Chief Nurse Lieutenant Archard pointed out that the only ship's rail was "a twisted wire"—a lifeline secured to the perimeter of the deck to which a person could cling to avoid being washed overboard—and it would be too easy for someone to fall asleep and roll into the sea.[15]

"Nobody got much sleep that night. Those of us who weren't sick were busy emptying and rinsing the helmets the girls were vomiting into," Molony remembered. "We hung the helmets from the hammocks by their chin straps. Our only consolation was the thought that we'd be on land again in twenty-four hours. But that was the longest twenty-four hours any of us ever lived through."[16]

In the morning, those nurses who were not sick went to the mess for breakfast. It would not take some of them long to regret this action. After breakfast, Archard emptied one woman's helmet and gave her water to wash her mouth out so she might feel a little better. "All of a sudden," Archard recalled, "I got a funny feeling in the pit of my stomach, and without any warning, my breakfast was gone. I had it! I closed my eyes and tried to forget the wretched stomach, but it was no use. Nothing could cure me now but a long rest under a sycamore tree."[17]

The women in the hammocks above and below Archard were also throwing up into their helmets. The entire cabin reeked, and the increasing heat as the day wore on made the stench even worse. "The thought passed through my mind: when the war is over and the powers that be decide Hitler's fate, the best punishment for him will be to keep him bobbing up and down on an LST until he dies. I could think of nothing worse," Archard remembered.[18]

At about 1600 that afternoon, the LST increased its speed and left the convoy. An hour later, it was in port at Licata on the southern coast of Sicily, and the nurses, glad to be on solid land again, climbed into ambulances and traveled to the area where their male officers and enlisted men waited for them. Every nurse eagerly anticipated cleaning up and changing into clothes that did not stink.

But when they arrived, they were disappointed to learn that there were no clean clothes, and very few supplies of any kind. Ninety percent of the 128th's equipment was on a ship somewhere between North Africa and Sicily. The enlisted men had put up the few ward tents they had so the nurses could sleep under canvas. There were no cots, so the travel-weary nurses pulled out the one blanket they had learned to carry in their musette bags, spread it on the ground, and stretched out, using their bags as pillows.

The next morning, they awakened to a male voice calling to them to come and get their rations. "We were delighted to discover they weren't C-rations," Molony said. "They were five-in-one rations [U-rations] and had a can of ham and scrambled eggs, some kind of mixed fruit bar, and instant coffee—they called it powdered coffee—and the whole thing tasted pretty good to a bunch of women recovering from almost terminal seasickness and still smelling like vomit."[19]

After breakfast, Colonel Norman Wiley, the 128th's commanding officer, informed the nurses that most of the unit's supplies had arrived, and the hospital would be leaving for Cefalù, on the north-central coast of Sicily.

"We were absolutely delighted to discover that dinner consisted of spaghetti and meatballs out of our five-in-one rations," Molony said. "It was amazing what came out of that one cardboard box: tomato soup, lemonade, spaghetti and meatballs, even toilet paper and a can opener. It was just wonderful after those awful C-rations. . . ."[20]

"We passed through lots of small towns as we wound through those mountains. . . . We lost sight of the other trucks as we made some of those hairpin turns," Molony went on. "Many of the buildings in the little towns had propaganda about *Il Duce* [Italian for "The Leader"], Mussolini, painted on them in Italian. Townspeople would stand beneath those slogans and shout, *'Viva Americani!'* as if they had always been one of our allies."[21]

Almost every house roof in the villages they passed had trays of dark red tomato paste spread out to dry in the sun, and on the ground in front were large wooden trays holding tomatoes that had been beaten to a pulp.

As darkness fell, the convoy moved forward in complete blackout conditions. Enlisted men walked beside the trucks. Molony remembered, "They shouted warnings to the drivers. Stay to your right. There's a three-hundred-foot drop to the left."[22]

Thirteen hours after they had left Licata, the trucks pulled to the side of the road at their new hospital site, five miles outside the coastal town of Cefalù. It was 0300 on 31 July, and sleepy and road-weary nurses climbed off the truck and tried to make out forms in the blackness. GIs pointed them toward their tents, warning them to watch out for a deep cement ditch that ran through the area. The tents were empty. The women, who had grown expert at coping, spread out one blanket each, removed their GI shoes, stretched out on the ground, and fell fast asleep.

That afternoon, the hospital admitted scores of battle casualties, and soldiers suffering from dysentery and malaria as well. Sick soldiers with a temperature above 101°F were admitted and infusions of normal saline solution started immediately. Those with fevers below 101° were treated briefly for "fever of undetermined origin" (FUO) and sent back to their units, where they were confined to quarters.

Many FUOs turned out to be the first signs of malaria and the men were brought back to the hospital in a matter of days. *Malaria* literally means "bad air," and for hundreds of years, people erroneously believed that inhaled swamp vapors caused the illness. This mosquito-born disease is prevalent in Latin America, Asia, and Africa, but military medical planners knew that malaria would be a threat to troops in Sicily and parts of Italy as well. The female *Anopheles* mosquito transmits malaria; when the mosquito bites its victim, it injects protozoa into the bloodstream. These protozoa multiply within the human body, invade the liver, and feed on the body's red blood cells, leaving cell debris behind.

Left untreated, malaria can become chronic and, in its most severe form, damages vital organs such as the brain and kidneys when cell debris lodge in capillaries and obstruct the blood flow to these vital organs. Malaria symptoms—fever, chills, headaches, and muscle pain—appear from twelve to thirty days after protozoa enter the body. The oral drug quinine is the treatment, and after twenty-four hours of therapy, the number of protozoa decreases, as do the malarial symptoms. Patients usually recover within three to four days.

In all of malaria-infested Sicily, there was only one mosquito control unit. At the rate the Seventh Army was moving, that unit could do little or nothing to combat the natural conditions that bred malaria-bearing mosquitoes from one end of the island to the other. Although Seventh Army strategists had planned a theaterwide control program, the Allies' initial assault and rapid advance across the island left no time or opportunity for measures to be implemented. The Seventh Army plan assigned responsibilities to nonmedical personnel at each army echelon, established malaria control units, and assigned a medical officer as malariologist.

Army engineers worked in collaboration with the plan and it was the engineers who carried out most of the malaria control projects. Foremost was the draining of standing water—the breeding ground for mosquitoes. The engineers filled in bomb craters and improved the outflow of water from blocked drainage ditches. This was no small task, since dikes, drainage systems, and water-pumping equipment had been thoroughly and systematically destroyed by the retreating German army. German engineers left in their wake large sections of once-reclaimed land now flooded; these quickly became acres of mosquito-breeding beds.

Preventive measures against malaria under these circumstances proved extremely poor and precautions instituted to avoid the disease depended almost wholly on an honor system of taking Atabrine (quinacrine hydrochloride). The small yellow antimalarial tablets were poured into large bowls and placed on tables near the entrances of the mess tents. Each soldier was to take a tablet and swallow it before leaving the mess. For the first several days of preventive treatment, Atabrine's side effects of nausea, vomiting, and diarrhea were so severe and disabling that most people preferred to take their chances with malaria. Much of the Atabrine picked up by the soldiers remained inside their shirt pockets, where heat and perspiration finally melted the small yellow tablets, leaving a telltale stain. In the Seventh Army, the rate of malaria would increase from 83 per 1,000 in September 1943 to 193 per 1,000 in October 1943.[23]

Malaria was taking its toll on the 128th Evacuation Hospital's doctors, nurses, and medical corpsmen as well. One day early in September, as Corporal Marcus Duxbury, a mail clerk, drove back alone to the hospital on his daily mail run, he had a sudden onset of malaria symptoms. "Coming home that afternoon about 1:00 P.M., it hit me hard. Some of the natives were hauling wine in big barrels on two-wheel carts with a little donkey pulling it. Coming around the curve, I could hardly see them, everything was blurry. But I was close to home, so I made it," Duxbury recalled. "I pulled my truck to a stop just before everything went black. When I woke up, I was a patient in my own hospital and I had malaria. I was there for three days, flat in bed before I could do anything or recognize anyone. They thought I was gone."[24]

Duxbury joined a growing list of 128th personnel who were being admitted as patients. The hospital was becoming more shorthanded every day and personnel were working longer hours.

By the afternoon the nurses reached Cefalù, most of the supplies had also arrived except for their clothing and personal items. The women would have to live and work in the same vomit-stained coveralls they had worn crossing the Mediterranean. After the second day, one of them produced a bottle of perfume from her musette bag and all the nurses used it liberally in hopes of covering up the stench that seemed to worsen each day in the unrelenting heat.

Despite the minor inconveniences, the 128th Evac had special gifts for which to be thankful. "We were lucky to have two brain surgeons and their teams assigned to us," Molony said. "We could operate on head wounds right there instead of sending them over miles of rough roads to get treated. We had a special tent—an eighteen-bed ward—just for brain cases."[25]

Of the hundreds of battle casualties that poured into the 128th Evac at Cefalù, one young man stood out in the minds of many of the nurses. He was admitted with a sucking chest wound. A fluoroscope revealed a shell fragment lodged between the patient's vena cava and aorta, two major blood vessels adjoining the heart. There was little chance that the fragment could be removed without killing the patient, but if it were left where it was, the razor-sharp fragment would erode the wall of either or both blood vessels, causing massive hemorrhaging and certain death.

The patient's surgeon, Lieutenant Frank Tropea, decided to wait until nighttime to operate since temperatures would be cooler. "All the doctors and nurses knew what was going on, what was at stake," Molony remembered. "The OR was so quiet you could have heard a pin drop." Lieutenant Tropea incised the boy's chest and went inside after the shell fragment. "Everyone seemed to hold his breath while the surgeon probed around the soldier's heart. Then, with a hand as steady as a rock, he withdrew the hemostat with the bloody fragment held tightly in its tip. That was quite a piece of surgery. It was touch-and-go for a few days afterwards." Several nurses specialed the young soldier and were glad to see him on the road to recovery and returned to the United States.[26]

At Cefalù, 3,776 wounded and sick soldiers were triaged and treated, and 1,466 were admitted within the second two weeks of August. The strain created by this relentless pace was becoming more and more evident in the faces of hospital personnel. One day in mid-August, Lieutenant Archard was surprised by a visit from a doctor she had known in the States. He was the first person from home she had seen since leaving for England.[27]

"Blankety, blankety, blank!" Edward Shannon exclaimed at the sight of Archard. "What in thunder have they done to you? You look like blazes!" Archard was as yet unaware of the major changes frontline nursing had wrought in her appearance; it would be another two weeks before she had access to a full-length mirror and the time to look at herself and see what Shannon meant: she'd lost twenty-five pounds; she was dehydrated from dysentery; her skin was yellow from Atabrine and malarial symptoms; and her brown, curly hair had turned gray.

"Ed Shannon, you don't look so hot yourself, but I'm glad to see you," Archard said.[28]

ON 30 JULY 1943, the men of General Troy H. Middleton's Forty-fifth Infantry Division captured the town of San Stefano on the north coast of Sicily, approximately forty miles west of the port of Messina. Since General Patton planned to use that division in the invasion of the Italian mainland, he pulled them off the line on 1 August and replaced Middleton's men with the troops of Major General Lucian K. Truscott Jr.'s Third Division on the north coast road.

By 7 August, troops of Patton's Seventh Army were approaching the next fierce place of battle on the San Fratello line. A small village on Sicily's north shore, San Fratello was one of the sites where German troops had dug in. It was located on a 2,200-foot mountain peak overlooking the coastal road. When the Americans realized that they could not gain San Fratello with frontal attacks, General Truscott led an outflanking movement inland. Given the rough terrain and the destruction of roads and bridges by the Germans during their withdrawal, Truscott had to use a fifteen-mule-pack train to carry in supplies and to evacuate the wounded. Casualties were heavy, and on 7 August the 93rd Evacuation Hospital was transferred to a site outside San Stefano to care for the wounded.

It was at this site on 10 August that General Patton slapped a young soldier and set events in motion that nearly cost him his military career. Colonel Donald E. Currier, Medical Corps Commanding Officer of the 93rd Evacuation Hospital, wrote the following memorandum to his superiors:

1. On Monday afternoon, August 10, 1943, at approximately 1330, General Patton entered the Receiving Ward of the 93rd Evacuation Hospital (Mtz) and started interviewing and visiting the patients who were there. There were some 10 or 15 casualties in the tent at that time. The first five or six that he talked to were battle casualties. He asked each what his trouble was, commended them for their excel-

American troops make their way across the rugged Sicilian terrain, 1943 (U.S. Army Signal Corps)

lent fighting; told them they were doing a good job, and wished them a speedy recovery. He then came to one patient who upon inquiry stated he was sick with a high fever. The General dismissed him without comment. The next patient was sitting huddled up and shivvering [*sic*]. When asked what his trouble was, the man replied, "It's my nerves," and began to sob. The General then screamed at him, "What did you say?" The man replied, "It's my nerves, I cant [*sic*] stand the shelling any more." He was still sobbing. The General then yelled at him, "Your nerves Hell, you are just a God damn coward, you yellow son of a bitch." He then slapped the man and said, "Shut up that God damned crying. I wont [*sic*] have these brave men who have been shot seeing a yellow bastard sitting here crying." He then struck at the man again, knocking his helmet liner off and into the next tent. He then turned to the Receiving Officer and yelled, "Don't you admit this yellow bastard, Theres [sic] nothing the matter with him." I wont have the hospitals clutteredup [sic] with these sons of bitches who haven't the guts to fight." He turned to the man again who was managing to sit at attention though shaking all over and said, "You're going back to the front lines and you may get shot and killed but you're going to fight. If you don't, I'll stand you up against a wall and have a firing squad kill you on purpose. In fact," he said, reaching for his pistol, "I ought to shoot you myself, you God damned whimpering coward." As he went out of the ward, he was still yelling back at the Receiving Officer to send that yellow son of a bitch back to the front lines.

2. All this was in such a loud voice that nurses and patients in adjoining wards had come outside to see what the disturbance was.[29]

By night, talk of the incident had spread all over the hospital. Lieutenant Vera Sheaffer, a 93rd Evac nurse from Harrisburg, Pennsylvania, had her own opinion of Patton's actions. "If that had been one of my patients General Patton slapped," Sheaffer recalled, "I would have hit Patton myself. Believe me, most of the nurses felt the same way."[30]

Within hours of the incident, it was determined that the young soldier Patton had struck was not, by virtually anyone's account other than Patton, a coward: he had volunteered for the army, and before Patton's unannounced arrival, had already requested that he be sent back to his unit on the front lines as soon as possible. Furthermore, he was found to be suffering from more than just nerves; he had malaria, a high fever, and bone-racking chills.[31]

Patton's next stop after leaving the 93rd Evac on that day was to General Omar Bradley's headquarters, where he spoke casually about the incident.

"Sorry to be late, Bradley. I stopped off at a hospital on the way up. There were a couple of malingerers there. I slapped one of them to make him mad and put some fight back in him."[32]

When news of the incident hit the United States, several loud calls were heard from Congress and the public to fire Patton, but his commander, General Eisenhower, decided instead to reprimand him severely, order him to apologize to the soldier and everyone at the 93rd Evac, and place him on probation. Eisenhower and Bradley both believed that Patton was under a great deal of stress himself during the Sicilian Campaign, and Eisenhower decided not to lose a brilliant military strategist because of a mistake. Patton was needed if the battle for Sicily were still to be won and the Germans and Italians pursued to their surrender. That battle was far from over.

In mid-August 1943, the fighting in the area became more intense as German troops did all in their power to slow down the Allies so they could get as many men and as much equipment as possible across the Straits of Messina to the Italian mainland. The closer Patton's army got to Messina, the fiercer the German defense grew. On 14 August, half of the 128th Evacuation Hospital, including Lieutenant Archard and twenty-one other nurses, was transferred to San Stefano to care for the increasing numbers of wounded and sick soldiers.

The drive from Cefalù to San Stefano was a mixture of beauty and desolation. Brightly colored geraniums grew along stretches of the roadside, but every so many miles their loveliness was replaced by scenes of bombed-out trucks and houses. The vivid colors of summer became the stark grays and charcoal-black of war, then changed again in a mile or two, all the way into San Stefano. Unlike the sandy beaches at Cefalù and pleasant lemon grove where the nurses' tents had been erected, San Stefano was rocky, oppressively hot, and boasted cacti instead of fruit trees.

When the nurses arrived, they found two ward tents filled with malaria patients who needed their immediate attention. These men were amazed to learn, when they questioned the nurses, that the women had landed with the invasion forces in North Africa more than nine months earlier, on 8 November 1942.

The fighting just ahead of San Stefano was the final battle of Messina, and it was clear to everyone that the Sicilian Campaign would end in favor of the Allies and very soon. Between the ferocity of the battle and the end of the campaign, however, many good men would be brought to the 128th Evac.

During the third week in August, a young litter bearer from the 26th Medical Battalion arrived as a patient in his own ambulance, missing his right forearm and with a bullet wound to the abdomen. He needed to be operated on immediately and was given blood plasma followed by whole blood. "When he returned from the operating room," Lieutenant

Archard recalled, "we were told he had only a slim chance. With the most vigilant care, and plenty of it, he might make it. We gave him that care, and when we found out how he had been hurt, our admiration was unbounded."[33]

The boy's captain had written the story in his medical record and recommended the young litter bearer for a citation for bravery. The soldier himself filled in parts of the story when the nurses spoke with him. "He and his fellow litter bearer had just placed a patient on a litter when a sniper's bullet got him just above the elbow," Archard wrote in *G.I. Nightingale*. The bullet shattered the bone and left the forearm hanging by a few shreds.

> "There was no pain," he told us later when we questioned him. "I just looked at it and knew I would have to tie a tourniquet around that arm and remove the forearm." He asked his friend to do it, but the poor boy couldn't. He would help tie the tourniquet, though. After this had been done, the wounded boy took his knife from his pocket and opened it, using his teeth. He then removed his hanging forearm. With his left hand he helped carry the other wounded man back to the ambulance, and as they were putting the patient into the ambulance, another bullet got the litter bearer in the abdomen. He came back to us in the role of a patient. . . . Homage and care he got from us—we could do no more, but we gave that gratefully.[34]

The fighting ended on 17 August, when Patton's army beat Montgomery's British Eighth Army to Messina that morning. Thirty-eight days after American and Allied troops had gone ashore in Sicily, hostilities ended. Soldiers of the Third Division's Regimental Combat Team 7 entered Messina at 1000 on 17 August. Although American newspapers would carry headlines of an Allied victory in Sicily, the campaign would prove a disappointment in that approximately 40,000 German troops and between 70,000 and 75,000 Italian troops escaped to the Italian mainland through the port of Messina and lived to fight in future battles. The Germans managed to flee with 9,600 vehicles, 47 tanks, 94 artillery pieces, and 18,000 tons of supplies and ammunition. They left behind approximately 12,000 killed and captured German soldiers, but succeeded in evacuating most of their wounded. The losses suffered by Italian troops were even greater: 145,000 killed or captured.[35]

In the battle for Sicily, 4,958 American and Allied were killed. A total of 20,734 American soldiers, 338 Allied troops, and 1,583 enemy soldiers were admitted to U.S. Army hospitals on Sicily. Of the U.S. troops who were hospitalized, 5,106 were battle casualties, 2,308 were injured, and 13,320 were diseased. Since the total number of hospital beds did not exceed 5,000, 20,828 additional troops were admitted "to quarters" rather than hospitalized; of these, 14,635 were diseased and 6,193 had minor injuries and wounds. Despite the preventive measures against malaria, malaria cases outnumbered the battle-wounded on Sicily. Evacuation from Sicily during the campaign numbered 5,391 to hospital ships and 5,967 by air—a total of 11,358 evacuees.[36]

With the end of hostilities, the 128th was transferred on 24 August to Trapani on the northwest coast of Sicily, five miles west of Castellammare del Golfo, to take care of a division. By this time, several of the doctors and nurses were in the hospital as patients, and Archard was beginning to feel the effects of another attack of malaria. For Archard and her nurses, hopes were high that since the Sicilian Campaign had ended, they would get at least a week's rest without patients to nurse themselves back to health. When she asked Colonel Wiley if that were possible, he told her that it was not. Although the nurses and doctors were obviously ill themselves, they would be needed to care for troops staging for the invasion of Italy.

Archard helped prepare sick corpsmen, doctors, and nurses for an evacuation train that would carry them the eighty miles to Palermo. But the ambulance taking them to the train went to the wrong station and they were returned to the 128th for the night. They would travel the eighty miles to Palermo's general hospital the next morning by ambulances and trucks.

When the time came to depart, it was discovered that Archard was running a high fever from malaria and was also suffering from fatigue and dysentery. Despite her objections, she was added to the patient evacuation list and sent to Palermo with the others. She was feeling guilty for not being able to get her nurses the rest they needed and the dental care they had gone without for months. "Missing back teeth were one thing," Archard wrote, "but when the front ones started to go, it was time to do something."[37]

When they arrived in Palermo, they were taken directly to the nurses' ward. The staff at Palermo was as kind and helpful as could be, but all Archard and her nurses wanted was sleep. "We were even too tired to eat," Archard remembered. That night a young nurse awakened Archard and the others to tell them to turn in their beds so that their heads were away from the wall, and to put their helmets on to protect them from falling debris in case a bomb should drop near the hospital. Archard could not believe what she was hearing. "I looked up at the tops of the walls and the ceiling," she wrote. "They were at least fifteen feet above me. The beds were flush with the wall. If those walls started to crumble, it was all over with us. So I righted myself in bed, left the helmet on the floor, and went to sleep. Why should we be afraid here when [in Tunisia] at Gafsa, Maknassy and El Guettar all that had been between us and the planes was a stretch of canvas?" Archard looked at the young nurse fresh from the States. "Please, Miss Johnson," she said, "don't wake us up again for enemy planes. We've been living under them for such a long time we're going to miss them."[38]

Two days later, Helen Molony and another nurse from the 128th, Margaret B. Stanfill, came to Palermo to visit Archard and the other sick nurses, wanting to know how soon they'd be back with the unit. "Archard said they were sending them further back so they could get some food and gain back some weight," Molony remembered.[39]

The next day, Archard and the other nurses were taken to the airport to be evacuated to North Africa to catch a hospital ship for America. There were fifteen other ambulatory patients on the plane. As Archard went aboard, a doctor whispered in her ear, "Keep an eye on the patient with crosses on his shirt—he's mental. He has decided he wants to be a chaplain and has made crosses out of some metal material and fastened them onto his shirt." Archard was shocked at the request. "I wondered what I was to do in case he started something. I hadn't energy enough left to kill a fly, much less struggle with a mental patient."[40]

It was difficult for people, even in a combat zone, to think of a nurse as a patient in need of care, and not an inexhaustible caregiver.

AT BIZERTE in Tunisia, Frenchie Miernicke, Ruth Hindman, and other members of the 2nd Auxiliary Surgical Group were enjoying some rest and relaxation even as they prepared for the next invasion that would follow the Sicilian Campaign. The personnel of the 2nd Aux had been together since March, and by the third week in August, they felt more and more like a large family. Nurses with one or more siblings back home now found that they had more than sixty sisters and each felt that she had the rights of a blood relative.

Nothing made this clearer to Frenchie than the day a cablegram arrived for her from the States. "I was on my way back to my tent after a short walk when all of a sudden, more than ten of my Army Nurse Corps family came running toward me," Frenchie said. "One of the girls was waving a piece of paper and the rest were running along beside her, like a flock of geese who were headed for dinner. All of them were shouting at the top of their lungs, 'Your sister had twins! Your sister had twins!' They were as thrilled as if they had just become aunts for the first time, and no one even questioned their right to open a cablegram addressed to me. After all, we were family and family looks out for each other. Cablegrams could mean bad news, and they felt it was better if I got bad news from my Army Nurse Corps sisters than from a piece of paper. When it turned out to be great news, they came running to share it with me. They were all my sisters and my new niece and nephew belonged to all of us."[41]

One of the nurses' favorite R&R pastimes was visiting navy ships for dinner while they were in port. The U.S. Navy had delicious food and the 2nd Aux nurses were always getting invitations and encouraged to bring a couple of others along.

During the last week in August, Lieutenant Anna K. McDonald invited Ruthie Hindman and another 2nd Aux nurse to join her aboard a navy ship where she had been invited for dinner. The food was wonderful, and the officers were gracious and attentive. These same officers, concerned for the nurses' safety, warned them that the Germans frequently bombed the ships in the Bizerte harbor around sunset, and that they would need to leave the ship well ahead of that time.

Hours later, when the dinner guests were departing, a small boat pulled alongside. The three army nurses, smartly dressed in class-A uniforms, made their way down the metal ladder and waited their turn to step into the barge as it and the ship were on the crest of the wave. Ruthie and the other nurse waved to the sailors lining the ship's rail, and took their places in the barge to wait for Lieutenant McDonald. McDonald was always a picture of perfection, her uniform spotless and her shiny dark hair pulled back in a bun. "All eyes were on Anna," Ruthie remembered, "and as she stepped from the ship's ladder to the barge, her timing was off about five seconds. She stepped out for the boat just as it sank to the bottom of the wave trough, and she missed the barge completely and went feet-first into the Mediterranean. For a few seconds, everyone was so shocked that time seemed frozen. Then Anna's head broke through the surface of the water, her uniform hat leaning to the right and her dark brown hair hanging in long soaked strands. Before she took a breath, ten or fifteen sailors standing on deck dove overboard to go to McDonald's aid. Between the sailors and the men on the barge, they finally got Anna out of the sea and into the boat. As it turned out," Ruth recalled, "the biggest problem she had getting into the boat was raising a leg high enough to climb aboard. Her girdle was so tight that it took a gargantuan effort to throw her leg up and on the barge. I laughed so hard I was doubled over and had tears running down my cheeks. It was a week before Anna forgave us for laughing at her 'major indignity.' " Ruthie smiled. "I'll bet no nurse has ever before or since had so many sailors jump overboard for her."[42]

In just two weeks, Ruthie Hindman and other nurses of the 2nd Aux would board another ship, headed for the invasion beaches of Salerno on the west coast of Italy.

THE NURSES of the 95th Evacuation Hospital remained stationed in Morocco and Algeria during the Sicilian Campaign in the summer of 1943. In mid-June in Oujda, Morocco, General Mark Clark invited the hospital's commanding officer, Colonel Paul K. Sauer; the chief nurse, Lieutenant Blanche F. Sigman; the assistant chief nurse, Lieutenant Carrie Sheetz; and several others to his headquarters' villa for supper. "The villa was beautiful," Claudine Glidewell remembered. "But the food was really terrific. The general had ham, roast beef, and anything else you could think of. After C-rations and K-rations, we thought we had died and gone to heaven." Before the evening ended, General Clark pinned campaign ribbons on the nurses and raised a toast to them and to victory with a bottle of brandy given to him by the Sultan of French Morocco. "It was a great evening," Claudine said. "The general even gave us permission to write home about it and promised that we would be the first American army nurses to land in Italy. None of us ever forgot that night or how nice General Clark was to all of us."[43]

On 8 July, the day before troops stationed at Oujda were to leave for the invasion of Sicily, an unusually high number of "accidental" gunshot wounds were brought to the 95th Evac at nearby Ain-el-Turk, Algeria, for surgery. "It was very surprising how many toes were shot off while their owners were cleaning their guns in preparation for the big jump," "Speedy" Glidewell recalled. "It was a busy night."[44]

General Clark had no way of knowing that the German Luftwaffe would keep him from making good on his promise to Glidewell and the others that they would be the first nurses to arrive in Italy. In September 1943, the 95th Evacuation Hospital would receive orders sending the nurses to Salerno, along with others from the 16th Evac and a handful from the 2nd Aux. Ninety-three nurses in all would board HMHS *Newfoundland* on 10 September and set sail for Salerno. The *Newfoundland* would never make it.

CHAPTER SIX

The Sinking of HMHS Newfoundland

ARMY MEDICAL TEAMS AT SALERNO

26 August–27 September 1943

*Painted white according to the Geneva [Hague] Conventions, with a broad
green band around the hull and plainly marked with red crosses, [British
hospital ships] sailed fully lit up during the hours of darkness, presenting a
sitting target to unscrupulous bombers. As those on board quickly came to
realize, the decision about whether to respect or ignore the conventional
immunity rested entirely with the individual Luftwaffe pilot above them at
the time.*

—*Brenda McBryde*, Quiet Heroines

THE SUN HAD BEEN UP for almost an hour and the air was already
thick with heat as nine teams of the 2nd Auxiliary Surgical Group
climbed aboard an old French train in Mateur, Tunisia, on 26 August
1943. The nurses and male officers settled themselves in seats covered
with stained, dust-filled cushions in cramped and dirty second-class cars.
The enlisted men of the 2nd Aux and a Negro Quartermaster Battalion
claimed space in the "forty-and-eight" boxcars at the rear of the train.
The French train was headed for Oran, Algeria, on the coast of the
Mediterranean Sea, one of several staging areas for the next planned
Allied invasion: Salerno, Italy.

After the Allied victory in Sicily in August, American and Allied top
decision makers debated what the next move should be. America was still

arguing for a cross-Channel invasion of France, while Britain favored further operations in the Mediterranean Sea. Whatever the decision, it would affect the entire conduct of the rest of the war. Current available Allied strength and equipment would not allow both operations in the same year, and a decision had to be reached quickly to allow for a new fall invasion against Axis-held territory.

The Allies did agree on several main issues: first, both the Americans and British agreed on the desirability of getting Italy out of the war. The Italian government had entered into secret negotiations for its surrender to the Allies during the Allied invasion of Sicily in July. If Italy surrendered, Germany would be compelled to recommit German troops now fighting on the eastern front to the southern front, Italy. This would provide the Russian people with a much-needed respite in their battle against Hitler's forces. Second, the surrender of Italy, which appeared imminent in the summer of 1943, might mean that the Allied invasion force would meet far fewer Axis troops during the crucial first two days following an Allied assault in the fall on mainland Italy.

On 26 June, the Allies decided to proceed with an assault on the Italian mainland. Allied forces would land on the southern coast of Italy with the objective of capturing Naples; the code name for the invasion was "Avalanche." British troops would land on the southwestern coast, the toe of the Italian boot, on 3 September, and Americans would assault the beaches near Salerno—northwest of the British landings—on 9 September and fight their way northwest to the port of Naples. Since military strategists—as a result of ongoing secret negotiations—were hoping to secure the surrender of Italy even before the initial Allied invasions of the Italian mainland, it was hoped that a demoralized and poorly equipped Italian army could halt or significantly slow the movement of German troops to the invasion sites during the crucial first days when American and British troops would be fighting to establish a firm foothold on the European continent. In preparation for the assault at Salerno, Allies were moving troops and field and evacuation hospitals, including the 2nd Auxiliary Surgical Group, to the coastal cities of French North Africa to stage for the Italian Campaign.

The train carrying the 2nd Aux to Oran pulled out of Mateur at about 0800. As it picked up speed, thick, oily clouds of dirt and soot spewed by the coal-burning engine flowed back into every car through the open windows and doors. Since the nurses' car was only two back from the engine, the nine women were the first to be covered in a gritty dust that left a black track below each nostril, stung their eyes, and filled their mouths with an oily, smoky taste.

In addition to the discomfort caused by heat, soot, and dirt, the nurses would make the six-hundred-mile trip in a carriage outfitted with straight-backed bench seats that stood row upon row on both sides of a narrow middle aisle that ran the length of the coach. They would have to ride and sleep in the same upright bench seats that grew more uncomfortable with each hour of the jarring four-day trip to their port of embarkation.

In the car behind the nurses, five doctors shared a private compartment, mopped sweat from their faces with gray-white handkerchiefs, and tried to ignore the heat that was pressing in on all of them. Luther Wolff and Trogler F. "Trogh" Adkins spent most of the day playing gin rummy in the compartment they shared with John Adams, George Donaghy, and Forrest "Frosty" Lowery.

Wolff and Adams had in common their southern tradition, a passion for surgery, and a love of fun. Luther had been raised in Columbus, Georgia, and hoped to return there to practice medicine after the war was won. John—Johnny to his friends—was a Virginian by birth, and looked forward to returning to Charlottesville when peace was finally declared.

Only hours after leaving Mateur, the nurses of the 2nd Aux discovered that the toilet in their car had stopped working, but since it was the only one available to them, they continued to use it. By noon the next day, after several meals of C-rations, gastrointestinal upsets and diarrhea were the rule, and the odor from the nurses' broken toilet had permeated as far as the doctors' car. By nightfall, sanitation had deteriorated even further. Nurses and doctors were covered in sweat and dirt, and their clothes, hair, and skin were saturated with the nauseating odor of overused and undercleaned toilets.

As nurses and doctors stretched out on seats and floors to sleep that night, a new and overpowering odor assaulted the doctors in Wolff's compartment. Wolff described the incident in his diary.

"Last night when bedtime came we were retired to our compartment. Frosty was on one seat, Adams on the other, Donaghy on the floor between them, and I in the aisle just outside the door. Soon Johnny started hollering, 'There is something dead in here!' The horrible stench soon engulfed me, also."[1]

They found flashlights and searched for the source of the nauseating odor. "One whiff of George Donaghy's feet and the mystery was solved.

With no baths or other bathing facilities, George had the worst case of bromidrosis (stinking feet) I have ever encountered. Water from canteens with some soap and scrubbing and jettisoning of his socks out the door enabled us to get some sleep, finally."[2]

The discomforts, aggravated by the train's slow pace and hours of waiting on sidings, continued over four days until they arrived in Oran at 1500 on 30 August. The doctors and surgeons staged to cross the Mediterranean to land with assault troops at Salerno on the initial day of the invasion, 9 September; the nurses would rejoin the 2nd Aux surgical team on D+3.

ON 8 SEPTEMBER, with D-Day less than twelve hours away, doctors of the 2nd Auxiliary Surgical Group and the 95th and 16th Evacuation Hospitals sat down to dinner aboard the 20,000-ton *Marnix*, a Dutch ship bound for the assault beaches off Italy's west coast. The public address system crackled to life and a voice announced that Italy had surrendered to the Allies. Luther Wolff and John Adams cheered with the rest of the men and talked about a speedier end to the war with the Italians now out of it.

"The fact that we were going ashore with only one unbloodied, inexperienced American division, i.e., the thirty-sixth . . . did not worry us in the least," Wolff wrote later. "After all, we were anticipating that we would have little or no resistance from the Germans now that Italy had capitulated."[3]

Fortunately for Operation Avalanche, Hitler, who was calling the shots for German commanders in the field, had made plans for repelling an Allied attack on Italy either before or after the Italian surrender that Germany expected, but hoped would not materialize. The Germans had not planned for what actually took place—Italy surrendered almost simultaneously with the Allied invasion at Salerno, Italy.

Only nine hours after General Eisenhower announced the Italian surrender to the U.S. Fifth Army and the world, the combat troops of Avalanche were storming Salerno's beaches. But Allied hopes for an easier invasion due to Italy's surrender were dashed: before Avalanche ended, thousands of American soldiers from the U.S. Third, Thirty-fourth, Thirty-sixth, and Forty-fifth Divisions on the Italian mainland would fight in some of the most bitterly contested battles of World War II.

The initial assault wave headed for the beaches at 0330 on 9 September. Unlike other amphibious invasions, there was no softening-up, pre-invasion naval shelling before the combat troops of the Thirty-sixth Division hit the beaches. Since Italy had surrendered, the Allies didn't pound the shores with the tons of shells that were customarily fired in previous assaults.

Captains Wolff, Adams, Adkins, Lowery, and Donaghy stood on deck in the early morning darkness on D-Day and watched the blinking tail-lights on LCIs as they moved steadily toward their assigned landing beaches. Finding a narrow strip of beach in total blackout was no easy feat; coxswains aboard the LCIs had to search out the color of the light blinking on pathfinder boats that had gone ahead to mark the landing areas. Wolff and his companions could see that no boats were headed for Yellow Beach since the Germans were showering it with a heavy steel rain of artillery shells. Bursts of yellow, orange, and white light dotted the blackness, disappeared, and were replaced by scores of others in what looked like a continuous string of thunder and lightning. It was clear to everyone on the water that an amphibious invasion and the guns that opposed it were terrifying, yet strangely beautiful.

The LCI carrying Luther Wolff and Johnny Adams stopped in front of Red Beach, lowered its bow ramp, and the crew waited impatiently as its passengers jumped into knee-deep water and made their way onto shore. Wolff and Adams shed their packs at a collecting point and proceeded toward the 602nd Clearing Station site at the southwest corner of the town of Paestum, about thirty miles south of Salerno. The infantry had moved on, but their wounded would be brought to the field and evacuation hospitals around Paestum's ancient Greek ruins.

The ruins were the remains of a Greek settlement that dated as far back as the fifth century B.C. One of the best-preserved sites was the Temple of Neptune; it stands on a three-stepped base and has six columns on the facade and thirteen on each long side. Construction in the settlement continued over the centuries, with a limestone amphitheater built during the first century B.C. between the reigns of Sulla and Caesar.

At nightfall, the 602nd Clearing Station was still being set up in a field of tomatoes two hundred yards from the beach. A few wounded were brought in, but since the surgical equipment was still not available for major surgery, they had to be evacuated to hospital ships offshore.

After exploring the nearby area, Wolff and Adams dug slit trenches to sleep in that night. They decided to go to the beach and "liberate" several navy life jackets to use as air mattresses. Laid out in a straight line and covered with a blanket, the life jackets made fairly comfortable beds. Several gas masks bunched together served as pillows and the doctors slept soundly until an air-raid warning awakened them about 0030 on 10 September. Allied antiaircraft guns blasted away at the German planes overhead for more than twenty minutes, then everything was quiet again.

Later in the daylight that morning, D+1, Wolff, Adams, Adkins, and Donaghy walked down the beach in hope of locating Joe Barrett, the anesthetist for Wolff's team who had not shown up at the 602nd Clearing Station. After about thirty minutes, Adkins and Donaghy sat down to rest while Wolff and Adams continued walking toward Green Beach. They had been walking for fifteen minutes when German planes flew overhead and strafed and bombed the area. The two surgeons dived for the only available cover, a spot on the sand where men off-loading landing craft had stacked bedrolls.

"We were just at the bow of one LST . . . and another LST lay perhaps fifty yards farther down the beach," Wolff recorded in his diary. "A bomb hit in the water directly between the two, only seventy-five to 100 feet from us, completely demolishing an LCA. . . . About the time we recovered our wits, the A.A. [antiaircraft guns] opened up again and we ran to the sand dunes, flopping in the foxholes in the middle of a morgue that contained about a dozen dead GIs." Less than one hundred yards from the doctors, two soldiers died after being wounded in the chest by shrapnel. The incident convinced Wolff and Adams that the beach was too dangerous, and they headed back to the clearing station. On the way, they passed a fig orchard where they sat among the trees and ate their fill of sweet, ripe figs before continuing their trip back to the 602nd.[4]

Later that afternoon, anesthestist Joe Barrett arrived at the clearing station. Barrett had not had an easy landing: his LCA had been hit by a bomb as the craft was landing, and cargo and passengers had been thrown into the sea. The struggling middle-aged doctor managed to escape the bombing uninjured but lost all his personal equipment.

About midafternoon, Johnny Adams received his first patient at the site—a GI with a serious leg wound. During the night, Luther Wolff got his first surgical case. The young soldier, seriously wounded, was from Anderson, South Carolina. Wolff noted in his diary:

"What a case! A rifle bullet through the left arm, left chest, lung, diaphragm, spleen, large and small bowel, and ending up somewhere in the left retro-peritoneal pelvic tissues, involving the nerves to the left

leg. I had to repair the sucking wound of the diaphragm, do a splenec-
tomy, repair the intestines, and do a transverse colostomy." Wolff operated using the equipment that belonged to the 602nd Clearing Station.
This severely injured soldier proved to be the first case of major surgery
done on the European mainland, and Wolff was nominated for the Legion
of Merit, a military decoration awarded to personnel of the U.S. military
and its allies for exceptionally meritorious conduct and fidelity.[5]

That night, Wolff and Trogh Adkins dug foxholes near their tent so
they would have some protection from the air raids that hit the area three
or four times a night. Wolff recorded that memorable incident, too: "The
early morning (4:00 AM) air raid caught Trogh and me rather unclothed
[like many GIs and officers of the day, Wolff and Adkins either slept in
their undershorts or in the nude when enjoying the luxury of a tent], and
we practically froze before it was over. I, at least, had my shorts on, which
Trogh did not. There he sat, shaking and shivering, his only clothing
being a helmet."[6]

On 12 September, when Wolff and Adams made rounds at the clearing
station, they found more than thirty-five soldiers who needed surgery as
soon as possible. All four operating tables were busy from noon until after
2300. When the last case was completed, Luther and Johnny were hungry
and remembered the fig orchard they had raided two days ago. They
decided that a return trip was in order before turning in for the night.
With a brightly shining moon, the orchard and the figs proved easy to
find. They climbed the trees and sat, bathed in moonlight, eating the
delicious fruit until they had had their fill.[7]

By 13 September, the 602nd Clearing Station was overflowing with
patients since battle conditions still made it too dangerous to evacuate
patients to hospital ships offshore. The German shelling and air raids
also made it impossible for hospital ships to come in close enough to
accept casualties.

ON 31 AUGUST, army nurses of the 2nd Auxiliary Surgical Group and
the 95th and 16th Evacuation Hospitals boarded HMS *Duchess of Bedford*
for transport to the Salerno beachhead, where they were scheduled to go
ashore on 12 September—D+3—in support of the Thirty-sixth Division, also know as the "Texas T-Patchers." The *Duchess of Bedford* had
been designated as the flagship for the invasion of Salerno.

Unfortunately, the captain of the ship was from the old British naval tradition and convinced that women aboard ship could only bring bad luck. During the next two days before leaving port, the captain spent a lot of time talking with British and Allied Headquarters, attempting to have the nurses reassigned to another vessel. He argued that a flagship was frequently the target of enemy action and that the nurses would be safer on any other carrier.[8]

While the nurses waited for their fate to be decided, they awoke to the traditional reveille on British ships: "Wakey! Wakey! Wakey! Rise and shine! Rise and shine! Hit the deck!" blared over the intercom each morning. On the second morning aboard, as they sat down to a British military breakfast of kidney pie, the rumors of the nurses' transfer to "any other ship" had gained in number and strength.[9]

About 1000 on 1 September, Lieutenant Neil Hansen, the 95th's adjutant, delivered mail to the nurses. Speedy Glidewell was happy to see mail from her former Sunday school teacher, "Mom" Appleby, and had just started to read the letter when the ships sirens began to sound, warning that a German plane was overhead. Glidewell stuffed the letter into her coverall's pocket and promptly forgot about it. It turned out that the German intruder was only a reconnaissance plane, but "the threat was enough for the captain to get us off his ship," she said.[10]

In less than ten minutes after the all-clear, the nurses were told to gather their equipment and board landing barges. They were taken to a cement pier in Oran where they perspired in the hot sun for hours, awaiting their next orders.

The nurses were finally picked up by a French tugboat and transported to a U.S. Army hospital ship, the *Acadia*. The nurses stationed on board treated their passengers as honored guests, helping them to settle into their temporary quarters and sharing perfume, cosmetics, nylons, and soap.

Speedy Glidewell, Bee Wee Wheeler, and Hut Walden explored the ship top to bottom, stem to stern. Compared to their tent hospital, the hospital on board the *Acadia* was luxurious. The ship had spacious wards, operating rooms, laboratory and X-ray departments; cozy, four-person living quarters for nurses; lounges and recreational areas. In addition, there were no blackout conditions to observe since the ship was not sailing in a convoy. Unlike the troopship that had carried the nurses from New York to Algeria, hospital ships were painted white and bore a broad green band that encircled the ship, as well as large red crosses on each side and on each smokestack. There were no rules forbidding throwing orange peelings or candy wrappers over the side as there were with regular ships of war. Since enemy submarines or warships could be alerted to the presence of Allied ships in the area by as little as a floating candy bar wrapper, passengers and crews were forbidden to throw anything—even a cigarette butt—overboard. Hospital ships were a different matter. Since information regarding their sailings and routes was routinely radioed to the enemy, and since the ships bore easily distinguishable and unique markings, no one on board a hospital ship had to worry about disclosing the vessel's location.

All of the *Acadia*'s markings were in accordance with the Hague Conventions—the international agreements that relate to the conduct of war and to the arbitration of international disputes—which also directed hospital ships to sail fully lighted at night. The special markings gave the nurses, medical personnel, and ship's crew a strong sense of security, despite traveling through a combat zone. That promise of safety also led hospital ships to sail in a straight line rather than in the zigzag pattern used by all other vessels at sea.

At dusk the *Acadia* got under way and, following a short and uneventful overnight trip, its passengers disembarked at Bizerte at 1200 on 2 September. Bizerte had suffered extensive damage during the North Africa Campaign, and the nurses rode through city streets lined with bombed-out buildings and houses reduced to rubble to their bivouac area with the 33rd Field Hospital just outside town. The 33rd Field Hospital had not been expecting the 2nd Aux, so empty ward tents were made to serve as the visiting nurses' quarters.

Supper that night was cold C-rations served in the officers' and nurses' mess. Before the meal ended, an officer announced that beginning with breakfast, visiting nurses would take their meals in the enlisted men's mess with the enlisted men and the Italian POWs—not in the officers' mess.

Later that night, German planes visited the area and nurses of the 95th and 16th Evacuation Hospitals experienced their first air raid. German planes dropped bombs, and American artillery teams sought German aircraft out with long beams of searchlights that combed the sky and held the intruders in their grip while ack-ack streaked toward the planes. Glidewell compared the strafing to a "gigantic fireworks display. . . . We stood and cheered our men as if it was a high school football game." As yet inexperienced in combat, she and the other nurses did not realize how dangerous it was to stand outside during an air raid. They watched the sky in awe and anticipation, yelling to the men manning the antiaircraft guns, "Get him! Shoot him down! Good shot!" Glidewell recalled the young male officer who threaded himself between and among the nurses-turned-cheerleaders, shouting: "Get back inside! This isn't a game. Get back inside before you get killed!" The following day, the same officer delivered a lecture to the women on why they should not stand outside in an air raid. "The huge pieces of flak from our own antiaircraft guns, as well as German bomb fragments, were his visual aids," Glidewell recalled.[11]

On 5 September, the nurses received permission to visit the nearby city of Tunis. Chief Nurse Lieutenant Blanche Sigman warned them to be careful what they talked about away from the bivouac area. With "There are lots of spies in Bizerte and Tunis" still ringing in their ears, they hopped rides with American soldiers driving jeeps and trucks to Tunis and back.[12]

In Tunis, nurses saw the burned-out hulks of German tanks and vehicles left behind by Rommel's retreating and captured troops, and large wire enclosures holding hundreds of German and Italian POWs. Despite this evidence of fierce and deadly battles, Tunis had been spared the almost total destruction that had left Bizerte in ruins.

THURSDAY, 9 September, brought long-hoped-for news to the Salerno invasion force. Loudspeaker systems aboard ships announced that Italy had formally surrendered. Hours after the doctors and corpsmen of the 95th and 16th Evacuation Hospitals landed at Paestum in the first waves of the invasion, the nurses of the 95th Evac Hospital received orders to board the British hospital ship HMHS *Newfoundland* at Tunis for transportation to Salerno. Trucks carried the nurses and their luggage to the dock, where they lined up in alphabetical order, dressed in herringbone twill coveralls, helmets, and full field packs, including field shovels for digging in on a beachhead. From a distance, they looked very much like combat soldiers as they climbed the *Newfoundland*'s gangplank, except that collapsible shovels for digging foxholes had been added, and the handles protruded from their field packs.

Like the *Acadia*, the *Newfoundland* was painted and marked as a hospital ship, as dictated by the Hague Conventions, and the layout and amenities of both ships were similar. The *Newfoundland* carried a regular complement of sixteen British nurses, known as "sisters"; one chief

HMHS Newfoundland (U.S. Army Signal Corps)

nurse, called a "matron"; several physicians; dentists; a chaplain; a crew of British naval officers; enlisted men who were responsible for the running and navigation of the ship; and a fourteen-year-old cabin boy.

As on the *Acadia*, the British sisters and crew welcomed the U.S. Army nurses and showed them to their quarters. Since the sisters and medical personnel occupied A Deck, and since the ship was not carrying patients on this trip, the nurses were made at home in the general hospital wards and in the units designated for the seriously ill on B Deck. Lieutenants Glidewell, Wheeler, and Walden shared one ward with Anita Foss, a young blond nurse, and thirty-eight-year-old Maryjane Shelver along with Red Cross worker Esther Richards.

Miss Richards had been an army nurse in World War I. When she tried to rejoin the Army Nurse Corps in World War II, she was rejected; the army considered Miss Richards, in her mid-fifties, too old for military service. But the Red Cross was glad to have the war-experienced nurse, as were the nurses of the 95th Evacuation Hospital.

Accommodations in the wards were a step up from the tents the nurses had occupied in North Africa: the women were delighted to find that they would be sleeping between sheets again instead of inside a bedroll. Their ward even offered a little privacy since each bed could be isolated by curtains that ran along heavy metal rods bolted to the overhead.

The next morning, Ruth Hindman and eight nurses from the 2nd Auxiliary Surgical Group, along with the nurses of the 16th Evacuation Hospital, boarded the ship. The 16th Evacuation Hospital was formed from the Michael Reese Hospital Unit in Chicago. Two of the nurses were sisters who had served together from the first day they joined in 1942: Lieutenants Madonna and Agnes Nolan, natives of Oakland, Illinois. "A Deck had comfortable lounge chairs, and a bar that was open several times a day," Madonna remembered. Agnes had similar memories: "The food was great and there was lots of it. We didn't miss the C-rations."[13]

The *Newfoundland* headed for Salerno, Italy. British sisters and American nurses exchanged stories and, like most soldiers who served in a combat zone, became good friends quickly, without the usual time and rituals that attend peacetime friendships. "We heard about the Blitz, and the different war experiences of the British nurses," Speedy recalled. "They were all about our ages, but they had seen a lot more of war and casualties than we had. I spent a lot of time talking to an Irish girl named Terry. We had a swell time."[14]

In between eating regular food and drinking Coca-Colas—scarce luxuries in wartime and a welcome break from C-rations—the women

British sisters and U.S. Army nurses aboard HMHS Newfoundland, *12 September 1943, one day before the Germans bombed the hospital ship* (Courtesy of Claudine Glidewell Doyle)

played cribbage. The weather was extremely hot, so everyone spent as much time as possible on the top deck in order to take advantage of any ocean breezes. Some of the nurses of the 16th Evacuation Hospital, including the Nolan sisters, even slept on deck in order to escape the still heat of their quarters. "It was so hot in the lower decks that most of the nurses slept in the nude," Madonna Nolan recalled. "Agnes and I decided to sleep on deck. We just put our life vests on, stretched out, and slept pretty well. At least the air was moving up there. Below was like a steam bath."[15]

At 1000 on Sunday, 12 September, the *Newfoundland* arrived off Paestum. The Gulf of Salerno was already crowded with battleships, destroyers, and two other British hospital ships, HMHC *St. David* and HMHC *St. Andrew*, waiting to pick up casualties from the beachhead and transport them to North Africa for more definitive treatment. The nurses were surprised to hear what they thought was thunder coming from the direction of shore. As the *Newfoundland* drew closer, they could see hundreds of individual black puffs of smoke against a clear blue sky. The German artillery was shooting at vessels in the gulf, and the battleships and destroyers were shooting back. It was clear the surrender of Italy had not curbed the fighting.

Lined along the rail, the nurses watched the battle. Every few minutes, a shell would fly past the *Newfoundland*, land in the blue-gray water, and send a white fountain of spray twelve to fifteen feet into the air. Conditions were not looking good for the scheduled landing, despite the fact that their luggage was lined up on deck and their hospital units were waiting for their assistance on shore. Suddenly, a German plane swooped down over the *Newfoundland* and a high, whistling sound filled the air, followed by an explosion and a tall waterspout just to the starboard side of the ship. The German pilot had released a bomb and it had narrowly missed the *Newfoundland*.

Speedy remembered her reaction: "We looked up and saw a German plane heading for Paestum. The damned fool had dropped a bomb and nearly hit us by mistake. We all had a lot to say about what poor shots the Germans were."[16]

The military command decided that the time was not right to land the nurses and ordered the three hospital ships to sea for the night. They were to sail about twenty miles out into the Tyrrhenian Sea in order to put more distance between them and the ships of war. The nurses felt safe, protected by the red crosses and Hague Conventions, as the hospital ships floated through the night lit up like three giant Christmas trees. Green, red, and white lights defined them clearly against the black skies, and there were no ships of war within twenty miles. With any luck, the nurses would be set on shore the next day.

But there was no need to waste their last evening aboard ship; 12 September was the birthday of the Irish sister, Terry, and Speedy Glidewell intended to help her celebrate with a birthday party complete with cake, sherry, piano music, and a group sing-along. A round of "Good Night Ladies" brought the party to a close around 2300, and Speedy and her bunkmates decided to play cribbage on deck to avoid the sweltering heat of their ward below deck as long as possible.

Several of the nurses of the 16th Evacuation Hospital chose to sleep on deck again. The Nolan sisters had already claimed space, stretched out, and were sleeping peacefully, lulled by the rocking of the ship and gentle night breezes.

At midnight, a naval officer told Speedy's group that they were talking too loudly and would have to keep it down. The group decided to call it a night and went below to their bunks. Again, the heat won out over orders and they stripped off most of their clothes to sleep. The cabin was filled with a red glow cast through the portholes from the red crosses. Speedy hung her map case containing photos, letters from her husband, Frank, and other personal items at the foot of her bed, along with her coveralls, and drifted off to sleep, hoping they would be able to join their hospital unit in the morning.

LIEUTENANT BLANCHE SIGMAN, chief nurse of the 95th Evacuation Hospital, awakened about 0500 the next morning and was pretty sure she had heard a bomb explode near the ship. "I got up and dressed and started up on deck," Sigman wrote later. "I met two girls [one was Lieutenant Mary Fischer], and they said they had not heard a bomb, so I decided not to awaken the others."[17]

Lieutenant Sigman was not the only person awakened at 0500. Lieutenant Martha Whorton, chief nurse of the 16th Evacuation Hospital, reported: "We were awakened by the noise of a bomb which had dropped very near us. We decided it wasn't anything to worry about, and we all went right back to sleep."[18]

Fifteen minutes later, a loud explosion rocked the *Newfoundland*. In flagrant violation of the Hague Conventions, a German plane had bombed the hospital ship.

Speedy recalled awakening to the weight of a curtain rod slammed across her face, and to the pain of one of the large screws that had held the rod to the overhead imbedded in her breast. They wouldn't dare, Speedy remembered thinking, as she felt a warm stream of blood gush from her nose. She stood up, put a hand to her bleeding nose, and, just before passing out, shouted: "Anyone got a Kleenex?" Her roommates tried for several minutes to revive her, but when she did not respond, they left her for dead and made their way out of the smashed ward.[19]

In the adjacent ward, nurses of the 16th Evacuation Hospital awakened to the violent rocking and shaking of the ship. There was no panic. They dressed in silence and waited for orders to tell them what to do next. In less than five minutes, a British sailor stuck his head into the ward and told the nurses to follow him. In the narrow passageway, they waded through warm, ankle-deep water, careful to avoid debris sticking out of the water or floating past on the surface. They entered the officers' dining room and the sailor told them to wait as he looked for an escape route to the top deck. While he was gone, the nurses sat and exchanged some light comments, avoiding any discussion of their situation. In less than five minutes, the sailor returned and led them to the ladder at the opposite end of the dining hall.

The explosion had rocked the nurses of the 2nd Auxiliary Surgical Group out of their bunks and set them to pulling on their clothes and looking for the fastest passage to the upper deck. Ruthie Hindman was the first to try the hatch leading out of the ward where they were quartered. She remembered pulling the metal hatch toward her and finding it did not give an inch. As she tugged harder with both hands, she saw that the bulkhead and frame were bent and twisted in against themselves. "The door is jammed. Somebody help me open it," Hindman remembered calling to her companions. Two nurses responded and all three pulled at the hatch. "It didn't give an inch. It was stuck tight," Hindman recounted. "I turned to look around the ward for an ax or hatchet, but couldn't see one."[20]

Several minutes passed. Suddenly, there was a scraping sound as a metal hatch along an inside bulkhead opened inward and a young British sailor stumbled into the ward. "You girls have to get out of here immediately," Hindman recalled him saying. "The ship is on fire. Follow me as fast as you can." He turned and disappeared through the hatch with a line of 2nd Aux nurses following him.[21]

As Ruthie Hindman moved toward the hatch, she noticed that Dorothy Fisher, a tall, slender, blond-haired nurse from Pittsburgh, was not moving. She was bent over her bunk and rummaging through her musette bag, Ruthie recalled. "I asked, 'What in the world are you looking for? We have to get out of here!' Dorothy said, 'My rosary beads!' 'Well, just forget them. You can get another,' I told her." Ruthie took Dorothy's arm and pulled her toward the hatch where the other nurses had already disappeared.[22]

"We followed the sailor through the boiler room which was beginning to fill with black smoke," Hindman recalled. "We climbed several metal ladders, and finally got to the top deck. It was covered with debris and smoke and we followed our sailor-guide to a lifeboat that was getting ready to launch. He told us to get into it and we climbed aboard just before it was lowered to the water. Dorothy was still complaining about her missing rosary beads so I told her she could get some new ones when we reached Rome."[23]

When the nurses of the 16th Evac reached the top deck, they discovered that the lifeboat at their station was already full and being lowered to the water. They would have to cross to the other side of the burning ship and hope for a lifeboat there.

AFTER TALKING to Lieutenant Blanche Sigman at 0500, Lieutenant Mary Fischer of the 95th Evac had returned to her ward, sat down on her bed, and had done a quick check on the location of her musette bag, bedroll, shoes, fatigues, and life jacket. Satisfied, she stretched out on her bed and drifted into sleep. When the bomb exploded at 0515, it jarred the ship and sent debris, wood, glass, and steel flying throughout the ward. "The first sensation," Fischer said, "was that of smothering. I threw up my hands and arms to brush away the debris that had fallen on me. A door had fallen on my legs. Everyone was coughing and choking."[24]

Fischer's fatigues had been blown six beds away and one of the nurses threw them to her. The only things left under her bed were her shoes. Everything else—musette bag, bedroll, even the socks in her shoes—had been sucked out by the bomb's concussion wave. She searched in the dark, managed to find her helmet and life jacket, and followed her fellow nurses out of the ward. "We had to hurry as we saw and heard the flames crackling away. We barely got up the steps when they collapsed. Then came a problem. . . . There were only two lifeboats that we could use, all the others were burning. . . . Some [nurses] jumped into the lifeboats and others of us had to get down the rope net. . . . If they [the *St. Andrew*] hadn't sent their lifeboats to our assistance, we would all have gone down, as we were packed in like sardines . . . ," Fischer recalled. The lifeboats were carrying more than seventy people in a boat intended to hold thirty-five.[25]

Below deck, the unconscious Glidewell regained consciousness slowly. Glidewell remembered opening her eyes and discovering that she was alone. "The air was thick with dust and smoke that made breathing in the stagnant heat even more difficult." Speedy remembered, "It reminded me

HMHS Newfoundland *after she was struck by a German bomb on 13 September 1943* (U.S. Army Signal Corps)

of the dust storms I had experienced as a child in Wichita, Kansas. The ship's exterior lights gave the cabin an eerie red cast, enough light to distinguish objects in the semi-darkness and I scanned the area looking for something to put on. I thought, I'll be damned if I'm going to drown completely naked." Two seconds later she spotted her coveralls and retrieved them from a debris-covered bed.[26]

Speedy recalled that she felt no panic, no fear. Shock had slowed and blunted what might be considered normal reactions. She walked toward the hatch and sat down on a pile of wood and metal. "I had once seen a movie where a ship sinks, and I could visualize the water in my cabin rising until it reached the ceiling," she remembered. "The next thing I knew, I was wondering how Frank, my mother, and my brother would react to the news of my death. Poor Frank! He'd be a widower. He'd probably marry again."[27]

The very thought of Frank's remarriage filled Speedy with new energy and resolve. She could hear crackling and popping sounds and noticed flickering orange and yellow shadows against the hatch. She remembered saying aloud to herself, "You idiot! We're on fire! You've got to get out of here."[28]

Suddenly, she saw a small space between the debris, the hatch, and the overhead, and carefully climbed toward it. In a matter of minutes, she squeezed through the opening and jumped to the other side. When she straightened up, she was face to face with Lieutenant Sigman and two of her fellow nurses. She learned later that they had been looking at the space above the hatch and deciding if they could get through it. Speedy recalled that at the time she felt stunned to see that everything on the other side of the hatch looked normal. She recounted that, for a moment, it seemed that the nightmare of the explosion was just a dream, and like Alice in Wonderland, she had passed through the rabbit hole into another world.

The illusion was gone in less than a second. She remembered shouting "We have to get out of here!" and running toward the nearest ladder. She stopped in her tracks when Lieutenant Marjorie Royal yelled, "You can't go that way! The stairs are on fire." Royal grabbed Speedy by the arm and pulled her back. "Let me go!" Glidewell demanded as she broke Royal's hold and started up the ladder. Glidewell had not climbed far when flames blocked her way and she had to turn back. The fire had a sobering effect. She was eye-to-eye with the chief nurse again. Speedy remembered Sigman's words: " 'You'll get the Purple Heart for this,' Sigman had said."[29]

Speedy wondered why Lieutenant Sigman would think so, but her own thoughts returned immediately to the idea of escape: "We have to get out of here," Speedy said again. Lieutenant Sigman handed Speedy a flashlight and told her, "Take this and go back in there to see if you can help the rest of the girls." Without another word, Lieutenant Speedy Glidewell, flashlight in hand, climbed back up the mountain of debris blocking the hatch and shined the flashlight into the cabin she had escaped from only minutes earlier. She moved the light around the room and confirmed what she already knew: the ward was empty. "Good," she remembered thinking. "I sure don't want to go back in there."[30]

As she climbed down, Speedy saw Bee Wee and Hut wrapped in sheets, walking down the passageway. "How did you get out? Where have you been?" Speedy remembered her surprised reaction and her friend's response. " 'We thought you were dead!' Hut said. She laughed with relief. 'Only you would ask for a Kleenex to clean up after a bombing.' "[31]

Speedy recounted that at that moment, Esther Richards—stark naked—came down the passageway. Her forehead was cut and dried blood had sealed the wound.

After conferring for several minutes, the group reentered their cabin through a large space left by a collapsed bulkhead. The dust and smoke in the ward had previously hidden it from Speedy's view. The visit was a quick one. Hut grabbed Maryjane Shelver's coveralls, Foss picked up an afghan, and Esther Richards found her field shoes, helmet, and field jacket. By this time the water on B Deck had reached their knees and they hurried back to the passageway just as a British sailor appeared and called for the group to follow him.

He led them toward the stern, through the laundry room, and up a narrow ladder to the top deck. As they stepped onto A Deck, they were immediately aware of a woman's screams. The sound was horrible, Speedy remembered. "I wondered why someone didn't go to the woman's aid." Black smoke billowed along the deck and flames lapped at the ship and its lifeboats. The nurses held wet clothes over their noses and mouths in order to make breathing easier. A British sister was handing out clothing to nurses in various stages of undress. When the sister saw Speedy, she stopped for a second and in a kind but absentminded voice said, "Oh, Ducky, your face!"[32]

Speedy returned to events of that terrible morning. " 'What is it?' I asked." The sister pointed to a broken mirror and Speedy looked at herself. Only her eyes, and the path taken by the flow of blood from her nose, stood out against her blackened face. There was no time to examine the damage further as the British sailor hurried them toward the lifeboats at midship.[33]

The sound of screaming grew louder as they walked, and as they approached two British sisters and the fourteen-year-old cabin boy, they saw the source of the awful sounds: a British sister was trapped in a burning cabin. The German bomb had struck the *Newfoundland* just above the wards shared by the 95th's nurses, hitting A Deck and the cabins beneath occupied by British sisters. Its explosion had killed all of the officers on the bridge, the ship's doctors, and six of the British sisters. The bomb that had killed the six British nurses outright had trapped one more in the same cabin. There was no hope of escape or rescue; the unfortunate victim was still alive. Each scream sounded less and less human, more and more tortured.

"Her head was sticking through the porthole, and her body was on fire," Glidewell said. "Her face was twisted with pain as she pleaded for help. The stench of burning skin was overpowering." A small group of people stood by helplessly in front of the burning sister as others hurried past. The anguished screaming, and knowing that no one could help, were horrible. Without a word, the young cabin boy stepped forward and walked toward the burning woman. He was crying softly as he bent and picked up a two-by-four from the debris-strewn deck. The boy brought the two-by-four down as hard as he could against the woman's head. The screaming stopped and the sounds of the young boy's weeping took its place. A British sister pried the bloody lumber from his hands, put her arm around his shoulders, and guided him down the deck toward the one remaining lifeboat.[34]

Other nurses described that unforgettable morning. Lieutenant Sigman reported: "Some of the girls would start down the ladders nude and sailors would pull them back and give them their pants. They were dressed in the strangest assortments of garments ever seen at sea."[35]

Mary Fischer remembered that with all officers dead, enlisted men orchestrated the details of abandoning ship. She described the exceptional courage of one man: "They towed us in. In the boat was one of the bravest men I had ever seen. How he hung on to that rope and commanded all the maneuvers, never thinking of himself. He had to be carried in on a litter when our rescue ship, the *St. Andrew*, finally picked us up. He had chest injuries and a fractured arm."[36]

FINALLY IT was time for Speedy and the other 95th Evac nurses to abandon the *Newfoundland*. News that one of the lifeboats had fallen earlier, injuring two of the nurses of the 16th Evac, reached the nurses of the 95th, and Speedy remembered praying silently that their boat would not meet the same fate. She was greatly relieved as the lifeboat settled on the surface of the Tyrrhenian Sea and made its way toward the *St. Andrew*.

As their small craft was lifted to *St. Andrew*'s top deck, dawn was claiming the night sky. Speedy, whose feet also had been injured when the heavy metal rod fell on her, was no longer able to walk. British sailors lifted her to a litter, carried her to a ward on C Deck, and gave her a large glass of lemonade-flavored glucose that was sickeningly sweet. Speedy noted, "I figured it was better than the IV they told me I'd have to have if I didn't drink all of that stuff." She went on: "Even worse was the claustrophobia I experienced when I realized my bed was up against the wall without a porthole in sight." She was trying to get comfortable in the bed when she noticed a lump in her coverall pocket. She reached in and pulled out what she hoped was her billfold, but it turned out to be the letter from her former Sunday school teacher, Mom Appleby, that she had shoved in her pocket three days earlier aboard the *Duchess of Bedford*. There was a white card attached to the letter. Speedy remembered that her heart beat faster as she read the message: "When thou passeth through the waters, I will be with thee; and through the rivers, they shall not overflow thee; when thou walkest through the fire, thou shalt not be burned, neither shall the flame kindle upon thee" (Isaiah 43:2).[37]

In about an hour, Bee Wee and Hut showed up in Speedy's ward, evaluated the situation, and told her they would be back to get her as soon as they found a place where all three could stay.

Speedy recalled that with the passage of time and the alleviation of shock, she became more aware of the wounds the bomb's explosion had dealt her. Her chest was black and blue, her mouth and nose were numb where the heavy rod had slammed against her face, and her hands and arms were covered with powder burns. The British doctor insisted on putting her left arm in a sling after diagnosing a fractured elbow. He was unimpressed with Speedy's protestations that her arm had been broken when she was six years old and was really fine now. She would take her arm out of the sling, and the doctor would put it back in whenever he passed her bed.

Finally, Bee Wee and Hut returned and, one on either side, spirited Speedy off to their quarters. They both slept in one bed so Speedy could have the other to herself. "You don't look so good yourself," Speedy remembered telling Bee Wee when she saw the myriad of powder burns all over Bee Wee's face. "You look worse than you did when you had the measles."[38]

The three shared the cabin all the way back to Bizerte. During the trip, the British sisters were hoping they would hear that their fellow nurses had been picked up by the *St. David* and were safe on board. Their hopes were dashed as lists of survivors were radioed between the ships and seven of their nurses were not accounted for. Among the dead were Speedy's friends, Terry and Helen, who had played the piano and led the singing at Terry's birthday party.

The Nolan sisters recollected their relief when each discovered the other was aboard the *St. Andrew*. Both lieutenants had suffered ruptured eardrums from the explosion. "We were so glad to see each other again our injuries didn't seem like much," Madonna Nolan recalled.[39]

One of the 16th's nurses, Lieutenant Gertrude Mills, had suffered a broken leg when her lifeboat fell to the sea, and Lieutenant Anna Mae Zigler had sustained severe rope burns on her hands, wrists, and forearms in the same fall. Zigler had been thrown from the lifeboat and dangled in the rope cargo net for more than thirty minutes, suspended between the top deck and the sea, as all attempts to free her failed. Finally, the net was pulled on board the burning *Newfoundland* and she was disentangled.[40]

When the *St. Andrew* docked in Bizerte harbor at 1400 on 14 September, the nurses were placed on trucks and taken to station hospitals where their wounds were treated. Then they were reequipped for their return to Salerno.

Nurses of the 16th Evac—including Ruth Hindman and the other nurses with the 2nd Aux who were assigned to temporary duty with that unit—were taken to a hospital in Bizerte. "I'll never forget our first trip to the hospital mess hall," Ruthie remembered. "We looked like drowned rats! We were dressed in whatever clothes we could borrow or were fortunate enough to save from the *Newfoundland*. We looked awful! But not one person asked us a thing about the sinking."[41]

The reception at the 74th Station Hospital in Mateur, Tunisia, was much the same. Speedy recalled that the admitting nurse took one look at the wound in her breast and said: " 'Good grief! I saw a woman hit like that in the breast, and she died from cancer six months later.' The remark didn't do much for my morale, but I chalked it up to a lack of tact," Speedy said.[42]

After two days as a patient, Speedy began experiencing pains in her buttocks. A physician's examination found three bomb fragments that were removed later that day.

Patients who arrived at the 74th Station Hospital from the 95th Evac in Salerno brought welcome news about the unit to the 95th's nurses. The patients seemed glad to be out of Salerno, but their stories only increased the nurses' desire to rejoin their hospital.

WHEN THE GERMANS bombed HMHS *Newfoundland*, General Mark Clark's promise that the nurses of the 95th Evacuation Hospital would be the first army nurses to set foot on the Italian mainland became impossible to fulfill. While the 95th's nurses were being reequipped and resupplied in North Africa on 15 September, the LST carrying the nurses of the 93rd Evac entered the Gulf of Salerno and got as close to shore as possible before it opened its bow doors and dropped its ramp. Lieutenants Evelyn Anderson, Vera Sheaffer, and the others waded ashore as they had on Sicily and took in the scene that surrounded them. Andy Anderson described what she saw: "All sorts of debris was floating in the greenish muddy water and we could see the still-burning hulks of two or three LSTs that had been bombed and strafed by the Germans. As we walked onto the beach, we could see American soldiers in foxholes all along the sand, and there were quite a few antiaircraft guns all along the coast." From the first moment the nurses set foot on shore, they were inundated with wolf whistles, catcalls, and cries of "Hubba-hubba" and "Hey, doll, welcome to Italy."[43]

The women continued up the beach to a single tree that promised more shade than it was able to deliver. Andy recalled, "There was a large manure pile nearby and the place stunk to high heaven. We had to wait there about two hours before trucks showed up and took us to the hospital area. When we arrived, we were mobbed by cameramen who claimed we were the first nurses to land in Europe since 1918." By that evening,

Nurses of the 93rd Evacuation Hospital arrive at their hospital site at Paestum, Italy, in September 1943 (U.S. Army Signal Corps)

the nurses of the 93rd Evac were caring for battle casualties in their own hospital tents.[44]

ON 22 SEPTEMBER, the nurses of the 95th Evac received orders to board an LST on the following day for transportation from Bizerte, Tunisia, to Salerno, Italy. When Speedy Glidewell got the news, she told her doctors she felt fine and wanted to rejoin her unit. Her act was convincing, and the next day, with Hut on one side and Bee Wee on the other, Speedy hobbled along the dock and up the gangplank.

They joined the nurses of the 16th Evac and 2nd Auxiliary Surgical Group, and settled in for their second trip to Salerno. It was a more experienced group of sea travelers who decided where and in what to sleep that night.

"I wasn't about to sleep below deck if I could help it," Ruthie Hindman remembered. "I had already liberated a hatchet that hung on the bulkhead of a gangway below and stowed it in my musette bag. That hatchet and I made our way topside and found a nice space in one of the gun lofts to spend the night. Some of the girls assured me that lightning doesn't strike in the same place twice, but I wasn't taking any chances. If the Germans would deliberately sink a hospital ship, they certainly wouldn't have any trouble attacking an LST."[45]

Speedy and several nurses of the 95th and the 16th Evacuation Hospitals had the same idea, and also claimed places on the top deck to sleep that night.

When they arrived at Salerno the next day, GI trucks transported the nurses to the hospital area where all the units were set up and receiving wounded. The same army nurses who had survived the bombing of the *Newfoundland* were back at work in the combat zone, determined to do whatever was necessary to save the lives of sick and wounded soldiers.

CHAPTER SEVEN

From Salerno to the Gustav Line

ARMY NURSES GOING WHERE THEY ARE NEEDED

29 September 1943–25 January 1944

Nurses are the most willing workers that anyone ever saw. . . . They are anxious and keen to get to the front in spite of the hard work. When they are there, they do not want to go back to the rear areas.

—*Lt. Col. Stewart F. Alexander, MC,*
Personnel Officer, Surgeon's Office,
Seventh Army, 14 July 1945

B Y THE LAST WEEK of September 1943, things had quieted down somewhat at Paestum for the 16th Evacuation Hospital and the 2nd Auxiliary Surgical Group assigned to it. The number of casualties arriving at the 16th had decreased dramatically since the 94th Evac had "leapfrogged" over the 16th Evac and moved twelve miles closer to the front lines. At that point, most of the planned hospital bed support—a total of 9,500 mobile and 7,000 fixed beds—was ashore and functional. With fewer battle casualties arriving, the personnel of the 16th Evac found themselves with a little off-duty leisure time—a few free hours in the evenings for letter-writing, card-playing, "shooting the bull," and drinking "yocky-docky," a potent homemade cocktail the doctors made of 95 percent ethyl alcohol mixed with lemonade powder. This respite, however, was soon to be interrupted.[1]

Nurses of the 93rd Evacuation Hospital hand-sewing a large red cross to mark their hospital site at Paestum (U.S. Army Signal Corps)

The weather in the Paestum area had been warm and dry throughout September, and 28 September dawned just as bright, warm, and dry as previous days. By 1930 that evening, card games and bull sessions were in full swing throughout the tented hospital area as doctors, nurses, and enlisted personnel told each other that they could easily get accustomed to such pleasant evenings. Moments later, without any warning, a gale-force wind and torrential rains struck the hospital. Within minutes, tents began collapsing, exposing patients to high winds and a heavy rain that was quickly freezing into hailstones.

Agnes Nolan recalled that she was in the OR tent with an emergency appendectomy patient in surgery when the mini-hurricane hit. The squall slammed into the tent with such force it buckled the canvas and began to uproot the tent pegs, threatening to unmoor the tent and blow it away like a loose sail. The surgeon had already made an incision through the fascia—a sheet of fibrous tissue beneath the skin that envelopes muscles or organs of the body—and the soldier's abdomen was wide open. In less than two minutes, the surgeon and OR team made a decision to send the anesthetized patient to the 95th Evacuation Hospital about a mile away to complete the surgery. They draped the soldier's abdomen with sterile sheets and rushed him to a waiting ambulance.

The two young sisters from Oakland, Illinois—Lieutenants Madonna

Lts. Madonna and Agnes Nolan of Oakland, Illinois, in Italy, 1943.
Both sisters were awarded the Purple Heart for wounds received
when Germans bombed the HMHS Newfoundland (U.S. Army
Signal Corps)

and Agnes Nolan—had completed St. Joseph's Nursing School in Elgin,
Illinois, within one year of each other, Madonna in 1940 and Agnes in
1941. Both joined the U.S. Army Nurse Corps the summer following
Agnes's graduation, and asked to be stationed together. They became
part of the original Michael Reese Hospital Unit out of Chicago, and
sailed for the war zone in mid-April after saying good-bye to their father
and friends. A little more than a year later, their younger brother,
William, enlisted in the army, and three silver stars hung on a flag in the
front window of their father's house in the small town where all three
grew up and their mother was buried years earlier.

"Once the ambulance was on its way," Agnes Nolan said of the night
of the hurricane, "we ran to the ward tents to help get the patients

Storm damage at the 16th Evacuation Hospital at Paestum, 1943 (U.S. Army Signal Corps)

out from under wet, collapsed canvas. We worked by flashlight and light-ning flashes to get the patients into ambulances for transportation to a tobacco warehouse several miles away." The tobacco warehouse had been taken over by the Supply Service as a barracks for their men.[2]

Word of the damage being done to the 16th Evac by hurricane-force winds and rain quickly spread, and brought personnel from adjacent hos-pitals to the 750-bed unit to help evacuate almost 1,000 patients to a place of safety. The medical staff moved the most seriously ill patients to a nearby farmhouse that quickly became a makeshift hospital for non-transportable casualties. The remaining sick and wounded were brought to the tobacco warehouse where bundles of tobacco leaves still hung from ceiling rafters to dry. Patients were placed on cots previously occupied by the supply company personnel, and given dry pajamas and blankets to help warm them as quickly as possible. "It was an odd sight," Agnes Nolan recalled, "to look down an aisle and see patients' cots lined up in rows under long tobacco leaves that hung from the rafters like golden-brown drapes."[3]

By 2140—only two hours after the storm had hit—all the patients had been moved out of the demolished hospital and were safe and dry in new quarters. In his diary, 2nd Aux Surgeon Luther Wolff praised the nurses and corpsmen for their quick and expert handling of the emergency. "The hospital was demolished, but they did a swell job of getting the patients evacuated. . . . It was terrible for some of the seriously ill, but fortunately no one was hurt further."[4]

The virtually total destruction caused by the storm was evident the next day, when nurses from the 8th Evacuation Hospital relieved the nurses of the 16th so they could return to salvage whatever personal belongings they could find. The site was a field of mud and standing pools of water. "Clothes, letters, cots, and Kotex were strewn over the area," Madonna Nolan said, "and you knew from your first glance that the chances for recovering anything usable were very slim."[5]

Whereas the 16th Evac had taken the brunt of the storm and been leveled by it, the 95th Evac, located about a mile south, was able to withstand the less severe winds and rain. On the evening of the storm, Speedy Glidewell recalled a corpsman coming to her tent and telling her to report immediately to the OR tent: an ambulance was on its way from the 16th Evac with a surgical patient.

When Speedy arrived in the OR minutes later and took her place at the head of the table to administer anesthesia, she was surprised to see the patient's open belly as the sterile sheets were removed. "I couldn't help thinking," Speedy recalled, "how surprised the soldier would be when he awakened from the anesthesia. He would have gone to sleep in the 16th Evac's OR and would wake up in the 95th Evac, which was about a mile down the road from where he started. He'd have quite a story to tell his grandchildren someday."[6]

NOT ALL INJURIES treated in the field and evacuation hospitals were battle wounds. Among the first wounded soldiers Glidewell recalled working with shortly after she rejoined her unit in Italy were three young soldiers tragically injured not in battle but while off duty. The three young men had decided to go swimming. Ignoring orders not to swim along a certain section of beach, the three were running toward the water when they stepped on a pattern of land mines. The explosions blew both legs off each boy, and they were brought to the 95th Evacuation Hospital for emergency surgery. All three survived. "They were making great strides in the development of prostheses," Speedy recalled, "but running on a sandy beach was a long way off. It's bad enough to see a soldier lose a

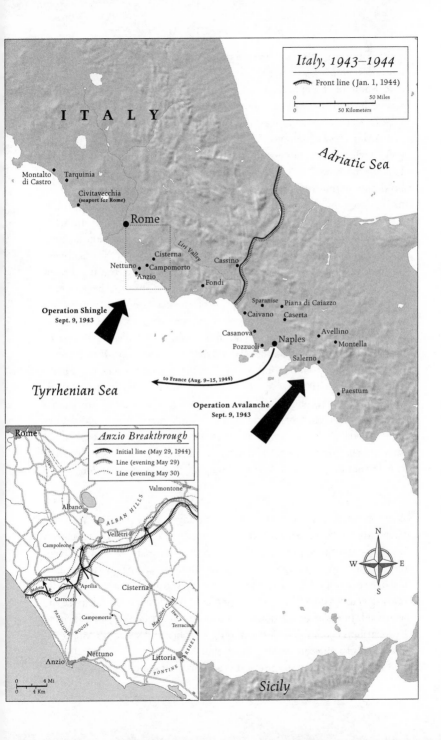

Italy, 1943–1944

🌊 Front line (Jan. 1, 1944)

0   50 Miles
0   50 Kilometers

ITALY

Adriatic Sea

Montalto di Castro
Tarquinia
Civitavecchia (seaport for Rome)
Rome
Cisterna
Liri Valley
Nettuno   Campomorto
Anzio
Cassino
Fondi

Operation Shingle
Sept. 9, 1943

Sparanise   Piana di Caiazzo
Caivano   Caserta
Casanova   Avellino
Pozzuoli   Naples   Montella
Salerno

Tyrrhenian Sea

to France (Aug. 9–15, 1944)

Paestum

Operation Avalanche
Sept. 9, 1943

Anzio Breakthrough
🌊 Initial line (May 29, 1944)
🌊 Line (evening May 29)
⋯ Line (evening May 30)

Rome

Valmontone
Albano
ALBAN HILLS
Velletri
Campoleone
Aprilia
Carroceto
Cisterna
Campomorto
Mussolini Canal
Terracina
Anzio
Nettuno
Littoria
PONTINE
PADIGLIONE WOODS

N
W   E
S

0   4 Mi
0   4 Km

Sicily

limb in battle, but these three were just acting like the kids they were
and it cost all of them their legs."[7]

A total of 2,443 casualties—1,223 surgical and 1,220 medical—
poured into the 95th Evac from the third week in September to the first
week in October as American and British troops fought their way closer
to securing their main objectives: Naples on the southwest coast of Italy,
along with a twenty-mile strip of the Volturno River north of the city.
The approach to Naples was treacherous: American and Allied troops
faced mountainous terrain as rugged as the American Rockies and made
all the more impassable by the bombed-out bridges and roads the Germans left behind in the wake of their withdrawal from southern Italy.[8]

On 2 October 1943, the Eighty-second Airborne Division entered
Naples, and moved carefully through the city to make sure it was free of
German rearguard troops and snipers. On 5 October, the capture of
Naples was made official, and Speedy recalled celebrating her twenty-
fourth birthday on that day, thinking of the capture of Naples as her
own special birthday present. Two days later, the 95th Evac near Paes-
tum received orders to close, pack, move about fifty miles northwest to
Naples, and set up outside the city to treat American and Allied forces.

Between 9 September and 6 October 1943, when Naples was finally
secured, the British X Corps suffered a total of 6,847 men killed,
wounded, and missing. In the same operation, the total of Americans
killed, wounded, and missing in action was 4,870: 727 American soldiers
were killed in combat, 2,720 were wounded, and 1,423 were reported
missing. Of that number, the Thirty-sixth Division alone lost 267 men
killed in action, 679 wounded in action, and 984 missing in action.[9]

As VI CORPS American and Allied troops advanced toward the Volturno
River, the distance between division clearing stations and evacuation
hospitals lengthened until they reached the excessive ambulance trip
of about one hundred miles seen in the Tunisian campaign. The longer
the distance from the front lines to a clearing station or evac hospital, the
more precious time it would take medics and corpsmen to transport the
wounded. In order to cut down on miles that must be traveled, the 93rd
Evacuation Hospital left Paestum on 2 October and set up in Montello,
about twenty miles northeast of Salerno.

Like Naples, Montello was situated in mountainous terrain in which many of the bridges and roads had been destroyed by German bombers even before the 93rd Evac went into operation there. As the bombing continued, more roads became impassable and the 93rd Evac became a little more isolated each day. Lieutenant Evelyn Anderson recalled their situation: "The place seemed plagued by bad luck. It rained steadily here and we waded in mud almost to our knees. Our sterilizing tent caught fire one night and presented a great target for the Germans. . . . " It was at Montello that one of the nurses, Lieutenant Decima McLaughlin, began running a high temperature and complaining of abdominal pain. One of the first diagnoses the doctors considered was acute appendicitis, but Decima reported that her appendix had been removed when she was in her early teens and she did have a surgical scar on her abdomen.[10]

Lieutenant McLaughlin's condition continued to deteriorate over several days. "We were all stunned and saddened," Vera Sheaffer recalled, "when Decima died on 7 October. . . . She was my tentmate. . . . We had

Nurses of the 93rd Evacuation Hospital, 1943 (Courtesy of Vera Sheaffer Skogsberg and Paul Skogsberg)

a religious service for her at the 93rd and they took her body back to
Paestum for burial."[11]

ON 9 OCTOBER 1943, a few days after the Allied occupation of Naples,
the 95th Evacuation Hospital opened its doors outside Naples proper in
an Italian hospital built on the crest of a hill that stood directly across
from Mount Vesuvius and overlooked the Bay of Naples. The legendary
beauty of the harbor was somewhat marred by the hulks of sunken
enemy warships and steel roadways built over them by American engineers, but it was still beautiful, and still lived up to its famous motto:
"See Naples and die!"

The Italian hospital consisted of a group of buildings named by the
Italians "The 23rd of March" in honor of the birth of fascism in Italy.
Mussolini had had the hospital built as a tuberculosis sanitarium. The
95th took over one building, while a British hospital unit occupied
another, and the Italians continued to use the other four buildings for
themselves. Each building was large and had long marble halls and reception areas. Those marble halls played a prominent part in Speedy's recol-
lection of the hospital: "I couldn't stop thinking about the song, 'I
Dreamt I Dwelt in Marble Halls,' and I sang it over and over until Bee
Wee and Hut threatened to murder me."[12]

As with all evacuation hospitals, the 95th was designed to work in
tents, and so buildings presented unaccustomed problems. The ground
floor of the 95th's building held the main OR; the receiving ward; and
the preoperative, postoperative, and X-ray departments. The generator
for the X-ray equipment was too large for the allotted space and had to be
placed outside. The technician had to line up each patient on the X-ray
table, then climb out a window, take the X-ray, and climb back inside the
building.

In addition, occupying a building meant that hospital personnel had
to police (inspect) and clean the rooms along with their regular hospital
duties. Since the Germans had destroyed the electric and water plants
before they withdrew, generators supplied electricity for the hospital and
Lyster bags (the portable waterproof bag used to supply troops with
purified drinking water) were set up at various places throughout the
building to supply hospital personnel and patients with usable, drinkable
water. With other hospitals leapfrogged ahead of them, the 95th Evac
operated as a station hospital while near Naples, and received accident

victims, sick soldiers, and battle casualties evacuated from hospitals closer to the front lines.

The day after the 95th arrived, 10 October, a gasoline truck and a jeep from the 95th Evac went into the city to pick up fuel for the unit. As the drivers of the two vehicles waited for their turn to take on gasoline, they parked in front of the main Naples Post Office. Suddenly there was a loud explosion: a time bomb planted in the post office by withdrawing German forces blew up, destroying the building and nearby vehicles. The driver of the truck, Corporal William Greene, was killed instantly, and Lieutenant Ray Berent, the driver of the jeep, was badly wounded. It was not the first German time bomb to go off in Naples and it would not be the last.

The next afternoon, Lieutenant Neil Hansen, the 95th's executive officer, told Bee Wee, Hut, and Speedy that they were looking pale from being indoors so much and advised them to leave the hospital for a few hours. The women had thought of going into Naples, but the city had

Col. Paul Sauer awarding the Purple Heart. Left to right: enlisted man; Lt. Claudine "Speedy" Glidewell; Lt. Isabelle "Bee Wee" Wheeler; and Lt. Ray Berent (U.S. Army Signal Corps)

been designated off-limits to military personnel: the Germans had destroyed the sewer system and raw sewage had gotten into the city's water supply, causing an epidemic of typhus and cholera. The women had nowhere to go but to other army installations.

When the three nurses returned to the 95th that evening, Lieutenant Hansen was waiting for them and said there was something in the basement he wanted them to see. The basement was damp and dark, but Hansen flicked on a large spotlight. The women were surprised to see a giant crater about two to three feet deep in the middle of the basement floor. As they stared at the crater, Hansen explained that the Germans had buried hundreds of pounds of dynamite in the ground, rigging the explosives with a delayed-action fuse to explode days later when American hospitals and their patients were settled into the building. "Lucky for us," Speedy said, "the Italians who lived nearby told some GIs about it, and they brought in the engineers to defuse and dismantle their time bomb. That's why Neil wanted us to go for a walk—just in case the thing went off while they were trying to take it apart."[13]

That evening, the 95th Evac showed a movie in the yard in front of the hospital building. Bee Wee, Hut, and Speedy were sitting on the ground enjoying the movie when the sound of planes overhead and the high piercing wail of air-raid sirens broke into the entertainment. Suddenly, tracer bullets from American artillery streaked through the night sky, and the whine and whistle of bombs could be heard around the outdoor movie theater. The three women dove for cover. "I didn't want to go inside a building," Speedy recalled, "and have it collapse on me. The *Newfoundland* had taught me how hard it was to get out of something hit by a bomb, so I dove for a nearby bush. I fell over a metal bucket someone had left there and since I didn't have my helmet with me, I put the bucket over my head." Speedy recalled that she lifted the bucket every couple of minutes to see what was going on. Suddenly the area lit up as if it were high noon, and Speedy peeked out from beneath her bucket-helmet to see that the Germans planes had dropped several large flares and they were floating down over the yard. "I was convinced that they had dropped the flares to light up their target for their bombs. I made a dash for the British hospital about twenty-five yards away."

As she entered the building, Speedy saw a young British soldier in a wheelchair moving in her direction. "Blimey!" Speedy recalled the young man saying, "I'd rather take my chances in the London Underground!" As she watched, the soldier and his wheelchair disappeared down a dark hallway. "When a Britisher is nervous in an air raid, you know the situation is pretty bad," Speedy remarked. She made her way to the basement and walked through the underground tunnel that connected the British hospital to the building housing the 95th Evac. By the time she reached her own unit, the air raid had ended.[14]

In mid-September, Speedy used some of her off-duty time to visit the nearby Italian civilian hospital. The hospital was filled to overflowing with civilian casualties that were the result of a seven-day civil war that had erupted just days before the Allied capture of Naples. During the weeklong civil war, anti-Nazi Italians had battled not only German soldiers but also fellow Italians who were Nazi sympathizers. Six hundred patients filled the hospital, which also served as a morgue for the approximately two hundred Italian civilians who had died in the battles.

An Italian nurse who spoke English showed Speedy around the wards. Medical and surgical supplies at the Italian hospital were all but nonexistent since the German troops had taken whatever they wanted with them as they withdrew from the city. American doctors, nurses, and corpsmen donated whatever medical supplies and medications could be spared, as well as some of their off-duty time. Speedy's tour finally ended in the operating room. She remembered that as she looked around, a supply table near one wall caught her attention. There was a tiny severed foot lying in an emesis basin. Speedy asked the Italian nurse why the child's foot had been amputated, and whether the child was okay. The nurse took her to the ward where the patient, a three-year-old girl with black, curly hair and large brown eyes, was lying in a crib. The child's foot had been run over by a U.S. Army truck and could not be saved. The nurse's next words rocked Speedy to the core: because the Germans had taken virtually all medical and surgical supplies with them when they left Naples, it had been necessary to amputate the youngster's foot without anesthesia or pain medication.

An American enlisted man who volunteered much of his off-duty time to the civilian hospital was standing to Speedy's right. Speedy asked the corpsman if he had been present during the surgery. When he replied that he had, Speedy asked why he had not requested anesthesia from the 95th Evacuation Hospital. Quite simply, the thought of borrowing anesthesia had not occurred to the American corpsman. For the next few seconds, Speedy's anger was directed toward the soldier. She felt her hands curl into fists and fought the desire to strike the young man. As she stared at the medic's face, she noticed that his eyes were filled with tears. The soldier was obviously deeply touched by the memory of the brutal surgery and was about to cry. Speedy's anger dissipated as she became aware of the soldier's pain. She reached out and placed a hand on his shoulder. She remembered her words as if she had spoken them yesterday: "If anything like this ever happens again, please come and ask me for whatever anesthesia is needed. I'll make sure you get whatever the patient needs for surgery."[15]

During the third week of October 1943, a group of nurses from the 95th Evac climbed in the back of a truck for an excursion to Mount Vesuvius and Pompeii. They carried a lunch prepared by the hospital mess for the occasion—Spam sandwiches on freshly baked bread, cookies, grapes, and lemonade. They climbed Mount Vesuvius in the morning, ate lunch, and traveled to the ancient ruins of Pompeii for a look at what one of Vesuvius' eruptions had done to a once prospering village. As they climbed the mountain, the nurses saw more than a half-dozen villages thriving on the side of the world-famous volcano.

Despite the fact that each village was picturesque and appeared peaceful, Speedy was convinced that she could never sleep a wink on the cliffs of a volcano that grumbled and spewed flames and hot lava into the sky day and night. "At night," Speedy remembered, "the German pilots used the glow from Vesuvius as a landmark to guide them over Naples and beyond to drop their bombs."[16]

Speedy, Bee Wee, and Hut got as close to the crater as they dared and stuck coins into cooling lava to coat them and keep for souvenirs.

The Italian guide who showed the women around Pompeii must have thought that nurses were not like other women since he enthusiastically showed them through rooms not open to the public, chambers that comprised Pompeii's "red light" district before Vesuvius put the entire city out of business in A.D. 79. The walls were covered with pornographic paintings. "All of us nurses thought the murals were thoroughly disgusting," Speedy recalled, "and talked among ourselves concerning the fact that some problems of cities and men never really changed."[17]

The problems of cities and men that the nurses discussed at Pompeii are the chronic, age-old problems of prostitution and venereal disease. Syphilis and gonorrhea had plagued the ancient armies of Greece and Rome, and were still ravaging the soldiers of the twentieth century. From the weeks following the first American landings in North Africa throughout the battle for Italy, venereal disease (VD) was an enemy with whom tens of thousands of American and Allied soldiers willingly consorted. Even before the Battle of Kasserine Pass in Tunisia, VD cases were being admitted to evacuation hospitals for treatment. Records from the 77th Evacuation Hospital in La Meskiana, Tunisia, indicate that of the first 1,000 surgical patients, there were 258 battle casualties and 120 patients with VD, more than half of whom suffered from new infections of syphilis. Despite the efforts of the U.S. military to prevent venereal disease, soldiers continued to contract gonorrhea and syphilis, the complications of which could be debilitating as well as deadly.

Caused by the spirochete *Treponema pallidum*, syphilis is a highly contagious and deadly disease spread by sexual contact. Left untreated, the disease, whose first signs are small, fluid-filled lesions (chancres) on the genitals, will eventually—within one to ten years after initial infection—kill its victim by destroying major blood vessels and organs, including the heart, liver, brain, bones, and/or stomach.

The other venereal disease common during World War II was gonorrhea. Caused by the *Neisseria gonorrhoeae* organism, gonorrhea is not fatal. But if left untreated, the infection, which begins in the urinary tract, will spread and may cause complications, including blindness.

Today, gonorrhea and syphilis are treated by penicillin. But penicillin would not reach the battlefields of World War II until late 1943. In the early years of the war, arsenic, sulfa, and bismuth were used to treat VD in protocols that were lengthy and often ineffective.

In an effort to prevent venereal disease among the troops, the U.S. Army set up prophylaxis stations. Whenever a man signed out to leave a military area on pass, he was issued a prophylaxis kit. Though the motto on the kit read "The safest way is to keep away," abstinence was not expected and the treatment in the kit was meant to be used after a soldier had engaged in sex. The remedy consisted, basically, of a syringe filled with Protargol, which a GI was to inject into the opening in the tip of his penis after having sex. Needless to say, soldiers were reluctant to self-administer this prophylactic treatment.[18]

To enforce use of the kit, the army conducted "short-arms" inspections, in which medical officers inspected the troops' penises for signs of venereal infections. Further, the military threatened to court-martial those soldiers who had contracted VD and did not use their prophylaxis kits. But the threat was essentially empty since the army never set up a way to ascertain whether or not an infected soldier used the kit. Instead, the soldier's word was all that was required for him to avoid penalty and keep his military record unblemished.

The American public was kept in the dark about the epidemic growth

of venereal disease among its fighting men. Though a designated VD officer at every headquarters and military hospital recorded the statistics for
the numbers of VD cases, the practice of listing such patients as "surgical cases" in official reports kept the truth about the high incidence of
VD in the military hidden.[19]

In French North Africa, two red light districts were legendary: in
Algeria, a brothel called "The Sphinx" that was located on the edge of
the Casbah in Algiers; and in Morocco, the fabled red light district in
Casablanca—a warren of streets enclosed by a high wall and filled
with brothels—called "The White City." French physicians regularly
inspected the prostitutes in both countries and issued them certificates
of health if the women were found free of syphilis and gonorrhea.

Once American and Allied troops reached Sicily and the Italian mainland, VD became much more difficult to control. With the surrender of
Italy and the Italian government in disarray, there was no organized medical inspection and treatment for prostitutes by government doctors as
there had been in North Africa. Thousands of women were the sole
source of support for children and families who were hungry or starving
because of the devastation of war, and many of these women turned to
prostitution to earn money for food. Italian women in all classes of society sought out soldiers for sex in exchange for money to purchase food on
the black market.

Cases of venereal diseases among American troops in Italy skyrock-
eted in the fall of 1943. The rate in September 1943 was 35 per 1,000; during December 1943, it increased to 101 per 1,000, a 180 percent increase
in just three months.[20]

Hospitals were faced with treating thousands of acute cases of sulfa-
resistant gonorrhea and syphilis, and charged with the mission of getting
the soldiers back to duty as quickly as possible. It was at this time that
physicians struggling to control this epidemic decided to use supplies of
a new wonder drug, just arriving in the theater, to treat patients infected
with VD: penicillin.

Penicillin was an antibiotic that had been overlooked on its initial
debut into the medical and scientific community in the late 1920s. It took
the worldwide conflagration of World War II to move penicillin from
under one researcher's obscure laboratory microscope to center stage
under the scientific, medical, and political spotlight that it deserved. In
1928, British medical researcher Alexander Fleming discovered the peni-

cillin mold. During 1929, Fleming, then forty-eight, experimented with the mold fluid from penicillin to the point of treating laboratory animals infected with the staphyloccus organism. Despite publishing two papers on his successful experiments with this penicillin mold fluid, the scientific community of that time ignored the discovery. During the 1920s and 1930s, British researchers considered that the idea of "chemotherapy of bacteria infections was absurd. . . . " The prevailing scientific community overlooked the data reported by Fleming.[21]

Years after Fleming's discovery, two other British scientists did recognize penicillin's potential, and appealed to the scientific community to study and produce penicillin. Oxford University's Howard Florey and Ernest Chain spearheaded this effort by publishing their ongoing experiments in *The Lancet*, the prestigious British medical journal, in 24 August 1940 and 16 August 1941. In June 1941, armed only with Florey's limited experience of treating a few patients with penicillin, they met with representatives of a British chemical company to discuss the possibility of growing and extracting penicillin for therapeutic use. Imperial Chemical Industries (ICI) started work on the project. By January 1942, six additional British pharmaceutical companies joined forces to produce penicillin by sharing their research. The scientists of these companies discovered that growing the mold by the "deep tank" fermentation method (using 5,000- to 7,500-gallon tanks instead of thousands of flasks) could increase the amount of penicillin extracted. The deep tank method, together with improvements in the extraction process (separating the penicillin mold from the mold fluid or "juice"), led this new industry to increase production of penicillin. By March 1943, Britain was producing at least 27 million units a week, and by 1945, 25 to 30 billion units a week.[22]

However, Florey and Chain realized the enormity of the project in the face of the hardships imposed by war—the regular, relentless bombings of London and other British cities by the German Luftwaffe made daily life difficult and hazardous. Fearing that British efforts would be stalled, Chain and Florey traveled in secrecy to the United States on 2 July 1941. With scientific colleagues in New York and New Haven, Connecticut, they discussed the urgent need for the United States to produce penicillin.

Plans quickly took shape. A committee of the National Regional Research Laboratory agreed to develop a culture medium for producing

large amounts of penicillin and to identify the strains that could be most
easily produced in large amounts by use of the deep tank method. These
companies worked with the U.S. government's Office of Scientific
Research and Development (OSRD). The OSRD's Committee on Medical Research, directed by Dr. Vannevar Bush of the Carnegie Institution
of Washington, D.C., did not hesitate to get involved. It assumed responsibility for the overall research and development of penicillin. The goals
of the Americans were different from those of their British colleagues.
The British researchers' clinical trials had focused on establishing the
minimal amount of penicillin that could be therapeutically effective. The
U.S. researchers decided to investigate "the breadth of penicillin's therapeutic potential and the wisdom (from an economic standpoint) of
embarking on its large-scale manufacture."[23]

At first the U.S. pharmaceutical companies, already involved in the
fermentation process, were concerned that the penicillin mold would
spread and contaminate their current products. However, they soon
plunged in.

With the full support of a number of U.S. pharmaceutical companies
and the development of deep tank fermentation, the production of penicillin gradually increased. Only twenty-two sanctioned investigators received small amounts of penicillin throughout 1942. These infectious
disease specialists treated various common infections with poor results.

By 1 January 1943, there was better news. Through a contract via Dr.
Chester Keefer with the Massachusetts Memorial Hospital, penicillin
was distributed to "responsible investigators" in return for clinical information of the results. Although twenty-two companies were sanctioned
to become involved—all agreeing to share their information—Abbott
Labs, Charles Pfizer & Co., Merck & Co., Squibb & Sons, and Winthrop
Laboratories produced all of the penicillin for these early clinical trials.
Among these trials was a case reported by Pfizer, which had pioneered
the deep tank fermentation of penicillin in the United States.

In September 1943, fifteen-year-old Shirley Carter of Macon, Georgia,
complained of a sore throat that quickly worsened to a raging 105°F temperature; the infection was caused by the streptococcus organism (a virulent strain of bacteria). So ill that she was hospitalized, Shirley failed to
respond to the treatment of the day—aspirin, ice packs, and sulfa. Her
family and her doctor despaired when her condition worsened and the
fever rose to 107°. Shirley, despite her perilous condition, remembered

reading an article in *Reader's Digest* about penicillin—the new miracle drug. She told her physician, Dr. Herbert Weaver, about it, and he agreed to use penicillin, if they could find it.

Joining a battle against time, the local newspaper, the *Macon News*, found Dr. Keefer of Boston, who quickly agreed to dispense the penicillin to Dr. Weaver in Georgia. The *Macon News* appealed to the Army Air Forces, which dispensed a B-24 Liberator to Boston immediately. On 5 September, with police escort sirens wailing, the precious penicillin was delivered and the first dose given to Shirley, by then close to death. On 21 September, two weeks later, she was discharged from the hospital, her condition miraculously improved. As if in repayment, Shirley Carter lived to graduate from the Medical College of Virginia; she practiced medicine in Richmond, married, and raised a family.[24]

With results such as these, all involved with the project were spurred on. During the first three years, the production of penicillin increased significantly:

June 1943, .425 billion units,

June 1944, 117.527 billion units,

June 1945, 646.817 billion units.[25]

By 31 December 1943, clinical trials in the United States demonstrated that penicillin was effective when injected into muscle tissue of patients with acute infections. Penicillin eliminated some of the most common and virulent bacteria, including streptococci that cause bacterial endocarditis—an inflammation of the outer layer of the heart; pneumococci that cause pneumonia; hemophilus influenzae that cause flu; and staphylococcal infections, which have an 85 percent death rate if untreated. Gonorrhea and syphilis, the two common venereal diseases, were treated successfully with penicillin. Since 5 percent (750,000) of the 15 million men who registered for the draft had one venereal disease or another, the U.S. government had much to gain with even the small amounts of penicillin distributed in 1943.[26]

The penicillin sent to the Mediterranean Theater of War was originally intended for the treatment of surgical cases and battle casualties. Colonel Edward Churchill was appalled at the redirection of medication intended for battle casualties to VD patients. "The hospitals were loaded with sulfonamide-resistant venereal disease," he wrote later. "The penicillin was used to treat those 'wounded' in the North African and Italian brothels and those wounded in 'combat' with the enemy had to wait."

The medical battles against venereal disease would continue throughout the war, but the American public would remain unaware of this vital conflict.[27]

ABOUT THIRTY MILES north of Naples at the 33rd Field Hospital near Dragoni, Captain Luther Wolff was struggling with another problem about which the American public was unaware—the lack of adequate equipment for surgery. On 25 October, Wolff made a lengthy diary entry on the Tables of Basic Equipment—the list of surgical equipment created by the Surgeon General's Office in the United States—as to what surgical equipment would and would not be included for field and evacuation hospitals. Wolff lamented: "There is so much junk sent that is never used and lifesaving things such as anesthetic machines, endotracheal tubes, Levin tubes, intestinal sutures, small hemostats, blood vessel sutures et cetera are all absent. . . . We have dozens of Miller-Abbott tubes [used for the treatment of obstruction of the small intestine] in our medical chests, but not one Levin tube. As far as I know, no one has ever needed the Miller-Abbott tubes, but we need Levin tubes in practically every belly case."[28]

But medical personnel were quick to improvise; Wolff also noted in his diary that the hospital staff was shortening the Miller-Abbott tubes by ten feet and cutting off the balloon end, effectively creating three- to four-foot Levin tubes—a nasogastric rubber tube passed through the nose into the stomach, used to suction the stomach contents out in preparation for, and following, gastrointestinal surgery.

Lack of surgical supplies continued throughout the Italian Campaign. Wolff noted his frustration with the army's inability to correct the supply problem: "Also we need suction machines desperately. Surely the Army Medical Supply should know what it needs after a year of battle casualties and could have done something about it by now! I don't like the army, particularly for this reason."[29]

Wolff had no way of knowing that the system for sending medical and surgical supplies to army hospitals in theaters of war was in a state of semichaos at this time. All medical and surgical supplies being shipped to the Mediterranean and European Theaters of War left the United States through the New York port of embarkation. The understaffed personnel at the port had several significant handicaps. Despite the fact that America had purchased surgical instruments from Germany before entering the war, a large percentage of the equipment purchased went to the United Kingdom under the Lend-Lease program. In the third week of June 1942, Colonel Francis C. Tyng, MC, chief of the finance and supply division at the Office of the Surgeon General, notified Major General Paul R. Hawley, chief surgeon of the European Theater of Operations and Services of Supply, that "We have a daily shortage of some 2,000 items at all times in our depots."[30]

Although the shortages were supposedly proportioned across the United States, the European and Mediterranean theaters felt the lack of equipment most acutely. Most of the packers at the port of embarkation were inexperienced and either failed to pack the appropriate supplies even when they were available, or mislabeled crates carrying the life-saving medical and surgical supplies. As a result, many "scheduled" supplies never reached their destination at all, and many crates arrived minus the surgical equipment theater surgeons needed for the smooth operation of surgical procedures. The majority of personnel available to Major General Hawley were without experience in services of supplies and seemed either to be surgeons with no administrative experience or administrators with little or no knowledge of medical and surgical equipment and supplies. On 31 December 1942, Hawley wrote in a letter to the Surgeon General of the United States, "I simply *have* to have fifteen good soldiers soon or this place is going to pot. . . . I'll stay here and pitch, but I've got to have someone who can bat in some runs." Those soldiers would be a long time coming to Hawley. Wolff and other medical personnel would continue to do their best for sick and wounded soldiers by improvising the surgical equipment and supplies that they lacked.[31]

ON 22 NOVEMBER, three miles south of Presenzano, at a site near the Volturno River, rain fell continuously as Ruth Hindman made her way from the nurses' latrine to her tent in the early evening darkness. Days of rain and weeks of winter weather had caused the Volturno to overflow its banks, turning the soil of the 11th Field Hospital into a thick sea of mud. Ruthie recalled using her arms to balance herself as she pulled her right foot out of the ankle-deep goo, stretched it in front of her as far as she dared, put it down again into the cold gluelike mess, and began the process anew with her left foot. The soft sucking sounds and flat *ker-plop* that accompanied each step beat a familiar cadence that had become as much a part of life at the Italian front lines as casualties and bandages.

As Ruthie headed for the tent she shared with three fellow nurses, she recalled that her group had a guest for the night—the renowned *Life* magazine photographer Margaret Bourke-White. Bourke-White was in Italy to do a spread on the war for the national weekly, as well as to gather information and photos for a book she was writing about life on the front lines of the Italian Campaign. When Ruthie entered the tent, she announced that the heavy rains and overflowing river had completely flooded the "powder room" and the nurses would have to dig a deeper trench around it in the morning. Her words were greeted with a collective groan from her sister army nurses and a shocked expression from Bourke-White. Ruthie recalled Bourke-White's words: "You don't really call that dilapidated tent a 'powder room,' do you? The place is a real dump." Ruthie assured Bourke-White that if she had seen the slit trenches the nurses had to use at their previous location, she would have more appreciation. "You get used to making do with the barest necessities when you follow the infantry through World War II's battlefields."[32]

The evening began in a routine way, as the women talked and went about their personal chores. Ruthie pulled out an empty plasma can, filled it with cocoa and water, and placed it on the stove in the middle of their

Lt. Ruth Hindman (Courtesy of Ruth Hindman Balch)

tent. Lieutenant Frances Mosher finished heating water for her bath in a salvaged apple butter can and, using a woolen scarf as a pot holder, poured the water into her helmet and started her bath with her face. All the while, Bourke-White asked questions, loaded new film into two cameras, listened to the conversation being exchanged in their tent, and wrote notes on a pad of paper. All of a sudden, the routine was interrupted by a deep roaring sound that seemed to be bearing down on their tent.

"Ours or theirs?" two of the nurses asked in unison. Ruthie answered, " 'Theirs!' I shouted and dove beneath my cot. My tentmates followed suit and fifteen seconds later, Miss Bourke-White was the only person in the tent who was not in a prone position. 'Get under your cot, Margaret,' I called to her."

As the women lay beneath their cots, Ruthie told Bourke-White what was happening: the Germans were most likely shelling the American artillery and not the hospital. "Unfortunately," Ruthie pointed out, "when the shells fell short, they landed in the tented hospital area, and you can be just as dead from a mistake as from a shell aimed at you."[33]

Ruthie recalled that the next thing she heard was Lieutenant Fran Mosher shouting to ask Bourke-White whether she was taking notes. Ruthie remembered Margaret's reply being short and to the point. "I don't think I'll need notes to remember this!"[34]

The shelling stopped. One by one the women crawled out from under their cots, stood up, and listened to the heavy rain beating against the canvas of their tent. Fran Mosher announced that the cocoa was ready, but the words were no sooner out of her mouth when the sound of artillery fire started again. "Here they come again!" Fran shouted. The cocoa was forgotten as all five women dove beneath their cots.[35]

Ruthie remembered that the roar grew louder until it seemed to be coming from inside her head. Suddenly, there was a loud thud, followed by an ear-splitting explosion and a strong concussion wave. Outside, chunks of earth, mud, and stones beat against the tent. Suddenly the lights went out and the five women had to resort to flashlights.

The shell had obviously struck the hospital area—and nearby. Ruthie remembered that she and Fran Mosher began pulling on their clothes so they could report to the OR tent and help with any wounded. Before they could start for surgery, a man called from outside to ask if Bourke-White was okay and whether she needed any help. The women recognized the voice of Corporal Jess Padgitt, a twenty-one-year-old infantryman from Des Moines, Iowa, who had been assigned to look after Bourke-White while she was at the front. Ruthie remembered Bourke-White requesting help getting her cameras together and finding the place where the shell had exploded so she could take some pictures. A few minutes later, Padgitt led the three women toward the damaged area. They walked in single-file with the aid of hooded flashlights to maintain blackout conditions.

Abruptly, Padgitt stopped and the three women ran into each other in a chain reaction. Ruth and Fran moved to Padgitt's side to see what was causing the holdup. Ruthie ran her flashlight over the area in front of them to reveal a waist-high tangle of electric wires directly in their path and a large, bowl-shaped crater about seven feet deep and twelve feet in diameter, off to the right where the hospital mess tent had stood. Ruthie recalled: "I remember praying that there were no soldiers in the mess tent when the shell hit. We all knew that we were lucky that the shell had hit around 2100 instead of an hour and a half later when the mess tent would have been crowded with night-shift personnel."[36]

The next morning, the wreckage of the mess tent looked particularly hideous in the daylight. The 170mm shell had landed directly on the officers' corner of the mess tent and left a crater where their table had stood. "We considered ourselves lucky to have survived another close call," Ruthie said. "Not as close as on the *Newfoundland*, but still too close for comfort."[37]

After a breakfast of cold K-rations, Bourke-White snapped a few more photographs, then climbed into a jeep with Corporal Padgitt and left the 11th Field Hospital for another view of the front lines. Ruthie reminisced, "She was very courageous—a great lady."[38]

ONE OF THE BENEFITS surgical teams at field hospitals enjoyed on the front lines was the opportunity to perform surgery on injuries not usually seen back in the States. The surgical patients who were brought to the OR rooms of a field hospital were essentially only the most unstable, critically wounded, those classified as "nontransportable" casualties. These were men so badly injured they could not be moved farther back from the front for fear they would die during the evacuation process. With such critical patients at extremely high risk, field hospital surgical teams had to devise creative ways of working to increase speed and efficiency.

At the 11th Field Hospital, the 2nd Aux teams practiced so that little time was lost in caring for a patient. While the team surgeon worked on

an anesthetized patient's wound from one side of the OR table, sometimes the 2nd Aux nurse would work on another of the patient's wounds
from the other side of the table. "Johnny Adams and the other doctors
would just say, 'Do whatever you think is needed while I work on his
chest,' or his belly or whatever," Hindman recalled. She remembered one
night, when casualties were particularly heavy, all four operating tables
were occupied, and patients were lined up on litters waiting their turn
for surgery. At one table, Johnny Adams was operating on a soldier while
Hindman, on the other side, was cleaning debris from a large gash in the
man's right thigh. Hindman recalled being mystified at finding three- and
four-inch bristles in the wound. " 'I don't know what I'm getting here,' "
she said. "I kept finding these bristles and continued to remove them for
about twenty minutes." The next afternoon when the patient was awake,
Hindman paid him a visit and asked if he had any idea where the bristles
had come from. "I had my shaving brush in my pants pocket," the soldier
told her.[39]

Not all stressful conditions were resolved so easily. One particular
source of stress for OR teams was the shelling that frequently occurred
while they were in the middle of surgery. At those times, one of the
corpsmen would go by each OR table and place a helmet on the head of
each doctor and nurse. The OR teams did not stop their work unless
absolutely necessary. Even then, they hit the ground while shrapnel was
coming through the canvas, then got up immediately and continued once
that particular danger had passed. "We all knew we could get killed,"
Ruthie recalled, "but none of us dwelled on the fact. We couldn't have
gone on working on the front lines if we got too concerned with getting
killed or wounded. You do what you need to do and if you get hit, that's
just the way it is."[40]

ONE FACTOR that made it possible for the 2nd Aux teams to work at
such a constant pace for days on end was the occasional rest and recuperation leave they were granted.

Hindman described an R&R leave at a fine old hotel in Sorrento, the
famous town on the Bay of Naples. Before each meal, the officers would
customarily gather outside the hotel dining-room doors fifteen minutes
before they opened. Each time, Ruth was the only female in a crowd of
male officers. One evening, she was waiting outside the dining room as
usual when General Mark Clark walked up, introduced himself to her, and

asked why there were no other nurses at the hotel. "That's what I'd like to know," Ruthie answered. General Clark turned to his aide, a full colonel, and told him to make sure that from then on, there were always to be at least three or four nurses in the hotel. Ruthie never forgot his words—"They need the R&R as much as our combat soldiers." Ruthie was delighted to hear the general acknowledge the nurses' frontline duty.[41]

The following day, Hindman met a handsome young captain while waiting to enter the dining room for lunch. The young man introduced himself and asked if Ruthie would like to attend a movie with him after lunch. The theater was next door and Ruthie gladly accepted the invitation. After the movie, they returned to the hotel for dinner. While they waited for the dining-room doors to open, several male officers began talking to them about books. One of the officers asked Ruthie's date, Captain Lewis, if his father happened to be Sinclair Lewis, the author. "I was totally surprised," Ruthie recalled, "when my date answered yes, and the conversation turned to his father's books. I'm sure that if that lieutenant hadn't asked, my captain would never have mentioned that fact. You just never knew who you were going to meet, and they were all the nicest people."[42]

One of the most fortuitous chance meetings Ruthie Hindman had during an R&R leave was with the adjutant general of the Fifth Army. Ruthie remembered meeting the general at a dance and telling him that she had always wanted to see Capri—the island on the southern rim of the Bay of Naples—but it was off-limits to U.S. military personnel. The general said that he and his group were using General Clark's Chris Craft to make the trip, and he invited her along. Ruthie explained that the 2nd Aux always did things as a team, so the general told her to bring her team with her. "When I went back to the hotel and told my team," Ruthie recalled, "I thought they'd flip. They thought they'd never get there. Everyone was so excited about seeing Capri that we were at our meeting place a half hour early the next morning."[43]

On 27 November, the 95th Evacuation Hospital left Naples and set up to receive patients near the town of Capua, about fifteen miles to the north. "The place seemed familiar to me," Speedy Glidewell recalled, "since I remembered my Latin book in high school talking about the Appian Way. Well, we were situated right by the thing. It was called Highway 6 now [actually Route 7 is the old Appian Way, a paved road extending from Rome to Brundisium begun in 312 B.C. by the Roman consul Appius Claudius Caecus], but it was the same route soldiers had traveled centuries ago." Speedy and her tentmates set up their tents— "Hut Two" and the "Fall Inn"—only ten yards from the ancient road. Traffic went by twenty-four hours a day, but it didn't bother the tents' occupants one bit.[44]

However, the proximity of the women's tents to Highway 6 did bother most of their hospital colleagues in neighboring tents. "The trouble started," Speedy recalled, "when we hung our laundry out to dry on our tent ropes. We hung our 'unmentionables' to dry along any of our tent ropes we could reach." With bras and panties hanging from tent ropes like gingerbread decorations on houses back home, "Hut Two" and the "Fall Inn" attracted a lot of attention from GIs traveling in trucks, jeeps, tanks, or on foot along Highway 6. Speedy remembered that the nurses and their laundry got so many horns blown at them, so many shouts of "Hubba-hubba," so many catcalls and whistles that it kept their colleagues in nearby tents awake and on edge. After two days and a night of a constant stream of GIs and their comments, the enlisted men of the 95th Evac got orders to move the nurses' tents to the rear of the camp, out of sight of passing traffic.[45]

The onslaught of severe winter weather in the Capua area and the mountainous territory surrounding it caused transport problems to and from the front lines. Rain, snow, and sleet turned the ground into knee-deep mud and made any traveling off the main highway a challenge for men and vehicles. By December, supplies were passing the 95th Evac on pack mules instead of trucks, but even these surefooted beasts found the going rough and tedious.

The same mules that brought ammunition and food to soldiers in the mountainous front lines were drafted by medics to help carry the wounded back to clearing stations and field hospitals. To the horror of medics, nurses, and doctors, evacuation from the front often took as long as twelve hours or more. In many areas in the mountains, even mules could not get to battlefields, and casualties had to be carried out by long stretcher relays. Lines of litter bearers would stand along evacuation routes from rugged mountains and literally hand-pass litter-borne casualties over their heads to the next pair of hands, which would pass it off to the next men in the living evacuation chain. Several places along this route, litter bearers and medics would have to use ropes to lower stretchers over high precipices to the next leg of the evacuation line. Adding to the tensions of getting wounded soldiers back to hospitals was the fact that medics and litter bearers, unlike infantrymen, did not have the winter clothes needed to protect them from the cold, inclement weather.

With or without warm winter clothing, battle casualties delivered to waiting hospitals often suffered from pneumonia, frostbite, trench foot, or overexposure to the cold, wet conditions. Too frequently, wounded soldiers would be left lying for hours in dirt and mud before a medic could even reach them. In a country such as Italy that had practiced agriculture and used manure for fertilizer for centuries, the soil was rife with bacteria. The bacteria would infect wounds and often led to gas gangrene, making amputation of limbs and death from abdominal gas gangrene far too frequent.

One bright spot was the 41st Hospital Train, which began running during the third week of November 1943 from Caserta to Naples, a distance of approximately twenty-five miles. The train offered wounded GIs a smoother trip back to hospitals near and in Naples, and eliminated a fifty-mile round trip by ambulance over bomb-damaged roads to drop off battle casualties.

The hospital train had fifteen cars and a staff of forty-eight: six army nurses, four physicians, thirty-three enlisted medics, and a train crew of five enlisted men who had worked on railroads in America—the Santa Fe, the Baltimore & Ohio, and the Jersey Central Railroad—before the war. The engine had been rescued from a demolished roundhouse, and the fifteen cars were salvaged from old and damaged Italian rolling stock. U.S. Army personnel remodeled the cars by tearing out seats, compartments, and heating systems, and installing triple-decked litter berths for a maximum load of 350 patients—the number of casualties that would require 87 ambulances.

Each morning, long lines of ambulances would pull up to the waiting train, which backed into the station at Caserta along the one expanse of track that was usable. Once loaded, the train would carry its precious cargo of wounded American and Allied soldiers, along with the occasional German prisoner of war, to base hospitals in southern Italy. The journey terminated at Naples. The train then traveled in reverse along the same twenty-five miles of track. New casualties were loaded for transport from Caserta to the base hospitals where they could receive more specialized treatment. All along the route, one could see sidings that were unusable because of bombed-out trains. The wreckage could not be removed without special heavy equipment and many hours of backbreaking work. Since neither the equipment nor the manpower was available to perform this cleanup job, the 41st Hospital Train had only the use of that section of track cleared between Caserta and Naples. (The 42nd Hospital Train was added on 12 May 1944 and ran between Sessa, about thirty miles northwest of Naples, and Naples.)

During the trip, patients were cared for by nurses, doctors, and medics who called the makeshift hospital train home. Several cars had been remodeled as quarters for the permanent staff and a hospital kitchen provided hot meals during the trip. Patients ate out of their own mess kits, or from mess kits that remained on the train. Each ward was heated by two potbellied stoves placed at both ends of each car for warmth. There was even an operating room in case emergency surgery had to be performed during the trip. All in all, the hospital train was a blessing for everyone concerned. It gave the wounded a fairly comfortable ride to hospitals behind the front lines and it helped free up Italy's clogged, narrow roads.[46]

DURING LATE NOVEMBER and December 1943, the objective of American and Allied troops was to capture Cassino, forty-five miles northwest of Naples, and gain entrance to northern Italy through the Liri Valley. This offensive was dubbed the "Winter Line Campaign." But first American and Allied soldiers would have to fight their way up rugged mountains and across the swiftly moving rivers covered by German guns and troops dug in along the high ground in heavy fortifications known as the "Gustav Line," a series of pillboxes (fortified gun emplacements) and intricate patterns of land mines. This was Hitler's main line of defense against the American and Allied advance toward Rome. The American/Allied plan was to drive the Germans out of their mountain strongholds and force them to withdraw farther north across the Rapido River, which at this point in its course ran south of Cassino. At the same time, the Allies were to exercise a wide flanking movement through the mountains northwest of Cassino.

The Allied attack started on 1 December 1943 with an assault on Cassino Hill—a mass to the south of the Mignano Gap, a pass in the mountains that was the gateway to the Liri Valley. The Thirty-fourth and Forty-fifth Infantry Divisions had been fighting their way to San Elia and Atina, towns located seven miles up a gorge from the Rapido Valley and about ten miles north of Cassino, since 29 November; by 4 December, after five days of brutal combat, the Thirty-fourth Division had gained only one mile and suffered 777 casualties. Casualty rates among the Forty-fifth were no better. It was obvious the Gustav Line was well planned, well executed, well defended, and contributed significantly to the number of American and Allied casualties.

The 95th Evacuation Hospital, northwest of Capua and just beyond the Volturno River, was inundated with patients. "In addition to doing surgery on our own soldiers," Speedy Glidewell noted, "we were operating on our Allies—Ghoumes from North Africa, Ghurkas from India, and Poles and New Zealanders. Of course we also got German POWs who were wounded." A visitor to the OR tent might hear four different patients counting in four different languages as they were inducted into anesthesia for their surgery.[47]

The Ghoumes, Arab nomads from North Africa, gained special notoriety in the OR tents. They were known for their fierceness and courage in battle and for a unique combat technique that often landed them in the hospital for repairs. When confronted in hand-to-hand combat, a Ghoume would use his left hand to deflect the thrust of an enemy bayonet. As a result, the bayonet often pierced the left hand through the palm

Personnel of the 95th Evacuation Hospital (Courtesy of Claudine Glidewell Doyle)

and extended one or two inches out the back of the hand. While his left hand acted as a shield to the enemy's bayonet, the Ghoume, with his right hand, would close with the German and cut his throat with the razor-sharp crescent-shaped knife that was part of each man's combat gear. "We spent hours in surgery repairing hands that had been run through with a bayonet," Speedy recalled. "Finding the ends of severed tendons and repairing the damage to small bones was a tedious and time-consuming process."[48]

In addition to the demands of such delicate surgery, the Ghoumes created problems in the wards that drove nurses crazy, as Speedy put it. Hut recalled that despite their numerous efforts, nurses were unable to make the Ghoumes understand the purpose of a urinal or bedpan. Ghoumes seemed convinced that the corners of ward tents existed as places for them to relieve themselves. "Another problem," Hut Walden recalled, "was convincing the Ghoumes that washcloths and towels were for bathing. We never did succeed at teaching them those facts. Each Ghoume considered the issue of a towel the personal gift of a clean, new turban. Some were creative enough to use the washcloths as turban decorations."[49]

THE CHRISTMAS HOLIDAYS and a regrouping of troops and plans on both sides coincided to produce a brief lull in casualties. Nurses and corpsmen decorated the wards with Christmas trees, complete with angels, stars, and Santas cut out of tin cans, and strings of rubber gloves, glass tubing, and empty penicillin bottles dipped in dye for color and Epsom salts for a touch of frost. Nurses and medics organized Christmas parties where small gifts like cigarettes, shaving lotion, and cologne were given out by an ill-dressed, underweight, yet recognizable Santa who wished everyone a "Merry Christmas" with a definite midwestern accent. Nurses had outdone themselves in supplying homemade fudge as part of the refreshments.

Speedy remembered that it seemed as if fudge was always cooking on their tent stove. When there was an air raid or a shelling, she and her tentmates would jump into the foxholes they had dug under their cots. They kept a suitcase nearby and pulled it over the opening of their foxholes to stop or slow down any shrapnel that might come their way. If anyone had to get out of her foxhole for any reason during the air raid or shelling, the other nurses would holler, "Stir the fudge!" This method worked fine and the nurses ended up with lots of fudge to share with their patients.[50]

THE NEW YEAR of 1944 began with Mother Nature raising a little hell of her own. Off-duty personnel had returned to their tents from quiet New Year's Eve parties and were either fast asleep or just drifting off when sleet, snow, and gale-force winds struck all along a twelve-mile area where hospitals were set up to support the Winter Line Campaign. All hospitals got some damage to their tents, but the 33rd Field Hospital near Presenzano was the hardest hit. As if summoned by a call to their battle stations, nurses, corpsmen, and doctors of the 33rd dressed in whatever clothes they could get their hands on and rushed into the blackness of the night to make sure patients were safe. For hours, the men and women of the 33rd, dressed in bathrobes, boxer shorts, undershirts, or pajamas, stood in the freezing rain struggling to hold down tent ropes and chains to keep canvas over the heads of the nearly one thousand patients while an evacuation operation was quickly put in motion.

"We were sidestepping tent poles and jumping over fallen electrical wires," Jessie Paddock recalled, "while we were getting the patients to trucks and ambulances. Nurses crawled through the mud from patient to patient, disconnecting intravenous lines and Wangensteen suctions so the patients could be moved."[51]

After several hours of backbreaking work, all but twelve of the one thousand patients had been moved several miles away to the safety of a warehouse. Now the real battle was about to begin. Each of the twelve remaining patients was critically wounded and could not be moved without serious risks to their lives. They would have to remain in a tent in the eye of the storm. Whether they lived or died was literally in the hands of the men and women who were holding tightly to ropes and tent-pole chains as the canvas was whipped by the cyclone-force wind and freezing rain. While doctors, corpsmen, and nurses held on to the tent, others crawled through the mud with flashlights tucked under their chins in order to keep their hands free for work. Teams of two or three carefully disconnected lines, tubes, and suction apparatuses, and gently lifted each wounded boy to a litter balanced on cinder blocks as close to the ground as possible. This done, they reconnected equipment needed by each patient and left a nurse or corpsman by his side as they moved on to the next wounded soldier.

The battle for the lives of these twelve boys continued throughout the night. A group of eight nurses, corpsmen, and doctors stayed behind. They spent the night holding on to the tent chains and ropes to keep the tent standing. In spite of suffering severe rope burns and lacerations, no one let go. As the first rays of daylight fell on the hospital, the winds subsided. For the first time in hours, the men and women could loosen the grip they had maintained on the tent through that long, cold night. Slowly, individuals got their first look at their comrades and the scene they had struggled through.

Smiles and laughter replaced much of the tension that had filled the hours of darkness. Hands hurt and bled as individuals relaxed the grip that had kept twelve brave and wounded boys safe. Nurses looked across at tentmates whose hair, always impeccably arranged, now hung down in straight, wet strands; at doctors, always the essence of dignity and decorum, in their muddy underwear or soaked and disheveled bathrobes, staring back in disbelief. Corporals and sergeants looked at lieutenants, captains, and majors with whom they had spent a memorable night; and everyone looked at the desolation around them: canvas, tent poles, personal belongings, and hospital equipment scattered in rivers of mud as far as the eye could see.

Then, as if by command, all eyes turned to a river of muddy water running through the area where the 33rd Field Hospital had stood. The water was moving downhill at a fairly fast rate of speed, and here and there along its surface was a half-cooked turkey floating peacefully in the wreckage and debris. Lieutenants Paddock and Farquhar counted at least twenty of the large waterlogged toms as they pitched and bobbed, then floated out of the area. "There goes our New Year's Day dinner!" Paddock shouted, and the weary group burst into gales of laughter.[52]

IN CONTRAST to New Year's Day in Italy, 1 January 1944 was a day of rest and celebration for the 128th Evacuation Hospital (the reorganized 48th Surgical Hospital) just newly stationed in England. In the late afternoon, hospital personnel sat down to a special holiday dinner at Tortworth Court near Chipping Sudbury in Gloucestershire—about ten miles north of Bristol—their home since 26 November 1943.

On 8 November, the hospital staff had boarded the USAT *Santa Paula* in Palermo, Sicily, one year to the day after they had waded ashore in America's amphibious landing on North Africa. With a year of combat medicine behind them, they were headed for another unknown destination. They waited three days aboard the *Santa Paula* before she finally headed out to sea. Helen Molony remembered the departure. "Of course we had no real idea about where we were heading but a few rumors said we were going back to the States."[53]

On 25 November, the *Santa Paula* docked at Newport, near Bristol, and the 128th Evacuation Hospital boarded a train for yet another unknown destination. It pulled into Charfield, Gloucestershire, in the early morning hours of the 26th, and personnel traveled to Tortworth Court, which was to be their home for a little more than seven months.

Many of the personnel of the 128th were suffering from malaria; more than seventy were too sick to march the last couple of miles and were loaded into trucks and driven to Tortworth. They arrived at 0330 and were met with hot coffee and sandwiches, and later shown to their rooms.

The contrast between the 128th's new hospital quarters at Tortworth Court, a stately castle, and the meager tents and ramshackle buildings that had housed the 128th throughout its year in the North Africa Campaign was startling. "This isn't bad," Lieutenant Martha Cameron remembered saying on her first morning, as she opened her eyes to the

Tortworth Castle, Gloucestershire, England—temporary home of the 128th Evacuation Hospital staff (Courtesy of Lt. Col. Martha Cameron, USAF, NC [Ret.])

first rays of daylight and looked around the large room she shared with eight other nurses. A fire was burning in a huge fireplace along one wall, providing a touch of elegance and beauty as well as some heat to the room. "They don't have anything like this in New Jersey," Cameron exclaimed. "Who would have guessed that a kid from Nutley would be living in a castle in England—even if it is temporary."[54]

The new assignment of the 128th Evac was to train novice hospital units preparing for the long-awaited invasion of Northern France. For a period of almost seven months, nurses, doctors, corpsmen, and other hospital personnel would train inexperienced U.S. Army hospital units in setting up, receiving, treating, and evacuating casualties from the front lines to hospitals in the rear areas. "We must have set up and torn down the hospital almost a hundred times while we were stationed at the Castle," Marte Cameron recalled. "There was always some hospital unit or visiting dignitaries who wanted a demonstration."[55]

The demonstrations were held in a large field just down the road from Tortworth Court. They included training on how to set a hospital up, as well as the best placement of wards in relation to X-ray, laboratory, and operating-room facilities to allow optimum movement of patients. They also discussed the placement of equipment, improvisation, patient care, special methods for adding light to the operating-room tents, and getting rid of mud on the OR floor. A year's worth of firsthand combat medicine was distilled to its essentials and passed on to the new hospital units that would follow the American and Allied troops who were to land on the beaches of Normandy.

A part of that training also included instructions on how to care for and repair hospital tents that were so often damaged by shelling or by severe rains and wind. Tent repair was a critical ongoing procedure in order to keep rain and cold wind off the patients. Oliver Sorlye, who worked in supply and transportation, remembered that when the 128th Evac first arrived at Tortworth Court, their own tents were in need of repair. Needles and thread were of no help repairing heavy canvas, so he used pliers to pull wire and heavy cord through the tenting to repair the hundreds of tears and holes shrapnel had made in the tents. For rips and holes that could not be sewn together, Sorlye used glue and canvas patches.[56]

During the brief periods when demonstrations were not being conducted, American doctors, nurses, corpsmen, and other hospital personnel were placed on temporary duty with British hospitals and medical units throughout England. American and British personnel would change places for a week or two while they learned the others' techniques and shared their lifestyle. More than a few American soldiers found the British food strange and unappetizing. Kidney pie for breakfast in British units would never be as popular with American GIs as bacon and eggs, and most looked forward to returning to their own hospital unit.

Lieutenant Martha Cameron remembered the on-the-job training in anesthesia she had received at the 250-bed 151st Station Hospital in Algeria. She recalled being surprised when she was told that she would be trained to give spinals, since in civilian hospitals only physicians were permitted to administer spinal anesthesia. This break with tradition concerned Marte enough that she went to the head nurse of surgery. Marte remembered the head nurse's response as if it had been yesterday: "She looked me in the eyes and said, 'You'll do whatever the chief of surgery tells you to do.' So I learned how to give spinals. The first time I hit the subarachnoid space and drew spinal fluid, I was hooked. I studied hard, read everything I could find, and loved my work."[57]

Life at Tortworth, however, was not all work. After a year of roughing it on the front lines in tents and in ill-equipped, dilapidated buildings in small towns few Americans had ever heard of, Tortworth Court seemed like the lap of luxury. "The Castle," as personnel of the 128th referred to their new temporary home, had approximately 80 rooms—each with its own fireplace—365 windows, and 12 doors. In order to protect the centuries-old tapestries, the U.S. Corps of Engineers had covered Tortworth's walls with plywood that went from floor to twelve or eighteen inches from the ceiling in each room. "We lived in a kind of semiluxury at the Castle," Marte Cameron remembered. "We were surrounded by plywood in an ill-heated castle that came complete with its own lake, fields, and formal gardens."[58]

Tortworth was close enough to Bristol and London to allow for passes and leaves to explore and enjoy some of England's treasures. Personnel made fairly frequent visits to the theater, the symphony, and sites such as St. Paul's Cathedral, Westminster Abbey, the Old Bailey, and Piccadilly Circus. Many visited Shakespeare's birthplace nearby at Stratford-on-Avon, and the town of Bath with its old Roman baths. On 22 January 1944, the 128th Evacuation Hospital held a costume ball at the Castle, complete with rented costumes and wigs.

Meanwhile, in Italy on that same day, troops of the Thirty-sixth Division were being slaughtered at the Rapido River and American troops were beginning to land on the beaches of Anzio-Nettuno, to engage in what would go down in history as some of the bloodiest battles of the entire war.

DURING THE FIRST week of 1944, the U.S. Fifth Army fought its way north along the Italian boot toward the fortified Gustav Line. German engineers had reinforced the natural defenses of the land—mountains, rivers, and valleys—with concrete gun pits, large dense fields of mines, and artillery emplacements on high ground. This field of fire was built by the Germans to cover all approaches to the Rapido, the final natural obstacle before the Gustav Line and the entrance to Italy's Liri Valley. At the heart of the Gustav Line was Monte Cassino, on the west side of the Rapido River. Monte Cassino, a fifth-century monastery founded by St. Benedict, was built across the river on the crest of the rocky slopes that overlooked the entrance to the valley and Highway 6. The highway and a double-tracked railroad ran northwest through the valley to Rome, approximately eighty miles away. The entrance to the Liri Valley lay through the Mignano Gap, a well-defended German observation point nicknamed "Purple Heart Valley" by the American troops. Purple Heart Valley was dominated by German-held mountain strongholds on each side of the mountain corridor and by the swiftly flowing Rapido River that lay between American and Allied troops on its east bank and the actual fortifications of the Gustav Line on the river's west bank.

During the first week in January 1944, British general Harold Alexander set a date for the amphibious invasion of Anzio, a small coastal resort town about thirty-five miles south of Rome, for 22 January. Code-named "Operation Shingle," the invasion of Anzio had as its ultimate objective the capture of Rome.

In preparation for the Anzio landing, the U.S. Third Division was ordered to bivouac near Naples to train for its role in Operation Shingle. None of the senior officers in charge of readying these American troops for the invasion of Anzio were prepared for the unexpected "assault" that took place at the bivouac camp during the first two weeks of January: "Prostitutes from Naples descended upon our encampment by the hundreds," wrote the surgeon of the Third Infantry Division in his annual 1944 report, "outflanking guards and barbed wire. . . . " The boldness of the women took the U.S. Army by surprise. Prostitutes gained entrance to the camp by posing as laundresses, while others set up for business in caves in the bluffs surrounding the area. The women were so determined to sell their wares that the infantry division surgeon reported that "each day several large truck loads of screaming, screeching prostitutes were collected in the Division area and delivered into the custody of the Italian police." At that time, Italian doctors estimated that half the available women in Italy had one or more forms of venereal disease, and that 95 to 100 percent of prostitutes in large cities had some form of venereal disease.[59]

While those preparing for the invasion of Anzio tried to stop the spread of VD, General Clark gave orders for the Thirty-sixth Infantry Division to cross the Rapido River. He ordered a direct frontal attack beginning on 20 January, thereby hoping to pull as many German troops as possible away from the Anzio area in order to better Operation Shingle's chances for success.

To prepare for the crossing of the Rapido, General Fred L. Walker, the commanding officer of the Thirty-sixth Division, ordered Colonel Oran Stovall, his division engineer, to make a reconnaissance survey of the proposed assault area and to give his findings on the best approaches for the crossing and the equipment that would be needed to carry out the mission. When Stovall presented his conclusions to the corps engineer, Colonel Leonard B. Gallagher, Stovall pointed out that there were no good approaches to the crossing sites. The Rapido itself was completely dominated by German artillery, machine guns, and small-arms fire. The Germans had sewn large fields of land mines all along the river's banks. Stovall said that in addition to the hazards posed by the German army, American and Allied forces lacked sufficient equipment and supplies to ensure the success of the mission. He predicted that the loss of American lives and the number of wounded would be staggering.

Armed with this new information, Walker urgently recommended to General Clark that the Thirty-sixth Division scrap the direct frontal attack across the Rapido in favor of a flanking maneuver. Walker believed this alternative plan would increase the chance for success and lessen the number of American and Allied casualties that could be expected in a frontal attack. In addition, Walker requested that Clark furnish the Thirty-sixth Division with twelve DUKWs (a six-wheeled, boat-shaped amphibious truck) to aid in getting his men across the rain-swollen Rapido.

Unfortunately for the men of the Thirty-sixth and the hospital personnel who would care for their wounded, General Clark's mind was made up. He issued the orders for a frontal attack on the Rapido. To make matters worse, available equipment and supplies were already committed to Operation Shingle at Anzio. Walker's requests were denied without further explanation. Clark seemed resolved to take whatever loses were in store for the Thirty-sixth Division in order to pull German forces from the Anzio area and improve Operation Shingle's chances for victory. Despite his heartfelt objections to the direct frontal crossing of the Rapido, General Walker obeyed his commander and gave orders to carry out Clark's plan. These orders would send American troops toward what, for all intents and purposes, would become a virtual suicide mission along the banks of the swiftly moving Rapido River.

American forces to support the Thirty-sixth Division in combat were also placed on the move. Beginning on the night of 17 January, engineers were ordered to survey the proposed crossing site areas. In addition, they were to clear paths through German minefields and mark those lanes with white tape, so that combat troops could move through the minefields and confront German soldiers defending the river and its west bank. On 19 January, a platoon of the 11th Field Hospital was moved up Highway 6, past Mignano. They set up in a high meadow one mile south of San Pietro and Mount Sammucro, and adjacent to the clearing station of the 111th Medical Battalion. On the way toward their new site, medical personnel passed through areas where the Germans had cut down trees and dug trenches to provide themselves with a clear field of fire.

At 1800 on 20 January, following an air and artillery barrage, the men of the 141st Regimental Combat Team (RCT) of the Thirty-sixth Division were led through cleared lanes in the German minefields to their river crossing points north of San Angelo. At the same time, the 143rd RCT moved to positions south of the town. German observation posts on the higher west bank had a good view of the entire river line and could blanket it at will with artillery shells, machine-gun, mortar, and small-arms fire. German engineers had left nothing to chance; they had pre-targeted possible crossing sites and strewn their approaches with densely planted land mines. The attack by the Thirty-sixth was no surprise to German defenders and they immediately sent a rain of steel along the entire course of the Rapido River.

As the Americans moved in darkness toward the rapidly flowing river, every fifth man was given a rubber raft to carry to the water. Private Charles Coolidge, a native of Signal Mountain, Tennessee, remembered, "By the time we got to the river, all of the rafts had holes in them. Some of our men swam across the river towing a strong rope that had been anchored on the east bank. Those who made it to the other side tied their end of the rope to a strong stationary object on the west bank so other soldiers could pull themselves across using the rope to guide and support them."[60]

American soldiers still on the east bank of the Rapido experienced increasing German artillery and mortar fire. As shells fell on the crossing sites, men dropped the rafts they were carrying and scattered to find any cover available. In the mad dash for safety, many soldiers left the cleared paths the engineers had marked days earlier. German shells destroyed the tape marking the safe lanes, and darkness and flying debris made any remaining tape difficult, if not impossible, to see. As men rushed unthinking into German minefields, they stepped on and triggered hidden mines, causing traumatic amputations, severe abdominal and head wounds, or immediate death. The fact that there were too few crossing sites and that hundreds of men were concentrated in a restricted area made the well-targeted German fire even more effective. The bleeding bodies of dead and wounded soldiers covered the ground like a carpet. Sandwiched between the sounds of whistling and exploding shells and mines came the agonized screams of dying men. Cries of "Mama!" and "Help me!" filled the night.

The cries drew corpsmen into the minefields to find, treat, and evacuate the wounded. Every few minutes, the sound of another mine exploding shot through the night as corpsmen inched their way forward through the profound darkness. The explosions were followed by new shouts of pain as corpsmen's hands rested on land mines and were ripped off by explosives.

Despite the hazards involved in treating and evacuating the wounded, 308 battle casualties were dragged from the minefields and from the east bank of the Rapido on the night of 20 January 1944. The wounded were carried by litter bearers and ambulances to the 111th Medical Battalion, where five medical officers triaged, treated, and evacuated the patients as quickly as their conditions allowed. Soldiers too badly wounded to survive evacuation were carried to the adjacent platoon of the 11th Field Hospital for immediate surgery. "We had six patients in shock and two in surgery. . . . The boys of the 36th Division are trying to cross the Rapido River and are taking a real shellacking . . . ," Captain Luther Wolff wrote in his diary. "Casualties severe and heavy."[61]

The Germans quickly pinned down the few men of the 141st RCT who did reach the west bank of the Rapido River. During the night when several hundred soldiers of the 143rd RCT joined them, they met the same fate. American wounded and dead were scattered only yards from the sites where they had stepped ashore. By 0700 on 21 January, the American troops who had made it across the Rapido were cornered and running out of ammunition. Daylight brought more German shelling and small-arms fire and added a new terror: German tanks joined the battle and rolled across American occupied areas, grinding the wounded and dead beneath their tracks. Private Coolidge of the 141st could see the German tanks rolling over his fellow soldiers on the west bank and recalled, "If you had a hole to hide in, you could survive the tanks rolling over you. But a lot of American soldiers didn't have any cover and the tanks ground them into the dirt."[62]

In another attempt to cross the Rapido on 22 January, 291 American casualties were brought to the 111th Medical Battalion Aid Station and the adjacent 11th Field Hospital. The five physicians at the battalion aid station were so overworked that it was obvious they would soon reach a point where they were no longer able to function. This was a grave problem since the only replacements for these men were physicians in fixed hospitals behind the front, and the majority of these had no frontline combat medical experience.

Only about forty men of the Thirty-sixth Division managed to cross back to the American side of the river. When casualties were totaled on 22 January 1944, the division had suffered 1,681—143 killed, 663 wounded, and 875 missing—in one 48-hour period.[63]

On 25 January, the Germans called for a three-hour truce, and American and German medics went into the battlefield to collect and remove the wounded and the dead. Between 1400 and 1700, medics and litter bearers worked feverishly to evacuate Americans back across the Rapido to the east bank. The Germans turned over twelve American wounded and informed the Americans that eighteen more casualties were patients in German hospitals and could be visited by U.S. medics during the truce.

Because time was limited and the wounded and dead so numerous, American corpsmen spent the entire three hours removing those who lay in the fields. When the truce ended at 1700, many dead Americans still remained on the Rapido's west bank, and American clearing stations and frontline hospitals were overflowing with the wounded.

CHAPTER EIGHT

Hell's Half-Acre—The Anzio Beachhead

AND IF I PERISH...

22 January–15 February 1944

The nurses were tremendous builders of morale at a time when it badly needed building. They went about their work wearing helmets and facing danger as great as anyone else on the beachhead. They worked with the doctors and in the operating rooms through bombardment of all kinds, day and night. It seemed to me that they were among the real heroes of Anzio.

—Gen. Mark Clark, commander, Fifth Army, Italy, 1944

On 21 January 1944, as American and Allied troops valiantly fought to cross the Rapido River and break through the Gustav Line at Cassino, the Allied troops of Operation Shingle began to move. Two hundred fifty warships, troop carriers, and other assorted ships, carrying fifty thousand soldiers, sailed out of Naples harbor just before dawn, at 0500 on 21 January. Their objective: Anzio, a town on the western Italian coast thirty-five miles south of Rome.

Along with the assault troops on board the warships and troop carriers were the male staff members—doctors, technicians, and corpsmen—of several American hospitals: the 93rd and the 95th Evacuation Hospitals; and the 33rd Field Hospital. These hospital units, minus their nurses, would land with the troops on D-Day; the nurses would go ashore to rejoin their hospital units several days later. Also on board was the VI Corps' indigenous medical support, the 52nd Medical Battalion. Three British hospital ships sailed in the convoy, too: the *St. David*, the *St.*

Andrew, and the *Leinster*. Each of these three carried, in addition to their British hospital teams, an American surgical team from the 2nd Auxiliary Surgical Group, comprised of male doctors, corpsmen, and women nurses.

Operation Shingle's ultimate objective was the capture of Rome, the Eternal City. Shingle, the amphibious landing at Anzio, was one arm of an Allied pincer movement; the other arm was the Allied charge across the Rapido River on the town of Cassino and its monastery, Monte Cassino, approximately sixty miles east of Anzio. Between Anzio and Cassino lay the Liri Valley. The plan was for the Americans and Allies to capture Anzio to the north and Cassino to the south. Then the Allied forces at Cassino would push the Germans north through the Liri Valley toward the Allied troops advancing from the Anzio beachhead. After defeating the German forces in this pincer movement, American and Allied troops would march on Rome.

That was the Allied plan, a deceptively clear and simple one: troops had to capture Monte Cassino, the monastery that was the chief obstacle to the capture of the Liri Valley; link up with troops at Anzio; and then drive northward thirty-five miles to capture their first European capital city. As simple as the plan may have appeared on paper, its execution, though ultimately successful, would prove a bloody campaign that cost many American lives. Monte Cassino would be taken, and so would Anzio, but the assault on the Rapido River and Cassino was a near-suicide mission that produced staggering numbers of American and Allied casualties, and the stalemate at Anzio would turn into one of World War II's biggest bloodbaths.

Now, under cover of darkness in the early hours of 21 January, Allied troops left the harbor at Naples headed for the beaches of Anzio and nearby Nettuno. The convoy—carrying the VI Corps that included the Third Infantry Division led by Major General Lucian Truscott Jr.; the First British Division (part of the British Eighth Army); Britain's 46th Royal Tank Regiment; and American Commandos, Rangers, and other support elements—turned south, rather than north, at Capri, the tiny island in the Bay of Naples. The ships' southern course was a deliberate maneuver by the Allies in an attempt to deceive the Germans as to the convoy's true destination; it was also meant to steer the convoy clear of German minefields.

As the 250 Allied ships made their roundabout way toward the beaches of Anzio, the troops on board tried to lose themselves in cards, dice, and conversation. In addition to the 50,000 men assigned to the convoy, the ships also carried 5,200 vehicles—jeeps, DUKWs, tanks, trucks—to be used in the invasion, and a ten-day supply of food and ammunition meant to keep the soldiers moving forward until the next supply convoy would arrive off the invasion beaches.

At 0100 on D-Day, 22 January 1944, the ships of the convoy dropped anchor several miles off the Anzio-Nettuno beaches and waited for the signal that would start troops loading into LCIs and LSTs and heading for shore. Ten minutes before H-hour, 0200, a short but heavy rocket barrage was fired at shore by several of the ships in the convoy, but there was none of the "softening-up" barrage that was usually fired by the escort ships.

Much to the surprise of American and Allied soldiers alike, the softening barrage was not needed: there was no return fire from Anzio's or Nettuno's beaches. The Germans had been taken completely by surprise. The first Allied combat troops went ashore and reached their cover of sand dunes without encountering any enemy opposition. What few enemy patrols did happen by the landing sites were quickly dealt with by American and British troops. Americans and Allied soldiers swiftly moved inland, dug in at their first defensive line, and prepared to repel enemy counterattacks.

By noon on D-Day, the VI Corps had achieved all of its primary objectives ashore, the capture of Anzio harbor and the town of Nettuno (the beachhead in the vicinity of Anzio), and had done so rapidly and with a minimum of casualties. The Albanese Mountains (Colli Laziali) were one objective that Major General John P. Lucas, commander of VI Corps, chose to ignore on the VI Corps' first days on the beachhead. Thirteen American soldiers had been killed; ninety-seven were wounded, and forty-four missing. The 52nd Medical Battalion, which had landed with the assault troops, treated the wounded on the beachhead and prepared them for evacuation to the three hospital ships.

By midnight of D-Day, 36,000 Allied soldiers were on shore, along with 3,200 vehicles and a large quantity of the allotted ten-day supplies. Within twenty-four hours of the initial landings, 90 percent of the convoy had been unloaded and the supplies placed ashore. By the following day, the Allies had established control of an area extending fifteen miles wide along the coast and seven miles inland. It would appear, then, that the Allies had the upper hand immediately following the invasion of

Anzio. But it was an advantage, some historians have argued, that was sadly squandered by the commander of the Anzio landing troops, Major General John P. Lucas.

In the first seven days following the 22 January invasion, Lucas chose not to move the troops beyond the initial beachhead line secured on D-Day. Instead, he had his soldiers dig in and secure the fifteen- by seven-mile beachhead and Anzio harbor against any potential German counterattack and to wait for further reinforcements. Lucas did not want to move his men immediately forward toward Rome without securing the beachhead, for fear the Germans would come behind the American and Allied troops and cut them off in the rear. It was also important to secure Anzio harbor to guarantee that the supply line for troops would be kept open.

Perhaps Lucas's strategy would have worked had reinforcements come. But reinforcements never came; in fact, Lucas's commander, General Clark, had never had any plans to send reinforcements to Anzio. Meanwhile, as the Allies, under Lucas's orders, stalled for a week digging in on the Anzio beachhead, the enemy had time to regroup. By 28 January, the Germans had pulled reinforcements, not up from the south at Cassino, but from the north—from France, Rome, and Albania—and mounted a ferocious counterattack. They hemmed the American and Allied troops on the beachhead, and throughout all of February and the second week of March pounded the men, who were trapped like sitting ducks.

But on D+1, 23 January, the dominating position at Anzio was held by American and Allied troops. The British hospital ship, HMHC *St. David*, with more than 150 on board, entered Anzio harbor at 1000 and anchored half a mile offshore. The passengers were British sailors, doctors, and nurses, as well as the American 2nd Auxiliary Surgical Group Team No. 4. This team was an orthopedic specialty unit, consisting of Major John E. Adams, surgeon; Second Lieutenant Ruth Hindman, surgical nurse; Second Lieutenant Anna Bess Berret, from Natchez, Mississippi, anesthetist; and Corporal Theron McComb, surgical technician.

Hindman, Berret, and Adams stood at the *St. David*'s rail on D+1 and watched as LCIs and motorboats launched from *St. David* pulled alongside and transferred seventy-eight wounded soldiers of the initial invasion force. Hospital ship staff settled these newly wounded soldiers into wards and triaged them for surgery, while Ruth Hindman and her team went to the operating room one deck down to begin work on the surgical cases.

Adams's team was in the midst of their first surgery when the ship's public address system announced that German planes had begun bombing the port of Anzio, Anzio harbor, and the beaches where the Allies were digging in to make their bridgehead more secure. Air-raid alarms continued all afternoon and the *St. David*, only half a mile offshore, was assaulted by low-flying German planes and their exploding bombs, and antiaircraft fire from American and British warships. During the air raids, the unloading of men, vehicles, and supplies had to be temporarily stopped.

The ship's operating room was to work around the clock, with surgical teams relieving each other as in a relay race. A British team relieved the Americans at 1800 and the 2nd Aux went to their cabins to rest before their next tour of surgery, scheduled to begin six hours later, at midnight. While the 2nd Aux team slept, the *St. David* and her two sister ships sailed twenty miles out to sea for the night. In accordance with the Hague Conventions, the three hospital ships cruised fully lighted and clearly marked, five miles from each other and at least twenty miles from any ship of war. When the 2nd Aux members were awakened at 2330 in preparation for their return to surgery at 2400, they found that the wind had picked up considerably and the sea was becoming rougher. Though most suffered severe seasickness, every member of Team 4 kept working.

At 1000 on 24 January, D+2, the *St. David* again sailed into the port of Anzio and anchored in the same spot she had occupied the day before. As the sea grew rougher, the ship's crew found it impossible to transfer wounded patients from shore to ship. At 1200, German planes appeared overhead and bombed and strafed the harbor, the port, and the beaches. Hindman, Berret, Adams, and McComb stood together at the rail watching American and British naval guns pounding away at the German positions on shore. They could see ack-ack racing toward German planes, hitting their marks, and sending enemy planes spiraling into the choppy Mediterranean or into the sand and brush of the Anzio beach.

With the winds rising and the seas getting rougher, it was obvious that no patients could be safely brought aboard any of the hospital ships. Nearby LCIs and small craft were bounced and tossed by the high seas and rough water, in danger of capsizing. At 1730, the three British hospital ships headed out to sea for the night. They sailed in total darkness until they were four miles out. At that point, they turned on their lights without fear of endangering Allied ships stationed off the Anzio coast. Brightly lit and with large red crosses clearly visible, they sailed in a straight line, five miles apart, until they reached a point twenty miles from any warship in the area.

With no new patients on board, the 2nd Aux team prepared for what they thought would be a relatively quiet night. In fact, had it not been for seasickness, this could have been a perfect opportunity for crew and hospital personnel to catch up on their sleep. Hindman, Berret, and Adams decided to accept an invitation by one of the British officers and stop at the ship's bar before turning in. Corporal McComb, who had been seasick all day, had avoided the mess and gone directly to his bunk on a lower deck. After talking with several British officers, the three team members left for the officers' mess.

They spent five minutes at the dining table, then all three decided to follow McComb's example. They pushed their untouched dinner plates aside and headed for their cabins in the hope of a good night's sleep and waking to a calmer sea in the morning. Their hopes were short-lived.

At 2000, a loud explosion and a violent rocking awakened cabin mates Ruth Hindman and Anna Bess Berret. "We had gone to sleep with our cabin lights on," Hindman remembered. "When we opened our eyes, it was in total darkness." A German plane—in clear violation of the Hague Conventions—had bombed the *St. David*. Hindman and Berret jumped out of bed. While Berret opened the hatch, Hindman grabbed their flashlights, life jackets, her shoes, and musette bag containing the hatchet she had kept with her since the sinking of the *Newfoundland* four and a half months earlier. Hindman led the way up a ladder leading to the next deck.

As the two women climbed, they were surrounded by the deafening noise of things crashing and people screaming. Through the passageways, they could see patients who were able to walk making their way toward the upper decks, while the more severely wounded were being carried up. Amid the pandemonium, crew members were shouting instructions to the more than seventy-eight patients, including three POWs, and each other on the best ways to reach the top decks.[1]

When Hindman and Berret reached the next landing, they met Major Adams. Adams helped Hindman into her life jacket and told her to get topside as quickly as possible. As Hindman turned to make sure Berret was behind her, she saw Adams climbing down the ladder toward the wards on the lower deck. "Where are you going?" Hindman shouted. "We have to get to the lifeboats, the ship's sinking!" Adams, turning his face to Ruth but without stopping his descent to the lower deck, said, "I'll be right behind you." Hindman remembered Adams's last words to her: "I have to check on a couple of patients to make sure they get out." He turned again and Hindman watched him disappear into a lower passageway.[2]

Hindman then turned quickly to Berret: "Hurry, Bess! We've got to get off this thing before it goes down." A minute later, the two women arrived on the boat deck and found the closest lifeboat already overflowing with patients and staff. Before Ruthie could decide which way to go next, the crew worked rapidly to lower the crowded boat to the water below. Suddenly, there was a loud crunching sound. Hindman looked up and saw the ship's mast rolling toward them. Several people screamed and someone yelled for everyone to jump. "In a matter of seconds," Hindman recalled, "I found myself under water." Hindman remembered her own surprise at her calmness. "Somehow I wasn't frightened. I kicked hard and swam upward. There was a strong jolt as my head ran into something hard and I began to feel the ship's suction pulling me down again." She recalled feeling as if she were watching herself sink farther into the ocean's depths and she had an almost overwhelming need to take a breath. "I told myself that I was a goner. 'This is it, Ruthie! You might as well take a deep breath and be done with it.' "[3]

Just as she was about to follow her own advice, her downward motion stopped, and without warning, the ship's suction released her and she was shooting upward like a bullet. "I gasped as my head broke the surface of the water, and I could see stars above me." There was screaming all around her, and objects floating by her in the darkness. Suddenly one man's voice cut through the cacophony: "Ruthie, is that you?" It was the British officer she'd met late that afternoon at the ship's bar.

She called back and he told her to grab on to something and hold on. "I stretched out an arm and closed my hand on a large piece of wood," Hindman recalled. "I figured it had been part of the *St. David*'s deck. Anyway, I hung on to that piece of wood and swam toward the officer's voice while he swam toward me. When we met, we used the plank as a makeshift raft for two patients who were in the water near us. Another officer joined us and we three held on to the planks and took turns waving the flashlight one of the officers had with him."[4]

Two hours passed without any sign of a rescue ship. The sea was cold and rough and the waves tossed the survivors around like corks. Every few minutes, a wave washed over Hindman and her small group, and she gasped for breath and forced her cold, numb hands to hold fast to the planks. Finally, the lights of a hospital ship came into view and every flashlight in the area waved frantically in its direction. Hearts sank as the vessel maintained its distance and sailed past the weary and desperate group in the water. "We were convinced that they hadn't seen our lights and were sailing on to look elsewhere," Hindman remembered. "In another minute or two, a second hospital ship came into view and stopped a good distance away from us. About ten minutes later, boats from the ship were in the water next to us and we were helping to get our two patients into the boat first."[5]

When it came time for the exhausted Hindman to be pulled into the lifeboat, she experienced an unforgettable sensation. "I thought I'd die when that air hit me . . . I have never been more uncomfortable in my life. I was so cold, I just thought I couldn't stand another minute." She remembered wrapping her arms about her body in an attempt to control her shaking and her chattering teeth. ". . . Being selfish human beings, you wanted to say, 'Take me back to the ship!' Then I thought about all those people in the water yet." Their lifeboat stayed out and rescued more people from the water before heading back for the ship.[6]

Forty minutes later, Hindman's boat pulled alongside the *Leinster*, which had also been hit by enemy bombing but was in no danger of sinking, and a sailor told the survivors to climb the cargo net to the deck. Only patients would be hoisted aboard. Hindman looked up at the railing and doubted her ability to make the climb. When it was her turn, she reached out and grabbed hold of the rope just as their lifeboat sank into a wave trough. "My feet were dangling in midair for about fifteen seconds," Hindman remembered, "as I hung on to the net for dear life. I didn't think I could continue to hold on when a man's voice called out, 'There she goes! She's going into the sea!' Well, that made me mad, and I grabbed on tighter and pulled myself up to the next wrung as I yelled back, 'Oh, no she is not!' and continued up the cargo net and onto the deck."[7]

The *Leinster*'s British crew wrapped Hindman and the others in blankets, fed them several shots of whiskey, and took them to the shock ward, where they slept the rest of the night. More than twenty-five people went down with the ship, two Q.A.s—sisters of Queen Alexandra's Imperial Military Nursing Service—several Royal Army Medical Corps

Lt. Ruth Hindman in class-A uniform (Courtesy of Ruth Hindman Balch)

officers, the *St. David*'s captain, fifteen patients who were U.S. military personnel, and Major Adams and Corporal McComb. McComb's body was recovered on the beach at Nettuno on 31 January.[8]

The next morning, the *Leinster* docked in Naples, and Hindman and Berret—now reunited—were taken to a hospital to be checked over and to await new orders. Lunchtime found the two army nurses sitting in the crowded hospital officers' mess, dressed in the same wrinkled and damp clothes they had been wearing when the *St. David* sank. Their hair hung down in long straight strands and their faces were pale. "Would you believe that not a soul asked us a question or said a word about the sinking?" Hindman remarked. "You'd think they got survivors from bombed hospital ships every day."[9]

It would be another two weeks before Hindman received orders to board another ship and return to Anzio. After surviving the sinking of two ships, she felt more than a little shaky at boarding yet another vessel. Her fears were not allayed by the greeting she received from the ship's rather misogynistic British captain. "I was scared anyhow to get on ships," Hindman recalled. "I'll never forget this captain as we were going aboard. The captain looked at my surgeon and said, 'Why do you have this damned black cat with you?' " The captain was referring to Hindman. "I know Britishers are superstitious," Hindman said, "but that didn't help my mind any. I thought, 'Maybe I am a jinx!' " Hindman was relieved when she disembarked at Anzio and was assigned with her team to a frontline hospital. "Somehow even the front lines seemed safer than life aboard a ship!"[10]

IN THE WEEK after D-Day, from 24 to 29 January 1944, American and Allied forces worked to consolidate their hold on the Anzio beachhead and planned a two-pronged attack to expand it. The high ground around the town of Carroceto, about ten miles north of Anzio harbor, was to be seized by the First British Division with support from the American First Armored Division. At the same time, the Third Division, enhanced by the attachment of Ranger forces, would strike toward Cisterna—about fourteen miles northeast of the Anzio harbor—seize the town, and cut off Highway 7. The Rangers would spearhead the attack and the Third Division would join them once the siege was well under way.

At 0130 on 30 January, the offensive to take Cisterna began. Men of the 1st and 3rd Ranger force, commanded by Colonel William O. Darby, made their way in silence across the western branch of the Mussolini Canal in the Pontine Marshes just outside the Allied eastern Anzio beachhead perimeter. In a long, single line, the men—now remembered as "Darby's Rangers"—hugged the side of the narrow Pantano ditch as they crept toward the town of Cisterna. When the first rays of daylight filtered through the night sky, the lead battalion was only eight hundred yards from their ultimate objective; they had, as yet, met no opposition. As daylight spread across the Pontine Marshes, the men leading the column emerged from the ditch. Without cover and in the bright glare of a new morning sun, Darby's Rangers stepped out, to be met by heavy German artillery and small-arms fire. They had walked into a German ambush. Although the men fought valiantly against an unseen and better-equipped enemy, the outcome was a devastating defeat for the ambushed Americans. Despite efforts of the 4th Rangers, the Third Battalion, and the Fifteenth Infantry, who fought desperately to reach their trapped comrades, the support troops were unable to break through the German defenses. Only 6 of the 767 ambushed Rangers escaped death or capture by the enemy.[11]

Fighting continued through that night and into the night of 31 January. In an effort to replace the hundreds of American troops already lost, commanders ordered the 39th Combat Engineers, who had been "delousing" bridges (removing explosives) in the beachhead area, to report to the front lines. Two young engineers found themselves and their outfit dug into the bank of the Mussolini Canal for the night, with orders to engage the enemy at first light. Private Berchard Lamar Glant, a native of Hammond, Indiana, who had celebrated his twenty-second birthday twelve days earlier, settled into his foxhole for the night. "Junior," as Berchard was known to his friends in the company, stood five feet four inches tall, weighed 122 pounds, and had an easygoing and cheery disposition.

Pvt. Berchard L. Glant (Courtesy of Berchard L. Glant)

Junior was sharing his foxhole that night with a buddy, Private First Class Billie L. Stone. Stone was a native of Arab, Alabama; he'd come to the 39th Combat Engineers as a replacement before the outfit left Sicily for Salerno in September 1943. Since Sicily, Junior and Billie had become fast friends, and had shared many foxholes together before occupying their current hole near the town of Littoria, in the Pontine Marshes.

The total blackness was an excellent backdrop for the tracer bullets, artillery shells, and exploding bombs that continuously lit the night sky, filling it with red, yellow, and white bursts of light. "Look at that, Billie!" Glant remembered saying, as he nudged Stone in the ribs to get his attention. "It's just like the Fourth of July back home." Stone did not move or even open his eyes. "Shut up and go to sleep!" was his only response to Glant's words.[12]

The first day of February was cold and sunny, a relief from days of rain, and the Germans wasted no time in using the new daylight to zero in on American positions. Stone and Glant returned fire with the 30-caliber air-cooled machine gun that the two manned in combat situations on the front lines. Glant aimed and fired while Stone fed ammunition belts into the weapon. A lull occurred in the fighting around 1700. After a half hour of silence, Stone and Glant climbed out of their hole in the canal bank to stretch their legs before the next exchange began. They were standing below the level of the canal bank. "We were both just standing there by our hole when a mortar came over the bank and exploded in front of us," Stone recalled. "The concussion knocked me to the ground and knocked several of my teeth out. When I looked over at Junior, I saw that his right arm was almost off, and blood was gushing from both of his legs. I knew that if I didn't stop the bleeding, he'd die."[13]

Stone yelled for a medic and scrambled to his knees at his friend's side. He removed his own belt and used it as a tourniquet above the wounds on Glant's left leg that were bleeding profusely. Billie "talked to Junior the entire time," telling him, " 'You're going to be all right.' " He unbuckled Glant's belt, pulled it free of the belt loops, and fastened it as a tourniquet on his friend's right leg. Next, Stone fumbled in the first-aid kit on his ammunition belt, found the sulfa, placed two tablets in Glant's mouth, and washed them down with a swallow of water from his own canteen. For a split second, he was aware that help had not arrived yet, and he shouted again for a medic. Without waiting, Stone found the packets of sulfa in his first-aid kit and poured the powder into his friend's wounds. As he finished this task, a medic slid to his knees beside the two young soldiers. Like Stone, the corporal, who appeared to be about the same age, talked to Glant as he examined the wounds and what Stone had done. Stone remembered the medic gave Glant morphine and used a marker to place a large red "M" on Glant's forehead to prevent other medics or hospital personnel from overdosing him. The medic next asked for help in getting the seriously wounded soldier to the battalion aide station on the other side of the canal.[14]

The Mussolini Canal was about twenty-five to thirty feet wide and filled with nine to ten feet of icy water; on the other side lay the 120th Medical Battalion Aid Station. The medic and Stone placed Glant on a litter; with the medic in the lead, the two men headed for a log that straddled the canal as a footbridge. As Stone stepped onto the log, the machine gun he was carrying over his right shoulder shifted its weight. For a second or two, Stone felt sure he was going to fall into the canal, where he knew the weight of the gun and the depth of the cold water would take both him and Junior to their deaths. "I knew if I fell, Junior would probably go into the canal too. We'd both be dead." He shuffled his feet, caught the machine gun between his arm and his body, regained his balance, and continued across the rain-soaked, slippery log. When they reached the opposite side, Stone and the medic lifted the litter up the seven-foot bank.[15]

Stone breathed a sigh of relief when all three were on solid ground again on the other side of the canal and he could put the stretcher down for a moment and resettle the weight of the machine gun. "For the first time, I was aware that my mouth was bleeding," Stone remembered, "and I spit blood and part of a tooth onto the ground as we started to carry Junior's litter again."[16]

The aid station personnel had pulled a jeep in close to the canal. Stone said good-bye to a semiconscious Glant as the stretcher was secured across the back of the jeep. "When Junior got hit, it was a blow to me. We were good friends . . . like losing one of your brothers. With all of those injuries, I figured he was gone. . . . I had a miserable few days until I got back." Stone headed back to his foxhole on the Mussolini Canal.[17]

As with the landings on Sicily and Salerno, only the male medical personnel—doctors, corpsmen, enlisted men—of the 93rd and 95th Evacuation Hospitals and the 33rd Field Hospital went ashore with the invasion troops on D-Day. The nurses of these medical units would follow later, after the personnel had set up each hospital.

On 28 January—D+6—at 1000, as scheduled, the LCI carrying 120 nurses approached Anzio harbor as a German air raid was assaulting the harbor and Allied positions on the beachhead. Glidewell, Walden, and Wheeler stood at the LCI's railing and watched German planes zoom overhead as American and British warships fired at them in an effort to knock the enemy planes down before they could discharge their payloads. Glidewell recalled looking up as a German plane swooped in over their ship and headed for Allied targets onshore. As she stared at the sky to get a better look, the wash from the low-flying plane caught Glidewell's unbuckled helmet and sent it plummeting into the gray water of the Mediterranean. She watched as her helmet filled with water and sank beneath the surface only seconds before a ship's officer shouted for the women to move away from the rail and take cover. The three ducked into a passageway and continued to follow the action as best they could.

The air raid went on for two hours, until 1200, when a lull allowed the LCI to pull into the beach and the nurses disembarked. "A convoy of trucks and a flock of newsmen were waiting for us," Glidewell recalled, "as we waded in and headed for our transportation to our hospitals. I was the only nurse without a helmet, and I felt naked as cameramen took our pictures as we climbed into the two-and-a-half-ton trucks."[18]

Little did Glidewell know that she would soon be seen on the silver screen back home. In the 1940s, movie theaters used to show, in addition to cartoons and film "trailers" of coming attractions, newsreels of current events before airing the feature film. In 1944, one of those newsreels contained footage of American nurses landing on Anzio Beach. "My mother saw that newsreel later at a movie theater at home," Speedy said. "She wrote me a letter asking why I was the only one without a helmet. At least she didn't have any trouble recognizing me."[19]

Three trucks assembled on the beach to carry the 120 nurses to their respective hospitals on the outskirts of Anzio. Lieutenants Glenda Spelhaug, La Verne "Tex" Farquhar, and Jessie Paddock, and the other 16 nurses of the 33rd Field Hospital, plus a number of the 2nd Aux nurses and some of the 95th's, loaded into one truck and headed for the hospital area; in another truck, 48 nurses of the 93rd, including Lieutenants Evelyn Anderson and Vera Sheaffer, piled in and headed for the 93rd. The third and last truck, which took on the remainder of the 95th Evac nurses, including Glidewell, Walden, and Wheeler, did not follow the first two vehicles. Instead, their truck headed up a picturesque road that wound along the coast of the Mediterranean.

It had gone about a quarter of a mile when a loud, whining sound caught their attention. A shell whistled overhead and dropped in the ocean about a hundred yards away. Less than thirty seconds later, another shell landed behind and to the right of the truck, sending a shower of dirt and stones into the air. Seconds later, a third shell whistled over and fell into the sea, creating a frothy white geyser that rose into the sky. "Since we were the only moving object in the vicinity," Glidewell recalled, "it was fairly obvious that they were aiming at us."[20]

Suddenly, the driver pulled the truck to the side of the road, walked to the rear, and told the nurses that they were to get out. Glidewell and Walden remembered trying to reason with the young man, who "looked scared to death and stammered as he spoke." He told the nurses that someone from the hospital would be by to pick them up, practically ran to the cab of his truck, climbed in quickly, and took off down the road "like a scared rabbit."[21]

The nurses found themselves on the edge of a plowed field. In the middle was a weathered and dilapidated chickenhouse. Glidewell suggested they sit outside the chickenhouse and rest their backs against the wall while they waited for someone to come by and take them to their hospital. After sitting and talking for about a half hour, enemy shells began whistling over their heads again, with two landing and exploding about two hundred yards from their makeshift shelter. The women ran into the chickenhouse for cover. There was a broken window in one side and they decided to use the jagged opening as an observation post.

After staring across a field of tall, dense grass for twenty minutes, the three women saw a line of British soldiers crawling toward the chickenhouse from the left, and a long line of American GIs, also crawling toward the chickenhouse, from the right. "We ran through the empty doorway and headed right for the Americans," Glidewell recalled. "When we were closer to our GIs, I called out and asked if they were there to pick us up and take us to the 95th Evacuation Hospital." At least ten GIs stood up and looked at the nurses as if they were crazy. One young sergeant seemed to speak for all of the men as they stared in disbelief. "What in hell are you women doing here?" Glidewell remembered the sergeant's words and his look of total astonishment. "We're the front line, and you're in front of us. That puts you in no-man's-land." The sergeant exchanged a few more words with the nurse, then contacted the 95th Evacuation Hospital on their behalf.[22]

Thirty minutes later, Lieutenant Neil Hansen showed up in a 2.5-ton truck with an enlisted man as the driver. "I don't think I ever saw Neil so angry before. He kept saying, 'Wait till I find that idiot driver! I'll have him court-martialed for leaving you girls out here.' " He finally calmed down, got the nurses into the truck, and took them to the 95th Evac, located next to a church on the outskirts of Anzio, where patients were waiting for their services. Nurses in the first two trucks had long since arrived and were already working. Casualties as of 28 January were light. Several nurses told Glidewell to hurry over to the OR tent where they were waiting for an anesthetist so they could put another surgical team to work. There was already a long line of wounded soldiers waiting their turn for an OR table. Glidewell worked in surgery until midnight, then returned to her tent for the night.[23]

Minutes after she had fallen off to sleep, German shells began whistling over the tented hospital area. Nurses jumped into the foxholes that had been dug for them inside their tents, pulled suitcases over their heads, and waited for the danger to pass. "All night long," Lieutenant "Si" Simonson recalled, "we'd hear this rumbling and roaring of big guns. We'd never heard anything like that before." Simonson had been in North Africa and Salerno, but never had her hospital been this close to the front lines. In North Africa, troops and hospitals had been spread further apart; here in Anzio, both troops and hospitals were confined within a fifteen- by seven-mile strip of beach. The shelling went on all night and after a short lull began again at breakfast.[24]

Bernice "Hut" Walden was not surprised that Bob Knecht, a pharmacy technician was as angry as Neil Hansen when he learned that a frightened truck driver had dropped the group of nurses off in no-man's-land. The two had begun dating in April 1943 when the 95th Evacuation Hospital was sailing for North Africa. There had been an instant attraction and neither was deterred by the fact that Knecht was an enlisted man and Hut Walden an officer. The more they dated, the more they liked each other, and it was only a matter of two months before the couple was engaged and making plans for life after the war was won and they were civilians again. Since the U.S. military officially frowned on dates between officers and enlisted personnel, Bob and Bernice kept their relationship hidden from all but their closest friends.

The lulls were few and spent in anticipation of the next shelling or air

95th Evacuation Hospital personnel on Anzio beachhead. Left to Right: "Bones" Mueller, Bob Knecht, Bernice "Hut" Walden, and two other pharmacy techs. Knecht was killed during the 7 February 1944 bombing (Courtesy of Claudine Glidewell Doyle)

raid. Simonson remembered how her tentmate, Lillie "Pete" Peterson, had planned ahead for the next raid. "One night, we popped popcorn. I don't know where we got it. We heard the whining of shells and had to get in our foxholes. Pete grabbed the bowl of popcorn, a flashlight, her hometown newspaper, and a blanket. She put those things in the foxhole that was underneath her cot and crawled in. She sat in there eating popcorn and reading the hometown paper during that air raid."[25]

On 28 January, after transportation delays, the 56th Evacuation Hospital landed on Anzio and set up about two miles east of Nettuno in a large field, bringing the bed strength on the beachhead to 1,750. This large field was designated to be the site not only for the 56th Evacuation Hospital but for all the other hospitals: the 93rd and 95th Evacuation Hospitals and the 33rd Field Hospital.

On 30 January, the 56th covered for the 93rd and 95th Evacs, taking in the wounded, in order to give the two hospitals time to break down their tents at Anzio, move to, and set up in the new hospital site outside Nettuno. "The night after we moved to the big field that was our new hospital location," Simonson recalled, "shells hit the church that was right next to our previous hospital site and demolished it completely."[26]

The new hospital area was about three miles east of Nettuno, on a sandy, flat stretch of beach. The location, like most of the land from the Italian coasts to the Alban Hills, was devoid of natural cover and consisted of reclaimed wetland where the water table was as close as one or two feet from the surface. This terrain frustrated hospital personnel who wanted to dig deep foxholes to protect patients and staff from shrapnel and bomb fragments. Frontline soldiers less than seven miles away were forced to spend their days and nights in foxholes with a foot or two of water constantly covering their muddy dirt floors.

The western sector of the beachhead was the only wooded area along the fifteen-mile-long and seven-mile-deep area and presented a real threat to the Americans and British. Not only did the woods provide cover to enemy snipers, but they also gave cover to infiltrators—those Germans whose excellent command of English allowed them to pose as British or American soldiers and infiltrate Allied troops to gather intelligence.

The new hospital area was completely in the open. Although as far from legitimate military targets as possible, it was not in a safe zone since the entire beachhead was under German observation, and every inch could be reached by German guns. Between the hospital area and the sea lay the only airstrip on the beachhead, and it was a regular target for enemy artillery and bombers. To the north, facing the front lines, were the VI Corps medium artillery guns that drew enemy counterbattery fire. A radar station lay on the east flank of the area, and on the west, a gasoline dump. German shells and bombs could, and regularly did, fall "short" or "long," in both events missing their legitimate military targets and hitting the hospital tents. And there was also the question of enemy fire being deliberately aimed at the hospitals.

Choosing another location was not an option. There was no way to place hospitals in a site safe from German guns and bombs, and there was no way to put legitimate military targets at a distance where shells that fell short or long did not threaten hospital patients, personnel, and equipment. The hospital compound could not be moved farther to the rear of the front lines because there was, effectively, no rear. As the historian Sidney Hyman put it later, the Anzio beachhead was "the front without a back. . . . The familiar margin of safety between front-line and rear installations was canceled by the tactical situation. In a beachhead fifteen miles wide at its base and seven miles deep there could be no retreat in depth from the range of enemy fire. A poverty of alternatives forced the location of the main medical installations only six miles from our forward outposts. . . ."[27]

The beachhead was a relatively easy target for the Germans: small, open, and densely populated with Allied troops. And right in the middle, at the "bull's-eye," lay the Nettuno hospital compound.

Aerial view of hospital area at Anzio, 1944 (U.S. Army Signal Corps)

Yet doctors, nurses, and hospital personnel were ordered to move to the new compound with assurances from American commanders that the site would be safe from shelling and bombing. These assurances were based on the expectation that Germany would honor the Geneva Conventions, which forbade all armed forces from targeting hospitals. Hospital personnel believed the assurances of their commanders, and commanders had no idea how wrong those assurances were. Glidewell remembered her sense of relief when the 95th Evac moved to the new site. "The officers who chose and planned the site told us that because the hospitals were all in one area, and every tent was clearly marked with a red cross, we would be so safe that we wouldn't even need foxholes. It sounded pretty good to all of us."[28]

On 31 January 1944, the 93rd and 95th Evacuation Hospitals opened for business in the new hospital compound. They joined the 56th Evacuation Hospital, which had been accepting patients there since 1300 on 30 January. By 0100 on 1 February, the 56th Evac had admitted 1,129 patients. The hospital area stretched over a half acre of flat, open land and in a matter of days would be christened "Hell's Half-Acre" by patients and hospital personnel alike. All throughout February and on through March and April, the hospital area would be continuously shelled and bombed; the wounded would be rewounded, and many doctors, nurses, corpsmen, technicians, and other hospital personnel would be wounded or lose their lives. No other hospitals in World War II took more bombings and shellings, or suffered as many injuries and deaths within their staffs of doctors, nurses, and enlisted men, as well as reinjuries of patients, than the hospitals on the Anzio beachhead.[29]

ON THE EVENING of 1 February, the 120th Medical Battalion Aid Station, on the easternmost perimeter of the Anzio beachhead, received a soldier who had been critically wounded during the advance on Cisterna. Private Berchard Lamar "Junior" Glant had wounds so severe that his foxhole mate, Billie Stone, the man who had helped to carry Junior out of the Mussolini Canal, counted Glant dead as he and the medic secured Glant across the back of a jeep for transport to the 120th. He expected never to see his friend again.

But Glant's journey was just beginning. At the 120th, Glant received 900 cc's of blood plasma and dressings for his wounds before he was lifted onto a stretcher and placed across the back of a jeep to be driven to the 93rd Evacuation Hospital farther back, at the Nettuno hospital site. The medical tag attached to Glant's wrist bore the following words under Diagnosis: "WIA [wounded in action]—Wound, compound [produces an open wound in the skin] comm. fracture [comminuted, i.e., bone splintered or crushed into small pieces] right arm—wound penetrating right and left knee, left forearm at waist, INC [incurred] Field, Feb 1, 1944, 1800 hours. Line of duty—yes—by enemy shell." At 1845, less than an hour after being injured, Glant left the 120th Medical Battalion Aid Station for the ten-mile trip to the Anzio beachhead hospital area.[30]

Medical records reveal that as soon as Glant was admitted to the 93rd

Evacuation Hospital, he was given 2 units of blood plasma to help fight shock. The next day, since his condition was not improved, he received 500 cc's of whole blood before being taken to the OR tent for debridement of all his wounds and the application of a shoulder spica cast (a figure-8 bandage with turns at the shoulder) to his right arm. The surgeon cut away dead tissue, trimmed the jagged edges, and placed the cast on the patient's right arm so that it was bent at the elbow and elevated. Glant was then taken back to the 93rd's shock ward, where patients' litters were placed in shock position (feet and legs elevated) by using sawhorses of different heights.[31]

Glant remembered regaining consciousness two days later. It was about 1600 on 4 February, and as he opened his eyes, the first thing he saw was his right arm and hand. "I could see that my hand was as black as the ace of spades," he recalled. "I felt my heart beat faster as I remembered stories I had heard about guys who developed gangrene after they were wounded. I was wondering if they'd have to amputate my arm when I fell back to sleep." The next day, surgeons removed Glant's right arm above his elbow. Glant would be evacuated to the 300th General Hospital in Naples as soon as he was well enough for the trip.[32]

That Glant's life was saved was due to the remarkably quick and effective medical protocols set up and honed in North Africa and now being put to the test in Italy: first, the immediate ministrations to the wounded on the battlefields by medics and soldiers; next, the quick transport of the wounded to a battalion aid station where medical teams could work to further stabilize patients; then, the transport to evacuation hospitals for more extensive treatments and surgery; and finally, the return of a healed soldier to the front, or his transfer to a hospital farther to the rear for a longer period of recuperation. In World War II, the survival rate for wounded soldiers who made it to a battalion aid station was a remarkable 95.86 percent; 85.71 percent were able to return to duty.[33]

LIEUTENANT GLIDEWELL adjusted her position on a three-legged stool at the head of one of four OR tables in one of the operating-room tents of the 95th Evacuation Hospital. It was 1545 on 7 February when anesthesiologist Captain Marshall Bauer entered the tent, handed Glidewell several letters he had carried over from the mailroom, and told her to take a break: "Here, Speed, sit on that stool and read your mail." He sat down in Glidewell's place to take over administering anesthesia on a patient undergoing surgery. "I'll watch your patient for you." She took the stack of letters Bauer was holding out and moved to an anesthesia stool to the right of her OR table. She sat with her feet on the legs of the stool and her elbows on her knees as she opened her mail and started to read.[34]

Glidewell and everyone else at the 95th Evac had been working around the clock since 31 January, when the first casualties from the Allied attack toward Cisterna came in. The Allies' Third Division had unexpectedly encountered "strongly manned and well-prepared [German] positions," and casualties were numerous. In addition to the continuous work was the stress from the almost constant noise of shells and bombs as Germans used the advantage of high ground in the Alban Hills to direct fire at ships in Anzio harbor. Even more nerve-racking was the sound of German shells and bombs directed at the military targets on land that surrounded the hospital area. "Short" and "long" rounds fell near the hospital day and night.[35]

Glidewell, Walden, and Wheeler developed a process of "calling the roll" after all explosions of shells or bombs that landed extremely close. After a shelling, the women would call out their names to each other to make sure each of them was unharmed. Since explosives fell at all hours of the day and night, "roll calls" were taking place around the clock. Chief Nurse Blanche Sigman got so tired of the practice, and so annoyed by roll calls that were as likely to occur at midnight or 0300 as at noon, that she had the enlisted men move her tent away from "Hut Two" and the "Fall Inn" so she would not have to hear the roll call as well as the shells and bombs. Glidewell remembered that at the time of Sigman's move, Glidewell and the other nurses in their two tents "figured that someone Sigman's age [thirty-six] was probably too nervous" and "too old" to remember what it was like to be young.[36]

Nurses and other hospital personnel had to get used to the almost constant whine and whistle of shells and bombs, and the ground shaking when these shells exploded anywhere nearby. Most hospital personnel adjusted to sleeping despite the almost continuous noise, but sleep, too, was interrupted by "unusually loud explosions" and everyone suffered from a sleep deficit. Glidewell "often wondered what it would be like to be in a quiet place again."[37]

Glidewell had been reading her mail for five minutes when, suddenly, a loud explosion and concussion threw her headfirst in a summersault off the stool and left her sprawling on the floor. "I could hear small objects—like hail—hitting the floor around me," she wrote later. "I looked up at the top of the OR tent and it looked like a sieve. I remember asking out loud 'What was that?' and Captain Bauer answering in a calm voice, 'That was a bomb. Put your helmet on.' " Glidewell reached for her helmet in its place beneath her OR table as Bauer left the tent to find out what had happened.[38]

A group of German fighter-bombers had made a raid on the harbor and airfield that afternoon. As British planes challenged the raiders, the Germans broke formation and headed back to their own airfields. According to eyewitnesses among hospital personnel who were watching from the ground, a British Spitfire pursued a single German fighter-bomber over the hospital area. In an effort to gain altitude and speed, the German pilot jettisoned his remaining load of five antipersonnel bombs. An antipersonnel bomb was an explosive packed with steel fragments designed to explode five feet above the ground and scatter shrapnel in all directions.

As hospital personnel watched in horror, the five bombs fell in a preset pattern—one after the other, so many feet apart—from the edge of the 95th Evacuation Hospital to its central tents. Bomb fragments—jagged pieces of steel—ripped through the administrative, receiving, and operating-room tents.

As Glidewell put her helmet on and rolled over to stand up, she saw small pieces of steel all over the floor. "On top of the Mayo stand [small instrument table] across my patient's chest was a piece of steel as large as an apple. That boy will never know how close he came to death." Glidewell returned to administering anesthesia while the surgeon quickly completed his work. The patient was moved out of the operating room as victims of the antipersonnel bombs that had just fallen on the hospital were brought inside.[39]

The first casualty was placed on Glidewell's table. His face was contorted and his skin a dusky-blue color. Despite the fact that he looked familiar, she could not recognize him. As she quickly opened her anesthetist's supply box and located the syringe with preloaded coramine—a cardiac stimulant—she kept in readiness for emergencies, she asked about the identity of her patient. "It's Bob Knecht, one of the pharmacists," someone answered. The information hit her like a hammer as she plunged the needle adeptly into the muscular upper arm of the unconscious man. Knecht and Walden, Glidewell's tentmate, had been dating for months and intended to get married. As Glidewell lifted Knecht's head and slipped her arm beneath his shoulders to adjust his position on the table, he gasped and then stopped breathing. It was too late for the coramine or any other help. Bob Knecht was dead.[40]

As she laid his head down on the table and her surgeon called for a corpsman to remove the body, Colonel Howard Patterson called for Glidewell to come and finish the anesthesia for his patient since Patterson's anesthetist had left to see about the bombing. Some minutes later, Captain Bauer stuck his head in the door of the tent and called out, "Sigman and Sheetz are dead. Colonel Sauer has been wounded." Bauer was referring to Chief Nurse Blanche Sigman—ironically, the nurse who disliked the roll calls after bombings—and Assistant Chief Nurse Carrie T. Sheetz.[41]

Lieutenant "Si" Simonson remembered the second casualty of the bombing who was brought into the operating room. He was the top sergeant, and a bomb fragment had lodged in his neck. Simonson recalled that as the man, covered in blood, was placed on the OR table, he cried out: "Doc, please save me!" She administered anesthesia and the surgeon went to work. The sergeant was a lucky man. Despite his injury, he lived.[42]

Simonson recalled that not everyone caught by the antipersonnel bombs was as fortunate. "There was a long line of wounded hospital personnel and rewounded patients. I don't remember how many, but there were a lot . . . I don't know how many we operated on. . . . We couldn't save them all. They were our co-workers, and some of them died. . . ."[43]

When every patient had been treated, nurses, doctors, and corpsmen left the operating room and headed for their own tents. Not far from the OR tent, Simonson passed a long row of litters holding the blanket-draped bodies of men and women who had been killed in the bombing. "I saw so many stretchers," Simonson said. "I saw two with nurses' shoes sticking out from under the blankets. I thought, 'Do I want to look?' and I thought, 'Well, I'm going to find out anyway.' I was hoping it wasn't any of my tentmates. . . . It was Sheetz and Sigman. I'll never forget that scene."[44]

Marjorie G. Morrow was left in critical condition by a fragment that severed her femoral artery; that evening, she died. Sigman, Sheetz, and Morrow had been survivors of the sinking of the *Newfoundland*.

In total, the bombing of the 95th Evacuation Hospital caused twenty-eight deaths; twenty-two were hospital personnel—three nurses, two officers, sixteen enlisted men, and one Red Cross worker. That Red Cross worker was former Army Nurse Esther Richards from San Francisco, who was also a survivor from the *Newfoundland*. Four hospitalized patients

Bomb damage to the 95th Evacuation Hospital on Anzio (U.S. Army Signal Corps)

were killed; and two other military personnel who were visiting patients in the hospital.

One of the two visiting soldiers who died was Private Robert P. Mulreaney, a member of an engineering unit. Mulreaney was visiting his brother, Private First Class Eugene A. Mulreaney, a member of Company A, 815th Engineers. Eugene Mulreaney had been carried to the 95th Evac after being wounded in action several days earlier, and Robert had come to visit him. When the bombs exploded, Robert covered the body of his wounded brother with his own body and was mortally wounded himself. Eugene escaped further injury and recovered from his combat wounds.

In addition to those killed, the 95th Evacuation Hospital suffered fifty staff wounded: ten officers, four nurses, and thirty-six enlisted men. Among the wounded were ten male officers, including the hospital commander, Colonel Paul K. Sauer from New York. Four army nurses were wounded: Second Lieutenant Ruth D. Buckley of Elmswood, Wisconsin, had shrapnel in both legs; Second Lieutenant Mary W. Harrison of Belyre, Ohio, had shrapnel in her arm; Second Lieutenant Fern H. Wingard of Omaha, Nebraska, had shrapnel in her right hand; Second

Lieutenant Ruby L. Hoppe had superficial wounds. Both Harrison and Hoppe, who remained on duty despite their wounds, were on temporary duty from the 21st General Hospital in Naples. Private Wesley Tanner, a litter bearer who was carrying a patient to the X-ray department when the bombs fell, was wounded in his back when he protected the patient with his body. Ten patients were also wounded.[45]

Throughout the bombing, 95th Evac personnel continued working at their assigned posts. They also helped remove the dead and evacuate all preoperative patients to the 93rd and 56th Evacuation Hospitals. Although wounded, Captains Henry A. Korda and Henry A. Luce, along with Technical Sergeant George J. Schuermann, Private First Class Donald E. Druck, and Private Wesley Tanner, remained on duty.

The bombing damaged twenty-nine ward tents, including two surgical, X-ray, and headquarters tents, and eight other tents along with all the equipment they contained. With the loss of X-ray and other equipment, the 95th Evac could now only receive and care for those medical cases and surgical patients whose procedures would not require X-ray studies prior to surgery.

Lieutenant Glidewell remembered her first meeting with her friend and tentmate Hut Walden after the bombing. Walden greeted Glidewell with a flat expression and the words spoken in a monotone: "Bob isn't dead." It was clear someone had already told Walden that her fiancé had been killed. Glidewell put her arms around Walden and said as gently as she could, "He died in my arms, Hut." Without warning, Walden pulled away and began running down the road near their tent. Glidewell ran after her and finally caught her in her arms. "I just held her while she cried like a baby," Glidewell recalled. "Telling her about Bob's death was almost as painful as the bombing itself."[46]

With Sigman and Sheetz dead, Helen Talboy, the only first lieutenant left among the 95th's nurses, was temporarily appointed chief nurse. A week earlier, news correspondents who lived in a nearby villa had invited several of the nurses including Talboy to visit them, giving them a few hours' reprieve from tent living. Jack Foisie of *The Stars and Stripes*, and Frederick Clayton, an American Red Cross correspondent, had noticed that the nurses seemed nervous and looked tired.

Several days later, but before the antipersonnel bombs fell on the 95th, the same correspondents were at the 95th Evac looking for the chief of surgery to get a story from him for the papers back home. First Lieutenant Talboy, charge nurse in the OR tent, volunteered to find Dr.

Christopher B. Carter, former faculty of Baylor University, and bring him back for an interview. Both correspondents watched as Talboy seemed to "wander indecisively out in the middle of the hospital area, talking disconnectedly about fear and recent close calls." The two correspondents felt that Talboy was trying to quell her growing fear. "She was not ashamed of it, nobody is ashamed of fear over here—she merely was trying to keep it from getting control of her."[47]

Fred Clayton commented to Foisie that Talboy "was in bad shape," that "she has been through enough" and was "about to go to pieces." Both correspondents wondered "what she would do in a sudden crisis."[48]

That crisis arrived just a few days later, when the antipersonnel bombs hit the 95th on 7 February. Talboy was on duty in the OR area, which was showered with bomb fragments. She took charge without hesitation. "She collected the surviving nurses, gave them bandages and first-aid equipment, and started them caring for the wounded, lying crumpled and moaning over the bloody hospital area." Talboy supervised first-aid operations and made sure that the dead were covered with blankets as quickly as possible. Her calm, orderly behavior brought "a semblance of order to the whole nightmarish scene."[49]

The same nurse who had appeared "jittery" and "near the breaking point" days earlier worked calmly and purposefully, bringing aid and assurance to the wounded, and whatever dignity could be brought to the dead.[50]

Clayton wrote in his report: "Nearby, I saw some men weeping, standing in small, shaken groups. Some of the nurses were crying, too, but soundlessly—the tears on their cheeks in the pale moonlight were the only sign."[51]

Talboy and her sister nurses had already survived the Sicilian and Salerno campaigns, the bombing of the British hospital ship *Newfoundland*, and now the bombing of their "protected" hospital area. Through it all, they continued to perform their duties as army nurses with the same courage and dedication expected of every member of the U.S. armed forces.

First Lieutenants Blanche F. Sigman and Carrie T. Sheetz were buried in the beachhead cemetery next to the GIs they had come to Anzio to care for. All told, the 7 February bombing of the 95th Evac killed twenty-eight patients and hospital personnel, and wounded sixty, including nine male officers of the hospital and three army nurses and one Red Cross nurse. Although the most deadly, the 7 February bombing of the 95th

Hospital was not, sadly, an isolated incident, but one of a continuing and constant string of bombings at the Nettuno hospital site.

ON THE NIGHT of 7/8 February 1944, German troops launched a new attack against the Anzio beachhead. The onslaught began with a heavy artillery barrage at 2100, followed by an infantry attack that was to employ a pincer movement to converge on Carroceto and Aprilia, two towns under the control of the First British Division located nine miles north of Anzio on the northern perimeter of the beachhead. Heavy rains had turned the surrounding farmland into a sea of mud, and enhanced the military value of a cluster of brick buildings located on a rise in Aprilia. The buildings had been designed at the direction of Benito Mussolini as a model farm, and U.S. troops dubbed the location "the factory." The factory stood at the juncture of a network of roads that were of primary importance to any combat troops who wanted to move soldiers and equipment to and from the front lines. The aim of the Germans was to seize Aprilia and use it as a base to launch a final victorious attack against the Anzio beachhead.

The British fought valiantly all through the night of 7 February and the next day, while the U.S. First Division engaged in close-in fighting with German forces attacking the frontline position being defended by the British. On 9 February, the German troops under their commander, General Eberhard von Mackensen, succeeded in driving the British out of the factory. American troops joined the battle in the Aprilia area in order to give British troops a chance to regroup and consolidate their positions for a counterattack against German forces now occupying the factory.

More and more aware of his precarious position on the beachhead, Major General John P. Lucas asked General Clark for an additional infantry division. Clark responded with irritation, telling Lucas that he did not have an infantry division that was not already committed in a vital location. Clark added that even if he did have such a division, he did not have the shipping capacity to maintain it with supplies on the Anzio beachhead.

Conditions at Anzio were growing more and more critical. Casualties were streaming into the hospital area for treatment, and patients were crowded into hospital tents. Because of the heavy fighting, the evacuation of wounded from the beachhead by sea slowed down and, in some cases, stopped. It was not unusual for patients sent in the morning to the

Anzio docks for evacuation to be returned to those same hospitals that evening. Hospital personnel were faced with the problem of having no beds for the returnees, having assigned the vacated beds to newly wounded and sick soldiers. Readmitting returned patients who had already been counted as evacuees to hospital ships caused overcrowding. As part of the effort to cope with the increasing number of patients, evacuation hospitals placed less seriously ill soldiers only partially inside hospital tents. Litters were set down on the ground so that the head and shoulders of these patients were inside the tent while the rest of their body lay outside the canvas.

With the hospitals under constant threat of shelling and bombing, patients did not feel safe under a canvas with a red cross painted on it. In fact, many soldiers, ironically, felt safer on the front lines than in the hospital area. "With all the shells traveling over the hospital, many of our patients decided it was safer on the front lines," Evelyn Anderson of the 93rd Evacuation Hospital recalled. "It wasn't unusual for less seriously wounded soldiers to go AWOL from the hospital and return to their units and their frontline foxholes." Hospital personnel began to question the prewar, civilian practice of lengthy hospitalizations and extended immobility following surgery when they learned that former patients who had rapidly gone back to their foxholes recovered quickly and without the complications of the more sedentary patients.[52]

At the 93rd Evac, Private Glant, recovering from the above-the-elbow amputation of his right arm and the treatment of the severe wounds to his legs, was surprised and somewhat entertained when a new patient placed across from him turned out to be a German POW. "He was about my age," Glant remembered, "and he had been hit in the neck by shrapnel. The guy spoke perfect English. The German guy would give me German chocolate and I'd give him cigarettes and talk to him a lot. When the nurse and a corpsman wanted to put him on a litter to take him to the operating tent for surgery, he refused to get on the litter. He insisted on walking to the OR tent."[53]

Ninety-third nurse Lieutenant Anderson recalled that it was not unusual for German soldiers to "show how tough they were" by refusing to lie down on the OR table, and by insisting on taking their anesthesia sitting up. Most of these troops were members of the SS or other elite German units, and the anesthetist would have to lay the men down on the table when they lost consciousness.[54]

In addition to caring for German "Supermen" and providing critical care for hundreds of recently wounded and acutely ill patients, the hospital staff was faced with the challenge of providing routine and maintenance care for all their patients. This care included such homely tasks as straightening pillows, scratching an itch that was out of reach, or providing wounded soldiers with a drink of water. Nurses and corpsmen elicited the help of less seriously wounded ambulatory patients to care for severely wounded soldiers who could not get out of bed or even lift a glass of water. Glant remembered receiving such help. "I had a hard time getting a drink of water. The nurse told this British guy in the bed on my left to 'help him out. He needs a lot of water.' And that Tommie helped me all he could."[55]

Glant also remembered that the boy in the cot next to the British Tommie was from his hometown, Hammond, Indiana. "We'd talk—holler—back and forth. He lived on the north side and I lived on the south side of town. He was in the Eighty-second Airborne and had been shot in the rear end and the leg. He lost his leg and he had to lie on his stomach. I was on my back with my arm and both legs bandaged. We couldn't see each other, but we talked all the time. His name was Hansie Lewandowski. He lived in the Polish section of town. I lost track of him when I got evacuated off the beachhead."[56]

The Germans continued to shell the Anzio beachhead every day. At 1400 on 9 February, Colonel Jarrett B. Huddleston, VI Corps surgeon, a 1916 graduate of George Washington University and veteran of World War I, was waiting outside VI Corps Headquarters for a jeep that was to carry him on a tour of medical installations on the beachhead. A 170mm shell fell nearby and a large fragment from that round struck and killed Colonel Huddleston where he stood. The U.S. Army and VI Corps lost an outstanding leader who had directed medical care on Salerno and Anzio from D-Day until his death. It is a testimony to Colonel Huddleston's leadership that the doctors, nurses, and personnel of the hospitals on Anzio would continue to give excellent care to sick and wounded soldiers in the days and weeks that followed.

ON 8 FEBRUARY, the day after the antipersonnel bombs fell on the 95th Evacuation Hospital, a group of enlisted men volunteered to dig foxholes for the nurses. They dug the foxholes inside the nurses' tents, under each nurse's cot so they would be easily accessible. There were more than a few raised eyebrows and ironic chuckles, as nurses reminded each other that "the brass" had said they would not need foxholes in this new hospital location. The brass had, however naively and misguidedly, expected the Germans to uphold the Geneva Conventions. Accordingly, the Allied military had even sent the exact map coordinates of the new hospital area to the Germans. Since the zone was at least a mile from any legitimate military target, Allied leadership expected that the hospital area would not be bombed or shelled. This proved to be wishful thinking. Bombing and shelling went on all hours of the day and night at the hospital compound.

All the nurses were glad to get foxholes inside or near their tents, despite the fact that the high water table made it necessary for the holes to be shallower than they would have preferred. No one went visiting on the beachhead without first making sure that their host's foxhole arrangements could accommodate company. In an effort to reduce the number of shrapnel injuries, personnel learned to "duck-walk" in a squatting position when traveling anywhere outside the tents during daylight hours.

If any doubt remained as to the need for foxholes, it was totally dis-

Nurses of the 33rd Field Hospital on Anzio. Left to right: *Lts. Sue Hancock, Jessie Paddock, and Eleanor Hulburt* (U.S. Army Signal Corps)

pelled by another bombing that the hospital site took on 10 February. At 1630 that Thursday, Lieutenant Glidewell, who was standing outside her tent, heard the sound of a loud explosion that was immediately followed by a strong concussion wave that knocked her to the ground. She got up, ran into her tent, and jumped into her foxhole. Bee Wee Wheeler, Neil Hansen, and Hut Walden, who had been sitting inside the tent talking, leaped into foxholes as the first explosion shook the ground. As the sounds of other shells exploding nearby roared through the air, the blast rolled through their tent, knocking them against the walls of their foxholes like rag dolls.

The waves of concussion created by the bombs were even greater across the road at the 33rd Field Hospital. As Second Lieutenant Jessie Paddock was walking toward her tent to spend some off-duty time with her tentmates, Glenda Spelhaug and LaVerne "Tex" Farquhar, she heard the sound of metal scraping on metal, and knew immediately that shells were about to fall on the hospital. "I could see our tent fifteen yards ahead," Paddock recalled, "and my heart beat wildly as I began to run toward it. I called out as loud as I could for Glenda and LaVerne to take cover. As I tried to run faster, my feet seemed to stick in the mud and slow me down." There was a loud explosion behind her and a strong wave of energy seemed to lift Paddock off the ground and propel her forward. She called out again to Spelhaug and Farquhar just before everything went black.[57]

The first 170mm shell hit the admissions tent and buried itself in the earth close to two male personnel. For some unknown reason, the shell exploded underground without sending shrapnel out of the hole. When the tent was inspected later, the only hole to be found was that made by the large-caliber shell as it entered the admission tent. Unfortunately, the rest of the 33rd Field Hospital was not so lucky.

Two of the 170mm shells were fired from the German railroad gun known to Americans as "Anzio Annie" or the "Anzio Express." The Germans mounted this huge gun on a railroad car, hid it inside a large tunnel when it was not in use, and brought it out only long enough to aim and fire. The limited exposure of the giant gun gave it protection from U.S. and Allied artillery and bombers. Two of the 170mm shells fired from "Anzio Annie" landed in the center of the cross arrangement of the ward tents of Unit C of the 33rd Field Hospital. Shrapnel flew in all directions, knocking out the unit generator and plunging the tents into darkness. Nurses and corpsmen went to work immediately, moving the most seriously wounded patients from their cots to litters on the floor. Before such moves could be made, intravenous lines and suction apparatus had to be disconnected. Nurses and corpsmen slashed the tents with scissors and pocketknives in order to admit daylight into the pitch-blackness of the wards.

As Lieutenant Paddock opened her eyes, she looked into the faces of hospital staff gathered around her as she lay on the ground. For several seconds, she fought to remember where she was and what had happened. Memory came flooding back as she looked at the remains of the tent that had been her home on the Anzio beachhead. What little was left hung in shreds or lay in debris-strewn mud. "Where are Glenda and LaVerne?" she asked. "What happened to them?" "Don't you remember?" the nurses around her answered. "You went into the tent before you passed out." Paddock could not then—and has never been able to since—recall entering the tent she shared with Glenda Spelhaug and LaVerne Farquhar. "Are they hurt bad?" Paddock asked. "Are they going to be all right?"[58]

One of the nurses put her arm around Paddock and spoke to her in a calm voice. "Paddy, they're dead. They both were killed instantly." Paddock remembered feeling as if she were going to faint again. She forced herself to stay conscious. By now she could feel the warmth of tears as they flowed down her face. She remembered that her own voice sounded as if it were coming from far away. "How were they killed?" The nurse tightened her grip around Paddock's shoulders and spoke quietly. "Let's talk about it after you get some rest. You can bunk in my tent."[59]

"No. Tell me now," Paddock insisted. "I have to know. They were my friends." Paddock did not recall who told her, but she never forgot what they said. "Glenda had been decapitated. LaVerne was eviscerated. I still don't remember seeing them like that. I just remember the good things about them."[60]

Paddock described some of those memories. "Glenda Spelhaug was the most caring person I'd ever met. Just two days before she was killed, she gave her helmet to a nurse who had lost hers. She really cared about all of us . . . and LaVerne—her nickname was 'Tex'—was one of the nicest people anyone could ever hope to meet. She was always trying to keep our morale up, always kidding, always smiling."[61]

LaVerne "Tex" Farquhar, a member of the 2nd Auxiliary Surgical Group who was assigned to the 33rd Field Hospital at the time she was killed, had been interviewed just days before her death. Rita Hume, a correspondent for the Red Cross, recorded Farquhar's words: "Our hospital area has been close to the firing line so many times that the dangers of strafing and bombing are not exciting any more. The exciting thing is the job. To see men so badly injured you don't know how they can live and save them—that's a thrill. There is not one patient who does not have to be built up out of shock for surgery. You should see the way we use blood plasma!"[62]

In addition to killing two nurses, the shelling wounded eleven other members of the staff—four male officers and seven enlisted men. Among the seriously injured was Lieutenant Colonel Samuel A. Hanser, commanding officer of the hospital, who subsequently returned to the United States with radial nerve paralysis. Shells were still falling in the beachhead area while patients were placed in ambulances and taken to nearby hospitals for care. Two nurses remained at their stations in the postoperative tent and calmly helped to evacuate the patients to safety: First Lieutenant Elaine A. Roe from Whitewater, Wisconsin, and Second Lieutenant Rita Rourke from Chicago. A third nurse, Lieutenant Mary Louise Roberts of Dallas, stayed on duty in the busy operating room during the shelling. These three nurses were the first U.S. Army nurses in World War II to be awarded Silver Stars for "gallantry in the face of enemy action."[63]

The courage of these three nurses was described in the April 1944 *American Journal of Nursing* and disseminated to their nursing colleagues. When the shelling began, Roe and Rourke refused to leave their patients, though the latter kept urging them to get out and seek safety. "Go to the foxholes," the wounded men told the nurses. "That's incoming mail. We know the sound and that's how we got wounded. Forget us and go." Roe and Rourke calmed them by saying, "Of course, we are not going. There is not a single nurse who will let this shelling of hospitals chase her off the beach. We are here to stay." The two nurses started immediately to evacuate forty-two patients by stretcher.[64]

In the busy operating room, red-haired Lieutenant Mary Roberts stayed with the surgeons throughout the thirty-minute attack. "I wanted to jump under the operating table," she admitted, "but before I could yield to the impulse, I had to help lower litter cases to the floor. Then I noticed that a patient on the operating table had his helmet near him, so I put it over his head to give him that much protection. Two of our enlisted medical men were hit and I just did not have time to stop working."[65]

The 56th Evac was also hit. Luckily, no patient was seriously wounded there, thanks in part to the quick action of nurses and corpsmen, who moved patients to litters on the ground as quickly as possible. One of those nurses was twenty-five-year-old Second Lieutenant Ellen G. Ainsworth from Glenwood City, Wisconsin. When the bombing of the Nettuno hospital site began on 10 February, Ainsworth was on duty in a surgical ward. For her gallantry and dedication to duty on that day, Ainsworth would later be awarded the Silver Star "for calmly directing the placing of surgical patients on the ground to lessen the danger of further injury during the enemy shelling of the hospital. By her disregard for her own safety and her calm assurance, she instilled confidence in her assistants and her patients, thereby preventing serious panic and injury."[66]

Also in the operating-room tent of the 56th Evac during the bombing of 10 February was Lieutenant "Frenchie" Miernicke of the 2nd Aux Surgical Group. Miernicke, who stayed at her post as flak fell throughout the OR and hospital area, was nominated for the Bronze Star for her actions that day: "Disregarding extreme danger, Lt. Miernicke continued to perform her duties in a cool and efficient manner."[67]

THE BOMBING of 10 February 1944 had a very sobering effect on the nurses and other staff of the 33rd Field Hospital. Nurses, doctors, and others dug foxholes inside their tents and developed a new and high regard for their helmets. The practice of going outside to watch the "Fourth of July show" whenever shells or planes were heard in the area halted immediately. At the first whine, whistle, or scraping sound of shells heading for the hospital, personnel who were not on duty put on their helmets and jumped into their foxholes. Those on duty stayed with their patients and tried to make them as safe as possible. Operating-room staff continued their work while a corpsman made the rounds of the tables, placing helmets on the heads of doctors, nurses, and technicians. Everyone was proud of the staff response to the shelling of 10 February. In less than twenty-four hours, they had cleared or repaired the damage and the 33rd was doing business as usual.

The personnel of the 95th Evacuation Hospital were not so lucky. The shells that hit the hospital on 10 February put the finishing touches on a unit that was already operating under severe handicaps. "Anzio Annie had done her work well," Glidewell recalled. "The generator and much of the hospital's remaining equipment were totally destroyed. Not even the dead on Anzio were safe from Anzio Annie. Two of the large shells plowed into the nearby cemetery and sent pieces of caskets and body parts in all directions."[68]

The 95th Evacuation Hospital was damaged beyond its ability to regroup and reopen on the beachhead. Top decision makers decided to replace it with the 15th Evacuation Hospital, which was stationed at Riardo, close to Cassino and the Benedictine monastery. Tents and remaining equipment were left in place at both sites, and hospital personnel with their own personal belongings exchanged locations. Teams that were attached to the 95th Evac were reassigned to hospitals that remained on the beachhead.

When the 15th Evac arrived on the beachhead on 11 February to replace the 95th, the nurses of the 95th visited neighboring hospitals to say good-bye to fellow nurses who had been kind enough to share their clothing and other personal belongings with them after the bombings. Then the 95th Evac nurses began packing what was left of their personal belongings.

Adeline "Si" Simonson was packing her musette bag when she heard that a nurse who had graduated from St. Luke's Hospital in Duluth, Minnesota, a year ahead of her, Lieutenant Gladys Mooney, was with the 15th Evac. Simonson got together with Gladys. "Gladys said, 'Why are you people leaving?' " When Simonson told her about the bombings, Mooney seemed unimpressed. A short time later, the Germans started shelling. Simonson headed for the foxhole she had shown Mooney a short time earlier. Soon, Gladys came running. "Here comes Gladys," Simonson recalled. " 'Si, for God's sake, move over! We've never had anything like this!' "[69]

At 1600 on 12 February, Glidewell, Simonson, and their sister nurses climbed onto trucks and traveled to the Anzio docks to board an LST bound for Naples. German shells whined and whistled overhead as the trucks make their way to the docks. When they were finally aboard the LST, Glidewell and others found their bunks, stretched out, and fell fast asleep. Their exhaustion was so complete that they were not awakened by artillery fire as the LST passed the mouth of the Gaeta River. "I was told later about the shelling," Glidewell remembered. "I was so tired, I slept right through the artillery barrage." She awakened as the LST sailed into Naples harbor. She went up on deck and looked at the scenery as they moved six miles west toward the town of Pozzuoli to disembark. "I thought about Carrie Sheetz, Blanche Sigman, Esther Richards, and Gertrude Morrow as we sailed through beautiful Naples harbor. I learned days after they were killed that each woman had had a premonition of her death. I'll never forget how Carrie talked about her home in Pennsylvania, or how lovingly she spoke about her daughter, Anne. Since she and her husband were both joining the military, Carrie left her daughter with her mother in Camp Hill, Pennsylvania. I'll never forget those four women."[70]

Back at Anzio, at 1830 on 12 February, German planes executed an unusually heavy attack on the harbor. During this raid that lasted more than an hour and a half, an antipersonnel bomb fell into the officers' living area of the 56th Evacuation Hospital. Nurse Ellen Ainsworth was sitting on her cot entertaining two other nurses when fragments from the bomb tore through her tent and sliced their way into her chest and

Bomb damage at the 56th Evacuation Hospital, 1944. Pvt. Robert Phillips from Jenks, Oklahoma, examines a shrapnel-torn hospital cot. (U.S. Army Signal Corps)

abdomen. The young nurse was taken immediately to surgery; in addition to a penetrating wound on the left side of her chest, Ainsworth suffered a tear in her left lung, lacerations of the right diaphragm and spleen, and a perforating wound of the stomach. She died four days later, without knowing she would receive the Silver Star.

BY 22 FEBRUARY—just one month after the landing on Anzio—German and Allied casualties had grown to almost 19,000. In only thirty days, Allied troops suffered approximately 2,000 killed, 8,500 wounded, and 8,500 missing in action. Together, the enemy and Allied forces lost almost 40,000 soldiers in just thirty days. And the fighting was far from over; in fact, it had just begun.[71]

CHAPTER NINE

Stalemate at Anzio Beachhead and Monte Cassino

NURSES ENDURE WITH THE REST OF THE TROOPS

12 February–15 May 1944

In no other theatre of the war was the resoluteness and fortitude of medical personnel more tried or indomitable courage greater displayed than during the early months of 1944 on the Anzio beachhead.

—Col. Rollin L. Bauchspies, MC, USA,
VI Corps surgeon, Italy, 1944
"The Courageous Medics of Anzio,"
Military Medicine (January 1958)

THROUGHOUT FEBRUARY 1944, the American and Allied troops made no headway at Anzio. They were locked in a bloody stalemate with the Germans and could not break out of the narrow confines of the Anzio beachhead to advance on Rome. The stalemate would last for several months, until the Allies finally managed to break through German defenses in late May.

Meanwhile, farther south at Monte Cassino, U.S. and Allied troops were locked in another stalemate: they were unable to break through the Gustav Line to join the Allied troops farther north and advance to Rome. At Anzio, what held the Allies back was a lack of troop reinforcements and supplies, coupled with a resistance by the Germans that was heavier than expected. At Monte Cassino, the story was a little different. What held the Allied troops back at this now-famous hill was not just the fierceness of the German resistance but, at least in part, the Allied high command itself—or, to be exact, the commitment on the part of the Allied high command to preserve a centuries-old monastery from destruction, even at the cost of American and Allied lives.

Monte Cassino is a hill just south of the Mignano Gap, the opening through the mountains into the Liri Valley that contained the direct highways and railway to Rome. In 1943, only one road led from the bottom of Monte Cassino to the top of the hill where the 1,500-year-old Benedictine monastery stood. The road was only six miles long, but it was the sole way up and over Monastery Hill, as Monte Cassino was called by the inhabitants, through the mountains, and on to Rome.

Its location on a strategic crossroads had put the monastery in the unfortunate path of many wars throughout history. It was built on the summit of Monte Cassino under the direction of St. Benedict in A. D. 529. In the sixth century, the Lombards destroyed the monastery; in the ninth century, the Saracens again destroyed it. It was rebuilt but fell into disrepair in 1071, due to the unsettled political situation in Italy. In the fourteenth century, an earthquake destroyed the buildings, but reconstruction started almost immediately. They were completed in the eighteenth century, but destroyed again in 1799 by French troops invading the independent Kingdom of Naples. Once again, the monastery was rebuilt to its former glory and, once again, in 1943, it found itself directly in the path of yet another attack.

It was here on Monastery Hill and in the mountains south of Cassino in late 1943 and early 1944 that the Germans mounted a fierce resistance to keep American and Allied troops out of the Liri Valley, thus blocking the routes to Rome. Although the Germans had given their word to the Italians that German troops would not enter the abbey on Monte Cassino or put it to any military use, it became clear that they had occupied it and were using it with devastating effect on Allied troops.

In early February 1944, twenty-four-year-old Corporal Joseph Samuel Tahan, a forward observer with the 977th Field Artillery Unit fighting at Monte Cassino, saw with his own eyes that the Germans were inside the abbey. Part of the job of a forward observer was to determine the coordinates for aiming large guns at selected targets. Once the coordinates had been determined for the day, Tahan would be sent up by his commander in a Piper Cub plane to observe German gunfire positions on Monte Cassino.

On one such reconnaissance trip during the first days of February, Tahan spotted a German forward observer positioned inside the monastery. Without hesitation, the bright young soldier radioed for artillery fire to knock out the German forward observation post, clearly set up inside the abbey itself.

After calling in the target coordinates over the radio, Corporal Tahan was shocked to hear the voice on the other end say, "No can do." "Why not?" Joe wanted to know. "The brass won't allow us to hit the abbey," the voice on the two-way radio replied. "The Germans have assured them and the Italians that they are not inside the monastery at all." Tahan remembered feeling angry and frustrated. "I'm flying over the abbey," Joe said, "and I can see the German forward observer inside the abbey. He's using the abbey to call down shells on our troops trying to take Monastery Hill. 'We can't fire on the abbey without approval from headquarters,' " Tahan remembered the officer on the other end of the radio telling him. "I thought the whole thing was crazy. Since when was a pile of stones and bricks worth more than the lives of American and Allied soldiers?"[1]

By 17 November 1943, after fifty-nine consecutive days of fighting, in the Third Division alone, 8,590 soldiers had been wounded or killed trying to battle their way up the slopes of Monte Cassino: 3,144 battle casualties and 5,446 nonbattle casualties. And Corporal Tahan's was not a lone voice. Reconnaissance flights were being made daily over Monastery Hill, repeatedly reporting the German presence. Moreover, survivors of the Allied debacle at the Rapido River in the foothills of Monte Cassino in January 1944 were well aware that the monastery was a German stronghold. Yet despite heavy troop losses, the Allied command was reluctant to destroy the abbey-turned-enemy-observation post.[2]

AT ANZIO, February was to see the launch of several heavy German offensives that would keep Allied casualties streaming into the hospital compound. Hospital protocol demanded that the most severely wounded be evacuated off the beachhead and taken, by ship, to hospitals farther in the rear. However, this was no easy task; daily German artillery shelling as well as air raids averaging up to one hundred sorties a day over Anzio harbor made the transport of wounded to hospital ships all but impossible.

In the weeks following Junior Glant's arrival at the 93rd Evac in the

Wounded on board an LCT being carried to the British hospital ship Leinster off Anzio, 1944. Hospital corpsmen and Red Cross workers accompany them. (U.S. Army Signal Corps)

Anzio beachhead hospital compound, the hospital administration made several failed attempts to get severely wounded soldiers off the beachhead and to a general hospital in the rear. "They'd take us on litters down to the harbor," Glant recalled, "so we could get on a hospital ship. The only trouble was that the harbor was full of ships and the Germans kept bombing and shelling the whole area. They'd finally have to take us back to the hospital. It wasn't much safer than the harbor. I made at least three round trips before I got off Anzio."[3]

For Glant, the fourth try was the charm. On 13 February, Glant and other wounded were placed on a flat-bottomed barge and taken out into the Mediterranean, where the British hospital carrier *Dinard* was waiting to take on casualties. Glant was swung aboard by a hoist that lifted each patient on his litter, one at a time. When he was finally settled below deck in a ward, he found his bed was next to that of a critically wounded soldier. The hospital ship had its hands full: more than two hundred wounded men were on board, tended by a staff of seven to eight Royal Army Medical Corps (RAMC) doctors, four to six sisters of Queen Alexandra's Imperial Military Nursing Service, and supporting RAMC technicians. "The doctors, nurses, and medics were all working like crazy," Glant remembered. "The guy next to me was Airborne and he'd been shot in the lung. They were working on him, but he looked as if he was dying. He looked over at me and said, 'It's hot in here,' and began pulling off his clothes. Well, it wasn't hot in there at all. It was February and the ward was warm enough to be comfortable. I felt sorry for the guy. He didn't look like he'd make it."[4]

Despite the ongoing commotion around him, Glant fell asleep. When he awakened more than an hour later, there was a different soldier in the bed next to him. "I asked a nurse what happened to the Airborne guy and she told me he didn't make it," Glant recalled. "That's the way war was. You could be alive one minute and dead the next. . . . I was pretty reli-

Wounded American and Allied soldiers on board a hospital ship evacuating them from Anzio, 1944 (U.S. Army Signal Corps)

gious and I didn't really think about dying myself. Even right after I was hit and bleeding like a stuck pig, I didn't think about dying. I always felt like I was going to make it."[5]

WITH GROWING EVIDENCE that the Germans were holding the monastery on Monte Cassino, the Allied command finally made the decision to bomb. A heavy, all-out air raid was set for 15 February. On the night before the bombing, Allied artillery fired twenty-five shells stuffed with leaflets into the sky over Monte Cassino. The leaflets were printed in Italian and English:

Italian Friends,

Beware!
   We have until now been especially careful to avoid shelling the Monte Cassino monastery. The Germans have known how to benefit from this. But now the fighting has swept closer and closer to its sacred precincts. The time has come when we must train our guns on the monastery itself.
   We give you warning so that you may save yourselves. We warn you urgently: Leave the monastery. Leave it at once. Respect this warning. It is for your benefit.

THE FIFTH ARMY[6]

The first wave of 37 B-17 bombers each carrying twelve 500-pound demolition bombs arrived over Monte Cassino at approximately 0925 on 15 February. They were the first of a four-wave attack scheduled to hit the monastery that day. The bombs plummeted toward the ancient stone buildings at 0928 and hit their target squarely. In all, 144 B-17s and 84 medium bombers would drop their bombloads before the day was over.

Charles Coolidge of the Thirty-sixth Division was within sight of Monastery Hill when the first bombs fell. "The Germans jumped out of the abbey," Coolidge recalled, "out of a window, after the bombers went over. I saw them jump out."[7]

At the 95th Evac Hospital set up in nearby Riardo in the old site of the 15th Evac, patients and hospital staff had an unimpeded view of Monte Cassino and the monastery. "The sky was black with bombers," Speedy Glidewell recalled. "We could see the ack-ack flying upward toward our planes. Every once in a while, one of the [American] bombers got hit and exploded. You could watch the burning pieces falling and floating toward the ground, and you knew it meant that another group of American boys had just been killed." Wave after wave of American bombers flew over Monastery Hill, dropped their bombs, and were replaced by other planes. "It was terrible to think that human beings were in the midst of that horrible devastation," Glidewell said, "but it also felt good to know that our troops would have an easier time getting to the summit. So many young boys had been killed or wounded over that one solitary hill. . . . Since that day, I've never been able to enjoy fireworks on the Fourth of July."[8]

Luther Wolff watched the destruction of the monastery from the 11th Evacuation Hospital on nearby Mount Lungo. "A sight to gladden the eyes today," Wolff wrote in his diary. "Seventy-two B-17s came over about 9:00 AM, very high, and knocked the monastery down. There were over 100 B-25s and B-26s that bombed this same area while some A-36s finished it off. Boy! Was that something to watch. It should have been done a month ago, though." Indeed, many agreed with Wolff; soldiers who survived the many battles to take Monastery Hill felt as Wolff did that the destruction should have come much sooner, before the lives of so many friends and comrades were needlessly lost. Since the bombing proved to be inevitable, the Allied command's delay could only be viewed as a futile and costly gesture.[9]

Ruth Hindman also watched the bombing from a nearby frontline hospital. "I was glad to see the monastery bombed," Hindman said, "because I thought it would cut down on our own casualties. We had seen so many critically wounded boys." Many soldiers at Cassino had stepped on land mines and been wounded all over their bodies, with lacerations on their legs, chests, arms, and backs. "Sometimes their legs were blown off completely," Hindman said. "We'd operate on all the wounds on the front of their bodies, then turn them over and operate on the wounds on their backs." Hindman especially recalled one American boy, who was brought into the operating room after a direct hit in the face: "I will never forget the image of that young man. His eyes and nose were gone. His mouth was lacerated and his ears were barely hanging on to his head. It was so sad to see him. He couldn't talk. We had to be careful about what we said around him because he could hear and understand. He tried hard to talk, but he mumbled in a voice that couldn't be understood."[10]

As a "floating" surgical nurse, moving rapidly from one hospital to another, Hindman could not recall which hospital she was in when she witnessed the bombing of Monte Cassino. Since the deaths of her team surgeon, Major Adams, and her corpsman, Corporal McComb, in the sinking of the *St. David* during the invasion of Anzio, Hindman had not been reassigned to one particular surgical team or hospital. Instead, she was assigned as a temporary replacement to any 2nd Aux team that needed a surgical nurse. She might be at one frontline hospital in the morning, and at another that night. Her reassignments were almost always in a direction closer to the front, and travel there often took place in the dead of night under complete blackout conditions. Whether she went to work immediately in the OR or got a few hours' sleep before reporting to her duty station, daylight would yield her first knowledge of the field hospital's surroundings. The only thing Hindman could be sure of as she traveled the front lines was that there would be scores of casualties awaiting her help. For all these reasons, she watched the bombing of Monte Cassino with the hope that it would result in a decrease in the number of American and Allied wounded.

ON THE ANZIO BEACHHEAD, the definitive defense line from which the Allies would not retreat was established by the end of February. This final line was virtually the same as it had been at the end of January, one week after the initial landing: basically no ground had been gained despite fierce fighting and heavy casualties, and no ground would be gained for several more months, until the Allied "breakthrough" for Rome in late May. The line started, in the northwest, at the Moletta River, ran east and then southeast across the fields of the central sector until it reached the Mussolini Canal, where it then turned back to the coast, south-southwest along the main canal until it reached the sea.

But many reinforcements were added to this line. During the second week of February, the 39th Combat Engineers strung barbed wire around the VI Corps' positions. In front of the barbed wire, the same engineers had laid a dense pattern of more than eight hundred land mines. Behind the barbed wire, they stretched coils of razor-sharp accordion wire. To further strengthen the final line of defense, all American and Allied artillery could be brought to bear on any part of the line within a minute's notice.

Several large German offensives were launched throughout February,

March, and April. One of the largest began at 0600 on 16 February
against the central beachhead front and lasted for five intensive days of
ground and air combat. In the midst of this onslaught, Second Lieutenant Ellen Ainsworth died of wounds she had received four days
before. The 56th Evac's chief nurse, First Lieutenant Dorothy F.
Meadors from Alma, Arkansas, selected Lieutenant Miernicke to prepare
Ainsworth's body for burial. The chief nurse's choice was based on the
fact that Miernicke had only been attached to the 56th Evacuation
Hospital since 11 February when Miernicke's 2nd Aux team was transferred. Chief Nurse Meadors assumed Miernicke was not a close friend of
Ainsworth.

As soon as Miernicke received her orders, she went directly to the
chief nurse to tell her that she and Ainsworth had become friends when
both were stationed at Camp Chaffee, Arkansas, during the winter of
1943. Miernicke asked that the assignment be given to someone else. Her
request was denied. "The chief nurse said someone had to do it, and I was
it." Under direct orders, Miernicke went to the tent that was used as a
morgue and located Ellen Ainsworth's body lying on a stretcher, covered
by a sheet.[11]

For forty-five minutes, Miernicke worked on Ainsworth's body. "It
was terrible," Frenchie recalled. "I have never forgotten that. I was alone
in the morgue tent with Ellen and ten or twelve dead GIs." Ainsworth's
body was swollen but rigor mortis had not yet set in. "She had been
through extensive surgery," Frenchie said, "and as I prepared her body, I
just naturally began talking to her. I said, 'Ellen, who would ever have
thought we'd meet again like this. I'm so sorry that this has happened to
you.' " As Miernicke talked to her dead friend, she struggled to get the
lifeless body into the uniform of the Army Nurse Corps Ellen had served
so proudly. "Ellen was a pretty girl and she was always careful about her
appearance. When I got her into her uniform, I combed her hair, put
makeup on her face, and lipstick on her mouth. I knew she would have
wanted that."[12]

That afternoon, 16 February, members of the 56th Evac who were not
on duty gathered for a funeral service. The chaplain was still speaking
when German bombers flew low overhead and the mourners were told to
return to their hospital area immediately. Crowds, even those gathered
to say good-bye to a fallen friend and comrade, were much too tempting a
target for enemy bombs and shells. Ellen Ainsworth was buried in the
American Cemetery at Anzio, along with five sister nurses also killed in

action on the beachhead. Ainsworth's Silver Star and Purple Heart decorations were awarded posthumously to her parents.

ON 14 FEBRUARY 1944, the hospital ship *Dinard* pulled into Naples harbor and her patients were taken by ambulance to the 300th General Hospital in the city. Junior Glant was carried to the second floor and placed in a large ward where the entire front wall was made of glass. "What was really neat," Glant remembered, "was that Mount Vesuvius was erupting and I could lie there and watch the whole thing. You could see the lava running down the side of the volcano."[13]

Glant's ward was filled with orthopedic cases. Like Glant, several had had amputations, and like Glant, they also had fractures that were still being treated. A large part of the treatment for amputees was debridment of stumps and wounds. Glant remembered the anxiety and pain that treatment brought with it. "I hated to have my bandages changed. They used to come in there and cut the dead skin off. The wound was wide open on the stump. The first time a doctor at the 300th General was working on me, I grabbed his hand to stop him because the pain was so bad. He looked at me with fire in his eyes and said, 'Boy, don't you ever touch my hand again!' For a minute I thought he was going to shoot me or something. But it turned out okay. Everybody there was real nice to all of us guys."[14]

AT ANZIO, American and Allied troops awoke on the morning of 18 February to a grisly sight. As the first rays of daylight fell along the beachhead's final line of defense, dead and dying German soldiers who had taken part in the previous night's attack hung tangled, bloody, and moaning in the barbed wire that stood less than fifteen feet from American and Allied foxholes. The attack, begun on the 16th, would last for five days. To give an idea of the enormity of this German onslaught, American forces suffered a total of 5,133 dead, wounded, and missing, an average of 1,000 casualties a day. Of these, 3,496 were battle casualties and 1,637 were nonbattle casualties—suffering from trench foot, exposure, and exhaustion. The enemy reported that they had taken 1,304 Allied prisoners.[15]

In the face of such extreme and close danger, rumors began to circulate in the hospital compound that the nurses were to be removed from the Anzio beachhead. These new stories followed an earlier rumor that nurses were to be issued side arms (.45-caliber automatics) for protection in the event that the enemy overran the beachhead. The rumors did not last long since American commanders decided that the nurses were far too valuable, both in the care of the wounded and as a morale factor for the troops, to be evacuated. "They decided that if they removed us from the beachhead," Lieutenant Miernicke remembered, "it would underscore the desperate position our troops were in, and send the morale of combat forces plummeting. They also decided not to issue us side arms in spite of the fact that the beachhead might be overrun, and that we were constantly expecting German infiltrators into our lines. I think that was a good choice since the Geneva Conventions don't allow medical personnel to carry weapons. If they gave us guns and we got captured, the Germans might not have considered us noncombatants."[16]

The heavy stream of incoming casualties to the hospitals kept personnel working round the clock. Unit A of the 33rd Field Hospital with about a hundred beds, which was located three miles inland close to the front line, reported that they received ninety-two critically wounded soldiers in a twenty-four-hour period between 15 and 20 February. "Our personnel worked day and night for three days with a minimum of sleep in order to care for them." There was little time for anything that did not involve direct patient care.[17]

Even taking the time to answer nature's call could seem like a dispensable luxury. One night after working many hours in the surgery tent and with many hours still ahead of her, Frenchie Miernicke decided she could no longer put off visiting the nurses' latrine. Her surgical team would have to do without her for ten minutes or so. Miernicke left the OR tent and, in dead of night under total blackout conditions, walked in the direction she thought the latrine would be. Ten minutes later, she still had not found it, and though surprised to hear a GI's voice call out, she was glad to have an opportunity for redirection.

"The GI guard called out, 'Who goes there?' I was supposed to answer with the password, but I couldn't remember it. I called back, 'I'm an American Army nurse. Just point me back to the 56th Evac Hospital.'" The GI got her headed in the right direction and she finally found the latrine. It was a two-holer: she went in and sat down. A few minutes later, she heard someone else come into the tent, sit down beside her, and was almost startled off her seat when a deep male voice cut across the darkness. "The baritone voice announced, 'This has been one rough night.' I didn't say a word and he didn't pursue a conversation. In about five minutes, he left. I gave him a couple of extra minutes to clear the area and then left myself. I never was more glad to get back to work as when I was safely in the OR tent again." After wandering around that night, she and many other nurses chose to use empty plasma cans in their tents and empty them in the morning when they could see where they were going.[18]

Other routines of daily life were also disrupted. There was little personal time for things like bathing and doing laundry. Even if the time had been available, water was not. The trip to the water point for the hospital was so dangerous that it was made only once a day. When an Italian civilian could be contracted to do laundry, the person hired—in tears and apologizing—would return with clean laundry riddled with holes from flak that had damaged the clothing while it was hanging out to dry on a clothesline.

Hair could be washed only when it rained. The nurses caught rainwater in plasma cans and buckets for that purpose. During the frequent, long spells without rain, nurses wore turbans fashioned from the Curity diapers originally intended to serve as Kotex pads. Turbans might keep fleas and lice out of one's hair, but they were no protection against shrapnel or falling flak.

Helmets took on a new significance as air raids and artillery barrages sent more and more shrapnel into the hospital area. The commanding officer of the 56th Evac, Colonel Henry S. Blesse, levied a $25 fine on anyone caught without his or her helmet.

The frequent air raids even affected the quality of air inside all hospital tents. When planes came over, it was necessary to close the dampers on the oil-burning stoves so that night-flying enemy aircraft could not spot the fires. Closing the dampers meant a buildup of smoke inside and difficult breathing conditions for patients and personnel alike.

By mid-February, American and Allied troops were suffering from weeks of fighting in freezing cold and rain and confinement in foxholes flooded with water. These conditions exacted a heavy toll. In addition to battle casualties, hospitals on the beachhead were now receiving large numbers of GIs suffering from pneumonia, bronchitis, and trench foot. During the Allied occupation of the Anzio beachhead, 2,196 cases of trench foot were reported. Trench foot, a term first coined in the trenches of World War I, is an injury of the skin, blood vessels, and nerves of the feet due to prolonged exposure to cold and moisture. Although not fatal, during the six-month period from October 1943 to

April 1944, the condition removed 5,752 soldiers, 7 percent of the troops in the Mediterranean theater of war, from the front lines as surely as if they were hit by a bullet.[19]

Conditions on the Anzio beachhead during the winter of 1943–44 were ideal for the development of trench foot. At the time, there was no waterproof GI shoe or boot. Soldiers stuck in frontline foxholes half-filled with water could not escape the freezing weather and almost perpetually wet living conditions. The cold caused blood vessels to contract, diminishing blood flow to the feet and damaging nerve endings. Wetness—whether standing water or perspiration—conducts heat away from the body and leads to further contraction of the blood vessels. These conditions, combined with the common GI practice of tying shoes and boots so tightly that circulation to the feet was further impaired, all too often led to trench foot.

The symptoms are similar to frostbite. The soldier's feet would swell, turn pale, and become clammy to the touch. Numbness and often agonizing pain rendered the man unable to walk. Hundreds of "foot soldiers" were sent to hospitals on Anzio for care and treatment of this debilitating medical condition. Treatment consisted of restoring warmth and improved circulation to feet, combined with the newly available "wonder drug," penicillin. At the first sign that gangrene was beginning in toes and feet, penicillin was added to the treatment. Left untreated, sufferers of trench foot could end up with gangrene that frequently necessitated the amputation of toes or even a foot.

Despite the danger, there were some soldiers who preferred the possibility of amputation to the perils of combat. "Patton slapped the wrong guy in Sicily," Sergeant Charles Coolidge said. "He should have seen some of the soldiers in the hospitals around Cassino. These guys would be hospitalized for trench foot and get treatment for it during the day. At night, they'd sneak out of the hospital and soak their feet in a bucket of water. Trench foot isn't going to get well as long as you're getting your feet wet, and as long as they had trench foot, they didn't have to go back to the front."[20]

Fortunately, by the early months of 1944, the armed forces were receiving about 85 percent of the nation's production of penicillin, and in 1944, the United States produced approximately 16,000 billion units. This production is all the more astonishing when you consider that just a year before, the total production of penicillin in the United States from January to May 1943 was a paltry 400,000 units. Penicillin was also used for the thousands of pneumonia and upper respiratory infections of soldiers who were brought to the hospitals from the front lines—and, of course, for the treatment of venereal disease.[21]

Administration of penicillin in early 1944 was no easy task. Doctors were still experimenting with dosages of the new antibiotic and frequent intramuscular injections were the rule of the day. Nurses sometimes suffered skin problems from the constant task of giving intramuscular penicillin. "We used a ten- or twenty-cc syringe to give penicillin," Lieutenant Vera Sheaffer of the 93rd Evacuation Hospital recalled. "We changed needles between patients. Each patient got one or two cc's of medication, but we used the same glass syringe. We didn't have many syringes. My hands and fingers broke out from the alcohol in painful blisters as a result of preparing and giving so many penicillin injections. Then the penicillin was ordered every three hours. I'd no sooner get done than it was time to start again." The nurse was accompanied by a corpsman and it was not uncommon for an armed guard to accompany nurses when they made their penicillin rounds. Rumors of the "miraculous" results produced by the drug had already made it a highly coveted item by enemy troops and those engaged in the black market.[22]

BY 20 FEBRUARY 1944, the enemy assault that had begun on 16 February was officially over. The VI Corps had won a significant victory in holding the beachhead's final line of defense. In just five days, German forces suffered at least 5,389 battle casualties as dead, wounded, and missing in action. Among this total were 609 German prisoners of war. In losing their all-out efforts to overrun the beachhead, the German Fourteenth Army also lost a great deal of prestige. When interrogated, German POWs showed signs of demoralization at the failure of their efforts to break through the Allied beachhead's final defense line.[23]

Along with waning morale, the German Fourteenth Army was suffering from a lack of organization and a sharp loss of men and equipment. The much-talked-about German secret weapon, the Goliath tank, had made its battlefield debut during this five-day assault and proved to be a miserable failure. The Goliath was a miniature, unmanned tank that was designed to function as an explosives carrier and container. It was powered by a large battery and controlled through electrical impulses sent over a long cable attached to Goliath's frame. The miniature tank was designed to go through minefields, barbed wire, and concrete walls. Captured German soldiers, members of the 813th Engineer Company, told Allied interrogators that the Goliaths were used only on the first day, when thirteen of the miniature tanks became bogged down in mud and proved impossible to extricate. Three of the Goliaths were destroyed by Allied artillery, and ten were dragged off the field of battle by the 813th Engineers and never introduced into combat again.

During the same five-day German attacks, the enemy inflicted approximately 5,000 casualties on American forces. The Forty-fifth Division suffered 400 killed, 2,000 wounded, and 1,000 missing. Twenty-five hundred additional American soldiers suffered nonbattle casualties that included exhaustion, pneumonia, upper respiratory infections, and trench foot.[24]

Anzio had reached a definitive point, but it was still a long way from being completed. American and Allied troops still faced almost three months of combat along the final line of defense, and the constant threat of German infiltrators, bombs, and shells in the hospital area.

THE MORNING OF 20 February was cold and clear as Frenchie Miernicke slipped into her newly acquired combat jacket and headed for the postoperative tent. She pulled the jacket collar up against the back of her neck as a frigid wind hurried her along. It was this kind of winter weather that had led Miernicke to ask her quartermaster friend, Junior Warshaw, a lieutenant from Myrtle Beach, South Carolina, if he could issue her a combat jacket. Only yesterday, Warshaw had delivered a brand-new jacket, along with an apology for the fact that it would be too large for Miernicke's small frame, despite the fact that it was the smallest size he had on hand.

The area was seldom, if ever, free of combat noise, and the sounds of bombs exploding in Anzio harbor had been rumbling through the hospital site for at least thirty minutes as Miernicke entered the postoperative tent and began her rounds. She had changed the dressing on one patient and was about to examine the bandage of the patient to her right when the roar of airplane engines vibrated through the tent. A moment later, the sound of machine-gun fire grew louder: a German and an American plane were engaged in a dogfight. As the two planes swept low across the hospital, Miernicke heard a whistling sound as .50-caliber machine-gun bullets ripped through the canvas wall. Almost immediately, she heard a short, soft cry on her left. When Miernicke turned, she faced the soldier whose dressing she had changed only moments earlier. The young man was staring motionless up at her. "His eyes were wide open and there was a look of surprise on his face," Miernicke recalled. "The blanket and sheet that covered his chest were bright red and blood was gushing from his neck. He had been killed instantly." When Miernicke turned toward the patient on her right, she saw a red, raw bleeding mass where his head had been. For a moment Miernicke thought she was going to pass out or throw up. Two corpsmen helped Miernicke screen off the area, then carried the bodies to the morgue. Miernicke went from cot to cot, reassuring the thirty remaining patients that the planes had left the area and that they were safe.[25]

She was shocked when a young soldier with a leg wound looked at her, shook his head, and laughed. "Well, Lieutenant," said the young soldier, "you're a fine one to talk about this hospital being safe." He reached up and pulled the right side of her combat jacket toward him. "Look here!" He poked his finger into a good-sized hole near the side seam. "I say that you're a pretty good argument against this hospital being safe from the Krauts. It looks to me like you're lucky to be alive." A .50-caliber machine-gun shell had missed her by millimeters as it traveled through the right side of her new jacket. Miernicke met the young man's eyes and said, "I guess if a bullet doesn't have your name on it, it doesn't have your name on it." She remembered the soldier's response: "He smiled and said, 'You're one lucky nurse, Lieutenant!' "[26]

Miernicke's next destination was the operating room, where her team was scheduled to go on duty for a twelve- to fifteen-hour shift. The 750-bed 56th Evac and all other hospitals' more than 2,000 total beds on the beachhead were filled to overflowing; many patients awaiting surgery had been brought in during the midmorning hours. The men were members of the Second Battalion of either the 157th Infantry or the Sixth Armored Infantry, who had fought valiantly on the north shoulder of the final defensive line since 16 February when the major German assault started. By battle's end on 20 February, from Company I of the 157th Infantry five officers and ninety-one enlisted men were killed in battle. For those who were fortunate enough to reach the hospital, everything possible was being done to save their lives. "We had never seen such severe wounds as these boys had suffered," Miernicke recalled. The men had called in their own artillery when German forces were moving up the ravines that led to the caves where they had taken a final stand. Between German artillery shells and "friendly" fire, "scores of these brave infantry men suffered severe shell fragment wounds and required long and extensive surgery."[27]

While the OR and hospitals worked feverishly, General Lucas summoned three army nurses to the flagpole area of the 56th Evac and awarded each a Silver Star for "conspicuous gallantry in the face of enemy action." The first citation went to Lieutenant Mary Roberts, chief nurse of the operating room. She became the first woman in the history of the U.S. Army to receive the Silver Star. The two other recipients that day were Second Lieutenant Elaine A. Roe and Second Lieutenant Rita Rourke.

On 22 February, one month after the landing on Anzio, General Clark removed Major General Lucas as commander of the VI Corps. In that first month on the beachhead, German and Allied casualties each numbered almost 19,000. Allied troops had suffered approximately 2,000 killed, 8,500 wounded, and 8,500 missing in action. Together, the enemy and Allied forces had lost almost 40,000 soldiers in just thirty days.[28]

General Lucas was not shocked at his removal, but he did consider himself a scapegoat for a thus far failed operation that had been undermanned and undersupplied from its inception. Lucas was to serve as General Clark's deputy for three weeks and then return to the United States to take stateside command.

ON 23 FEBRUARY 1944, Major General Lucian K. Truscott Jr. commander of the Third Division, replaced Lucas as the commander of the VI Corps. Truscott was no newcomer to the Mediterranean theater. He had led his division in the campaigns in North Africa, Sicily, and southern Italy, and had the respect and admiration of his troops and American and Allied commanders.

Truscott brought a new style of command. One of his first changes was to move VI Corps Headquarters from the underground wine cellar in Nettuno to a location above ground. He met with commanders on the beachhead and helped work out a coordinated fire plan for Allied weapons on the beachhead and offshore naval guns. Truscott made frequent visits to troops living in foxholes along the final line of defense. Slowly but surely, the general feelings of desperation and depression on the beachhead began to change.

After inspecting the hospital area and speaking with staff and patients, Truscott ordered combat engineers to dig the hospital in and

U.S. Army engineers "digging in" the tents on Anzio, 1944 (U.S. Army Signal Corps)

make it as safe as possible from shrapnel and bomb fragments. "When General Truscott saw how we had to operate with no protection," Miernicke recalled, "he had the engineers dig deep ditches all around the operating-room tents and sandbag the outside walls high enough to be above our heads. The sides of the OR tents were pretty well protected, but if anything came from the top of the tent, you just had to hope it wouldn't hit anybody."[29]

Everyone knew that there was no protection against direct hits from either shells or bombs, but with the ditches in place, hospital staff felt considerably safer from bomb fragments and shrapnel. To add to their safety when traveling between tents, they either duck-walked or crawled on all fours. The sight of a nurse, doctor, or enlisted man crawling or duck-walking to the latrines or another tent was not at all uncommon.

On 26 February, the first U.S. Army blood bank in the Mediterranean theater opened in Naples and began to supply whole blood to the wounded troops of Cassino and the Anzio beachhead. Like the advent of penicillin, the arrival of whole blood into the operating tents of frontline hospitals was another giant step in military medicine. It was a step very slow in coming, however, due in part to bureaucratic and military log-jamming.

With tales of life and death on the Anzio beachhead making their rounds among VI Corps staff, people automatically divided themselves into "those who had served on Anzio" and "those who had not served on Anzio." Doctors and nurses who had not yet set foot on the beachhead began to think of themselves as "outsiders" or "uninitiated" when discussing Anzio in the presence of those who had lived and worked in the crucible that promised to be one of the bloodiest battlefields of World War II.

One doctor who would soon count himself among the "initiated" was Captain Richard V. Hauver of the 2nd Auxiliary Surgical Group. Hauver had graduated from Jefferson Medical College in Philadelphia in 1931, and practiced medicine and surgery in civilian life until he joined the U.S. Army Medical Corps in September 1941. Hauver left his home near Hagerstown, Maryland, for his first military assignment at Lawson General Army Hospital in Atlanta. Then he was assigned to the 2nd Auxiliary Surgical Group, which left Camp Kilmer, New Jersey, aboard HMS *Andes* for an unannounced duty station in a war zone. On 9 March 1943, Hauver disembarked at Oran in Algeria. Now, one year later, 3 March 1944, Hauver landed on the Anzio beachhead and was attached to the 93rd Evacuation Hospital.[30]

As March wore on, more and more shells and enemy planes flew over the hospital site. German bombers that used to come in mainly at night began making more appearances in broad daylight. Ack-ack and artillery shells flew over the tents almost continuously and staff became even more proficient at distinguishing the sounds of various shells. The "crying cat" sound of the 88mm shells, the low roaring of 170mm shells, and the screeching brake of metal-on-metal from shells fired by railroad guns, all became familiar to the men and women living and working on the beachhead. They also learned to predict from the shell's sound in flight whether it would fall on the hospital area or fly past the "protected" but vulnerable tents. They could even tell how all these sounds were affected by clear weather or low-lying clouds. The period from mid-February to mid-March 1944 became known as a period of near misses. But as March passed its midpoint, the near misses were gone and direct hits became the order of the day.

One struck at 0400 on 21 March when several shells, believed to be 88mms fired from a German tank, fell in an open field near the 15th Evac area. The shrapnel killed five patients and rewounded eleven at the site, and wounded an enlisted man at the 52nd Medical Battalion.

In the midst of all the bombing and shelling, medical administration staff had to begin to consider the coming malaria season. The beachhead was located in the middle of a breeding area for malaria-carrying mosquitoes. When plans had been made to land at Anzio in winter, no one thought American and Allied troops would still be on the beachhead by spring. As it became obvious that they would still be there for the malaria season, medical planners put the antimalaria program into effect. Responsibility for malaria control was placed squarely with each battalion and company of the divisions. About 2,011 officers and enlisted men underwent training, with at least six hours of class instruction, in the control of mosquito-breeding areas and the use of protective measures and clothing.

On 26 March, suppressive therapy with the drug Atabrine began. Planners hoped that the adverse effects that accompanied the first use of Atabrine in North Africa and Sicily in 1943 would not be repeated. Doctors had learned more about dosages, and instead of two Atabrine tablets taken once a week, it was now a half-tablet daily for the first seven days, then one tablet a day thereafter. Supervision rested with the antimalaria control officer in each unit. Troops did tolerate this new medicine regimen, and the debilitating side effects of diarrhea, nausea, vomiting, and loss of appetite were minimized or eliminated.

In late March, staff at VI Corps Headquarters considered how they would increase the safety of the hospital compound, including the possibility of moving it to a different site. But reconnaissance studies had shown there was no safer place on the beachhead. The only viable option was to "dig in" even more effectively. In order to make this a little easier, and to increase the number of beds available on the beachhead to 3,500, the 94th Evacuation Hospital and the 402nd Collecting Company were brought to the beachhead on 28 March. At the same time, the Thirty-fourth Division of the Fifth Army came to relieve the Third Division, whose men had seen sixty-seven days of continuous frontline duty.

The 94th Evacuation Hospital set up its four hundred beds east of the hospital site, separated from the 93rd Evac by a deep ditch. On 29 March, the 94th Evac opened for admissions and took in most new cases in order to give the other hospitals some relief while the digging-in process was carried out.

At 2100 that same night, a long and heavy German air raid occurred over the harbor and beachhead area. Second Aux Surgeon Hauver and others not on duty hurried to the OR and wards to see if they were needed. In the 93rd Evac's OR tent, Captain Howard B. Shorbe was the only surgeon busy with a patient, and as Hauver quickened his pace toward the tent, a loud explosion and strong concussion wave hit the area. Hauver immediately fell to the ground and crawled to nearby sand-bags for safety. Several more explosions occurred nearby and flames could be seen coming from the roofs of tents of the 93rd Evac and the nearby 56th. A German plane was dropping large fragmentation-incendiary bombs that not only sent flak flying but also sprayed streams of highly flammable phosphorus that, in the heat of the explosions, ignited fires. "I run to Ward 14," recorded Hauver in his diary, "where [a] bomb has demolished and set fire to it. It is a shambles with live and dead patients lying all around and trying to get out." Hauver and others worked to put the fire out, but secondary explosions spewed phosphorous all over, which covered the would-be rescuers. Luckily, no one was injured, and when the fire was extinguished, Hauver ran to the OR tent. Captain Shorbe had been wounded; "small foreign body in abdominal wall," Hauver's diary entry reads. "One patient and one ward boy dead. Many injured."[31]

At the same time the 93rd was hit, three of the six fragmentation-incendiary bombs fell on the 56th Evac. One landed outside Surgical Ward 8; one hit directly in the center of the fifty-foot Geneva Red Cross marker near Ward 26; and the third hit the officers' area. When staff not on duty got out of their foxholes, they found that the bombs were still splattering and spraying fire. Three pyramidal and three small wall tents had been leveled. Personal belongings, hospital forms, and letters were strewn everywhere, entangled with shattered tent poles and torn canvas. The 56th Evac fire crews used sand to extinguish the flames. All told, four patients were killed and nineteen wounded; and twenty hospital staff were wounded, including two nurses. First Lieutenant Helen McCullough, a nurse, suffered a torn right lung and sucking chest wound and was evacuated to the 300th General Hospital in Naples on 3 April. Equipment damaged included forty-two tents.

The next day, 30 March, the 39th Engineers began digging in the hospital tents. They excavated approximately three feet of dirt in each tent, piled it outside the canvas walls to create revetments, then reinforced the revetments with chicken wire and sandbags. In addition to these improvements, the OR tent was reinforced with a roof of thick mahogany wood.

The engineers were interrupted frequently by German air raids and shelling. The entire hospital area was not completely dug in until after the hospitals had left the beachhead.

Even when dug in and reinforced, the compound continued to be a treacherous site for both patients and personnel. Most of the staff slept in cramped conditions in their foxholes when they could sleep at all. Air raids and shelling that used to come at predictable hours in the early days of the beachhead now occurred at any hour of the day or night. Nurses spent much of their time calming the fears of patients who were convinced that life on the front lines was safer than life in the Anzio hospital area. While doctors, nurses, and corpsmen may have agreed, they never let on how much they themselves wished to get off the beachhead.

After two months of combat, hospitals began to receive greater numbers of soldiers suffering from what was then called "battle fatigue"— now known as post-traumatic stress disorder. Psychiatric trauma patients could not be treated in a frontline hospital compound so close to the combat conditions that had psychologically wounded them. Previous studies conducted by army psychiatrist Captain Frederick R. Hanson in 1943 near Maknassy, Tunisia, indicated that neuropsychiatric patients had to be evacuated away from the front in order to avoid being returned to their units, which they surely would be if they were treated close to the front lines. To protect patients from further psychological damage, and to hasten their return to duty, Hanson developed a treatment protocol: heavy sedation would be administered to the traumatized soldier at the clearing station; he would then be transferred to an evacuation hospital, where the sedation was continued for three days. During this time, patients were to be awakened only for food and toileting. The vast majority of these patients would then be evacuated to hospitals farther to the rear.

Between 9 September and December 1943, 2,749 cases of battle fatigue were treated; only 26 percent returned to duty. The remaining 74 percent of these patients were evacuated out of the combat zone. These men would be discharged from the army on a "Section 8"—the psychiatric clause stating reasons for discharge from the armed forces. Despite the perils of combat, the majority of American soldiers preferred physical wounds to battle fatigue. At Anzio and Cassino, the number of neuropsychiatric patients rose sharply. Exposed to almost constant bombing, shelling, and combat, 4,786 cases occurred at Anzio and Cassino between

January and April 1944. The peak was reached during February, when 1,910 cases of battle fatigue occurred in troops of the Fifth Army engaged at Anzio and Cassino.[32]

Psychiatric casualties, however, were not limited to frontline combat soldiers. Occasionally, hospital staff also fell victim to the anxiety and stress of living under combat conditions. Lieutenant Miernicke remembered witnessing the mental breakdown of one doctor. It occurred during one of the daily, near-routine German shellings; shells had been falling near the hospital for about thirty minutes and were still landing every minute or so around the site. Miernicke, on duty in the OR tent, left to go to the adjacent supply tent for an item that was needed immediately. "As I walked into the supply tent," she recalled, "I saw one of the hospital's surgeons cowering in a corner of the tent. He was sitting on the floor in a modified fetal position and he was dressed in a surgical gown and gloves. He was seated on a metal bedpan and had placed a bedpan on his head. He was hugging his shoulders and had a bedpan over each elbow. His eyes were wide open and staring into space. I was so shocked and so moved by his condition that I didn't say a word. I took what I had come for and returned to the OR. Several days later that surgeon was evacuated from the beachhead."[33]

On another occasion involving the possible evacuation of a nurse for psychiatric problems, Miernicke intervened on the nurse's behalf. Miernicke felt that an undiagnosed physical illness, rather than a psychiatric disorder, could be the underlying cause for her unorthodox behavior. When Colonel Forsee visited the 56th Evacuation Hospital, Miernicke stopped him outside the OR tent and told him of her concern. "After I expressed my thoughts," Miernicke remembered, "Colonel Forsee said he had heard about the nurse and was planning to evacuate her on a Section 8. I said, 'Oh no, you can't do that without having her examined for a physical cause for her behavior. I think she may be physically ill.' " Colonel Forsee listened and had the nurse sent to an army hospital in Naples for a physical. The medical review revealed that the patient was severely anemic. After treatment, she was able to return to her duties as a 2nd Aux nurse.[34]

In the last days of March, Colonel Rollin L. Bauchspies, VI Corps surgeon, visited the officers' mess tent at the 56th Evac. During that visit, Bauchspies observed that "the usual cheerful spirit and feeling of physical well-being of the personnel . . . were definitely diminished." He noticed that the staff wore "haggard and weary expressions on their faces or had no expressions at all." Men and women appeared listless and there was no laughter or joking between staff. In the chow line, they took very little food, and at their tables, they pushed it around on their plates but ate very little. There was no longer the usual chatter that had been ever present in mess tents during the early days on the beachhead, and this behavior was becoming more and more common.[35]

Bauchspies recommended to General Joseph I. Martin, the Fifth Army surgeon, that the 56th and 93rd Evacuation Hospitals be replaced on the beachhead as soon as possible. Bauchspies did not discuss his request with individual hospital commanders since he knew through almost daily contact that each would say he and his personnel were "ready and willing to stick it out."[36]

On 3 April, the 56th Evac personnel were playing a baseball game when German shells landed on the ball field. Everyone naturally "hit the ground" and watched as a shell struck the patients' mess kitchen. The blast killed Private Estes, a well-liked soldier who brought sandwiches and coffee to the OR tent every morning around 0300.

Three days later, enemy shells again fell in the hospital area. A direct hit destroyed the Post Exchange tent at the 56th, while another direct hit struck the enlisted men's area, killing one man and wounding a second.

Minutes before the bombing, Miernicke and her team had left the OR to get some rest. She and her tentmate, Esther Henshaw, the team's anesthetist, were walking toward their tent when a German incendiary bomb dropped just outside their canvas home. "We ran to the tent," Miernicke said, "and jumped into our foxhole for cover. Another bomb fell and the sides of the foxhole collapsed on top of us. We were coughing up dust and dirt when the tent pole snapped and it and the canvas fell on top of us." Miernicke could hear Major Howard Bos, their team surgeon, screaming: " 'Where are the girls? Where's Frenchie? Frenchie?' " Miernicke and Henshaw tried to call back, but their mouths were full of dirt and dust. The next thing they heard was several people digging through the rubble and dirt. "We were so glad," Miernicke recalled, "when they reached us that we almost flew out of that hole. . . . That was one close call. I can honestly say that being buried alive is no fun."[37]

On Easter morning, 9 April 1944, the 38th Evacuation Hospital arrived at Anzio to exchange places with the 56th Evac. In only a few hours, the staff of the 56th had turned over all responsibility for patients and equipment to the 38th Evac and were aboard an LST headed for the port of Naples. The 56th was to take over the 38th's former hospital site at Nocelleto, set up to support troops at Cassino. That night was the first in more than two months that 56th Evac staff would sleep without having to jump into a foxhole, or go to the aid of wounded colleagues or re-wounded patients.

Word reached the 93rd Evac Hospital that it, too, would be leaving Anzio in a matter of days. But for the 2nd Auxiliary Surgical Group teams assigned to the 56th and 93rd Evac Hospitals at Anzio, the story was different. They were reassigned to other hospitals on the Anzio beachhead. Miernicke, Major Hauver, and all other 2nd Aux members were reassigned to the newly arriving hospitals and stayed in the same hospital tents. Although the 2nd Aux team members had been through the same tragedies as the members of the 56th and 93rd Evac Hospitals, their expertise could not be replaced. They would continue to work under fire at Anzio until the Allied troops made the breakthrough—then follow them to Rome, and beyond.

ON 12 APRIL, Glant was evacuated from the 300th General Hospital in Naples to the 43rd General Hospital in North Africa. He made the trip on the U.S. Army hospital ship *Seminole* and arrived at the 43rd General three days later. The hospital was set up in Quonset huts and Glant was placed in an orthopedic ward. "I had a nurse I really liked," Glant recalled. "Her name was Lieutenant Tillie and she was a real nice lady. She buzzed around the ward singing and making all the patients feel good. She was always singing, 'I'm going back to where I came from/ Where the honeysuckle smells so sweet it darn near makes you cry.' She'd always sing that."[38]

Glant found himself next to a young soldier called Alfred Billings-worth who was a former divinity student. Billingsworth taught Glant and a young Italian ward boy who spoke almost no English how to play chess. Glant remembered that Billingsworth "got tickled at the two of us playing chess. All we knew were the moves, but somehow we managed to communicate."[39]

While he was at the 43rd General Hospital, Glant's spica cast on his leg was removed and replaced with a long leg cast. "The reason they changed the cast," Glant recalled, "was that I was complaining about severe pain in my heel and asking for pain pills. My heel was really killing me. Well, when they removed the cast from my heel, the skin on my heel came off with it. I had a bad pressure sore that went all the way to the bone."[40]

About a week later, one of the ambulatory patients, a large, red-haired man who had been a professional ice skater in civilian life and had lost one of his legs in combat, decided to take Glant for a ride in his wheelchair. The two went visiting around the Quonset huts but got bogged down in the rocks and gravel between the metal buildings. They finally flagged down some help, were retrieved from the rocks, and returned safely to their own ward.

AT 1000 on 16 April, the 11th Evacuation Hospital arrived on Anzio to relieve the 93rd Evac. By 1130, the 93rd was aboard an LST and headed for Naples and Casanova, thirty-five miles outside Naples and the former site of the 11th Evac. With hospital tents already set up and patients waiting, the 93rd would step in to take over the treatment of soldiers from the battle for Cassino. Evelyn Anderson recorded in the 93rd Evacuation Hospital nursing report: "It was a beautiful sunny day and just before we started on our journey down 'Purple Heart Highway,' Highway 6, a few shells landed nearby. 1130 found us a tired group of nurses aboard an LST, which would carry us away from the 'Dante's Inferno' that had been ours. . . . It was with pleasure that we rode through the streets of Naples. It seemed like heaven after our experiences." Staff of the 93rd again would enjoy nights with movies instead of blackouts, and days of swimming at the nearby beaches without fear of being strafed, shelled, or bombed.[41]

For Vera Sheaffer, the move from Anzio was a double relief. Her ward master, Private Joe R. Perez, had died during the bombing of 29 March while on duty in the ward they shared. Then surgeons diagnosed Vera with appendicitis. She had witnessed the death of her tentmate, Decima McLaughlin, six months earlier from what turned out to be acute appendicitis. Nevertheless, the doctors wanted to wait until the hospital was ordered off Anzio before performing the appendectomy on Sheaffer. Although she was not in acute pain, Sheaffer was sore and anxious. After the 93rd had moved to Casanova and about three weeks after her symptoms had first appeared, the surgery was successfully completed.

Colonel Bauchspies had considered replacing the 33rd Field Hospital and the 52nd Medical Battalion also. Both units had spent more than sixty days on the beachhead and were badly in need of rest. However, because these units were actually assigned to VI Corps, they were left in place to carry out their primary objective of caring for the soldiers of that corps.

In mid-April, after three months of intensive fighting, Allied troops were still unable to advance to Rome. The Fifth Army was stalled in two places: divisions were penned in on the Anzio beachhead, while other divisions was unable to break through the Gustav Line at Cassino. Plans for the Allied invasion of France—Operation Overload and Dragoon—had already been made. But these plans could not proceed without the U.S. Army first being in position in Rome.

CHAPTER TEN

Breakout and Pursuit

THE U.S. ARMY ENTERS ROME

15 May–5 June 1944

It is my opinion that combat nurses, frontline nurses, should be rotated every 18 months, because they are under constant grind and pressure and they are worked every minute. These girls really look old, they have aged, and many now have white hair. It has been a hard campaign, and they are right up there under fire and hardship.

—Lt. Col. Bernice Wilbur, director of nursing,
Mediterranean Theater of Operations, U.S. Army

DURING THE FIRST WEEK in April 1944, General George C. Marshall, Chief of Staff of the U.S. Army, informed General Mark Clark that Clark was to fly to Washington, D.C., for a top-secret military meeting to discuss the Fifth Army's situation on Anzio. Marshall was quick to point out that the Fifth Army needed to be in Rome before the fast-approaching Allied invasion of France, scheduled—depending on weather conditions—for a window opening that ran from 31 May to 7 June.

At 0300 on 11 April, General Clark landed under cover of darkness outside Washington and was greeted by Marshall. He was quickly ushered away to a waiting car, where Mrs. Clark greeted her husband. Secrecy would not permit Clark to go to his own home, so he was whisked off to General Marshall's home in nearby Fort Myers, Virginia.

The next morning, Clark was permitted to write a letter to his mother, who lived in D.C. The letter was delivered by special messenger.

It told Clark's mother "to put on her hat" and meet him and his wife at a military airport outside the District. Mrs. Clark followed orders, and in a matter of hours, she was on a plane with her son and daughter-in-law headed for White Sulphur Springs, West Virginia. The U.S. Army had taken over the Greenbrier Hotel and turned it into the U.S. Army Ashford General Hospital. The hospital had several guest cottages; Clark was settled into one for several days of rest and relaxation.[1]

As it happened, President Roosevelt was spending a few days at the estate of Bernard Baruch, a well-known multimillionaire businessman, in South Carolina, and after a couple of days of rest Clark was flown to Baruch's estate to discuss Fifth Army plans with the president. FDR offered several suggestions and surprised Clark with his knowledge of what was going on at Anzio and Cassino. It was agreed that Rome had to be taken before the invasion of France; such a decisive victory in Italy, the Allies believed, would persuade Turkey to defect from the Axis and join the Allies for the duration of the war.

The die was cast: the push from Anzio and Cassino to Rome was planned to start before the last week of May. It was code-named "Operation Buffalo."

BEFORE CLARK returned to Italy, Mrs. Marshall asked him to deliver letters and packages to her two sons who were serving with Clark's troops in the Cassino area. The two young men, General Marshall's stepsons, had been fighting on the front lines for months, and Clark was only too happy to carry out her request.

Not all soldiers were so fortunate as to have their letters and packages carried out in person. When Lieutenant Miernicke's sister sent her a birthday cake for her birthday on 25 April, it took longer than she had hoped to reach Miernicke at the front. The package was delivered in the evening: it was clearly a birthday cake, but in the dim light of her tent not much more could be determined. Frenchie suggested they wait until morning to cut the cake, but her tentmate, Esther Henshaw, insisted on eating a piece there and then. Miernicke gave her permission and then Henshaw cut a large slice and began to eat. "It's a marble cake and it's delicious," Miernicke remembered Henshaw saying as she wolfed it down. The next morning, both women saw the situation clearly. "It wasn't a marble cake at all," Miernicke remembered. "The cake was covered and filled with green mold. I wasn't about to eat any of it." It did, however, arrive packed in popcorn. Despite the fact that the popcorn was stale from its long trip, Miernicke decided it had some promise. "I heated the popcorn in a plasma can on our tent stove and we ate it gratefully. Even stale, it tasted pretty good," she remembered.[2]

MUCH OF APRIL 1944 on the front lines at Anzio continued in a stalemate. Germans and Allies watched each other's positions from observation posts and with reconnaissance patrols, but there was little if any exchange of territory. The German army was reinforcing its defensive positions, while American and Allied troops were preparing for their final push on Rome.

On 1 May 1944, Clark met with his senior officers at Caserta to work out any last-minute problems with the overall plan to take Monte Cassino, break through to the Liri Valley, merge with American and Allied troops at Anzio, and begin the final attack to capture Rome. On 5 May, Field Marshal Sir Harold Alexander issued Operation Order No. 1, Allied Armies in Italy, for the drive through the Gustav Line to Rome, and the pursuit of the enemy to the Rimini-Pisa line north of the Eternal City.

Lt. Gen. Mark Clark awarding the Bronze Star to Lt. Frances "Frenchie" Miernicke, 1944 (Courtesy of Maj. Frances Miernicke Plenert, ANC [Ret.])

On 10 May, Clark awarded the Bronze Star to Lieutenant Frances "Frenchie" Miernicke. She was cited "for heroic achievement in action on 12 February 1944 . . . during an enemy bombing . . . when Lt. Miernicke remained at her post of duty in the operating room, even though considerable flak was falling throughout the hospital, many fragments piercing the operating tents. . . ."[3]

AT 2300 on 11 May, the drive to Rome opened with a tremendous artillery barrage at Cassino and Anzio. Approximately one thousand American and Allied artillery weapons began firing simultaneously at specific targets along the Gustav Line. For hours, a rain of Allied steel fell on German headquarters, command posts, and communication centers from Cassino to the west coast. In the first twenty-four hours of the attack, Allied guns fired 173,941 shells at German targets. Added to this heavy barrage, the U.S. and Allied air forces began flying the first of more than fifteen hundred sorties over roads and trails where the enemy was most likely to try to mass troops and reinforcements. The Allied air raids demolished the German Tenth Army Headquarters and General Albert Kesselring's headquarters. The Germans were not only surprised by the force of the attack, they were rocked by the speed with which it fell on key command positions. On the night of 13–14 May, German forces withdrew to new defensive positions in a delaying action designed to give their troops time to escape the massive assault.

Despite German efforts, by 17 May, U.S. and Allied troops had captured more than three thousand prisoners of war. On 18 May, Monte Cassino fell to Allied troops and the route through the Liri Valley to Rome was finally open. That same day, Clark ordered the Thirty-sixth Division, which had been held in reserve, to move to the Anzio beachhead in preparation for a concentrated push toward Rome.

On 19 May, the II Corps captured an important highway junction at Itri. On 20 May, it took Fondi and turned southwest toward Terracina. At Terracina, Highway 7 ran straight across the Pontine Marshes to Asterna, the Alban Hills, and Rome.

ON 23 MAY, Private Berchard "Junior" Glant was waiting in Battle Creek, Michigan, for the first visit with his parents after his long journey home. Glant had been evacuated on 4 May to the United States by way of the U.S. Army hospital ship *Acadia*. Patients aboard the *Acadia* were put in bunk beds and Glant had been assigned to a bottom bunk. There was not much space, but Glant discovered that when he held on to the top bunk just right and swung one leg over the side of his lower bunk, he could pull himself up and stand on one leg. "It might not sound like much," Glant said, "but it was a real big thing to me. I could actually stand on my own. It gave me all kind of hope for the future."[4]

After ten days at sea, the *Acadia* docked in Charleston, South Carolina, on 14 May. Glant was admitted to the army's Starke General Hospital for five days, and during that time the army arranged for each newly arriving patient to call home. "My mother was real excited when she heard my voice," Glant recalled. "I wasn't too excited, but she was real excited about having me home."[5]

On 19 May, Glant and other patients were taken by ambulance to a hospital train that would be their home for two days. "We had a whole train full of us guys," Glant remembered. "We had nurses and doctors just like in a hospital. Most of us were getting well enough by then that we could horse around and give everybody a bad time. Everybody wanted a back rub and all that stuff. Before, you were too sick and didn't care whether you got anything or not. We were all beginning to get a little life."[6]

Glant was admitted to the Percy Jones General Army Hospital in Battle Creek, Michigan. The hospital had an authorized bed capacity of 3,414 and specialized in the areas of neurology, amputations, neurosurgery, and deep X-ray therapy. The building had been reconverted to army use from a civilian TB sanitarium.

Glant had met up with Corporal Pete Bentley and Sergeant Danny Polonski at the 300th General Hospital in Naples. Bentley, a former corpsman from the Anzio beachhead, lost both legs when the Germans bombed the beachhead in February 1944. Polonski, who had been with the Third Division, lost his right arm and right leg when he was hit by a shell on the beachhead. The three severely wounded soldiers had gradually formed strong and deepening friendships as they traveled together on the long journey to Battle Creek, the closest army hospital to their homes. Twenty-three-year-old Polonski was from Cleveland and twenty-four-year-old Bentley grew up in the Minneapolis–St. Paul area.

The three men made a deal: they agreed that none of them would have to be alone with visitors, whether family or friends. The agreement offered each soldier the protection of "someone who really understood what it was like to be an amputee."[7]

When Glant's parents and hometown girlfriend arrived at Percy Jones, they found a long line waiting to be cleared to visit their relatives and friends. Glant remembered that first visit. "My mom just broke the line and came running in. Nobody said a word or tried to stop her." She hugged, kissed, and talked with her son in his hospital room while they waited for his dad and girlfriend to get through the line. Then the Glants decided to take their son for a ride around the hospital. "My father had just started pushing my wheelchair when I said, 'Hey, somebody push these other two guys.' So my mom pushed Danny and my old girlfriend pushed Pete."[8]

FROM 22 JANUARY to 22 May 1944, U.S. Army hospitals on the beach-head had cared for a total of 33,128 patients: 10,809 wounded in battle,

A night out from the Percy Jones General Army Hospital, Battle Creek, Michigan, 1944. Left to right: *"Whitey," corpsman on Glant's hospital ward; Dan Polonski; photographer; Junior Glant; "Whitey's" girlfriend; and John Serrin* (Courtesy of Berchard L. Glant)

4,245 nonbattle injuries, 18,074 ill from diseases, plus an unknown number of civilians. The British hospitals had treated a total of 14,700 troops.[9]

Finally, on 23 May, four months and one day since landing on Anzio, American and Allied troops launched Operation Buffalo—the breakout from the Anzio beachhead and the push to Rome. The first objective of the VI Corps at Anzio was to capture Valmontone, where the Allies could cut off Highway 6 to the northward-fleeing Germans and block them from entering the Sacco Valley. The German Tenth Army would then be trapped between Valmontone and Cassino.

During the long months the Allies spent on the Anzio beachhead, the GIs were treated to German propaganda via the radioed broadcasts of "Axis Sally," Germany's answer to Japan's "Tokyo Rose" radio broadcasts. These broadcasts continued during Operation Buffalo. One evening, when Private First Class Billie Stone of the 39th Combat Engineers and his unit were preparing to go behind enemy lines to blow up a church in whose belfry and steeple German soldiers had set up an observation post, Stone and his fellow GIs heard "Axis Sally" telling the Americans that the Germans knew they were coming and would be ready and waiting for them.

This was not the first time "Axis Sally" and the Germans seemed to have foreknowledge of American troop movements; Stone and his unit had been in several previous situations when the Germans just seemed to be lying in wait for the Americans to arrive. The ambush that "Darby's Rangers" had walked into three months earlier at the Mussolini Canal, which had cost the Rangers seven hundred lives, had been one such prescient piece of planning by the enemy.

GIs wondered where "Axis Sally" got her information. As Stone and the 39th Combat Engineers fought their way out of the Anzio beachhead area, they captured a German military hospital and took about fifteen prisoners with them as they moved forward. The first German bivouac area the 39th Combat Engineers reached was at a crossroads, and presented a gruesome sight. American artillery had caught the German forces as they were trying to withdraw: German troops and vehicles were bunched along the roads where American artillery shells had zeroed in on them. Wrecked and destroyed equipment was scattered everywhere, along with the burned and torn bodies of German soldiers.

The engineers set up in the wrecked German campsite for the night. The following morning, the 39th awakened to German artillery shelling. "Everybody in the unit was mad about the shelling of our troops and were talking pretty bad about the Germans," Stone recalled. "We had found some chocolate in the old German mess area at the site, but were afraid to eat it since the Germans were known for poisoning or booby-trapping what they left behind." Stone and his unit decided to get the German POWs to eat some of the candy to see if it were free of poison. "We had to kinda talk ugly to them to get them to eat any of the candy. While this was going on, one of our men went berserk. He started shooting at us with his rifle and shouting in German. That's when we discovered that he was a German spy planted in our outfit. He'd been with us from the beginning and we figured that some of the ambushes our people—especially the Rangers at the Mussolini Canal—walked into had something to do with him."[10]

The men of the 39th Combat Engineers were shocked and furious at the idea that this man they had treated like a buddy was an infiltrator and had been betraying them to the enemy all along. "The guy's buddy was a big ole Irishman," Stone recalled, "as big as Junior and me put together—about 6 foot 2 inches and built like a wrestler. He was the first one who got to this spy. He knocked the guy unconscious and was going to beat him to death if we didn't pull him off. And believe me, some of the guys didn't want to stop him." The German spy was interrogated by Army Intelligence and sent off to prison. "They didn't execute him," Stone remembered. "Just kept him in prison for a long time. Anyway, none of the Germans we forced to eat the chocolate got sick, so we ate the rest later."[11]

Casualties on 23 and 24 May were extremely heavy. Captain Richard Hauver and his 2nd Aux team, assigned to the 94th Evac with its staff of 40 officers, 40 nurses, and 240 enlisted men, worked twelve hours straight through the night, from 2000 to 0800, operating on 8 seriously wounded patients. Hauver returned to the OR after only six hours of rest at 1400 on the 24th and worked fourteen hours straight, treating 20 patients, including 4 amputations, before taking a break at 0400 the next morning. That night, Major Hauver, Lieutenant Mary A. Matlock, Lieutenant Anne K. Brix, and the rest of his team operated on 17 patients—all German POWs. By 26 May, four 2nd Aux teams—Hauver's and three others: 8 physicians, 4 nurses, and 4 surgical technicians—at the 400-bed 94th Evac were operating on an average of 125 patients a day. Hauver noted in his diary that all the other hospitals were just as busy. On 27 May, he wrote: "Never have been so tired even after a day's sleep. Two very hard belly cases and a lot of other stuff. Still they come. Six miles from

Rome. . . . Twelve to fourteen hours daily. . . . Three field and eight evacuation hospitals now here with one more evac coming."[12]

THE TERRAIN SOUTH of the Liri Valley and its Sacco River north of Cassino was rugged and mountainous, making medical support for Allied troops there extremely difficult. Medical supplies were carried into the area by jeeps, mules, hand-carries, and sometimes by parachute drops from small planes. Casualties had to be carried out by mules, jeeps, and hand-carries that stretched for miles. In several cases, it was deemed more advantageous to keep casualties at forward aid stations until advancing troops secured the nearby roads. This way, medical personnel hoped to avoid the long litter journeys that were arduous and took their toll on patients and medical personnel alike.

The 310th and 313th Medical Battalions that were organic to the Eighty-fifth and Eighty-eighth Divisions each received an assignment of one hundred extra litter bearers before the drive began, but that number soon proved inadequate, and both medical battalions drew additional bearers from service and headquarters' troops. The Eighty-fifth Division had approximately seven hundred litter bearers above its normal complement, and the Eighty-eighth Division had almost as many assigned to it.

Two of the six surviving Darby's Rangers attached themselves to the evac hospitals at the Cassino front. They worked with the litter bearers to evacuate casualties in the Cassino area. "They were wonderful," Frenchie Miernicke remembered. "They helped the medics bring in the wounded. Because the mountain slopes were so rocky, they brought the casualties down on mules."[13]

The Allies were not the only ones to use mules and horses to carry the wounded back to evacuation hospitals, and to transport supplies to the front lines. Due to a shortage of gasoline, German forces also used horses and mules, not only to transport casualties but to move large guns and supplies from one defensive position to another.

Like soldiers and hospital staff in the area, many mules and horses were wounded by shells, land mines, small-arms fire, or shrapnel. And like wounded soldiers and hospital staff, wounded animals needed medical care. By April 1944, the number of mules and horses being used and cared for in the area of the Fifth Army rose from 986 horses and 4,136

Mule train used to deliver supplies to front lines and help evacuate the wounded to rear hospitals in Italy (U.S. Army Signal Corps)

mules in January 1944 to 2,023 horses and 110,433 mules. During the four months between January and April 1944, 608 U.S. and Italian animals were admitted to the U.S. Army 17th Veterinary Evacuation Hospital and the French Veterinary Hospital that cared mainly for animals assigned to the French Expeditionary Corps, which had its own facilities to treat animal casualties.[14]

Italian veterinarian hospitals were also used. When the Italians surrendered to the Allies in September 1943, the German army moved quickly to destroy any horses and mules not needed by German forces. On Sardinia, about 185 miles northwest of Sicily, prompt action by Italian troops who were garrisoned on the island saved 5,000 mules, 1,500 horses, 3,000 saddles, and thousands of metal shoes from destruction by German soldiers. These animals went on to serve in Italy and saved many American and Allied lives by transporting casualties to medical help.[15]

ON 25 MAY 1944, Unit A of the 33rd Field Hospital moved out of the Anzio beachhead in support of the Third Division. Two days later, Units

B and C also left the beachhead to support advancing American and Allied troops.

Support also came from Casanova, where the 93rd Evacuation Hospital had cared for 1,087 patients since April. On 26 May, the 93rd Evac was ordered to Fondi to help treat casualties on the rapidly advancing front lines; and the Third Division Clearing Station reinforced with Unit A of the 33rd Field Hospital set up south of Cori and began accepting casualties.

By 27 May, Highway 7 was the main axis for the Eighty-fifth and Eighty-eighth Divisions, and medical installations tended to be located along this highway. Once the Gustav Line was broken, troops and medical support moved more quickly, but a platoon of the 11th Field Hospital always remained behind to care for nontransportable patients. As the Eighty-eighth Division cut across roadless mountains between 24 and 27 May to Priverno, litter carries ranged up to fourteen miles between the advancing front lines and the rear at Fondi.

On 29 May, units of the 19th Field Hospital were assigned to clearing stations of the Third, Eighty-fifth, and Eighty-eighth Divisions. Traveling north toward Rome, combat troops and hospitals were confronted by flooded fields and seas of mud caused by deliberate German flooding designed to slow down the pursuing American and Allied troops.

The next day, despite the water and mud, Units B and C of the 33rd Field Hospital set up near the Thirty-fourth Division Clearing Station south of Velletri and began accepting wounded.

The final push toward Rome began on 1 June 1944, with major moves by the Third and Thirty-sixth Divisions. During the day of 1 June, the Third Division took Valmontone and cut Highway 6. That same day, the Thirty-sixth penetrated the eastern slopes of the Alban Hills without encountering any serious opposition. By the evening, the Thirty-sixth Division held commanding positions above Velletri and German positions inside the town were no longer tenable.

On the morning of 4 June, American troops of the Thirty-sixth Division and the First Armored Division reached the outskirts of Rome. That afternoon, they entered the city with uneven resistance from the German rear guard that remained behind to slow down the American/Allied pursuit of German forces. Close-in and hand-to-hand combat took place at various locations around the city. By nightfall, all German troops had cleared out of the area south of the Tiber River from the junction of the

Tiber and Aniene rivers above Rome, to the sea. Rome was in American and Allied hands.

Daylight south of Rome was only two hours old on 5 June when Richard Hauver, Mary Matlock, Anne Brix, and the 94th Evac personnel climbed aboard trucks and began their long-awaited trip to the Eternal City. When the convoy wound its way through the streets of Anzio, the overriding feeling for many was sadness. Shells and bombs had turned the once beautiful resort city into slag heaps of brick, stone, wood, and mud. Mountains of rubble were everywhere, and mixed in with the bricks and mortar were the remnants of civilian life on the beachhead before the war came to Anzio.

As the convoy left the town, it followed Highway 7—the old Appian Way. The convoy passed through flattened towns and alongside disjointed railroad tracks that lay in two-foot lengths of twisted metal leading nowhere. Trees were tossed here and there; roads were pockmarked with bomb and shell craters; and torn and burned-out tanks and vehicles were scattered over the desolate landscape. Foxholes with pieces of blood-stained clothing and discarded equipment littered the fields as far as the eye could see, but the ravages of war went far beyond that. "No bodies seen but there is odor of dead and decaying flesh at places," Hauver described the trip in his diary, "probably animals (hope so). Lines of areas that are cleared of mines, piles of mines along the road and endless streams of army vehicles going in both directions plus civilians with push carts and donkeys going south and begging for food and cigarettes." After four and a half months of living in Hell's Half-Acre, the Allies approached Italy's capital city as liberators, but it was clear victory came at a high price.[16]

On 5 June, American combat troops and hospital personnel, including the convoy of the 94th Evac, officially entered the Italian capital city as victors. They were the first army to conquer Rome from the south in fifteen centuries. After months in the fields in water-filled foxholes and tents riddled by shrapnel, victorious Americans marched along Rome's ancient streets, past the ruins of the historic Colosseum where, centuries earlier, Romans had thrown Christians to the lions. Amazingly, the streets were untouched by the ravages of World War II; there were no piles of rubble, crater-pocked streets, burned-out tanks and vehicles, no bloodstained clothing, no odor of death. Troops and hospital personnel marveled at the absence of the signs of war.

American soldiers and army nurses being welcomed to Rome. The Colosseum is in the background, right (Courtesy of Maj. Frances Miernicke Plenert, ANC [Ret.])

Italian civilians wearing their Sunday best lined the streets, cheering the American forces, throwing flowers in their path, offering them bottles of wine, hugging and kissing the American liberators as they moved slowly toward the heart of the capital and beyond, where they would set up bivouac areas and hospitals to care for newly wounded as the pursuit of the German army continued north toward the Arno River. Lieutenants Matlock and Brix riding with their 2nd Aux teams were swept up in the welcome along with the men.

From the time of the Anzio landing on 22 January 1944 to the capture of Rome on 4 June 1944, the VI Corps had suffered over 29,200 combat casualties: 4,400 killed; 18,000 wounded; 6,800 POWs or missing; and 37,000 noncombat casualties. Included among these dead and wounded were men and women of the Army Medical Department: 92 killed, including 6 nurses; 387 wounded; 19 captured; and 60 missing in action. A total of 558.[17]

The advances in combat medicine—improvements in battlefield surgical techniques; better management of shock; the introduction of penicillin and whole blood, to name only a few—were hard-won in Tunisia, Sicily, Salerno, Cassino, and Anzio. They came at a high cost and often too late for many of the casualties suffered there. But the knowledge and experience gained by veteran medical personnel would be passed on to rookie doctors, nurses, and corpsmen who were training in England for the next planned Allied offensive in the European theater soon to be launched: Operation Overlord, the invasion of Normandy.

PART THREE

The Liberation of France

On 6 June 1944, the invasion of Normandy was launched. Approximately 150,000 Allied troops stormed beaches on the northern coast of France. Hundreds of thousands of reinforcements followed. In June, July, and August, the Allies routed the Germans from France and chased them to the German border. A second invasion in Southern France landed 150,000 troops on the shores of the French Riviera on 15 August. Driving north, these troops consolidated the Allied drive to the German border. Paris was liberated on 25 August 1944.

By the end of August, 35,000 medical personnel, including 6,640 nurses, were ashore in Europe, right behind the troops.

In September, October, and November, the steady forward drive of the Allies ground to a halt on Germany's western border, as the Germans dug in to keep the Allies out of the fatherland.

CHAPTER ELEVEN

The Invasion of Normandy

ARMY NURSES IN NORTHERN FRANCE

6 June–21 August 1944

When I was in England, I spent some time with the army's Medical Corps, and witnessed some of our preparations for tending wounded soldiers. The sight of surgeons being taught to operate at the front, of huge warehouses filled to the roofs with bandages, or scores of hospitals built for men then healthy who would soon be wounded—seemed shocking and morbid to me.

—Ernie Pyle, *war correspondent*,
Brave Men

A T FALMOUTH in Devonshire, at 2000 on 7 June 1944, Lieutenant Helen Molony and her sister nurses inched their way toward and up the gangplank of USAT *William Pendleton*. As always, the nurses lined up for boarding in alphabetical order. Being an "M," Molony had a good view of the front of the line as the "As" through "Gs" climbed the gangplank and disappeared into the hold of the ship that would carry personnel of the 128th Evacuation Hospital to the shores of Northern France. The *Pendleton* was headed for the beaches of Normandy, where the long-awaited Allied battle to liberate France from the Germans—code-named "Operation Overlord"—had begun.

It was a massive offensive, on a scale never seen before in the history of warfare. Two days earlier, in an Allied naval convoy of over 5,000 ships, approximately 150,000 men—70,000 out of a planned 87,000 American soldiers and paratroopers, and 75,215 Canadian and British troops—

Personnel of the 128th Evacuation Hospital leave Tortworth Castle, England, on their way to Normandy in June 1944. Left to right: Capt. Kathryn Helm, Lt. Margaret B. Stanfill, Capt. Michael P. DeVito, Lts. Helen Molony, Edna Browning, Martha Cameron, Frances Farabough, Gladys Martin, Margaret E. Hart, and Doris Brittingham (Courtesy of Lt. Col. Martha Cameron, USAF, NC [Ret.])

stormed the shores of Normandy at two beaches dubbed "OMAHA" and "UTAH."[1]

The assault on OMAHA Beach would prove to be one of the most gruesome battles of World War II. Only five miles wide, OMAHA Beach was a tidal flat bordered at the high-water mark by an embankment of loose pebbles known as shingle. The beach was backed on the east by sand dunes, and on the west by a four- to five-foot-high wooden sea wall. Beyond the shingle were bluffs—low-lying yet too high to be negotiated by vehicles—that would block the advance of Allied troops. These bluffs were mined and defended by German troops dug into pillboxes on and in front of the bluffs. From the vantage point of the bluffs, the Germans had American troops landing on the beach clearly in their sights: as GIs attempted to land, heavy machine-gun fire cut them down, many before they even left the bow ramps of their landing craft. Those GIs lucky enough to make it onto the beach crawled across the sand dragging the wounded and leaving weapons and equipment to be swallowed up by the rapidly advancing sea. Tragically, as the unwounded dragged the wounded out of the dangerous reach of the incoming tide, they pulled themselves and the injured toward the enemy instead of back toward the water's edge and away from enemy fire.

The 116th Infantry Company alone sustained 105 casualties at the water's edge. Medical supplies went up in flames as German artillery shells fell on landing craft and the beach area, claiming new casualties and further disfiguring the dead American bodies densely strewn from the water to the shingle pile. "Face downward as far as eyes could see in either direction," Major Charles E. Tegtmeyer, MC, regimental surgeon of the Sixteenth Infantry, described in his diary, "were the huddled bodies of men living, wounded, and dead, as tightly packed together as a layer of cigars in a box. Some were frantically but ineffectually attempting to dig into the shale shelf. . . ." Of the 70,000 Americans who landed on D-Day—34,000 soldiers at OMAHA, 23,000 troops at UTAH, and 13,000 paratroopers—5,000 were killed or wounded in the first twenty-four hours.[2]

Unlike D-Day North Africa, no field or evacuation hospitals went ashore with the landing troops. They followed shortly after: the 13th and 51st Field Hospitals without their complement of nurses followed the troops ashore a day later, landing at OMAHA Beach on 7 June. The 42nd and 45th Field Hospitals, again without their nurses, landed on UTAH Beach on 8 June. Scheduled to land there on 10 June was the 128th Evacuation Hospital, with its forty-two nurses, including Helen Molony. These women would be among the first to land in Normandy.

Boarding the *Pendleton* on 7 June, the nurses of the 128th were dressed in full battle gear, including helmets and full field packs. From a distance, they could easily have been mistaken for male soldiers, except that these "soldiers" carried no rifles slung over their shoulders. As soon as the women set foot on board, they were directed to their quarters on a lower deck. Along with the usual directions, the women were given additional instructions: "Don't let the boys know you're women." The nurses took the instructions to heart and confined themselves to the areas of the ship permitted to them. Whenever they went to the top deck, they stayed on their side of a partition that had been erected to keep them segregated from the First Army troops who were on board and headed for Normandy.[3]

Military medicine had undergone a trial by fire in the North African, Sicilian, and Italian campaigns, and the lessons learned there were now

Personnel of the 128th Evacuation Hospital boarding the USS Pendleton *for the voyage to Normandy, June 1944.* Left to right: Lts. Edna M. Atkins, Doris Brittingham, Edna Browning, and Martha Cameron (Courtesy Lt. Col. Martha Cameron, USAF, NC [Ret.])

going to be put to good use. The shortage or lack of medical supplies and equipment—especially in the first critical hours of an invasion—had been problems in Algeria, Sicily, and Italy. Hopefully, these problems would not be repeated in Normandy. Operation Neptune—the code name for the medical side of the invasion that would provide for the care of wounded and sick soldiers from their first moments on the beach until field and evacuation hospitals could be brought in—came up with ways to remedy that problem.

On D-Day, the Eighty-second and 101st Airborne Divisions dropped special canisters of medical and surgical supplies at various locations in Normandy. Additionally, each soldier going ashore on D-Day carried medical supplies and equipment along with his regular field pack and weapons. The soldiers dropped the medical supplies and equipment on the beachhead, to be picked up later by battalion medics for use in treating the wounded at "rough-and-ready aid stations" near unit command

North Sea

ENGLAND
London
Dover
Portsmouth

HOLLAND
GERMANY
Antwerp
BELGIUM
Maastricht
Aachen
Feb. 7
Cologne
Brussels
Liège
Eupen
Namur
Huy
Spa
Malmedy
Meuse R.
Manhay
Houffalize
Hotton
Koblenz
Ettelbruck
ARDENNES
FOREST
Bastogne
Frankfurt
am Main
Sedan
Luxembourg

English Channel

D-DAY
(Operation Neptune)
June 6, 1944

Cherbourg
COTENTIN
PENINSULA
Ste-Mère-l'Église
Utah
Omaha
Gold
Juno
Sword
Le Havre
Aug. 25
Carentan
La Cambe
Reims
Verdun
Metz
Vibersviller
Périers
Saint-Lô
July 24
Caen
Paris
Nancy
Sarrebourg
Saint-Malo
Falaise
Argentan
Lunéville
Strasbourg
Brest
Mortain
Colmar
Épinal
Plombières
Sept. 25–Nov. 22
Mulhouse
Lorient
Aug. 25
F R A N C E
Dijon
Rioz
Sept. 15–25
Besançon
Belfort
Saint-
Nazaire
Aug. 23
Nantes
SWITZERLAND
Lausanne
Saint-
Amour
Geneva

ATLANTIC OCEAN

Ambérieu
Lyon
Aug. 31–Sept. 25
Rives
Voiron
Grenoble
ITALY
Bordeaux
Rhône R.
Crest
Montélimar
Sisteron
Sault
Aug. 26
Aug. 18
Nice
Toulouse
Barjols
Aug. 22–31
Draguignan
Saint-Raphael
Fréjus
Sainte-Maxime
Aug. 15–16
Saint-Tropez
Istres
Marseilles
Toulon
Plan de la Tour
Aug. 16–22
Cap
Cavalaire

Allied
Landings
August 15

SPAIN

Mediterranean Sea

France, 1944

⌒⌒⌒ Front line (date)

← Route

0 _____ 100 Miles
0 _____ 100 Kilometers

N
W   E
S

posts until field hospitals could be brought ashore and set up. The evacuation hospitals would follow them ashore a few days after the initial assault.[4]

Aboard the *Pendleton*, the nurses lived in crowded quarters, slept in multitier bunks, ate C- and K-rations out of cans, and remained in the same clothes they had been wearing since they departed from Tortworth Castle on 6 June. The two-day trip was accomplished with the nurses' presence kept a secret to all but their own hospital staff and a limited number of the crew. Why such precautions were necessary was never explained to the nurses.

On the afternoon of 9 June, the *Pendleton* and the two other ships in her convoy reached a rendezvous point off the Isle of Wight, five miles southwest of the coastal city of Portsmouth. The *Pendleton* with its convoy waited more than an hour for a larger convoy they were to join. When the larger convoy failed to show up, the *Pendleton*'s captain decided that their three ships should proceed alone across the Channel to Normandy. As the afternoon wore on and the three-ship convoy sailed toward France, several submarine alerts were sounded and passengers and crew were put on heightened alert should a torpedo attack force them to abandon ship.

At about 0315 the next morning, the watch crew, several medical officers, and the CO of the 128th Evac, Colonel Norman Wiley, noticed the reflection of a large fire on the water about six miles astern. Later, the men learned that an oil tanker with the larger convoy, now in their wake, had been torpedoed by a German submarine, caught fire, and sunk.

With that news came an increased awareness of the possibility that the *Pendleton* might not reach her appointed unloading station off the coast of Normandy. Still, no one on board had any idea that the ship had entered dangerous waters as she pulled closer to the French shore and ran parallel to the beach. After sailing twenty minutes along this new course, the watch crew and medical officers on the upper deck became aware of an American motorized launch running alongside the vessel.

The crew of the launch informed the ship's captain that their ship was sailing parallel to OMAHA Beach, not UTAH Beach, where she was scheduled to anchor. Further, the *Pendleton* was now in an area of water in which the Germans had placed many mines. With the navy launch guiding him, the *Pendleton*'s captain altered course and sailed out of the minefield toward UTAH Beach. The *Pendleton* had wandered into the minefield and sailed out of it while most of her passengers were still fast asleep.

An hour later, the vessel was alerted for possible air attacks. As they approached UTAH Beach, high-flying German planes dropped bombs on the three-ship convoy. Several fell and exploded near the *Pendleton*, causing damage on one side and a leak in a water tank. About 0530, low-flying German aircraft overflew the convoy and dropped several more bombs.

Helen Molony, who had awakened earlier and had made her way to the head facilities on the top deck, was on her way back to her bunk when she heard a swishing sound overhead and looked up in time to see a low-flying German plane release a glider bomb headed for her ship. "There was a terrible sound of wood splintering and metal buckling at the right-front [starboard bow] of the ship," Molony remembered. "The bomb hit our ship but, thank God, it was a dud. It didn't explode." Now, damaged for the second time, the *Pendleton* was listing slightly, and Molony decided to stay topside just in case the ship should begin to sink. In their sleeping quarters, other passengers heard the sound of metal buckling and wood splintering.[5]

Belowdecks, Lieutenants Marte Cameron and Doris Friedlund and their sister nurses were just beginning to respond to an order for all nurses to go topside. "We dressed except for our helmets," Cameron remembered. "As we started toward the ladder to the top deck, Doris Friedlund pulled me aside. She looked worried and was carrying her helmet by the strap like a bucket. 'Marte, what should I do?' Friedlund asked. 'I didn't want to go all the way to the top deck last night, so I peed in my helmet. What am I going to do if they tell us to put them on?' It only took me a second to decide," Cameron said. "I opened a porthole that was right by us and took Friedlund's helmet, dumped it, and handed it back to her. 'Just follow instructions like a good soldier,'" Cameron told her companion as the two continued their climb toward the upper deck.[6]

When they reached the top deck, no one seemed to be in a hurry to get off the ship. Though the dud bomb had done a fair amount of damage to the starboard bow, the *Pendleton* was still seaworthy. As the nurses lined up along the rail, they were astounded by the sight before them. Hundreds of ships were anchored offshore or waiting for their turn to come in closer and unload. Above the vessels floated hundreds of barrage balloons tethered to steel cables attached to the ships' decks. The balloons looked like large, silver-colored dirigibles, complete with tailfins. They formed a canopy over the vessels to block German pilots from swooping low and strafing Allied ships bringing in personnel and supplies. "It looked like the 'bridge of ships and umbrella of power' Winston Churchill had talked about in some of his speeches," Marte Cameron later wrote in a letter.[7]

German artillery shells were hitting the waters around the ships and exploding every few minutes. In the gray-green water floated enemy mines that could be detonated magnetically or by collision. Allied minesweepers were still working to clear sealanes in order to expand the beach area so more ships could approach the shore to unload their cargos.

About 1530, the 128th Evacuation Hospital received orders to disembark into landing barges for the trip to shore. For Helen Molony and the majority of nurses with the 128th, the trip over the side of the ship and down the cargo net was a reminder of landings in Arzew and Sicily. For others who had joined the 128th as replacements—including Marte Cameron, Normandy was their first amphibious landing. "Rope ladders aren't as difficult as they look," Cameron wrote. "The shelling and occasional bombing gave you something to think about besides getting down the net to the barge."[8]

The first landing barge—carrying Molony, Cameron, Edna M. Atkins, Doris Brittingham, Frances M. Farabough, and Margaret B. Stanfill, and some of the men of their unit—pulled in and stopped about thirty yards from shore. The young barge operator encouraged everyone to leave the craft and get to the beach as quickly as possible. "The tide's coming in fast," he shouted above the surf and the noise of artillery guns. "You better get off and walk in from here, or you'll have to swim in if the water rises fast."[9]

As the nurses jumped off the landing craft and entered the cold water that reached to their waists, the veterans of the first landing at Arzew naturally compared the Normandy landing to the North African one. The first thing that Molony noticed was several bloated bodies of dead GIs floating facedown in the incoming tide, bobbing like corks, submerging and reappearing in the cold gray water of the English Channel. "At least Arzew didn't have dead bodies floating offshore," Molony said. "But at Normandy, the water was only waist-high instead of reaching my shoulders as it did in Arzew."[10]

When they reached the beach, Cameron turned to look back in the direction of the *Pendleton*, expecting to see more of the unit's nurses close behind them on a landing barge. Instead, she saw the nurses loading onto a DUKW from the *Pendleton*. Cameron and her group hesitated on shore, deciding to wait for the other nurses to arrive. In doing so, they caught the attention of the beachmaster, an MP. "He shouted at us, 'Get moving, get moving!' " Cameron recalled. "We didn't know where we were going. Neither the CO nor the chief nurse was ahead of us. We felt very much alone. And the faces of the MPs were so grim. They'd always been so dapper in England, but here, they looked as if they'd been through hell."[11]

Within minutes, the DUKW reached the shore and caught up with Cameron and Molony and the other four, and they climbed onto the crowded vehicle. "Molony got on the back and I sat on the front fender, holding on to the headlight," Cameron said. They drove inland a short distance and the DUKW dropped them off. There, they pulled off their stiff, gas-impregnated clothing—men's shirts and trousers. Cameron's clothing was wet from wading ashore, and she fumbled, trying to open the fly of the pants. "I always had trouble opening the flies on our GI clothes—they were six-button flies. I don't know how we got through that war with the men's trousers having a six-button fly."[12]

The nurses of the 128th Evac were assigned temporary duty at the 42nd Field Hospital, located about three miles inland. When they reached the 42nd, they realized immediately that they were ahead of its own nurses. "We didn't find anybody in the wards where the patients were in the beds," said Cameron. "There was one dead one; another one—the IV had run out. And all these urinals and bedpans were on the floor." The nurses immediately set to work, caring for patients and cleaning up the ward.[13]

When they had finished, Cameron took a look around and found doctors and corpsmen in the operating room, doing surgery. Outside, wounded men waited their turn for surgery on litters on the ground near the entrance to the OR tent. Some of the more alert, lightly wounded men saw Cameron and smiled at her. "Up to that point, we hadn't seen anything but grim faces. I guess they were saying, 'Women are here. Everything's going to be okay.' They must have felt much safer all of a sudden." Since their equipment still had to be off-loaded, the nurses bivouacked with the 42nd Field Hospital; the nurses of the 42nd arrived several hours later.[14]

Meanwhile, corpsmen of the 128th Evac were to set up the hospital site. The first job the men faced on 10 June was getting their hospital equipment and vehicles off the ships and onto UTAH Beach. As the LSTs dropped their bow ramps as close to dry land as possible, the enlisted men started their vehicle engines and drove their trucks or jeeps into the gray sea that stretched between them and the beachhead. The vehicles had been painstakingly waterproofed while they were in England and their rubber hoses replaced with flexible tubing. "The Germans were strafing us the whole time," 128th Evac staff member Corporal Oliver Sorlye said of the trip from the *Pendleton* to the beach. "My buddy, Charlie Thorson, drove a truck . . . I was his assistant. The truck was loaded with medical supplies and the water was almost to our necks. . . . I could look down the beach and see all these other trucks coming in too, and guys were standing on top of the cabs. We had about two city blocks to travel before we hit dry land."[15]

Corporal Marcus Duxbury had been assigned to drive a jeep—loaded with an empty water tank for drinking water—from the landing barge to the shore. "When we drove off the barge, the water was only as high as the hubcaps. We just got going pretty good when—*woo-woo*—down we go into a shell hole. The water rose up to my shoulders, but we kept going and made it to the beach."[16]

Some of the drivers were not so lucky. "Some of those guys [with other units] went down into a shell hole with their vehicle and sank like rocks," Duxbury said. "They drowned because no one could get to them to help get them out. You just had to keep your eyes front and keep moving for the beach."[17]

The 128th Evacuation Hospital did not make it very far inland by late afternoon. While their nurses were working with the 42nd Field Hospital, some of the men of the 128th drove a couple of miles inland and settled in for the night. They found the stench of decaying flesh unbearable. "The area was a mess," Sorlye remembered. "There were dead cattle and horses everywhere and we had to pull them aside so we could bivouac for the night. The next morning, we collected quite a few dead bodies, put them in mattress covers, and stored them in one area for the graves [registration] units who would be following us."[18]

At midnight that night, twenty-four-year-old Lieutenant Edna Browning of Cumberland, Maryland, made her way from the hospital ward at the 42nd Field Hospital where she had worked since coming ashore earlier that day. Browning was a replacement, new to the 128th and new to the war. She had been at Tortworth Castle just long enough to spend one night before departing for Normandy. Now, she headed toward the area where she was told the 128th Evac nurses were settled in for the night. "It was pitch-black, blackout conditions and you couldn't see your hand in front of your face," Browning remembered. "Some of the other nurses were old-timers; they had gone to bed. Finally I yelled, 'Where am I supposed to sleep? I can't find you.' One of the nurses yelled back, 'We're over here in a foxhole.' " Browning still could not see a thing. " 'What foxhole? I don't see anything.' " The same voice yelled again, " 'We're here by the fence.' " Browning cautiously made her way forward until she bumped into something that turned out to be an empty pup tent. "I crawled inside with all my field gear . . . and the stuff I had on when we waded in—it was now five days. I was beginning to smell. I called back, 'I found a pup tent. Goodnight.' "[19]

At 0200 on UTAH Beach the next day, fifteen enlisted men of the 128th Evac were curled up against the walls of the slit trench they had claimed for the night, completely unaware that the incoming tide was steadily making its way toward their accommodations. The cold gray sea crept silently toward the edge of the trench and began spreading out along its dirt floor. Men squirmed in their sleep as cold water surrounded their warm, relaxed bodies. Suddenly, two awoke and began cursing the incoming tide just seconds before all fifteen scurried out, damning their luck and looking for a new place to sleep until their hospital equipment arrived.

The following morning, Oliver Sorlye and the 128th Evac's enlisted men who had spent the night inland assessed the area in broad daylight for its suitability as a hospital site. The ground was heavily pockmarked with shell holes and littered with dead cows and horses; shells still fell. Among the debris and dead animals was the occasional body of a dead American GI not yet picked up by graves registration. Colonel Wiley, the hospital's CO, decided to look farther inland for a more suitable location. He settled on a site near Boutteville, about five miles from the coast and an equal distance from the frontline fighting.

The new site was not much better than the old one, but it did have fewer shell holes. "We still had to move dead cows and horses out of the way," Oliver Sorlye said. "We had to carry a lot of bodies." Many of the bodies were those of American paratroopers caught in nearby trees and hedgerows. Sorlye along with other corpsmen of the 128th Evac placed the bodies in a temporary morgue until graves registration could claim them. "One dog tag was left on the body and the second one went back to Washington. Each body was wrapped in a mattress cover."[20]

These paratroopers were some of the thirteen thousand soldiers of the U.S. 82nd and 101st Airborne Divisions who had either jumped or ridden in small, motorless gliders to land behind enemy lines just after midnight on D-Day, 6 June. The troops had come by air into the Cotentin Peninsula countryside while amphibious forces were still making their way to assembly points off the northern French coast. As a result of strong winds, navigation errors, and enemy fire, paratroopers and glider passengers were scattered in disorganized groups throughout the countryside. Now, several days after this massive air assault, incoming ground troops and support personnel were still recovering bodies of the less fortunate paratroopers.

While the enlisted men set up the new hospital, nurses of the unit continued to live and work with the 42nd Field Hospital. On the morning of 11 June, Browning went to breakfast with a veteran of the 128th Evac, Lieutenant Carrie Smith. Browning was assigned to work with Smith on the preoperative ward all that day. "My mother was a Smith so I felt like I had a cousin," Browning recalled. "Carrie would be at one end of the ward, and I'd be at the other." As a field hospital, the 42nd received casualties directly from battalion aid stations at the front lines. "They'd come in in groups. The ambulances would pull up one after another," said Browning. At the 42nd's receiving tent, incoming wounded were triaged by the admitting physician; of those needing surgery, some were sent to Browning and Smith's preoperative tent.[21]

This preop ward was made up of two large tents laced together. In the center of the ward where the tents met, a large open wooden box holding supplies sat on two wooden sawhorses. "That was the nurses' station," Browning said. "My job was to assess the patient's condition, and tell the doctor when he'd come through." As a nurse who had only recently come into the army from civilian nursing, Browning was surprised at first by the weapons that came along with the new admissions. "I had a sack of guns, metal, things like that. When the sack got filled up, I took it to the first sergeant and asked why no one had gone through their uniforms and gear [at reception]."[22]

Later that day, Browning received a soldier who had a leg injury as well as a dressing on his left shoulder. "You never knew when you pulled a dressing down, what you would see. I pulled that dressing down and saw a little metal bullet." She removed the bullet with a forceps, cleaned and covered the wound with a small dressing, then gave the bullet to the GI. "Here's your lavalier. If you'd have gone to surgery, they'd throw this out."[23]

At 1930 that night, the nurses of the 128th joined their unit at Boutteville, and by 2115 the 128th Evac received its first patients on Nor-

Lt. Martha "Marte" Cameron at the 128th Evacuation Hospital in Boutteville, France, June 1944 (Courtesy of Lt. Col. Martha Cameron, USAF, NC [Ret.])

mandy. By midnight, less than three hours later, 123 battle casualties had been admitted to the 400-bed hospital. The fighting was fierce as the glidermen and paratroopers of the 101st Airborne Division fought desperately to drive an elite German parachute regiment out of Carentan, five miles from the hospital tents at Boutteville. By midnight of the following day, 12 June, after five days of struggle by the Allies to take Carentan and thus join the two beachheads—OMAHA and UTAH—the 128th's census had more than doubled, to 284. Twelve officers and twelve enlisted men from the 3rd Aux Surgical Group were attached for duty to help care for the increasing numbers of surgical patients.[24]

On 16 June, the 96th Evacuation Hospital arrived on the beach, and the 128th sent ten trucks to transport the officers and nurses of the 96th to the 128th to help care for the ever-increasing numbers of battle casualties. By midnight the next day, the 128th Evac had 487 patients for its 400 beds and was anticipating the arrival of other evacuation hospitals to help manage the workload. In a letter to her father dated 25 June 1944, Cameron wrote: "The only thing that is hard to take is seeing a never-ending stream of nastily wounded boys. . . . My only message is a plea for no more wars."[25]

During the month of June, a total of 27,392 casualties from Normandy would be evacuated to U.S. Army hospitals in England. It was obvious to everyone caring for wounded at the 128th Evac that the sooner other evacuation hospitals arrived on the beachhead, the better.[26]

THE 67TH EVACUATION Hospital landed on OMAHA Beach on D+10, 16 June. The hospital's 31 officers, 40 nurses, and 130 enlisted men spent their first night in Normandy bivouacked near the beachhead. "It was strange to think that we were walking up that beach and over the sand hills behind it without a moment's thought of any possible danger, when just a few weeks [ten days] before, men had died in hundreds as they fought their way through all the cruel obstacles and heavy fire," Mandie, a nurse with the 67th Evac, wrote later.[27]

On 17 June, the 67th Evac left OMAHA Beach by truck and set out for their hospital site at Sainte-Mère-Eglise. They passed long lines of dirty, tired soldiers as their trucks crawled along the road. When they reached the town of Sainte-Mère-Eglise, the nurses could see parachutes hanging in trees and off the roofs of buildings. Their hospital was set up four miles west of the town in two pastures separated by hedgerows. Shortly after the hospital opened at 1200 on 19 June, a steady stream of ambulances rolled in bearing scores of wounded GIs as American and Allied troops fought to expand the beachheads of the Cotentin Peninsula and free it from the Germans.[28]

On 21 June, two days after opening, the 67th Evac had 275 admissions lying on the ground near the receiving tent because the evacuation system had come to a standstill. Air evacuation planes were grounded due to bad weather. Land and sea evacuation had ground to a halt because the bridge to Carentan was out, blocking evacuation of the wounded by truck and ambulance to the beach for pickup by ships and transport to England. When the situation became acute, doctors instructed nurses of the 67th

Evac to use their own initiative in giving plasma, intravenous transfusions, and blood to the ever-growing numbers of wounded. "It is no exaggeration to say that many lives were saved because of this procedure," wrote Captain Jean Truckey, chief nurse of the 67th Evacuation Hospital. "Many patients who had left the operating room in good condition fell into shock an hour or so after returning to the ward, and her [the nurse's] trained eye found him at once and then the precious bottles of blood or plasma would be given, tiding him over the crisis." Before they left Sainte-Mère-Eglise ten days later, the staff of the 67th Evacuation Hospital would receive and treat more than 5,300 casualties and operate on more than 2,600 of them with a death rate of 1.2 percent—only 32 deaths.[29]

AT 0355 on 18 June, the 44th Evacuation Hospital received orders to proceed to Southampton, England, where they would board two LCIs for transport to Normandy. The 44th Evac had been stationed at Maidenhead, twenty-seven miles west of London, for little over half a year, since Thanksgiving Day, 26 November 1943. In that time, the 35 male officers, 193 enlisted men, 2 Red Cross workers, and 40 army nurses had trained for the Normandy invasion. They attended classes and seminars in such subjects as aircraft identification, map reading, and how to care for wounded during bombing or shelling attacks.

During this training period, the staff also visited the seasoned 128th Evacuation Hospital at Tortworth Castle to observe and learn the process of setting up and tearing down a tent hospital, and how to improvise in combat areas when necessary medical and surgical equipment was not delivered with supplies as scheduled. The chief nurse of the 44th Evac, First Lieutenant Martha Nash, was determined that her nurses, corpsmen, and OR personnel would learn as much as possible from a veteran evacuation hospital that had cared for battle casualties from North Africa to Sicily.

Lieutenant Nash brought an unusual personal history to her hospital. At age twenty-four, she gave orders to, and made decisions for, nurses who were older than she and had more nursing experience before joining the Army Nurse Corps. But not one of her nurses at the 44th could match Nash's personal history and motivation for volunteering for duty overseas. In September 1940, when twenty-year-old Martha was working as a nurse in Yonkers, New York, she was visited by her older sister, Sec-

ond Lieutenant Frances Nash, who was in New York to board an army
ship that would carry her to a tour of duty in the Philippine Islands. It
was during this brief visit that Frances convinced her younger sister that
she, too, should join the Army Nurse Corps and serve her country.
Though the United States was not yet at war in 1940, Frances felt it was
but a matter of time before the country would be pulled into the worldwide conflagration.

Only weeks after the USS *Grant* carried Frances to the Philippines,
Martha visited the Fisher Federal Building in New York City, took and
passed her army physical examination for the nurse corps, raised her
right hand and swore the oath of an army nurse. While Lieutenant
Frances Nash practiced her profession in the Philippines, Lieutenant
Martha Nash worked on wards in station hospitals at Fort Bragg, North
Carolina, and Camp Croft, Spartanburg, South Carolina.

When the Japanese attacked Pearl Harbor, Frances Nash was serving
as the operating-room supervisor at Fort William McKinley, seven miles
from Manila. In the months following the attack on Manila, the Nash
family lost all contact with Frances. Unbeknownst to them, Frances was
captured by the Japanese in May 1942. She and sixty-six other U.S. Army
nurses were placed in a prisoner of war camp in Manila. Not until the end
of the war would these U.S. prisoners of war's struggle against starvation
and brutality at the hands of the Japanese become known.

Meanwhile, Martha was transferred to work in the chief nurse's office
at Fort Jackson, South Carolina. It was here that she became aware that
the 44th Evacuation Hospital was looking for a chief nurse to supervise
thirty-nine army nurses and two Red Cross workers who would take part
in the Tennessee maneuvers and, soon after, be shipped overseas. Not
knowing if her sister were dead or alive, twenty-three-year-old Martha
Nash volunteered for the job and got it.

At the time Nash took over, the women under her command were
wearing outdated World War I uniforms consisting of military jackets
and skirts. One of Nash's first priorities was to get her nurses into uniforms more serviceable for frontline hospital duty. With no one in her
office but herself—she did her own "hunt and peck" typing of reports
and requests—she succeeded in getting the blue Army Nurse Corps
uniform, complete with slacks, issued for her nurses.[30]

The blue slacks were especially welcomed when Nash obtained permission for her nurses to fire a carbine and a .45 Colt automatic on the firing range. "We took a large picture of Adolf Hitler out to the firing range

and had the boys put it up as a target for the nurses," Nash said. "They nailed the picture to a tree and I was the first to shoot at it. I aimed the .45 automatic at Hitler's heart and squeezed the trigger. The bullet struck right between his eyes. Everyone thought that I was a fantastic shot. I never mentioned that I had been aiming at his heart."[31]

When Martha Nash set sail for England with the 44th Evac on 17 November 1943, the Nash family still had not learned what had become of Frances. She was listed as missing in action.

The Nash family had sent both of its daughters to war, but that was not all; it had also sent its only son. Lieutenant James Nash was a gunner with the Third Armored Division, which would fight its way from Normandy to the German surrender in 1945. Both he and Martha felt that being a part of the U.S. Army fighting against the Germans and the Japanese was one of the best ways to honor their sister missing in action. "There wasn't a day that went by," said Martha, "when I didn't say a prayer for my sister's safe return to our family back home in Georgia. Our brother, Jimmy, did the same. All three of us were raised in a family where love of country and a strong belief in the power of prayer was as natural as breathing."[32]

At 1200 on 19 June, D+13, a convoy with two LCIs carrying the 44th Evacuation Hospital arrived off OMAHA Beach in Normandy. A storm that would reach near-hurricane proportions was approaching; the Channel was roiling, with large waves and deep troughs caused by a north-westerly gale increasingly gathering strength and moving toward the beach. The LCIs had difficulty trying to approach the man-made dock called a mulberry, set up for disembarking and unloading ships at the OMAHA beachhead. The first LCI, carrying forty-four hospital personnel, managed to get close enough to disembark passengers during the late afternoon. The second LCI, carrying most of the male officers and nurses, waited hours for its chance while it pitched and bobbed on the stormy sea. About 1900, the nurses' LCI tied up at the mulberry dock; as the doctors and nurses walked across the metal causeway to the beach, some stopped and vomited over the side of the causeway as it, too, rocked and bounced in the pitching sea. Only hours later, the dock and causeway would be completely destroyed by the storm.

On the beach, wrecked vehicles still burning or smoking hours after they were hit by German shells and bombs cluttered the sand. The personnel of the 44th Evac traveled eight miles inland. They spent the night at the 45th Evacuation Hospital in the town of La Cambe, about fifteen miles north of Saint-Lô. The next morning, the 44th Evacuation Hospital team set up their own tented hospital one and a half miles west of La Cambe, along the Bayeux-Carentan-Cherbourg Highway, opposite the newly opened Twenty-ninth Division Cemetery. The cemetery was to be the resting place for hundreds of the Twenty-ninth Infantry Division and other divisions fighting in the Saint-Lô area.

ON 3 JULY, two days after organized resistance of Cherbourg ceased, the 128th Evacuation Hospital at Boutteville was notified to prepare to receive large numbers of casualties the following day. A new American offensive in the hedgerows for which the Normandy countryside was renowned was beginning in the early morning hours of 4 July and would continue for many bloody days to follow.

The famed hedgerows of Normandy—parallel rows of trees planted on top of two- or three-foot-high mounds of earth—were created centuries ago by farmers to delineate the boundaries of their irregularly shaped farms. The branches of these trees grew up and toward the next parallel hedgerow, frequently meeting to form a canopy over the sunken roads that ran between the tall, dense rows of trees and other vegetation. When the branches met and intertwined, dark green tunnels were created that gave a soldier the sense of fighting inside impenetrable tubes that crisscrossed the area like a gigantic maze.

The Germans knew the terrain and had worked their defense into the intricate patterns of troughs and hedgerows. However, the Americans and Allies were unprepared to do battle on this terrain. In the weeks of intense and bloody hedgerow fighting, casualties would run high: the 128th Evacuation Hospital alone would receive 2,851 casualties between 4 and 18 July.

By midnight on 6 July, just two days after the opening of the offensive, the 128th Evac had received 808 casualties. The hospital's census had risen from 10 patients on midnight 3 July to 480 by 6 July. More medical personnel were needed to handle the overload: on 4 July, the 501st Medical Collection Company of four officers and seventy-three enlisted men were attached for duty; and the next day two surgical teams of the 4th Auxiliary Surgical Group—four officers, four nurses, and four enlisted men—were attached to assist with the casualties requiring surgery. The operating-room tables worked nonstop, around the clock.

Lieutenant Marte Cameron was working twelve- to fifteen-hour shifts administering anesthesia to the wounded, who included not only American and Allied troops but German POWs as well. The hospital was receiving large numbers of patients with facial and neck wounds caused by glider crashes, gunshot wounds, and shell fragments. These facial and neck wounds required special care. Cameron remembered one young American soldier brought to her OR table who had been hit in the left jaw by an exploding high-powered bullet. The young man's lower jaw hung down like an unhinged gate. In addition, his left facial nerve had been severed and his left lower ear had been lacerated and was hanging loosely by a narrow band of skin. Several of the patient's upper and lower front teeth had been fractured at various distances from the gum line and displaced about an inch to the left.

"I felt a special compassion for these young men with torn-up faces," Cameron said. "The wounds one could see were often less severe than the psychological injuries they brought with them. My heart went out to each of them." With maxillofacial wounds—wounds that involved the mouth, jaw, and teeth in addition to other areas of the face—anesthesia

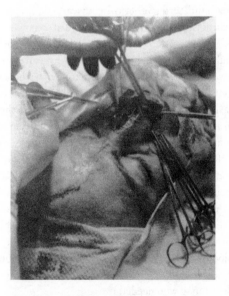

An American soldier wounded in the face undergoing facial and reconstructive surgery (Courtesy of Gilbert Smith)

was a special concern. Since surgeons would be working on or around the mouth and nose, the usual method of anesthesia—drop ether or nitrous oxide applied by a mask constructed of wire mesh and gauze placed over the nose and mouth—could not be used.[33]

Instead, endotracheal anesthesia was used. The patient was given morphine to begin to sedate him, and atropine to lessen or stop the normal production of fluids in the mouth and throat. The injured area was covered with sterile gauze soaked in sterile saline to protect the open areas and keep them moist. Intravenous Pentothal could not be given initially to put the patient to sleep because Pentothal often caused spasms of the larynx—the muscle and cartilage that forms a portion of the patient's airway and is crucial to breathing. If the larynx went into spasm, the contracting of the muscles would halt normal breathing and endanger the patient's life. So ether was given initially, but only for as long as it took to put the patient to sleep. As soon as he was under, the mask was removed and a doctor would insert an endotracheal tube through the mouth to keep the airway open and allow for ether to be administered without using the mask.

Since masks could not be used for this type of surgery, a system was improvised for administering ether using discarded plasma cans. "As soon as the endotracheal tube was in place, we would attach what was known as the 'Flagg can,' " Marte Cameron said. "You had a hose connected to the endotracheal tube, and the other end of it went into an empty plasma can and had adhesive tape cross-hatched on the top with a hole in the middle to put the tube through. Then you'd have a half-inch of ether in the bottom [of the plasma can]. You'd let the patient breathe. If the case went on for six hours or more, you added more ether to the bottom of the can."[34]

Items such as blood pressure cuffs and oxygen tanks were stretched thin in busy OR tents. Usually, there was only one blood pressure cuff for the entire tent, which nurse anesthetists had to share. When administering anesthesia, it is crucial that an anesthetist continually monitor a patient's blood pressure and other vital signs. With only one cuff in the tent, an anesthetist would monitor her patient's pulse by placing her finger over an artery; if the pulse began to increase, the nurse would retrieve the blood pressure cuff, take the patient's pressure, and adjust the anesthesia accordingly. She would then return the cuff to the supply table for the next nurse who needed it.

Oxygen tanks were also scarce. "Normally every case had Pentothal," Cameron explained, referring to the fact that some surgical patients received sodium Pentothal as an anesthetic. "[Y]ou carried them [the patient] with no oxygen. You gave them oxygen if they got a little dusky [indicating a lack of oxygen]. And you put it [the oxygen tank] back so someone else might use it."[35]

Lieutenant Cameron and Sergeant Loren Butts at the 128th remembered the outstanding work of one maxillofacial surgeon, Major Michael P. DeVito. DeVito had graduated from, and practiced surgery at, Harvard University before entering the Army Medical Corps. "He was an amateur photographer and he took pictures [of the patient] before and afterward," Butts said. "They built a stool for him to stand on when he operated because he was only five feet one or two, and he needed the extra height that the box provided in order to see and work better."[36]

Cameron, DeVito, Lieutenant Frances Farabough—the scrub nurse—and a corpsman named Darcy liked to work together as a team. "We were the perfect team together. Mike [DeVito] was fast. He knew how to get those shell fragments out quicker than anybody. They would always call him for injuries from the neck up." On one occasion, when DeVito was busy with a case, another surgeon decided to work on a patient who was waiting his turn for DeVito's surgical skills. The surgeon told DeVito that he would handle this waiting patient. "Mike gave him a look over his mask," Cameron said, "and said to me, 'Isn't he confident?' " In a little while, the surgeon threw up his hands. When DeVito had completed the case he was working on, he turned his attention to this patient. "It seemed as if he [DeVito] reached for a shell fragment with a Kelly clamp," Cameron said, "and *wham*, the operation was over. Mike was fast."[37]

Most maxillofacial surgeries took four to six hours or longer, since the patient usually required several specialists to operate on his wounds. A dentist would work on fractured teeth and help in realigning the patient's jaw. An ear-nose-throat surgeon might be next to take care of a nasal passage or an eye wound. Finally, the plastic surgeon would come in to reconstruct and reshape the soldier's battered face. Hours in the OR were long and tedious.

Unique problems in maxillofacial surgery occurred when an eye was seriously involved in the wound. Surgeons in frontline hospitals were very conservative about enucleation (removal) of an eye. However, there were occasions when they had no choice. Whether the removal was due to nonbattle injuries or battle wounds, or if the soldier was someone who had been inducted into the army on limited duty because he had only one eye, these men needed artificial eyes. At that time, artificial eyes were made of glass and they presented their own set of problems. Glass eyes required many weeks to manufacture and, once fitted, frequently caused irritation and infection. Even if these two problems were avoided, the eye itself was a fragile thing. If dropped, it broke like any glass object, and that could leave a soldier with an empty eye socket for up to the two months it took to create and fit another glass eye.

While the 128th Evac was in England in November 1943, a staff ophthalmologist requested that a dental officer, Captain Stanley F. Erph, who had been experimenting in the creation of artificial eyes using the same clear acrylic resin that was used in dentures, make an artificial eye for a patient. The acrylic could be colored and painted to match the soldier's remaining eye, which gave him a good psychological boost. The acrylic eye could be created, colored, painted, and fitted in no more than four days. Furthermore, the eye could be made with ordinary dental equipment; it did not cause the irritation and infection that were common with glass eyes; and it was not as easily broken.

By the end of 1943, the theater surgeon reviewed the results of Captain Erph's new acrylic prosthetic eye, contacted the theater's ophthalmology consultant, and adopted use of the eye throughout the European theater. In January 1944, Captain Erph began teaching a two-week course for dentists, but it was discontinued in May in deference to the upcoming invasion of Northern France. Later that year, a school to teach dentists these techniques opened at the two central dental laboratories in the European theater. On the basis of the performance of Captain Erph's acrylic eye, the U.S. War Department then adopted the acrylic in place of the glass eye throughout the military. The U.S. War Department also transferred Captain Erph back to the United States in June 1944 to set up and supervise training personnel who would be sent to all theaters of war to provide this new artificial eye.

AFTER WORKING BEYOND her twelve-hour shift one evening in the OR tent, Marte Cameron came off duty well after midnight, but was not expected back on duty until 1200. At about 0700, she awakened out of a sound sleep to the aroma of frying bacon. Despite the fact that she had only been asleep for four hours, her appetite won out, and she dressed and went to the officers' mess tent for breakfast. The mess tent was crowded. After going through the line and receiving two scrambled eggs and three strips of crisp, well-done bacon, she spotted the closest empty place at the nearest long table and sat down between two male officers, who were already enjoying their bacon and eggs.

Cameron had just taken her first bite of the delicious bacon when the male officer on her left said, "Guten Morgen." Lieutenant Cameron, still a little groggy from lack of sleep, swallowed her food and looked at the handsome blond man to her left. He was wearing a German naval uniform and smiling as if they were old friends. Before she could respond to the man on her left, another male voice on her right said, "Guten Morgen," and she turned to see another blond German officer on her right. "My first thoughts were, 'We've been captured while I was asleep!' " Cameron recalled. "Then I realized that the rest of the people in the mess tent were Americans with the 128th." As she was sorting out her surroundings, the young naval officer on her left continued speaking to her, but this time in English. He explained that he was a surgeon in the German navy and that his friend to her right was a physician in the German army; they had been captured at Cherbourg several days earlier. The two had been selected and assigned to an area of the 128th Evac to help care for wounded German POWs. "They both spoke pretty good English, and after the shock wore off, I talked with them as we finished our breakfast," Cameron said. She learned later that these surgeons were not permitted to operate, but were assigned to manage the postoperative patients on the POW unit.[38]

ON THE NIGHT of 14 July, Marte Cameron was working in the 128th's OR when she got word that a relative of hers, Lieutenant Colonel Crawford MacNeeley, had been hit outside the town of Saint-Lô. In England, Cameron had met with Colonel MacNeeley, her cousin's husband, once while both were preparing for D-Day. MacNeeley was the CO of the Eighth Infantry's Battalion B. "He sent a lieutenant to the place where I was staying and he escorted me to dinner," Marte Cameron recalled. "Here I was—a second lieutenant, and nobody at dinner would sit down until I sat down—all those high-ranking people."[39]

Marte saw MacNeeley again after arriving at Boutteville when he came to see her. She followed his progress, getting news of him whenever she could. "When anybody from the Eighth Infantry came through, I would ask about Colonel MacNeeley. They'd say, 'He's okay, he's okay.' " Then, during her twelve-hour tour on 14 July, she heard that he had been injured. When her own CO, Colonel Wiley, made rounds through the OR tent that night, Cameron asked him to inquire about Colonel MacNeeley for her. Wiley "came back on his next rounds and told me that he'd give me his jeep and driver when I got off at 0800 to go to a field hospital." Cameron visited MacNeeley and learned that he had been hit by a mortar. "I think that he was more upset about being out of the war than he was about losing his leg. The only thing I could think to take him was a loaf of bread because the cooks and bakers in our outfit made good bread. He could have cared less about a loaf of bread . . . there were no flowers or anything you could take anybody."[40]

The casualties coming into the 128th Evacuation Hospital included not only American and Allied soldiers and German prisoners but also civilians. A very small girl was brought into the OR one day. An explosion from a hand grenade had blown off all of the fingertips on one hand and she was crying. Because Cameron spoke French, the child was brought to her OR table. Surgeon Major Frank M. Burton, a physician from Hot Springs, Arkansas, planned to close the open wounds with sutures. It was necessary to put the child to sleep during the process. "Major Burton was kind and patient and did everything he could to reassure the little girl," Cameron said. "She wanted to wash the wounds herself." Burton watched the child cry as Cameron attempted to clean the bloody fingers. "He told me to let her do it herself, so I gave her a little basin of soapy water and a little four-by-four square of sterile gauze. She didn't cry anymore, and she carefully washed each tiny stump with the gauze. I was touched," Cameron said. "I would never have thought to have her wash her own hand." Then Cameron put her to sleep and Major Burton sutured and dressed her wounds.[41]

More than forty thousand casualties streamed into surrounding hospitals over a seventeen-day period that ended on 19 July. On that day, the battle-weary men of the Twenty-ninth Infantry Division entered the demolished town of Saint-Lô and placed the body of their dead CO, Major Thomas D. Howie, on the debris-cluttered steps of the town's destroyed church.[42]

IN WAR, death by enemy fire is tragic but expected. But death by "friendly fire" is not expected and perhaps all the more heartbreaking for its irony. On 18 July 1944, General Omar Bradley traveled to Great Britain to work out battle plans for the Eighth and Ninth Air Forces.

Plans called for the two forces to use heavy and medium bombers to destroy German troops, communications, and reserves around the Périers–Saint-Lô road. Bradley and Army Air Forces commanders agreed that the ground troops of Bradley's First Army would withdraw approximately 1,200 yards from their positions along the road in order to avoid the possibility of being hit by their own bombs. It was agreed that the road itself would be the dividing line between friend and foe. Unfortunately, Bradley and the Army Air Forces generals disagreed on the angle of approach for the bombers: Bradley wanted the bombers to approach their target parallel to the road, while the Air Forces wanted to approach perpendicularly. Sadly, each left the meeting believing that his position had been chosen for the attack.

Operation Cobra, as this offensive was called, began on 24 July. As a result of the misunderstanding between Bradley and the Air Forces generals, one of the three hundred American bombers that flew in this raid dropped its load in the First Army area. Bombs fell on the Thirtieth Infantry Division, resulting in over 150 casualties. A follow-up attack against the Germans was needed if the German forces were to be severely disabled; with this in mind, Bradley approved a second Air Forces attack for 25 July. The second raid involved 1,500 heavy bombers, 380 medium bombers, and 550 fighter-bombers. Unfortunately, pilots and bombers could not see the Périers–Saint-Lô road due to drifting dust created by the bombs dropped from preceding planes. Several of the bombloads fell short of the target. Once again, American soldiers became casualties of "friendly fire": 111 men were killed, including the chief of army ground forces, Lieutenant General Lesley J. McNair, who was present to observe in action the troops he had trained in the United States. Hundreds of others were wounded in the attack and brought to nearby hospitals for treatment of their wounds.[43]

IN JUNE, while the 44th Evacuation Hospital was set up near La Cambe, a 90-millimeter antiaircraft battery was set up in a field next to them. As hospital staff took care of casualties from the Twenty-ninth and Thirtieth Infantry Divisions, the Second Armored and other XIX Corps units were firing at German planes, which were making fewer and fewer appearances as the days rolled forward. There was virtually no air resistance from the Germans. By the last week of June 1944, the Allies—Americans,

British, and Canadians—overwhelmingly ruled the skies and had virtually broken the back of the German Luftwaffe. A combined effort in
bombing German military and industrial targets and shooting down German fighter-planes had gutted the Luftwaffe.

One evening just before dark, an American P-38 Lightning came in
low over a nearby airfield and tried to land. Martha Nash and several
other 44th Evac nurses watched in stunned silence as American antiaircraft guns shot the plane from the sky. "We couldn't figure out why we
would shoot down our own plane," Nash said as she recalled the incident.
As soon as possible, the nurses asked the men of the antiaircraft battery
why they had shot down an American plane. The men explained that the
airfield personnel had contacted the P-38 pilot by radio with the password, and asked him to give the countersign. When the P-38 crew failed
to answer several contacts and flew low over American positions, the AA
battery shot it out of the sky. American soldiers who arrived at the crash
site found two German officers who had somehow captured the P-38 and
flown it over American lines. The Germans were taken prisoner, treated
for their injuries in the crash, and sent to a POW enclosure for further
questioning.[44]

Subterfuge and sabotage of another sort was also being used by the
Germans. Martha Nash recalled working in the OR assisting Major
Rainey, an orthopedic surgeon, in removing several bullets lodged near
the femur of a wounded soldier. Major Rainey pulled a wooden bullet
about an inch and a half in length with a tapered point from the soldier's
wound. "The bullet had a pinkish cast and Major Rainey told me that he
was willing to bet it had been soaked in some kind of poison before it was
loaded into a rifle and fired at our troops," Nash recalled. Surgeons and
nurses at the 44th Evac felt certain that the teakwood bullets had a dia-
bolical purpose. "We figured the Germans thought they would splinter
when they hit a bone and it would take an OR team quite a time to get all
of it out of a wound." While the team took longer on one casualty, other
soldiers would die and fewer would be sent back to duty on the front line
once they had recovered. As far as Nash knew, their theory was never
investigated further since no one had the time to send the wooden projectiles to a lab for analysis.[45]

When nurses of the 44th Evac were off duty, they were requested by
the U.S. Army to go to the U.S. Cemetery across the road to see if they
could identify any of the dead GIs found without identification. "The
Germans either stole or threw away the dog tags on quite a few of our

men, and nurses were routinely asked to look at the dead to help identify them since the divisions had been stationed near the hospitals in the past," Martha Nash said. "It was an awful experience. Nobody liked having to look at those poor dead boys and it was even worse when you did recognize one or two you had met." Nash had no way of knowing at the time that her POW sister, Frances, had undergone a similar experience on Bataan when Frances visited a common gravesite for American and Filipino dead looking for articles of clothing that might be salvageable for use by destitute troops.[46]

ON 1 AUGUST 1944, the 67th Evacuation Hospital put up the ward and personnel tents of their hospital at a new site four miles east of Saint-Lô, but the setup was not in the usual pattern. The apple orchard where the personnel had spent the night in bivouac was riddled with shell holes, and ward and personnel tents had to be erected in a pattern that took these large craters into consideration. The entire area was permeated by the nauseating stench of stiff and decaying bodies of dead cows and dead U.S. and German soldiers. Corpses were scattered throughout the rows of broken and twisted apple trees where hospital personnel had spent their first night on the new site. While several groups of enlisted men set up hospital tents, other groups of soldiers used large bulldozers to dig huge graves, push the rotting cow carcasses into the holes, and then cover them with freshly dug earth.

While animals were being buried, small detachments of privates and corporals loaded the bodies of dead soldiers into trucks and delivered them six miles to the rear, where graves registration units were recording the names of the dead and placing them in military cemeteries. As the dead were being buried, teams of combat engineers explored the large field next to the hospital site for unexploded German mines. When the engineers completed their work, they marked safe paths with white tape, and posted signs stating that mines had been cleared from the field.

The following day, the sound of a nearby explosion jarred the 67th Evac and sent off-duty personnel toward the site of the explosion. It soon became clear that an ambulance belonging to the 502nd Medical Collecting Company had driven over a mine in the "cleared" field, triggering an explosion and setting the ambulance on fire. Two sergeants assigned to the ambulance were lying on the ground near the wrecked vehicle; one was screaming in pain while the other lay motionless. Several corpsmen of the 67th Evac rushed to the aid of the wounded men and were blown into the air when one of them stepped on another German land mine. Doctors and nurses not on duty watched the unfolding tragedy as yet another group made their way toward the injured. "Our warrant officer was in the group; and he too stepped on a Teller mine," Truckey wrote in her journal. The mine "exploded into the air but failed to detonate at the customary level. He is still pale and has not grown an inch since then."[47]

The accident was one that hospital personnel would not soon forget. "As a result of this accident, we had one death and fourteen casualties," Truckey noted. "One of our men suffered a chest wound with a nick in the heart, but he made a successful recovery."[48]

Severely burned tank crewmen made up a large number of the wounded received by the 67th Evac at Saint-Lô. Many of these wounded suffered such extensive burns that they were completely wrapped in bandages with openings only for their eyes and mouths. Frequently their lips were so blistered that it was difficult for them to use even a drinking tube for liquids.

Frontline hospitals often worked under staggering patient workloads. On 8 and 9 August, the number of wounded treated at the 67th Evac set new records even for that hospital. Between 1000 on 8 August and 0600 on 9 August—less than twenty-four hours—the 400-bed hospital received 700 new patients. The 67th already had 200 wounded, and casualties were continuously arriving from General Courtney Hodge's First Army, which was fighting near Vire, about fifteen miles to the south. Every bed was full, and the less seriously wounded had to be placed on litters and blankets beneath the trees. Even with the huge numbers of incoming patients, triage was lightning-quick and only 412 men were actually admitted to the hospital, while the rest were evacuated to hospitals in the area.

On 9 August, the surgical backlog stood at an astounding 295 patients waiting for necessary surgical procedures. Hospitals strove to maintain a zero backlog; no one wanted patients waiting in line for surgery. To the credit of the 67th, by midnight, all major surgeries had been completed; twenty-four hours later, all needed surgeries, both minor and major, had been performed and the surgical backlog stood at zero. This meant that approximately 300 surgeries were performed in forty-eight hours by about 25 surgeons, with the help of 40 nurses and 136 corpsmen—a feat that would be astonishing under the best of circumstances in state-of-

the-art operating rooms, and something just short of miraculous in the
rudimentary conditions of the 67th's tented operating rooms.[49]

BY AUGUST, it was clear that the Allies had gained the upper hand in
Normandy, not only on the D-Day landing but throughout the weeks of
fighting that followed. In early August, Hitler and Field Marshal Günther von Kluge had to decide on the best path for the German Seventh
Army to take to regain the strength they felt they had possessed before 6
June 1944. Field Marshal von Kluge received a direct order from Hitler on
4 August instructing him to use eight of the nine Panzer Divisions in
France to attack the Allied forces still fighting to gain a secure lodgment
in Northern France. Hitler's order ran completely counter to von Kluge's
advice to the Führer: von Kluge wanted to withdraw all German forces
eastward behind the line of the Seine River in order to save the army
from destruction, and to regroup and fight a battle where German victory was more likely. If von Kluge followed Hitler's plans, he would use
the Panzer Divisions to drive west between Vire and Mortain, about ten
miles apart, to the Gulf of Saint-Malo on the Atlantic coast. There the
army was to regroup all the German forces in France and with a sweep to
the northeast, push the Allies into the English Channel.

On the part of the British, General Bernard Law Montgomery
planned to have Canadian forces leave the JUNO and GOLD Beach areas
on the Normandy coast and advance to the town of Falaise, about
twenty-five miles southeast of their present location. While the Canadians were moving in on Falaise from the north, General Bradley's Twelfth
Army Group would advance toward Falaise from the west and help encircle the German Seventh Army in the Argentan-Falaise area. Since General Patton's Third Army had already encircled the Germans in the
French coastal cities of Brest, Lorient, and Nazaire, the majority of Patton's army would advance to Le Mons, then turn sharply northwest and
encircle German troops near Mortain.

By 14 August 1944, most Allied troops were in place and thousands of
German forces were caught in a pocket that extended forty-eight miles in
length—east to west—and twelve to fifteen miles in width—north to
south. All that remained was for Bradley to move his Twelfth Army
northeast, seal the pocket off completely, and block the final avenue of a
German retreat eastward. That avenue between the American Twelfth

Army and the Canadian forces was twenty-five miles wide. However, Bradley determined not to seal the pocket for fear of friendly fire between Canadian and American troops. The Argentan-Falaise pocket in which the Germans were contained was an easy target for American Air Forces and artillery fire. American and Allied troops fired shells and dropped bombs with increasing frequency, knowing that anything that exploded within the pocket was bound to wreck or destroy something German.

By 21 August 1944, American and Allied forces had killed approximately 10,000 Germans and had taken more than 50,000 prisoners of war. Before General Bradley's men sealed the Falaise pocket on 18 August, approximately 35,000 German soldiers escaped through the opening between American and Canadian troops. The more than 10,000 German dead left behind in the Falaise pocket were strewn across the ground in various stages of decomposition. General Eisenhower described the carnage: "Forty-eight hours after the closing of the gap, I was conducted through it on foot, to encounter scenes that could be described only by Dante. It was literally possible to walk for hundreds of yards at a time, stepping on nothing but dead and decaying flesh."[50]

ON 15 AUGUST, the 128th Evacuation Hospital was ordered to close and move from its second site, one mile northwest of Tessy-sur-Vire on the western edge of the Falaise-Argentan pocket, to Haleine, a town on the southern border of the pocket about ten miles southeast of Argentan. Battle casualties from the Falaise-Argentan area were increasing hourly, and American hospitals would be needed to care for wounded American and Allied soldiers as well as German POWs. The town of Falaise was taken on 16 August, and the 128th Evacuation Hospital opened its doors to patients at 1700 on the 17th.

The patient census grew rapidly as casualties from the Falaise pocket were received. "On 21 August, our hospital received large numbers of German POWs," Marte Cameron said. "The Germans had been surrounded for three days and the wounded had lain in the field for at least that long. That meant that infections were gaining hold because they ran out of medical supplies. The Germans had run out of everything: medical supplies, ammunition, gasoline—everything."[51]

Cameron remembered that physician Captain Edward Rosenbaum, Lieutenant Vilma Vogler, and two enlisted men were the only ones in the unit who spoke fluent German, so they did most of the interpreting. "Ironically," Cameron said, "three of the four personnel were Jews . . . and we'd see them walking around chatting with the prisoners and the two German surgeons who were assigned to the care of the POWs. Many of the Germans were stony-faced. You realized how much propaganda there was." Despite the fact that many POWs were rude and hostile to Americans, personnel of U.S. Army hospitals treated them like any other patients. On 21 August alone, the 128th received, treated, and evacuated 515 wounded German POWs; admitted 126; and had a midnight census of 313 patients. Sixty-six ambulances and five 2.5-ton trucks were used to send the Germans to POW enclosures and hospitals farther behind the front lines.[52]

THE NORMANDY CAMPAIGN had a high cost: 125,847 U.S. casualties; of these, 20,838 were killed and 94,881 wounded. Due to the difficulties presented by the hedgerows, 90 percent of battle casualties were from the infantry rifle companies. The British and Canadian forces reported 83,825 casualties; of these, 16,138 were killed and 58,594 wounded. The remainder were the results of accidents. German losses totaled about 200,000, including 91,000 POWs. Airplane and crew losses included 2,036 Royal Air Force planes and 8,178 aircrew; 2,065 U.S. planes and 8,536 aircrew; and 3,656 German planes.[53]

By the end of this period, 35,000 medical personnel were ashore in Europe and caring for patients, including a total of approximately 6,640 nurses. Even with the high number of casualties, less than 1 percent of the wounded men treated by medical units in Normandy and evacuated to England died.[54]

With the invasion of Northern France progressing rapidly, the planned second invasion that would take place in Southern France was approaching its own D-Day.

CHAPTER TWELVE

Operation Dragoon and the Battle of the Rhône Valley

COMBAT MEDICINE IN SOUTHERN FRANCE

15 August–15 September 1944

A year ago, practically the same group of nurses had traveled in trucks through Sicily and Italy, laughing at hardships, singing all the songs they knew, wisecracking with each other, making a gay picture as they rolled merrily along. This year, they waited quietly to climb into the trucks, sat quietly and only occasionally a nurse was heard humming to herself.

—Lt. Evelyn F. Anderson,
"Report of the Nursing Activities for the Year of 1944,"
93rd Evacuation Hospital Report, December 1944

O N THE MORNING of 19 August 1944, the hospital ship *Marigold* dropped anchor off the coast of Southern France near the famed resort town of Saint-Tropez. On board were many of the nurses of the Seventh Army, including nurses of the 93rd and 95th Evacuation Hospitals, the 10th Field Hospital, and the 2nd Auxiliary Surgical Group teams that were assigned to the 10th Field Hospital.

Like all hospital ships, the *Marigold* lay several miles offshore, as mandated by the Hague Conventions, and began preparation for unloading her passengers. At about 1000, the nurses were loaded into landing barges for the trip to the beachhead. The French Riviera in late August was warm; the sky was clear, with a few white, puffy clouds, and the sun was shining. As destroyers and several battleships from the invasion convoy lay offshore, many Liberty ships were unloading troops, and LCTs were unloading supplies and equipment—about four thousand to five thousand tons of cargo a day—onto the beach. When the LCTs emptied, large groups of POWs, the only sign of the German resistance, were herded onto the vessels. On the beach, army combat engineers searched for enemy land mines, the only known remaining German threat to invaders of Southern France. White tapes marking the sections cleared of mines provided soldiers with a safe area for travel without threat of hitting a mine.

Compared to the landing nurses went through in Normandy two and a half months earlier on D+4, 10 June, the nurses of the Seventh Army in Southern France found their landing at Saint-Tropez on D+4, 19 August, uneventful, orderly, and relatively peaceful. At UTAH Beach in Northern France, the nurses of the 128th Evac had seen bodies of dead GIs floating in with the tide, and damaged and abandoned vehicles in the surf. The beach had been littered with clothing and equipment laying near gaping craters left by enemy shells or bombs. At Normandy, the nurses were hurried inland away from the beach by tired-looking MPs. In Southern France, troops were unloading landing craft and barges in the warm sunshine of a clear, bright day. A greeting party that included several hospital COs stood near their vehicles waiting for the nurses to arrive on shore.

Captain Evelyn E. Swanson, chief nurse of the 95th Evacuation Hospital, was the first army nurse to set foot in Southern France. Earlier that year, in April, Swanson had been appointed chief nurse following the deaths of Lieutenant Blanche Sigman and assistant chief nurse Lieutenant Carrie Sheetz in the 7 February 1944 bombing at Anzio beachhead. Now, some six months later, Swanson leaped out of the landing craft before its stern line was tied to the dock. The nurses were to join the advance echelons of their units who had landed with the invasion forces on D-Day, four days earlier. On that day, an 855-ship convoy had landed 151,000 troops, including the U.S. Seventh Army and the French army, on the sandy beaches of three towns: Saint-Tropez, Sainte-Maxime, and Saint-Raphael—for the invasion of Southern France, code-named "Dragoon."[1]

That the invasion of Southern France occurred two months after the invasion of Northern France—or, for that matter, occurred at all—was the result of an Allied military strategy that took months of debate to

Capt. Evelyn Swanson, chief nurse of the 95th Evacuation Hospital, leaping from a landing barge to become the first U.S. Army nurse to set foot in Southern France, August 1944 (U.S. Army Signal Corps)

decide. Originally, the military strategists for Overlord—the invasion of Normandy—had planned the invasion of Southern France (then called Operation Anvil) to occur simultaneously with the cross-Channel invasion of Northern France on 6 June. The Anvil plan was dropped because of stiff opposition from Prime Minister Churchill, and the lack of an adequate number of landing barges to put troops ashore in Northern and Southern France at the same time.

However, the Americans never gave up the idea, and on 24 June 1944, Anvil was resurrected under the code name "Dragoon." The Americans felt the capture of Southern France was crucial since France's largest port, Marseilles, and the nearby port of Toulon could provide a pipeline on the Mediterranean for the additional supplies and personnel needed by an advancing army. Holding the southern part of France would allow the Allies to rehabilitate the badly bombed and shattered railroad system that fed the Rhône Valley to the north. Railroad cars could hold three to four times the equipment that could be placed in a single GI truck. Needed supplies could be brought in through the southern ports of France and delivered to the north by railway far more quickly than by truck convoy.

American military strategists also believed that the invasion of Southern France would allow the veterans who had fought so well in North Africa, Sicily, and Italy to join with the less experienced soldiers of Operation Overlord who had landed in Northern France. Together, the two forces could move more quickly into Germany. Churchill, however, argued for an Allied invasion of the Balkans, with an eye to limiting the Russians' future claims and possible territorial expansion. In the end, Eisenhower made the decision and Operation Dragoon was on. Churchill came to greet the Allied invasion forces as they departed from Naples and he later traveled to the southern coast of France to witness the beginning of the invasion.

On 15 August, 151,000 troops of the Seventh Army led by Lieutenant General Alexander M. Patch, including men of the U.S. Third Infantry, Forty-fifth and Thirty-sixth Divisions, along with equipment—1,375 landing craft; 21,400 trucks, tank destroyers, bulldozers, and so on—hit the beaches of the French Riviera. The invasion also included pre–D-Day bombings by the XV Air Corps, an early morning D-Day drop of para-troopers and glider forces, and commando and French partisan activi-ties—all tactics designed to delay German troop movements.[2]

D-Day in Southern France was a clear, bright, sunny Mediterranean morning, with calm seas and the bright sliver of a moon overhead. Troops that were going ashore heard shells overhead and the loud boom of the naval guns firing from American destroyers that lay offshore. American fighter planes droned overhead as engineers exploded land mines on shore. Off the coast of Cape Cavalaire about ten miles west of Saint-Tropez, Major Richard Hauver with the 2nd Auxiliary Surgical Group team watched troops unloading from his ship. On 15 August he reported in his diary, "At 0900 all very quiet and we are slowly going for-ward towards shore. . . . News [is] ahead of schedule and little resistance." The men of the 93rd Evacuation Hospital who came ashore at Sainte-Maxime at H+4, 1200 (H-hour, the hour of an invasion, in this case was 0800), were surprised and relieved that they had no enemy resistance. They watched infantrymen marching German POWs down paths toward the beach. An occasional enemy shell scattered the barges and speedy destroyers that patrolled the waters. Although three ships had struck enemy mines, things were going smoothly.[3]

Off the coast at Fréjus about ten miles northeast of Sainte-Maxime, Sergeant Charles Coolidge with the Thirty-sixth Division compared the lack of serious German resistance to his first amphibious assault at Salerno, Italy, in September 1943. At Salerno, he and his squad climbed over the side of the landing barge when the bow ramp failed to open. At 0330, under cover of darkness and in a hail of enemy gunfire from shore, Coolidge dropped down into cold water up to his armpits, weighed down by 100 pounds of equipment, including a 30-caliber machine gun. "We lost 13 percent of our division during its Salerno landing," Coolidge said. At Fréjus at 0800, Coolidge made sure that he and his men got off their boat onto solid ground. He had made a deal with the barge pilot: if the pilot got Coolidge and his troops off on dry ground, they would push his barge back into the water. "Every one of my men got off on dry ground—we never lost a man right then. . . . And we kept our part of the deal. We tugged and pushed and finally got the landing barge out into the water." Compared to the rough landing of the Thirty-sixth Division at Salerno, with a loss of about two hundred of its men, the smooth landings without enemy resistance in Southern France were a blessed relief.[4]

AFTER ROME fell to the Allies in June 1944, fighting continued in Italy, but some of the troops and hospitals began staging for the next invasion. From 1 to 12 June, the nurses of the 95th Evacuation Hospital continued to work at their hospital site at Cisterna di Littoria, about twenty-five miles southeast of Rome and twenty miles northeast of Anzio. On 13 June, the 95th moved to Montalto di Castro, on the Italian coast fifty-five miles northwest of Rome, following U.S. troops that had driven German forces out of Rome and were continuing to drive them north. When the 95th Evac received orders to prepare for a new invasion, the hospital moved on 15 July to a staging area near Sparanise, twenty-five miles north of Naples. A week before leaving for the new front, the nurses were granted passes. The women used the time to visit Naples and attend the opera, take in the sights, and shop for souvenirs to mail home to family and friends.

Nurses also found time, just before shipping out for the invasion of Southern France, to attend the wedding of Lieutenant Adeline "Si" Simonson to Capt. Marvin Williams of the Thirty-fourth Infantry Division. The two had met at a dance in North Africa and, after a year of dating, decided to get married. In compliance with military rules, they applied to their respective COs for permission; requests were also submitted to the chaplain as well. Usually the only marriage requests that were disapproved by the army were marriages between a female officer and an enlisted man, as this violated the military's nonfraternization policy.

The wedding took place at one of the few Protestant chapels in Naples. Before the ceremony, the couple realized they had not had time to obtain a wedding ring and were glad of Speedy Glidewell's offer to lend them hers for the time it took to take their vows. Claudine "Speedy"

Capt. Marvin Williams and his bride, Lt. Adeline "Si" Simonson, leave for their honeymoon after their marriage and reception in Naples, 1944 (Courtesy of Adeline Simonson Williams)

Glidewell was now assigned to the 300th General Hospital in Naples. Chronic respiratory problems had taken her off frontline hospital duty and she was reassigned to a nonmobile hospital. Glidewell was glad for the chance to spend some time with her original overseas "family," especially Bee Wee Wheeler, Hut Walden, Pete Peterson, and Si Simonson.

The reception, held at the well-known "uptown" Orange Grove Restaurant, offered the guests a chance to indulge in local Italian food. The restaurant was famous for its delicious dishes, and guests from the 95th Evac and Thirty-fourth Infantry Division ate heartily despite the general order not to eat the local food. The chocolate eclairs were a big hit with everyone and nobody gave a thought to the unpasteurized milk products that went into them.

When the reception ended, the guests followed the bride and groom to a waiting jeep with JUST MARRIED on the rear bumper. The couple drove off for a five-day honeymoon in Rome, and the guests went back to their units. The next morning, wedding guests who had enjoyed the eclairs were running high temperatures and suffering from diarrhea and nausea. Glidewell was admitted to her own hospital in Naples with a temperature of 105°, abdominal pains, and a diagnosis of salmonella.

By 14 August, everyone who had eaten the eclairs had recovered and had received orders that they would ship out shortly for a combat zone. Captain Evelyn Swanson, the new chief nurse of the 95th Evacuation Hospital, and Wheeler, Walden, Peterson, and the newlywed Simonson-Williams—just back from her honeymoon—visited the 300th General to say good-bye to Glidewell. They talked for hours and sipped a local wine. The women toasted "the success of the upcoming invasion, wherever it may be," and "the health" of each of the nurses present.

Late on the night of D-Day, 15 August, the nurses of the 95th and the 93rd Evacuation Hospitals were awakened by the sound of many planes flying over Naples, the bay, and beyond. The XV Air Forces was returning from bombing raids in Southern France. "I said a prayer for all my buddies with the 95th Evac," Glidewell remembered. "It wouldn't be long before they too were traveling out of the Bay of Naples. I also bemoaned the fact that I wouldn't be with them."[5]

In the daylight hours the following morning, the nurses of the 95th and 93rd lined up alphabetically and waited their turns to board the *Marigold* for its maiden voyage as a newly refitted hospital ship. Since the crew was celebrating this special event, the vessel offered many more amenities than the average hospital ship could manage. The women were directed to their quarters on a lower deck; each was surprised and delighted to find herself sharing a six-bed ward with clean, white sheets and spreads, and a radio to listen to the armed forces network. "Everything was perfect on the *Marigold* and we took full advantage of its luxuries," Evelyn Anderson said. "In addition to each ward having its own radio, each bed had its own reading light."[6]

After North Africa, Sicily, and Italy, the *Marigold* was nothing less than exquisite for women who had lived in muddy combat zones under German shelling and bombing. Most of the army nurses coming ashore in Southern France were veterans of at least one other amphibious landing, and like combat veterans everywhere, they knew how to enjoy luxury when it was offered to them. Compared to their ill-fated voyage from North Africa to Salerno in September 1943, this was a real pleasure. Although German submarines lurked beneath the surface of the Mediterranean, the survivors of the bombed *Newfoundland* took full advantage of the *Marigold*'s amenities. In addition to comfortable living quarters, the *Marigold* had her own orchestra, which played the latest tunes from America every night from 1800 to 2000. The ship also had the best food the United States could provide. "We had food from the stores in the States," said Vera Sheaffer. "We had candy bars and ice cream. We had an orchestra on board, too. Oh, it was fancy." Before she had left the United States, the *Marigold* had been stocked with fresh eggs, frozen vegetables, fresh steaks and roasts, and fresh tomatoes. To add to these comforts, meals were served on china set on white linen tablecloths. In contrast to the experiences of other army nurses headed into invasions, the nurses on the *Marigold* were alone on board, with only the ship's crew and the physicians and corpsmen of the hospital unit that was assigned to the ship. There were no military troops on board.[7]

Even the exchange was something special. "The ship's post exchange had carried large quantities of Coca-Colas and we drank them as often as our thirst needed quenching," Swanson, the chief nurse, wrote in her annual report. "This was our first experience overseas where we could have such luxury in unlimited amounts and needless to say, this opportunity was embraced by all the nurses." But not even the luxuries offered by the *Marigold* could banish the reality of war. "The reminders of war were ever present, for it was the grim business of war that had made this trip necessary," Swanson added.[8]

Now, after a rather luxurious three-day crossing from Italy via Corsica to France, the nurses of the 95th Evac found themselves seated in the back of a truck headed for their hospital site near Gonfaron, about fifteen miles west of Saint-Tropez. The tented wards were crowded with patients—mostly French civilians and members of the Free French Forces (FFI—Forces Françaises de l'Intérieur), a group of French resisters to the German occupation which was founded in February 1944.

All but a few French resistance groups belonged to the FFI, which was commanded by General Pierre-Joseph Koenig in London. At the beginning, the FFI was made up of about thirty thousand lightly armed men and women, most of whom were in contact with members of British intelligence—the Special Operations Executive (SOE)—or American intelligence—the Office of Strategic Services (OSS). By the time Allied and American troops landed in Normandy, membership in the FFI had swelled to approximately 200,000 men and women. The resistance contributed mightily to the success of the Normandy landings by wrecking or destroying railroads and telephone lines used by the Germans. They were especially active and effective in Southern France, in the coastal towns of Toulon and Sète, where FFI groups disrupted German efforts to destroy port areas. Several larger groups also helped Americans capture Grenoble in seven days rather than the ninety days predicted by D-Day planners. In September 1944, approximately 137,000 FFI members were inducted into the First French Army to replace French North African troops, who were returned to North Africa.[9]

ON 19 AUGUST 1944, D+4, the hospital ship *Ernest Hinds* dropped anchor off the coast of Saint-Raphael and discharged its passengers into landing craft for the ride to shore. Like the USAHS *Marigold*, the USAHS *Ernest Hinds* was a World War I army transport that had been recently converted into a hospital ship, and sent to support the invasion of Southern France along with the *Marigold* and ten other hospital ships. The *Hinds* carried the nurses of the 11th Field Hospital and those of the 2nd Aux Surgical Group attached to that hospital. She had traveled in the same convoy with the *Marigold*, and arrived in France the same day as the *Marigold*; but there the similarities between the two ships ended. Compared to the luxurious *Marigold*, the *Ernest Hinds* was one of the smallest hospital ships, only about 373 feet in length and with a weight of 4,858 tons, whereas the *Marigold* was 522 feet in length and 10,533 tons. The *Hinds* had no special amenities—no Coca-Cola, shipboard band, fine china, or table linen—and had long ago celebrated her maiden voyage.[10]

When the nurses from the *Hinds* waded ashore at Saint-Raphael, a reception party from the 11th Field Hospital met the women and transported them to their hospital sites at Saint-Raphael and Le Muy, about ten miles farther northwest. The 11th Field Hospital was now functioning as three separate hospitals or platoons—two 120-bed hospitals and one 160-bed hospital. Each of these three units—designated as 11th Field Platoon #1, #2, and #3—was more mobile because of its smaller size, and would be able to "leapfrog" in order to keep up with the Seventh Army troops. Each 11th Field platoon with teams of the 2nd Auxiliary Surgical Group attached had six nurses assigned to provide postoperative care. The 2nd Aux teams were completely mobile; their

U.S. Army nurses wading ashore in Southern France, August 1944 (Courtesy of Maj. Frances Miernicke Plenert, ANC [Ret.])

assignments to the 11th Field platoons and other hospitals supporting the American and French troops of Dragoon could change daily or hourly as needs dictated.

Like all hospital staff, each new arrival was wearing an armband— called a *brassard*—on his left arm, bearing an American flag. All U.S. forces in the army hospitals wore flags on their sleeves since the FFI were active in the area and had given their allegiance to the Americans. "If you weren't wearing that American flag," Frances "Frenchie" Miernicke said, "the FFI would just as soon take a shot at you as not." The French liked the Americans, but bore a grudge against the British that went back to 1940 when the British sank the French fleet at Mers-el-Kebir.[11]

From the time the nurses arrived at the 11th Field Hospital on D+4, Lieutenant Miernicke's 2nd Auxiliary Surgical Group team and the other assigned 2nd Aux teams worked sixteen-hour shifts to help clear the surgical backlog. German artillery shells flew overhead and landed in the sea or fell short and landed near the hospital area at Draguignan, a small town about fifteen miles inland from the beach and about five miles northwest of Le Muy. However, the enemy was unable to concentrate its forces because of Allied air and naval coverage, and German attacks on the American beach forces were not as heavy as anticipated by medical planners.

The Allied invasion of Southern France met poorly organized and ineffective German defenses. The Germans' rapid retreat up the Rhône Valley was interrupted only by several pockets of stiff resistance in the cities of Toulon, Marseilles, and Montélimar. Compared to the invasion of Normandy in Northern France, where Americans and Allies suffered high casualties at the hands of Germans who launched heavy resistance from well-defended, dug-in positions, the Allied forces that invaded Southern France took far fewer casualties. U.S. casualties on D-Day alone in Northern France were 5,000; in Southern France, it took a month of fighting from D-Day to D+30 to wrack up 4,500 American casualties.[12]

After the beachhead was secured, the Forty-fifth Division moved north rapidly, meeting only scattered German resistance along the way. By 22 August, only one week after D-Day, the Forty-fifth had crossed the Durance River and expanded the Allied beachhead to at least sixty miles deep at its narrowest point. The fast-moving Thirty-sixth Division headed for territory twenty miles north of Sisteron, located about sixty-five miles north of Saint-Raphael. One corps of General Jean-Marie de Lattre's French army surrounded the enemy occupying the ports of Mar-

Lt. Evelyn "Andy" Anderson and the enlisted men on her OR team, 1944 (Courtesy of Evelyn Anderson Blank)

seilles and Toulon. On 28 August, D+13, both port cities fell into Allied hands. The Allied army was moving rapidly and the Nineteenth German Army was in retreat.

ON 22 AUGUST 1944, the 93rd Evacuation Hospital moved forty-five miles north from Plan de la Tour to Barjols. Barjols, about thirty miles northeast of Marseilles, was a "quaint French town," Anderson wrote. "Life for us was rather monotonous. Our recreation consisted of walks and occasional rides on a French train."[13]

The German Nineteenth Army was retreating rapidly, with American troops in hot pursuit. Since two field hospitals, the 10th and the 11th, and the 9th Evacuation Hospital were located near Montélimar, and were caring for casualties resulting from a battle for that town, the 93rd Evac's patient load was light. Anderson and the other 93rd Evac nurses were veterans of other extremely challenging campaigns and dangerous living conditions such as those on the Anzio beachhead. To these seasoned army nurses, the Southern France invasion, so far, was not a serious challenge. A total of 1,216 patients received care in fifteen days from the 93rd Evac team while it was located near the French Riviera.[14]

The tables turned a bit against the Allies toward the end of the first week after the invasion: at Montélimar, up the Rhône Valley about ninety miles north of Marseilles, the Germans mounted a strong resistance. For nine days, from 21 to 29 August, the Thirty-sixth Division fought a heated battle. Two of the 11th Field Hospital platoons were supporting the combat troops, and for a time found themselves in "extremely uncomfortable" positions. "For two days we were surrounded by the enemy on three sides, and the one road leading to the units was under constant artillery fire," the chief nurse of the unit, Captain Margaret W. Sydel, wrote later. "It was most fortunate for the mental well-being of my nurses that they were too busy with the battle casualties to have any time to think of personal danger. I can never praise sufficiently their courageous attitude and devotion to duty evidenced during this hazardous experience."[15]

Doctors, nurses, and corpsmen had to deal not only with the stress of almost constant artillery fire but also the stress of listening to threatening German radio broadcasts by the propagandist known as "Axis Sally." During the fighting at Montélimar, "Axis Sally" tried to instill fear in the Allies with taunts that German victory was imminent. She began directly addressing hospital personnel—the nurses in particular—in her radio broadcasts, and described to the doctors and nurses what the Germans would do to them when hospital staff were captured.

One nurse not likely to be easily demoralized or frightened by "Axis Sally" was Frenchie Miernicke. Frenchie was a veteran of "Hell's Half-Acre," Anzio beachhead. She had ministered to countless soldiers, some grotesquely wounded; she had survived months of artillery fire and shelling on the beachhead; she had prepared the body of a fellow nurse and friend, Ellen Ainsworth, for burial at Anzio. There was not much that a radio propagandist could say that would deter Miernicke from performing her sworn duties.

On 24 August, Miernicke was working with the 11th Field Hospital platoons at Crest, about twenty miles northeast of Montélimar. "Supplies weren't coming in very fast," Miernicke said. "We were going through our stores pretty fast. Even the boys on the line weren't getting the ammunition they needed. Well, all of a sudden, Axis Sally began telling hospital personnel that they would be among the first prisoners taken by the Germans in Southern France. Worse yet, she said, 'All you nurses will soon be on the arms of German generals who will show you off just like the war trophies you'll be.' "[16]

Miernicke and others noted that for hours that day American antiaircraft guns had been eerily silent. The skies were dominated by frequent flyovers of German Messerschmitts whose pilots flew them so low their wings almost scraped the tops of the hospital tents. No one could be sure that "Axis Sally" was not speaking the truth when she predicted that German victory was close at hand. Tension ran high among patients and staff at the hospitals, and Miernicke found it hard to concentrate on her work in the OR tent.

All of a sudden, as if by a coordinated signal, a number of nurses and other medical personnel abruptly walked out of the OR tent and joined others in their unit who were leaving the hospital area and their patients. "They left their [OR] tables," Miernicke recalled. "They took to the hills. There we were, our one little five-person team, alone in the OR tent." Apparently, those who had suddenly chosen to leave and run for the hills did so to avoid the German capture that "Axis Sally" kept broadcasting was imminent. "My surgeon [Major Howard Bos] said, 'We don't leave patients, and we don't stop working even if it means we're captured. And if we're captured, we'll still continue our work,' " Miernicke said. "I was scared. I was always afraid of being raped and I sure didn't want to be taken prisoner. I used to pray that I'd go home in one piece, or I wouldn't go home at all."[17]

Despite their fears, Miernicke and her team stayed at their posts and continued to assist Bos with surgery. About fifteen minutes later, the tank guns of Task Force Butler, a fast-moving armored force under the command of Brigadier General Frederick B. Butler, broke the hours-long eerie silence with an Allied armored barrage aimed at German positions beyond the hospital. Shortly after the Allied tank attack began, the nurses and medical personnel who had fled reappeared and went back to work. Without a word to Miernicke's team, the 11th Field staff brought new patients into the OR tent, and all five tables were busy again. "I don't remember that anyone ever brought up their 'desertion' with them, but they worked steadily for the rest of the night," Miernicke recalled. "I could understand their embarrassment. Like Howard said, we don't leave our patients even if it means that we're captured by the enemy."[18]

During the Battle of Montélimar, the medical units admitted 2,174 patients—840 battle casualties, of whom 411 were POWs. The Thirty-sixth Division took 3,700 German prisoners, fully one fifth of the Nineteenth German Army strength, at Montélimar. The Americans suffered about 100 casualties.[19]

LIKE ALL of the 2nd Auxiliary Surgical Group nurses in each hospital in every campaign, Miernicke was attached to her team: they were "family"—"all in it together." When the men on her team went onto the beaches of Southern France on D-Day without her or the other nurses, Miernicke found ways to help them even in her absence. Technical Sergeant Ernest Tignanelli particularly disliked one duty that fell to him when Miernicke was not with the team—threading suture needles. " 'Whenever I have to thread a suture needle,' Tignanelli would say, 'I want to do it like my mother did when she was getting ready to sew,' " Miernicke recalled Tignanelli's words. " 'She'd put the thread in her mouth to make it wet so the end would form a point and be easier to get through the needle's eye.' " In order to help him, Miernicke threaded a supply of sterile suture needles and pushed the needles through a sterilized gauze sponge and included them in presterilized suture packs. "When I saw him on 19 August, one of the first things he said was, 'You saved my life! Thank you for threading the needles. I really appreciate it.' "[20]

On their 2nd Aux team, the favors went both ways. As Miernicke recalled, "Tignanelli always seemed to know when I wasn't feeling very well. At times like that, I didn't look forward to digging a foxhole at a new location. Tignanelli would see me digging and come take the shovel out of my hands. 'You go into your tent and rest,' he would say. 'I'll dig the foxhole.' When I objected because nurses were supposed to dig their own foxholes, he'd say, 'Yes, and corpsmen should thread their own suture needles.' Families share what's tough for them as well as the good times. We're a family!"[21]

One person Miernicke at first felt would never be "family" on their close-knit team was a new assistant surgeon, Captain Ross Hobler, who joined them in late August 1944. Hobler was a battalion surgeon with the Forty-fifth Division when he finally received his requested transfer to

2nd Auxiliary Surgical Group Team #12. Left to right, standing: *Major Frank Norris, Capt. Ross Hobler, Lt. Frances "Frenchie" Miernicke, Major Howard Bos.* Kneeling: *Tech-5 Frank Kempner and Tech-4 Ernest Tignanelli* (Courtesy of Maj. Frances Miernicke Plenert, ANC [Ret.])

the 2nd Auxiliary Surgical Group. At the time his transfer came through, the Forty-fifth Division was located near the 11th Field Hospital. Hobler left the division and joined the 2nd Aux team. The chief surgeon of the team, Major Howard Bos, knew Hobler personally from back home; he had worked with him in Chicago before the war. Hobler was a Phi Beta Kappa and he was from New York, and Bos was impressed with both of these facts. The 2nd Aux chief surgeon was happy to have his old friend and colleague join their General Surgical Team #12.

On the first day Hobler was scheduled to work in the OR, Bos had a day off. Hobler took over as chief surgeon, and he and Miernicke worked together for the first time. Like all surgical teams, the 2nd Aux team members usually carried on friendly conversations among themselves during surgery. Miernicke noted that from the moment Hobler entered the OR and all throughout surgery, the surgeon would not condescend to speak to any members of the team except to bark out orders. Worse than his giving the team the cold shoulder, Hobler threw away a chest tube that Miernicke had scrounged and improvised to create. "He just threw the tube in the bucket at the side of the table and asked for another one," Miernicke said. "I told him that we didn't have another tube and he told me to go and find one. His entire manner was degrading and snarly. I made up my mind at that instant to talk to Howard that night about Captain Hobler."[22]

Miernicke was not one to tolerate condescension silently. When their twelve-hour shift ended, she went straight to Major Bos's tent. "I'm glad you'll be back tomorrow because I'm not scrubbing with Captain Hobler again until he apologizes to me for his rude, obnoxious behavior," Miernicke said. Bos listened attentively as Miernicke went on about Hobler. "You need to talk to him and he'd better get off of his high horse because we're a team and we work together. He thinks he's a prima donna or something special from New York." Miernicke explained that she had nothing against New Yorkers but thought that there must be others who were a lot nicer. "You can just tell him that I don't go back to the OR until he apologizes to me for throwing the tubing away, and talking to me like I was his servant."[23]

Later that night, there was a knock on Miernicke's tent flap. It was Hobler, and he walked into Miernicke's tent and sat down. "He sounded different than in the OR that morning," Miernicke said. " 'I had a long talk from Howard and he told me that you all are a team and that you work together. He said I'd have to fit in with the team to survive. I'm very sorry that I threw away the tubing and that I talked to you as if you were not part of the team. I apologize.' " Miernicke said, "That's fine. I accept your apology. As long as you treat me with respect and are polite to me, everything will be okay."[24]

Miernicke had learned early in her career to stand up for herself and to demand that she be treated as an equal in the OR and when off duty. Even as a young civilian nurse, Miernicke had not been afraid to speak up for herself or others. While working at St. Luke's Hospital in Duluth, Minnesota, before America's entry into the war, Miernicke was assigned as scrub nurse to a German-born physician who was legendary among hospital personnel for his harshness. "He was a well-built, tall man and I had to stand on a box in order to pass him instruments from a parallel height," Miernicke said. This surgeon had a bad habit of using the retractor—an instrument used during surgery to separate incisions and hold back organs or internal tissue in order to expose the operative area—to slap interns on their gloved hands during surgery. The blow was so painful that many of the young doctors would faint.

Finally, Miernicke could take no more of the surgeon's sadistic behavior. "Doctor, you keep doing that, and I'm leaving the operating room," Miernicke said. "Well, he did it again, and I walked out. He covered the surgical field with sterile towels and came after me." The doctor called after Miernicke, "Come back, Nurse. I didn't mean it. I didn't mean it." Miernicke turned and looked up at the flustered surgeon. "If you promise not to do it again, I'll come back. But if you do it one more time, I will not scrub with you again."[25]

Although the surgeon did not hit another intern, it was not the last time he locked horns with Miernicke. One morning, he had completed an operation and they were getting ready to close the patient's incision. Miernicke was accounting for the instruments and sponges used in the case to be sure that none was left in the operative area—inside the patient. "Don't close!" Miernicke said. "The sponge count is off by one. There is a sponge missing." The surgeon continued his movement to close the incision until Miernicke put her gloved hand in his way. "I'm sorry, Doctor, but there is a sponge missing and my name goes on the sponge count as a record. You cannot close until we find the missing sponge." Without a word, the surgeon pulled out the sponge he had hidden under the edge of a sterile sheet. Despite some minor backsliding, the surgeon and Miernicke got along in an atmosphere of mutual respect after that incident.[26]

Miernicke was the only woman on her 2nd Aux Group team. The team consisted of Major Howard Bos, the chief surgeon; Captain Ross Hobler, assistant surgeon; Major Frank Norris, anesthesiologist; two surgical technicians, Tech-4 Ernest Tignanelli and Tech-5 Frank Kempner; and Miernicke herself, surgical nurse. "We were like brothers and sister," Miernicke said. "I had lots of brothers to look out after me, and they had a big sister to watch their backs. We were family."[27]

Being the only woman on the team did have some drawbacks. There was no other woman with whom Miernicke could form a buddy system, which left her alone when it came to a seemingly simple matter— "answering nature's call." However, after Miernicke and Hobler had spent hours working together in the OR, coping with difficult living conditions and surviving the ever present dangers of war, they forged a strong bond of friendship. Once, in early morning darkness and only five miles from the front lines, as they both were leaving the OR tent after long hours of surgery, Miernicke told Hobler, "I have to go to the bathroom. It's dark out here and I can't find my way around this hospital in pitch darkness. Promise you won't leave me alone." Hobler said that he promised. In a few minutes, the two reached the nurses' latrine. "How will I know where you are in the dark?" Miernicke asked Hobler, who responded, "Hold my hand and I'll go in with you." "Okay, but don't look," Miernicke said.[28]

By 1 September, the ports of Toulon and Marseilles were under Allied control. In just two weeks, the Allies had captured 57,000 prisoners in Southern France and put the Germans into full retreat, while suffering 4,000 French casualties and 2,700 American. The number of battle casu-

Nurses of the 95th Evacuation Hospital waiting for transportation to their hospital site. Left to right: Lts. Ruth Buckley, Bernice "Hut" Walden, and Isabelle "Bee Wee" Wheeler (Courtesy of Claudine Glidewell Doyle)

alties for the Normandy invasion from 6 June to 24 July 1944 totaled 63,360—vastly more than the number of casualties suffered in General Alexander Patch's Seventh Army in Southern France.[29]

THE 95TH EVACUATION Hospital left Gonfaron on 3 September with orders to set up at a site fifty miles north. But before the hospital reached its new site, a change of orders arrived, directing the 95th Evac to continue on to Saint-Amour, more than three hundred miles north of the landing sites in Southern France. After bivouacking one night with the Third Division Clearing Station near Ambérieu, the 95th Evac set up at Saint-Amour at 0900 on 5 September. Elements of the Seventh Army had already marched through this country and were now at Besançon, ninety miles north of Saint-Amour. The 95th Evac became the first group of Americans to bivouac near the town. "The people were wonderful to us," Lillie "Pete" Peterson said. "They greeted us as liberators and brought all kinds of food as gifts—chickens, eggs, ducks, and rabbits."[30]

This area of Southern France had been fairly isolated from the war. Due to the bombing of the railroads, townspeople were unable to ship produce and other food products to markets in large French cities. They found themselves with surpluses of food that they shared freely with the hospital. "On Sunday, the French civilians showed up at the hospital with wine, cheese, eggs, and butter as gifts for the patients and hospital personnel," Peterson said. "All of us were sad when in less than two weeks in this land of plenty, we received orders to move again. Our troops were on the move once more, and where the soldiers went, our hospital was soon to follow."[31]

Since the 95th Evac was the most forward evacuation hospital, it received a heavy load of battle casualties from the Doubs River and Dijon areas. The four hundred beds were soon overflowing because the chain of evacuation to the rear had been disrupted. Wounded could not be moved by hospital trains because French railroads had been bombed and left in twisted heaps. Evacuation by air was also at a standstill due to rain and fog.

Finally, on 9 September, the weather cleared and air evacuation began again from Ambérieu, northwest of Lyon, to Istres, an airfield twenty-five miles northwest of Marseilles. These evacuees either stayed at rear hospitals in the Rhône River delta or were flown on to hospitals in Italy. From 22 August to 7 November, 17,255 casualties of the Seventh Army would be evacuated by air from airfields in Southern France to Istres, with 7,377 of these continuing on by air to hospitals in Italy. Compared to the difficulties of evacuating 33,063 patients from the Anzio beachhead—rough seas and German air raids with strafing of the beachhead and bombing of ships in the harbor—the evacuation from Southern France went relatively smoothly. Effective pre-invasion planning and weak enemy resistance made a vast difference.[32]

ON 31 AUGUST 1944, the 93rd Evacuation Hospital moved two hundred miles farther north to Rives, and set up on a plateau about three miles from the town. "This is the first time any evacuation hospital in the Mediterranean Theater of Operations has been called up to move such a long distance, without aid of borrowed vehicles, keep two hospitals functioning at the same time, and do it on such brief notice," Colonel Donald Currier, CO of the 93rd Evacuation Hospital, wrote. Moving a four-hundred-bed hospital on sixteen hours' notice under blackout conditions over two hundred miles of winding, narrow mountain roads that had to be shared with other military and civilian traffic was no easy feat.[33]

It was 1600 on 30 August when Currier received the order to move one of four echelons at 0830 the next morning. With about six hours of daylight remaining, hospital personnel activated their well-practiced plan. First, patients were moved to other wards in order to clear one section of the hospital. Each of the thirty-four trucks was assigned a specific load and moved into loading position. Equipment inside the tents, such as patients' cots and the nurses' supply chest, were removed, collapsed, and loaded according to specifications. Tents were struck, collapsed, and packed into one of the eighteen one-ton trailers that belonged to the 93rd Evac. By dark around 2300, the convoy was ready to roll.

The next day, 31 August, at exactly 0830, Colonel Currier gave the signal and the convoy moved forward on its two-hundred-mile trip north. Fortunately, the weather was clear and warm. "The ride was one of the most beautiful we had in Europe," Evelyn Anderson wrote. "We wound around mountainous roads and looked over verdant valleys in which nestled quaint little French villages. These looked like miniature settings under Christmas trees, with the red roofs and church steeples glistening in the sun."[34]

When the convoy arrived at 1900 that evening, the staff found their standard plan had been laid out ahead of time by an advance team. Each tent area was clearly marked so that the truck drivers knew where to unload. The first section of the hospital was set up before dark and patients began arriving several hours later. The trucks, now empty, were ready to leave in the morning, roll south to the original site, and repeat the process all over again until the entire hospital was moved.

All four sections of the hospital were open on 3 September. The hospital supported troops of the Forty-fifth Division who were fighting south of Lyon. While at Rives, the 93rd would care for 1,053 patients in the first two weeks of September.[35]

American and Allied soldiers were continuing to move quickly toward the borders of Germany. On 11 September, troops of Operation Dragoon coming up from Southern France met up with troops of Operation Overlord coming from Northern France in Saulieu, twenty-five miles north of Autun, which was ninety miles northwest of Lyon in eastern France. There, troops waited for the delivery of fuel and prepared for new orders that would carry them and the hospitals supporting them to Belgium and Germany.

On 13 September, tanks of the Third Armored Division of the VII Corps pushed forward and crossed the German border ten miles south of Aachen at Rotgen. By the evening of 14 September, four divisions of General Patton's Third Army crossed the Rhine River, but it was a supply-starved force that took up positions on Germany's doorstep. As predicted, Patton had outrun his supply lines, and General Courtney Hodge's First Army had to wait for supplies to catch up before launching a new offensive.

By the time the Allied troops from Southern France had reached the border of Germany, they had liberated the ports of Marseilles and Toulon and the city of Lyon, rid all of Southern France of the enemy after four years of German occupation, and advanced four hundred miles into central France. Allied troops had captured about 63,000 Germans and killed about 7,000; German wounded were estimated at 21,000. Many of these were treated at U.S. Army hospitals supporting the Seventh Army.[36]

By the end of Dragoon, the medical installations of the Seventh Army had admitted more than 28,000 soldiers from 15 August to 30 September. Of these, 13,000 were evacuated to Southern France or Italy; 9,000 were able to return to duty; and 6,000 remained hospitalized. By September 1944, the Seventh Army had 5,000 hospital beds near the front lines for the 140,000 troops positioned in the field. Though the invasion of Southern France was comparatively less bloody than the invasions at Anzio and Normandy, the death toll was still considerable: 7,301 American/Allied dead.[37]

The Americans and their Allies showed their mettle in France: the invasions in Normandy and Southern France were staggering victories. In less than three years, a militarily unprepared America had drawn itself up to launch two massive amphibious invasions that not only put 198,400 military vehicles and 1,080,000 American soldiers on French soil in less than two months, but kept those soldiers well fed and well supplied with both equipment and top medical care.[38]

But after almost three years of war, everyone was sick of it—soldiers, officers, doctors, nurses, civilians—sick and tired. America and the Allies were primed to get to Germany and to get there fast, to put an end to this war, and go home. "Everyone knew and accepted that the road home led through Berlin," Anderson wrote, "and believe me, none of us wanted to waste one minute getting to Hitler's capital city. Our hearts were already knocking on Berlin's door."[39]

CHAPTER THIRTEEN

Confronting the Siegfried Line

MEDICINE UNDER CANVAS

15 September–15 December 1944

When you see the sights we see and work with for twelve to fourteen hours a day, you come off duty tense and tired—you feel like blood, you smell like blood—it is in your hair and on your clothing—you need something to make you forget.

—*Capt. Mamie Miller,*
"A Nurse in Normandy," Army Life (July 1944)

L IEUTENANT "FRENCHIE" MIERNICKE looked at the young German SS trooper on her OR table and knew it was time to make a decision. Outside the surgical tent of the 11th Field Hospital, now set up in the small town of Saulx in eastern France, Frenchie could see a long line of wounded soldiers lying on litters in the mud and freezing rain waiting for surgery. It was the last week in September 1944, and a heavy stream of battle casualties had been pouring into the hospital from the Lunéville-Nancy area since the 18th, when the Germans had launched a ferocious counterattack against the steadily advancing Allies. Unexpectedly, the strength of the German defense was growing fiercer the closer the Allies drew to the German border, and the Allies were getting very close. The 11th Field Hospital had quickly moved to Saulx on 21 September to keep up with the rapidly advancing troops. As a forward unit, the 11th Field was among those mobile hospitals set up closest to the front lines to receive battle casualties from division clearing stations and serve as the first links in the evacuation chain.

These casualties included not only American and Allied men but wounded prisoners of war as well. The wounded soldier seated on the OR table before Miernicke was a German POW. He was, however, not a regular foot soldier of the Wehrmacht. This POW was an SS officer, one of Hitler's elite. And that was the problem facing Miernicke: this soldier would not lie down on the OR table. As one of the elite of a superior race, the SS officer considered it beneath him to cooperate with his "inferior" captors, even if his life depended on it. Though bleeding and in need of surgery, he obstinately refused to lie down so that Major Frank Norris could administer anesthesia. For ten minutes—a long and precious ten minutes considering the line of wounded outside the OR tent—Miernicke tried to talk the SS officer into lying down. "We'd get SS troopers as patients and they were tough," Miernicke said. "They would just as soon raise up off the table and do something to you. They were hard to put under. They were real nasty." Miernicke finally decided that the man would need an injection of morphine to knock the fight out of him and keep him calm for surgery. "They just fought anything that you did for them," Miernicke said, "trying to get them under anesthesia . . . we had to give them more anesthesia, maybe morphine—you had to knock them out. We only had a couple of them, but you never forget." These uncompromising patients would spew their propaganda at anyone who would listen: the Germans were going to win the war, Americans were weak and made bad soldiers. "At least anesthesia shut them up for an hour or two," Miernicke remarked.[1]

Soldiers and POWs were not the only battle casualties. Sometimes wounded French civilians were brought to field hospitals. One day an old French bus delivered a group of injured men, women, and children. The bus had stopped wherever injured civilians appeared along the road or near small villages, picked them up, and delivered them to the closest hospital. Among the wounded were two curly-haired sisters, ages three and six years. They were brought to Miernicke's OR table for surgery. "They looked so little on the table compared to the SS 'Supermen,' " Miernicke said. "The two only spoke French and every American doctor who could speak French spent time talking to the girls. They were just adorable. Their whole family was gone." The doctors were so touched by these tiny victims of war that several wanted to adopt them and send them home to America. "Our hospital tried to locate the bus driver to find any relatives the girls might have, but with no success," Miernicke said. "The driver who brought them in could not be found, nor did anyone know their names or the name of their village. He had found them sitting at the side of the road, crying and holding on to each other."[2]

With hundreds of soldiers and civilians lined up for their turn in surgery, Miernicke was not able to keep track of the girls. American physicians did not adopt them, and Miernicke could only hope they were reunited with family members or anyone who would love and care for them. Everyone at the 11th Field, including the 2nd Aux Surgical teams, knew that there was no way to keep the children with either unit. The units were constantly on the move and too frequently the target of German strafing or shelling. "You went where you were called," Miernicke said. "I think we moved twenty-one times in one month. We lived out of our bedrolls."[3]

Even on the move, hospital staff were often the target of German pilots. German Messerschmitts would fly low over convoys of ambulances and strafe them, in flagrant disregard of the large red crosses against white circular backgrounds painted on the roofs and doors of the cars. "We had to dump ourselves out, get into a ditch, and lie on the ground as flat as you could get," Miernicke said. "I don't care what people say. It was intentional."[4]

The weather in Northern France also was a formidable foe. Late autumn in France 1944 was already showing signs of the unusually severe winter that lay ahead. Temperatures were unseasonably cold and the rain was constant; the two together produced an ever present damp cold that penetrated clothing, skin, and muscle, right down to the bone. The heavy rains turned roads and fields into rivers and pools of deep, sticky mud. Both troops and hospital personnel had to slog through mud that often ranged from ankle- to knee-deep and clung to people and equipment with an almost conscious tenacity. Equipment bogged down: cars, ambulances, jeeps, trucks, trailers, tanks struggled slowly, if they moved at all, through the muck.

With the front lines advancing so rapidly and the mud making roads all but impassable, problems developed in the supply system. The distances between supply dumps and frontline troops that needed new supplies of all kinds were growing in length every day. Priority items like gasoline and ammunition were harder and harder to move from the rear to the front two hundred or three hundred miles away. Shortages in supplies also affected the mobile hospitals—especially the most forward ones, like the 11th Field, which were constantly moving in step with the frontline troops.

One shortage that hit the 11th Field Hospital hard was in foods that could be tolerated by patients requiring a soft or liquid diet. The hospital mess had plenty of C- and K-rations, but even healthy, uninjured soldiers found these difficult to digest. Soldiers with stomach or abdominal wounds needed a liquid diet or soft, low-fiber foods that did not tax the stomach and intestines until the soldiers recovered sufficiently to handle solid food. Like most field and evacuation hospitals, the 11th Field did not have the luxury of an assigned dietician. Those duties therefore fell on the nurses. The women improvised a solution: from gift packages sent to them from home, they donated items for soft and liquid diets—canned soups, juices, and powdered Jell-O among them. Although the hospital had a large quantity of canned juice, it was primarily unsweetened grapefruit juice, which most seriously wounded soldiers could not tolerate. The nurses at first thought that their improvisation was a temporary solution, but the army never did send the items needed. Nurses would continue until the end of the war to depend on food packages from home to create their patients' special diets.

WITH THE END of the first three months of fighting following the two invasions of France, the Germans were clearly put to rout by the Allies and frantically retreating. The Allies had broken the back of the German Nineteenth Army, which suffered a total of 1 million dead, wounded, and missing in action.[5]

In September, General Eisenhower began to reorganize his armies in preparation for a major fall assault on one key barrier blocking entry into the German fatherland: the Siegfried Line. Extending from the Netherlands in the north to Switzerland in the south, the Siegfried Line—also known as the West Wall—consisted of hundreds of pillboxes with interlocking fields of fire supported by an extensive system of command posts, observation posts, and troop shelters. Along with the German troops stationed all along the line were minefields and large areas of dragon's teeth—large concrete barriers—set so close together that it was impossible for vehicles, even tanks, to cross the area.

The fall offensive would involve General Patch's VII Army Group, VI Corps; General de Lattre's First French Army Group, I and II Corps; and General Bradley's Twelfth Army Group. Eisenhower believed that the strength of these combined forces—1 million men—would break through the German defenses of Hitler's West Wall without facing strong resistance, especially since Germany had taken approximately a million casualties since D-Day.[6]

However, breaching the Siegfried Line would prove to be difficult. The remaining German troops in the area would fiercely defend Hitler's West Wall to the last man and the last bullet. Allied armies met increasingly stiffer resistance as they drew closer and closer to Germany's western border.

On 17 September 1944, the forces of British general Montgomery, including American paratroopers from the 101st and Eighty-second Airborne Divisions, jumped or rode gliders into the city of Arnhem in Holland, a part of the fortifications of the Siegfried Line, located about eighty miles west of, and inland from, the North Sea. Code-named "Market- Garden," Montgomery's offensive had as its objective the capture of three bridges that led into Germany's heartland. The Germans planned to destroy those bridges to slow down the Allied advance. Fierce fighting went on for days, causing heavy casualties on both sides.

Since the Allies had no port on the northern coast of France or the Low Countries, the wounded were evacuated mainly by air. Planes were brought in as close as possible to nearby fighting in order to work swiftly. As usual, air evacuation flights used whatever planes they could commandeer, and this made it necessary that the planes be unmarked, since the same aircraft were used in both military flights, such as bringing supplies to the front, and medical evacuation flights.

The unseasonably cold temperatures and constant rain plagued air transport. Because of icy rain and wind, many flights, including air support for Market-Garden and air evacuation flights, were canceled. Furthermore, American and Allied fighters and bombers remained grounded instead of carrying out missions to destroy German defenses along the Siegfried Line. Wounded American and Allied soldiers along with wounded German POWs were evacuated to First Army hospitals stationed behind Market-Garden's front lines, but evacuation to England by plane was erratic at best. Transporting the wounded overland was not a good alternative: distances from the front to the port of Cherbourg on the northwest coast of France were long; ground transport through rain, snow, and mud was slow; and trucks and ambulances required more gasoline than was available. Moreover, land transport was hard on the wounded.

In hopes of opening up a sealane to England closer to the front, Eisenhower ordered Montgomery to capture the North Sea port of Antwerp in northern Belgium. While Montgomery pounded his way to Antwerp, Bradley and Devers had to make do with what limited supplies were available. Hodge's First Army continued its march toward the Belgian-German border south of Aachen, while General William H. Simpson's Ninth Army captured Brest on the west coast of France, then took up a position between Hodge's First Army and Patton's Third Army. Patton's army, short on fuel, continued its battle in the Lorraine area of eastern France, and contained the German counterattack near Lunéville-Nancy in southern Lorraine from 19 to 29 September.

Farther to the north, beginning on 29 September, little by little, American and Allied forces were encircling the ancient German city of Aachen and recovering from the losses suffered in Market-Garden. The Eighty-second Airborne Division had lost 1,432 men either killed or missing; the 101st Airborne Division, 2,100 killed or missing. After three weeks of fierce fighting, American troops finally broke through the section of the Siegfried Line east of Aachen, about 5 miles from the Belgian border. At the same time, American and FFI forces captured the French city of Nancy, about 150 miles south of Aachen.[7]

By 21 September, the Third Army, XV Corps, had crossed the Moselle River and was planning for an attack on the Rhine River, one of the last obstacles between American and Allied forces and the German fatherland. Two days later, the 180th Infantry of the Forty-fifth Division took the town of Epinal, in eastern France. On 24 September, all but one of the Seventh Army hospitals had moved close to the main highway that stretched about seventy miles from Besançon north to Epinal. The 51st Evacuation Hospital lacked indigenous trucks and trailers and therefore stood stranded, packed and waiting at Draguignan for transportation. Forward movement by the Allied frontline troops was so swift that both indigenous battalion hospitals and field and evacuation hospitals were having trouble keeping up, especially because of the shortages in the supply of gasoline and trucks.

On 26 September, the second echelon of the 93rd Evacuation Hospital, including the unit's nurses, arrived at Plombières, fifteen miles south of Epinal. The move was the hospital's fifth in six weeks as it followed the rapidly advancing American and Allied troops. The day was cold, with a heavy, drizzling rain. Despite the mud and rain and the long lines of wounded, the sight of distant snowcapped mountains imparted a quiet, if ironic, air of beauty and peace to the area. "The distant trees and hills were picturesque in their white mantle," Lieutenant Evelyn Anderson wrote, "and brought many memories of snow at home."[8]

The following morning, the 93rd Evac opened for business at Plombières. Hospital personnel were working twelve-hour shifts when, on 1 October, the 93rd was ordered to expand its bed capacity for the month of October from 400 to 450 to accommodate the high number of casualties. Though the patient load had been increased, orders came during the second week in October from headquarters to the 93rd informing the hospital that the total strength of its enlisted personnel was to be reduced from 217 to 207, a real blow. The corpsmen were being pulled from hospital duty to replace infantrymen, or litter bearers. Active hospital personnel had already been dwindling in numbers due to illness: between overwork and the constant rain and cold, many doctors, corpsmen, and nurses themselves became ill with upper respiratory infections. The increase in patient load by fifty beds and the decrease of ten corpsmen, combined with the growing list of staff too sick to work, meant a heavier workload for the remaining hospital members.[9]

Hospital administration officials hired French civilians to haul rock and pebbles to fight the rising mud in the ward and service tents. Engineers worked twenty-four hours a day until drainage ditches, walkways, and roads were built to lift the 93rd Evac out of the mud. During snowstorms, a special work detail had to scrape heavy, wet snow off the tents to keep them from collapsing under the weight onto patients. Inside, staff hung blankets around the doorways to cut down on the cold wind and protect patients from drafts. By the third week in October, eleven nurses from other units were sent to the 93rd Evac to fill in for nurses who were too ill to work and now were hospitalized in a newly created nurses' ward.

As October drew to a close, Lieutenant Evelyn Anderson and her nurses planned a Halloween dance to offer much-needed relaxation to hospital staff and combat troops bivouacked in the area. But at 2330 the dance came to an abrupt halt when scores of battle casualties—men of the Thirty-sixth Division—arrived from the Vosges Mountains area. The dance ended abruptly without the singing of "Good Night Ladies." An announcement went out to all hospital personnel to report to their duty stations immediately.

The combat in the Vosges Mountains and its resultant casualties had started several days earlier. Company M, 141st Infantry of the Thirty-sixth Division, ran into the enemy in that area on 24 October. Sergeant Charles Coolidge, the survivor of the debacle at the Rapido River in Italy in January 1944, led a section of heavy machine guns up a slope in the Vosges with the mission of guarding the right flank of the Third Battalion and supporting its combat action. Coolidge went forward with a sergeant from Company K to choose a position to coordinate the fire from heavy and light machine guns. The two met a German force in the woods and Coolidge decided that he and the other sergeant would bluff the group into surrendering. The Germans declined and asked the two to surrender themselves to the Nazi forces. When the Americans refused, the Germans called up tanks to support them. "The German spoke better English than I did," Coolidge said. "That's when I got out two cases of grenades. I stood up. The tank was about twenty-five to thirty-five feet away and I looked him straight in the face and said, 'I'm sorry, Mac, but you've got to come and get me.' He closed the turret of the tank and turned that barrel—that 88 [-millimeter gun]—right at me. He fired and the first shell hit a tree and the shrapnel cut a gash right across the top of my toes." Luckily, only the leather in Coolidge's boot got hit. The tank fired at Coolidge four more times. "When he went to the right, I crawled to the left behind another tree. When he went to the left, I crawled behind a tree to my right."[10]

Their platoon was not far behind. Since no officer was with the platoon, Coolidge took charge, guiding his men, many of whom were replacements and without combat experience. "My men and I kept firing at the Germans," Coolidge stated, "until we ran out of ammunition. That's when I told my men to withdraw." After four days of nonstop fighting, Coolidge got all of his men out except for a machine gunner and a medic, who were taken prisoner. Coolidge had managed to hold the German force through 24 and 27 October. His superior leadership, conduct, and actions were seen as "above and beyond the call of duty," and Coolidge was awarded the Medal of Honor several months later.[11]

BY OCTOBER, it was obvious to Eisenhower that although the Allies had initially put the Germans on the run, the war would not end, as hoped, before Christmas 1944. Rather, as the Allies hit the Siegfried Line and Germany's western border, the Germans looked to be well dug in and planning to fight for every inch of their country.

General Paul R. Hawley, the chief surgeon for the European theater of operations, had already begun in July to prepare for a longer war. He planned to bring several more large general hospitals into France to care for the thousands of wounded who were yet to fall. This was difficult because of the lack of ships in July. As things stood in October 1944, despite the problems with logistics and delays due to the shortage of ships and inter-Allied politics, 18,000 nonmobile general and station hospital beds were already operating on the continent. The lives of the wounded depended on how fast they were transported from field and evacuation hospitals working at the front lines to the general and station hospitals in the rear. The best hope for the wounded, then, was to back up the mobile field and evacuation hospitals with more general hospitals in France and Belgium, thereby shortening the evacuation process. Hawley planned to open up approximately 14,250 additional hospital beds on the continent. These beds would be divided into seventeen new general and station hospitals that would operate in France, Belgium, and Germany. Because the hospitals would be large—approximately 1,000 beds each—they would, of necessity, be nonmobile, since it would not be easy to rapidly pack, move, and set up such large hospitals to follow the front lines as they advanced up to and into Germany.[12]

For the evacuation chain to operate at an optimal level, whole blood would have to be delivered to frontline hospitals. Having learned from the experiences in the Mediterranean theater, the medical strategists for the European theater of operations had carefully planned for the distribution of whole blood well before D-Day, 6 June 1944. Operation Neptune—the medical arm of the Normandy invasion—put refrigerated trucks of the 152nd Station Hospital ashore at OMAHA Beach and UTAH Beach on 7 June and 9 June, respectively, fully loaded with whole blood. Early in the invasion, LSTs delivered about three thousand more pints of blood. As soon as an airfield was operational on the Cotentin Peninsula, the blood bank that had been set up at Salisbury in England sent daily planeloads of whole blood packed in insulated cans designed originally to preserve food items. Refrigerator trucks distributed the blood to clearing stations and field and evacuation hospitals near the front lines. By the last week of July, the blood supply plan was fully operational.

Medical strategists had anticipated a high casualty rate and a correspondingly high need for whole blood in the first two months of combat following the invasion of Northern France. But the need for whole blood was even higher than expected: in the forward hospitals, for every four casualties, 1 pint of blood was needed, and the ratio of whole blood to plasma was 1:1, instead of the anticipated 1 pint of whole blood to 2 pints of plasma.[13]

During June and July 1944, General Hawley monitored the amount of blood being used by theater surgeons. By the end of June, the First Army alone was consuming 500 pints a day. This was the entire daily production capacity of the Salisbury blood bank. In the first six weeks of the invasion, Allied battle casualties totaled 63,360; of these, 43,221 were wounded or injured in action. Even though the Allies had succeeded in driving the Germans out of France, the resistance and resilience of the determined German army was growing fiercer throughout September and October the closer the Allies drew to the Siegfried Line. Thus it became clear that the casualty rate might climb higher than first anticipated. A major Allied assault on the Siegfried Line was planned for the fall of 1944. General Hawley realized that the amount of blood that could be processed and shipped by the Salisbury blood bank would not be enough.[14]

To make up for shortages of whole blood in early August 1944, some of the field and evacuation hospitals set up their own blood banks. Hospital personnel and the lightly wounded became sources of whole blood

A flight nurse helps deliver whole blood to wounded soldiers at the front. (U.S. Army Signal Corps)

for these hospital blood banks. When wounded POWs were among those hospitalized, German POWs working in the hospitals, or lightly wounded POWs gave blood for their severely injured comrades. This ad hoc collection of blood from the wounded themselves was obviously not the best solution for boosting the blood supply. It was clear to Hawley that another source had to be found, and quickly. He looked to the United States.[15]

More than a year had passed since Colonel Edward Churchill, chief surgical consultant for the Mediterranean theater, had made his appeal to the U.S. Army, the American National Red Cross, and U.S. Surgeon General Norman T. Kirk for a system to supply much-needed whole blood, in addition to plasma, to the fighting forces on the front lines. Now, in July, with Allied troops advancing on Germany, General Hawley came face to face with the same issue Dr. Churchill had struggled to address: lack of an adequate supply of whole blood. Kirk and others in the United States who had been in a position to make changes during 1943 and the spring of 1944 had failed to break away from the misguided but deeply entrenched belief that plasma alone could be used to manage shock.

After final discussions with his consultants on 28 July 1944, General Hawley requested, by radiogram and then in writing, daily U.S. airlifts of up to one thousand pints of whole blood via transatlantic airlift. Hawley had already arranged for long-range C-54s of the Air Transport Command to take on the mission. Unwilling to take no for an answer, he sent an envoy of emissaries—his chief surgical consultant, Colonel Elliott C. Cutler; the director of the Salisbury blood bank, Major Robert C. Hardin; and a veteran evacuation hospital commander, Colonel William F. MacFee, MC—to Washington by air to expound on the urgent importance of immediately setting up whole blood airlifts. On 12 August the trio of experts left Scotland for the United States.

In the meantime, during the first week of July, Surgeon General Kirk had already reviewed the facts and made a personal trip to the front lines. By the time he received Hawley's request in late July by radiogram, and before the three envoys arrived, Kirk had turned his thinking 180 degrees and was working out the details of shipping whole blood to the European theater of operation. On 21 August, thirty-two months after America entered World War II, the transatlantic blood airlift began with 258 pints of whole blood airlifted from New York to Prestwick, Scotland. The plan was to increase the shipments to 1,000 pints a day by September 1944. Blood for the airlift was collected from volunteer donors in the east coast and midwest sections of the United States and processed by the American National Red Cross.[16]

In order to decrease the weight of the refrigeration equipment in each load, a preservative—Alsever's solution—was added in equal amounts (a 1:1 ratio) to that of the blood. It was stored and transported without refrigeration in 1,000 cc bottles. In the beginning, flights went to the blood bank in Salisbury; but late in October, flights carrying whole blood went directly to Orly Field near Paris.[17]

MARTHA "MARTE" CAMERON of the 128th Evacuation Hospital managed to secure the driver's-side rear seat in the 2.5-ton truck carrying the nurses from France to a small town in Belgium only a handful of miles from the German border. Cameron and the rest of the 128th Evacuation Hospital were winding along Belgian country roads en route to Baelen, near Eupen, in support of the advancing American and Allied troops of General Hodge's First Army. The front lines were rapidly approaching the German border: Baelen, Belgium, was only fifteen miles south of Aachen, Germany.

Eight days earlier, on 5 September, Cameron had visited Paris: "Yesterday, I went to Paris for a visit," she wrote to her father in a letter, ". . . arrived there fairly early and had the whole day. We passed by the Palace of Versailles on the way—it was huge. The Eiffel Tower was the next thing we spotted and that was a real thrill. We saw all the sights. . . . Later, after lunch in an army officers' mess, we went shopping . . . mostly window shopping for me. . . . I bought a little perfume but otherwise things I purchased were little things I happened to need. . . . Stores were huge but nearly empty, food scarce . . . few places to eat. . . . The people friendly and very glad to see us."[18]

Cameron had hoped to visit Paris again, but little more than a week after her one-day leave in the City of Lights, she and the rest of her hospital team were leaving France for Belgium. Moving the 128th Evac approximately 360 miles was no small task. The trucks left in groups of three at ten-minute intervals and the entire hospital was in transit for about two days. As everyone in the unit agreed, "It was at least in the right direction."

However, moving in the right direction did not rule out a wrong turn or two. On the last night of their journey, one of those turns took the nurses and their convoy of three trucks down a small country road, and eventually led to an incident that caused a nurse to be reassigned. Two or three miles down the road, one of the nurses was sure she heard German voices. Since their trucks had taken a wrong turn several miles back, and the German Nineteenth Army was scattered and retreating pell-mell from France eastward toward Germany, it was quite possible that the voices were those of German soldiers. As the truck was making a 180-degree turn to find its way back to the right road, the nurse started talking in a loud voice. "This nurse got very upset," Cameron said. "She sort of blew her top. It was sort of an hysterical reaction." The outburst presented a real and immediate threat to the 128th. On this particular occasion, the hysterics caused no harm to her hospital, but they could not take a chance that the nurse might respond this way again. The very next day, she was transferred to a general hospital far behind front lines. No one could afford to have a soldier, male or female, prone to hysterics anywhere in the vicinity of the front lines. Hospital personnel understood perfectly why the nurse was sent to the rear. "Why would you take someone like that deeper into the war?" Cameron said.[19]

IN LATE SEPTEMBER, the 67th Evacuation Hospital also left France and headed to a site closer to the German border: Lentzweiler, in Luxembourg, about 10 miles north of the city of Luxembourg and only 20 miles east of the German border. The 200-mile move from their old site between Paris and Rheims took the 67th Evac through several of the battlefields of World War I. The truck convoy rolled through Château-Thierry about 50 miles east of Paris, and across the Marne to nearby Belleau Wood. Belleau Wood was the site of a famous battle in May 1918 against the Germans and now contained a large, well-kept World War I American military cemetery. The rows of white crosses cast somber thoughtfulness over the 67th's personnel. "It filled us with a sense of futility," Chief Nurse Captain Jean Truckey wrote in her journal, "that once more our young men were fighting here and new cemeteries were dotting the countryside with their countless rows of white crosses."[20]

The convoy rolled on through mile after mile of vineyards and vast farmlands that stretched to the horizon. The trucks stopped long enough for passengers to eat a lunch of K- or C-rations and then drove on across the border into Belgium. "It was evident that we were in a new country," Captain Truckey noted. "The roofs instead of being red tile were gray slate and the houses were of heavier construction. [The terrain] was very hilly with heavy forests and small farms. Every home was decorated with the gay Belgian flag of black, orange, and red."[21]

On 24 September, the 67th Evac crossed the border into Luxembourg and reached their new site at Lentzweiler. Due to the constant rain, the site was a vast sea of mud. "It was raining now, and it never stopped raining during our entire stay," Truckey wrote. "Our hospital tents soon were in a mire of mud." The mud was so thick and deep it sucked objects in like quicksand: combat engineers laid wire netting as a foundation, but in less than two hours, the rivers of mud it was meant to bridge had swallowed up the netting. The engineers next laid bales of straw up to two feet thick over the muddy paths. The straw sank into the mud, and for a time, nurses and hospital personnel were able to walk along the tops of straw bales as they made their way around the hospital.[22]

At night, in blackout conditions, the pathways of baled straw were very difficult to see. It was not uncommon for someone to miss and end up with a foot stuck in the omnipresent sea of mud. People who had only one foot off the path might well be able to free themselves and continue, but for several who left the path entirely, they actually fell into the sticky, chocolate-colored marsh. "A nurse slipped in a rut and floundered until two people came along to pull her out," Truckey wrote. One afternoon, a cow wandered into the hospital area and got firmly stuck up to her knees in the mud. The cow mooed louder and louder as she tried to free herself. Finally, several GIs figured out a way to liberate her from her sticky prison. The soldiers—farm boys among them—got a mattress off an empty cot, and after much pulling and pushing, worked the mattress under the cow's ample belly. Three teams of GIs and a 2.5-ton truck took turns pulling and pushing the cow to an island with a path that was only ankle-deep in mud. It took about forty-five minutes, but finally the cow, still mooing loudly, reached a spot where she could walk on her own. She turned herself around and set off quickly back in the direction of her nearby pasture.[23]

The thick, deep rivers of mud fouled up the ambulance and road-vehicle evacuation process throughout the frontline area. General Hawley had already ordered hospital trains into service as soon as bombed and sabotaged rail systems could be repaired. In September 1944, five hospital trains were operating on the continent—two in the Normandy area to Cherbourg, and three running from front lines to airfields in Paris. Though hospital trains provided a partial solution for getting casualties to rear-area hospitals, air evacuation could perform the job even faster.

Flying was clearly the most rapid means of getting an injured soldier to a hospital where definitive surgery could be performed and intricate medical treatments applied.

With this in mind, General Hawley requested that the Ninth Carrier Command assign two hundred C-47s to medical evacuation each day until the backlog of patients awaiting evacuation was cleared. When the Carrier Command told the general they had to turn down his request, Hawley asked for fifty C-47s a day. That would allow the theater to air-evacuate two thousand patients a day. Again, this request was turned

Flight nurse Aleda E. Lutz cares for wounded soldiers on a medical air evacuation flight. Lt. Lutz was later killed when her flight on 1 November 1944 crashed into the side of a mountain during foul weather near Saint Chamond, Central France. The USAHS Aleda Lutz was named in her honor. (U.S. Army Signal Corps)

down. The Carrier Command did offer Hawley twenty UC-64s and their crews to be at his call for evacuation purposes. These planes—single-engine, high-wing monoplanes—were originally designed to carry freight and passengers in the Canadian Arctic. The planes had been used for observation, liaison, and light cargo, but had not proved satisfactory for any of these missions. For air evacuation, the UC-64 could carry three litter cases, two or three ambulatory patients, and a quantity of medical supplies. Hawley accepted the planes gladly; in the next three months, the twenty UC-64s would carry 1,100 casualties, 30,000 pints of whole blood, and approximately 460 tons of other medical supplies.[24]

It was not long before Hawley received another proposal from Ninth Carrier Command. It was customary protocol for planes of all types to report in, upon arrival, to Carrier Command to receive their assignments. If General Hawley agreed, he could use these planes for several air evacuation trips "before they reported in" and were assigned to a unit and a specific job. Hawley agreed to the plan, and "unassigned" planes that were still in transit were used to help get casualties evacuated to the rear.

Along with his UC-64s and "unassigned" C-47s, Hawley took advantage of any flights he could get for the theater. C-47s carrying supplies to the front lines would also fly specially trained nurses—flight nurses—and specially trained corpsmen to the front to pick up loads of casualties and bring them to rear-echelon military hospitals. Every flight nurse was a double volunteer—she had volunteered for the Army Nurse Corps, and then volunteered again to be trained and assigned as a flight nurse. Since air evacuation was carried on in whatever aircraft was available to them, the planes had no special markings and were legitimate targets for enemy planes and artillery.

On 27 September 1944, Lieutenant Reba E. Whittle and her surgical technician, Sergeant Hill of the 813th Medical Air Evacuation Squadron, were flying across Northern France and Belgium to pick up wounded near the front and deliver them to hospitals in England. Reba Whittle unbuckled her seat belt as the plane completed its takeoff and settled into its assigned altitude for the trip to the front lines of Belgium and Germany. It was Wednesday morning, and twenty-four-year-old Whittle was looking forward to being back in England the following day, Thursday, her scheduled day off. She and her boyfriend, an officer with the IX Air Forces, planned to see the sights and take in a USO show. As the plane took off, Whittle sprawled across several empty seats next to her, and drifted quickly into sleep.

Hours later, when the plane began tossing from side to side, Whittle awakened abruptly to the noise of metal tearing around her, explosions close by, and the whistle of a cold wind blowing through a large hole in the fuselage. As she sat up, she looked across the aisle and saw that Sergeant Hill was bleeding profusely from the calf of his left leg. Almost at the same instant, Whittle realized that the explosions around the plane were ack-ack rounds fired at their plane by Germans on the ground. The plane sank and rose like an elevator gone mad, and everything not tied down tossed about the cabin. Whittle grabbed the back of the seat next to her and hung on for dear life. It was patently clear that she and her sergeant would not be returning to England that night with a planeload of patients.

A native of Texas, Whittle had volunteered for flight training because she felt it would be an exciting facet of war nursing. She and her group had made it through the flight nurses' training course at Bowman Field in Kentucky months ago and had been flying on medical evacuation flights since graduation in early 1944. Planes and pilots were scarce, and flight nurses and their corpsmen flew on whatever planes they could get to the front to pick up wounded and sick soldiers. On return flights, a nurse and a corpsman routinely would care for as many as twenty patients on litters and ten or more ambulatory cases en route to a large station or general hospital in England. Every flight nurse knew the extra dangers they would be exposed to when they volunteered for flight school and each had accepted the additional perils: flights over enemy territory, antiaircraft fire from the ground, enemy planes shooting at your aircraft, inclement weather, engine trouble, and the real prospect of just plain getting lost.

Those dangers had been brought soundly home to army flight nurses when, in November 1943, a C-54 on its way to pick up wounded in Bari, on the east coast of Italy, had veered off course and crash-landed behind German lines in Albania. Thirteen flight nurses and twelve corpsmen had to hike out of enemy territory, with the German army never far behind. It had taken the British OSE and the American OSS to help get the group back into Allied-held territory. The trip of approximately eight hundred miles through the snow-covered mountains of Albania in winter lasted almost two months for the majority of the group, and an extra two months for three of the army nurses trapped in a German-occupied town. The incident made the newspapers in England and America, and stimulated deep discussions among flight nurses. In the end, every nurse had already accepted the many dangers involved in bringing air-evacuated wounded to hospitals in the rear.[25]

Now, almost a year after the Albanian crash landing in enemy territory, Whittle, her sergeant, and the plane's crew faced a similar prospect. The sounds of antiaircraft fire and tearing metal grew louder as the plane shook and began to lose altitude. Whittle looked out the window and realized that the left engine was on fire. She began to cry and scream and was glad when Sergeant Hill, wounded leg and all, crossed the aisle and sat in a seat next to her. He put his arm around her and said that crying would not help. Whittle rested her head against Hill's shoulder and began to gain control over her tears. Just as she was beginning to calm down, a large piece of flak hit the sergeant in the left arm. Whittle was so shocked by how close the flak had come to her head that she stopped crying immediately. She sat in silence as the plane went into a dive and crashed nose-first into the ground. The force of the crash threw Whittle into the navigator's compartment, about five feet from her seat. The plane was on fire and the fuselage was peppered with holes. Whittle watched as several of the crew crawled through the top hatch and left the plane. Both she and Sergeant Hill followed quickly.

"Immediately, we saw soldiers not many yards away," Whittle wrote later in her diary. "At first we thought they were British soldiers." It only took a second glance to realize that the soldiers were Germans, and they were pointing rifles at the Americans. They had "surprised look[s] on their faces when they saw a woman. . . ."[26]

Whittle was startled as a German soldier put his rifle down, took a bandage from a pouch on his belt, and wrapped it around her head. Only then did she realize that she was bleeding from the forehead. That German soldier also gave first aid to Sergeant Hill and the pilot, First Lieutenant Ralph Parker. When he finished, they motioned for the group—which included Second Lieutenant David Forbes, co-pilot; Sergeant Harold Bonser, crew chief; and Corporal Chester D. Bright—to walk ahead of them down a road. After traveling about a quarter of a mile, Whittle saw a sign that read: AACHEN 4 KILOMETERS. When they reached Aachen, Whittle was surprised to see that it was about 99 percent evacuated. She spotted "only a couple of civilians and occasionally an army vehicle and soldiers running around. Naturally all glaring at us."[27]

The group walked on a further three or four miles and then was ordered inside a neat brick house close to the road. They were taken into a room where five German officers were seated, working on papers. Whittle and the American men waited while the German guards and the officers engaged in conversation. One of the officers poured a glass of wine and handed it to Sergeant Hill, a concession to the sergeant's painful, wounded leg. In about five minutes, the group was taken outside and told to sit on the ground while they waited. "There we sat on the ground shivering as it was rather cold with no coats," Whittle wrote. "We had to sit outside there for some time—until a queer-looking truck came up and they motioned for us to get in." The back of the enclosed truck was loaded with junk and Whittle and her companions squeezed in as ordered. "At least [we were] out of the wind," Whittle noted.[28]

In about an hour, they arrived at a large village, their first stop in a long chain of intermediate way stations during a nine-day journey that would end with their final place of confinement as prisoners of war. A few minutes later, a German officer walked into the barn and introduced himself in perfect English. He interrogated each individual while the others sat by and watched. Each American gave his name, rank, and serial number, in accordance with the Geneva Conventions. A German soldier came into the barn with a basket half-filled with pears. "They tasted very good as we had had nothing to eat all day," Whittle said. After the German officer finished his questions, he directed the group into the kitchen of a nearby house. The group was served coffee and large slices of black bread and butter. "It seemed heavenly to have a bit to eat and be a little warm," Whittle wrote in her diary.[29]

While they ate, four more German officers entered the kitchen, looked at the group of Americans, and went through the identification papers collected while they were still at the crash site. The newcomers talked, glanced at the group, then back at the identification papers. "Everyone [was] taking a good [look at us] and saying 'swester' which means 'nurse,' " wrote Whittle.[30]

An elderly German woman who was eating with her family in the kitchen brought Whittle a cup of hot soup. She was "afraid to eat it at first," but the woman insisted. When Whittle still refused, the old woman added some kind of sauce to the soup, took a sip from the cup, smiled at Whittle, and said, *"Gut!"* With this reassurance, Whittle ate the soup and found that it did indeed taste very good.[31]

About thirty minutes later, the group was ushered onto an old bus and driven forty miles to their next destination. Whittle noticed several horse-drawn wagons traveling in the opposite direction in the darkness. When the bus pulled past a high metal fence, the Americans were escorted into a large office where four German officers were working on military papers. About five minutes later, a German enlisted man entered with a large container of cold stewed potatoes. Since Whittle had eaten a quantity of black bread and butter at their last stop, she had a difficult time getting a plate of them down. When the group finished the meal, they were escorted upstairs to sleep. Whittle was given a room to herself while the four men were placed in another room nearby. When the guard left, Whittle took the thin mattress off her bed and pulled it into the adjacent room where the men were settled into four bunk beds.

The five were awakened about an hour and a half later by another German officer speaking perfect English and asking the same questions his fellow officers had asked at earlier stops. Suddenly, an air-raid siren sounded. The German officer rose immediately and walked toward the door. His hand was on the doorknob when he turned and spoke to the Americans. "Well, too bad [but] you know, you might be bombed by your own people."[32]

At about 1100 the following morning, an old truck pulled up and the captured American group was told to climb in the back. Since the truck was piled high with wood chips, the group seated themselves at various heights on top of wood chip piles. The truck moved at a snail's pace and Whittle and her companions were surprised to learn that it burned wood chips for fuel. In a country at war with most of the world, wood-burning trucks and horse-drawn wagons existed side by side with V-1 rockets and the giant Tiger tank.

In that same country of contradictions, the Wehrmacht and the German people could sometimes treat POWs with thoughtfulness, good food, a clean place to sleep, and no physical or emotional abuse. At least, it was that way with Whittle and her comrades. It would be known at the war's end how cruel and inhumane the SS and the Gestapo could be toward Allied POWs as well as the civilian inmates of the concentration camps. Even so, the regular foot soldier in the Wehrmacht was sometimes far removed from the heartless and merciless elite German units.

The truck slowly crawled along while an assistant to the driver shoveled wood chips into a fuel box to keep the motor running. The next stop was at a German military hospital, where a German doctor, again speaking perfect English, examined each captive and treated their wounds.

When he had completed Whittle's treatment, he said, "Too bad [being] a woman, as you are the first one, and no one knows exactly what to do [with you]."[33]

After a meal of a warm sauerkraut mixture and thin slices of black bread brought to them by nuns working in the hospital, the group was brought outside to wait for the wood-burning truck to complete its unloading and reloading. The weather was very cold and a brisk wind added a frigid touch that went straight through the Americans' uniforms. Whittle was shivering when an elderly nun brought her a wooden chair to sit on. Thirty minutes later, the POWs were on their way again and did not stop until 0200, when they reached an old railroad station. There, they were directed to a cellar under the waiting room where there were other American and British POWs. While they waited, the American soldiers shared food from Red Cross packages given them by the Germans. These supplemental food packages were sent monthly by the Red Cross to Allied POWs and internees. Each package contained a small can of tomatoes, meat spread, cheese, bacon, margarine, condensed milk, soda crackers, sugar, tea, a bar of chocolate, and a piece of soap.

Generally, German soldiers delivered these packages on a regular basis to American and Allied POWs. Despite the fact that the same sort of packages were sent by the Red Cross to POWs and internees held by the Japanese, army nurses at Santo Tomas and Los Banos internment camps in the Philippine Islands never received them. The delivery or lack of delivery of those Red Cross packages was partly responsible for the difference in the survival rate between German and Japanese POWs: 27 percent of POWs died in Japanese hands, while only 4 percent died in German hands.[34]

At 0500, all the POWs waiting in the cellar were placed on a train and taken deeper into the heart of Germany. Most reached their final destination at Frankfurt, 115 miles east of the German/Luxembourg border and 125 miles southeast of Aachen. Finally, on 1 October, Whittle and the men who had accompanied her inside Germany were separated. The men went to a nearby *Stalag*—German POW camp.

On 6 October, carrying a boxed lunch provided by the nuns, Whittle was transported to an American and Allied hospital. The next day, she reached a POW *Stalag* in Meiningen, about 135 miles northeast of Frankfurt. Over a period of several days, Whittle was integrated into the hospital care of wounded and ill POWs. She would remain at this duty until February 1945, when she was sent to Portuguese South Africa and placed aboard a Red Cross exchange ship, the *Grisholm*, for repatriation arranged by the International Red Cross.

ON 29 SEPTEMBER 1944, the First U.S. Army began a new offensive to capture the German cities of Düren and Cologne, about twenty miles and forty miles east of Aachen, respectively. Before the First Army could accomplish its assigned objectives, it would have to capture Aachen— the all-but-empty city Whittle and her crew had been taken to as POWs the day before. The ancient city stood squarely in the First Army's path. General Courtney Hodges ordered his forces to begin the siege of Aachen by encircling it completely, thereby preventing the escape of German soldiers garrisoned inside.

Despite the fact that Aachen had no particular military or manufacturing advantages, the city held a prominent place in the hearts of the German people and the mythology of the Nazi Party. In the last one thousand years, thirty-two emperors and kings had been crowned at Aachen. One—Charlemagne—had been born inside Aachen's walls and now, centuries later, his body rested within the historic city. Moreover, Aachen—situated virtually on the western border—represented the gateway into the German fatherland. No foreign soldier had set foot on German territory during a time of war since Napoleon. Should the historically venerated city of Aachen fall into the hands of the Allies, the near-sacred inviolability of German soil would be broached after more than two hundred years. The psychological and mythological value of Aachen could not be overestimated in the eyes of the Germans.

With these sentiments in mind, Hitler ordered that Aachen was to be held at all costs. Defense of the city was to become a symbol of German resistance to the entire world. With the armies of Russia threatening from the east, three Allied armies threatening from the west, and more than seventy-five air raids launched against Aachen and its environs during the preceding six weeks, approximately 40 percent of its buildings had been destroyed. Another 40 percent had been seriously damaged by bombs and artillery, and debris covered much of the city. Aachen was virtually empty; in compliance with Hitler's direct orders, most of its civilian population had been evacuated on 14 September.

Now, in the final days of September, American and Allied forces were closing in a circle around the ancient city. Aachen's natural terrain of thickly wooded hills made it difficult going for the Third Armored Division unless it advanced through the Stolberg corridor, a portion of the surrounding countryside that was relatively flat. The commander, Major General Maurice Rose, directed the division to approach through the corridor and head for the cities of Düren, twenty miles east, and Eschweiler, about ten miles northeast, thereby outflanking many of the West Wall fortifications that protected Aachen and the fatherland. After weeks of fighting, the venerated city finally fell on 21 October.

With the fall of Aachen, the prevailing attitude among the Americans and the Allies was that Germany did not have the strength for another serious offensive. U.S. and Allied strategists planned a very serious winter offensive that would take place in November 1944. In preparation for this offensive, and to care for wounded and ill soldiers already engaged on the Siegfried Line, army hospitals were ordered forward once again. On 31 October, the 67th Evacuation Hospital mobilized and moved from its bivouac area in Stavelot, Belgium, eight miles east to Malmédy, a small town fifteen miles from the German border. The 67th would remain at Malmédy for the next six or seven weeks.

The 44th Evac was already in Malmédy, having arrived on 1 October. The patient load had been relatively light throughout October, but rumors had it that a big push was soon to begin in November. "We had heard rumors that American and Allied troops were going to launch a big push against the Siegfried Line in November," said Lieutenant Martha Nash, chief nurse of the 44th. "Since it was already 1 November, we didn't figure we'd have long to wait." Rather than being set up in their usual tents, the 44th was operating out of a deserted schoolhouse. Hospital personnel were also given a much-welcomed break from tent living; they occupied vacated Belgian homes. "We were glad to move into such clean and comfortable houses," Nash said. "The German sympathizers who had vacated them only a day or two before were no doubt looking for new quarters in a town not in immediate danger of being captured by Americans."[35]

As with many hospital sites throughout Belgium that fall and early winter, the 44th had to deal with the problem of mud, which obstructed the movement of army vehicles delivering or transferring patients. But even given the mud, Malmédy was better in other respects than certain earlier sites of the 44th. "At Malmédy, the mud was bad," Lieutenant Nash recalled, "but compared to the minefields around Saint-Lô in June and July 1944, it was a lot easier." But the land mines in Normandy had not stopped Martha Nash. Headstrong and self-initiating, she had cleared her own path of mines even before engineers had cleared all the mines in the Saint-Lô area. "I got to kidding one of those young GIs who was working at detecting the land mines and placing white tape to mark the cleared paths," Nash said. "I told that GI that I had already cleared a path from my tent to the hospital and walked on that path every day. He laughed and said he was glad that I had luck on my side."[36]

In Malmédy, Nash noticed a new type of German weapon: the buzz bomb. "When we were in Malmédy, it was the first buzz bombs I'd ever seen in my life—like Buck Rogers," Nash said. Nicknamed "buzz bombs," the new-fangled high-tech rockets flying over the hospital (prototypes for today's intercontinental ballistic missiles) looked like something from outer space. "We were in Malmédy and those V-1 and V-2 rockets came rushing across," Nash said. "You feel so helpless. I believe I could meet up with the enemy and [if] I had my own weapon, I'd feel different, but those things, I felt so helpless . . . and everybody else did too."[37]

The rockets had the appearance of small airplanes with fire streaming out of the tails. The V-1 made a roaring noise as it flew; when the roaring stopped, the rocket fell to the ground and exploded. The V-2 rockets, on the other hand, made no sound at all, but they were more frightening to onlookers because they appeared suddenly without a sound in the sky, stopped their forward motion, then fell steeply to the earth and exploded.

Hitler had ordered that V-1 and V-2 rockets be targeted at civilian areas—large cities, towns, and villages—in order to strike fear into people's hearts and break their morale. Naturally, if military personnel happened to be in or near the targeted location, the weapons wounded and killed them as easily as they did civilians. But civilians were the selected target, and they accounted for most of those wounded by Hitler's vengeance weapons. The civilians were brought to the 44th Evac and to other hospitals in the area.

By November, Martha Nash finally learned the fate of her sister, Frances Louise Nash, the army nurse who had been missing in action in the Philippines since the fall of Corregidor in May 1942. One day during the second week in November, her brother, James Nash of the Third Armored Division, visited Martha at the 44th Evacuation Hospital at Malmédy. He had exciting new information: Frances was alive. She was a prisoner of war at the Santo Tomas Internment Camp in Manila. "He never did find out through the government," Martha said. "He wrote to the [International] Red Cross in Geneva, Switzerland, and found out that she was a POW. That was in 1944. She was taken prisoner in 1942 and it took all those years to find out." Frances, the oldest sibling, had been the first in the Nash family to volunteer for duty in the war. She had blazed the trail; she was the inspiration, the path setter for her younger sister, Martha, and her brother, James. All three siblings shared the same traits of tenacity, self-initiative, and commitment to duty.[38]

THE SURRENDER of Aachen on 21 October dealt a strong blow to the German army and the Führer. It also served to buoy the morale of the Americans and Allies. However, the ongoing battle in the Hürtgen Forest, which had begun in September, was a punishing and demoralizing one for American soldiers and resulted in staggeringly high numbers of casualties.

The geographical features of the forest made it an especially treacherous battlefield. Located south of Aachen along the Belgian and German border, the Hürtgen was fifty square miles of hilly, ravine-filled, densely wooded forest. Foliage was so tightly packed that sunlight seldom pierced through it to reach the forest floor, casting the trees into a perpetual deep green darkness. German troops who had trained in the Hürtgen had placed their artillery where it would be the most hidden and do the most harm to Allied forces. In fact, German artillery forces had developed a special technique of shooting into the tops of the hundreds of fir trees, thereby bringing about a deadly shower not only of shrapnel but of large splinters of wood that broke off and fell to the forest floor like wooden spears. Large splinters pierced many an American soldier; it required hours of tedious surgery to remove and repair organs the splintered wood had torn or penetrated.

In what would turn into a six-month-long battle for this forest—a battle that stretched from September 1944 to February 1945—eight infantry, two armored divisions, and several smaller U.S. military units marched into the Hürtgen to find and dislodge the German forces controlling it. Rifle company after rifle company entered the forest and suffered a 50 percent casualty rate. Two groups, the Ninth Division's Sixtieth Regiment and the Fourth Division's Twenty-second Regiment, suffered 100 percent casualties. In all, in six months of bloody battle,

American and Allied losses totaled thirty thousand. Many later questioned why U.S. troops were not ordered to bypass the area and leave the Germans in a pocket that could be cleaned up afterward. However, bypasses and detours were not the order of the day.[39]

Lieutenant Paul Skogsberg with the Reconnaissance Battalion, First Division, was one of the men who made it out of the Hürtgen Forest alive and unwounded. "We went to the Hürtgen Forest before Thanksgiving. . . . It was dense forest. It was so dense, that one night I got up—it was cloudy and rainy the whole time we were there—it was so dark that I couldn't find my way back to my tent," Skogsberg said. "So I stood where I was until I heard something. I moved in that direction and it was headquarters. Then I found my way back. It was pitch-black." Not everyone was as fortunate as Skogsberg.[40]

ON 16 NOVEMBER 1944, the 128th Evacuation Hospital at Baelen, Belgium, got word to be ready to receive a significant number of casualties the following day. The weather continued to bring rain, snow, sleet, and freezing temperatures to regions around the border. American and Allied troops did what they could to keep warm—chopped up and burned furniture when no other fuel was available, or cut down trees and brush to build fires against the freezing temperatures.

Marte Cameron looked into the plasma can of ice she had placed on the stove in her tent. After ten minutes, the ice was melting slowly but it still had a long way to go to fill the can with warm water for washing. As she had done many times in different hospital sites, Cameron used the toe of her right combat boot to lift the lid on the Sibley stove, and added another lump of coal so that it would put out more heat. The Sibley was a portable, three-piece metal stove with a drum on the bottom, a bridge across the middle, a can on top, and a chimney. The stovepipe went through the corner of the tent; if it were not properly positioned, the heat could ignite the tent canvas and cause a fire.

Cameron sat on her cot, took a deep breath, and studied the burn mark on the toe of her right combat boot. She had learned from weeks of living in cold combat areas that the burn spot on the toe of a soldier's combat boot was a sure sign that the owner was a veteran. "People who had been up front for a while all had burned toes and melted welts because the toes of their boots had been used to open the Sibley stove,"

Cameron remembered. Another way of identifying veteran frontline personnel was by the condition of the leather strap on their helmets. Nurses used their helmets to heat water for washing. "If anybody had a complete strap on their helmet, they had not been over there very long. The strap would fall off and get burned on the hot stove."[41]

By November 1944, the record-breaking cold with subfreezing temperatures was taking a toll on combat troops. Foxholes and trenches were hardly adequate shelter against a cold so bitter it often led to frostbite or trench foot. One night in mid-November, a corpsman brought a severely wounded soldier to Cameron's OR table in the 128th Evac. The young man was one of many being carried out of the Hürtgen Forest by a very busy group of litter bearers. "He was one of the most seriously injured men I had seen," Cameron said. "A large shell fragment had hit him in the head and a large piece of his skull was missing. You could actually see his brain. Unfortunately, the head wound wasn't his only problem. The soldier also had severe frostbite to both hands and feet." The surgeons worked on him for more than two hours before he was moved to a postoperative ward. "They had to amputate his hands and feet and part of his lower legs and arms," Cameron said. "I heard that when he went to the postoperative ward, he vomited and died. I can remember thinking that it was probably a blessing since he had severe brain injuries in addition to the amputations. I can still see him at times—whenever bad memories come to mind."[42]

With the ongoing Battle of the Hürtgen Forest and a new push toward the Rhine, all frontline hospitals began losing from ten to twenty of their enlisted men as the army took these GIs from their hospitals to replace fallen soldiers either as litter bearers in the forest or as infantrymen on the front lines. By midnight of 18 November, the 128th Evacuation Hospital had a reduced staff but an overload of patients: 514 in its 400-bed hospital. Even with the best of planning, not every contingency had been covered by the medical brass. Unusually severe weather conditions and a stronger than anticipated German defense were causing higher than expected casualties, disruptions in supply, and an overload at many frontline hospitals.[43]

On the morning of 19 November, several personnel of the 128th Evac noticed something new in the sky above the hospital. It looked like a plane, but it moved faster than any plane the Americans had seen or heard about to date. "It was a German jet aircraft," surgical technician

Gilbert Smith said. "I think that if they'd started it a year earlier, things might have been different. It seemed miraculous to see a plane move that fast. We had no idea what it was."[44]

SHARING THE FRONTLINE dangers and experiences of soldiers created a special, strong camaraderie among nurses and hospital personnel. Just as soldiers were proud of their unit's history and proud to wear the ribbons and battle stars awarded to them for their service, so, too, were nurses and hospital personnel proud of their awards, medals, and ribbons. Nurses of the 128th Evac who had started with the 48th Surgical Hospital and landed on the beaches of Algeria with assault troops on D-Day, 8 November 1942, now held six battle stars. Whenever a soldier had earned five battle stars, the U.S. Army replaced the five gold stars with one silver star. When the soldier took part in another battle, a gold star was awarded and placed next to the silver star. Military personnel who had earned the right to wear those battle stars knew and respected what they stood for.

Colonel Florence Blanchfield, chief of the U.S. Army Nurse Corps for the entire United States, visited hospitals throughout the European theater. During one visit to the 128th Evac, Colonel Wiley, the 128th's CO, ordered his nurses to be present at a reception for Colonel Blanchfield. Since the casualties were relatively low at that point, nurses were able to attend. Dress uniforms were worn, and, as awards were always worn on dress uniforms for special occasions, the nurses were proudly displaying their battle stars. "When we went through the reception line," Cameron said, "Colonel Blanchfield remarked on the battle stars worn by her nurses—us. She didn't win any points when she congratulated me for the four battle stars on my uniform and encouraged the veterans with one silver and one gold star to keep up the good work—that getting through two battles was a wonderful achievement. All of us were really surprised that the chief of the entire U.S. Army Nurse Corps who held the rank of colonel didn't know how to read the ribbons and battle stars earned by her nurses."[45]

On 28 November, the 128th Evac was ordered to move to a new location in Brand, Germany, just four miles southeast of Aachen. The hospital opened and received its first patients on 6 December; the census by midnight that first day was only sixty-nine, an unusually low figure. Since there were fewer patients, the commanding officer, Colonel Wiley, decided to allow a number of hospital staff forty-eight-hour passes, plus travel time to visit Paris. The general consensus of opinion was that the war would end not long after Christmas. Americans felt certain that the back of the German army had been broken and surrender was only weeks away.[46]

On 8 December, Chief Nurse Kathryn Helm of the 128th Evac asked the nurses who were not on duty to attend a dance being given by an infantry unit. Cameron said she could not attend because her hair was a mess and needed washing. When the chief nurse made a special request, Cameron gave in and washed her hair. Since she no longer had enough bobby pins to set it in pin curls, she used white muslin rags obtained from the OR to make curls and had a friend iron her hair dry, curl by curl. "I got the idea from *Mrs. Wiggs of the Cabbage Patch* [a children's book]. It always impressed me when I was a kid, when they ironed one of the character's braids," Cameron said. "The dance was more fun than I thought it would be." Spirits were high and most Americans looked forward to being home before the end of January 1945.[47]

PARIS WAS NOT HOME to Frenchie Miernicke, but on a three-day pass plus travel time, the Normandy Hotel offered several of the luxuries Miernicke thought of when she thought about home. The first was a private room and bath. "I took two baths that night," Miernicke remembered. "When you saw a mirror for the first time and you took off your boots for the first time . . . you had a 'high-water mark' here and a 'high-water mark' there. . . . Oh, my heavens! Is this me?" Miernicke shampooed her hair, manicured her nails, and climbed into bed and relaxed. "Everyone else went on a date, but not me. I stayed in and it was wonderful."[48]

The next night, Miernicke and the other three nurses from the 2nd Aux all had dates and all four couples went together to the same nightclub. "Oh my, that was a liberal education. . . . It was a three-hour floor show of nude gals. The army officers we were dating wanted us to see this 'wonderful show,' " Miernicke said. "The show included dinner and the French food was excellent. But that floor show was one big bore for all four of us women."[49]

The following evening, Miernicke asked the concierge for the name of a good French restaurant patronized mainly by French people who lived in the area. She was delighted with the food and a *chanteuse* who played the piano and sang. "I met a wonderful French couple who had the table next to mine," Miernicke said. "The man was a champagne dealer and spoke perfect English. It was a very enjoyable evening."[50]

On their last day, the four nurses and their dates went on a sight-seeing tour around the city. "We visited the Eiffel Tower, Notre Dame Cathedral, and spent a couple of hours walking through the beautiful city of Paris." When Miernicke, refreshed and relaxed, returned on 17 December to 2nd Aux headquarters to join her team on the southern end of the Siegfried Line, she had no idea that the Germans had launched a massive stealth attack through the Ardennes Forest and were rapidly advancing miles into the American front lines.[51]

What happened in the Ardennes on 16 December caught the Americans and Allies completely by surprise. During the first two weeks of December, Hitler had secretly amassed 1,322,000 troops in the Ardennes, the frontline area most sparsely manned by the Americans and Allies. This buildup put the Germans at a three-to-one advantage—and a ten-to-one advantage in assault areas—when the Germans launched their surprise attack on 16 December.[52]

No one expected a counterattack of such strength; no one thought that the Germans had the troops and equipment to mount such an attack. With Christmas only nine days away, the world of the U.S. armed forces was turned upside down. All thoughts and hopes of being back in the United States before the end of January 1945 were completely dashed. The Germans were attacking in force. It would take a major American and Allied defense to stop them, and a major offensive action to drive them back across the German border.

That meant that no one was going home any time soon. The war and the future of the world hung in the balance.

PART FOUR

The Conquest of Germany

The war of attrition that was fought throughout the fall and early winter of 1944 came to an abrupt end on 16 December, when the German army shocked the Americans with a massive surprise offensive in the Ardennes Forest—the infamous Battle of the Bulge. The Germans not only broke through the Allied front but took the greatest toll in American lives of any single battle fought since the Battle of Gettysburg before the Allies successfully halted the German advance.

In March 1945, the Allied armies crossed the Rhine River—a feat no invading army had accomplished since Napoleon invaded Germany in 1805. It signaled the beginning of the end. German troops fought desperately as American and Allied troops pushed their way into and across the German heartland. As the Third Reich fell, GIs trained for fighting became prison guards for POWs, as hundreds of thousands of German troops surrendered.

After Germany's surrender, army nurses not only continued to care for wounded Americans and German POWs but also entered German concentration camps to care for the starving and brutalized inmates.

CHAPTER FOURTEEN

The Battle of the Bulge

ARMY NURSES MEET THE CHALLENGE

16 December 1944–15 January 1945

The commanding officer informed me that it would be necessary for five nurses to remain behind to help in the OR and to care for the non-transportable patients. I gathered them [the nurses] together and told [them] the story. Before the words were entirely out of my mouth, there were so many hands raised that I was speechless.

> —*Capt. Jean Truckey, chief nurse,*
> *67th Evacuation Hospital,*
> *Malmédy, Belgium, December 1944*

AT 1530 on 16 December 1944, Lieutenant Martha "Marte" Cameron took another look at herself in a full-length mirror, adjusted the brass on the lapels of her class-A uniform, and returned to her cot to pick up her helmet. She glanced out her third-floor window in the former SS Nazi barracks and headquarters building that served as the nurses' quarters for the 128th Evacuation Hospital now set up in Brand, Germany, four miles south of Aachen. She saw an American command car about a quarter of a mile down the road heading for her barracks. In the car was Cameron's date, a lieutenant colonel from a nearby artillery unit, coming to pick up the nurse to take her to a dance in Maastricht, Holland. The nurse and colonel settled in to a comfortable ninety-minute drive from Brand to Maastricht, complete with a flask of Scotch, a loaf of brown bread, a slab of sharp Cheddar cheese, and the car's heater kicked into high gear against the freezing cold outside. Neither could have known that on that very morning a massive German offensive had begun that would produce the largest number of American casualties in any single offensive in America's military history.

Cameron and the colonel cannot be accused of complacency or negligence in their duties. No one—neither Eisenhower, Bradley, nor the GIs in the frontline trenches—was expecting the massive winter German offensive that would be dubbed the "Battle of the Bulge" by American media within days after it began on 16 December 1944. No one saw it coming and no one expected it to erupt where it did: at the center of the American line, in the Ardennes Forest. A densely wooded plateau, deeply ridged and cut by many streams extending from northeastern France through northern Luxembourg and southern Belgium into Germany, the Ardennes was least expected by U.S. military intelligence to be the site of a German offensive. The trees were too dense, the roads too few and narrow, and in the winter mud and snow made it barely passable. Such a terrain did not allow for the quick deployment of troops, tanks, and artillery. And in fact, throughout November and the first two weeks of December, the Ardennes was quiet, as expected, while north and south of it the First and Third Armies, respectively, were on the offensive against the Germans.

But that quiet would prove to be deceptive. As early as September, Hitler had begun secretly preparing for a major offensive in the Ardennes: German forces began amassing men and equipment in the Eifel Forest that lay in Germany, between its western border and the Rhine River and adjacent to the Ardennes Forest of Belgium, for an attack the Führer felt could turn the war in Germany's favor. In this heavily forested area along the Belgium-Luxembourg-German border, the Germans amassed three armies with 1,900 artillery pieces and 1,000 armored fighting vehicles, grouped into 25 armored and infantry divisions. Using clandestine troop movements under cover of darkness by night and dense forest by day, the massive buildup remained virtually invisible to Allied air and ground reconnaissance. On December 15, more than one and a quarter million German troops were positioned in the Ardennes.[1]

While German troops were stealthily pouring into the Ardennes, American troops maintained on this front were, by comparison, few and far between. Eisenhower had been dealing with a shortage of infantry

Germany, 1944–45

〰 Front line (date)

0 — 100 Miles
0 — 100 Kilometers

DENMARK

Baltic Sea

North Sea

N
W E
S

●Hamburg

●Bremen

HOLLAND

●Amsterdam

GERMANY

Arnhem

Dec. 15, 1944

Rhine River

Ruhr River

Nordhausen●

Leipzig●

Krombach●

t. 15, 1944

●Antwerp
BELGIUM
Brussels

Eschweiler
Düren
●Cologne
Bonn
●Olpe

Erfurt●

amur
Liège
Aachen
Härtgen Forest
Euskirchen
Remagen

Meiningen●

Verviers
Malmédy●

St. Vith

Frankfurt
am Main
●

Römershag●

ARDENNES FOREST
Bastogne
(LUXEM-BOURG)

Moselle River

Kircheim●

Dieburg●
Würzburg●

Nürnberg●

Mannheim●
Adelsheim●
Bartenstein●

Heidelberg●

Meuse R.

Rur R.

FRANCE
●Metz

Hornbach●

Dieuze●

Sept. 15, 1944

Nancy●
Moselle R.
Strasbourg●

Bischwiller●

Stuttgart●

Rambervilliers●

Augsburg●
Einsbach
●Dachau

Epinal●

Landsberg●

Plombières●

Rhine R.

●Freiburg

Munich

Mulhouse●
●Belfort

Rioz●
Sept. 15, 1944

●Besançon

SWITZERLAND

(**AUSTRIA**)

forces for more than two months, and American and Allied troops were spread very thin along miles and miles of frontline positions. Since the Ardennes was quiet throughout October, November, and the first two weeks of December, new divisions just coming to the front were often sent there to gain some frontline experience. Hence, many of the American troops guarding the western front in this area were replacements just out of high school, with little or no combat experience.

Isolated reports from American reconnaissance troops warning of a possible German buildup along the Ardennes had trickled into Supreme Headquarters, Allied Expeditionary Force (SHAEF), during November and December, but top brass nonetheless remained convinced that the German army had neither the manpower nor the resources for another major offensive. Complacency, denial, and wishful thinking had somehow overcome vigilance and reality-based planning at SHAEF. At the front, many American soldiers, lulled by a lack of recent battles and enemy contact during the previous two months, spent a great deal of time thinking and talking about Christmas and going home. Even a few days after the German winter offensive began, U.S. military leaders and troops had a hard time seeing it for what it was—a massive lightning strike that would push a large pocket, a "bulge," into the center of the thinly defended Allied line, which, if successful, could change the course of the war.

At 1915, only fifteen minutes after arriving at the dance in Maastricht on 16 December, Marte Cameron's date was called away to the side of the hall that the Red Cross had decorated for that night's dance. When he returned in ten minutes, his news was not good. "He looked very serious," Cameron said. "He said that the Germans had made a breakthrough along the Belgian border. He had to go to work and so did I." The two said good-bye quickly and the lieutenant colonel's driver drove her back to the 128th Evac in Brand.[2]

When she arrived at about 2100, there were as yet no signs of a German breakthrough. "A half hour later, a V-1 rocket exploded about two miles away from our location. That night, enemy planes flew over the hospital quite a bit. Enough for us to realize that something different was going on." During the night of the 16th, American trucks, tanks, and infantry moved past the 128th Evac toward the rear. It looked like a retreat and panic was in the air; nurses not on duty got a chance to ask the GIs what was going on. "Some of those GIs were recent replacements," said Cameron. "They said the German infantry and tanks had broken through our lines near the Belgian border. 'They've pushed at least ten miles behind our line,' one of the soldiers told me. 'It looks like they've got us on the run.' Believe me, his words were not at all consoling. We began to wonder when they'd move us and our patients to the rear. We'd ask, 'Aren't we going to move today?' And they'd say, 'No, no orders from headquarters yet.' "[3]

AT 0545 on 16 December, nurses and other military personnel at the 67th Evacuation Hospital in Malmédy, about five miles west of the front lines, were awakened by the sounds of exploding shells in the distance. Most 67th personnel, experienced in reading the sounds of artillery fire for the telltale signs that indicated close danger, turned over and went back to sleep. Less than five minutes later, a loud explosion nearby awakened everyone and sent nurses dressed in nightgowns, pajamas, and steel helmets into the hallway to see what was going on and whether they would be needed on the wards. Again, most went back to bed. When another round of shells fell at 0800, everyone decided to get up and dress. Word filtered back to the nurses that the shells were from 170-millimeter German railroad guns and had fallen outside the local Catholic church just as parishioners were leaving early-morning mass. The wounded civilians were being brought to the 67th Evac. There were two American soldiers who had attended the mass, and during their attempts to help the wounded civilians, each was hit by shrapnel and killed.

This shelling was part of the opening salvos of the battle for the Ardennes. Soon, wounded troops from the front lines were being carried into the 67th for treatment. Many had suffered head wounds and were in critical condition. As Captain Jean Truckey, the chief nurse, helped to prepare two seriously wounded soldiers for surgery, she caught sight of the Christmas tree that had been set up and decorated in the preoperative ward. With a score of wounded young men on litters lined up and waiting in view of the tree with its tinfoil angels and five-pointed stars, Truckey noted, "It became an incongruous thing to enter a ward full of seriously wounded men and see the tree that had been so pretty and gay a few days earlier. It meant nothing now."[4]

Wounded soldiers who had been stationed ten or more miles ahead of the 67th Evac arrived all morning and afternoon. Over and over, these soldiers repeated the same story about fierce German attacks coming out of the Ardennes: tanks, artillery, and infantry were streaming out of the densely wooded areas of the Ardennes and rolling past U.S. troops as if they were not there at all. Unfortunately, these American troops were made up mostly of inexperienced replacements filling companies built around only five or ten men who were combat veterans. Caught completely by surprise and totally off guard, many of the green troops were breaking and running, leaving weapons and equipment behind.

By the afternoon of 16 December, American forces and headquarters personnel were having a difficult time evaluating and responding to the German attack. For many hours, Americans saw the offensive as isolated firefights and attached no major significance to them. Within forty-eight hours, however, U.S. and Allied military leaders would do an about-face and rush support troops, artillery, and equipment to the area to counter the very real German threat. But in those first two days, German tanks and infantry, breaking through Allied lines along an eighty-mile front that spanned territory from southern Belgium south to Ettelbruck, Luxembourg, would, for the most part, roll and walk through the sparsely manned American lines with little or no opposition, making their way farther westward. The German objective was to swing north and capture the port of Antwerp in Belgium, thereby driving a wedge between the American and Allied armies stationed north and south of the Ardennes and thus causing friction between the Allies. Hitler felt that this friction would eventually lead to a break in the united Allied front. Germany would, if not win the war, at least gain an advantage by that break and perhaps establish a favorable truce.

By the following day, 17 December, the U.S. Seventh Armored Division was mobilized and en route to the Ardennes. The division left Heerlen, Holland, about ten miles north of Aachen, and headed for St. Vith, Belgium, in the Ardennes about forty miles south of Heerlen. The men were to help rescue the 106th Division, which was encircled by the enemy. The convoy moved uneventfully through the town of Malmédy. However, just south of Malmédy, at an intersection near Baugnez, they confronted a long line of German tanks also rolling toward the intersection. The tanks were an advance unit of *Kampfgruppe Peiper* of the First SS *Leibstandärte Adolf Hitler* Panzer Division, commanded by SS Ostbf. Joachim Peiper, a veteran of the Russian front with a reputation for ruthlessness.

The Germans opened fire on the small convoy, and in less than thirty minutes, the Americans surrendered. As the captured GIs stood with their hands above their heads, a German SS trooper who spoke good English welcomed them to Belgium. The captors herded the Americans along with their unarmed medics and their wounded into an open field near the Café Bodarwé by the intersection on the outskirts of Malmédy. There were approximately seventy-two Americans in the group of captives. According to several of the twelve men who survived, the Germans lined the soldiers up and began looting watches and rings. The Germans then brought in machine guns and swept the Americans with continuous machine-gun fire. Several survived by falling beneath a dying comrade and playing dead while SS troops walked around the field and shot any man still breathing, moaning, or moving.

News of the massacre traveled around American troops so quickly that, within twelve hours, men in foxholes on the new front lines heard that the SS had killed U.S. prisoners. The news brought two main reactions in American troops: No one who heard the story was about to surrender to SS troops no matter what the circumstances; and U.S. troops would wreak revenge on the SS for what they had done to their comrades. If the GIs captured SS who were wearing American paratrooper boots, the SS soldier was shot with no questions asked. If an SS soldier was captured wearing U.S. combat boots, the SS men were forced to take off their boots and socks, roll up their pant legs, and walk around in the snow until they could no longer feel their feet or react to a knife prick on either foot. This done, the SS troopers were sent back to U.S. field hospitals where, more than likely, both feet would have to be amputated.[5]

IN BRAND, wounded continued to arrive at the 128th Evacuation Hospital on 17 December while retreating American troops and tanks continued to flee past the hospital toward the rear. Sixty-four new casualties arrived that day, bringing the census to 260 and filling over half of the hospital's beds. That night, V-1 rockets and German planes overflew the 128th Evac and rumors of Germans in the vicinity were rampant. "We were told no one was to go outside alone," Cameron said. "The word was that German paratroopers were dropped close by our hospital area and they didn't want anyone picked off by them."[6]

The hospital was placed under strict blackout conditions that evening. "We had blankets taped over our windows in our building," Corporal Oliver Sorlye said. "I pushed the blanket to the side at night. I could hear a lot of noise and I looked out. The whole sky was lit up with artillery fire. I turned to two of the guys and said, 'We've got to get out of here.' " Sorlye's alarm was not that of an untried rookie. As a veteran who had had enough frontline military service, starting in North Africa, to recognize the sounds, flashes, and explosions of a dangerous combat situation, he also had enough experience to sense that danger was getting closer.[7]

Six nurses and four doctors from the 25th Ohio General Hospital had been ordered on detached service with the 128th Evac about a week before Christmas. One of the nurses, Lieutenant Agatha Dohr from Cincinnati, had joined the Army Nurse Corps with the Ohio General Hospital Unit. Now she was working with veteran staff of the 128th. "At Brand," Dohr said, "I was a little apprehensive because the [hospital occupied] a former barracks for SS troops. We [staff from 25th General Hospital] had been there a few days when a plane went over the center of the building, strafing the place."[8]

What neither Sorlye nor any of the 128th Evac staff knew was the size and determination of the German troops pushing their way toward and through American forces that lay in the German path to Antwerp. Sorlye would learn days later that his brother, who was serving with the 106th Division and was hauling 155-millimeter shells to the front lines, had been taken prisoner by advancing German troops.

Hitler had chosen well the time and place of his winter offensive. Freezing temperatures kept most American troops huddled in their foxholes or, if they were more fortunate, in buildings, for warmth. Rain, fog, sleet, and snow kept the Army Air Forces out of the skies for days at a time, forcing American GIs to depend on their own isolated units for any combat support and reconnaissance they needed. The Führer was also right in thinking that it would take the Americans some time to figure out what was happening and to present an effective defense. What Hitler had not foreseen were the American units here and there that would dig in and fight to their last bullet. Nor had he foreseen the quick response of General Eisenhower in getting reinforcements to the front to stop, then push back the German winter offensive. Hitler's gamble would fail, but it triggered the most costly battle of any war in which Americans fought in the twentieth century.

TWO HOSPITALS were located in Malmédy on 17 December—the 67th Evacuation Hospital and the 44th Evacuation Hospital. As the number of GIs streaming past toward the rear increased, it was clear that both hospitals would soon have to retreat as well.

During the afternoon of 17 December, the commanding officer of the 67th Evac, Colonel John L. Crawford, called the nurses together and told them to pack immediately for an emergency departure. They could take only what they could carry with them. Nurses covered the wards for each other as they took ten or fifteen minutes to throw a few personal belongings into a bedroll and add them to a growing pile outside, which GIs would collect and throw onto a 2.5-ton truck.

Before the withdrawal, Colonel Crawford informed Chief Nurse Truckey that it would be necessary for five of the 67th Evac's nurses to remain behind to work in the OR and to care for nontransportable patients. Truckey was to select the five nurses who would stay, and she could not include herself in their number. The news hit Truckey like a punch in the stomach. Commanding officers had to make life-and-death decisions for their people almost every day, but on the whole, chief nurses were spared those kinds of choices. The CO and Truckey both knew that there was a good possibility that the five nurses left behind would be killed or captured by the Germans. The news of the nearby massacre of sixty of the seventy-two men of the Seventh Armored Division had not escaped the notice of the nurses. Truckey and her staff had discussed the recent atrocity and understood the message it held for future SS captives. There was no reason to believe that the SS would be any kinder to captured nurses than they had been to captured wounded soldiers and medics.

The SS were a breed unto themselves. By late 1944, most of these elite troops were very young—in their early or mid-twenties. Indoctrinated in Naziism since early childhood, these youths were fervent disciples of Hitler, brutal in the discharge of what they perceived to be their duty to the Führer and the fatherland.

Truckey decided to call her nurses together and ask for five volunteers to remain. If no one volunteered, she herself would have to choose the five. She sent word for an immediate meeting, and began developing the criteria for those she would order to stay. Standing before the group, Truckey explained the need for volunteers to stay behind, the dangers involved, and the chances the women left behind stood of making it back to their unit. Before she could finish, many of the nurses had raised their hands. The room was filled with strong, determined voices: " 'I'll stay behind,' 'Let me stay!' 'Count me in!' " Truckey wrote later. Truckey could not have been more proud of her nurses, or more honored to be a member of the Army Nurse Corps. She chose the five and called their names: First Lieutenants Anna M. Aslakson, Nina L. Bareham, Sally J. Casement, Ethel Gilbert, and Elizabeth C. Stuber.[9]

A much less difficult decision faced the remaining women before they could leave Malmédy for the rear—what to do with the special Christmas packages of food from home. The nurses had stored their personal parcels in order to share them with patients and the rest of the staff on Christmas Day. So as not to allow food and gifts from home to fall into German hands, the nurses gave an impromptu party in one of the nurse's rooms. Presents were opened, admired, and many of the edible goodies eaten. Some of the cookies, cake, and fudge had to be left behind. It was hoped that American infantry troops, and not the Germans, would be the victors of the battle and thus the recipients of the Christmas treats.

An hour later, all but a skeletal crew of corpsmen, doctors, and the five nurses selected to remain behind were dressed in their heaviest clothes, seated in the backs of trucks, and moving down the highway toward the rear area. The going was very slow because in addition to the military who were using the roads, scores of civilian refugees with their children, carts, animals, and belongings flowed along in a westerly direction as they too sought to get out of the reach of the advancing Germans.

When the convoy reached the 4th Convalescent Hospital at Spa, Belgium, about ten miles west of Malmédy, personnel were provided with hot meals and cots for the night. At breakfast the next morning, 18 December, they were delighted to see the five nurses who had been left behind at Malmédy join them. All of the patients at Malmédy had been evacuated, including the German POWs. "One Nazi had been a bit irritating because of his loud laughter each time a German shell exploded," Truckey wrote.[10]

The 44th Evac was not far behind the 67th Evac in retreating to the rear. On the night of 18 December, the forty-two nurses of the 44th Evac left Malmédy in the back of a truck and were driven northwest to Spa, where they were to spend the night with the 4th Convalescent Hospital, just as the 67th Evac had done the day before. "Spa was about seventeen kilometers from Malmédy, and after we reached our destination, they told us that we had been surrounded by Germans," 44th Evac Chief Nurse Martha Nash said. "I asked them, 'Well, how in the world did we get through there?' The men said they [the Germans] didn't want to waste their ammunition on one truck, but if they had known that there were forty-two nurses in the truck, they would have killed us for sure."[11]

Just the day before, Technical Sergeant Donald Pickard and several other corpsmen from the 44th Evac had each driven trucks in a convoy to a field hospital at Waimes, about four miles east of Malmédy. Their mission was to pick up equipment from the field hospital and bring it back to the 44th Evac at Malmédy. All the corpsmen except Pickard arrived at the field hospital in Waimes; apparently, Pickard had fallen behind during the drive without the corpsmen driving the other trucks noticing his absence. Each of the men loaded their trucks with equipment belonging to the field hospital and headed back for the 44th Evac. Along the way back, the convoy was stopped by a small unit of Germans that suddenly appeared from nowhere. The entire group was taken prisoner and held for about forty-five minutes. But before the Germans had time to evacuate or kill their prisoners, an American half-track appeared, fired a few shots, and sent the German unit into a speedy retreat without their prisoners.

The 44th Evac corpsmen thanked the half-track crew, climbed quickly into their trucks, and headed to Malmédy as fast as the roads would permit. When they reached the 44th Evac, they immediately asked if Sergeant Pickard had returned to the outfit. The news was not good—no one had seen or heard from Pickard since he left the 44th Evac for Waimes. A special detail of officers and enlisted men was dispatched to search for Pickard along and near his known route to the field hospital at Waimes. The search turned up nothing; there was no sign of Pickard or his truck. When the detail returned to the hospital, Sergeant Donald Pickard was officially listed as missing in action.

Approximately a month later, after the Germans had been pushed out of the Malmédy-Waimes area, GIs discovered a 2.5-ton truck in a densely wooded area some distance off the main road between Malmédy and Waimes. Pickard's body was slumped against the front seat with a large-caliber wound to the chest. Staff speculated that he may have driven off the main road to avoid German soldiers, or to avoid coming under enemy fire. "Everybody was sad when they found Donnie," Martha Nash said.

"They found him in his truck. He'd been shot by the Germans. We were all sad about his death. Donnie was a nice-looking young fellow from Virginia. Everybody called him 'Rebel.' " The U.S. Army buried Sergeant Donald Pickard in Henri Chappel Cemetery near Verviers, Belgium. About a week later, the chaplain of the 44th Evacuation Hospital held a well-attended memorial service for "Rebel."[12]

ON 19 DECEMBER 1944, Allied commanders meeting in Verdun decided to halt all offensive action north and south of the Ardennes— offensives that were pushing toward the Rhine—and concentrate instead on reducing the enemy salient in the Ardennes. The number of casualties decreased for the next five or six days while divisions moved toward the line for the new offensive.

The Third Armored Division left Stolberg, Germany, a town about ten miles north of Aachen, at 1700 on 19 December, heading south to the Ardennes. Now, more than twelve hours later, the division was dealing with heavy snow, freezing temperatures, and blackout conditions as it made its way toward the area where they expected to meet German forces.

"Toward the area where they expected to meet German forces" was about as good as information got concerning the location of the German tanks and infantry in Belgium. American units were still trying to gather information on German troops who had caught them completely by surprise. Surprise and some of the worst weather Belgium had seen in recorded history was making information about the enemy extremely difficult to gather. Due to the constant heavy sleet, rain, and snow, air reconnaissance patrols could rarely be flown. Without accurate intelligence, it was all but impossible to precisely calculate a hard target. Tankers and infantrymen accustomed to having detailed maps and up-to-the-minute information to aid them in battle were now making their way along narrow, muddy roads in pitch darkness, in the middle of a heavy snowstorm, with only educated guesses and probabilities to guide them. Bitterly cold temperatures and lack of sleep only added to the hazards of the journey and coming battle.

As daylight penetrated the snow and fog on 20 December, Private First Class Jim Vance of the Third Armored Division, a twenty-year-old native of Mississippi, put his hands out quickly to steady himself as his Sherman tank slipped in the snow-covered mud and slid off the narrow road that led toward Manhay, Belgium. He could see two lines of tanks in the distance on the left and right flanks of his division. "There was no way of knowing whether the tanks were American or German," Vance said. "But in about ten minutes, one of the tanks fired on us and a shell hit our .50-caliber machine gun and tore it off our tank. We never did find out if it was German or friendly fire. We were just glad the shell didn't damage our tank any worse than tearing the machine gun off."[13]

The Third Armored Division's Task Force Kane, which included Company D to which Vance belonged, reached the outskirts of Manhay that morning, and late on the afternoon of 20 December they waited to receive further orders. That night, a young lieutenant, a replacement fresh from the States who had been in command of Company G for only about a week, ordered one of Vance's fellow tankers, Private Fred Headrick from Chattanooga, Tennessee, on temporary duty with Company G, to walk to the command post and bring him back a blanket. Given the company's lack of information about the lay of the area and the location of enemy troops, a walk to a command post a mile away in total blackout conditions could very well be a death sentence. "I was surprised that he'd give

Tech-5 Fred Headrick with the Third Armored Division, 1945 (Courtesy of Fred Headrick)

me such an order," Headrick said. "But a private doesn't have the authority to tell a lieutenant that he's given him a stupid order that might just get him killed."[14]

To find the command post that was about a mile from where the tanks were stopped for the night, Headrick had to wander around in pitch darkness. When he stumbled upon the post, the two officers on duty were shocked to see a GI out in the night fog and snow. "One asked me, 'What in the hell are you doing here?' and I told him," Headrick said. "The two officers had a few choice words about a stupid stunt and told me, if I got back alive, to tell the lieutenant that they 'don't have any damn blankets.' "[15]

On his way back, Headrick was stopped by a sentry and challenged for the password. When the sentry recognized Headrick and learned what he was doing out at night in an area that could have enemy troops just looking for someone to take back and question, the guard cursed and told Headrick that he hoped he made it back alive.

Headrick survived the unnecessary danger this officer had put him in that night, but others in Headrick's outfit would not be as lucky just a few days later. Task Force Kane pulled out of Manhay and headed for the town of Hotton on 26 December. Fred Headrick was in the lead tank, and as the convoy of tanks approached a crossroads near the town of Soy, he spotted several German tanks in the distance. "The tank commander radioed the lieutenant and told him we needed to call in tank destroyers or artillery because we couldn't get a clear shot through the trees that were all around us," Headrick recalled. "The lieutenant said he could shoot out the branch of a tree that was in the way so we could fire on the Germans without calling for help." Before he could respond, the lieutenant ordered the third tank in the column—the tank in which the lieutenant himself was riding—to shoot at the offending branches.

Just like Headrick, who had followed the lieutenant's orders to go to the command post to get the officer a blanket, the gunner in the third tank did what he was told. The branch exploded into a thousand splinters and fell to the ground in front of Headrick's tank. Seconds later, an 88-millimeter shell hit the third tank, killing everyone except the assistant driver and the lieutenant, who managed to get out before it burst into flames. The lieutenant's orders to shoot at the trees had revealed the position of Task Force Kane's tanks to the Germans. Now, armor-piercing shells bounced in front of Headrick's lead tank. The tank commander gave an order to immediately move out. "I didn't think that this boy who was driving could cross a ditch to our left," Headrick said, "but he turned that tank right over the ditch and got on across and out of there." Later, Headrick learned that the assistant driver of the third tank was not about to let the lieutenant who had foolishly brought about the crew's deaths off the hook. "The assistant driver was so mad at the lieutenant for giving the Germans a perfect target by firing at the tree," Headrick recalled, "that he cursed him and said he'd kill him the first chance he got. About a month later, they sent the lieutenant back to the States."[16]

Military officers were trained to avoid actions that would unnecessarily endanger their men. Unfortunately for Headrick and the men of Company G, their lieutenant, newly arrived, did not appear to have absorbed that lesson as well as he should have.

The next day, 27 December, two of the infantrymen who were trying to keep warm in the frigid weather asked Headrick if they could get inside the tank for a few minutes to warm up. Headrick and his crew made room, and the two soldiers climbed into the belly of the tank. After ten minutes, both men said they were going back outside because "it's colder inside the tank than it is outside." Private Headrick could have told the soldiers as much, but he doubted that they would have believed him. "I had stolen a blowtorch from maintenance," Headrick said, "and we'd light that blowtorch up at night and pass it around trying to warm our feet with it. I found some sheepskin. I lined my shoes with all that sheepskin. It was about twenty to thirty degrees below zero down there at that time."[17]

Many of the tankers wounded during the German winter offensive and delivered to frontline hospitals suffered second- and third-degree burns that often covered their bodies from the waist up. Tank fires happened far too easily because of the Sherman tank's thin armorplating and the American use of gasoline instead of the less volatile diesel fuel, which the Germans used. When a shell hit a Sherman tank, it ignited like a match. It was no wonder that many soldiers referred to the Shermans as "Ronsons"—a popular cigarette lighter. Given that the Sherman was prone to explode into flames instantly, some of the injured tankers suffered extensive burns, involving up to 60 percent of the surface of their skin. In addition to the extent of surface burned, the severity, or degree, of the burn was a critical factor. Some of the injured had less severe, second-degree burns that resulted in blistering, while others had third-degree burns that caused necrosis, or death, to the involved skin and tissues beneath. To treat the burns, fluid lost from a burn victim's body because of seepage through the burn sites had to be replaced intravenously; penicillin and sulfa had to be administered to prevent infection; and the wounds had to be debrided to remove foreign matter and dead tissue. In addition, a new method of treatment consisting of the use of compression bandages to stop or at least slow the rate of fluid loss was being tried. It was hard to predict whether a burn victim would live or die, but a soldier with more than 60 percent of the surface of his body burned was not likely to survive. If a soldier with serious burns lived, he usually faced months or even years of painful treatment and plastic surgery. He had also to adjust psychologically to disfigurement and disability.

British medicine had been dealing with the problems of serious burns in combat before America entered World War II. Many British pilots who were part of Churchill's "precious few" who saved England during the Battle of Britain in 1940 suffered serious and disfiguring burns when their planes were hit by enemy fire. British medicine had pioneered plastic surgery at a specialized hospital center located in Basingstoke in Surrey.

ON 22 DECEMBER 1944, an advance echelon of the 128th Evacuation Hospital was loaded at Brand into trucks for the trip to a new hospital site at Verviers, Belgium, about fifteen miles southwest of Aachen. Unfortunately, VII Corps activity on the roads in the area forced the echelon to return to Brand for the night. The next morning brought better luck; the 128th Evac moved by infiltration—one or two trucks at a time. "During the retreat from the Bulge," Lieutenant Agatha Dohr said, "the patients had already been evacuated and we traveled on trucks. We found out what was going on from the soldiers who were coming through."[18]

The hospital was set up in buildings in Verviers. The new site was not out of German reach as V-1 rockets flew over all day and night. One never knew when a V-1's motor would cut out and the weapons would fall and explode near or on the hospital site. "We watched the buzz bombs go over," Lieutenant Dohr said. "When the taillight went out, we rushed for the shelters."[19]

Hospital personnel worked the entire day before Christmas completing the hospital setup. At 0800 on Christmas Day, the 128th Evac officially opened to receive casualties. One hundred eighty-three wounded and ill soldiers were brought in that day. By midnight on Christmas night, the 128th Evac had a patient census of 189—far below its 400- to

450-bed capacity. This moderate patient load allowed hospital staff to carry out their plans for a traditional turkey dinner for all personnel and patients who were well enough to enjoy it. "It was wonderful to get the chance to celebrate Christmas in the midst of so much carnage and death being dealt all around us," Martha Cameron said. "It was a way of reaffirming for all of us still alive that life is for the living." Patients and staff sang Christmas carols together, shared the Christmas meal, participated in a mass, and exchanged small gifts mostly created from personal items donated by the nurses.[20]

However, the relatively light patient load on Christmas Day changed abruptly overnight. The next day marked the beginning of a period in which the number of wounded received and treated by the 128th Evacuation Hospital reached a record high: in the last week of December 1944, 1,890 patients were received, and 595 of these underwent surgical procedures. "The 128th had the most patients they had ever had," Sorlye said. "Patients were lined up two abreast for at least a mile." The combat wounded from engagements on the northern shoulder of the bulge in Belgium were being brought to Verviers and lined up on litters along the hallways and directly outside the admission ward. Litter bearers were at a premium; even Sergeant Loren Butts, the first sergeant, was called out of headquarters along with anyone else who could be spared. "Everybody turned to," Butts said, "and carried litters all night. The numbers were overwhelming. My shoulders and back ached from carrying so many litters for so many hours."[21]

The OR worked around the clock on wounds that were among the worst ever seen by 128th Evac personnel. A number of the wounds were from land mines, complicated by exposure to mud, snow, and below-freezing temperatures. "Many of them resulted in amputation," Marte Cameron recalled. One night during the last week of December, she arrived in the OR around 2000 to find eight patients each lying on a makeshift table—individual litters supported by two sawhorses—with one or both legs elevated in preparation for surgery. "When the shifts changed, the new people coming on duty—us—inherited these eight wounded soldiers who were prepped and waiting to be operated on. That's the only time I really felt like getting out of there. 'Enough of this,' I told myself. I didn't want to go home necessarily, I just wanted to get out of the OR."[22]

In a letter to her father dated 28 December 1944, Marte made no mention of the amputation surgeries that day or any other day in the operating room. Her words were meant to reassure him and prevent him from worrying about her: "The news of the month probably made you worry [newspapers in the U.S. were filled with the combat action of the Battle of the Bulge], but if you did, I'm sorry 'cause we've been as safe as usual."[23]

Unfortunately, amputations were far too frequently the only remedy for thousands of Allied and German troops who suffered severe frostbite in the subfreezing temperatures of the European winter of 1944–45. On 28 December, Lieutenant Edna Browning had her first experience with surgery that involved an amputation. One of the regular nurse anesthetists had become ill and was unable to report for duty. Browning was tapped to assist with the major surgery, something with which she had little experience. Though she had previously filled in for other nurses in the operating room, until that day she had only helped with minor procedures. This time, Browning was to give drop ether while surgeons amputated a German POW's right leg below the knee. The POW was the victim not only of a severe wound that included multiple fractures of his lower right leg but of frostbite as well. He had lain in snow exposed to the freezing cold for hours before he was discovered and rescued by U.S. Army medics. "I'll never forget that German. His leg was so mangled," Browning said. "There were bones protruding out of wounds in at least three places. All they could do was take the leg off." Browning had to focus on her job as an anesthetist and struggle not to pass out or to be overcome by nausea.[24]

The surgeon used a scalpel to make an incision in the skin and underlying tissues. Once the bleeding arteries were tied off, he folded the skin up toward the knee. This process ensured that sufficient skin would remain to serve as a flap that would be used, some four months to a year after the amputation, to actually close the stump permanently. The surgeon then asked for the sterile surgical saw; after determining the desired angle of the cut, he began sawing the exposed bone about an inch or so higher than where he had made the original incision. The sound of the saw moving back and forth, deeper and deeper into the bone, filled the OR. Finally, there was a crack as the bone was completely cut through. The surgical technician who had been holding the leg in place on the amputation block lifted it away, wrapped it in several surgical towels, and placed it in a bucket at the side of the operating table. The surgeon then tied off any remaining bleeders and folded the skin around the open wound of the stump. He sewed it in place with "staying" sutures (minimum sutures to keep the skin flap in place) and dressed the wound with gauze and roller bandage. The German soldier and Edna Browning both survived the amputation.

Lieutenant Agatha Dohr worked in the orthopedic postoperative ward at the 128th Evac. "I worked where I was needed including heavy orthopedics," Dohr said. "They called it that because the casts on some of these patients were so heavy." Patients on Dohr's unit had casts that involved a broken leg and sometimes a pelvis, or casts that stabilized an arm and shoulder, and often a lower limb as well. "Most of these guys were hurt badly enough that they went right on home because they needed more surgery or longer treatments. I helped take care of them until they were well enough for evacuation."[25]

One of the wards that frequently needed extra help was the maxillofacial ward. Dohr spent a good deal of time working to care for these casualties, too. "One of the things that I liked in the army," she recalled, "was the way they grouped patients. We had a ward with all the same types of injuries—all broken legs or all broken jaws that were wired shut as part of their treatment." This practice of placing patients with like injuries together had advantages for the staff. They could quickly learn the specific nursing care that all of the patients needed. Patients with wired jaws had special problems eating. Moreover, staff had to be prepared for one particular danger that could threaten the life of a patient with his jaws wired shut: should the patient vomit, he could choke to death. "On every bed hung a pair of pliers in case a patient started to throw up," Dohr said. "If one of the soldiers got sick to his stomach and vomited, there was no way he could open his mouth to get rid of it." In such a situation, the staff member closest to the patient would use the pliers to quickly cut the wires and turn or move the patient so that he would not choke or aspirate the vomited material into his lungs. The patient's airway would be suctioned if necessary. If vomited material did reach the lungs, pneumonia would develop and complicate the soldier's recovery. "Unfortunately," Dohr said, "having to cut the wires holding the jaw usually meant another trip to the OR to get the jaw rewired."[26]

THE RAPID MOVEMENT of American infantry troops and armored divisions to meet the German onslaught, along with several clear days of good flying weather for American fighters and bombers, stemmed the tide of the Allied retreat and turned the Ardennes campaign around. By 26 December 1944, the German thrust forward was halted short of the Meuse River and over seventy miles short of Antwerp. Eight days later, on 3 January 1945, an American/Allied counterattack began along with a week of constant snowfall and temperatures that hovered around zero degrees Fahrenheit. Two days of snow were classified officially as "blizzards." Despite the freezing temperatures, snow, and large number of casualties already suffered, the Americans fought on with courage and determination.

For several days near the end of December and the beginning of January 1945, as the Germans attempted to regroup and U.S. troops reorganized along the front lines for a planned American offensive, the number of incoming casualties decreased dramatically. Several of the 128th Evac nurses took advantage of the lull by making appointments to get their hair shampooed, curled, and arranged at a beauty shop not far from the hospital. "My hair was long," Dohr said. "We had those hairpieces that we called 'rats.' They were like tubes and you flipped your hair over them. My hair looked so good when we left the shop, that I decided to carry my helmet back to the hospital instead of wearing it." All military personnel were ordered to wear a helmet in the combat zone. About ten minutes after arriving back in her room, Dohr was summoned by the chief nurse, who had seen the nurses returning from their visit to the beauty shop. Dohr thought that she was in some kind of trouble, but did not connect it to her new hairdo. "As it turned out," Dohr said, "I was confined to quarters because I had my hair done and carried my helmet back instead of wearing it. I didn't get to go anywhere with my new hairdo."[27]

Since the lull in the hospital workload continued through New Year's Eve, the officers and nurses held a dance in one of the larger buildings. A dance indoors was a particular treat for the unit's veterans. They remembered the difficulties trying to dance on the floor of a canvas tent or on the temporary flooring they had felt lucky to use back in North Africa. An orchestra made up of GIs from companies stationed nearby provided the music.

Martha Cameron walked into the dance at 2000. She was wearing a black, floor-length evening dress that her friend and roommate Frances Farabough had carried in her bedroll since landing in North Africa. For almost four hours, Cameron danced around the floor with her date, Major Michael DeVito, and other officers. Then, suddenly, like Cinderella, she dashed out of the dance. She rushed to the second-floor room she shared with Farabough and passed the dress off to her roommate. Farabough had a date in ten minutes. She donned the dress and ran to meet her artillery captain from a nearby detachment, who told her, as he guided her onto the dance floor, that she looked very beautiful.

By 1 January 1945, the 12th Field Hospital with its eighteen nurses was assigned to duty in Namir, a Belgian city located on the west bank of the Meuse River and a major railroad line. While at Namir, the large 910-bed 12th Field Hospital functioned in several different capacities: as a field hospital, as a station hospital, and as a holding unit. As a field hospital, the 12th received large numbers of American casualties from the vicinity of Huy, Belgium, about fifteen miles northeast of Namir—casualties from the Ardennes. Many of these wounded who required longer periods for convalescence could remain at the hospital since 400 of its 910 beds were designated as a station hospital and another 100 beds were reserved for nontransportable patients. As a holding unit, the 12th Field Hospital used a large number of its beds to treat patients being prepared for evacuation.

As an evacuation hospital, the 12th was charged with evacuating thousands of American soldiers by railroad and by air. Ninety percent of the first nine thousand soldiers evacuated in the first nine days of 1945 were suffering from trench foot or severe frostbite. "It was a common sight," said Captain Harold M. McGreevey, commanding officer of the 12th, "while walking through the corridors of the hospital, to see in the adjacent wards long lines of patients with their feet uncovered, and all suffering from the ailments [frostbite or trench foot]. . . ."[28]

The lack of waterproof boots in the American combat uniform was costing the U.S. Army dearly in the thousands of combat troops pulled off the front lines suffering from trench foot or frostbite or both. In the Mediterranean theater, 5,700 combat troops had fallen victim to trench foot during the winter of 1943–44. Unfortunately, the lessons learned there had not been transferred to the European theater. Many commanding officers, including General Bradley, had hoped that the war would end before cold weather set in. Faced with limited space for the shipment of supplies from the United States, commanding officers had ordered gasoline and ammunition instead of warm clothing and winter boots. When requests for winter clothing were finally submitted, there was not enough time to permit their delivery before the onset of Western Europe's worst winter on record. Frontline soldiers paid a high price for this serious mistake. Many men would lose toes, a foot, even both feet.[29]

Trench foot cost U.S. troop strength 14,505 men during the fall and winter of 1944. Before the winter months of January, February, and March 1945 were over, the number of troops suffering from trench foot would reach a grand total of 29,389 casualties in the European theater.[30]

On 28 January 1945, the "bulge" had been eliminated and the American and Allied front lines stood in a slightly better position than they had been on 16 December 1944 before the German winter offensive began. Prime Minister Winston Churchill summarized the victory in the Ardennes very well in his address to the House of Commons on 18 July 1945: "This is undoubtedly the greatest American battle of the war and will, I believe, be regarded as an ever-famous American victory."[31]

The battle produced the largest number of American casualties since the Civil War battle at Gettysburg, and to the end of the twentieth century. American losses during the Battle of the Bulge were staggering. From 16 December 1944 to the third week in January 1945, there were at least 81,000 casualties; this number includes 19,000 killed in action and 16,900 missing in action or taken as prisoners of war. Approximately 800 tanks and tank destroyers were lost. During the same period, Allied estimates of German casualties were 90,000; after the war, the Germans put their estimated losses at 100,000 casualties from the Bulge. They also lost about 800 tanks and 1,000 planes.[32]

CHAPTER FIFTEEN

Battle of the Rhineland

ARMY NURSES PERSEVERE

15 January–23 March 1945

The consensus of public opinion held that American nurses were shirking their patriotic duty and not volunteering for war service.

—*Col. Mary T. Sarnecky, USA, ANC (Ret.),*
A History of the U.S. Army Nurse Corps

L IEUTENANT "PETE" PETERSON of the 95th Evacuation Hospital dropped more ether onto the gauze mask covering her patient's nose and mouth and nodded to the surgeon, signaling that he could begin his incision. Like hundreds of other battle casualties arriving on Peterson's OR table over the past six days, this soldier had been wounded during the battle for the Colmar pocket, the northern perimeter of which was located about forty miles south of the 95th Evacuation Hospital's location at Sarrebourg, in northeast France, about forty miles west of the Rhine River.

By the end of January 1945, with the tide of war turned back in favor of the Allies, General Eisenhower began to focus on a plan for a broad sweep eastward across Germany. Since the front that extended from the North Sea southward to the northern border of Switzerland was ragged, it needed to be straightened and thereby shortened so that it would be easier to manage and defend. On the southern end of the western front, there remained a fifty-mile gap along the Rhine River near the town of

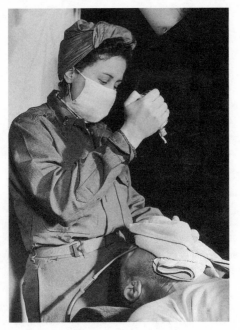

*Lt. Lillie "Pete" Peterson administering drop ether to an
American soldier during surgery* (Courtesy of Lillie
Peterson Homuth)

Colmar that formed the edge of an 850-square-mile pocket of German
forces. This was the Colmar pocket.

General de Lattre, of Jacob Devers's Sixth Army Group, had
attempted to eliminate the pocket early in December, but alone, his
forces were too weak to drive out the Germans. General Devers appealed
to SHAEF Headquarters, requesting reinforcements for his group. He
was promised two additional divisions: the Tenth Armored Division and
the Twenty-eighth Infantry Division. On 20 January 1945, a simultaneous Allied attack on two sides of the Colmar pocket began. The battle
would last until the German forces were defeated on 5 February. Some of
the 8,000 U.S. and the 16,483 German casualties were carried to the army
hospitals that were supporting the troops, including the 95th Evac at
Sarrebourg.[1]

Now, at 0130 on 27 January, Peterson watched as the surgeon cut through the abdomen of a young German POW, and called for retractors to open the incision wider. As the bright light of the overhead OR lamp lit up the dark interior of the soldier's exposed abdomen, an eerie, almost surreal scene emerged: masses of five-inch-long white worms slithered wildly around the man's belly. Like the majority of German patients with abdominal wounds, the patient on Peterson's OR table was infested with parasites. "No matter how many times I saw those worms crawling around in patients' bellies, I never got used to the sight," she recalled. Amid the worms, the surgeon searched for shrapnel and began to repair the damage the razor-sharp metal had done to the intestines and stomach. "The surgeon mostly worked around the worms sewing up tears and closing off bleeders in the patient's abdomen," Peterson said. "But every now and then, several of the worms crawled into the area where he was working and one of the surgical technicians would scoop them out with a clamp and drop them in the bucket at the side of the OR table. They looked just as ugly in the bucket but not quite as eerie as they looked inside the patient."[2]

In addition to dealing with worms, the surgical team had to explore every wound for debris such as pieces of clothing that were often wet and caked with mud. If the threads from clothing were not cleaned out, infection was sure to follow in a hurry. "There was a lot of sulfa powder used in the wounds," said Peterson, "and plenty of penicillin given following surgery."[3]

The OR teams worked twelve-hour shifts, and in order to cut down on the amount of linen being used, doctors did not always change their gowns between operations. However, they did put on new sterile gloves for each case. When not actually on duty elsewhere, nurses were expected to help in the sterilizing tent, rolling plaster bandages for casts, patching rubber gloves, or sharpening needles to prepare them, with the syringes, for sterilization.

After long evenings of work in the OR, nurses, doctors, and corpsmen would go by the mess tent for something to eat. Sergeant Larry Schweitzer, the hospital's baker, would always have pie and cake ready for tired and hungry OR personnel. Schweitzer had attained quite a bit of fame for his breads, biscuits, cakes, and pies. Even General Clark loved Schweitzer's raisin pie. Back in Italy when the 95th Evacuation Hospital was assigned to the Fifth Army, Clark had tasted Schweitzer's handiwork at a dinner at the 95th. Clark later wrote a letter to Sergeant Schweitzer

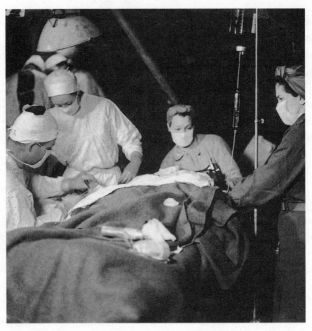

Personnel of the 95th Evacuation Hospital at work in the OR tent. The nurse on far right is Lillie "Pete" Peterson. (U.S. Army Signal Corps)

complimenting the baker, and in return, Schweitzer sent the general a freshly baked pie. The brass and the hospital personnel were not the only ones to enjoy Schweitzer's skills. The sergeant was the baker for the entire hospital, wounded included. Hungry, cold, sick, and wounded soldiers who were admitted into the hospital after meal hours were always assured of something good to eat, if the admitting doctor approved. The food available at any hour of the day or night was usually a bowl of hot soup, rolls, and a slice of Schweitzer's pie.

DURING THE THIRD week in January 1945, Frenchie Miernicke and her 2nd Auxiliary Surgical Team traveled through the Vosges Mountains in northeast France with the 11th Field Hospital to Vibersviller, thirty miles north of Strasbourg. Even in good weather during peacetime, these roads were dangerous for travelers. "We were traveling in an ambulance,"

Miernicke said. "Tig [Corpsman Tignanelli] drove with me in the Vosges Mountains up on the rim, near the front lines. You'd look down . . . [there were precipitous drop-offs] and there were huge potholes. That kid was as cool as a cucumber. We were in the Lord's hands."[4]

Now, in the midst of war in the coldest European winter on record, the mountain roads were truly treacherous. The thermometer rose and fell between +30° and −30° Fahrenheit, with the temperature, on average, hovering around zero degrees. The bitter cold combined with weeks of snowfall brought continuously rising mounds of snow and created a thick layer of ice that covered the roads. "We passed several locations where the German army had set up defensive positions about a week earlier," Miernicke said. "The [German] soldiers were still at their posts as we drove by. The men were frozen in place"—leaning forward against a log or a rock, their eyes still on the road, their hands still on their rifles. "They must have frozen to death while waiting for the Americans and Allies to come up the narrow road. It was sad to see that."[5]

The same numbing cold that had claimed the German rear guard made life for Miernicke and her team at the 11th Field Hospital at Vibersviller very difficult. Water froze solid wherever it collected. "Even our Lyster bags of drinking water turned to ice," Miernicke said. "You'd fill your canteen when you could get to flowing water, and in a matter of an hour, your canteen and the water were frozen into one solid unit. They had to put the Lyster bags and the main tank of water inside a heated tent to keep it liquid. You'd put water in your helmet to bathe, and before you were finished, the water had ice floating in it. I have never been as cold again as I was that winter."[6]

Up until this time, mainly wood-burning stoves had been used to heat the hospital tents in the Mediterranean and European Theaters. But at some point during the war, Congress back in Washington passed legislation replacing some of the wood-burning stoves with oil-burning substitutes. The reasons for this change remain obscure to this day. Sadly, U.S. congressmen and senators had not taken into consideration the effects of freezing temperatures on oil. "Someone in Congress decided we needed oil-burning stoves, not wood," Miernicke said. "The oil would thicken and freeze, leaving us with another problem—something else to thaw out."[7]

Hospital personnel were billeted in sheds and barns during their first days at the Vibersviller site. The sheds in which the male officers were housed along the edge of the hospital area had vestibules in which farm

animals were kept. One had to pass through these vestibules to reach the
rooms in back in which the officers slept. Of course, with the farm animals came large manure piles. "The odor was terrific on the way in,"
Miernicke said. "The men said they got used to it after a time and didn't
notice the odor at all."[8]

When the nurses first arrived, their tents had not yet been pitched, so
they were housed in various stables around the hospital. "They put us
right by the cows. The first evening we were bedding down in straw. All
of a sudden that night, one of the nurses sharing my stall thought she
heard something or someone moaning. She whispered in my ear, 'Somebody's in here,' and I whispered back, 'It can't be,' " Miernicke said. "As
it turned out, it was just one of the cows, but we were so far up front and
we knew Germans had infiltrated the area before, so we were scared most

Lts. Frances "Frenchie" Miernicke and Celia Allison going for water at their
hospital site in Alsace-Lorraine, France, 1945 (Courtesy of Maj. Frances
Miernicke Plenert, ANC [Ret.])

of the time. But we never let it interfere with our work of taking care of wounded and sick soldiers."[9]

ON 6 JANUARY 1945, President Roosevelt gave his State of the Union address. As part of that address, the president declared that the nation was in dire need of twenty thousand additional army nurses. So pressing was the need, Roosevelt said, that he had asked Congress to immediately pass legislation that would impose a draft upon American women between the ages of nineteen and forty-five who were graduate registered nurses. The address was heard by millions of Americans over their home or business radios. As a result, the American public feared its wounded GIs were not getting the nursing care they needed and deserved.

In fact, the public was misled, drawing the conclusion that registered nurses were failing to volunteer in adequate numbers for military service and thus shirking their patriotic duty. The truth of the matter was far more complicated. To begin with, the question of whether a shortage of army nurses existed at all, and in what numbers, was debatable, as we have seen. In April 1944, the U.S. Surgeon General had ordered the American National Red Cross to stop recruiting and appointing nurses for the military because the quota needed for the Army Nurse Corps was 40,000 and there were already 39,671 nurses on active duty. When the War Department raised the ceiling to 50,000 on 30 June 1944, a shortage of 10,000 nurses was created overnight.[10]

Yet in late November and early December 1944, the director of the Army Nurse Corps, Colonel Blanchfield, visited the army hospitals in the European theater and found that staffing was adequate. Upon her return, Blanchfield announced that a draft of nurses was not needed. However, she was being pressed to testify in Congress against her convictions and in support of the draft; rather than compromise herself, Blanchfield found a reason to travel out of the country and therefore made herself unavailable to testify.[11]

When President Roosevelt proposed legislation to draft nurses in his address on 6 January, he surprised the U.S. Surgeon General, the War Department, and the director of the Army Nurse Corps by asking for not 10,000 but 20,000 women—double the number the War Department had estimated the war effort needed—a figure that would ensure an Army Nurse Corps of 60,000.[12]

Whether or not a shortage of nurses actually existed, several factors had been working to severely inhibit, if not outright prohibit, nurses from volunteering for the military throughout 1943 and 1944. For one, a vicious slander campaign on the home front that depicted not just military nurses but all women in the military as whores, lesbians, and husband-stealers had effectively discouraged women, including nurses themselves, from volunteering.

The military also actively discriminated on the basis of sex: male registered nurses were prohibited from serving in either the Army or the Navy Corps. The American Nurses Association strongly held the position that these men should be considered. But men would not be accepted in the Army Nurse Corps until 9 August 1955, when Representative Frances P. Bolton of Ohio introduced a bill to authorize the commissioning of male nurses in the U.S. Army Reserve. The Congress passed it and President Eisenhower signed it. Edward Lyon, a nurse anesthetist from Kings Park, New York, entered active duty on 10 October that year.[13]

Racial discrimination was also practiced by the army: the military restricted the recruitment of African-American registered nurses, holding to a quota of only 185 in mid-1941. Not only was the quota extremely low, but segregation was enforced. The twenty-two African-American nurses who were on active duty in 1941 at Fort Bragg, North Carolina, and Camp Livingston, Louisiana, were segregated and rarely worked with white troops.

One young black nurse who enlisted in the Army Nurse Corps in 1942 was twenty-two-year-old New Jersey native Lieutenant Alice McKoy. Discriminatory and segregation practices were distasteful to all blacks serving in the U.S. armed forces, but Lieutenant McKoy was determined to do something about the regulations that rankled all black troops. One army regulation she found particularly insulting was a rule that demanded that all black military personnel enter and leave military buses by the back door. A simple bus ride across a military post required black troops—enlisted and officers alike—to exit a bus that was about to enter a military reservation and reboard the same bus by the back door for the ride on the military post. Alice McKoy remembered those times: "It was ridiculous and humiliating to have to exit and reenter the bus by the back door before it proceeded to enter a military post. We nurses discussed the regulation and I decided to lodge an official complaint with the commanding officer of the post." Despite warnings from her sister nurses that the army would not like anyone complaining, Lieutenant McKoy wrote and submitted a formal complaint. "It didn't actually change the rule but at least the army knew how we felt about it," McKoy said.

McKoy was clear about why she had volunteered to serve in a military that treated her and other blacks like second-class citizens. "No matter what segregation the military had, it wasn't as bad as what blacks faced every day in civilian life. Besides, our country was at war and I wanted to do my part to help win that war. All the women I served with felt the same way. As corny as it may sound, I guess you could say we were patriots."[14]

Despite requests for the elimination of the quota from a representative of the National Association of Colored Graduate Nurses to President Roosevelt, progress was slow. By December 1944, 302 black nurses were on active duty in the Army Nurse Corps. Some of them were ordered to England, where they were assigned to take care of German POWs, a restrictive assignment that was hard on their morale. In the United States, African-American nurses were rotated every six months to relieve white nurses who were assigned to POW camps. The Army Nurse Corps would not be integrated until 1948, when President Harry Truman mandated Executive Order No. 9981, which integrated the entire U.S. armed forces.[15]

Morale in the Army Nurse Corps also suffered due to the fact that the corps was unable to offer incentives to recruits as attractive as those offered by a newly formed branch of the military: the Women's Army Corps. The organization was established in 1942 as the Women's Army Auxiliary Corps (WAAC), and became the Women's Army Corps (WAC) one year later. Women who volunteered for the WAAC/WAC worked in all areas of the military except combat: they were cryptographers; drivers; attachés; mechanics; spies; medics; photographers; and clerks. Though the Army Nurse Corps was the oldest of the women's military corps—established on 2 February 1901, forty-one years earlier than the WAAC—the base pay of a second lieutenant army nurse in September 1942 was $90 per month, compared to the $125 per month paid to a WAAC officer of comparable rank. WAAC/WAC officers were granted permanent rank from the beginning of the existence of the WAAC in 1942 while the Army Nurse Corps officers only had relative rank, which came with less pay, benefits, and respect.[16]

In addition to the WAAC/WAC, several other new women's military organizations had been formed at approximately the same time: the

WAVES—Women Accepted for Volunteer Emergency Service, an organization for women serving in the U.S. Navy; the SPARS—based on the motto *Semper paratus*—an organization for women in the Coast Guard; and the women Marines. All of these brand-new organizations offered permanent commissions right from their inceptions. Even the Navy Nurse Corps, established in 1908 and the country's second oldest women's military organization after the Army Nurse Corps, had gotten regular commissions for its nurses by February 1944. That same month, Representative Bolton proposed a bill that would have corrected this and other inequities—such as conditions of duty, retirement, dependents' allowances—and improved the lot of army nurses, but the War Department spoke out against the bill, and it was abandoned. Finally, in June 1944, the relative rank in the Army Nurse Corps was elevated to regular rank, with full pay and other attendant benefits, but this was instituted only as a temporary measure—commissions were granted only for the duration of the war plus six months. It would take another three years, on 16 April 1947, before army and navy nurses were granted permanent commissions equal to those of the other branches of the military, albeit with a ceiling that prohibited nurses from attaining any rank higher than lieutenant colonel.[17]

Not only were WAC officers granted permanent rank, but they were on a faster track for promotion. "Army nurses around the world," wrote Major Edith Aynes, assistant to Colonel Blanchfield, "were wondering why the newly organized Women's Army Corps with its fully commissioned Officer Corps could rate rapid promotions but nurses in overseas hospitals, even some of those on the Anzio beachhead, were still second lieutenants after two and three years in the service."[18]

Armed with these incentives—higher base pay, permanent commissions in the military, and a rapid path to promotions—the WAC set out to recruit eight thousand women as medical and surgical technicians. The WAC was also given a budget of $3 million and a staff for war recruitment. The Army Nurse Corps had neither; though the corps had been charged with the responsibility to recruit nurses, it was given neither a budget nor a staff with which to implement a recruitment program. The staff of the WAC running the recruiting advertisements used savvy advertising techniques. One example is an article that appeared in the *Toledo* (Ohio) *Blade* on 18 January 1945, under the headline "WACs Replace Skilled Nurses in Hospitals, More Needed":

Toledo women may enlist with Sergeant Purcell for medical assignment to an army hospital. Due to insufficient numbers of nurses and
the urgent need for medical WACs, high school entry requirements
have been lowered from four to two years. Applicants must be at least
twenty.[19]

Whether through intent or ignorance, the article implied that women
without a high school education could join the WAC and replace nurses in
army hospitals.

In the midst of this confusion, nurses "were called unpatriotic and
selfish; accused of not wanting to nurse the sick and wounded," Aynes
wrote later. On top of these spurious accusations, the supposed deficit in
army nurses was suddenly doubled, from ten thousand to twenty thousand, a number not supported by any evidence. "Despite this 'tremendous need,' " continued Aynes, "the Army had still not appropriated a
nickel [to the Army Nurse Corps] for nurse recruitment. . . ."[20]

Army Nurse Corps recruiting efforts were also made difficult due to
the War Manpower Commission, which classified all civilian nurse positions as "essential." This meant that civilian nurses could not change
their job or place of employment without government permission. As a
result, many civilian nurses who wanted to join the Army Nurse Corps
were prohibited from leaving their civilian jobs for any reason other than
health or dire family circumstances. "It was like holding a person with
one hand and beating him over the head with the other," Aynes wrote.[21]

On Christmas Eve 1944, the assistants to the secretary of war drew
up the wording for a bill that would draft women nurses between nineteen and forty-five years of age. The bill used the Selective Service Act of
1940 as a framework for "the registration, selection, induction" process
and the "same exemptions, rights and obligations" for those nurses
drafted under its provisions. The bill was introduced into the House of
Representatives by Andrew J. May of Kentucky. The War Department
was now firmly behind the bill. Secretary of War Henry L. Stimson asked
President Roosevelt for support; hence Roosevelt's appeal to the American public in his State of the Union address in January 1945.[22]

The 1945 bill was not the first brought before Congress for drafting
women. In 1943, the Austin-Wadsworth bill to make war service compulsory for all American women was defeated by Congress. In the
United Kingdom, women had lived with compulsory National Service

since 1939, but National Service that allowed each woman to select the organization in which to fulfill her obligation. British women could choose service with a branch of the armed forces or with the Land Army, whose members worked on farms in place of men who had been called into military service. The same bill also authorized British women to select work with an ambulance company or in an industrially related war job.

The backers of the Austin-Wadsworth bill thought that American women should be just as accountable in defending their country as the women of the United Kingdom. Those who opposed the bill believed there was no room in America for any bill that compelled women to enter the military or industrially related war work. Organized labor was opposed to this legislation. When the bill was defeated, many of its supporters looked for other ways to accomplish their objective of compulsory military service or work-related war production for all American women. The push in 1945 to enact a bill to draft army nurses could be seen as a first step toward a larger draft for all women.

During the second week of January 1945, the colonel in charge of personnel in the Surgeon General's office telephoned Major Aynes and told her to stop all recruiting of nurses. When Aynes asked the colonel why, he responded that the office wanted the bill for drafting nurses to pass. When Aynes pointed out that it seemed to her it was better and faster to get nurses who would volunteer rather than be drafted, and that the American Nurses Association (ANA) would never agree to no recruitment of nurses, the colonel asked: " 'What is the ANA?' " "The American Nurses Association," Aynes replied. "You know, like the American Medical Association. . . ." " 'Never heard of them,' was the personnel chief's honest answer."[23]

In the end, organized nursing "went along with the draft as a first step to the drafting of all women," as Major Aynes wrote.[24]

On 7 March 1945, the U.S. House of Representatives passed the draft bill and sent that bill to the Senate for its approval. The Senate would now decide whether graduate registered nurses would be that first occupational group, and the first American women, to be drafted into the U.S. armed forces. The opinion expressed by Martha Cameron in a letter to her father dated 24 February 1945 was typical of most army nurses of the day: "The hospitals at home must be full of veterans. . . . If they draft for the A.N.C. . . . that's fine and I wouldn't be sorry if Helen [Cameron's younger sister, who was a registered nurse] had to go—it is her duty as much as anyone's."[25]

In fact, the war in Germany came to an end before the bill was voted upon by the Senate, and it was abandoned.

ON 9 FEBRUARY 1945, Lieutenant Martha Nash and the rest of the 44th Evacuation Hospital moved southeast of Aachen to a former German barracks in Brand, Germany. During the second week in February, the 44th's patients were predominantly medical in nature rather than war casualties. The exceptions were mainly soldiers suffering from wounds inflicted by German shoe mines. The German shoe mine or s-mine was designed so that it could not be detected easily, if at all. Unlike other German mines constructed of metal, which could be located with mine-detecting equipment and thus removed, the shoe mine was made entirely of wood and could not be found with metal detectors. It consisted of a narrow wooden box with an open and slightly raised top. When a soldier stepped on the box, forcing the lid closed, the explosive charge was ignited. Amputation of a foot, or leg, or both was usually required to save the soldier's life.

Other frequent patients were those injured in truck or jeep accidents. On an unusually warm afternoon on 14 February, when the temperature was well above freezing, a young soldier born and raised in the Southwest, a first-generation Mexican-American, was stretched out asleep on the roof of the cab of an army truck. When the driver climbed behind the wheel, drove down the road, and turned sharply onto a secondary road, the young soldier rolled off and fell onto the rocky road. The driver heard the man scream and stopped to see if he was hurt. The injured soldier complained of abdominal pain and was taken to the 44th Evac for evaluation and treatment. In less than thirty minutes, he was in the OR undergoing surgery for a ruptured spleen.

"When the surgeon, Major Whitlock, opened up the patient's abdomen, a forceful stream of blood shot from the splenic artery and hit the major's eyeglasses. It blinded him and he couldn't see anything," Martha Nash recalled. "So I grabbed one of those Oxman clamps and clamped that artery and saved the soldier's life." For Nash and many nurses working on the front lines, taking charge in an emergency was by now standard operating procedure.[26]

On 22 February, life at the 44th Evac changed drastically with the beginning of an artillery barrage that shook the hospital and heralded the next American offensive—the crossing of the Roer River. The hospital was moved over the Roer River and set up in tents to support the troops that were establishing a bridgehead across.

On 14 March, the 44th set up at an airstrip in Miel, Germany, ten miles east of Brand. "It was at Miel that we became the first hospital to receive patients brought in on gliders," Nash recalled. "Two gliders crash-landed on the airstrip and each had twelve patients from across the Rhine on board." Since gliders did not have motors, the only way they could be landed was in a modified version of a crash. The expertise of a good glider pilot kept those crash landings from inflicting further injury on already wounded soldiers.[27]

Also at Eudenbach airfield, Nash and other hospital personnel cared for patients stopping at Eudenbach but destined elsewhere. "Light casualties were on their way to hospitals in France," Nash said. "Medium casualties were on their way to hospitals in England. Patients who required long-term care were headed for hospitals in Paris until they could be sent back to the United States."[28]

BETWEEN 10 and 18 March 1945, the 128th Evacuation Hospital was set up in buildings formerly used as a reformatory one mile northeast of Euskirchen, thirty miles southeast of Aachen, and fifteen miles west of the Rhine River. "We were the first evacuation hospital to be set up in support of the Remagen bridgehead," Lieutenant Martha Cameron recalled. Cameron and other hospital personnel got to see the effects of combat before anything major was done to correct them. "The casualties we received were pretty severely wounded," Cameron said. "We received several young American soldiers who had literally 'lost face.' Direct hits had left them in such a bloody mess that their own mothers wouldn't have recognized them."[29]

On 22 March, the 128th moved by truck convoy to Duenstekoven, Germany, and set up in tents. "On 24 March, we started getting wounded who told us that we were in the process of fighting our way across the Rhine River at the Remagen Bridge," Martha Cameron recalled. The Rhine represented not only the last major obstacle to entry into Germany but, psychologically, the barrier that ensured the security and inviolability of the German people. It was the sacred line no enemy could cross.

"Soon we were getting wounded who said, 'We have some men across the Rhine.' An hour later, we received wounded who said, 'We have a platoon across the Rhine.' An hour or so after that, some of the wounded were telling us, 'We have a company across the Rhine.' It was like a newsreel. Finally the word arrived with a newly wounded soldier with a broken ankle: 'We have a bridgehead across the Rhine—we're over!' "[30]

The last obstacle to the heart of Germany had been crossed. Two years, four months, and sixteen days after landing with assault troops on the beaches of North Africa, the personnel of the 128th Evacuation Hospital stood on German soil, poised to follow American troops across the Rhine and into the heart of Germany. After 866 days of following and caring for combat troops on the front lines, personnel of the 128th Evac could truly see the end of the war in Europe at hand. It would take more American blood and lives to get the German armed forces to sign an unconditional surrender, but the 128th Evac staff were only three hundred miles from Berlin—and victory.

At the time, they had no way of knowing that the worst horrors the German army had visited on the human race were still to pass before their eyes.

CHAPTER SIXTEEN

The Surrender of Germany

ARMY NURSES AT DACHAU AND NORDHAUSEN

29 April–8 May 1945

A guard showed us how the blood had congealed in coarse black scabs where the starving prisoners had torn out the entrails of the dead for food. Eisenhower's face whitened into a mask. Patton walked over to a corner and sickened. I was too revolted to speak.

—*Gen. Omar N. Bradley*, A Soldier's Story

B Y APRIL 1945, after successive Allied victories at the Colmar pocket, Cologne, and the Remagen Bridge, it was clear that the German war machine had been broken. German troops were fleeing or surrendering in the tens of thousands, as the Allies advanced swiftly toward Berlin and a victory that was all but assured and imminent. The hospitals moving in the wake of the front lines were also advancing rapidly— sometimes so rapidly that they became cut off from supplies and relief from the rear.

During the first week of April, Frenchie Miernicke and her 2nd Auxiliary Surgical Group found themselves in just such a situation. Attached to the 11th Field Hospital, they had followed the front lines across the Rhine to Adlesheim, Germany, thirty miles east of Heidelberg in west-central Germany. For seventy-two hours straight, Frenchie and her surgical team worked in the operating room with no relief. "We were somewhere near Adlesheim and we had moved forward with the front so fast that headquarters had lost touch with us," Miernicke recalled. "They had no idea where we were, and had no way to replace a team that was lost somewhere on the front lines." Usually, surgical teams relieved each other in twelve-hour shifts. But at Adlesheim, there was no other surgical team to relieve the six members of Frenchie's team. "That meant we continued to work as long as battle casualties and surgical cases were coming into the OR," said Miernicke.[1]

For three days, wounded arrived in a steady stream. The team had to work continuously, breaking only for the few moments it took to remove one patient from the OR table and replace him with the next. "It seemed like one long nightmare," Miernicke recalled. "After so many hours, it

Lt. Frenchie Miernicke and Capt. Ross Hobler after they had worked in surgery for seventy-two hours without relief. Their 2nd Auxiliary Surgical Group team was "lost" on the front lines in Germany, April 1945 (Courtesy of Maj. Frances Miernicke Plenert, ANC [Ret.])

seemed like an out-of-body experience. You didn't have time for coffee or anything. They couldn't find us to send in a relief team. Those were the kinds of things that you had to do and you just did it."[2]

ON 11 APRIL 1945, the Third Armored Division entered the outskirts of Nordhausen in central Germany, forty miles north of Erfurt and seventy miles west of Leipzig. The town contained a former German military barracks that had been converted by the Nazis into a forced-labor camp filled with multinational political prisoners, including Allied POWs. Tankers from the Third Armored Division who entered the area were stopped in their tracks by what they saw. "Hundreds of corpses lay sprawled over the acres of the big compound. More hundreds filled the great barracks. They lay in contorted heaps, half stripped, mouths gaping in the dirt and straw: or they were piled naked, like cordwood, in the corners and under the stairways," according to the official account of the Third Armored Division.[3]

The prisoners who were still alive lay mingled with the dead in crowded, three-tiered bunks on mattresses soaked in diarrhea. The men, clad in striped uniforms, were nothing more than living skeletons, bones covered with a thin sheet of almost translucent skin—"emaciated, ragged shapes whose fever-bright eyes waited passively for the release of death. . . . " The area had a "terrible odor" of decomposing flesh and a depressing atmosphere of hopelessness. "The combined cries of these unfortunates rose and fell in weak undulations. It was a fabric of moans and whimpers, of delirium and outright madness."[4]

Outside along the road to the barracks, corpses were piled, and "here and there a single shape tottered about, walking slowly, like a man dreaming." The Third Armored's medical officer, Major Martin L. Sherman, predicted that even with immediate medical attention, only about half of these victims, so severely starved and gravely ill, would survive.[5]

The following day, 12 April, the division reached Dora, an elaborate factory and forced-labor camp about two miles north of Nordhausen. At Dora, they found a crematorium with ovens for the burning of human bodies. Apparently a shortage of fuel had halted the cremations: piles of bodies lay stacked, or buried in shallow mass graves. In addition to the ovens, Dora housed a V-1 and V-2 rocket plant built underground in two, two-mile-long tunnels that were crisscrossed by shorter tunnels. The tunnels held precision machinery for the construction of the rockets.

The political prisoners at Nordhausen—Poles, Hungarians, Germans, members of the French intelligence, Belgians, males of all ages—were forced to work in the rocket factory in Dora. Each day, they were awakened at 0400 and marched the two miles north to the camp at Dora, where they worked in the underground tunnels until dusk. Each man was fed a mere 4 ounces of black bread and a bowl of thin soup: this was an inmate's entire daily food allotment. Prisoners told the Third Armored men that the SS guards regularly beat them. In one incident, the SS had made an example of thirty-two of the prisoners who were singled out as "slackers" or "saboteurs." The emaciated prisoners were hanged while their comrades were forced to watch and then carry the bodies to the crematory ovens. Prisoners spoke of others of their comrades who had been assigned to work on the new, secret V-3 rocket and then were killed to assure that the secret would be kept. "[They] were segregated and finally murdered to preserve the secret of that which they had seen."[6]

During the construction of Nordhausen, an average of one hundred inmates died each day. Of the sixty thousand prisoners interned at the forced-labor camp at Dora, thirty thousand perished during their internment.[7]

The memory of the liberation of Nordhausen would remain with the men of the Third Armored Division, not because it involved the heaviest fighting of their sweep across the Rhineland but because of the horror that they witnessed. They considered Nordhausen a "hell-hole" and felt heart-wrenching pity for the prisoners. ". . . You'd never forget the look in their eyes. It was almost enough to make up for all the weary days and the fear and the hell of battle. They were so thankful to the liberators, and they looked at the Yanks with that special gaze reserved for deities. . . ."[8]

On 13 April, as the tanks of the Third Armored Division continued to push farther into Germany, two escapees from a satellite concentration camp, Langenstein-Zwieberge, caught up with the column and flagged it down. Both were eighteen-year-old Jews, a German named Eddie Willner and a Dutchman named Mike Swaab. Both had been inmates at Auschwitz concentration camp in Poland, and after five years there had been moved away from the oncoming Russian troops and into Germany. In Germany, they worked on the V-1 and V-2 rocket projects. As orders came down from the high command to kill all prisoners and destroy all evidence of the camps, SS prison guards had taken five hundred prisoners outdoors to march them to a destination where they would be killed. Willner and Swaab, who were among the five hundred, determined to escape and find the advancing American troops. On the second day of the death march, under cover of darkness during an Allied air raid and strafing, the young prisoners escaped. They listened for the sound of American artillery and moved in that direction. After three days of hiding and waiting, the two boys watched the advancing Third Armored Division tanks come into view. When the tanks rolled closer, "[W]e jumped up and threw our hands up in the air," Willner said. "The first tank stopped and Mike and I showed them the number tattoos on our arms."[9]

The commander of Company D, First Lieutenant Elmer Hovland, who had ordered the tanks to stop, gave the boys a ride. "They could have just thrown us K-rations and moved on," Willner said.[10]

Both boys were starving and painfully emaciated—Willner weighed only 75 pounds. The two were to stay with Company D for the next six months, working in the kitchen and helping out wherever they could. "Our unit kind of adopted the two teenagers," Tech-5 Fred Headrick recalled. "They were given American army uniforms minus the insignia, and fed all the American food they could hold."[11]

In mid-April, the 44th Evacuation Hospital, including Lieutenant Martha Nash, was transferred to the outskirts of Nordhausen. On 16 April, Nash asked to be shown around the prison camp. Nothing she had seen during twelve months of service on the front lines had prepared her for what she was about to witness. "They had Italians and Russians and Americans out there and they were so skinny they could hardly walk. They had been starved and overworked too long to be saved. I will never forget the sight of those human skeletons." Nash's tour uncovered other grisly sights. "We went into this room where they [German SS guards] had this enamel-looking thing . . . where they had extracted their [prisoners'] teeth that contained gold then stuck them [the prisoners] into an autoclave [crematory oven] and burned them to ashes. I have a picture of a pile of bones. I couldn't help but think of my sister, Frances, and wonder what horrors she had lived through in a Japanese prison camp."[12]

By the last week in April, news of the conditions at Nordhausen labor camp made its way among American troops. Personnel of the 95th Evacuation Hospital, located at Würtburg, seventy miles northeast of Mannheim, from 8 to 25 April cared for liberated Nazi prisoners of many nationalities, including recovered Allied military personnel (RAMPs). "The RAMPs were suffering various stages of malnutrition," Pete Peterson recalled, "but most were in much better condition than the prisoners liberated from the Nordhausen camp. It was probably a good thing that we didn't know what we would run into at a concentration camp near Munich." Only a few weeks later, Peterson and the 95th would arrive at that concentration camp near Munich—Dachau—and find conditions as severe as, if not worse than, those at Nordhausen.[13]

DURING THE SECOND week of April, the 128th Evacuation Hospital set up at Kromback, about forty miles east of Cologne and a few miles south of Olpe, in support of the First Army fighting in the Ruhr pocket. American soldiers were only a small number of the patients admitted to the 128th Evac in the first three weeks of April. "We were getting patients who were displaced persons, German POWs, and finally large numbers of recovered Allied military personnel who had been held in German POW camps," Lieutenant Edna Browning recalled. "We heard stories of large groups of displaced persons making their way around and through Germany." German control of civilians was minimal. There was little law enforcement as tens of thousands of people roamed the countryside looking for food and shelter.[14]

ON 12 APRIL 1945, President Franklin Delano Roosevelt died of a cerebral hemorrhage. The nation was plunged into sorrow and grief. Millions of citizens mourned the fact that FDR, their beloved and trusted leader for the entire duration of the war thus far, had not lived to witness the final moment of victory. Roosevelt had been president for twelve years; for many Americans, including the large numbers of young troops fighting in Europe and the Pacific who were under the age of twenty-five, he was virtually the only president they had ever known. When word of FDR's death reached American troops fighting abroad, memorial services for the president and commander in chief of the U.S. armed forces were held at military posts and frontline locations throughout the world. Vice President Harry S. Truman was quickly inaugurated as president and vowed to continue FDR's battle strategies to bring the war to an end.

ON 18 APRIL, German resistance in the Ruhr pocket in northern Germany collapsed and German troops surrendered by the tens of thousands. The U.S. military had expected to take 150,000 POWs by the end of the third week in April. They were stretched to their limits of POW care when the actual number of German soldiers surrendering reached 325,000. By the end of April 1945, the First Army alone had taken 389,000 POWs.[15]

On about 20 April in Kromback, two unusual surgical cases came in to the OR at the 128th Evacuation Hospital. Two wounded American soldiers with unexploded bazooka shells lodged in their bodies were brought in for surgery. Designed primarily as antitank weapons, bazooka shells were explosives shot from portable rocket launchers. Corporal Gilbert Smith worked with the surgical team who treated both patients. "They brought in a patient with a rocket from a bazooka stuck in him. It had gone all the way through the patient and the shell's fins were sticking out four inches from his lower back. He was still alive and this rocket was still alive too. We had to dig it out of him," Smith recalled. The surgeons called in the demolition men. "The bomb squad came in there to tell us what to touch and what not to touch while we removed the live bazooka shell." Although the shell was recovered successfully, the soldier succumbed to shock and died of his wounds. The second soldier had a bazooka shell lodged in his thigh; he recovered fully once the unexploded weapon was removed.[16]

Unexploded bazooka shell removed from the body of a wounded American soldier at the 128th Evacuation Hospital in Germany, 1945 (Courtesy of Gilbert Smith)

On 22 April, the 128th moved again, following the First Army farther east.

THE LAST WEEK of April 1945 found American and Allied troops steadily advancing toward Munich and Berlin. On its way to Munich, the Seventh Army liberated a concentration camp near Landsberg on the Lech River about twenty-five miles west of Munich. As a battalion surgeon with the Seventh Army, Major Brendan Phibbs followed the American soldiers to the camp. About a mile before he reached the concentration camp, Phibbs saw bodies lying along the side of the muddy road. At one point, he stopped his jeep and walked toward a body lying facedown near the center of the road. The corpse was little more than bones clad in filthy blue-and-white-striped pajamas. Phibbs turned the body over and drew back in shock and horror at the dead man's face. The eyes were large circles of unseeing glass, the nose was as sharp as a razor, and the mouth was frozen wide open. As a physician, Phibbs saw what the average onlooker did not see. "The soft tissues of the face were collapsed right onto the bone, and the only structures still full-sized, the teeth and the eyes, were bared in frozen agony, a terminal sustained scream."[17]

As Phibbs's jeep moved into the camp, he noticed U.S. Army graves registration units carrying badly burned corpses on litters. The long rows of huts in the camp were also burned. In speaking with the litter bearers, Phibbs learned that German soldiers—engineers sent to destroy any evidence of the atrocities of the camps—had ordered the camp inmates into the huts, "thrown gasoline on them," and set the huts on fire. Graves registration units found many of the bodies lying half-in and half-out of the charred huts. Other bodies, with bloodstained stab wounds in the chest and abdomen, lay twisted in holes that had been gouged out under the hut walls. Claw marks were still visible, scratched into the frozen mud: it was clear that the inmates, trapped in the burning huts, had attempted to dig their way out with their bare hands through the mud and dirt that supported the walls. The German soldiers had bayoneted all who escaped the gasoline-fed flames. The pajama-clad dead were the first Nazi atrocities Phibbs witnessed, but they would not be the last.[18]

ON 29 APRIL 1945, soldiers of the Forty-fifth and Forty-second Divisions fought their way through the barbed-wire gates of Dachau concentration camp, located twelve miles northwest of Munich. German troops fired at them from guard towers. On a railway track near the SS guard barracks, the men found a parked forty-car train. When they opened the boxcar doors, hundreds of skeletal corpses were piled on top of each other like logs. The train was apparently carrying the last evacuees from Buchenwald to Dachau for final elimination. In spite of all the carnage they had seen on the battlefield, many combat-hardened American veterans wept and vomited at the sight of the corpses in the boxcars. Many would continue to have nightmares about Dachau for decades following the war.

Helen Richert and Frenchie Miernicke of the 2nd Aux arrived at Dachau a day or two after it was liberated. Richert went through Dachau on 30 April. "Bodies were still burning," Richert wrote. "I felt a dark cloud around me for a long time after that."[19]

Miernicke arrived on 2 May and found a camp filled with the dead and dying. "We had no idea what we would see there before we arrived, no warning," she recalled.[20]

As they entered the Dachau camp, American and Allied military and news media personnel were dusted with DDT powder applied with a "flit can"—a small, hand-held metal container equipped with a plunger that pumped in and out to spray the DDT onto the targeted area. Since typhus is contracted by inhaling dried louse feces, the DDT was necessary to kill body lice and fleas that carried the typhus *Rickettsia prowazekii* organism. Typhus was endemic in Dachau. Hundreds of inmates suffered its ravages, along with the effects of starvation, which only served to make them more susceptible to typhus as well as other illnesses and infections. It causes high fever, nervousness, low blood pressure, frightful dreams, deafness, stupor, delirium, coma, macular rash, cough, pneumonia, muscle pain, peripheral vascular collapse, and finally death. The mortality rate of adults with untreated typhus is about 60 percent.

Major Phibbs described the symptoms of typhus from a physician's point of view: "Invasion of the central nervous system produced a peculiar agitation, followed within hours by delirium. [People with typhus] would suddenly begin babbling wildly, trying to lift themselves from the cot, so weak they needed only a hand or finger to restrain them." Phibbs goes on to: ". . . Within a day or two, a shock-like state would produce deadly cold, a weak, rapid, thready pulse, a blue color to lips and earlobes, and gasping, wheezing death. . . ." Just before their deaths, patients commonly "drew up in a terrifying position called opisthotonus, commonly seen in the last stages of tetanus, when the body is arched like a drawn bow, only the heels and the back of the head touching the bed, muscles drawn to unbelievable rigidity."[21]

Penicillin could not defeat the organism and there was no other antibiotic or antibacterial in existence at the time. The drugs of choice— tetracycline, doxycycline, and chloramphenicol—would not be discovered until years after the end of World War II, so the only weapon available with which to fight typhus was food. With proper nourishment, the patient's immune system might rally to help the body overcome the disease.

The struggle by U.S. hospital teams to save starving and dying inmates had just begun, and it was clear that it was going to continue for several months. By 3 May 1945, the U.S. Army Medical Department had organized a coalition of army hospital personnel to work inside Dachau on a weekly rotation basis. Medical commanders believed that human beings could not deal with the horrific conditions of the camp for more than a few days at a time without acquiring psychological scars that would affect them far into the future.

Lieutenant Peterson of the 95th Evacuation Hospital was a member of the first coalition hospital team. When she arrived at Dachau, the army was feeding the inmates GI rations cooked into soups or served in other ways. "The patients got six small meals a day during the first ten days after the camp was liberated," Peterson recalled. "When they heard the food carts coming and smelled food, the patients who could walk had to be restrained from grabbing the food from the cart. They swallowed the food as fast as they could and would beg for more. Many of them would vomit after eating because their shrunken stomachs just couldn't handle the food. They would also try to steal food from each other."[22]

THE THIRD REICH, which Hitler said would last a thousand years, fell within only a matter of days as German commanders began surrendering their forces en masse. On 29 April, in the town of Caserta in southern Italy, representatives of General Heinrich von Vietinghoff signed the unconditional surrender document for all German troops in Italy. The surrender was to go into effect on 2 May 1945.

News of the surrender reached Adolf Hitler in his Berlin underground bunker along with the report of Mussolini's execution by the Italian people. By many accounts, the execution of Mussolini dealt a heavy psychological blow to the Führer, especially the report that Mussolini's body and that of his mistress had been taken to Milan and hanged upside down in a city square. Mussolini's fate horrified Hitler, who was determined not to meet the same end at the hands of the rapidly advancing Russians—or of his own people.

Nine months earlier, on 20 July 1944, Hitler had survived a major assassination attempt in Rastenburg plotted by a group of his own generals. A bomb left in a briefcase exploded under a map table where Hitler and members of his military staff were discussing future war plans. As luck would have it, only minutes before the explosion, one of the officers happened to reposition the briefcase in order to have greater access to the maps. When the bomb exploded, several Germans officers were killed, but Hitler escaped with only minor physical injuries. The Führer ordered the execution of approximately five thousand people he believed had taken part in the plot.[23]

Now, on 29 April 1945, a physically and emotionally diminished Führer—his body racked by tremors that gave rise to the speculation he may have been suffering from Parkinson's disease—was plagued with fears concerning the disloyalty and traitorous acts of the top officers of his armed forces and closest associates. These fears were exacerbated by the news of the surrender of German troops in Italy, the death of Mussolini, and the Russian army fighting its way toward the city of Berlin.

With his end clearly approaching, Hitler began to execute a plan for his own death and cremation. He wrote out a political testament. In that testament, he expelled Field Marshal Hermann Goering and Heinrich Himmler from the Nazi Party on grounds of disloyalty to the Reich and their Führer. He also announced the creation of a new government, with Grand Admiral Karl Dönitz as president and Joseph Goebbels as chancellor. Finally, he gave orders that Berlin was to be destroyed by the German army—a punishment to the German people for not living up to his plans for the Third Reich.[24]

That same day was also the day Adolf Hitler married his longtime mistress, Eva Braun, as a reward for her unswerving loyalty. Braun had traveled to Berlin in order to be with Hitler in the bunker and refused to leave in order to save herself.

On 30 April, their marriage barely a day old, Hitler and Eva Braun committed suicide—she by biting into a cyanide capsule, and he by cyanide capsule and a gunshot to the head. In accordance with Hitler's instructions, the two bodies were taken to a courtyard behind the Reich

Chancellery building, placed in a shallow ditch, soaked with gasoline, and set on fire. The remains were then buried in a shallow grave where they would stay until the Russians discovered them approximately a week later.

On 3 May, Soviet forces coming from the east reached the Elbe River west of Berlin, and made contact with soldiers of the U.S. First and Ninth Armies. The British army entered Hamburg, Germany, and the U.S. Seventh Army took Innsbruck, Austria, while other U.S. troops marched toward Salzburg, Austria.

On 4 May, Grand Admiral Karl Dönitz sent envoys to General Montgomery's headquarters in Lüneberg, Germany, and they agreed on the surrender of German forces in Holland, Denmark, and northern Germany. The surrender became effective at 0800 on 5 May 1945. Also on 5 May, German forces in Haar, Bavaria, surrendered to British forces.

The following day, General Patton received orders to stop his Third Army advance at the newly taken town of Pilsen in Czechoslovakia, and the Allies allowed the Soviets to occupy the rest of the country. U.S. forces were also halted only miles from Berlin in order to allow the Soviets to take the city they had had under attack since 16 April.

On 7 May, Admiral Hans von Friedeburg and General Alfred Jodl signed an unconditional surrender to end all hostilities. The surrender was signed at Reims, France. Military operations were to cease at 2301 on 8 May and the surrender was to go into effect at 0001 on 9 May. General Eisenhower sent a message that the mission of the American and Allied forces in Europe was completed in the early morning hours of 7 May 1945.

News of the final German surrender exploded across headlines and over radio waves across the United States and around the world. Civilians and armed forces personnel cheered, sang and danced in the streets, hugged and kissed each other to the accompaniment of church bells, car horns, and whistles on a day that would go down in history as Victory in Europe Day—VE-Day. For a brief moment, no one thought of the war that was still raging in the Far East and what it would cost America and Allies before Japan signed a surrender agreement.

No one, that is, except frontline army hospital personnel, whose reaction to the news of Germany's surrender was much more restrained. Even on VE-Day, doctors, nurses, and corpsmen were still on duty fighting to save the lives of wounded and sick U.S. and Allied soldiers. Many had been performing this essential mission on the front lines in North

Africa, Italy, France, and now Germany. For the thousands serving in frontline army hospitals, the reaction to the news of Germany's surrender was mixed: a quiet relief that it was over, blended with an ambivalence at the thought of leaving the "families" of their hospital units. "When I heard the news," Oliver Sorlye recalled, "I cried. We had been living and working together for so long, it seemed almost impossible to believe that we'd soon be going in different directions. We had been family for a long time and it would be sad to leave family even to return home."[25]

For Lieutenant "Pete" Peterson, the news brought gladness that the war was ended in Europe, but also questions about where their hospital would be sent next. "We all knew they would be sending more troops and hospitals to the Far East for the assault on Japan," Peterson recalled. "Most of us were pretty tired and wondering if our luck would hold out through another campaign."[26]

Frenchie Miernicke echoed Peterson's concerns. "Of course everyone was glad the fighting in Europe was over," Miernicke remembered. "But we all knew that it meant some of us would be going to the Far East to take part in the invasion of Japan. That didn't make any of us happy. Most people who had survived North Africa, Sicily, Italy, France, Belgium, and Germany figured that their luck couldn't hold out forever."[27]

Hospital staff who had served in the Mediterranean and European theaters were members of an elite group of trained and experienced veterans who could not be easily replaced. Because the supply of such highly trained medical personnel was limited, many of the tens of thousands of nurses, doctors, and medics who had served for months or years on the front lines in North Africa and Europe would now be sent on to serve in the Pacific to support an assault on the Japanese homeland. The nurses' draft bill had not been needed for Europe, but would it be needed for the Far East and Japan? Even if the draft were passed, or thousands more registered nurses volunteered for the war against Japan, there was no substitute for the experience and expertise of those who had been on the front lines through one, two, three, and more bloody campaigns.

A WEEK AFTER Dachau was liberated, the U.S. Army quartermaster in the area issued a stunning order: inmates and patients in the camp hospital could no longer be fed GI rations. The unreasoning bureaucracy of commanders who had spent their military tours in the United States or far behind front lines "discovered" an army regulation that forbade GI rations being used for civilians. The interpretation went on to say that civilian inmates must be fed with the captured food in German warehouses. Unfortunately for the inmates of Dachau, the key to the food warehouse was in a U.S. Army general's pocket and the general had left the vicinity.

Meals at Dachau dropped from six a day to two a day and consisted of a cup of milk and two crackers from a GI ration kit. Inmates could not understand why the Americans who had liberated them had suddenly stopped feeding them. Major Phibbs took it upon himself to solve the problem by speaking to his commanders and explaining what they apparently did not understand: the inmates of Dachau and the camp hospital were starving to death before the eyes of medical personnel. That patients were being allowed to die for want of food that was available and on hand was unacceptable—an intolerable situation—to nurses, doctors, and corpsmen. Phibbs told the commanders that since news had gotten around the camp that he spoke German, inmates would call him aside, explain that they were hungry, and beseech him to do something to get them more food. The inmates seemed sure that if the Americans learned that they were not getting enough food, they would immediately remedy the problem. "They're starving," Phibbs told Major Karff, the commanding officer of the camp. "These people are really starving to death. Right in this United States hospital."[28]

When the CO responded that "starving is a strong word," and said something about "supply problems," Phibbs suggested that, with some help, he could do something to supply food for the inmates and inmate patients. "I have a carbine and sixty rounds of ammunition in my ambulance," Phibbs told the commanding officer. "Give me some men from the mess crew and I'll bring in all the fresh meat we can use."[29]

The CO was horrified when he learned that Phibbs's source of fresh meat were to be the cows and pigs grazing on local German farms. Major Karff protested that "the U.S. Army didn't steal property." Phibbs suggested it could be considered "foraging" and stated that all armies had this right. Karff retorted that "foraging" was only allowed so the army could feed itself. At last admitting defeat in this futile and absurd exchange, Phibbs left the commanding officer's office angry and depressed by the callousness of this by-the-book officer. The food shortage at

Dachau continued, and liberated inmates continued to die of starvation. Whether they would have died anyway is a question that cannot be answered, but clearly, the food shortage did not do the inmates any good.[30]

MANY TROOPS and hospital personnel began staging for Japan only weeks after the declaration of victory in Europe. Some were placed on ships to sail directly to Japan, while others were ordered back to the United States to go through U.S. Army redistribution centers. These centers, located at various points around the country, would screen returning European troops to ascertain their fitness for duty in Operation Downfall—the planned invasion of the Japanese home islands.

As with most things in the U.S. military, redistribution centers were geared mainly toward men. The U.S. Army had made arrangements for wives to join their husbands in places like the Grove Park Inn in Ashville, North Carolina, where couples would share a week or two of vacation while the army was deciding its soldiers' next assignments. Returning troops were allowed to use the telephone freely; some even had phones in their rooms, a distinct luxury in 1945.

U.S. Army nurses like Frenchie Miernicke met a different experience at the redistribution centers. "We weren't too happy when male officers and enlisted lectured us nurses that it was time to become 'ladies' again," Miernicke recalled. "They actually told us nurses that it was time to put on dresses, watch our language, and act like ladies again. This attitude made many of us nurses furious. We had never stopped being ladies." In addition, the nurses were not allowed to make any telephone calls for two weeks after their arrival. No reason was given for this restriction.[31]

This was not the first time the nation tried to "put women back in their places" after extreme situations had allowed them to breach the boundaries of their traditional roles as mothers, wives, and homemakers. For example, in the 1800s, women who helped settle the American West became in many situations, of necessity and sometimes by choice, pioneers who acted on a par with and even independently of men. But after running homesteads, and fighting outlaws and hostile Indians, these women were expected to return to traditional roles at home and hearth once the West was settled.

So, too, at the end of World War II; in mid- to late 1945 and 1946, women were expected to return to their previous status. They were not encouraged to pursue careers in the armed forces. The G.I. Bill, which offered all veterans a chance at a free education, was available to women veterans as well, but they were not openly urged to take advantage of it and few of them did.

No one thought of these women as veterans—not even the women themselves. There were few records of these women by their maiden names, and no effort was made to systematically keep track of their name changes and whereabouts. Because the Veterans Administration and other government agencies kept few and haphazard records, many of the women virtually disappeared when they married and took their husbands' names.

Americans in future generations would grow up not knowing who these women were and what part they had played in winning the peace in World War II.

Epilogue: Forgetting and Remembering

ALL TOLD, 59,283 army nurses volunteered to serve in World War II; more than half of these—almost 30,000—volunteered for, and served in, combat zones on the front lines of every American battlefield of the war. Sixteen army nurses were killed by enemy action; 201 lost their lives to illness or in accidents; more than 1,600 were decorated for meritorious service and bravery under fire. Nurses won the Distinguished Service Medal, the Silver Star, the Distinguished Flying Cross, the Soldier's Medal, the Bronze Star, the Air Medal, the Legion of Merit, the Army Commendation Medal, and the Purple Heart.

After three and a half years of war, it was time for these women to come home. Most Americans were looking forward to a "return to normalcy"—civilian life as they knew it before America entered World War II. This meant that these women—as well as the women on the home front who had taken over men's jobs in factories and offices "for the duration"—were expected to return to their old roles as wives, mothers, and homemakers.

The majority of women veterans from World War II were eager to do just that. However, returning to the norm was just not possible. During the war, large numbers of women received the opportunity to discover and use talents they may never have otherwise had the chance to explore. A change—however ambivalent and no matter the rebound to old norms for several years after the war—had occurred in the perception of what a woman could be or do.

When Captain Edward E. Rosenbaum, MC, starting down the cargo net into a landing barge for the invasion of North Africa on 8 November

1942, looked to his side and saw Lieutenant Vilma Vogler, an army nurse, descending the net with him, a paradigm shift occurred in his own mind and heart. "At that moment, she and the other nurses had ceased to be 'the women.' We were all comrades in equally dangerous footing, trying to survive the insanity of combat."[1]

That paradigm shift was to spread and grow stronger across each new battlefield of World War II. It deepened as army nurses, medical personnel, and soldiers fulfilled their missions on the front lines of combat zones together. From the young wounded GI looking up from a blood-stained floor in a makeshift hospital in Algeria and hearing an American woman's voice asking him about his injuries—"Holy cow! An American woman! Where in the world did you come from?"—to General Eisenhower's recognition of how important it was to have army nurses in combat zones; to sending the surviving army nurses from the sinking of the *Newfoundland* back to the battlefields of Salerno; to leaving army nurses on the bloody beachhead of Anzio when the going was at its roughest; to the return of the surviving army nurses of the *St. David* to the combat zones in Italy; to assigning army nurses to the front lines of France, Belgium, and Germany, the paradigm shift continued. The future was forever changed.[2]

That change in the way America saw its women and how American women saw themselves was nothing short of revolutionary for the 1940s. Young women, most of whom had never traveled farther from home than their nursing schools, willingly volunteered to travel halfway around the world into harm's way in order to help save the lives of wounded and sick American and Allied—and enemy—soldiers. The great majority of these women surely had no idea how profoundly their actions would change them and the world forever. They were simply doing their duty.

And when they came home, no one—including, for the large part, the women themselves—recognized them as the veterans they were. In those frontline army hospitals, the roles of women nurses had expanded, as roles tend to do in every national or local emergency, but following the war, those roles contracted. Male war veterans were encouraged to use the G.I. Bill to pick up their education where they had left off to jump-start their lives after the war, whereas very few women took advantage of the bill. Veterans Administration hospitals were totally unprepared for female veterans; their medical staffs did not include gynecologists and had no way to diagnose or treat exclusively female health problems. Neither were the VA hospitals prepared to treat women veterans with gen-

eral health problems if those problems required the patient to be hospitalized. There was no such thing as a women's ward; in fact, there were
no designated women's bathrooms or bathing facilities in inpatient units.
If, by rare chance, a woman veteran was admitted to the hospital, there
were no hospital pajamas in women's sizes and only an occasional staff
member—usually a VA nurse who had served in the Army Nurse
Corps—knew anything about the contributions women had made to
achieving victory in World War II.

Women veterans also found that many of the largest veterans' service
organizations, such as the Veterans of Foreign Wars and the American
Legion, did not accept women as members. One of the few exceptions to
this rule was the Military Order of the Purple Heart. "I joined the Purple
Heart Service Organization in Chattanooga, Tennessee," Ruthie Hindman Balch recalled. "I was the only woman member and the boys were
just wonderful to me."[3]

If a woman veteran applied for educational benefits, a home loan, or
other veterans' benefits, she was more likely than not to be greeted by
VA employees who knew little or nothing about women's military service
during World War II, and who might ask her, "Where is the veteran?"

Indeed, these same problems were still facing women veterans in
the late 1980s and early 1990s. Not until 1983 did Congress establish the
National Women Veterans Advisory Council. And not until 1985 did the
VA mandate the appointment of Women Veteran Coordinators at VA
medical centers and regional offices in order to ensure that former military women would receive the information, help, and care that have been
provided to male veterans for decades.

Women veteran army nurses—including Frances Nash—who had
been prisoners of the Japanese for more than three and a half years discovered quickly that the Veterans Administration knew little or nothing
about what Army and Navy Nurse Corps POWs had endured during
World War II. The final straw came in 1980, when a VA research study of
former POWs did not include women because there were, in the opinion
of the researchers, too few women POWs to consider. Former POW
Colonel Madeline Ullom of the Army Nurse Corps had had all the
inequality of benefits she could take and volunteered to testify before
Senator Dennis DeConcini's (D-Ariz.) Veterans Affairs Subcommittee on
Oversight and Investigation in 1982. This testimony was a benchmark in
the battle by women veterans to gain equal access to benefits they had
already earned.

But the struggle for recognition of women's contributions in World War II is not just a matter of winning medical and pay benefits. It has far larger ramifications. In the early 1970s, the Georgia League of Women Voters was working to get the Equal Rights Amendment (ERA) passed by the Georgia legislature. Only one state was needed for ratification and Georgia was an important pivotal state. Rosemary (Neidel-Greenlee), then a volunteer with the league, was to speak with state Senator Jim Tysinger in an attempt to get his vote for the passage of the ERA. He listened to arguments about equality and justice, then gave his response. "Why should women have equal rights? They never went to war for this country. They never got shot at by the enemy. I was on Guadalcanal and there were no women there."

Rosemary was at a loss for words. She had not yet done the research that would reveal the fact that U.S. Army and Navy nurses served on Guadalcanal. Flight nurses did fly into the combat zones in unmarked planes to evacuate wounded marines and GIs. What difference might it have made for the fate of the ERA if the contributions of the women who served on the front lines in World War II had been written down and passed on as part of the nation's history? What difference will it make to the country's future if the frontline service of army nurses in World War II is not made part of the national memory? What is known as history is vitally important to every American. Those who write our histories and preserve our stories have a tremendous effect on our futures. If a person can write your résumé, he can control what jobs you will be allowed to hold in the future. If history is not recorded and made known—if the contributions women made to the freedom of America by serving on the front lines of World War II are not recorded and remembered—women could be doomed to a gigantic board game in which each new generation must return to "start" and prove itself anew.

The truth is that both men and women of the Greatest Generation paid the price for the freedom we enjoy today, and like all national heroes, these women deserve our gratitude and a place in our national memory and hearts. The words Aeschylus wrote in *Prometheus Bound* centuries ago still ring true today: "Memory is the mother of all wisdom."

WE WOULD LIKE TO finish by summarizing what became of many of the nurses and soldiers whose stories you've just read:

Lieutenant Jimmy Nash was transferred to Okinawa before the war

Captains James Nash, Martha Nash, and Frances L. Nash after the war (Courtesy of Martha Nash Jones)

ended and was wounded by the Japanese. When the medics found him, they thought he was dead and began rolling him up in a GI blanket. "He couldn't speak because he had lost so much blood," his sister Martha recalled. "All he could do was wiggle his little finger. Thank God, the corpsmen saw it and recognized their mistake. He was taken to a hospital where he recovered from his wounds. It was 1947 before he got home and saw Frances."[4]

Former Lieutenant Claudine "Speedy" Glidewell Doyle and her husband, Frank, settled in the New England area after the war and raised a family. "Not quite six months after the war ended, I was talking to a man about repairing the well pump at our new home when lightning struck the corner of the house," Speedy recalled. "Without a word, the repairman and I hit the dirt. When we got up, the repairman said, 'Well, ma'am, I can see you were in the army too.' "⁵

Lieutenant Isabelle Wheeler and Lieutenant Neil Hansen got married shortly after leaving the army. They celebrated their forty-second wedding anniversary before Bee Wee died in 1987.

Bernice "Hut" Walden married and left the army in 1945. She and her daughter still attend the 95th Evacuation Hospital reunions.

Lieutenant Lillie "Pete" Peterson Homuth married shortly after the war ended. Her husband, Ernest, had been a corpsman with the 95th Evac. She and her children and grandchildren live in the Midwest.

Evelyn "Andy" Anderson married shortly after the end of the war and eventually retired to Florida.

Vera Sheaffer married Paul Skogsberg after World War II, raised a family, moved to Florida, and remained close friends with Evelyn "Andy" Anderson until Evelyn's death in 2000. Vera died in September 2002.

Lieutenant Ruth Hindman met her future husband, a U.S. Navy officer, while serving at England General Army Hospital in Atlantic City, New Jersey, near the end of the war. Her husband, the Reverend Lee Balch, was ordained an Episcopal priest and was rector of Grace Episcopal Church in Chattanooga, Tennessee, until he retired. Reverend Balch died in 2001 and Ruth now lives in the Washington, D.C., area. Two of her most recent neighbors were Senator Jesse Helms and his wife. During lunch one day, the subject of difficulty with hearing came up. "The senator told me how he lost some of his hearing," Ruthie recalled. "And I told him how mine was damaged when the Germans sank the second hospital ship I was on—the *St. David*. He hadn't realized before our conversation that U.S. Army nurses had been aboard hospital ships attacked by the German air force."⁶

Lieutenant Frances "Frenchie" Miernicke learned at the end of the war that three of her four brothers had survived the war. "My mother was a five-star mother," Miernicke said. "One brother was in England with the Eighth Air Force; Roman and Tony were in the U.S. Navy. Another— my second oldest brother, Steve—was a sergeant major in the regular army. He had been on the Bataan Death March and a POW for three years.

Steve was put on a ship [a Japanese 'hell ship'] in Luzon Bay. It was unmarked and got bombed by the U.S. Navy. Using the GI Bill, Frenchie earned a B.S. in Nursing. During the Korean War, she was recalled to active duty until 1952. Later, she met and married James W. Plenert, a World War II army veteran. She retired from the U.S. Army Reserve in 1964. She lives in Georgia and is active in Army Nurse Corps functions.[7]

During the war, Lieutenant Alice McKoy married Lieutenant John R. Ishmael who was serving with the U.S. Army in Europe. After the war, they settled in New Jersey and raised four daughters, one of whom chose the army as a career. "My youngest daughter, Lauren, is a career officer in the army and she doesn't have to put up with the discriminatory practices. I'm glad I lived to see these rules changed."[8]

Alice McKoy Ishmael died on 3 October 1991. Her youngest daughter, Lieutenant Colonel Lauren Ishmael, who had been stationed at the Pentagon, retired from the army in 2001.

Former Corporal Berchard L. "Junior" Glant was discharged from the U.S. Army and moved to Chattanooga, Tennessee, where he married and raised a family. He is active in the Medal of Honor Museum in Chattanooga and in various veterans' organizations.

Former Sergeant Billie Stone returned to Alabama after the war. He attended and graduated from Auburn University, married, and raised a family. Billie and Junior Glant have remained good friends over the years. Once, not long after the war, while visiting Billie and his family, Junior found that Billie's preschool-age son was fascinated by Junior's new "Utah" arm, the latest thing in prosthetics for veterans who suffered amputations of an upper extremity. When the day came for Junior to leave, Billie walked him to his car and noticed that in place of the Utah arm, Junior was wearing a prosthetic hook. "Where's your new arm?" Billie asked as they reached Junior's car. "I almost fell over when Junior said, 'Little Billie liked it so I left it for him to play with.' " "Oh no you don't!" Billie told Junior. "You wait right here and I'll get your arm."[9]

Former Tech-5 Fred Headrick returned to Chattanooga after the war and went into the restaurant business. He is active in the Medal of Honor Museum in Chattanooga and in various veterans' groups. At the reunion of the Third Armored Division in Falls Church, Virginia, in 2002, Fred, its organizer, helped honor the Third Armored's special guest: one of the two teenaged survivors from Dachau, who is now a prosperous U.S. citizen. Eddie Willner is a major, USA (Ret.), with a

wife, Johanna, six children, and eleven grandchildren. Three of the Will-
ners' six children are in the military and one son teaches at the U.S. Military Academy at West Point. Eddie Willner feels he owes his life to the
men of the Third Armored Division, who adopted him as an eighteen-
year-old escapee from a German concentration camp. Mike Swaab also
came to the United States after World War II ended. He and Eddie
remained close friends until Mike's death in 1990. In memory of Mike,
Eddie uses his friend's concentration camp number as the license plate
number on his car.

Colonel James Vance, USA (Ret.), used the G.I. Bill to obtain a college
degree and rejoined the army during the Korean War. Colonel Vance lives
in Georgia and has a son who is a nurse anesthetist in the U.S. Army
Nurse Corps.

*Oliver Sorlye, Jesse Flynn, and Charlie Thorson. Jesse Flynn is the son of two 48th/128th
Evacuation Hospital members, Lts. Gladys Martin Flynn and John Flynn.* (Courtesy of Jesse
Flynn)

Sergeant Charles Coolidge returned to Tennessee and his family's business. He married and raised a family. His son, air force General Charles Coolidge, is the vice commander, Headquarters, Air Force Material Command, Wright-Patterson Air Force Base in Dayton, Ohio.

Former lieutenant Martha "Marte" Cameron transferred to the U.S. Air Force in 1947 and then left when she married a career air force officer. Later, Marte rejoined the U.S. Air Force and retired in 1965 as a lieutenant. She is active in her local theater group in Florida.

Former U.S. Army Nurse Corps members at a reunion of the 48th Surgical/128th Evacuation Hospital in 2001 in Louisville, Kentucky. Left to right: Martha Cameron, Edna Marie Browning, Evelyn Kemer Slotwinski, Agatha Dohr Griebel, Doris Brittingham Simion, and Helen Molony Reichert (Courtesy of Jesse Flynn)

Lieutenant Ruth G. Haskell was discharged from the U.S. Army Nurse Corps due to back problems stemming from the fall from her ship's bunk while on her way to the invasion of North Africa in 1942. She lived in Maine and remained in close contact with Helen Molony, visiting her several times at her home in Florida in the years after the war. Ruth died in 1970.

Captain Theresa Archard returned to the United States in 1943; after regaining her health she was assigned as an instructor in the U.S. Army Nurse Corps School for basic training at Camp McCoy, Wisconsin.

Lieutenant Edna Browning remained in civilian nursing after World War II. She died in 2002.

After the war, Lieutenant Jessie Paddock married and moved to Pennsylvania.

Lieutenant Helen Molony married an army pilot, Hugh "Rick" Reichert, and raised two sons in Florida. She remained close friends with Martha Cameron and Ruth Haskell. Helen died in December 2002.

Lieutenant Adeline "Si" Simonson married army officer Marvin Williams, who was with the Forty-fifth Infantry Division and served at Kasserine Pass in Tunisia in 1943. Marvin's career took the Williams family on various foreign assignments. They settled in Atlanta, Georgia. Si survived her husband, and died in December 2002.

To all the U.S. Army nurses who served during World War II, we give our thanks and our respect. We are truly honored to have spoken with hundreds of these women and communicated with thousands of military nurses and other women veterans between 1988 and 2003. It is our sincere hope that America will claim and treasure the history that these women of the Greatest Generation have passed on to all Americans. Perhaps more Americans will look into their family histories and remember and honor the women who contributed their own not insignificant page to one of the largest and most important chapters in the nation's history.

We can look to the example of one American, Taylor Wheeler, who did just that. Taylor is the great-grandson of Speedy Glidewell Doyle. In 2002, Taylor's fifth-grade class at Kimball School in New Hampshire was given the assignment to write a paper about a woman in history. Ten-year-old Taylor was assigned Cleopatra as his subject. Without hesitation, he raised his hand and asked his teacher, Madelaine Barry: "Is it all right if I write my paper about my Grandma Doyle instead of Cleopatra? My Granny took care of wounded soldiers in World War II."[10]

Ms. Barry gave her permission and Taylor informally interviewed his Granny—he had heard her stories many times—and wrote and submitted his paper. When the paper was returned to Taylor a week later, it received an A.

*Former army nurse Lt. Claudine "Speedy" Glidewell
Doyle and her great-grandson, Taylor McKenzie Wheeler*
(Courtesy of Claudine Glidewell Doyle and Taylor
McKenzie Wheeler)

Rosemary and Evelyn would like to go on record by giving their own
A+ to Ms. Barry and Taylor. We hope both are only the beginning of a
long line of Americans who will recognize and cherish the history of the
thousands of U.S. Army and military nurses who went to war not as
draftees but as volunteers, and who marched to battle not to conquer but
to heal.

NOTES

INTRODUCTION

1. Col. Florence Blanchfield, letter to Mrs. Ellen Gertrude Ainsworth, Glenwood City, Wisconsin, February 1944.

PROLOGUE

1. Edith Aynes, *From Nightingale to Eagle* (Englewood Cliffs, N.J.: Prentice-Hall, 1973), 6.

2. Lt. Frances Nash, "Georgia Nurse's Own Story . . . My Three Years in a Jap Prison Camp," *Atlanta Journal Magazine*, 15 April 1945, 6.

3. Ibid.

4. Ibid.

5. Lt. Frances Nash, address to Grady Memorial Hospital staff, Atlanta, Georgia, 1945.

6. Ibid.

7. Alfred A. Weinstein, MD, *Barbed-Wire Surgeon* (New York: Macmillan, 1947), 16.

8. Nash, address.

9. Ibid.

10. Nash, "Georgia Nurse's Own Story," 7.

11. Maj. Jeanne Holm, *Women in the Military: An Unfinished Revolution* (Novato, Calif.: Presido Press, 1982), 12.

PART ONE

CHAPTER ONE: OPERATION TORCH— U.S. ARMY NURSES IN THE INVASION FORCE

1. Edward D. Churchill, MD, *Surgeon to Soldiers, Diary and Records of the Surgical Consultant Allied Force Headquarters, World War II* (Philadelphia: J. B. Lippincott, 1985), 123–24.

2. Charles Whiting, *Kasserine: The Anatomy of a Slaughter* (New York: Stein & Day, 1984), 23.

3. Ibid., 67.

4. Helen Molony Reichert, interview with authors, Atlanta, Georgia, September 2001.

5. Ibid.

6. Helen Molony Reichert, interview with authors, Louisville, Kentucky, August 2001.

7. Ibid.

8. Lt. Ruth G. Haskell, ANC, *Helmets and Lipstick* (New York: G. P. Putnam's Sons, 1944), 101; Reichert interview, September 2001.

9. Haskell, *Helmets and Lipstick*, 107.

10. Ibid., 108.

11. Ibid.

12. Ibid., 111.

13. Ibid., 112; Reichert interview, September 2001.

14. Haskell, *Helmets and Lipstick*, 112; Reichert interview, September 2001.

15. Haskell, *Helmets and Lipstick*, 116.

16. Ibid.; Reichert interview, September 2001.

17. Haskell, *Helmets and Lipstick*, 117; Reichert interview, September 2001.

18. Haskell, *Helmets and Lipstick*, 117; Reichert interview, September 2001.

19. Reichert interview, September 2001.

20. Ibid.

21. Ibid.

22. Capt. Theresa Archard, NC, USA, *G.I. Nightingale: The Story of an American Army Nurse* (New York: W. W. Norton, 1945), 10.

23. Ibid.

24. Reichert interview, September 2001.

25. Ibid.

26. Ibid.

27. Ibid.

28. Ibid.

CHAPTER TWO: NURSES AT THE BATTLE OF KASSERINE PASS

1. Lt. Ruth G. Haskell, ANC, *Helmets and Lipstick* (New York: G. P. Putnam's Sons, 1944), 148; Helen Molony Reichert, interview with authors, Louisville, Kentucky, August 2001.

2. Reichert interview.

3. Haskell, *Helmets and Lipstick*, 151; Reichert interview.

4. Reichert interview.

5. Ibid.

6. Haskell, *Helmets and Lipstick*, 156; Reichert interview.

7. Reichert interview.

8. Ibid.

9. Ibid.

10. Haskell, *Helmets and Lipstick*, 156; Reichert interview.

11. Haskell, *Helmets and Lipstick*, 156–57; Reichert interview.

12. Haskell, *Helmets and Lipstick*, 156–57; Reichert interview.

13. Reichert interview.

14. Haskell, *Helmets and Lipstick*, 162; Reichert interview.

15. Haskell, *Helmets and Lipstick*, 159–60; Reichert interview.

16. Haskell, *Helmets and Lipstick*, 161; Reichert interview.

17. Reichert interview.

18. Ibid.

19. Ibid.

20. Capt. Theresa Archard, NC, USA, *G.I. Nightingale: The Story of an American Army Nurse* (New York: W. W. Norton, 1945), 73; Reichert interview.

21. Archard, *G.I. Nightingale*, 78; Reichert interview.

22. Archard, *G.I. Nightingale*, 78–79; Reichert interview.

23. Archard, *G.I. Nightingale*, 79.

24. Haskell, *Helmets and Lipstick*, 175.

25. Ibid., 176.

26. Ibid., 177–78; Reichert interview.

27. Haskell, *Helmets and Lipstick*, 178; Reichert interview.

28. Ibid.

29. Charles Whiting, *Kasserine: The Anatomy of Slaughter* (New York: Stein & Day, 1984), 184–85.

30. Loren E. Butts, interview with authors, Atlanta, Georgia, January 2002.

31. Ibid.

32. Ibid.

33. Ibid.

34. Haskell, *Helmets and Lipstick*, 193; Reichert interview.

35. Ibid.

36. Haskell, *Helmets and Lipstick*, 194; Reichert interview.

37. Haskell, *Helmets and Lipstick*, 195; Reichert interview.

38. Ibid.

39. Haskell, *Helmets and Lipstick*, 198–99; Reichert interview.

40. Charles M. Wiltse, *The Medical Department: Medical Service in the Mediterranean and Minor Theaters* (Washington, D.C.: Department of the Army, 1965), 126; "World War II's Human Toll," *VFW Magazine* (November 1991), 38.

41. Haskell, *Helmets and Lipstick*, 198–99; Reichert interview.

42. Reichert interview.

43. Helen Molony Reichert, interview with authors, Atlanta, Georgia, September 2001.

44. Ibid.

45. Haskell, *Helmets and Lipstick*, 201.

46. Reichert interview, September 2001.

47. Haskell, *Helmets and Lipstick*, 202; Reichert interview, September 2001.

48. Haskell, *Helmets and Lipstick*, 204; Reichert interview, September 2001.

49. Haskell, *Helmets and Lipstick*, 205; Reichert interview, September 2001.

50. Haskell, *Helmets and Lipstick*, 206; Reichert interview, September 2001.

51. Ibid.

CHAPTER THREE: THE ALLIED PUSH TO BIZERTE AND TUNIS

1. Capt. Theresa Archard, NC, USA, *G.I. Nightingale: The Story of an American Army Nurse* (New York: W. W. Norton, 1945), 83; Helen Molony Reichert, interview with authors, Louisville, Kentucky, August 2001.

2. Archard, *G.I. Nightingale*, 83; Reichert interview.

3. Archard, *G.I. Nightingale*, 84; Reichert interview.

4. Archard, *G.I. Nightingale*, 86; Reichert interview.

5. Charles Coolidge, interview with authors, Atlanta, Georgia, April 2002.

6. Archard, *G.I. Nightingale*, 93; Reichert interview.

7. Archard, *G.I. Nightingale*, 94.

8. Jodie Harmon, interview with authors, Atlanta, Georgia, March 2002.

9. War Diary, 48th Surgical Hospital: 10 February 1941–1 May 1943; 128th Evacuation Hospital: 1 May 1943–1 June 1945; 28 March 1943 entry, authors' archives, Atlanta, Ga.

10. Archard, *G.I. Nightingale*, 94; Reichert interview.

11. Ibid.

12. Reichert interview.

13. Ibid.

14. Ibid.

15. Archard, *G.I. Nightingale*, 96; Reichert interview.

16. Gilbert Smith, interview with authors, Atlanta, Georgia, January 2002.

17. War Diary, 48th Surgical Hospital, 28 and 29 March 1943 entries.

18. Archard, *G.I. Nightingale*, 98; Reichert interview.

19. Gerald Taylor, interview with authors, Atlanta, Georgia, January 2002.

20. Edward D. Churchill, MD, *Surgeon to Soldiers, Diary and Records of the Surgical Consultant Allied Force Headquarters, World War II* (Philadelphia: J. B. Lippincott, 1985), 51–52.

21. Ibid.

22. Ibid.

23. Archard, *G.I. Nightingale*, 100; War Diary, 48th Surgical Hospital, 31 March 1943 entry.

24. Archard, *G.I. Nightingale*, 110.

25. Ibid., 111.

26. Ibid., 115.

27. Helen Molony Reichert, interview with authors, Atlanta, Georgia, September 2001.

28. Ibid.

29. Archard, *G.I. Nightingale*, 116–17; Reichert interview, September 2001.

30. Archard, *G.I. Nightingale*, 118; Reichert interview, September 2001.

31. Archard, *G.I. Nightingale*, 120.

32. Archard, *G.I. Nightingale* 121.

33. Ibid.

34. Ibid.

35. Ibid., 122.

36. Ibid.

37. Ibid., 124.

38. Ibid.

39. Ibid., 124–25.

40. Ibid., 125–26.

41. Ibid.

42. Ibid., 126–27.

43. Ibid., 128; Reichert interview, September 2001.

44. Archard, *G.I. Nightingale*, 129; Reichert interview, September 2001.

45. War Diary, 48th Surgical Hospital, 6–23 August 1943 entry.

46. Peter R. Mansoor, *The GI Offensive in Europe: The Triumph of American Infantry Divisions, 1941–1945* (Lawrence: University Press of Kansas, 1999), 89, 92, 96.

47. Archard, *G.I. Nightingale*, 132.

48. Ibid., 133.

CHAPTER FOUR: STAGING FOR ITALY

1. Col. Mary T. Sarnecky, USA (Ret.), *A History of the U.S. Army Nurse Corps* (Philadelphia: University of Pennsylvania Press, 1999), 129.

2. American National Red Cross, *Uncle Sam Needs Nurses*, Washington, D.C., August 1942, ARC 779. Authors' archives, Atlanta, Ga., 204.

3. Ibid.

4. Col. Robert V. Piemonte, ANC, USAR, and Maj. Cindy Gurney, ANC, eds., *Highlights in the History of the Army Nurse Corps* (Washington, D.C.: U.S. Army Center of Military History, 1987), 13–15.

5. Claudine Glidewell Doyle, interview with authors, Atlanta, Georgia, August 2000.

6. Evelyn Anderson Blank, interview with authors, Atlanta, Georgia, July 1989.

7. Claudine Glidewell Doyle, interview with authors, Atlanta, Georgia, February 2002.

8. Mary Elizabeth Carnegie, *The Path We Tread: Blacks in Nursing, 1854–1984* (Philadelphia: J. B. Lippincott, 1986), 168–73.

9. Doyle interview, August 2000.

10. Doyle interview, February 2002.

11. Claudine Glidewell Doyle, interview with authors, Atlanta, Georgia, December 2001.

12. Ibid.

13. Ibid.

14. Claudine Glidewell Doyle, interview with authors, Atlanta, Georgia, January 2002.

15. Ibid.

16. Claudine Glidewell Doyle, interview with authors, Atlanta, Georgia, October 2001.

17. Ibid.

18. Ibid.

19. Doyle interview, January 2002.

20. Ruth Hindman Balch, interview with authors, Arlington, Virginia, August 2001.

21. Ibid.

22. Doyle interview, January 2002.

23. Doyle interview, December 2001.

24. Ibid.

25. Ibid.

26. Evelyn Anderson Blank, interview with authors, Atlanta, Georgia, July 1989.

27. 93rd Evacuation Hospital Summary—History: June 1941–December 1943, National Archives, Washington, D.C., RG 112.

PART TWO

CHAPTER FIVE: NURSES IN THE SICILIAN CAMPAIGN

1. Evelyn Anderson Blank, interview with authors, Atlanta, Georgia, July 1989.

2. Ibid.

3. Ibid.

4. Ibid.

5. Ibid.

6. Ibid.

7. Ibid.

8. Ibid.

9. Evelyn Anderson, Annual Report of the 93rd Evacuation Hospital, Nursing Report, 1943: "Adventures of the 93rd Evacuation Hospital Nurses," National Archives, Washington, D.C., RG 112.

10. Helen Molony Reichert, interview with authors, Atlanta, Georgia, June 2001.

11. Ibid.

12. Charles M. Wiltse, *The Medical Department: Medical Service in the Mediterranean and Minor Theaters* (Washington, D.C.: Department of the Army, 1965), 165.

13. Reichert interview.

14. Ibid.

15. Capt. Theresa Archard, NC, USA, *G.I. Nightingale: The Story of an American Army Nurse* (New York: W. W. Norton, 1945), 149.

16. Reichert interview.

17. Archard, *G.I. Nightingale*, 150.

18. Ibid.

19. Reichert interview.

20. Ibid.

21. Ibid.

22. Ibid.

23. Wiltse, *The Medical Department*, 165.

24. Marcus Duxbury, interview with authors, Atlanta, Georgia, January 2002.

25. Reichert interview.

26. Helen Molony Reichert, interview with authors, Atlanta, Georgia, July 2001.

27. War Diary, 48th Surgical Hospital: 10 February 1941–1 May 1943; 128th Evacuation Hospital: 1 May 1943–1 June 1945; 6–23 August 1943 entry, authors' archives, Atlanta, Ga.

28. Archard, *G.I. Nightingale*, 160.

29. Col. Donald E. Currier, Medical Corps Commanding Officer, 93rd Field Hospital, Memorandum to Surgeon, II Corps, 12 August 1943, authors' archives, Atlanta, Ga.

30. Vera Sheaffer Skogsberg, interview with authors, Atlanta, Georgia, February 2002.

31. Edward D. Churchill, MD, *Surgeon to Soldiers, Diary and Records of the Surgical Consultant Allied Force Headquarters, World War II* (Philadelphia: J. B. Lippincott, 1985), 479.

32. Omar N. Bradley, *A Soldier's Story* (New York: Modern Library, 1999), 160.

33. Archard, *G.I. Nightingale*, 166–67.

34. Ibid., 170.

35. Peter R. Mansoor, *The GI Offensive in Europe: The Triumph of American Infantry Divisions, 1941–1945* (Lawrence: University Press of Kansas, 1999), 99–110.

36. Wiltse, *The Medical Department*, 165–67; "Sicily: The U.S. Army Campaigns of World War II" (Washington, D.C.: U.S. Army Center of Military History, 1965), pub. 72–16, 25.

37. Archard, *G.I. Nightingale*, 170.

38. Ibid., 176–77.

39. Reichert interview, June 2001.

40. Archard, *G.I. Nightingale*, 172.

41. Maj. Frances Miernicke Plenert, ANC (Ret.), interview with authors, Augusta, Georgia, July 2001.

42. Ruth Hindman Balch, interview with authors, Chattanooga, Tennessee, July 1991.

43. Claudine Glidewell Doyle, interview with authors, Atlanta, Georgia, October 2001.

44. Claudine Glidewell Doyle, "Oh, My Knocking Knees!," authors' archives, Atlanta, Ga.

CHAPTER SIX: THE SINKING OF HMHS *NEWFOUNDLAND*

1. Maj. Luther H. Wolff, *Forward Surgeon: The Diary of Luther H. Wolff, M.D., Mediterranean Theater, World War II, 1943–1945* (New York: Vantage Press, 1985), 2.

2. Ibid.

3. Ibid., 5.

4. Ibid., 9.

5. Ibid.

6. Ibid., 10.

7. Ibid., 11.

8. Claudine Glidewell Doyle, "Oh, My Knocking Knees!," authors' archives, Atlanta, Ga.

9. Ibid.

10. Claudine Glidwell Doyle, interview with authors, Atlanta, Georgia, September 2000.

11. Claudine Glidwell Doyle, interview with authors, Atlanta, Georgia, May 2000.

12. Ibid.

13. Madonna Nolan, interview with authors, Atlanta, Georgia, September 1989; Agnes Nolan, interview with authors, Atlanta, Georgia, August 1989.

14. Doyle interview, September 2000.

15. Madonna Nolan interview.

16. Doyle interview, September 2000.

17. Blanche Sigman, "History of the 95th Evacuation Hospital," National Archives, Washington, D.C., RG 112, 8.

18. Martha Whorton Black, interview with authors, Atlanta, Georgia, July 1989.

19. Doyle, "Oh, My Knocking Knees!"

20. Ruth Hindman Balch, interview with authors, Atlanta, Georgia, March 2002.

21. Ibid.

22. Ibid.

23. Ibid.

24. Capt. Mary H. Fischer, ANC (Ret.) [Report of the Bombing of the *Newfoundland*], National Archives, Washington, D.C., RG 112, 2.

25. Ibid., 3–4.

26. Doyle interview, September 2000.

27. Ibid.

28. Ibid.

29. Ibid.

30. Ibid.

31. Ibid.

32. Ibid.

33. Ibid.

34. Ibid.

35. "British Rescued U.S. Nurses on Hospital Ship," Report, National Archives, Washington, D.C., RG 112.

36. Fischer report, 4.

37. Doyle interview, September 2000.

38. Ibid.

39. Madonna Nolan interview.

40. Nursing Report of the 16th Evacuation Hospital, National Archives, Washington, D.C., RG 112, 18.

41. Ruth Hindman Balch, interview with authors, Atlanta, Georgia, November 2001.

42. Doyle interview, January 2001.

43. Evelyn Anderson Blank, interview with authors, Atlanta, Georgia, August 1989.

44. Ibid.

45. Balch interview, March 2002.

CHAPTER SEVEN: FROM SALERNO TO THE GUSTAV LINE

1. Charles M. Wiltse, *The Medical Department: Medical Service in the Mediterranean and Minor Theaters* (Washington, D.C.: Department of the Army, 1965), 225.

2. Agnes Nolan, interview with authors, Atlanta, Georgia, August 1989.

3. Ibid.

4. Maj. Luther H. Wolff, *Forward Surgeon: The Diary of Luther H. Wolff, M.D. Mediterranean Theater, World War II, 1943–45* (New York: Vantage Press, 1985), 20–21.

5. Madonna Nolan, interview with authors, Atlanta, Georgia, September 1989.

6. Claudine Glidewell Doyle, interview with authors, Atlanta, Georgia, July 2001.

7. Ibid.

8. 95th Evacuation Hospital Annual Report and Historical Record, 1 January 1944, National Archives, Washington, D.C., RG 112.

9. "Salerno: American Operations from the Beaches to the Volturno: 9 September–6 October 1943" (Washington, D.C., U.S. Army Center of Military History, 1990), pub. 100–7, 93.

10. Evelyn Anderson Blank, interview with authors, Atlanta, Georgia, July 1989.

11. Vera Sheaffer Skogsberg, interview with authors, Atlanta, Georgia, February 2002.

12. Claudine Glidewell Doyle, interview with authors, Atlanta, Georgia, August 2000.

13. Ibid.

14. Ibid.

15. Ibid.

16. Claudine Glidewell Doyle, interview with authors, Atlanta, Georgia, April 2000.

17. Claudine Glidewell Doyle, interview with authors, Florence, Kentucky, September 2000.

18. Graham A. Cosmas and Albert E. Cowdrey, *The Medical Department: Medical Service in the European Theater of Operations* (Washington, D.C.: U.S. Army Center of Military History, 1992), 145.

19. Edward D. Churchill, MD, *Surgeon to Soldiers, Diary and Records of the Surgical Consultant Allied Force Headquarters, World War II* (Philadelphia: J. B. Lippincott, 1985), 201.

20. Wiltse, *The Medical Department*, 259.

21. Gladys L. Hobby, *Penicillin: Meeting the Challenge* (New Haven: Yale University Press, 1985), 125.

22. Ibid., 140.

23. Ibid., 141–42.

24. Jeffrey L. Rodengen, *The Legend of Pfizer* (Fort Lauderdale, Fla.: Write Stuff Syndicate, 1999), 62.

25. R. D. Coghill and R. S. Koch, "Penicillin in Wartime Accomplishment," *Chemical and Engineering News* 24 (December 1945), 2310.

26. Hobby, *Penicillin*, 154.

27. Churchill, *Surgeon to Soldiers*, 204.

28. Wolff, *Forward Surgeon*, 32–33.

29. Ibid., 33.

30. Cosmas and Cowdrey, *The Medical Department*, 51.

31. Ibid., 46.

32. Ruth Hindman Balch, interview with authors, Atlanta, Georgia, October 2001.

33. Ibid.

34. Ibid.

35. Ibid.

36. Ibid.

37. Ibid.

38. Ibid.

39. Ibid.

40. Ibid.

41. Ruth Hindman Balch, interview with authors, Chattanooga, Tennessee, December 1991.

42. Ibid.

43. Ibid.

44. Doyle interview, September 2000.

45. Ibid.

46. Sgt. Burgess H. Scott, "Hospital on Rails: First Ambulance Train in Italy Carries Wounded GIs Out of Fighting Zone," *Yank Magazine* (January 1944), 9.

47. Doyle interview, September 2000.

48. Ibid.

49. Bernice Walden Thibodeau, interview with authors, Florence, Kentucky, September 2000.

50. Claudine Glidewell Doyle, interview with authors, Atlanta, Georgia, November 2000.

51. Jessie Paddock, interview with authors, Atlanta, Georgia, October 1990.

52. Ibid.

53. Helen Molony Reichert, interview with authors, Louisville, Kentucky, August 2001.

54. Lt. Col. Martha Cameron, USAF, NC (Ret.), interview with authors, Louisville, Kentucky, August 2001.

55. Ibid.

56. Oliver Sorlye, interview with authors, Atlanta, Georgia, January 2002.

57. Cameron interview.

58. Ibid.

59. Wiltse, *The Medical Department*, 258.

60. Charles Coolidge, interview with authors, Atlanta, Georgia, May 2002.

61. Wolff, *Forward Surgeon*, 66.

62. Coolidge interview.

63. Martin Blumenson, *The Mediterranean Theater of Operations: Salerno to Cassino* (Washington, D.C.: U.S. Army Center of Military History, 1993), 346.

CHAPTER EIGHT: HELL'S HALF-ACRE—THE ANZIO BEACHHEAD

1. Ruth Hindman Balch, interview with authors, Chattanooga, Tennessee, December 1991; 1st Lt. Sidney Hyman, MSC, "The Medical Story of Anzio," Report by Historian, Medical Section, HQ Fifth Army, National Archives, Washington, D.C., RG 112.

2. Hindman interview.

3. Ibid.

4. Ibid.

5. Ibid.

6. Ibid.

7. Ibid.

8. Brenda McBryde, *Quiet Heroines* (London: Chatto & Windus/Hogarth Press, 1985), 153; Col. James H. Forsee, MC, Memorandum to Commanding General Medical, NATOUSA, 27 October 1944, National Archives, Washington, D.C., RG 112; Maj. Owen Elliot, AGD, Assistant Adjutant General, Memorandum to Commanding General, U.S. Armed Forces, "Determination of Status of Casualty," 26 May 1944, National Archives, Washington, D.C., RG 112.

9. Balch interview.

10. Ibid.

11. Col. Rollin L. Bauchspies, MC, "The Courageous Medics of Anzio," Part I, *Military Medicine* (January 1958), 62.

12. Berchard L. Glant, interview with authors, Chattanooga, Tennessee, October 2000.

13. William Stone, interview with authors, Atlanta, Georgia, March 2002.

14. Ibid.

15. Ibid.

16. Ibid.

17. Ibid.

18. Claudine Glidewell Doyle, interview with authors, Florence, Kentucky, September 2000.

19. Ibid.

20. Claudine Glidewell Doyle, "Oh, My Knocking Knees!," authors' archives, Atlanta, Ga.

21. Doyle interview; Bernice Walden Thibodeau, interview with authors, Florence, Kentucky, September 2000.

22. Doyle interview.

23. Ibid.

24. Adeline Simonson Williams, interview with authors, Atlanta, Georgia, June 2002.

25. Ibid.

26. Ibid.

27. Hyman, "The Medical Story of Anzio."

28. Claudine Glidewell Doyle, interview with authors, Atlanta, Georgia, October 2000.

29. 56th Evacuation Hospital Medical Historical Report, 5 October 1944, National Archives, Washington, D.C., RG 112.

30. Berchard L. Glant, U.S. Army Medical Record, 1943–45, authors' archives, Atlanta, Ga.

31. Ibid.

32. Glant interview.

33. See Bauchspies, "The Courageous Medics of Anzio," Part I, 55.

34. Doyle, "Oh, My Knocking Knees!"

35. *Anzio Beachhead: 22 January–May 1944* (Washington, D.C.: U.S. Army Center of Military History, 1990), 53.

36. Claudine Glidewell Doyle, interview with authors, Atlanta, Georgia, April 2001.

37. Ibid.

38. Doyle, "Oh, My Knocking Knees!"

39. Ibid.

40. Doyle interview, September 2000.

41. Doyle, "Oh, My Knocking Knees!"

42. Adeline Simonson Williams, interview with authors, Atlanta, Georgia, June 2001.

43. Ibid.

44. Williams interview, June 2002.

45. Helen Wharton, Director of Nurses, Fifth Army, letter to Lt. Col. Bernice Wilbur, Director of Nursing Mediterranean Theater, 16 February 1944, U.S. Army Military History Institute, Carlisle, Pa.—Early 1940s File; Lt. Col. Hurbert L. Binkley, 95th Evacuation Hospital Report and History, 1944, National Archives, Washington, D.C., RG 112.

46. Doyle interview, April 2001.

47. Fredrick Clayton, unpublished paper, U.S. Army Military History Institute, Carlisle, Pa.—Early 1940s box.

48. Ibid.

49. Ibid.

50. Ibid.

51. Ibid.

52. Evelyn Anderson Blank, interview with authors, Atlanta, Georgia, July 1989.

53. Glant interview.

54. Blank interview.

55. Glant interview.

56. Berchard L. Glant, interview with authors, Atlanta, Georgia, July 2002.

57. Paddock interview.

58. Ibid.

59. Ibid.

60. Ibid.

61. Ibid.

62. Ruth B. White, "At Anzio Beachhead," *American Journal of Nursing*, 44 (April 1944), 370–71.

63. Hyman, "The Medical Story of Anzio."

64. White, "At Anzio Beachhead," 71.

65. Ibid.

66. Citation for Silver Star Medal, Lt. Ellen Ainsworth, NC, USA, World War II Casualties Lists, Department of Defense, 1965, U.S. Army Military History Institute, Carlisle, Pa.

67. Gen. Mark W. Clark, Memorandum to 2nd Lt. Frances A. Miernicke, "Award of Bronze Star," 10 May 1944, authors' archives, Atlanta, Ga.

68. Doyle interview, September 2000.

69. Williams interview, June 2002.

70. Doyle interview, September 2000.

71. Martin Blumenson, *The Mediterranean Theater of Operations: Salerno to Cassino* (Washington, D.C.: U.S. Army Center of Military History, 1993), 424.

CHAPTER NINE: STALEMATE AT ANZIO BEACHHEAD AND MONTE CASSINO

1. Joseph S. Tahan, interview with authors, Atlanta, Georgia, October 2001.

2. Peter R. Mansoor, *The GI Offensive in Europe: The Triumph of American Infantry Divisions, 1941–1945* (Lawrence: University Press of Kansas, 1999), 115–16.

3. Berchard L. Glant, interview with authors, Chattanooga, Tennessee, October 2000.

4. Brenda McBryde, *Quiet Heroines* (London: Chatto & Windus-Hogarth Press, 1985), 146; Glant interview.

5. Glant interview.

6. The Fifth Army letter to Italian Friends, Imperial War Museum, London.

7. Charles Coolidge, interview with authors, Atlanta, Georgia, March 2002.

8. Claudine Glidewell Doyle, interview with authors, Florence, Kentucky, September 2000.

9. Maj. Luther H. Wolff, *Forward Surgeon: Diary of Luther H. Wolff, M.D. Mediterranean Theater, World War II, 1943–1945* (New York: Vantage Press, 1985), 77.

10. Ruth Hindman Balch, interview with authors, Atlanta, Georgia, November 2001.

11. Maj. Frances Miernicke Plenert, ANC (Ret.), interview with authors, Atlanta, Georgia, January 2002.

12. Ibid.

13. Glant interview.

14. Ibid.

15. *Anzio Beachhead: 22 January–25 May 1944* (Washington, D.C.: U.S. Army Center for Military History, 1990), 88–89.

16. Maj. Frances Miernicke Plenert, ANC (Ret.), interview with authors, Augusta, Georgia, July 2001.

17. Capt. Robert R. Levine, MC, Unit "A" Report—33rd Field Hospital, Annual Historical Review 1944, National Archives, Washington, D.C., RG 112.

18. Plenert interview, January 2002.

19. Charles M. Wiltse, *The Medical Department: Medical Service in the Mediterranean and Minor Theaters* (Washington, D.C.: Department of the Army, 1965), 453.

20. Coolidge interview.

21. Gladys L. Hobby, *Penicillin: Meeting the Challenge* (New Haven: Yale University Press, 1985), 196.

22. Vera Sheaffer Skogsberg, interview with authors, Atlanta, Georgia, February 2002.

23. Clayton D. Laurie, "Anzio: The U.S. Army Campaigns of World War II, United States Army" (Washington, D.C., U.S. Army Center of Military History), pub. 72–19, 20.

24. Martin Blumenson, *The Mediterranean Theater of Operations: Salerno to Cassino* (Washington, D.C.: U.S. Army Center of Military History, 1993), 423–24.

25. Plenert interview, July 2001.

26. Ibid.

27. Ibid.; Col. Rollin L. Bauchspies, MC, "The Courageous Medics of Anzio," Part IV, *Military Medicine* (April 1958), 270.

28. Blumenson, *Mediterranean Theater of Operations*, 424.

29. Plenert interview, July 2001.

30. Richard V. Hauver, MD, "Diary February 22, 1943–September 20, 1945," U.S. Army Military History Institute, Carlisle, Pa.—Late 1940s box, 26 February 1944 entry.

31. Ibid., 29 March 1944 entry.

32. Wiltse, *The Medical Department*, 255.

33. Plenert interview, July 2001.

34. Ibid.

35. Col. Rollin L. Bauchspies, "Courageous Medics of Anzio," Part V, *Military Medicine* (May 1958), 358.

36. Ibid.

37. Plenert interview, July 2001.

38. Glant interview.

39. Ibid.

40. Ibid.

41. 1st Lt. Evelyn Anderson, Report of the Nursing Activities for the Year of 1944, 93rd Evacuation Hospital, National Archives, Washington, D.C., RG 112, 3.

CHAPTER TEN: BREAKOUT AND PURSUIT

1. Gen. Mark W. Clark, *Calculated Risk* (New York: Harper & Brothers, 1950), 336.

2. Maj. Frances Miernicke Plenert, ANC (Ret.), interview with authors, Augusta, Georgia, July 2001.

3. Gen. Mark W. Clark, Memorandum to 2nd Lt. Frances A. Miernicke, "Award of Bronze Star," 10 May 1944, authors' archives, Atlanta, Ga.

4. Berchard L. Glant, interview with authors, Chattanooga, Tennessee, October 2000.

5. Ibid.

6. Ibid.

7. Ibid.

8. Ibid.

9. Charles M. Wiltse, *The Medical Department: Medical Service in the Mediterranean and Minor Theaters* (Washington, D.C.: Department of the Army, 1965), 278.

10. Billie Stone, interview with authors, Atlanta, Georgia, March 2002.

11. Ibid.

12. Richard V. Hauver, MD, "Diary February 22, 1943–September 20, 1945," U.S. Army Military History Institute, Carlisle, Pa.—Late 1940s box, entry for 27 May 1944.

13. Plenert interview.

14. Wiltse, *The Medical Department*, 263–65.

15. Ibid., 265.

16. Hauver Diary, 5 June 1944 entry.

17. Wiltse, *The Medical Department*, 278.

PART THREE

CHAPTER ELEVEN: THE INVASION OF NORMANDY

1. Graham A. Cosmas and Albert E. Cowdrey, *The Medical Department: Medical Service in the European Theater of Operations* (Washington, D.C.: U.S. Army Center of Military History, 1992), 201–4; William H. Hammond, "Normandy: The U.S. Army Campaigns of World War II" (Washington, D.C., U.S. Army Center of Military History), pub. 72–18, 5.

2. Tegtmeyer quoted in Cosmas and Cowdrey, *Medical Service in the European Theater of Operations*, 211.

3. Helen Molony Reichert, interview with authors, Louisville, Kentucky, August 2001.

4. Cosmas and Cowdrey, *Medical Service in the European Theater of Operations*, 204.

5. Reichert interview.

6. Lt. Col. Martha Cameron, USAF, NC (Ret.), interview with authors, Louisville, Kentucky, August 2001.

7. Lt. Martha Cameron, letter to her father, Mr. E. H. Cameron, Nutley, New Jersey, 3 July 1944, France.

8. Ibid.

9. Lt. Col. Martha Cameron, USAF, NC (Ret.), interview with authors, Atlanta, Georgia, October 2002.

10. Reichert interview.

11. Cameron interview, October 2002.

12. Ibid.

13. Ibid.

14. Ibid.

15. Oliver Sorlye, interview with authors, Atlanta, Georgia, January 2002.

16. Marcus Duxbury, interview with authors, Atlanta, Georgia, January 2002.

17. Ibid.

18. Sorlye interview.

19. Edna Marie Browning, interview with authors, Louisville, Kentucky, August 2001.

20. Sorlye interview.

21. Browning interview.

22. Ibid.

23. Ibid.

24. War Diary, 48th Surgical Hospital, 10 February 1941–1 May 1943; 128th Evacuation Hospital, 1 May 1943–1 June 1945; 12 June 1944 entry, authors' archives, Atlanta, Ga.

25. War Diary, 17 June 1944 entry; Lt. Martha Cameron, letter to Mr. E. H. Cameron, Nutley, New Jersey, 25 June 1944, France.

26. Cosmas and Cowdrey, *Medical Service in the European Theater of Operations*, 218, 247, 257.

27. 2nd Lt. Mandie, letter to unnamed recipient (copy to Lt. Mary Eaton, MDD), 15 August 1944, U.S. Army Military History Institute, Carlisle, Pa.—Early 1940s box.

28. Cosmas and Cowdrey, *Medical Service in the European Theater of Operations*, 211.

29. Capt. Jean Truckey, Chief Nurse, 67th Evacuation Hospital, "American Nurses on European Battlefields," U.S. Army Military History Institute, Carlisle, Pa.—undated, Early 1940s File; 67th Evacuation Hospital, Annual Report, 1944, National Archives, Washington, D.C., RG 112.

30. Martha Nash Jones, interview with authors, Atlanta, Georgia, January 1992.

31. Ibid.

32. Ibid.

33. Cameron interview, October 2002.

34. Ibid.

35. Cameron interview, August 2001.

36. Loren Butts, interview with authors, January 2002, Atlanta, Georgia.

37. Cameron interview, October 2002.

38. Cameron interview, August 2001.

39. Ibid.

40. Ibid.

41. Ibid.

42. Hammond, "Normandy," 39.

43. Charles B. MacDonald, *The Mighty Endeavor: The American War in Europe* (New York: Da Capo Press, 1992), 332–34.

44. Jones interview.

45. Ibid.

46. Ibid.

47. Truckey, "American Nurses on European Battlefields."

48. Ibid.

49. The 67th Evacuation Hospital Annual Report, 1944.

50. MacDonald, *The Mighty Endeavor*, 347; Gen. Dwight David Eisenhower, AUS (Ret.), *Crusade in Europe* (Baltimore: Johns Hopkins University Press, 1997), 279.

51. Cameron interview, October 2002.

52. Cameron interview, August 2001; War Diary, 128th Evacuation Hospital, 21 August 1944 entry.

53. Omar Bradley, *A Soldier's Story* (New York: Modern Library, 1999), 380; Cosmas and Cowdrey, *Medical Service in the European Theater of Operations*, 224–25, 234, 293; Christopher Argyle, *Chronology of World War II* (New York: Exeter Books, 1980), 167.

54. Lt. Col. Ida W. Danielson, ANC, Director Nursing Service, ETO, Annual Report of the Army Nurse Corps—1944, Office of the Chief Surgeon European Theater of Operations, 1944, National Archives, Washington, D.C., RG 112, data calculated from enclosure #1, 12.

CHAPTER TWELVE: OPERATION DRAGOON AND
THE BATTLE OF THE RHÔNE VALLEY

1. "Southern France: The U.S. Army Campaign of World War II" (Washington, D.C., U.S. Army Center of Military History), pub. 72–31, 9.

2. Ibid.

3. Maj. Richard V. Hauver, Diary of World War II: February 22, 1943–September 30, 1945, U.S. Army Institute of Military History, Carlisle, Pa.—Late 1940s box, 15 September 1944 entry; 93rd Evacuation Hospital Annual Report 1944, National Archives, Washington, D.C., RG 112.

4. Charles Coolidge, interview with authors, Atlanta, Georgia, April 2002.

5. Claudine Glidewell Doyle, interview with authors, Florence, Kentucky, September 2000.

6. Evelyn Anderson Blank, interview with authors, Atlanta, Georgia, August 1989.

7. Vera Sheaffer Skogsberg, interview with authors, Atlanta, Georgia, March 2002.

8. Capt. Evelyn Swanson, 93rd Evacuation Hospital Nursing Report, 1944, National Archives, Washington, D.C., RG 112, 4.

9. I. C. B. Dear and M. R. D. Foot, eds., *Oxford Companion to World War II* (New York: Oxford University Press, 2001), 275–76.

10. Emory A. Massman, *Hospital Ships of World War II* (Jefferson, N.C.: McFarland & Company, 1999), 43, 53, 67, 125, 188.

11. Maj. Frances Miernicke Plenert, USA, NC (Ret.), interview with authors, Augusta, Georgia, July 2001.

12. Graham A. Cosmas and Albert E. Cowdrey, *The Medical Department: Medical Service in the European Theater of Operations* (Washington, D.C.: U.S. Army Center of Military History, 1992), 202; "Southern France," 30.

13. Lt. Evelyn Anderson, 93rd Evacuation Hospital Annual Nursing Report 1944, National Archives, Washington, D.C., RG 112.

14. Ibid.

15. Capt. Margaret W. Sydel, "An Account of the Nursing Service of the 11th Field Hospital," 1944, National Archives, Washington, D.C., RG 112.

16. Plenert interview.

17. Ibid.

18. Ibid.

19. Peter R. Mansoor, *The GI Offensive in Europe: The Triumph of American Infantry Divisions, 1941–1945* (Lawrence: University Press of Kansas, 1999), 175; "Southern France," 24.

20. Plenert interview.

21. Ibid.

22. Ibid.

23. Ibid.

24. Ibid.

25. Ibid.

26. Ibid.

27. Ibid.

28. Ibid.

29. Charles B. MacDonald, *The Mighty Endeavor: The American War in Europe* (New York: Da Capo Press, 1992), 352; W. Victor Madej, *The U.S. Army Order of Battle: Mediterranean and Europe, 1942–1945* (Allentown, Pa.: Game Publishing Co., 1984), 104.

30. Lillie Peterson Homuth, interview with authors, Florence, Kentucky, September 2000.

31. Lillie Peterson Homuth, letter to authors, 15 October 2000.

32. Charles M. Wiltse, *The Medical Department: Medical Service in the Mediterranean and Minor Theaters* (Washington, D.C.: Department of the Army, 1965), 279–80, 398.

33. 93rd Evacuation Hospital History and Report, 1944, National Archives, Washington, D.C., RG 112.

34. Anderson, Annual Nursing Report, 1944.

35. Ibid.

36. "Southern France," 30.

37. Wiltse, *The Medical Department*, 395; Madej, *U.S. Army Order of Battle*, 105.

38. Christopher Argyle, *Chronology of World War II* (New York: Exeter Books, 1980), 163; "Southern France," 11–12.

39. Anderson, Annual Nursing Report, 1944.

CHAPTER THIRTEEN: CONFRONTING THE SIEGFRIED LINE

1. Maj. Frances Miernicke Plenert, USA, NC (Ret.), interview with authors, Augusta, Georgia, July 2001.

2. Ibid.

3. Ibid.

4. Ibid.

5. "Rhineland: 15 September 1944–21 March 1945" *The U.S. Army Campaigns of World War II* (Washington, D.C.: U.S. Army Center of Military History), pub. 72–25, 8.

6. Graham A. Cosmas and Albert E. Cowdrey, *The Medical Department: Medical Ser-*

vice in the European Theater of Operations (Washington, D.C.: U.S. Army Center of Military History, 1992), 354.

7. "Rhineland," 12.

8. Evelyn Anderson Blank, 93rd Evacuation Hospital Annual Nursing Report, 1944, National Archives, Washington, D.C., RG 112.

9. Carl A. White, ed., "93rd Evacuation Hospital During World War II," National Archives, Washington, D.C., RG 112, 28–30.

10. Charles Coolidge, interview with authors, Atlanta, Georgia, May 2002.

11. Ibid.; *Medal of Honor of the United States Army* (Washington, D.C.: Government Printing Office, 1948), 301.

12. Cosmas and Cowdrey, *Medical Service in the European Theater of Operations*, 266–67, 326–27, 336, 441.

13. Ibid., 348.

14. W. Victor Madej, *The U.S. Army Order of Battle: Mediterranean and Europe, 1942–1945* (Allentown, Pa.: Game Publishing Co., 1984), 104.

15. Cosmas and Cowdrey, *Medical Service in the European Theater of Operations*, 350.

16. Ibid., 351.

17. Ibid.

18. Lt. Martha Cameron, letter to Mr. E. H. Cameron, Nutley, New Jersey, 6 September 1944.

19. Lt. Col. Martha Cameron, USAF, NC (Ret.), interview with authors, Atlanta, Georgia, November 2001.

20. Capt. Jean Truckey, Chief Nurse, 67th Evacuation Hospital, "American Nurses on European Battlefields," U.S. Army Military History Institute, Carlisle, Pa.—Early 1940s box, 22.

21. Ibid.

22. Ibid.

23. Ibid.

24. Cosmas and Cowdrey, *Medical Service in the European Theater of Operations*, 332.

25. Evelyn M. Monahan and Rosemary Neidel, *Albanian Escape: The True Story of U.S. Army Nurses Behind Enemy Lines* (Lexington: University of Kentucky Press, 1999), 21.

26. Rheba Whittle Tobiason, Diary, U.S. Army Military History Institute, Carlisle, Pa.—Early 1940s box, 2.

27. Ibid., Lt. Col. Mary E. V. Frank, AN, "The Forgotten POW: 2nd Lt. Reba Z. Whittle, ANC," U.S. Army War College, Carlisle Barracks, Pa.—February 1990, 11.

28. Tobiason, Diary, 3.

29. Ibid.

30. Ibid.

31. Ibid., 3–4.

32. Ibid., 4.

33. Ibid.

34. *Prisoners of War Bulletin*, 3 (1945), American Red Cross, Washington, D.C.

35. Martha Nash Jones, interview with authors, Atlanta, Georgia, January 1992.

36. Ibid.

37. Ibid.

38. Ibid.

39. Charles Whiting, *The Battle of Hurtgen Forest* (New York: Da Capo Press, 2000), xi.

40. Lt. Col. Paul Skogsberg, USA (Ret.), interview with authors, Atlanta, Georgia, March 2002.

41. Lt. Col. Martha Cameron, USAF, NC (Ret.), interview with authors, Lexington, Kentucky, August 2001.

42. Lt. Col. Martha Cameron, USAF, NC (Ret.), interview with authors, Atlanta, Georgia, November 2002.

43. War Diary, 48th Surgical Hospital, 10 February 1941–1 May 1943; 128th Evacuation Hospital 1 May 1943–1 June 1945; 18 November 1944 entry, National Archives, Washington, D.C., RG 112.

44. Gilbert Smith, interview with authors, Atlanta, Georgia, January 2001.

45. Cameron interview, August 2001.

46. War Diary, 128th Evacuation Hospital, 6 December 1944 entry.

47. Cameron interview, August 2001.

48. Maj. Frances Miernicke Plenert, USA, NC (Ret.), interview with authors, Augusta, Georgia, July 2001.

49. Ibid.

50. Ibid.

51. Ibid.

52. Stephen E. Ambrose, *Citizen Soldiers: The U.S. Army from the Normandy Beaches to the Bulge to the Surrender of Germany* (New York: Simon & Schuster, 1997), 185.

PART FOUR

CHAPTER FOURTEEN: THE BATTLE OF THE BULGE

1. Graham A. Cosmas and Albert E. Cowdrey, *The Medical Department: Medical Service in the European Theater of Operations* (Washington, D.C.: U.S. Army Center of Military History, 1992), 393.

2. Lt. Col. Martha Cameron, USAF, NC (Ret.), interview with authors, Atlanta, Georgia, November 2002.

3. Ibid.; Lt. Col. Martha Cameron, USAF, NC (Ret.), interview with authors, Louisville, Kentucky, August 2001.

4. Capt. Jean Truckey, Chief Nurse, 67th Evacuation Hospital, "American Nurses on European Battlefields," U.S. Army Military History Institute, Carlisle, Pa.—Early 1940s box, 8.

5. Stephen E. Ambrose, *Citizen Soldiers: The U.S. Army from the Normandy Beaches to the Bulge to the Surrender of Germany* (New York: Simon & Schuster, 1997), 354–56.

6. Cameron interview, November 2002.

7. Oliver Sorlye, interview with authors, Atlanta, Georgia, January 2002.

8. Agatha Dohr Greible, interview with authors, Louisville, Kentucky, August 2002.

9. Truckey, "American Nurses on European Battlefields," 9.

10. Ibid., 10.

11. Martha Nash Jones, interview with authors, Atlanta, Georgia, January 1992.

12. Ibid.

13. Col. James Vance, USA (Ret.), interview with authors, Decatur, Georgia, November 2002.

14. Fred Headrick, interview with authors, Chattanooga, Tennessee, October 2000.

15. Ibid.

16. Ibid.

17. Ibid.

18. Greible interview.

19. Ibid.

20. Cameron interview, August 2001.

21. Sorlye interview; Loren Butts, interview with authors, Atlanta, Georgia, January 2002.

22. Lt. Col. Martha Cameron, USAF, NC (Ret.), interview with authors, Atlanta, Georgia, October 2002.

23. Lt. Martha Cameron, letter to Mr. E. H. Cameron, Nutley, New Jersey, 28 December 1944, Belgium.

24. Edna Browning, interview with authors, Louisville, Kentucky, August 2001.

25. Greible interview.

26. Ibid.

27. Ibid.

28. Annual Report of the 12th Field Hospital, 1945, National Archives, Washington, D.C., RG 112, 5.

29. Cosmas and Cowdrey, *Medical Service in the European Theater of Operations*, 489.

30. Col. John Lada, MSC, USA, ed., *Medical Statistics in World War II* (Washington, D.C.: Office of the Surgeon General, Department of the Army, 1975), 540, 1190.

31. I. C. B. Dear and M. R. D. Foot, eds., *Oxford Companion to World War II* (New York: Oxford University Press, 2001), 39–40; Danny S. Parker, *Battle of the Bulge: Hitler's Ardennes Offensive 1944–1945* (Conshohocken, Pa.: Combined Books, 1999), 297; Charles B. MacDonald, *The Mighty Endeavor: The American War in Europe* (New York: Da Capo Press, 1992), 452.

32. MacDonald, *The Mighty Endeavor*, 451–52; "Rhineland: 15 September 1944–21 March 1945" (Washington, D.C., U.S. Army Center of Military History), pub. 72–25, 8; Cosmas and Cowdrey, *Medical Service in the European Theater of Operations*, 395–96.

CHAPTER FIFTEEN: BATTLE OF THE RHINELAND

1. Jeffrey J. Clarke and Robert Ross Smith, *The European Theater of Operations: Riviera to the Rhine* (Washington, D.C.: U.S. Army Center of Military History, 1993), 533–35, 555–57.

2. Lillie Peterson Homuth, interview with authors, Louisville, Kentucky, August 2001.

3. Ibid.

4. Maj. Frances Miernicke Plenert, ANC (Ret.), interview with authors, Augusta, Georgia, July 2001.

5. Ibid.

6. Ibid.

7. Ibid.

8. Ibid.

9. Ibid.

10. Major Edith Aynes, USA, NC (Ret.), *From Nightingale to Eagle* (Englewood Cliffs, N.J.: Prentice-Hall, 1973), 268.

11. U.S. Army Nurse Corps, Chief Nurse Diary for the Months of October–December 1944, U.S. Army Military History Institute, Carlisle, Pa.—Early 1940s, box 3, and entry for 11 December 1944; Ayres, *From Nightingale to Eagle*, 269.

12. Ayres, *From Nightingale to Eagle*, 268.

13. Col. Mary T. Sarnecky, USA, (Ret.), *A History of the U.S. Army Nurse Corps* (Philadelphia: University of Pennsylvania Press, 1999), 316; Col. Robert V. Piemonte, ANC, USAR, and Major Cindy Gurney, ANC, eds., *Highlights in the History of the Army Nurse Corps* (Washington, D.C.: U.S. Army Center of Military History, 1987), 30–31.

14. Alice McKoy Ishmael, interview with authors, Atlanta, Georgia, November 1990.

15. Mary Elizabeth Carnegie, *The Path We Tread: Blacks in Nursing, 1854–1984* (Philadelphia: J. B. Lippincott, 1986), 168–173; Sarnecky, *A History of the Army Nurse Corps*, 171.

16. "Nurses' Pay Cause Backed: Eberharter to Offer Bill to Equalize Rate," *New York Times*, 24 September 1942, 1.

17. Piemonte and Gurney, eds., *Highlights in the History of the Army Nurse Corps*, 17, 20; Sarnecky, *A History of the U.S. Army Nurse Corps*, 291.

18. Aynes, *From Nightingale to Eagle*, 266.

19. Quoted in ibid., 263.

20. Ibid., 269.

21. Ibid.

22. An Act to Insure Adequate Medical Care for the Armed Forces, 9 January 1945, National Archives, Washington, D.C., RG 112.

23. Aynes, *From Nightingale to Eagle*, 269.

24. Ibid., 272.

25. Lt. Martha Cameron letter to Mr. E. H. Cameron, Nutley, New Jersey, 24 February 1945, Belgium.

26. Martha Nash Jones, interview with authors, Atlanta, Georgia, January 1992.

27. Ibid.

28. Ibid.

29. Lt. Col. Martha Cameron, USAF, NC (Ret.), interview with authors, Louisville, Kentucky, August 2001.

30. Ibid.

CHAPTER SIXTEEN: THE SURRENDER OF GERMANY

1. Maj. Frances Miernicke Plenert, ANC (Ret.), interview with authors, Augusta, Georgia, July 2001.

2. Ibid.

3. *Spearhead in the West: The Third Armored Division, 1941–45* (Nashville, Tenn.: Battery Press, 1980), 148.

4. Ibid.

5. Ibid.

6. Ibid.

7. I. C. B. Dear and M. R. D. Foot, eds., *Oxford Companion to World War II* (New York: Oxford University Press, 2001), 241.

8. *Spearhead in the West*, 149.

9. Michael Hoover, "Falls Church's U.S. Army Major (Ret.) Eddie Willner Reunites with Soldiers Who Saved His Life in WWII," *Falls Church* [Virginia] *News-Press*, 19 September 2002, 12.

10. Tamara Jones, "Thanking 'the Boys' Who Gave Him Life," *Washington Post*, 16 September 2002, A18.

11. Fred Headrick, interview with authors, Chattanooga, Tennessee, October 2000.

12. Martha Nash Jones, interview with authors, Atlanta, Georgia, January 1992.

13. Lillie Peterson Homuth, interview with authors, Florence, Kentucky, September 2001.

14. Edna Browning, interview with authors, Louisville, Kentucky, August 2001.

15. Graham A. Cosmas and Albert E. Cowdrey, *The Medical Department: Medical Service in the European Theater of Operations* (Washington, D.C.: U.S. Army Center of Military History, 1992), 561.

16. Gilbert Smith, interview with authors, Atlanta, Georgia, January 2002; 128th Evacuation Hospital Surgical Report, 1945, National Archives, Washington, D.C., RG 112.

17. Brendan Phibbs, MD, *The Other Side of Time: A Combat Surgeon in World War II* (Boston: Little, Brown, 1987), 315.

18. Ibid., 317.

19. Helen Richert, questionnaire, U.S. Army Military History Institute, Carlisle, Pa.—Early 1940s box.

20. Plenert interview.

21. Phibbs, *The Other Side of Time*, 326.

22. Lillie Peterson Homuth, letter to the authors, 15 October 2000.

23. Martin Gilbert, *The Second World War: A Complete History* (New York: Henry Holt, 1989), 555–59.

24. Walter C. Langer, *The Mind of Adolf Hitler: The Secret Wartime Report* (New York: Basic Books, 1972), 266.

25. Oliver Sorlye, interview with authors, Atlanta, Georgia, January 2002.

26. Lillie Peterson Homuth interview.

27. Plenert interview.

28. Phibbs, *The Other Side of Time*, 328.

29. Ibid., 329.

30. Ibid., 330.

31. Plenert interview.

EPILOGUE: FORGETTING AND REMEMBERING

1. Edward Rosenbaum, MD, former Captain, U.S. Army Medical Corps, "Wartime Nurses: A Tribute to the Unsung Veterans," *New Choices* (July 1989), 24–25.

2. Lt. Ruth G. Haskell, ANC, *Helmets and Lipstick* (New York: G. P. Putnam's Sons, 1944), 112.

3. Ruth Hindman Balch, interview with authors, Atlanta, Georgia, November 2000.

4. Martha Nash Jones, interview with authors, Atlanta, Georgia, January 1992.

5. Claudine Glidewell Doyle, interview with authors, Atlanta, Georgia, October 2000.

6. Balch interview.

7. Frances Miernicke Plenert, interview with authors, Augusta, Georgia, July 2001.

8. Alice McKoy Ismael, interview with authors, Atlanta, Georgia, November 1990.

9. Billie Stone, interview with authors, Atlanta, Georgia, March 2002.

10. Claudine Glidewell Doyle, interview with authors, Atlanta, Georgia, September 2002.

BIBLIOGRAPHY

An Act to Insure Adequate Medical Care for the Armed Forces, 9 January 1945, National Archives, Washington, D.C., RG 112.

"Action at Anzio: Mud and Mountains in Italy." *Tank Magazine*, 17 March 1944, 12–13.

Allen, Max S. *Medicine Under Canvas: A War Journal of the 77th Evacuation Hospital.* Kansas City, Mo.: Sosland Press, 1949.

Allen, Thomas B., and Norman Polmar. *Code-Name Downfall: The Secret Plan to Invade Japan—and Why Truman Dropped the Bomb.* New York: Simon & Schuster, 1995.

Ambrose, Stephen E. *Citizen Soldiers: The U.S. Army from the Normandy Beaches to the Bulge to the Surrender of Germany.* New York: Simon & Schuster, 1997.

American National Red Cross, *Uncle Sam Needs Nurses*, Washington, D.C., August 1942, American Red Cross, pamphlet 779, authors' archives, Atlanta, Ga.

Anderson, Lt. Evelyn. Annual Report of the 93rd Evacuation Hospital, Nursing Report, 1943: "Adventures of the 93rd Evacuation Hospital Nurses," National Archives, Washington, D.C., RG 112.

———. Report of the Nursing Activities for the Year of 1944, 93rd Evacuation Hospital, National Archives, Washington, D.C., RG 112.

———. Annual Report of the 93rd Evacuation Hospital, Nursing Report 1944, National Archives, Washington, D.C., RG 112.

Annual Nursing Report of the 16th Evacuation Hospital, National Archives, Washington, D.C., RG 112.

Anzio Beachhead: 22 January–May 1944. Washington, D.C.: U.S. Army Center of Military History, 1990.

Archard, Capt. Theresa, ANC. *G.I. Nightingale: The Story of an American Army Nurse.* New York: W. W. Norton & Company, 1945.

Argyle, Christopher. *Chronology of World War II.* New York: Exeter Books, 1980.

"Army Nurse Receives Purple Heart for Salerno Action." *Denison* [Kansas] *Herald*, 16 January 1944, 8.

Astor, Gerald. *The Greatest War: D-Day and the Assault on Europe.* New York: Warner Books, 2001.

Aynes, Edith. *From Nightingale to Eagle.* Englewood Cliffs, N.J.: Prentice-Hall, 1973.

Badsey, Stephen. *Normandy 1944.* Oxford: Osprey Publishing, 1990.

Bauchspies, Col. Rollin L., MC, USA. "The Courageous Medics of Anzio," *Military Medicine* (January–June 1958), a six-part series.

Benz, Wolfgang, and Barbara Distel, eds. *Dachau Review: History of Nazi Concentration Camps. Studies, Reports, Documents.* Vol. 1., Wemding, Germany: Appl, Wemding, 1988.

Binkley, Lt. Col. Hurbert L. 95th Evacuation Hospital Report and History, 1944, National Archives, Washington, D.C., RG 112.

Birdsall, Steve. *Log of the Liberators.* Garden City, N.Y.: Doubleday & Company, 1973.

Blumenson, Martin. *The Mediterranean Theater of Operations: Salerno to Cassino.* Washington, D.C.: U.S. Army Center of Military History, 1988.

Bourke-White, Margaret. *Purple Heart Valley: A Combat Chronicle of War in Italy.* New York: Simon & Schuster, 1946.

Bradley, Omar N. *A Soldier's Story.* New York: Modern Library, 1999.

"British Rescued U.S. Nurses on Hospital Ship." Report, National Archives, Washington, D.C., RG 112.

Cameron, Lt. Martha. Letters from the ETO to Mr. E. H. Cameron, Nutley, N.J., from 1 January 1944–19 March 1945.

Carnegie, Mary Elizabeth. *The Path We Tread: Blacks in Nursing, 1854–1984.* Philadelphia: J. B. Lippincott, 1986.

Churchill, Edward D., MD. *Surgeon to Soldiers: Diary and Records of the Surgical Consultant Allied Force Headquarters, World War II.* Philadelphia: J. B. Lippincott, 1972.

Clark, Gen. Mark W. *Calculated Risk.* New York: Harper & Brothers, 1950.

Clarke, Jeffery J., and Robert Ross Smith. *The European Theater of Operations: Riviera to the Rhine.* Washington, D.C.: U.S. Army Center of Military History, 1993.

Clayton, Frederick. Unpublished paper, U.S. Army Military History Institute, Carlisle, Pa.—Early 1940s box.

Coghill, R. D., and R. S. Koch, "Penicillin in Wartime Accomplishment," *Chemical and Engineering News,* 24 December 1945.

Cosmas, Graham A., and Albert E. Cowdrey. *The Medical Department: Medical Service in the European Theater of Operations.* Washington, D.C.: U.S. Army Center of Military History, 1992.

Costello, John. *Virtue Under Fire: How World War II Changed Our Social and Sexual Attitudes.* Boston: Little, Brown, 1985.

Currier, Col. Donald E., MC, USA, Commanding Officer of the 93rd Evacuation Hospital, Memorandum to Surgeon, II Corps, 12 August 1943, authors' archives, Atlanta, Ga.

Danielson, Lt. Col. Ida W., ANC. Annual Report of Army Nurse Corps—1944. Office of the Chief Surgeon European Theater of Operations, 1944, National Archives, Washington, D.C., RG 112.

Dear, I. G. B., and M. R. D. Foot, eds. *The Oxford Companion to World War II.* New York: Oxford University Press, 2001.

D'Este, Carlo. *Fatal Decision: Anzio and the Battle for Rome*. New York: HarperCollins, 1991.

————. *World War II in the Mediterranean, 1942–1945*. Chapel Hill, N.C.: Algonquin Books of Chapel Hill, 1990.

Doyle, Claudine Glidewell. "Oh, My Knocking Knees!," authors' archives, Atlanta, Ga.

Eisenhower, Gen. Dwight David. *Crusade in Europe*. Baltimore: Johns Hopkins University Press, 1997.

Elliot, Maj. Owen, AGD, Assistant Adjutant General. Memorandum to Commanding General, U.S. Armed Forces, "Determining of Status of Casualty," 26 May 1944, National Archives, Washington, D.C., RG 112.

"Ferndale Nurse Describes Hospital Ship Sinking." *Johnstown* [Pennsylvania] *Tribune*, 27 January 1944.

The Fifth Army letter to Italian Friends (leaflet). Imperial War Museum, London.

Fischer, Capt. Mary H., ANC, USA (Ret). Personal account of 95th Evacuation Hospital, National Archives, Washington, D.C., RG 112.

Frank, Lt. Col. Mary E. V., ANC. "The Forgotten POW: 2nd Lt. Reba Z. Whittle, ANC," U.S. Army War College, Carlisle Barracks, Pa.—1 February 1990.

Gilbert, Martin. *The Second World War: A Complete History*. New York: Henry Holt, 1989.

Goodenough, Simon. *War Maps: World War II, from September 1939 to August 1945, Air, Sea, and Land, Battle by Battle*. New York: Crescent Books, 1988.

Hammond, William M. "Normandy: The U.S. Army Campaigns of World War II," Washington, D.C.: U.S. Army Center of Military History, pub. 72–18.

Hapgood, David, and David Richardson. *Monte Cassino*. New York: Congdon & Weed, 1984.

Harrison, Gordon A. *Cross Channel Attack*. Washington, D.C.: U.S. Army Center of Military History, 1993.

Haskell, Lt. Ruth G. *Helmets and Lipstick*. New York: G. P. Putnam's Sons, 1944.

Hauver, Maj. Richard V., USA, MC. "Diary February 11, 1943–September 20, 1945," U.S. Army Institute of Military History, Carlisle, Pa.—Early 1940s box.

Hill, Martin. "Stranded on Anzio Beach," *Retired Officer Magazine* (April 1994), 44–49.

Hobby, Gladys L. *Penicillin: Meeting the Challenge*. New Haven: Yale University Press, 1985.

Holm, Maj. Jean. *Women in the Military: An Unfinished Revolution*. Novato, Calif.: Presido Press, 1982.

Hoover, Michael. "Falls Church's U.S. Army Major (Ret.) Eddie Willner Reunites with Soldiers Who Saved His Life in WWII," *Falls Church* [Virginia] *News-Press*, 19 September 2002, 1.

"Hospital Ship Is Sunk After Nazi Air Attack." *New York Times*, 9 October 1944.

Howe, George F. *The Mediterranean Theater of Operations: Northwest Africa: Seizing the Initiative in the West*. Washington, D.C.: U.S. Army Center of Military History, 1993.

Hyman, 1st Lt. Sidney. "The Medical Story of Anzio." Report by Historian, Medical Section, HQ Fifth Army, National Archives, Washington, D.C., RG 112.

Jeffcott, Col. George F., D.C., USA. *United States Army Dental Service in World War II.* Washington, D.C.: U.S. Army Center of Military History, 1955.

Jones, Tamara. "Thanking 'the Boys' Who Gave Him Life," *Washington Post,* 16 September 2002, A1.

Kendrick, Brig. Gen. Douglas B., MC, USA (Ret.). *Blood Program in World War II.* Washington, D.C.: U.S. Army Medical Service, 1964.

Lada, Col. John, MSC, USA, ed. *Medical Department of the United States Army: Medical Statistics in World War II.* Washington, D.C.: Office of the Surgeon General, Department of the Army, 1975.

Langer, Walter C. *The Mind of Adolf Hitler: The Secret Wartime Report.* New York: Basic Books, 1972.

Laurie, Clayton D. "Anzio: The U.S. Army Campaigns of World War II, U.S. Army." Washington, D.C., U.S. Army Center of Military History, pub. 72–19.

Lehman, Sgt. Milton. "Anzio Guns Duel; MAAF Downs 93," *Stars and Stripes,* 28 February 1944.

————. "23 Killed in Bombing of American Hospital," *Stars and Stripes,* 8 February 1944.

Levine, Capt. Robert R., MC. Unit "A" Report—33rd Field Hospital, Annual Historical Review 1944, National Archives, Washington, D.C., RG 112.

"Lt. Laura Hindman, Survivor of 2 Sinkings, Tells Experiences in Broadcast from Italy." *Johnstown* [Pennsylvania] *Democrat,* 31 January 1944.

MacDonald, Charles B. *The Mighty Endeavor: The American War in Europe.* New York: Da Capo Press, 1992.

Madej, W. Victor. *The U.S. Army Order of Battle: Mediterranean and Europe, 1942–1945.* Allentown, Pa.: Game Publishing Co., 1984.

Majdalany, Fred. *Cassino: Portrait of Battle.* London: Cassell & Co., 1957.

Mandie, Lt. Letter to unnamed recipient (copy to Lt. Mary Eaton, MDD), 15 August 1944, U.S. Army Military History Institute, Carlisle, Pa.—Early 1940s box.

Mansoor, Peter R. *The GI Offensive in Europe: The Triumph of American Infantry Divisions, 1941–1945.* Lawrence: University Press of Kansas, 1999.

Massman, Emory A. *Hospital Ships of World War II: An Illustrated Reference.* Jefferson, N.C.: McFarland & Company, 1999.

McBryde, Brenda. *Quiet Heroines.* London: Chatto & Windus/Hogarth Press, 1985.

Medal of Honor of the United States Army. Washington, D.C.: Government Printing Office, 1948.

Miller, Capt. Mamie. "A Nurse in Normandy," *Army Life and United States Army Recruiting News,* 26 (July 1944).

Monahan, Evelyn, and Rosemary Neidel. *Albanian Escape: The True Story of U.S. Army Nurses Behind Enemy Lines.* Lexington: University of Kentucky Press, 1999.

"Mrs. Balch Recalls Terrifying German Bombing Attacks." *Chattanooga News–Free Press,* 18 September 1983, B6.

Mullins, Col. William S., MSC, USA, ed. *Medical Training in World War II.* Washington, D.C.: U.S. Army Center of Military History, 1974.

Nash, Lt. Frances L. "Georgia Nurse's Own Story . . . My Three Years in a Jap Prison Camp," *Atlanta Journal Magazine,* 15 and 22 April 1945.

Natkiel, Richard. *Atlas of World War II.* New York: Bison Books, n.d.

"Needed: 50,000 Nurses." *New York Times Magazine,* 12 April 1942.

"Northern France: U.S. Army Campaign of World War II." Washington, D.C.: U.S. Army Center of Military History, pub. 72–31.

"Nurses' Pay Cause Backed: Eberharter to Offer Bill to Equalize Rate." *New York Times,* 24 September 1942, 1.

"Nurses to the Colors!" *American Journal of Nursing* 42, no. 8 (August 1942).

Parker, Danny S. *Battle of the Bulge: Hitler's Ardennes Offensive, 1944–1945.* Conshohocken, Pa.: Combined Books, 1999.

Peterman, Ivan H. "The Medics Also Fought." *Liberty,* 26 February 1944.

Phibbs, Brendan, MD. *The Other Side of Time: A Combat Surgeon in World War II.* Boston: Little, Brown, 1987.

A Pictorial History: Navy Women, 1908–1988. N.p.: WAVES National, 1990.

Piemonte, Col. Robert V., ANC, USAR, and Maj. Cindy Gurney, ANC, eds. *Highlights in the History of the Army Nurse Corps.* Washington, D.C.: U.S. Army Center of Military History, 1987.

Prisoners of War Bulletin 3 (1945), American Red Cross, Washington, D.C..

Pyle, Ernie. "American Medics on Battlefield Duty and Telephone Linemen Get Well-Earned Tribute for Noble Efforts." Syndicated column, 1943, National Archives, Washington, D.C., RG 112.

———. *Brave Men.* New York: Henry Holt, 1944.

———. *Here Is Your War: Story of G.I. Joe.* New York: World Publishing Company, 1943.

———. "Veteran Nurses in Hospital Close Behind Tunisian Front Line Just Work, Sleep, Sit, Write Letters." Syndicated newspaper column, 1943, National Archives, Washington, D.C., RG 112.

Reister, Frank A. *Medical Statistics in World War II.* Washington, D.C.: Office of the Surgeon General, Department of the Army, 1975.

Richert, Helen. Questionnaire, U.S. Army Military History Institute, Carlisle, Pa.—Early 1940s box.

Rodengen, Jeff. *The Legend of Pfizer.* Fort Lauderdale, Fla.: Write Stuff Syndicate, 1999.

Rosenbaum, Edward E., MD. "Wartime Nurses: A Tribute to the Unsung Veterans." *New Choices* (July 1989).

"Salerno: American Operations from the Beaches to the Volturno: 9 September–6 October 1943," Washington, D.C., U.S. Army Center of Military History, 1990, pub. 100–7.

Sarnecky, Col. Mary T., USA (Ret.). *A History of the U.S. Army Nurse Corps.* Philadelphia: University of Pennsylvania Press, 1999.

Scott, Sgt. Burgess H. "Hospital on Rails: First Ambulance Train in Italy Carries Wounded GIs Out of Fighting Zone." *Tank Magazine* (January 1944).

Scott, Col. Raymond, MC, USA. "Eleventh Evacuation Hospital in Sicily." *American Journal of Nursing* 43, no. 10 (October 1943).

Shortz, Capt. Gerald, USA, MC. "Anesthesia in the Combat Zone." *Bulletin of the U.S. Army Medical Department* 79 (August 1944).

Sigman, Blanche. "History of the 95th Evacuation Hospital." National Archives, Washington, D.C., RG 112.

"Southern France: The U.S. Army Campaign of World War II." Washington, D.C., U.S. Army Center of Military History, pub. 72–31.

Spearhead in the West: The Third Armored Division, 1941–1945. Nashville, Tenn.: Battery Press, 1980.

Swanson, Evelyn. 93rd Evacuation Hospital Nursing Report, 1944., National Archives, Washington, D.C., RG 112.

———. 93rd Evacuation Hospital Nursing Report, 1945. National Archives, Washington, D.C., RG 112.

Sydel, Capt. Margaret W. "An Account of the Nursing Service of the 11th Field Hospital," 1944. National Archives, Washington, D.C., RG 112.

To Bizerte with the Corps: American Forces in Action Series, 1943. Washington, D.C.: U.S. Army Center for Military History, 1990.

Tobiason, Rheba Whittle. Diary, U.S. Army Military History Institute, Carlisle, Pa.—Early 1940s box.

Tomblin, Barbara Brooks. *G.I. Nightingales: The Army Nurse Corps in World War II.* Lexington: University of Kentucky Press, 1996.

Truckey, Capt. Jean, Chief Nurse, 67th Evacuation Hospital, "American Nurses on European Battlefields," est. date 26 December 1944, U.S. Army Military History Institute, Carlisle, Pa.—Early 1940s box.

"Two Army Nurses Survive Injuries." *Terre Haute* [Indiana] *Tribune,* 16 September 1944, 2.

Untitled accounts of U.S. Army Nurses in the European Theater of Operations Concerning D-Day and D+ Patients Arriving in England, est. date June 1944, U.S. Army Military History Institute, Carlisle, Pa.—Early 1940s File.

U.S. Army Nurse Corps, Chief Nurse Diary for the Months of October–December 1944, U.S. Army Military History Institute, Carlisle, Pa.—Early 1940s, box 3.

War Diary, 48th Surgical Hospital: 10 February 1941–1 May 1943; 128th Evacuation Hospital: 1 May 1943–1 June 1945; authors' archives, Atlanta, Ga.

Weinstein, Alfred A., MD. *Barbed-Wire Surgeon.* New York: Macmillan, 1947.

Wharton, Capt. Helen. Director of Nurses, Fifth Army, letter to Lt. Col. Bernice Wilbur, 16 February 1944, U.S. Army Military History Institute, Carlisle, Pa.—Early 1940s box.

White, Carl, ed. "93rd Evacuation Hospital During World War II." National Archives, Washington, D.C., RG 112.

White, Ruth B. "At Anzio Beachhead." *American Journal of Nursing* 44 (April 1944).

Whitehead, Don. "U.S. Nurses So Seasick They Ignored Bombs South of Rome." *Stars and Stripes,* 31 January 1944, 2.

Whiting, Charles. *Kasserine: The Anatomy of Slaughter.* New York: Stein & Day, 1984.

———. *The Battle of Hurtgen Forest.* New York: Da Capo Press, 2001.

Williams, Mary H. *United States Army in World War II, Special Studies: Chronology 1941–1945.* Washington, D.C.: Department of the Army, 1960.

Wiltse, Charles M. *The Medical Department: Medical Service in the Mediterranean and Minor Theaters.* Washington, D.C.: Department of the Army, 1965.

Winter, George. *Freineux and Lamormenil: The Ardennes.* Winnipeg, Manitoba: J. J. Fedorowicz Publishing, 1994.

Wolff, Maj. Luther H. *Forward Surgeon: The Diary of Luther H. Wolff, M.D. Mediterranean Theater, World War II, 1943–45.* New York: Vantage Press, 1985.

"World War II's Human Toll." *VFW [Veterans of Foreign Wars] Magazine* (November 1991).

"Wounded Hour in Sea After Ship Sank: Nurses Cling to Raft in Wreckage." *Daily Herald*, 28 January 1944, 4.

Young, Brig. Peter, ed. *The Cassell Atlas of the Second World War.* London: Weidenfeld & Nicolson, 1999.

INTERVIEWS

Balch, Ruth Hindman. Interview with authors, Chattanooga, Tennessee, December 1991.

———. Interview with authors, Arlington, Virginia, August 2001.

———. Interview with authors, Atlanta, Georgia, November 2001.

———. Interview with authors, Atlanta, Georgia, March 2002.

Barnett, Agnes Nolan. Interview with authors, Atlanta, Georgia, June 1989.

———. Interview with authors, Atlanta, Georgia, August 1989.

Black, Martha Whorton. Interview with authors, Atlanta, Georgia, July 1989.

Blank, Evelyn Anderson. Interview with authors, Atlanta, Georgia, July 1989.

———. Interview with authors, Atlanta, Georgia, August 1989.

Browning, Edna Marie. Interview with authors, Louisville, Kentucky, August 2001.

Butts, Loren E. Interview with authors, Atlanta, Georgia, January 2002.

Cameron, Lt. Col. Martha USAF, ANC (Ret.). Interview with authors, Louisville, Kentucky, August 2001.

———. Interview with authors, Atlanta, Georgia, November 2001.

———. Interview with authors, Atlanta, Georgia, October 2002.

Coolidge, Charles. Interview with authors, Atlanta, Georgia, April 2002.

———. Interview with authors, Atlanta, Georgia, May 2002.

Cousins, Madonna Nolan. Interview with authors, Atlanta, Georgia, June 1989.

Doyle, Claudine Glidewell. Interview with authors, Atlanta, Georgia, May 2000.

———. Interview with authors, Atlanta, Georgia, August 2000.

———. Interview with authors. Florence, Kentucky, September 2000.

———. Interview with authors, Atlanta, Georgia, October 2001.

———. Interview with authors, Atlanta, Georgia, November 2001.

———. Interview with authors, Atlanta, Georgia, December 2001.

———. Interview with authors, Atlanta, Georgia, January 2002.

———. Interview with authors, Atlanta, Georgia, February 2002.

Duxbury, Marcus. Interview with authors, Atlanta, Georgia, January 2001.

Glant, Berchard L. Interview with authors, Chattanooga, Tennessee, October 2000.

Greible, Agatha Dohr. Interview with authors, Louisville, Kentucky, August 2001.

Harmon, Jodie. Interview with authors, Atlanta, Georgia, March 2002.

Headrick, Fred. Interview with authors, Chattanooga, Tennessee, October 2000.

Homuth, Lillie Peterson. Interview with authors, Florence, Kentucky, September 2000.

Ishmael, Alice McKoy. Interview with authors, Atlanta, Georgia, November 1990.

Jones, Martha Nash. Interview with authors, Atlanta, Georgia, January 1992.

Paddock, Jessie. Interview with authors, Atlanta, Georgia, October 1990.

Plenert, Maj. Frances Miernicke, USA, ANC, (Ret.). Interview with authors, Augusta, Georgia, July 2001.

———. Interview with authors, Atlanta, Georgia, January 2002.

Reichert, Helen Molony. Interview with authors, Atlanta, Georgia, March 2001.

———. Interview with authors, Atlanta, Georgia, June 2001.

———. Interview with authors, Atlanta, Georgia, July 2001.

———. Interview with authors, Louisville, Kentucky, August 2001.

———. Interview with authors, Atlanta, Georgia, September 2001.

Skogsberg, Vera Sheaffer. Interview with authors, Atlanta, Georgia, February 2002.

———. Interview with authors, Atlanta, Georgia, March 2002.

Skogsberg, Col. Paul, USA (Ret.). Interview with authors, Atlanta, Georgia, February 2002.

———. Interview with authors, Atlanta, Georgia, March 2002.

Smith, Gilbert. Interview with authors, Atlanta, Georgia, January 2002.

Sorlye, Oliver A. Interview with authors, Atlanta, Georgia, January 2002.

Stone, Billie. Interview with authors, Atlanta, Georgia, March 2002.

Tahan, Joseph. Interview with authors, Atlanta, Georgia, October 2001.

Taylor, Gerald C. Interview with authors, Atlanta, Georgia, January 2002.

Thibodeau, Bernice Walden. Interview with authors, Florence, Kentucky, September 2000.

Vance, Col. James, USA (Ret.). Interview with authors, Decatur, Georgia, November 2002.

Williams, Adeline Simonson. Interview with authors, Atlanta, Georgia, June 2001.

———. Interview with authors, Atlanta, Georgia, May 2002.

ACKNOWLEDGMENTS

We wish to express our thanks to everyone who gave their time and energy to share their World War II experiences with us, or who helped put us in touch with veterans who shared their stories.

A special thanks to: Claudine "Speedy" Glidewell Doyle, Martha "Marte" Cameron, Frances "Frenchie" Miernicke Plenert, Laura "Ruthie" Hindman Balch, Jesse Flynn, Fred Headrick, and Berchard L. Glant.

A special thanks also to our agent, Mary Tahan of Clausen, Mays & Tahan Literary Agency, for her passionate commitment: she had unswerving faith in us and our project. Not only did she find the perfect home for our book, but she read and commented on the manuscript as we were writing it, chapter by chapter. Her insights were invaluable. Our heartfelt thanks to her for traveling the beaches and battlefields of World War II with us. Two authors could not have asked for a more faithful comrade. Our gratitude also goes to Mary's partner at the agency, Stedman Mays, who provided us with guidance and support as well.

Our heartfelt and deepest thanks go to our editor and champion, Jane Garrett. Jane's encouragement has spanned nearly a decade and began when writing the story of what American military nurses did in World War II was only an idea in our heads looking for a form of expression. Without her early encouragement and suggestions, those ideas may never have made it into the pages of three books. But it is this book, *And If I Perish*, which clearly bears the gifted editing and talented teaching of Knopf's Jane Garrett. The knowledge and experience that Jane brings to the editing process are visible on every page. The wisdom and caring she shared with us are the backbone and fabric that made this book possible. We cannot imagine a more gifted editor and teacher, nor could we have asked for a more devoted champion or truer friend. She is our hero.

INDEX

Abbott Labs, 214
Acadia (ship), 180–3
Adams, Capt. John, 175–9
Adams, Maj. John E., 140, 221, 241–4, 246, 283
Adkins, Capt. Trogler F. "Trough," 175, 177–9
Aeschylus, 461
African-Americans, 127–8, 136–7, 434–5
Afrika Corps, 92
Ainsworth, Lt. Ellen G., 6–7, 272, 274–5, 284–5
Air Force, U.S., 466
Air Medal, 458
Albania, 241, 389–90
Alexander, Col. Stewart F., 198
Alexander, Field Marshal Harold, 233, 305
Allen, Gen. Terry, 152
Allison, Lt. Celia, *illus. 432*
American Broadcasting Company (ABC), 5
American Legion, 3, 4, 460
American National Red Cross, 103–5, 121, *illus. 122*, 263, 383–4, 433; Harvard Medical Field Hospital Unit, 31; Nursing Service, First Reserve of, 121–3
American Nurses Association, 121, 123, 128, 434, 438
American Revolution, 9
amputations, 422–3, 439
Anderson, Lt. Evelyn "Andy," 125–6, 144, *illus. 150*, 205, *illus. 361*, 463; at Anzio, 251, 266, 301; in France, 350, 357, 361, 370, 379; landing at Salerno of, 195; in Sicilian Campaign, 149, 151–3

Andes (ship), 294
Anvil, Operation, 352
Anzio beachhead, 235, 238–75, *illus. 256, 276, 283–302, illus. 293, 304–9, 314–16, 362, 372*; evacuation of wounded from, 278–81, *illus. 279, 280, 370*; shelling and bombing of hospital site at, 253–69, *illus. 262, 272–5, illus. 274, 287, 293–7, 299*; landing at, 233, 234, 239–41, 247, 250–1, 267, 315; sinking of hospital ship at, 241–7, 283, 459, 463
Appleby, "Mom," 125, 180, 193
Archard, Lt. Theresa, 50–1, 94, 99, 467; at Kasserine Pass, 54–5, 60–1, 69–74; in Sicilian Campaign, 157, 158, 162–3, 166–9; in Tunisia, 88–91, 96–7, 106–20
Ardennes Forest, Battle of, 402, 403, 405–26
Army, U.S., 39, 71, 143, 147, 308, 335, 344, 383, 416, 454–5, 468; blood supply of, 103, 105, 293; British attitude toward, 150; Corps of Engineers, 232; graves registration units of, 449; hospitals of, 308, 332, 349, 371 (*see also specific hospital units*); hospital ships of, *see specific ships*; hospital trains of, 224; Intelligence, 310; medals awarded to nurses in, 271, 400; Medical Department, 14, 27, 315, 451; Medical Corps, 17, 25, 56, 163, 294, 319, 339; redistribution centers of, 456; Reserve, 434; in Rome, 302; segregation of, 128; Signal Corps, 125; trench foot in, 425–6; venereal disease prevention efforts of, 211; *see also specific battalions; corps; divisions*

Army Air Forces, 70, 136, 215, 342–3, 348, 412; Air Transport Command, 383; Eighth Air Force, 342, 463; IX Air Force, 388; Ninth Air Force, 342; Ninth Carrier Command, 387–8; XV Air Force, 353, 356

Army Commendation Medal, 458

Army Nurse Corps, 6, 27, 50, 120, 170, 284, 334, 414, 427, 433–8, 463–6, *illus. 466*; draft proposed for, 433, 437–8; establishment of, 121; European theater hospital visits by head of, 400; flight nurses in, 388; male nurses excluded from, 121; Michael Reese Hospital Unit, 200; Ohio General Hospital Unit, 412; racial discrimination in, 434–5; recruitment for, 121–3, *illus. 122*, 433–4, 436–7; relative rank of officers in, 123–4, 435–6; School of, 467; Veterans Administration and, 460; volunteers for, 9, 19, 138; weight requirements for, 125–6; in World War I, 183

Army Reorganization Act (1920), 14, 123

Arnest, Col. Richard T., 74

Arnim, Gen. Jurgen von, 57, 62, 68, 118

Ashford General Army Hospital, 304

Aslakson, Lt. Anna M., 414

Atabrine, 295

Atkins, Lt. Edna, 40–1, 43–4, 46–7, *illus. 322, 326*

Atlanta Chamber of Commerce Military Affairs Task Force, 4

Auburn University, 464

Auschwitz concentration camp, 445

Austin-Wadsworth bill, 437–8

Avalanche, Operation, 176

"Axis Sally," 309, 362, 363

Aynes, Maj. Edith A., 9, 436–8

Ayres, Lt. Ginny, 63, 110–11

Bair, Lt. Cecile "Teddy," 94, 111

Balch, Lee, 463

Balch, Ruth Hindman, *see* Hindman, Lt. Ruth

Balkans, 353

Bareham, Lt. Nina L., 414

Barrett, Joe, 178

Barry, Madelaine, 467–8

Baruch, Bernard, 304

Bataan Death March, 463

battalion aid stations, 29

battle fatigue, 106, 297–8

Battle of the Bulge, *see* Ardennes Forest, Battle of

Bauchspies, Col. Rollin L., 276, 298–9, 301

Bauer, Capt. Marshall, 258–61

Baylor University, 264

bazooka shells, 448 *and illus.*

Belgium, 378, 381, 384–6, 395, 406, 409–11, 421, 425, 454, 459

Bell Telephone, 132

Belleau Wood, Battle of, 385

Benedict, St., 277

Bentley, Pete, 307–8

Berent, Ray, 207

Berret, Lt. Anna Bess, 140, 241–4

Billingsworth, Alfred, 300

Blake, Lt. Henry S., 105

Blanchfield, Col. Florence, 6–7, 400, 433, 436

Blesse, Col. Henry S., 287

blood supply, 102–5, 293–4, 381–4, *illus. 382*

Bolton, Frances P., 434, 436

Bonser, Harold, 390

Borgmeyer, Capt. Henry, 40, 41, 43, 44

Bos, Maj. Howard, 299, 363–8, *illus. 365*

"Bouncing Betty" antipersonnel mines, 99, 107

Bourke-White, Margaret, 218–20

Bowman Field (Kentucky), 389

Bradley, Gen. Omar, 110, 119, 165–6, 342–3, 347–8, 376, 406, 442

Braun, Eva, 452

Breckenridge, Camp (Kentucky), 131–2

Brenner, Lt. Mary, *illus. 122*

Brigham, Lt. Amy, 89

Bright, Chester D., 390

Britain, 20, 316, 328, 342; Battle of, 420; bombing of, 213; evacuation of wounded to, 377–8, 388, 389; Land Army in, 438; Lend-Lease program for, 217; Harvard Medical Red Cross Field Hospital Unit in, 31; National Service in, 437–8; penicillin production in, 212–13; Special Operations Executive (SOE) of, 358, 389; U.S. Army hospital personnel in, 229–32, 332, 340, 435

British forces: in Crimean War, 9; Eighth Army, 57, 152, 153, 167, 239; Eighth Infantry, 341; First Division, 239, 247, 265; 46th Royal Tank Regiment, 239; in Germany, 453; hospital ships, 180–95 (see also *Dinard; Leinster; Newfoundland; St. Andrew; St. David*); in Italian Campaign, 156, 167, 174, 204, 206, 208–9, 233, 251, 252, 255, 260, 267, 309; 95th General Hospital, 140; in Normandy invasion, 319, 344, 347, 349; in North African Campaign, 32, 33, 36, 48, 49, 62, 63, 66–8, 74, 103,

114, 140; as POWs, 393; Queen Alexandra's Imperial Military Nursing Service, 245, 280; Royal Air Force, 349; Royal Army Medical Corps (RAMC), 245–6, 280; Royal Navy, 33; in Southern France invasion, 360; X Corps, 204

Brittingham, Lt. Doris, *illus. 320, 322, 326, 466*

Brix, Lt. Anne K., 310, 314, 315

Bronze Star, 6, 147, 272, *illus. 305,* 306, 458

Brooklyn Navy Yard, 135–6

Browning, Lt. Edna Marie, *illus. 320, 322,* 330, 422, 447, *illus. 466,* 467

Buchenwald concentration camp, 450

Buckley, Lt. Ruth D., 262, *illus. 368*

Buffalo, Operation, 304, 309

burn victims, 419–20

Burton, Maj. Frank M., 342

Bush, Vannevar, 214

Butler, Gen. Fredrick, 363

Butts, Loren, 77–8, 339, 421

buzz bombs, *see* V-1 and V-2 rockets

Cable Network News (CNN), 5

Calcaterra, Cpl., 79

Cameron, Helen, 438–9

Cameron, Lt. Martha "Marte," *illus. 331,* 400–1, 405–6, 424–5, 438–40, 466 *and illus.,* 467; during Ardennes Forest offensive, 408–9, 411–12, 421–2; in Belgium, 384–5, 398–9; in England, 230–2, *illus. 320;* in Normandy invasion, *illus. 322,* 325–7, 336–42, 348

Canadians, 319, 344, 347–9

Carnegie Institution, 214

Carney, Capt. Henry J., 38, 44, 46, 55, 111, 114–16

Carter, Christopher B., 264

Carter, Shirley, 214–15

Casement, Lt. Sally J., 414

Chaffee, Camp (Arkansas), 284

Chain, Ernest, 213

Charlemagne, 394

chemical weapons, 134–5

Churchill, Col. Edward D., 56, 103–5, 215, 383

Churchill, Winston, 33, 326, 352, 353, 420, 426

Civil War, 9, 106, 426

Claiborne, Camp (Louisiana), 138

Clark, Gen. Mark, 33, 36, 171, 221–2, 234–5, 238, 241, 265, 292, 303–6, *illus. 305,* 429–30

Clark Field (Philippines), 15

Clayton, Frederick, 263, 264

clearing stations, 29, 177–8

Coast Guard Women's Reserve (SPARs), 19, 436

Cobra, Operation, 343

collecting companies, 29, 226, 245

Colosseum, 314, *illus. 315*

Columbia Broadcasting System (CBS), 5

Commandos, U.S. Army, 239

concentration camps, 445–7, 449–51, 454–5, 464–5

Congress, U.S., 5, 14, 19, 121, 165, 431, 433, 434, 437, 460

Coolidge (ship), 15

Coolidge, Charles, 93, 235–6, 281, 380, 466

Coolidge, Gen. Charles, Jr., 466

Cooper, Everett, 124, 125

Cowell, Gen. Ernest M., 73–4

Crawford, Col. John L., 413

Crimean War, 9

Currier, Col. Donald E., 163–5, 370

Cutler, Col. Elliott C., 383

Dachau concentration camp, 447, 449–51, 454–6, 464

Darby, Col. William O., 152, 247, 309, 311

Darlan, Adm. Jean, 32

Davis, Col. Benjamin O., 136

Davis, Gen. T. J., 107–8

DeConcini, Dennis, 460

Devers, Gen. Jacob, 428

DeVito, Capt. Michael P., *illus. 320,* 339, 424

D-Day: Anzio, 240–1, 247, 251, 267; Normandy, 319–22, 330, 341, 347, 358, 377, 381; North Africa, 3, 20, 25–55, 137, 150, 151, 166, 229, 321, 400; Salerno, 176, 177; Sicily, 149–51

Dinard (ship), 279, 285

displaced persons, 447

Distinguished Flying Cross, 458

Distinguished Service Medal, 6, 458

Dohr, Lt. Agatha, 412, 420, 423–4, *illus. 466*

Don Passage, Camp (Morocco), 142

Donaghy, George, 175–8

Dönitz, Adm. Karl, 452, 453

Dora labor camp, 444–5

Downfall, Operation, 456

Doyle, Claudine Glidewell, *see* Glidewell, Lt. Claudine

Doyle, Lt. Frank, 128–32, 135, 186, 190, 463

Dragoon, Operation, 302, 350–54, 360, 371

Druck, Donald E., 263
Duchess of Bedford (ship), 179–80, 193
Duckworth, Col. J. W., 16–18
Duxbury, Marcus, 161, 328

Ebbert, Capt. Charles A. "Chuck," 60–1, 94
Egypt, 57
8th Evacuation Hospital, 137, 202
Eighteenth Infantry Division, 36
Eighty-second Airborne Division, 142–3, 204,
    267, 322, 329, 377, 378
Eighty-fifth Division, 311, 313
Eighty-eighth Division, 311, 313
813th Medical Air Evacuation Squadron, 388
815th Engineers, 262
Eisenhower, Gen. Dwight D., 36, 143, 151,
    165–6, 176, 348, 353, 376–8, 380, 406, 412,
    427, 434, 453, 459
11th Evacuation Hospital, 156, 282, 301
11th Field Hospital, 156, 217–20, 235–7,
    358–65, 373–6, 430–2, 442–4
El Guettar, Battle of, 99, 101, 139
Elisofon, Eliot, 74
Ellis, Lt. Pearl T., 130
endocarditis, bacterial, 215
England General Army Hospital (Atlantic
    City), 463
English, Lt. Helen, 106
Equal Rights Amendment (ERA), 461
Ernest Hinds (ship), 358–9
Erph, Capt. Stanley F., 340
Ester, Queen, 21
Estes, Pvt., 299
European Theater of Operations (ETO), 216,
    217, 380–1, 431
evacuation hospitals, 30; *see also specific hospitals*
eyes, artificial, 339–40

Farabough, Lt. Frances, *illus. 320*, 326, 339,
    424–5
Farquhar, Lt. La Verne "Tex," 229, 251, 269–71
fevers of undetermined origin (FUOs), 160
field hospitals, 29–30, 220; *see also specific
    hospitals*
Fifth Army, 176, 222, 233, 238, 295, 298, 299,
    302, 303, 311, 429
XV Corps, 378
15th Evacuation Hospital, 111, 256, 273, 281,
    294–5
Fifteenth Infantry, 248
51st Evacuation Hospital, 378
51st Field Hospital, 321

51st Medical Battalion, 63
52nd Medical Battalion, 238, 240, 295,
    301–2
54th Medical Battalion, 136
56th Evacuation Hospital, 254, 257, 263,
    271–2, *illus. 274*, 274–5, 284, 286–7, 291–2,
    296, 298, 299–300
59th Evacuation Hospital, 157
First Armored Division, 62, 68, 70, 71, 77,
    247, 313
First Army, 321, 343, 346, 371, 377, 378, 382,
    384, 394, 406, 447–9, 453
First Infantry Division, 52–4, 58, 62, 63, 68,
    75, 98, 118, 126, 152, 265; Reconnaissance
    Battalion, 398
1st Medical Battalion, 63
Fischer, Lt. Mary, 186, 188, 189, 192–3
Fisher, Lt. Dorothy, 188
Fisher, Lt. Vaughn, 85
501st Medical Collection Company, 336
502nd Medical Collection Company, 345
509th Parachute Infantry Regiment, 142
Fleming, Alexander, 212–13
Florey, Howard, 213
Flynn, Jesse, *illus. 465*
Flynn, John, 465
Foisie, Jack, 263, 264
41st Hospital Train, 224–5
42nd Field Hospital, 327, 328, 330
42nd Hospital Train, 225
43rd General Hospital, 300
44th Evacuation Hospital, 333–6, 344, 395–6,
    413–16, 439–40, 446
45th Evacuation Hospital, 335
45th Field Hospital, 321
Forty-fifth Infantry Division, 163, 176, 225–6,
    290, 353, 360, 364–5, 371, 378, 467
47th Armored Medical Battalion, 82
48th Surgical Hospital, 50, *illus. 58*, 88–91,
    illus. 100, 106–7, 111, 113, 229, 400, *illus.
    466*; in Algeria, 52–5, 88–94, *illus. 92*; at
    Kasserine Pass, 56–8, 60–3, 69–73, 75,
    77–8, 82, 83, 85–7; landing in North Africa
    of, 20, 25–32, 40–9, 120, 137, 151; in
    Tunisia, 94–102, 107–11; *see also* 128th
    Evacuation Hospital
Forbes, Lt. David, 390
forced labor camps, 444–5
Ford, Sgt. John, 111–16
Forsee, Col. James H., 140, 298
Foss, Lt. Anita "Foo," *illus. 134*, 142, 183
4th Auxiliary Surgical Group, 336

4th Convalescent Hospital, 414–15

Fourth Division, 397

402nd Collecting Company, 295

France, 3, 241, 277, 406, 453, 459; advance through, 375–402; invasion of, 174, 231, 302, 303, 304, 350–72 (*see also* Normandy invasion); map of, 323; North African colonies of, 32–3, 36, 39–41, 46, 49, 50, 57, 69, 138, 212; surrender to Germany of, 20; *see also* Free French forces

Francis, Lt. Mary, 85

Fredendall, Gen. Lloyd R., 63, 86

Free French forces (Forces Françaises de l'Intérieur; FFI), 32, 358, 360, 378

French Expeditionary Corps, 312

French Foreign Legion, 41, 47, 53, 57

"friendly fire" incidents, 342–31

Friedeburg, Adm. Hans, 453

Friedlund, Lt. Doris, 39, 66, 325

G.I. Bill, 456–7, 459

Gabès, Battle of, 139

Gallagher, Col. Leonard B., 234

gangrene, 73

general hospitals, 30; *see also specific hospitals*

Geneva Conventions, 18, 20, 49, 50, 60, 70, 173, 256, 268, 286, 296, 391

George Washington University, 267

Georgia League of Women Voters, 461

German forces, 32, 33, 219, 277, 315, 317, 354, 357, 375; at Anzio, 234, 235, 239–43, 248, 251, 253, 255, 256, 259, 265–9, 273–6, 279, 283–5, 289–91, 294–7, 299, 305–7, 309–10, 370; Ardennes Forest offensive of, 401, 403, 405–26; defense of Siegfried Line by, 373, 376–8, 380–5, 389, 394–401; on eastern front, 174; Gestapo, 392; along Gustav Line, 225, 226, 233, 276, 306, 313; horses and mules used in Italy by, 311–12; hospital ships bombed by, see *Newfoundland; St. David;* Luftwaffe, 171–3, 213, 344; medical personnel captured by, 390–3; at Monte Cassino, 276–8, 281; at Naples, 204–10; in Normandy, 320, 321, 324–6, 328, 332, 335–7, 341–9; in North Africa, 32, 33, 52, 57–62, 67–72, 74–5, 77, 79, 82–6, 88, 91, 95, 105–9, 116–18, 140, 141, 170, 182; Panzers, 74, 118, 347, 411; at Rapido River, 235–7; at Salerno, 177, 178, 185; in Sicily, 149, 152, 157, 161, 163, 166, 167; in Southern France, 351, 354, 360–4, 368,

371; SS, 141, 266, 374, 392, 405, 411–13, 445, 446, 450; submarines of, 136, 324; Wehrmacht, 141, 374, 392; in World War I, 134

Germany, 33, 36, 86, 371, 459; chemical weapons of, 134–5; declaration of war on U.S., 19, 51, 122; fall of France to, 20; map of, 407; invasion of, 353, 372, 427–8, 439–41; liberation of France from, 317, 319, 358; propaganda of, 309, 349, 363; surgical instruments from, 216; surrender of, 335, 442–57; and surrender of Italy, 174, 176; VE-Day in, 3, 453; Vichy French and, 32, 33

Gettysburg, Battle of, 426

Ghoumes, 226–7

Ghurkas, 226

Gilbert, Lt. Ethel, 414

Giraud, Gen. Henri, 33

Glant, Berchard L. "Junior," *illus. 248,* 248–50, 257–8, 266–7, 278–81, 285, 300–1, 306–8, *illus. 308,* 464

Glidewell, Lt. Claudine "Speedy," 120, 124–33, *illus. 127, 134,* 135, 136, 281–2, 463, 467, *illus. 468;* aboard *Newfoundland,* 183, 185–7, 189–95; at Anzio, 251–3, 256–61, 263, 272–3; awarded Purple Heart, *illus. 207;* in Italy, 202, 204, 206–10, 222–3, 226, 227, 355–6; in North Africa, 137, 142–3, 171–2, 180–2; transported to Salerno, 196, 197

Glidewell, Hazel, 124–5, 190

Glidewell, Stuart, 124–5, 190

Goebbels, Joseph, 452

Goering, Field Marshall Hermann, 452

GOLD Beach, 347

gonorrhea, 210–11, 215

Gordon, Lt. June, 126, *illus. 134,* 135

Gorion, Madame, 113, 114

Grady Memorial Hospital School of Nursing (Atlanta), 9, 11, 17

Grant (ship), 334

Grant, Camp (Illinois), 128

Great Depression, 11

Greene, William, 207

Griebel, Agatha Dohr, *see* Dohr, Lt. Agatha

Grisholm (ship), 394

Grove, Captain Samuel A. C. "Chappy," 87, 94, 110

Guadalcanal, Battle of, 461

Gustav Line, 225–6, 233, 238, 276, 302, 305, 306, 313

Hague Conventions, 173, 181, 182, 185, 187, 242, 350

Hancock, Lt. Sue, *illus. 268*

Hansen, Isabelle Wheeler, *see* Wheeler, Lt. Isabelle

Hansen, Lt. Neil, 136, 180, 207, 208, 253, 269, 463

Hanser, Col. Samuel A., 271

Hanson, Capt. Frederick R., 106, 297

Hardin, Maj. Robert C., 383

Harmon, Jodie, 95

Harrison, Lt. Mary W., 262, 263

Hart, Lt. Margaret, *illus. 320*

Harvard University, 339; Medical Red Cross Field Hospital Unit, 31

Haskell, Carl, 27, 44, 51

Haskell, Lt. Ruth G., 27–8, *illus. 28*, 37–47, 51–2, 58–60, 63, 66, 75–87, 120, 466, 467

Hauver, Capt. Richard V., 294–6, 300, 310–11, 314, 353–4

Hawley, Gen. Paul R., 217, 380–3, 386–8

Hay, Camp (Philippines), 15

Headrick, Fred, *illus. 417*, 417–19, 446, 464

Helm, Capt. Kathryn, *illus. 320*, 401

Helms, Jesse, 463

Henry, Lt. Leona, 30

Henshaw, Esther, 299, 304

Hill, Sgt., 388–91

Hill 609, Battle of, 117

Himmler, Heinrich, 452

Hindman, Lt. Laura Ruth, 138, 140, 169–71, 183, 187–8, 194, 196–7, 217–22, *illus. 218*, 241–7, *illus. 246*, 282–3, 460, 463

Hitler, Adolf, 20, 158, 334–5, 372, 397, 410, 451–2; Ardennes Forest offensive of, 402, 406, 412–13; death of, 452–3; defense of Aachen ordered by, 394; Gustav Line of, 225; during Normandy invasion, 347; Russians and, 174; SS and, 374; V-1 and V-2 targeting of civilians ordered by, 396; West Wall of, 377

Hobler, Capt. Ross, 364–8, *illus. 365*, 443

Hodge, Gen. Courtney, 346, 371, 378, 384, 394

Hodges, Lt. Evelyn, 49

Holbrook (ship), 15

Homuth, Ernest, 463

Homuth, Lillie Peterson, *see* Peterson, Lt. Lillie

Hoppe, Lt. Ruby L., 263

Hornback, Margaret, 63

House of Representatives, U.S., 438

Howie, Maj. Thomas D., 342

Hoyland, Lt. Elmer, 446

Huachuca, Fort (Arizona), 128, 464

Huddleston, Col. Jarrett B., 267

Hulbert, Lt. Eleanor, *illus. 268*

Hume, Rita, 270

Hürtgen Forest, Battle of, 397–9

Husky, Operation, 144, 150

Hyman, Sidney, 155

Imperial Chemical Industries (ICI), 213

influenza, 215

Inkpen, "Inky," 108

Irwin Army Community Hospital (Kansas), 126

Ishamel, Alice McKoy, *see* McKoy, Lt. Alice

Ishmael, Col. Lauren, 464

Ishmael, Lt. John R., 464

Italy, 3, 20, 147, 198–237, 292, 304, 321–2, 350, 353, 357, 380, 389, 453, 459; map of, 203; surrender of, 176, 177, 182, 185, 451; declaration of war on U.S. by, 51, 122; and North African Campaign, 32, 33, 36, 47, 52, 57, 60, 73, 105, 118, 141; *see also* Anzio beachhead; Monte Cassino; Rome; Salerno; Sicilian campaign

Jamison, Capt. William E. (Jamie), 62, 63

Japan, 309, 335, 453, 454, 456, 462; declaration of war, 19, 122; Pearl Harbor attacked by, 15, 19, 20, 27, 50, 51, 124, 138, 334; Philippines captured by, 15–19; POWs of, 5, 9, 19, 304, 334, 393, 396–7, 446, 460, 463–4

Jefferson Medical College, 294

Jews, 349, 445

Jodl, Gen. Alfred, 453

John Erickson (ship), 140

JUNO Beach, 347

Karff, Maj., 455

Kasserine Pass, Battle of, 56–88, 91–2, 100, 153, 210, 467

Keefer, Chester, 214, 215

Kelly, Lt. Marie, 40, 41, 43, 44, 46, 47, 72, 117

Kempner, Frank, *illus. 365*, 367

Kesselring, Gen. Albert, 306

Kessler, Lt. Artemese, 128

Kilmer, Camp (New Jersey), 294

Kimbrough, Emily, 135

King, Gen. Edward, 19

Kingston, Capt. Louis G., 76, 78

Kirk, Gen. Norman T., 105, 383

Kluge, Field Marshal Günther von, 347

Knecht, Bob, 253, *illus. 254*, 260–1, 263

Koenig, Gen. Pierre-Joseph, 358
Korda, Capt. Henry A., 263
Korean War, 4, 465
Krist, Cpl., 75, 79
Kruzic, Lt. Genevieve, 63, 68, 114

Langenstein-Zwieberge concentration camp, 445
Lattre, Gen. Jean-Marie, 360, 376, 428
Lawson General Army Hospital (Atlanta), 294
Legion of Merit, 6, 179, 458
Leinster (ship), 239, 245–6, *illus. 279*
Lend-Lease program, 217
Levine, Sgt. David "Squeaky," 108
Lewandowski, Hansie, 267
Lewis, Captain, 222
Lewis, Joe, 127–8
Lewis, Sinclair, 222
Libya, 57
Locke, Lt. Jessie, 131
Long, Perrin, 103
Los Banos internment camp (Philippines), 393
Louis-Philippe, King of France, 53
Lowery, Capt. Forrest "Frosty," 31, 175, 177
Lowery, Kenneth, 31
Lucas, Gen. John P., 240–1, 265
Luce, Capt. Henry A., 263
Lutz, Lt. Aleda E., *illus. 387*
Luxembourg, 385, 406, 410
Lyon, Lt. Edward, 121, 434

MacArthur, Gen. Douglas, 15–16
MacFee, Col. William F., 383
Mackenbrock, Maj. Frederick, 82–3, 95
Mackensen, Gen. Eberhard von, 265
MacNeeley, Col. Crawford, 341–2
malaria, 160–1, 163, 165, 295
Marigold (ship), 356–9
Marine Corps Women's Reserve, 19, 436
Mariposa (ship), 136
Market-Garden, Operation, 377, 378
Markham, Capt. Blackwell, 40, 90
Marnix (ship), 176
Marshall, Gen. George C., 150, 303–4
Martin, Lt. Gladys, *illus. 100, 320, 465*
Martin, Gen. Joseph L., 299
Massachusetts Memorial Hospital, 214
Mast, Gen. Charles Emmanuel, 33
Matlock, Lt. Mary A., 310, 314, 315
maxillofacial surgery, *illus. 337*, 337–9, 423
May, Andrew J., 437
McBryde, Brenda, 173

McCollough, Lt. Helen, 296
McComb, Theron G., 140, 241, 242, 246, 283
McCoy, Camp (Wisconsin), 467
McDonald, Lt. Anna K., 170–1
McGreevey, Capt. Horace, 425
McKinley, Fort (Philippines), 14, 334
McKoy, Lt. Alice, 434–5, 464
McLaughlin, Lt. Decima, 205–6, 301
Meadors, Lt. Dorothy F., 284
Medal of Honor, 380
Medal of Honor Museum (Chattanooga), 464
Mediterranean Theater of Operations, 215–17, 370, 383, 431
Meese, Gen. Giovanni, 118
Mellies, Col. Chester J., 52, 58, 60, 62, 70–2, 77, 90, 94
Merck & Company, 214
Mexico (ship), 149
Meyers, Lt. Mary E., *illus. 80*, 80–1, 84, 109
Michael Reese Hospital (Chicago), 184, 200
Middleton, Gen. Troy H., 163
Miernicke, Lt. Frances A. "Frenchie," 138, 169–70, 304–5, 311, *illus. 365*, 454, 456, 463–4; at Anzio, 272, 284, 286, 290–3, 298–300, 362; Bronze Star awarded to, 272, *illus. 305*, 306; at Dachau, 450; in France, 360, 362–8, 373–5, 401–2; during invasion of Germany, 442–3, *illus. 443*; in Rhineland, 430–3, *illus. 432*
Miernicke, Roman, 463
Miernicke, Steve, 463–4
Miernicke, Tony, 463
Military Order of the Purple Heart, 460
Miller, Capt. Mamie, 373
Miller, Lt. Louise, 28–9, 40, 59, 63, 80–1, 83, 84, 87
Mills, Lt. Gertrude, 194
Molony, Lt. Helen, 19, *illus. 26*, 47, 230, *illus. 320, 466 and illus.*, 467; in Algeria, 52–5; at Kasserine Pass, 56–63, 66–9, 80–1, *illus. 80*, 83–5; landing in North Africa of, 20, 25–7, 32, 36–40, 120; in Normandy invasion, 319, 321, 325–7; in Sicilian Campaign, 157–9, 162, 169; in Tunisia, 97, 109, 156
Monarch of Bermuda (ship), 25, 31
Monte Cassino, 233, 239, 276–8, 281–3, 293, 297–8, 300, 302, 304–6, 309, 311, 316
Montélimar, Battle of, 364
Montgomery, Gen. Bernard Law, 57, 153, 167, 347, 377, 378, 453
Mooney, Lt. Gladys, 273
Moorhead, John J., 103

Morrow, Lt. Marjorie G., 261, 274

Mosher, Lt. Frances, 219

Mueller, "Bones," *illus. 254*

Mulreaney, Eugene A., 262

Mulreaney, Robert P., 262

Mussolini, Benito, 159, 206, 265, 451–2

mustard gas, 134–5

Nash, Capt. Frances Louise, 8–14, *illus. 12*, 16–21, 333–5, 345, 396–7, 446, 460, 462 *and illus.*

Nash, Capt. James, 335, 396–7, 461–2, *illus. 462*

Nash, Capt. Martha, 333–5, 344–5, 395–7, 415, 439–40, 446, 462 *and illus.*

National Association of Colored Graduate Nurses, 128, 435

National Broadcasting Company (NBC), 5

National Nursing Council for War Service, 123

National Regional Research Laboratory, 213–14

National Salute to Women Veterans of World War II, 4, 5

Navy, U.S., 14, 48, 149, 170, 436, 463, 464; Pacific Fleet, 15; Nurse Corps, 5, 11, 121–3, *illus. 122*, 434, 436, 460, 461

National Women Veterans Advisory Council, 460

Nazism, 209, 394, 405, 413, 414, 444, 446, 449, 452

Needleman, Lt., 93

Negro Quartermaster Battalion, 173

Neidel, Lt. Anna, *illus. 122*

Neptune, Operation, 322, 381

Newfoundland (ship), 172, 182–95, *illus. 183*, *184, 189,* 197, 200, 208, 220, 243, 261, 264, 357, 459

Nickles, Lt. Amy, 72, 73, *illus. 100*

Nightingale, Florence, 9

Ninth Army, 378, 453

Ninth Division, 397

9th Evacuation Hospital, 63, 77, 96, 107, 108, 361

XIX Corps, 343

93rd Evacuation Hospital, 136–7, *illus. 150*, *205,* 289, 313, 350, 356; at Anzio, 250, 251, 254, 257–8, 263, 266, 278–9, 294–6, 299–301; in France, 354, 361–2, 370, 378–9; Patton slapping incident at, 163–6; Salerno vicinity hospital sites of, 195–6, *illus. 196*, *199,* 204–5; in Sicilian Campaign, 149, 151–2; staging for Italy of, 137, 144–5, 156

94th Evacuation Hospital, 198, 295, 310, 314

95th Evacuation Hospital, 131–7, *illus. 134*, 176, 179–81, 195, *illus. 226*, 350, 356–7, *illus. 368*, 429–30, *illus. 430*, 446–7, 463; aboard *Newfoundland*, 183, 186, 188, 192, 193; at Anzio, 238, 250–7, *illus. 254*; bombing of, 258–65, *illus. 262*, 267–9, 272–3; at Dachau, 447, 451; during invasion of Germany, 427–9; in Italy, 199, 202, 204, 206–10, 222–3, 226, 281, 354, 356; in Southern France, 351, *illus. 352*, 358, 369; staging for Italy of, 137, 141–3, 171–2; transported to Salerno, 196–7

96th Evacuation Hospital, 331–2

977th Field Artillery Unit, 277

Nolan, Lt. Agnes, 184–6, 194, 199–201, *illus. 200*

Nolan, Lt. Madonna, 184–6, 194, 199–200, *illus. 200,* 202

Nolan, William, 200

Nordhausen labor camp, 444–7

Normandy invasion, 231, 316, 317, 319–49, 358, 360, 369, 372, 381

Norris, Maj. Frank, *illus. 365,* 367, 374

North African Campaign, 23, 141, 150, 181, 210, 212, 215, 230, 258, 292, 295, 353, 357, 424, 454; D-Day, 3, 20, 25–55, 166, 229, 321, 326, 400; Kasserine Pass, 56–88; Allied push to Bizerte and Tunis, 88–119, 140

Office of Scientific Research and Development (OSRD), U.S., 214

Office of Strategic Services (OSS), U.S., 358, 389

Okinawa, Battle of, 461–2

OMAHA beach, 320–1, 324, 335

101st Airborne Division, 322, 329, 331, 377

106th Division, 410

109th Medical Battalion, 63, 82

111th Medical Battalion, 236, 237

116th Infantry Company, 321

120th Medical Battalion, 250, 257

128th Evacuation Hospital, 111, *illus. 331,* 405, 422–3, *illus. 466;* during Battle of the Bulge, 408, 411–12, 420–2, 424; in Belgium, 384–5, 398–401; in England, 229–31, *illus. 230, 320,* 340; during invasion of Germany, 440–1, 447–9; in Normandy invasion, 319, 321, *illus. 322,* 324, 327–33, 340–2, 348, 351; in North Africa, 115–19; in Sicilian Campaign, 156–63, 166, 168–9; *see also* 48th Surgical Hospital

141st Regimental Combat Team, 235–7
143rd Regimental Combat Team, 237
151st Station Hospital, 232
157th Infantry, 291
168th Infantry Regiment, 71, 77, 82
Orbita (ship), 25, 31
Overlord, Operation, 302, 316, 319, 352–3, 371
Oxford University, 213

Paddock, Lt. Jessie, 228–9, 251, *illus. 268*, 269, 270, 467
Padgitt, Cpl. Jess, 219–20
Parker, Lt. Ralph, 390
Patch, Gen. Alexander, 369, 476
Patterson, Col. Howard, 261
Patton, Gen. George S., 86, 93, 95–6, 110, 150, 152, 153, 156, 163–7, 347, 371, 378, 453
Pearl Harbor, Japanese attack on, 15, 19, 20, 27, 50, 51, 103, 124, 138, 334
penicillin, 212–15, 288–9, 420, 451
Pennsylvania, University of, 138
Pentagon, 464
Percy Jones General Army Hospital (Battle Creek, Michigan), 307–8, *illus. 308*
Perez, Joe R., 301
Peterson, Lt. Lillie "Pete," *illus. 134*, 142, 254, 356, 369, 427–30, *illus. 428, 430*, 446–7, 451, 453, 463
Pettingill, Janet, 86
Pfizer, Charles, & Company, 214
Phibbs, Maj. Brendan, 449–51, 455
Philippines, 8, 11–20, 334; Japanese capture of, 15–19; POWs in, 5, 9, 19, 334, 345, 393, 463–4
Phillips, Robert, *illus. 274*
Pickard, Donald, 415–16
plastic surgery, 420
pneumonia, 215, 287, 289
political prisoners, 445
Polonski, Danny, 307–8, *illus. 308*
post-traumatic stress disorder, 106, 297
Power, Lt. John J., 55, 94, 106, 110
prisoners of war (POWs), 444, 446; American, 5, 9, 19, 334, 304, 315, 364, 390–3, 396–7, 411, 426, 446, 460, 463–4; Arab, 50; British, 393; French, 50; German, 60, 105–6, 117, 118, 141, 182, 224, 226, 266, 289, 337, 341–2, 348–9, 351, 354, 364, 371, 374, 377, 383, 414, 422–3, 429, 435, 447–8; Italian, 60, 105, 118, 141, 181, 182
Proffitt, Maj. William E., Sr., 68, 119
Propea, Lt. Frank, 162

Purple Heart, 6, 147, 200, *illus. 207*, 285, 458
Purple Heart Service Organization, 460
Pyle, Ernie, 74, 319

racial discrimination, 128, 434–5
Rainey, Maj., 344
Rangers, U.S. Army, 52–4, 118, 152, 239, 247–8, 309–11
Rapido River, Battle of, 232, 234–8
Ray, Lt. Edna G., 142
recovered Allied military personnel (RAMPs), 446
Red Cross, 50, 54, 70–2, 183, 261, 264, 270, 279, 296, 333, 334, 393, 394, 397, 408; American, *see* American National Red Cross
Reichert, Helen Molony, *see* Molony, Lt. Helen
relative rank, 13–14, 123–4
Rhineland, Battle of the, 427–8, 439–41
Rhône Valley, Battle of, 369–72
Richards, Esther, 183, 191, 261, 274
Richert, Lt. Helen, 450
Riley, Fort (Kansas), 125, 126, 128, 130
Ringer, Col. Merritt G., 37, 40, 52
Roberts, Lt. Mary Louise, 271, 292
Roberts, Sgt., 69
Rodenburg, Lt. Luella, 117
Roe, Lt. Eleanor A., 271, 292
Rome, capture of, 239, 302–15, *illus, 315*, 354
Rommel, Field Marshal Erwin, 57, 62, 88, 91–2, 118, 182
Romohr, Lt. Gladys, 117
Roosevelt, Eleanor, 120
Roosevelt, Franklin Delano, 20, 36, 304, 433, 435, 437, 447
Rose, Gen. Maurice, 395
Rosenbaum, Capt. Edward E., 25, 348–9, 458–9
Rosten, Lt. Othelia "Oats," 142
Rourke, Lt. Rita, 271, 292
Royal, Lt. Marjorie, 190
Russians, 174, 353, 394, 411, 445, 452, 453

Said, Fort (Morocco), 143
St. Andrew (ship), 185, 189, 193, 194, 238–9
St. David (ship), 185, 194, 238, 241–7, 283, 459, 463
St. Luke's Hospital (Duluth), 273, 366
Salerno, invasion of, 147, 172–97, 264, 267, 316, 357, 459
Salter, Lt. Alys, 30, 37, 39, 40, 54, 59, 63, 66, 68, 78, 80, 83–7, 110, 111
Santa Paula (ship), 25, 31, 229–30

Santo Tomas internment camp (Philippines), 393

Saracens, 277

Sarnecky, Col. Mary T., 427

Sauer, Col. Paul K., 171, *illus. 207*, 261, 262

Schick General Hospital (Iowa), 130–1

Schuermann, Sgt. George J., 263

Schwade, Lt. Leonard J., 106

Schweitzer, Larry, 429–30

Scott (ship), 15

Scott, Col. Raymond, 149

Scripps-Howard newspapers, 74

Second Armored Division, 343

2nd Auxiliary Surgical Group, 29–31, 137–40, 222, 283, 298, *illus. 365*, 401–2, 442, *illus. 443*; aboard *Newfoundland*, 183, 187, 188, 194; at Anzio, 239, 241–2, 251, 270, 272, 284, 294–96, 300; and capture of Rome, 310, 315; at Dachau, 450; French civilians treated by, 374–5; in invasion of Germany, 430–2, 442–3; at Kasserine Pass, 70, 71; OR techniques of, 220–1; at Paestum, 198, 201; in Southern France, 350, 353, 358–9, 364–8; staging for Italian campaign of, 169–76, 179, 181; transported to Salerno, 196

2nd Medical Supply Depot, 63

segregation, racial, 128, 434–5

Selective Service Act, 437

Self, Lt. Gladys, 117

Seminole (ship), 300

Senate, U.S., 438; Veterans Affairs Subcommittee on Oversight and Investigation, 460

Serrin, John, *illus. 308*

VII Corps, 420

Seventh Armored Division, 410

Seventh Army, 150, 152, 156, 160–1, 163, 198, 351, 353, 359, 369, 371, 376, 378, 449, 453

17th Veterinary Evacuation Hospital, 312

74th Station Hospital, 195

77th Evacuation Hospital, 49, 53, 63, 85, 93, 96, 107, 108, 211

Shanks, Camp (New York), 133, 134

Shannon, Edward, 162–3

Sheaffer, Lt. Vera, 165, 195, 205–6, 251, 289, 301, 357, 463

Sheetz, Anne, 274

Sheetz, Lt. Carrie, 171, 261, 263, 264, 274, 351

Shelby, Camp (Mississippi), 51

Sheldon, Priscilla, *illus. 122*

shell-shock, 106

Shelver, Lt. Maryjane, 183, 191

Sherman, Camp (Ohio), 128

Sherman, Maj. Martin L., 444

Sherman tanks, 416–19

Shingle, Operation, 233–5, 238, 239

Shorbe, Capt. Howard B., 296

Sicilian Campaign, 147, 149–74, *illus. 164*, 212, 264, 292, 295, 316, 321–2, 350, 353, 357, 454; map, 154–5; staging in North Africa for, 110, 119, 137–45

Siegfried Line, 376–8, 380, 382, 395

Sigman, Lt. Blanche F., 132, 133, 137, 171, 182, 186, 188, 190–2, 259, 261, 263, 264, 274, 351

Silver Star, 6, 147, 271, 272, 275, 285, 292, 458

Simion, Doris Brittingham, *see* Brittingham, Lt. Doris

Simonson, Lt. Adeline "Si," *illus. 134*, 136, 142, 143, 253–5, 261, 273, *illus. 355*, 355–6, 467

Simpson, Gen. William H., 378

VI Corps, 204, 238–40, 255, 267, 276, 283, 292, 294, 295, 298, 302, 309, 315, 376

Sixth Armored Infantry, 291

Sixth Army Group, 428

16th Evacuation Hospital, 140–1, 176, 179, 181–8, 186, 193, 194, 196–202, *illus. 201*

Sixteenth Infantry Division, 36, 321

16th Medical Battalion, 70

16th Medical Regiment, 63

67th Evacuation Hospital, 332–3, 345–7, 385–6, 395, 409–10, 413–15

602nd Clearing Station, 177–9

Skinner, Cornelia Otis, 135

Skogsberg, Lt. Paul, 398, 463

Skogsberg, Vera Sheaffer, *see* Sheaffer, Lt. Vera

Slotwinski, Evelyn Kemer, *illus. 466*

Smiley, Cpl., 79

Smit, Lt. Jennette "Jan," 142

Smith, Gilbert, 100–1, 400, 448

Smith, Lt. Carrie, 330

Snyder, Col. John, 71

Soldier's Medal, 458

Sorlye, Oliver, 91, 231, 328, 412, 453, *illus. 465*

Spanish-American War, 13

Spelhaug, Lt. Glenda, 251, 269, 270

Squibb & Sons, 214

Sramcik, Lt. Margaret, 96

Stanfill, Lt. Margaret B., 169, *illus. 320*, 326

staphylococcus, 213, 215

station hospitals, 30; *see also specific hospitals*

Index

Sternberg General Hospital (Manila), 13
Stimson, Henry L., 437
Stone, Billie L., 249–50, 309–10, 464
Stotsenberg Army Hospital (Philippines), 15
Stovall, Col. Oran, 234
streptococcus, 215
Stuber, Lt. Elizabeth C., 414
sulfa drugs, 420
Sullivan, Lt. Mary Ann, 31, 71
Supreme Headquarters, Allied Expeditionary Force (SHAEF), 408
Surgeon General, Office of, 216–17
Swaab, Mike, 445–6, 465
Swanson, Capt. Evelyn E., 351, *illus. 352*, 356
Sydel, Capt. Margaret, 362
syphilis, 210–11, 215

Tahan, Joseph Samuel, 277–8
Talboy, Lt. Helen, 263–4
Tanner, Wesley, 263
Task Force Butler, 363
Taylor, Gerald, 91
Tegtmeyer, Maj. Charles E., 321
Tenth Armored Division, 428
10th Field Hospital, 156, 350, 361
Third Armored Division, 371, 394, 396, 416–18, *illus. 417*, 444–6, 464, 465
Third Army, 347, 371, 378, 406, 453
3rd Auxiliary Surgical Group, 331
Third Battalion, 248
Third Division Clearing Station, 369
Third Infantry Division, 163, 167, 176, 233, 239, 247, 259, 278, 292, 295, 312, 353
13th Field Hospital, 321
Thirtieth Infantry Division, 343
33rd Field Hospital, 181, 216, 228–9, 238, 250, 251, 254, *illus. 268*, 269–72, 286, 301–2, 312–13
Thirty-fourth Infantry Division, 62, 71, 77, 176, 225–6, 232, 295, 313, 355, 356
Thirty-sixth Infantry Division, 93, 176–7, 179, 204, 234–7, 281, 306, 313
38th Evacuation Hospital, 48, 299–300
39th Combat Engineers, 248–9, 283, 309–10, 353, 362, 364, 379–80
Thorson, Charlie, 328, *illus. 465*
300th General Hospital, 258, 285, 296, 300, 356
310th Medical Battalion, 311
311th Medical Battalion, 311
Truman, Harry S., 435, 447
Tignanelli, Ernest, 364, *illus. 365*, 367, 431

Tillie, Lt., 300
"Tokyo Rose," 309
Torch, Operation, 20, 25–55,
transfusions, *see* blood supply
trench foot, 287–8, 425–6
Truckey, Capt. Jean, 333, 346, 385, 413–14
Truscott, Gen. Lucian K., Jr., 163, 2., 292–3
tuberculosis, 13
Turkey, 304
Tuskegee Airmen, 136
Twelfth Army, 347–8, 376
12th Field Hospital, 425
21st General Hospital, 263
25th Ohio General Hospital, 412
26th General Hospital, 113–14
26th Medical Battalion, 166
Twenty-eighth Infantry Division, 428
Twenty-ninth Infantry Division, 336, 342, 343
II Corps, 62–3, 68, 70, 74, 93, 96, 110, 306
Tyng, Col. Francis C., 217
typhus, 450–1
Tysinger, Jim, 461
Tyson, Camp (Tennessee), 30

Ullom, Col. Madeline, 5–6, 460
UTAH beach, 320, 321, 324–5, 327, 329, 351

Vance, Col. James, 416–17, 465
VE-Day, 3, 453
venereal disease (VD), 210–12, 215–16, 234, 289
Veterans Administration, U.S., 3, 4, 457, 459–60
Veterans of Foreign Wars (VFW), 3, 4, 460
Vichy French, 32, 33, 43
Vietinghoff, Gen. Heinrich von, 451
Virginia, University of, 140
Vogler, Lt. Vilma, 25, 106, 117, 348–9, 459
V-1 and V-2 rockets, 396, 408, 411, 420, 444, 445

Wainwright, Gen. Jonathan, 19
Wakefield (ship), 26
Walden, Lt. Bernice "Hut Sut," 133, *illus. 134*, 135, 136, *illus. 368*, 463; at Anzio, 251–3, *illus. 254*, 259, 260, 263, 269; in Italy, 206–8, 210, 227, 356; aboard *Newfoundland*, 183, 191, 193–4; in North Africa, 137, 142, 180; transported to Salerno, 196

11/04

n. Fred L., 234

een, Owen Harding, 102

artment, U.S., 14, 90, 101, 102, 108, 124, 130, 340, 433, 436, 437

anpower Commission, 437

eurosis, *see* battle fatigue

haw, Junior, 290

nstein, Alfred A., 17

st Point, U.S. Military Academy at, 465

heeler, Lt. Isabelle "Bee Wee," 133, *illus. 134*, 135, 136, *illus. 368*, 463; at Anzio, 251, 252, 259, 269; in Italy, 206–8, 210, 356; aboard *Newfoundland*, 183, 191, 193–4; awarded Purple Heart, *illus. 207*; in North Africa, 137, 142, 180; transported to Salerno, 196

Wheeler, Taylor McKenzie, 467–8, *illus. 468*

Whitlock, Maj., 439

Whitside, Camp (Kansas), 126

Whitt, Glenna, 63

Whittle, Lt. Reba E., 388–93

Whorton, Lt. Martha, 186

Wilbur, Col. Bernice, 110, 303

Wiley, Col. Norman H., 94, 99, 108–11, 119, 159, 168, 324, 329, 341–2, 400–1

William Pendleton (ship), 319, 321, *illus. 322*, 324, 326

Williams, Adeline Simonson, *see* Simonson, Lt. Adeline

Williams, Lt. Marvin, 355 *and illus.*, 467

Willner, Maj. Eddie, 445–6, 464–5

Wingard, Lt. Fern H., 262

Winter Line Campaign, 225, 228

Winthrop Laboratories, 214

Witte, Lt. Doris E., 142

Wolff, Capt. Luther, 175–9, 201–2, 216, 217, 236, 282

Women Accepted for Volunteer Emergency Service (WAVES), 19, 436

Women's Army Auxiliary Corps (WAAC), 19, 435

Women's Army Corps (WAC), 435–7

Women Veterans Advisory Committee, 5

Woolbine, Capt., 70

World War I, 9, 14, 19, 106, 121, 128, 134, 183, 267, 334, 358, 385

Wright-Patterson Air Force Base (Dayton), 466

Zigler, Lt. Anna Mae, 194